THE GERMANS

European Perspectives

European Perspectives
A Series in Social Thought and Cultural Criticism
Lawrence D. Kritzman, Editor

European Perspectives presents English translations of books by leading European thinkers. With both classic and outstanding contemporary works, the series aims to shape the major intellectual controversies of our day and to facilitate the tasks of historical understanding.

The Germans

Power Struggles and the
Development of Habitus in the
Nineteenth and Twentieth Centuries

NORBERT ELIAS

edited by
Michael Schröter

Translated from the German
and with a Preface
by Eric Dunning and Stephen Mennell

Columbia University Press
New York

English translation © Polity Press 1996

First published in German as *Studien über die Deutschen*
by Suhrkamp Verlag © Norbert Elias 1989.
Edited by Michael Schröter.

This translation first published in 1996 by Polity Press
in association with Blackwell Publishers Ltd.

Published with the financial support of Inter Nationes, Bonn.

The publishers wish to thank Dr. Rosemary Breger for her help in the preparation
of this translation.

Columbia University Press
New York

Library of Congress Cataloging-in-Publication Data

Elias, Norbert.
    [Studien über die Deutschen.   English]
    The Germans : Power struggles and the development of
habitus in the nineteenth and twentieth centuries / Norbert Elias :
edited by Michael Schröter : translated from the German and with a
preface by Eric Dunning and Stephen Mennell.
        p.   cm.
    Translation of: Studien über die Deutschen.
    ISBN 0–231–10562–2
    1. Germany—Politics and government—1789–1900.   2. Germany—
Politics and government—20th century.   3. National
characteristics, German.   4. Nationalism—Germany.   5. Political
culture—Germany.   I. Schröter, Michael.   II. Dunning, Eric.
III. Title.
DD197.5.E4513   1996
943.08—dc20   95–46443
                                                                                    CIP

∞

Casebound editions of Columbia University Press books
are printed on permanent and durable acid-free paper.

Printed in Great Britain

c   10   9   8   7   6   5   4   3   2   1

Contents

WITHDRAWN

vi *Contents*

Preface

Eric Dunning and Stephen Mennell

1

Studien über die Deutschen is the most important book by Norbert Elias since *The Civilizing Process*. Its publication in English is thus a sociological event of some significance. The German edition was the last of Norbert Elias's books in any language to be published during his lifetime and with his own seal of approval. The book deals with issues about which he had been thinking and writing – but publishing relatively little – for decades. It is the late product of what is perhaps one of the most remarkable pieces of non-quantitative comparative or cross-cultural sociological research to have been carried out in recent years. At the time of his death at the age of 93 in 1990, Elias was an international intellectual celebrity, but fame had come to him extraordinarily late in his long life. His reputation has continued to grow since his death, and is likely to be still further enhanced by the appearance in English of *The Germans*. At the same time, this book will serve to clarify certain points on which his work, especially the theory of civilizing processes which he regarded as the linchpin of his sociological contribution overall, continues to be widely misunderstood.

Studien über die Deutschen was published in 1989, exactly fifty years after *The Civilizing Process*[1] and one year before Norbert Elias's death. Its publication owed much to the zeal, energy and editorial skill of its German editor, Michael Schröter. It is not a continuous text on which Elias had worked in the two or three years preceding publication but rather a selection of essays and lectures on which he had been working, in some cases for as long as thirty years. For example, the essay on 'The Breakdown of Civilization' was stimulated by the trial of Adolf Eichmann in Jerusalem in 1961 and there is still in existence a lengthy manuscript dating from that time written in Elias's characteristic English and containing numerous hand-written alterations by the author. However, what is printed in *The Germans* is our translation of the German text, which is longer and different in several ways from the English version. It was evidently worked on by Elias perhaps together with Michael Schröter and/or one of his (Elias's) assistants.

For all that the origins of the book lay in separate essays and lectures, with some inevitable overlap between them, it amounts to a chronologically almost continuous account of German social development, especially from the Enlightenment to the present. Elias writes that it would be 'a rather nice task to write the "biography" of a state-society, for instance Germany' (p. 178 below). That is because, he suggests, 'just as in the development of an individual person the experiences of earlier times continue to have an effect in the present, so, too, do earlier experiences in the development of a nation.' *The Germans* amply bears out this proposition. Thus, through skilful interweaving of empirical evidence and theoretical reasoning, Elias points to many of the ways in which those features of German habitus, personality, social structure and behaviour which combined to produce the rise of Hitler and the Nazi genocides can be understood as having grown out of Germany's past. Elias draws particular attention to such features of German history as: the devastation wrought in the seventeenth century by the Thirty Years War; Germany's late unification compared with countries such as Britain and France which became unified much earlier and enjoyed, as a result, a much less discontinuous pattern of history and social development; and the fact that, in the German case, unification took place through a series of wars under the leadership of the militaristic ruling strata of Prussia, a process in the course of which large sections of the middle classes abandoned the humanistic values which had hitherto predominated in their social circles, and adopted instead the militaristic and authoritarian values of the hegemonic Prussians. Elias describes Germany's Second Empire – the unified *Kaiserreich* of 1871–1918 – as a *satisfaktionsfähige Gesellschaft*, a term which it is impossible to translate directly into English but which means a society orientated around a code of honour in which duelling and the demanding and giving of 'satisfaction' occupied pride of place. According to Elias, Germany's unification thus involved a 'brutalization' of large sections of the middle classes, a process in which the student fraternities in the universities played a crucial role.[2]

Elias goes on to discuss the weakening of state control in Germany after the First World War and how, in that context, the private armies of the *Freikorps* emerged, destabilizing the fledgeling Weimar Republic and contributing to a terrorist movement which was opposed to the 'talking shop' of the Weimar parliament and which strove for the restoration of authoritarian rule. (He also shows how terrorists after the Second World War such as the Baader–Meinhof group arose from a structurally similar situation.) However, Elias's point is not that the rise of Hitler and the Nazi genocides grew inevitably out of such structural sources but rather that these internationally stigmatizing events occurred as a result of decisions made in a context of national crisis by ruling groups which enjoyed widespread popular, especially middle-class, support and which were acting in terms of what were – and to some extent still are – deeply sedimented aspects of German habitus, personality, social structure and behaviour.

By 'habitus' – a word which he used long before its popularization by Pierre Bourdieu[3] – Elias basically means 'second nature' or 'embodied social learning'. The concept is not in any way essentialist; in fact it is used in large part to overcome the problems of the old notion of 'national character' as something fixed and static. Thus Elias contends that 'the fortunes of a nation over the centuries become sedimented into the habitus of its individual members' (p. 19 below), and it follows from this that habitus changes over time precisely because the fortunes and experiences of a nation (or of its constituent groupings) continue to change and accumulate.[4] A balance between continuity and change is involved, and nowhere is this more clearly demonstrated than in Elias's essay on 'changes in European standards of behaviour in the twentieth century' (part IA below). This is Elias's considered response to the extended debate, particularly among Dutch sociologists, about whether and in what ways the informalizing spurt of the 1960s and 1970s (including the rise of the so-called 'permissive society') represents a reversal of the main trend of the European civilizing process as described by Elias, and in what ways it is a continuation of it.[5]

The fact that Elias was able so perceptively to write a 'biography' of the Germans was clearly dependent to a large extent on his own biography. So is the fact that *The Germans* is replete with comparisons of German patterns of habitus and social development with the patterns in other European countries, particularly Britain, France and Holland. The book draws on the kinds of intimate and detailed knowledge of and feel for these countries and their developing patterns of culture and social structure which can only come from living and working in them and learning to speak, read and write their languages. (Dutch was the only one of these languages which Elias never learned.) Elias was born of German Jewish parents in Breslau in 1897 (it is now Wrocław in Poland), fled to France in 1933 and travelled to Britain in 1935. One reason why Elias waited for some seventeen years after the end of the Second World War before writing about the genocides and the collapse of German civilization under the Nazis may have been his struggle to come to terms with the fact that his mother had been murdered in the gas chambers of Auschwitz – whilst he had escaped to Britain. He became a naturalized British citizen and, apart from two years (1961–3) in Ghana, taught sociology, mainly at the University of Leicester. In 1978 he moved back permanently to the continent, teaching and writing in Germany and Holland, finally retiring from teaching to live and write in Amsterdam, where he died on 1 August 1990.

In part, *The Germans* can be seen as expanding on and developing the triangular comparison between the development of Britain, France and Germany which runs through *The Civilizing Process*, notably in an 'Excursus on some differences in the paths of development of Britain, France and Germany'.[6] His central point is that the ease and speed with which centralized states emerged in Western Europe depended, *ceteris paribus*, on the size of the social formations involved and thus on the extent of the geographical and social divergences which existed within them.[7] He shows how the colossal 'German-Roman' (or 'Holy Roman') Empire – the First Reich – crumbled away for centuries at its borders, particularly in the West and South, a process which was only partly compensated for by colonization and expansion to the East. This trend was continued, he argues, in the diminution in the size of Germany's territory after 1866, when the war between Prussia and Austria led to Austria's exclusion from the German Confederation and the so-called *kleindeutsche Lösung* (small Germany solution) to the problem of the national unification of the German-speaking peoples. There was a further diminution after 1918 in consequence of the territorial losses suffered by

Germany through defeat in the First World War. In *The Germans*, Elias goes on to show how a major consequence of Germany's defeat in the Second World War was yet another continuation of this trend towards territorial diminution. That is to say, there occurred yet another split, this time between the Federal (West German) and Democratic (East German) Republics.

The essays in this book were written before the collapse of the Communist states of Eastern Europe, and not long before he died, Elias explained that one of his aims in writing *Studien über die Deutschen* had been to try to reconcile the German people to the probability that the split between East and West would prove a permanent one. Ironically, he lived to see the end of the Cold War and German re-unification. Along with most other people, he had failed to grasp the weakness of the former Soviet Union and its eventual collapse. Elias appreciated – and indeed laughed about – the irony of his failure in this regard. One of the central points of his sociology more generally is that, whilst 'every explanation makes possible predictions of one kind or another', this does not by any means imply that it is possible on the basis of sociological models to 'prophesy' future events.[8] Perhaps if Elias had applied his model in detail to the former Soviet Union, it would have been possible to diagnose the structural weakness of the Soviet 'empire', if not perhaps the timing of its demise.[9] Elias certainly reached such a diagnosis regarding the former British Empire as early as 1939.[10]

The Germans must also be seen as part of a series of books and articles by Elias, growing out of the excursus in *The Civilizing Process* and comparing the trajectories of state-formation and civilization of Britain, France and Germany. The French trajectory is examined in detail in volume II of *The Civilizing Process* and in *The Court Society*;[11] the German trajectory is examined in *The Germans* and *Mozart: Portrait of a Genius*;[12] and the British trajectory is examined in *Quest for Excitement*, especially in Elias's 'Introduction' and his 'Essay on Sport and Violence'.[13] The British trajectory is treated further in his 'Studies in the genesis of the naval profession'.[14] Together these constitute a set of detailed and developmental cross-national comparisons.

2

We are writing this preface in 1995, the year in which the fiftieth anniversary of the ending of the Second World War is being celebrated and when the media are focusing regularly on the Nazi genocides. The murder of some six million Jews, Gypsies, Slavs and others is also coming into prominence once again as a subject of academic debate. *The Germans* makes a contribution to two related disputes: the issue of the causes of the genocides, and the issue of the validity of Elias's theory of civilizing processes.

Of all the events which have occurred so far in the twentieth century, the Nazi genocides is the one which has represented the greatest shock to the self-image of European people, so heavily permeated by the idea of 'civilization'. Whatever else it may have been, and even though it involved the use of 'civilized' techniques such as 'rational' bureaucratic forms of administration, the genocides cannot by any stretch of the imagination be described as a 'civilized' affair. It was, in fact, extremely 'uncivilized' and occurred in the context of what Elias described as a 'breakdown of civilization' (see especially part IV). Of course, as Elias maintained and as has more recently been pointed out by Edward Said among others,[15] the view of European people of themselves as 'civilized' and 'superior' always implied that there were other people whom they stigmatized as 'uncivilized' and 'inferior'. Nevertheless, knowledge of the fact that European people could act in such 'uncivilized' ways towards fellow Europeans as the Germans had acted in the 'Holocaust' came as a profound shock, and the Nazi genocides have remained the central image of evil for most people in the West. The 'Holocost' has certainly remained the central image of evil for most social scientists at least since the trial of Adolf Eichmann in 1961 and probably since the Nuremberg trials.

For some twenty or thirty years after the Second World War, most discussion by historians, psychologists, sociologists and other social scientists which was directly or indirectly relevant to the Nazi genocides focused on Germany – on its society, its history and the psychology of its people. There were sociological studies of the sources of electoral support for the Nazis[16] and historical discussions of Prussian attitudes and their spread.[17] In his *Society and Democracy in Germany*, Ralf Dahrendorf sought persuasively to show the Nazis as unwitting agents in a modernization process which they accomplished by destroying old elites and institutional structures.[18] Even works in which more ostensibly general theses were proposed, such as Arendt's *The Origins of Totalitarianism*[19] and Adorno et al.'s *The Authoritarian Personality*[20] were, at bottom, Germanocentric in their focus.

From the 1960s onwards, however, more and more people began to become aware that genocide is a continuing problem in the modern world.[21] First, attention focused on Stalin, who killed more people than did Hitler, and over a longer period. Then there followed a whole series of appalling episodes – Uganda, Cambodia, Rwanda, Bosnia, to name but a few – which seem likely to continue and which have added to the vocabulary of the twentieth century terms such as 'ethnic cleansing'. Nevertheless, any comparison which seemed to diminish the enormity and deny the uniqueness of the Nazi atrocities remained highly controversial, not least in Germany itself. In 1986, the historian Ernst Nolte sparked off a heated debate among German historians. He argued that the Final Solution could not be understood without relating it to the Soviet terror, which had served as a precedent for the Nazi one. In some sense, the 'Holocaust' had been based on the model of an Asiatic mode of killing. Nolte's thesis was vigorously opposed by other German academics, including Jürgen Habermas. They pointed to differences, if not in scale then in kind, between Hitler's and Stalin's killings; in particular, they pointed to the 'planned purposefulness and the European-wide aspirations of Nazi genocide' and the fact that

> The regime rounded up people in Westerbork, Saloniki, Warsaw, collected them from all over and brought them to places where they were to be killed. In many cases they were not even used as labour. The victims were selected by virtue of their group identity. Behaviour was irrelevant.[22]

Above all, however, those who opposed Nolte's interpretation objected that, if it did not excuse genocide, then it at least made the Nazi genocides less exceptional; the effect of Nolte's thesis was in some sense to bracket the Final Solution, and re-establish a continuity in 'normal' German politics and social life before and after the Nazi aberration.[23]

Some sociologists, however, have been less hesitant in placing the 'Holocaust' in a wider category of modern genocide. Recent theorizing has tended towards the depressing view that genocide is endemic in the societies of the modern world, that it is one of the hallmarks of 'modernity'. Perhaps the most prominent and extreme expression of this view is provided by Zygmunt Bauman in his *Modernity and the Holocaust*.[24] The core of Bauman's argument is that 'modern', 'rational' societies produce conditions under which the effects of individual actions are removed beyond the limits of morality. Bauman's book stands near the opposite end of a continuum from those who wish still to focus on German exceptionalism: it minimizes what may be called the peculiarity of the Germans. In *The Germans*, Elias takes a position somewhere around the middle of the continuum. On the one hand, he works with ideas of general application, such as his recognition of the dominance of warrior classes and warrior values in agrarian states,[25] the connections he traces between industrialization and the rise of nationalism, his observation that what he calls 'half-educated' people have placed their stamp on all 'modern' societies and his concern with processes and consequences of 'group charisma' and 'group disgrace'. (Shame and related emotions are central to *The Germans* as they were in *The Civilizing Process*; T.J. Scheff, partly under Elias's influence, has further elaborated the role of 'shame–rage spirals' in nationalism.)[26] On the other hand, he also stresses the particular conjuncture of circumstances which arose in German history to produce, for instance, a resurgence of warrior values when a more unilinear theory might have led to the expectation of their decline. Also traced by Elias to this conjuncture were the concomitant desire for a return to 'strong-man' rule; the widespread contempt for parliamentary democracy; the rise to political dominance of a 'half-educated' group; and ultimately how the deeply troubled German people of the 1930s came under the thrall of Hitler, a 'political medicine man', with his chiliastic promise to fulfil the age-old German dream of a European Reich in which Germans would enjoy – with no effort on their part – the prestige increment of belonging to the so-called 'Aryan master-race'.

Bauman's book is also, among other things, a sustained polemic against Elias's theory, though it is easy to miss how central a misunderstood Elias is to Bauman's case because he is mentioned directly only a few times.[27] This is not the place to examine Bauman's arguments at length, but perhaps it is not inappropriate to comment that, *pace* Bauman, *The Civilizing Process* is not a 'celebration' of the everyday, taken-for-granted notion of 'civilization'. It begins[28] by considering the varied connotations acquired by the word 'civilized', and reaches the conclusion that they can only be understood through studying the term's *functions*. It had come to express the self-image of the West. It expressed the sense of superiority first of members of upper classes over the lower orders in Western societies, and then of Western nations as a whole in relation to peoples in other parts of the world whom they had conquered, colonized or otherwise come to dominate. Their own attitudes, feelings and modes of behaviour had come to seem inherent and 'natural' – second nature – to them. By the nineteenth century, the ways in which people in the West used the *word* civilization – except in Germany, where 'civilization' was rejected in favour of the more particularistic term 'culture' – showed that they had already largely forgotten their own *process* of civilization: for them it was completed and taken for granted, even 'something' they had 'naturally' (that is, 'racially' or genetically) inherited. In the rest of the book, Elias seeks to recover the structure of that half-forgotten process. In *The Civilizing Process*, as much later in *The Germans*, Elias makes a connection between state-formation and other processes of development on the 'macro' level, and changes in the habitus of individuals on the 'micro' level. In a nutshell, his key proposition is that:

> if in a particular region, the power of central authority grows, if over a larger or smaller area the people are forced to live in peace with each other, the moulding of affects and the standard of the drive-economy [*Triebhaushalt*] are very gradually changed as well.[29]

But *The Civilizing Process* was written against the background of the Third Reich in Elias's country of birth, and under the looming threat of another World War. Far from celebrating the permanent achievement of a final state of 'civilization', this early work is shot through with a sense of foreboding. Elias warned that

> The armour of civilized conduct would crumble very rapidly if, through a change in society, the degree of insecurity that existed earlier were to break in upon us again, and if danger became as incalculable as once it was. Corresponding fears would soon burst the limits set to them today.[30]

In a later work, he wrote that 'our descendants, if humankind can survive the violence of our age, might consider us as late barbarians'.[31] The publication of this translation of *The Germans* will inevitably help to correct the misperception of the theory of civilizing processes as an 'optimistic', 'unlinear', 'progress' theory of human history, and promote a wider recognition of the place of *de*civilizing processes within the overall theory. Elias recognized clearly that civilizing and decivilizing processes can occur simultaneously in particular societies, and not simply in the same or different societies at different points in time.

3

In translating *Studien über die Deutschen*, we have tried to keep to a minimum the use of untranslated German words, but we have not been able to avoid it altogether. We have already referred to the difficulties of translating *satisfaktionsfähige Gesellschaft* directly into English. What we have done, although such a solution is far from perfect, is to translate the term where it first appears in the text, using the German words thereafter. We have similarly used the German 'Reich' (and derivations such as *Kaiserreich*), partly because most English speakers will be familiar with it in the form of Hitler's 'Third Reich' but also because, as Elias points out, Reich has connotations which are different from 'empire' in English and French. More particularly, it refers to the idea of an empire in Europe as opposed to overseas and is heavily imbued with romantic yearnings for a lost past.

Many people have helped us with this translation. Ros Shennan and Sue Smith undertook with unfailing cheerfulness and skill the laborious task of typing drafts of the manuscript through its various stages. Joop Goudsblom read through the entire translation, and also this preface, offering much valuable advice. Helmut Kuzmics helped us to construe some of the idiomatic German which appears in the letters from which Elias quotes in part IV. Thanks are also due to the following: Alan Farncombe, Richard Kilminster, Julie Marriott, Barbara Mennell, Pat Murphy, Jeremy Noakes, Harry Redner, Jill Redner, Hugh Ridley, Michael Schröter, Ken Sheard, Walter Veit and Ivan Waddington. They have all helped us in numerous practical ways as well as by their support.

Acknowledgements

The author and publishers wish to thank the following for permission to use copyright material.

Macmillan Press Ltd and W. W. Norton & Company, Inc. for extracts from Emily Anderson, ed., *The Letters of Mozart and his Family*, Vol. II, 3rd edition. Copyright © 1966 by The Executors of the late Miss Emily Anderson. Copyright © 1985 by The Macmillan Press, Ltd;

Ewan MacNaughton Associates on behalf of The Telegraph plc for 'Fall of Goa stuns Lisbon: Radio Dirges for end of an Empire', *The Daily Telegraph*, 20.12.61. Copyright © The Telegraph plc 1995;

Times Newspapers Ltd for extracts from 'On Britain's Conscience', *The Times*, 20.2.78;

Time Inc. for a short extract from 'America's new manners' by Letitia Baldridge, *Time*, 27.11.78. Copyright © 1978 Time Inc.

Every effort has been made to trace all the copyright holders, but if any have been inadvertently overlooked the publishers will be pleased to make the necessary arrangement at the first opportunity.

Introduction

1

Standing half-hidden in the background of the studies published here is an eyewitness who has lived for nearly ninety years through the events concerned as they unfolded. The picture of events formed by someone personally affected by them usually differs in characteristic ways from that which takes shape when one views them with the detachment and distance of a researcher. It is like a camera, which can be focused to different distances – close up, middle distance and long distance. Something similar holds for the point of view of a researcher who has also lived through the events he is studying.

Many of the following discussions originated in the attempt to make understandable, to myself and anyone who is prepared to listen, how the rise of National Socialism came about, and thus also the war, concentration camps and the breaking apart of the earlier Germany into two states. Its core is an attempt to tease out developments in the German national habitus which made possible the decivilizing spurt of the Hitler epoch, and to work out the connections between them and the long-term

---

This introduction, like the book as a whole, owes a great deal to my collaboration with Michael Schröter.

process of state-formation in Germany. Tackling such a problem entails certain difficulties.

It is easier from the outset to recognize the shared elements of the national habitus in the case of other peoples than it is in the case of one's own. In dealings with Italians or British people, Germans often fairly quickly become aware that what at first seem to be differences in personal character actually involve differences in national character. 'That was typically Italian, typically British' they will say. It is different with the nation to which one belongs oneself. To become aware of the peculiarities of the habitus of one's own nation requires a specific effort of self-distancing.

Furthermore, in the case of the West Germans, any consideration of the national habitus trespasses into a taboo zone. The hypersensitivity towards anything that recalls National Socialist doctrine results in the problem of a 'national character' being largely shrouded in silence. But perhaps precisely because of this, it is advisable to bring this and related topics into the realm of calm discussion within the social sciences. It then soon becomes evident that a people's national habitus is not biologically fixed once and for all time: rather, it is very closely connected with the particular process of state-formation they have undergone. Just like tribes and states, a national habitus develops and changes in the course of time. No doubt there are also inherited, biological differences between the peoples of the earth. But even peoples of similar or identical racial composition can be quite different in their national habitus or mentality – that is, the way in which they relate to one another. One can meet people in Holland or Denmark who would probably have been considered to be prototypically German in the Goebbels era; but the national habitus of the Dutch and the Danes has a markedly different stamp from that of the Germans.

2

If someone were to ask me which peculiarities of the German state-formation process seem to me to be of particular significance in understanding the German habitus, and by extension the change in habitus during the Hitler period, then from the knot of interwoven part-processes, I would emphasize four.[1]

The *first* concerns the location of and structural changes in the people who spoke Germanic languages, and later German, in relation to neighbouring societies speaking other languages. The Germanic-speaking tribes, who settled in the European lowlands west of the Elbe and in a wide area between the Elbe and the Alps throughout the centuries of the migration of the peoples [*Völkerwanderung*], found themselves embedded between tribes whose language was derived from Latin, and eastern tribes speaking Slavonic languages. These three groups of peoples fought over the borders of their areas of settlement for more than a thousand years. Sometimes the borders were pushed in favour of the western and eastern groups, sometimes in favour of the Germanic- or German-speaking middle bloc. The transformation of parts of the Germanic Frankish kingdom into the state we now know as France is just as much an example of the struggle between latinized and Germanic groups as is the gallicization of Alsace-Lorraine hundreds of years later, or the continuing conflicts between the Walloons and the Flemings in Belgium today. Similarly, the penetration of groups of German-speaking peoples back across the Elbe shows that the tension between groups of Germanic and Slavic origins remained active. It was expressed once again, perhaps for the last time, in the redrawing to the west of the border between Germany and the two Slavic countries of Russia and Poland as a consequence of the Second World War.

The process of state-formation among the Germans was deeply influenced by their position as middle bloc in the figuration of these three blocs of peoples. The latinized and Slavonic groups time and again felt threatened by the populous German state. Time and again, the representatives of the nascent German state felt threatened from different sides at the same time. Each group quite ruthlessly exploited every chance to expand that offered itself. The forces within this figuration of states led to a constant breaking off from the centre of areas around the rim, regions which separated from the group of German states and established themselves as independent states. The development of Switzerland and of the Netherlands are early examples, the creation of the German Democratic Republic a late one. The latter testifies to neighbouring states' continuing fear of the hegemonial position held by a German state – a fear that had found new incitement in Hitler's war.

3

The *second* aspect of the process of German state-formation that left its peculiar mark on the German habitus is very closely connected with the first. Up to now, in the development of Europe and indeed of humankind, a central role has been played by elimination contests between groups, whether integrated at the level of tribes or of states. It is possible that today humankind is approaching the end of elimination contests in the form of wars, but one cannot yet be certain of that. Quite often state or tribal social units have been defeated in these violent struggles and have had thenceforward to live with the certain knowledge that they will never again be states or tribes of the highest rank; that probably for all time they will be social units of lower rank. They live in the shadow of their greater past.

It may be tempting to say, 'So what? Who cares whether one's own state is a first-, or second- or third-rate centre of power?' I am not talking here about wishes and ideals. Up till now in the course of human history, it is a proven fact that the members of states and other social units which have lost their claim to a position of highest rank in the elimination struggles of their day often require a long time, even centuries, to come to terms with this changed situation and the consequent lowering of their self-esteem. And perhaps they never manage it. Britain in the recent past is a moving example of the difficulties a great power of the first rank has had in adjusting to its sinking to being a second- or third-class power.

One recurrent reaction in this case is to deny the reality of one's decline. People behave as if nothing has happened. Then, when they can no longer conceal from themselves that their society has lost any chance of a position in the topmost ranks of the hierarchy whether of tribes or states, and thereby has at the same time lost some of its independence, then the habitus of that society's members usually shows signs of depression. A phase of mourning over lost greatness begins. Think of Holland or Sweden. In the seventeenth century, Holland could still defy Britain as a naval power. Until the eighteenth century, Sweden was embroiled in elimination struggles with Russia, and lost. Currently, Europe as a whole is losing the monopoly of world leadership claimed by its member states since about the seventeenth century. How the Europeans will cope with this situation remains to be seen.

For Germans, such a life in the shadow of a greater past is anything but unknown. The medieval German empire and particularly some of the more notable medieval emperors long served as symbols of a Great Germany which had been lost – and thereby secretly also as symbols of an aspiration towards supremacy in Europe. Yet it was the medieval phase of the German state-formation process in particular that contributed significantly to the fact that in Germany this process did not keep pace with the processes of state-formation in other European societies.

In the case of countries like France, England, Sweden or even Russia, the medieval society of feudal estates underwent a continuing process of transformation into states of the more tightly integrated absolute monarchy type, which were usually stronger in power struggles. In Germany, the power balance gradually tilted away from the level of integration represented by the emperor towards that of the regional princes. In contrast to the growing centralization of other European countries, the German (Holy Roman) Empire experienced a decay of central power. The case of the Habsburgs shows very clearly how their power as emperors came to depend more and more on the resources which their own allodium or family power base put at their disposal. In the course of centuries, the medieval imperial state increasingly lost its function. Already by the eighteenth century elimination struggles were flaring up within its boundaries between the kings of Prussia and the Habsburg rulers of Austria. Prussia under Bismarck took them up again in the nineteenth century. Quite clearly, the struggles were about hegemony within the inherited boundaries of the old German empire. When Prussia won the war of 1866, the Austrian rulers dissolved their ties with the German Confederation; they discarded the useless shell of the old German (Holy Roman) Empire and thenceforward identified themselves as emperors of Austria.

In its early stages, the Holy Roman Empire of the German Nation legitimated itself as a kind of reincarnation of the western Roman Empire. During these early phases of state-formation, the German rulers, whether Franks, Saxons or Hohenstaufens, enjoyed a position of pre-eminence in the realm of the Roman church, which more or less encompassed what is known nowadays as 'Europe'. It was an expression of this position that they were the first to fight the battle for power between warriors and priests – a battle between those who had monopolized access to physical violence as a means of power and those who controlled access to the invisible spiritual world and the means of power bound up with it. Possibly the non-German European states' fear of the power potential of the German bloc of people was already then beginning to have its effects. The peculiarities of German state-formation are due in no small part to the practice of the non-German states of hitting out whenever the empire in their midst showed any signs of weakness, usually as a counter-offensive against its claims to hegemony.

At a time when many neighbouring states were being transformed into quite effective centralized and internally pacified monarchies, the loose integration of the German (Holy Roman) Empire proved to be one of the major weaknesses of its structure and an invitation to invasion. Following the internal clashes between reigning Protestant regional princes and the Catholic imperial house, and the smouldering religious wars of the sixteenth century, in the seventeenth century Germany became a major arena of war where the rulers and armies of other Catholic and Protestant countries fought out their battles for supremacy. And the armies of regional magnates fought each other in German territories, too. They all needed quarters, and food from the fields. Insecurity grew. Bands roamed the land, burning and murdering. A great proportion of the German populace became impoverished. Experts reckon that during the Thirty Years War Germany lost a third of its population.

In the context of German development, these thirty years of war represent a catastrophe. They left permanent marks on the German habitus. In the memories of the French, English and Dutch, the seventeenth century is pictured as one of the most brilliant in their development, a period of great cultural creativity and of increasing pacification and civilization of the people. For Germany, however, this century was a time of impoverishment, including cultural impoverishment, and of a growing brutality amongst the people. The peculiar drinking customs of the Germans, which survived as student drinking rules and rituals in the nineteenth and twentieth centuries, had precursors in the seventeenth century (and probably still earlier) and were then to be found at princely courts large and small. They enabled individuals to get drunk and intoxicated in good company. At the same time, they taught the individual to control himself even when heavily inebriated, thus protecting both the drinker himself and his companions from the dangers of losing all inhibitions.

Social customs which encourage heavy drinking and at the same time accustom the drinker to a certain amount of discipline in drunkenness indicate a high degree of unhappiness: apparently, a social plight which is painful but inescapable is made more bearable in this way. It is frequently pointed out that the delayed formation of a modern unitary state is one of the basic characteristics of German development. It is perhaps less clear that the relative weakness of their own state, compared with other states, entails specific crises for the people involved. They suffer from physical danger, begin to doubt their own intrinsic worth, feel humiliated and degraded, and are prone to wishful thinking about the revenge they would like to take on the perpetrators of this situation.

In the later seventeenth century, it was the troops of Louis XIV who fought in battles for supremacy against imperial troops on German soil. The burning of the castle at Heidelberg in this struggle is still remembered. In the nineteenth century, Napoleon's revolutionary armies invaded Germany in his attempt to unify Europe under French overlordship. Again, the weakness of Germany compared with the more effectively centralized neighbouring states was demonstrated. The Queen of Prussia, who fled from the approaching French army, became for a while a symbol of German humiliation. German students formed *Freikorps* or corps of volunteers who harassed Napoleon's occupying troops. One of them, Theodor Körner, sang the praises of 'The Sword at my Side' in a famous poem, at a time when representative poets in France, Britain, Holland and other more stable states seldom took up military themes.

The structural weakness of the German state, which constantly tempted foreign troops from neighbouring countries to invade, produced a reaction among Germans which led to military bearing and warlike actions being highly regarded and often idealized. It is highly typical that a relatively young German regional state, whose ruling house had worked its way up through a series of risky but in the end successful wars, became the standard-bearer of Germany's military catching-up with the rest of Europe. The dynamics of the inter-state elimination struggles pushed the ruling house of Brandenburg-Prussia, when it became the ruling house of Germany, into the thick of the contest for supremacy in Europe. A few years after it had achieved victory in the internal German struggles, it engaged France, the strongest rival on the next highest integration level, in battle and won. The victory in the 1870–1 war could have meant the end of the drive to catch up. But Germany was still at its core an absolute monarchy. The stage of state development meant that dynastic rivalries continued to be decisive factors in relations among the great powers. In this way, the politicians, chosen by the Kaiser, steered unexpectedly towards a new war, without apparently asking themselves if Germany had any chance of winning if America were also to enter it on the side of the Western allies.

For many Germans, the defeat of 1918 was an unexpected, highly traumatic experience. It hit a raw nerve in the national habitus, and was felt to be a return to the time of German weakness, of foreign armies in the country, of a life in the shadow of a greater past. The entire catching-up process in Germany was at stake. Many members of the German middle and upper classes – perhaps the large majority – felt that they could not live with such humiliation. They felt they ought to prepare themselves for the next war, with a better chance of a German victory, even if at first it was not clear how this could be done.

In understanding Hitler's rise to power, it is not unimportant to keep in mind that the groups supporting the Weimar Republic were quite restricted from the very beginning. They included above all the mass of social democratic workers. They also included the diminishing group of liberal middle classes, including many Jews. The larger part of the middle and upper classes stood on the other side. For both young and old members of these traditional ruling classes, communication with the masses remained rather difficult. On their own, they had no chance of starting a broad movement in favour of rescinding the Treaty of Versailles and in the end bringing about a revanchist war. In order to mobilize some sections of the masses, they required a man whose rhetoric and battle strategies were more in accordance with the needs of those groups. Thus, they gave Hitler his chance. But, when it came to the crunch, he outmanoeuvred them.

Again, there beckoned the hope of escaping from the shadow of a greater past. There beckoned the fulfilment of a dream in which, after the first medieval (Holy Roman) Empire of the German Nation, and after the second [*Kaiserreich*] created by Bismarck and shattered in 1918 in defeat in war, a third empire – the Third Reich – would follow under the leadership of Adolf Hitler. This hope was also crushed.

4

However else one may regard the end of Hitler's Reich, it shows very clearly a *third* structural peculiarity of the German state-formation process which was crucial in the development of the German habitus. Its distinctive mark becomes evident when state-formation processes in several countries, and perhaps civilizing processes too, are compared with each other.

Compared with other European societies, for example the French, British or Dutch, the development of the state in Germany shows many more breaks and corresponding discontinuities. A first impression of this difference is gained by looking at the capital cities of the three states of France, Britain and Germany. London was one of the major bases of William the Conqueror. Over a thousand years ago he built a fortress there: almost every English dynasty has left its mark on the Tower of London, where even today the Crown Jewels are kept. This continuity of London as national capital mirrors the continuity of the development of the British state, and the relatively high stability of the development of British culture and civilization which is linked with it. The same holds for Paris as capital of France. There, the medieval cathedral of Notre Dame, and equally the Louvre with the glass pyramid built this century standing in front of it, are symbols of the unbroken, living tradition of the country.

Elsewhere, I have examined with some precision the process of state-formation in France.[2] It is astonishingly continuous and direct. The central rulers of the embryonic French state had to contend with few defeats. By chance the kings of Paris and Orleans were gradually able to extend their areas of rule through successful military operations and favourable marriage alliances, and through their efforts to round them off with borders strategically well chosen for defence. Certainly, the French Revolution represented a break in the continuity of the national tradition. But by this stage, the French language and habitus were, in general, already so stable that, despite the break with the *ancien régime*, in many fields continuity of development remained. This held for the strong centralization of the state apparatus, as well as for cultural production. The court-aristocratic character of the French language was not lost when the French bourgeoisie became the model-setting power group. The similarity between Proust's novels and Saint-Simon's memoirs is difficult to overlook. I know of French poems of the nineteenth century which recall the great poets of the Pléiade in the sixteenth century, but which are nevertheless quite unambiguously creations of their time. The spokesmen of the German classical period seemed to find their Baroque forerunners unbearable. The court civilization of the eighteenth century hardly entered at all into the formation of the German habitus.

Compared with Paris and London, Berlin is a young city. It gained its importance as capital city of the area ruled by the Hohenzollerns. Their victories internally and externally, combined with diplomatic skill, raised the city's importance, especially in the eighteenth century and the nineteenth, when it eventually became the capital of the *Kaiserreich* – the second German empire. A single defeat of the Prussian king in the struggle with his Habsburg rivals could possibly have halted the rise of Berlin forever. During the Seven Years War, Frederick II often came close to this fate. Perhaps it is useful to add that in the period of the Habsburg emperors, Vienna often functioned as capital city of the German empire. Prague also served in this role for a time. Vienna was a city of the German empire long before the Habsburgs held court there.

Walther von der Vogelweide belonged to the court of the Babenbergs there at the end of the twelfth century. All this adds up to a pattern of development full of breaks.

Another example of this peculiarity is that the ways of life and the achievements of the self-governing German cities of the Middle Ages are hardly any longer seen as an important component of national development with which Germans nowadays can identify. Richard Wagner attempted to show these urban merchant strata to better advantage in his *Die Meistersinger*, but the success of his opera did little to change the fact that in the self-image of the Germans the urban culture of the Middle Ages plays a relatively small role today. With the partial exception of the Hanseatic cities, the tradition was broken. The extent of this break can perhaps be better recognized if German development is compared with that of a country in which a similar tradition of self-governing cities has remained alive continuously up to the present day. I am referring to the tradition of the Netherlands.

5

In the seventeenth century, the Dutch cities and the lands belonging to them, after having successfully defended their independence against the claims of the Spanish Habsburgs, left the loose association of Germanic states which the Holy Roman Empire had now become once and for all. Under the leadership of Amsterdam, they formed the only republic in Europe besides Venice and the Swiss cantons. All the other states were absolute monarchies. In the Netherlands, by contrast, despite the self-government of the cities, there developed at the same time an overall government which was primarily responsible for foreign policy, but which was not without influence on the internal affairs of the seven provinces. This republican central organ, the States-General, mostly comprised members of the respective city patriciates.

There were analogous urban merchant strata in Italy, Germany and England. In Germany, however, the rise of the more highly centralized absolute monarchies and of the courtly aristocracy, into which members of the old warrior nobility were being incorporated, by and large put an end during the sixteenth and seventeenth centuries to the beginnings of parliamentary self-government which had existed in the cities before. In Florence, the corresponding middle strata were made subject to the Medicis even earlier. When Charles I of England wanted to use armed force to compel the obedience of non-compliant Members of Parliament, the leaders of London's citizenry mobilized the train-bands (i.e. militia) of the city and, together with the middle-class officers and crews of the merchant ships and the navy,[3] came to the aid of the Members of Parliament. But in Britain – as in Germany and other European monarchies – these top groups of urban merchants remained people of second rank. They were inferior to the princes and the topmost ranks of the court aristocracy, and sometimes also to the provincial aristocracy. Only in Holland, and perhaps in parts of Switzerland, did such groups of merchants form the highest ranks in the social hierarchy. They governed not only their own cities, but also the entire republic, thus continuing the medieval tradition of self-government. Representative group portraits of men of this stratum, probably the most famous example of which is Rembrandt's *The Night Watch*, manifestly testify to their pride and self-confidence.

In the course of their national development, the Dutch city merchants provided an exemplary case for the solution of the problem of how civilians can protect themselves from violent external attack without being dominated by their own military helpers. Their naval captains right up to the admirals were in large part from the middle and petit-bourgeois strata, in accordance with the special nature of maritime warfare, which demanded above all technical expertise. On land, the Dutch fought for and maintained their independence as a Protestant republic mainly with the help of mercenaries, who were commanded by members of a Protestant noble dynasty, the House of Orange. In time, a relationship of trust gradually formed between these noble *Stadholders* and the merchant patricians, who took care of the business of governing in the States-General. It was by no means free from major disputes, but was stable enough to survive such conflicts.

At the Congress of Vienna, the allied monarchs who had thwarted Napoleon's attempts to gain hegemony also decided on a new order in Holland. For Metternich, the abrogation of republics and their replacement with absolute monarchies as a counter-measure to the French Revolution became a leading principle. Holland therefore became a monarchy, with the previous hereditary *Stadholders* as kings. There may have been cases where a ducal palace was turned into a civic town hall, but in Amsterdam the town hall now became the palace – probably the only occurrence of this type in Europe. The centuries-old relationship between the House of Orange, which has remained the Dutch royal family to this day, and all other groups of the population is a sign of the continuity and unbroken nature of Dutch development.

Although the formal change of the Netherlands into an absolute monarchy narrowed the area of responsibility of the States-General, at the same time they retained quite considerable power. People from a patrician and in the broader sense merchant middle-class tradition still played an important role in the country's affairs. There was certainly no lack of attempts to increase the prestige of military attitudes and values, and Dutch colonial rule strengthened these tendencies. In their colonies, the Dutch behaved like all colonial masters: harshly and oppressively. But all that happened far from home, where the uninitiated knew little about it.

As model-setting classes, urban merchant patricians founded a markedly different tradition of behaviour and values from that of a ruling military nobility with leading middle-class groups orientated towards them. The States-General were a type of parliament where members endeavoured to influence each other with words and not with weapons. Thus, the townspeople of cities such as Amsterdam or Utrecht brought their heritage into the development of the Dutch state and into that of the Dutch habitus. The art of governing with the help of negotiation and compromise was passed on from the city to the state. In Germany, on the contrary, military models of command and obedience smothered on various levels the urban models of negotiation and persuasion.

A striking example of this difference in traditions and of the strength with which it affects the social standard of behaviour and feeling over the generations is the relationship between parents and children in the two countries. It is widely said – and observation confirms this – that the Dutch allow their children more freedom than do the Germans. As Germans would put it, Dutch children are naughtier.

In this area, as in others, the highly bourgeois character of Dutch development is expressed in the insistence and intensity with which the equality of human beings has become the watchword of the Dutch. This attitude becomes easier to understand when one remembers that, in other countries in seventeenth-, eighteenth- and nineteenth-century Europe, an upper stratum of bourgeois patricians had to fight constantly to be accepted as equals by the ruling court and military aristocracies. But these very same people were careful about preserving their own high status as patricians, that is, maintaining the inequality between them and strata who, in their own country, were lower than themselves. The paradoxical situation of having an upper class composed of urban merchants has left deep marks in the habitus of the Dutch. Fostering equality is of prime importance. It is apparent, for example, in the relatively tolerant treatment of Catholics and Jews in a predominantly Protestant land. Even nowadays it is evident in the aversion to symbols of human inequality. But in spite of all this, patrician cultivation of inequality, which is not orientated towards military models, has not disappeared. It is kept discreetly alive by the sons and daughters of old patrician houses as a covert or unconscious demand which is justified by their own behaviour, by propriety and reserved friendliness in relations with other people. The German nobility legitimized their claims to superiority mostly through unbroken lines of descent as untainted as possible by burgher elements. In contrast, the tacit claim of Dutch patricians – as is also the case among the British aristocracy – found legitimation in special behaviour. The feeling that 'A Dutchman wouldn't do that', that the claim to a higher social status entails an obligation for the individual, remains strongly pronounced.

6

To this day, it is obvious how very much the habitus of the Dutch – despite their physical relatedness to the Germans – differs from the traditional German habitus. Especially after 1871, military models were incorporated in the latter to a much higher degree. But the penetration of the German middle classes by such models, which are particularly characteristic of Prussian development, did not occur all at once. It was the result of a process – the *fourth* part-process in German state-formation – which deserves attention in this context.

The classical period in German literature and philosophy represents a stage in the social development of Germany during which the antagonism between the middle class and the court nobility ran high. Rejection of military attitudes and values by this middle class was correspondingly sharp. Furthermore, unless they numbered among the middle-class people who served as advisers to one of the many monarchs, great and small, within the German (Holy Roman) Empire, the mass of the middle class was almost totally cut off from access to political and military activity.

The conflicts between the middle class and court-aristocratic strata in Germany in the eighteenth century, which I have discussed at greater length in the first part of *The Civilizing Process*,[4] were an expression of a veritable class conflict. This is sometimes overlooked today, because the idea of such a conflict is largely shaped by the economic conflicts between the bourgeoisie and the working class in the nineteenth and twentieth centuries. In the older case it is less easy to tease out the collision of economic interests, which certainly played a role, from the entire complex of oppositions between nobility and middle classes. In the framework of the absolute monarchies of the eighteenth century, these conflicts were at one and the same time conflicts of a political, civilizational and economic character. Frederick II's contemptuous rejection of contemporary bourgeois literature is well known: Goethe's *Götz von Berlichingen* made him shudder. It is possible that the older, classical Goethe also regarded his youthful work rather disapprovingly. He was one of the few spokesmen of the middle-class elite of his time who succeeded in rising to a ministerial position at the court of a prince – at a fairly small court in a fairly small state. As a rule, representatives of the German classical movement were denied access to key positions in politics. This outsider position is reflected in their idealism.

For a while, the idealistic humanism of the classical movement had a determining influence upon the political endeavours of the German middle-class opposition. On the whole, two streams of middle-class politics can be recognized in the nineteenth and early twentieth centuries, one idealistic-liberal and the other conservative-nationalistic. In the early nineteenth century, one of the main points in the programmes of both was the unification of Germany, putting an end to the plurality of numerous small states. It was of great significance for the development of the middle-class German habitus that these plans failed. The shock caused by this was deepened when one prince, the King of Prussia with his adviser Bismarck, managed to satisfy the craving for a united Germany militarily, through a successful war, when the middle classes had failed to do so by peaceful means. The victory of the German armies over France was at the same time a victory of the German nobility over the German middle class.

The Hohenzollern state had all the hallmarks of a military state which had risen through successful wars. Its leading men were quite open to the necessity of increasing industrialization and, in the broader sense, of growing modernization. But the bourgeois industrialists and owners of capital did not form the ruling, the upper stratum of the country. The position of the military and bureaucratic nobility as the highest-ranking and most powerful stratum of the society was not only preserved, but also strengthened by the victory of 1871. A good part, though not all, of the middle class adapted relatively quickly to these conditions. They fitted into the social order of the *Kaiserreich* as representatives of a second-rank class, as subordinates. The family of Max and Alfred Weber proves that the liberal middle-class tradition had not disappeared, but it should not be forgotten that, in the years before 1914, it was difficult to imagine what sort of regime could replace the imperial one. At that stage, wide circles of the German middle class adjusted to the military state and adopted its models and norms.

A particular variety of middle class thus came on to the scene: bourgeois people who adopted the lifestyle and norms of the military nobility as their own. This was associated with a clear distancing from the ideals of the German classical period. The failure of their own class's efforts to realize their ideal of uniting Germany, and the experience of this having been achieved under the leadership of the military nobility, led to an outcome which can perhaps be described as the capitulation of broad circles of the middle class to the aristocracy. They now turned decisively from classical bourgeois idealism to the apparent realism of power. This is also a testament to the discontinuous nature of German development: a change in habitus which can be very precisely assigned to a specific phase in the development of the state. In this case the break was especially significant, because the aristocratic models adopted were often misinterpreted. Noble officers were usually subject to the constraint of a fairly deeply imprinted civilizing inheritance. The sense of how far one could go in applying aristocratic models in practice was quite often lost in their appropriation by middle-class groups. They came to support the boundless use of power and violence.

I have treated the expansion of military models into parts of the German middle class somewhat more precisely because I believe that National Socialism and the decivilizing spurt which it embodied cannot be completely understood without reference to this context. A simple example of the appropriation and then coarsening of aristocratic models is the requirement that every 'Aryan' had to prove him- or herself as such through a specific number of 'Aryan' ancestors. Above all, however, the unbridled resort to acts of violence as the only realistic and decisive vehicle of politics, which was at the centre of Hitler's doctrine and the strategy used already in his rise to power, can be explained only against this background.

7

Hitler's end meant yet another break in the development of Germany. Two heavy defeats certainly do not remain without consequences. It shows the resilience of the Germans that they emerged from these shocks as a viable and capable nation. It can only be hoped that their future development will be less plagued by breaks and discontinuities than it has been up to now. One can only wish Germany a more linear and continuous pattern of development in the future.

Let us step back a little and examine the German scene from a greater distance. There is Germany. Two lost wars have not stamped the Germans as a declining, humiliated and despised group of people. Instead, we find an affluent, even flourishing country, which on the whole enjoys the respect of the other states of the world, not least the enemies of yesterday. Many of them are now allies of West Germany, on the one hand, or East Germany, on the other. Perhaps people do not often think about this; but it certainly says a great deal for the relatively high standard of civilization of contemporary humankind that, after two bitter and destructive wars which Germany fought – partly with a claim to natural, racially determined superiority – West Germany at least can lead a fairly normal existence as a well-off industrial state. This fact is symptomatic of the high global interdependence of nations. It was in the interests of the victors to help the half-destroyed western regions on to their feet again. But it does not make their help any the less astounding and remarkable that, directly after the Nazi threat had disappeared, it was in their own interests not to abandon the defeated people to poverty and hunger. I remember a statement by a leading National Socialist in a phase during the last war when the allied troops were steadily advancing from both the West and the East; I probably read it in Chatham House in London where, right up to 1945, Nationalist Socialist newspapers were put out for the use of members, often on the day of publication. Whether it was by Goebbels or Goering or one of the others, the statement remains in my memory: 'If once more we lose this war, it will be the end of Germany.' It was not the end.

But coming to grips psychologically with what happened is not easy for many Germans. Generations come and go. They have to struggle again and again with the fact that the we-image of the Germans is soiled by the memory of the excesses perpetrated by the Nazis, and that others, and perhaps even their own consciences, blame them for what Hitler and his followers did. Perhaps one should draw from this experience the conclusion that the perception of oneself as a completely independent individual is false. One is always a member of groups, whether one wants to be or not. The language one speaks is a communal language. One is jointly responsible, one is made to be jointly responsible, for the actions of the group. For centuries, churches have made my Jewish ancestors responsible for the crucifixion of Jesus. It is quite useful to ask oneself whether one does not have disparaging images of other groups in one's own head and whether, when one meets individual members of these groups, one does not involuntarily seek proof that the stereotyped group picture in one's head is correct.

Already in the past, due to the brokenness of German development, there was great uncertainty about the value and meaning of being a German man or woman. Nowadays, it is greater than ever. The difficulty is exacerbated because this problem is seldom spoken of in public. The problem of national pride remains undiscussed. The memory of the distorted form of national pride prevalent under the National Socialist regime has made this topic unmentionable. I think one should not hesitate to grasp the nettle. There are indeed forms of national pride which are dangerous and insulting. But the question is not whether one thinks national pride is a good or a bad thing. The fact is that it exists. If one looks around disinterestedly, it is evident that people in all states in the world have to come to terms with the problem of national pride; and people at the tribal (or pre-state) stage of development have to come to terms with tribal pride. For example, so humiliated have the Argentinians been over the Falklands that no Argentinian politician can dare assert that Argentina has a rewarding future to look forward to, even if its statesmen are not in a position to rectify either by military or peaceful means the lost war over the control of the Falkland Islands and their English-speaking inhabitants. Another vivid example of national pride is seen in the United States, where there has been an astounding degree of success up till now in transforming immigrants from all over the world into Americans. Service in the forces, the cult of the American flag, teaching programmes in schools – a wide variety of institutions contribute to immigrant outsider groups learning over the generations to identify with the American nation and with the national pride of the Americans.

Even in the most powerful countries, national pride is and remains a sore spot in the personality structure of the people concerned. This is particularly true of countries which have sunk in the course of time from a higher to a lower position within the pyramid of states. I have already spoken about this. Even Britain and France have to contend today with problems of national pride. In Holland, once a mighty maritime power, people have to a large extent become accustomed to the loss of power, but a slightly depressive note, a scarcely verbalized sorrow about their more glorious past, pervades their national habitus in many ways. They love their nation. They are proud of the achievements of Dutch people from Rembrandt to Van Gogh. The twinges of conscience left by the era of Dutch colonial rule are not too bad. But they nevertheless remark with a touch of self-irony, 'Well, we are just one of the smaller nations now.'

The Danes are an illuminating example of a small nation which has coped with the problem of national pride rather well. After the defeat in the war of 1864 with Germany, and the enforced relinquishing of Schleswig-Holstein to Austria and Prussia, the existence of Denmark was seriously threatened.[5] A number of reforms were necessary to keep the nation alive. Today, the Danes have regained their equilibrium. They think that they are a nice nation, that it is pleasant to be a Dane. Particularly after the Second World War, using the familiar form of 'you' instead of the formal form became widespread amongst the population: it was an expression of the intimacy within the Danish nation and its relative contentedness with itself. Once when I was walking with a Danish acquaintance, we encountered a Danish couple who were unknown to him. A small shriek by the woman, a short exchange of words in Danish, indicated to me that something had happened. I asked, and was told that she had exclaimed, 'He is a Dane and uses the formal "you" with me.'

8

The fortunes of a nation become crystallized in institutions which are responsible for ensuring that the most different people of a society acquire the same characteristics, possess the same national habitus. The common language is an immediate example. But there are many others.

In the first chapter of this book, I examine the duel, which was particularly strikingly developed in Germany, as a prime example of the habitus-shaping influence of institutions. The duel is an institution common to Europe as a whole which goes back to the international culture of the nobles. In other countries it increasingly lost its significance with the rise of the middle class. But in Germany the duel developed in an almost opposite direction. With the adoption of aristocratic models in middle-class circles after 1871, and possibly already before then, duelling became a potent and widespread institution even among non-aristocratic students. Two of my senior schoolteachers had duelling scars on their faces. I have chosen the duel as a symbol of a specific cultural syndrome. It is a symbol of a particular human attitude, a socially regulated fostering of violence. Students and officers were the main exponents of the duelling culture. They were accustomed to a strictly hierarchical order, and hence to an emphasis on inequality between people. If one asks how Hitler was possible, one cannot help concluding that the spread of socially sanctioned models of violence and of social inequality are among the prerequisites of his advent.

From this example it can perhaps be seen that the present work opens a wide area of research which has hitherto been largely evaded. The central question is how the fortunes of a nation over the centuries become sedimented into the habitus of its individual members. Sociologists face a task here which distantly recalls the task which Freud tackled. He attempted to show the connection between the outcome of the conflict-ridden channelling of drives in a person's development and his or her resulting habitus. But there are also analogous connections between a people's long-term fortunes and experiences and their social habitus at any subsequent time. At this layer of the personality structure – let us for the time being call it the 'we-layer' – there are often complex symptoms of disturbance at work which are scarcely less in strength and in capacity to cause suffering than the individual neuroses. In both cases it is a matter of bringing back into consciousness, quite often in the face of strong resistance, things which have been forgotten. In the one as in the other, such an undertaking requires a certain self-distancing, and may, if successful, contribute to the loosening of rigid models of behaviour.

It is not yet common practice today to link the current social and national habitus of a nation to its so-called 'history', and especially to the state-formation process it has experienced. Many people seem to have the unspoken opinion that 'What happened in the twelfth, fifteenth or eighteenth centuries is past – what has it got to do with me?' In reality, though, the contemporary problems of a group are crucially influenced by their earlier fortunes, by their beginningless development. This points to one of the tasks sociology has not yet coped with – and at the same time to a method which can help a nation in coming to terms with its past. One of the functions of this book is to pave the way intellectually and practically in handling such problems. Perhaps it may have a cathartic effect if the relationship between past and present is seen in this way, and people may, through understanding their social development, find a new understanding of themselves.

9

It is an open question whether and to what extent the Germans have digested their own past, and particularly the experiences of the Hitler era. It is not easy to distance oneself from these events. One often has the impression that the Hitler boil has not yet burst. It throbs, but the pus does not come out. The following studies are primarily concerned with problems of the German past. Perhaps they may be of some help in coming to terms with Hitler's legacy. But a people's past also points forward: knowledge about it can be of direct use in forging a common future.

Hitler was still completely tied up in the problems of the old Europe and its battles for supremacy. With dogged determination, he sought to establish Germany's hegemony in Europe at a time when the hegemony of Europe over the rest of the world was obviously coming to an end. Europe was now increasingly exposed to the pressure of competition from other regions of the world. Had Hitler achieved his goal, then the suppression of neighbouring nations by Germany, as well as their inevitable attempts to liberate themselves, would have considerably reduced Europe's power. Today, this power can manifest itself fully because Europe is an association of free nations. But it is not easy to strike a balance between solidarity and competition in the relationships of the European nations with each other as well as with the other nations of the world. It is clear that humankind as a whole is now threatened by the destruction of the environment and the possibility of atomic wars. In this way, vital issues are raised which go far beyond the problem of Hitler.

The problem of the past is important. In many respects, it is still completely unsolved. But over and above this, today we are standing at a turning point when many of the problems, including those of habitus, are losing their relevance, and new tasks for which there are no historical parallels are appearing on all sides.

I
Civilization and Informalization

A Changes in European Standards of Behaviour in the Twentieth Century

1

It is not possible adequately to discuss changes in standards of behaviour which are observable in the twentieth century in European societies in general, and in Germany in particular, without a preparatory examination of certain structural changes in society as a whole that occurred in the same period. Of these, I would like to mention briefly five aspects which seem to me to be relevant to what I have to say about behavioural changes.

1 In the twentieth century, the gross national product of most European countries has increased to an extent and at a rate which is almost unique. The astonishing thrust in this direction began slowly around the middle of the eighteenth century, and accelerated, with fluctuations, in the twentieth century, especially after the Second World War. Thus, for example, the gross national product in the countries of the European Economic Community grew at an average annual rate of between 3 and 4 per cent per head of the population in the years between

Section A outlines the questions which gave rise to the conceptualization in Section B of the *satisfaktionsfähige Gesellschaft* under the second German empire or *Kaiserreich*. [German editor's note]

1951 and 1976, which works out as an increase of approximately 100 per cent. This rate has been exceeded perhaps only by states in the early phase of industrialization, such as Britain in the nineteenth century, or Russia in the twentieth. But in countries in these earlier phases of industrialization, the growth was used mainly for capital investment, whereas at the later stage it went mostly into improving living standards.[1]

In these societies, the solution of old problems has allowed new problems to surface. In them, even the poorer parts of the population are relatively well safeguarded against hunger and malnutrition; to a similarly large extent all men and women have been freed from heavy manual labour; a degree of physical security unprecedented in the history of humankind has been achieved (within state boundaries, although wars between states remain a threat); labour-saving devices are uniquely abundant, and there is a growing reduction in working hours. All this has brought new human problems to light, problems arising out of people's life together in society which are hidden in less affluent societies by the harshness of daily toil, by the shortness of life, and also by the greater gap between the masses of poor people and the minority of the affluent and rich. Some of these new problems, characteristic of the later phase of industrialization with its accent on growing consumer markets, are discussed below.

2   A second aspect of the structural changes in society as a whole in the twentieth century which may contribute to understanding the simultaneous changes in the code of behaviour and feeling is the series of emancipatory movements the century has witnessed. These movements are about changing balances of power between established and outsider groups of the most diverse kinds. During the course of them the latter become stronger and the former weaker in power. These emancipatory movements have, in one particular case, led to a reversal of the power-ratio in favour of the upwardly mobile outsider group which went so far that the former monopoly group ceased to play any role as an independent power factor in the interplay of forces within its own society. I am referring to the relationship of the middle class to the aristocracy. The course of development in Germany can serve as an example.

Let us not forget that in the first eighteen years of the twentieth century the Kaiser and his court were still the centre of the German establishment. Members of the middle class – and with some hesitation the working class – were first really granted access to the topmost offices of the state and civil service only in the Weimar Republic.[2] The nobility could now bring their weight to bear only as allies of middle-class groups. Nevertheless, the highest military and diplomatic positions still remained largely in the hands of the aristocracy. It was the leaders of the National Socialist experiment who really put an end to this remnant of the old supremacy as well, and thus played the final stroke, perhaps without intending to, in the centuries-long class struggle between aristocracy and middle class which can be traced far back into the Middle Ages. This then is the one great emancipatory movement of the twentieth century where the rise of a class which was once an outsider group led to the disappearance, to all intents and purposes, of the previous establishment. For the continuity as well as for the transformation of the code of behaviour this outcome was of major significance.

3   In the case of all other emancipation movements in the twentieth century which have similarly had consequences of some significance for the form of social life, not least for people's behaviour and feelings in their dealings with each other, the established groups did not disappear; rather the power gradient between stronger and weaker groups decreased. I shall list only a few examples. During the twentieth century, the power differential between the following groups has lessened:

 - in the relationship between men and women;
 - in the relationship between parents and children, or, put more generally, in the relationship between the older and younger generations;
 - in the relationship between the European societies and their former colonies, and indeed the rest of the world;
 - in the relationship between rulers and ruled – with qualifications.

When viewed in this summary way, the strength of these movements for the emancipation of formerly weak outsider groups is certainly astonishing. I shall not presume to explain this structural change here. Nevertheless, two of its consequences must be mentioned.

4   A change in the power relations of so many diverse groups inevitably brings with it a widespread feeling of uncertainty to many people who are caught up in the turmoil of change. The conventional code governing behaviour between groups, which was attuned to a more strictly hierarchical order, no longer corresponds to the actual relationships of their members. It will only be possible for another code of

behaviour to emerge gradually through many experiments. All in all, this is a century of increasing *status uncertainty*. With such a transformation of power relations, the problem of social identity also becomes much more explicit than it is in a society where the pace of change has not become so accelerated. With increasing status insecurity and an increasing search for identity, worries grow. There is no doubt that the twentieth century is an unsettling century, and not only because of the two World Wars.

5   The sources of this disquietude, which have played an increasing role, especially in the second half of the twentieth century, include the fact that the mainly unplanned decrease in the power-ratios between all the groups mentioned above has brought the extent of these power-ratios, and the problem they pose to us, to many people's conscious attention for the very first time. I should like to demonstrate this with a single example.

We are nowadays more strongly than ever aware that an enormously large part of humanity live their entire lives on the verge of starvation, that in fact there are always and in many places people dying of hunger. This is most certainly not a new problem. With few exceptions, famine is a constantly recurring feature of human societies. But it is a peculiarity of our times that poverty and high mortality rates are no longer taken for granted as a God-given condition of human life. Many members of richer countries feel it to be almost a duty to do something about the misery of other human groups. To avoid any misunderstanding on this point, let it be said that in actual fact relatively little is done. But conscience-formation has changed in the course of the twentieth century. The feeling of responsibility which people have for each other is certainly minimal, looked at in absolute terms, but compared with before it has increased.

I am not saying all this in order to express any judgement about what is good or bad, but simply presenting a factual observation: hand in hand with the small shifts in power to the disadvantage of former established groups, and to the advantage of former outsider groups, goes a change in conscience-formation for both.

2

As will perhaps be evident, I am not attempting to look at the behaviour of people in isolation, as currently prevailing theories of behaviour do.

The changes in codes of behaviour with which I am going to deal are inseparably entwined with massive structural changes in the societies in question. Conventional subject compartmentalizations which assign to psychologists the examination of human behaviour and to political scientists the examination of power relations seem to me for that reason not to be quite in accordance with the observable facts. Let us look for instance at the behaviour of people in their relationship to each other as ruler and ruled, as illustrated in an eighteenth-century source.

In August 1778, Mozart's father, who had long been the Deputy *Kapellmeister* (or deputy director of music) at the Salzburg court, directed an appeal to his archbishop for promotion to the post of *Kapellmeister*, which had become vacant on the death of the previous incumbent. It ran as follows:

Your Most Gracious Highness!
Most Worthy Prince of the Holy Roman Empire!
Most Gracious Prince of the Realm and Lord Lord!
I prostrate myself most humbly at Your feet, Your Most Gracious Highness, and seeing that *Kapellmeister* Lolli has passed over into eternity, that he drew only the salary of a Deputy *Kapellmeister*, that, as Your Most Gracious Highness is aware, I have been serving this worthy Archbishopric for thirty-eight years, and that since the year 1763, that is, for fifteen years, I have been performing and still perform without reproach as Deputy *Kapellmeister* most of the services required, and indeed nearly all of them, I humbly beseech Your Most Gracious Highness to allow me to recommend myself to you and to remain with the deepest homage
the most humble and obedient servant of
Your Most Gracious Highness,
Most Gracious Prince of the Realm,
and Lord Lord
Leopold Mozart[3]

Mozart himself used a similar, if not quite so servile, style when he directed a petition to his Salzburg lord and master. He also addressed him as 'Imperial Prince, Most Gracious Prince of the Realm', and, to our ears especially odd-sounding, as 'Lord Lord'. How should one describe this language and the type of behaviour it expresses: as 'formalism', as 'formalistic' or as 'formal'? In whichever case, the ceremonial which the lower-ranking person is forced to follow in his dealings with the higher-ranking person when approaching him as petitioner reflects the power gradient. In his dealings with those of higher rank, the lower-ranking person must constantly display his own low position, his submission to higher-ranking people, by observing a formal ritual.

But this strict formalization of behaviour certainly did not extend to every aspect of people's life in those times. Indeed, if a ritual formality exceeding any formality in the multi-party industrial societies of today is evident in the above quotation, there was nevertheless at the same time in other areas of the same society a code of behaviour and feeling which far exceeded our own in *in*formality, if one may so express it. Thus, Mozart suggests to his father that he would like to have made in his name a target for the crossbow-shooting competition in Salzburg on which the instructions made socially acceptable by Goethe's *Götz von Berlichingen* were illustrated.[4] Mozart was able to call a spade a spade – unlike the author of an academic text today. What emerges here is not a personal shortcoming of Mozart's,[5] but rather a different code of convivial-social behaviour and feeling in the social group to which he belonged. Animalic human functions, which today especially in mixed company of men and women can be talked about at most marginally, in passing, and with decently lowered voices, could, in Mozart's circle, still be referred to very directly. These references were regarded as mild violations of taboo, deliberately used by both men and women to increase the convivial hilarity; and in doing so, they could use expressions which today would cause feelings of unease, shame and embarrassment not only in mixed company, but even in men-only groups.

The society of Mozart's time was thus characterized simultaneously by a formality in contact between people of socially higher and lower standing which in its ceremonial severity far exceeded any corresponding formality of our times, and an informality within one's own group which likewise far exceeded what is now possible in social intercourse with people of relatively equal status. This aspect of the civilizing process deserves to be more precisely formulated. In all more differentiated societies, as in many simpler ones, there are categories of social situation in which the social code demands of members raised in the society that they behave in formal ways – or, to use a noun, it demands *formality* of behaviour; and there are other categories of social situation where, according to the code, informal behaviour – that is, a more or less high degree of *informality* – is appropriate. In order to examine this aspect of civilization, a clear conceptual means of orientation is required. What must be worked out sociologically is, to put it in a nutshell, the *formality–informality span* of a society. This relates to the operation of both formal and informal behaviour-regulation in a society at the same time; or, to express it differently, it concerns the *synchronic* gradient between formality and informality. This is different from the successive informalization gradients observed in the course of social development, the *diachronic gradient of informalization.*

Everyone in present-day societies ought to be more or less familiar with what I mean by this; for everyone has been invited somewhere as a guest where things are a bit stiff – all those present are reticent, extremely polite and consider carefully every word they speak. Then we go home, where we can be more relaxed, can let ourselves go a bit more. The same people are, so to speak, flexed between formal and informal areas of social life. Currently, the formality-informality span in many of the more advanced industrial states is relatively small, and among people of the younger generations perhaps smaller than ever before. But people are not fully conscious of this; they are unable to see themselves as it were in the mirror of earlier phases of society, or of other contemporary societies corresponding in structure to an earlier phase of their own society. The small example I gave from the time of Mozart may help in this. It shows not only that there is a synchronic gradient in the parameter of formality, but also that it can change, and in fact has changed. Perhaps the stages of this change have not totally disappeared from the memory of the living.

At the time of the great European monarchies, the Habsburgs, Hohenzollerns and Romanovs before the First World War, the gradient between formality and informality was no longer quite as steep as in the eighteenth century, but it was still much steeper than during the Weimar Republic. It increased again under the Nazis, and decreased further in the post-war years. Arising from that, it seems to me as well that there is a noticeable difference between the older generations, who lived a substantial part of their lives before the war, and the younger generations who were born only after the war. The latter have been endeavouring quite consciously to break down the formality of behaviour still further. There is possibly less awareness of the fact that at the same time the scope for informality in the key areas of informal behaviour has decreased. The tendency – partly unintended, partly intended – is towards the same behaviour in all situations. The experiments with extreme degrees of informality made by the younger generations among themselves perhaps obscure the difficulty which stands in the way of efforts to achieve total absence of formality and norms.

The relaxation of previously formal behaviour extends, however, far beyond the circles of younger people.[6] Examples are obvious. For instance many of the previously customary polite set phrases have disappeared from routine letters. Where one formerly used in German '*Mit vorzüglicher Hochachtung Ihr sehr ergebener . . .*' ['With deep respect your most obedient servant . . .'], the simple '*Mit freundlichen Grüßen*' ['With friendly greetings'], which is similar to the British 'Yours sincerely' and the American 'Yours truly', has become more commonplace. Even in letters to high officials, to ministers and presidents, or kings and queens, Mozart's 'I throw myself most respectfully at your feet' would be unthinkable – but, *mutatis mutandis,* so also would be the expression 'Your Majesty's most humble servant', which was still used at any rate in correspondence with Wilhelm II. Or consider the strictness of the ritual around the frock coat and top hat in Wilhelmine society, and the gradients which led from it to the ritualized male boisterousness of the officers' and students' club nights, or the witty joviality of the regulars in the pub. This shows at a glance how much greater a polarization between formal and informal behaviour there still was in the reign of the Kaiser, the *Kaiserzeit,* at the beginning of this century, and how it has been reduced by degrees – allowing for the relapse of the Hitler era. At the same time, it is evident that the process of functional democratization – the thrust towards diminishing the power gradient between rulers and ruled, between the entire state establishment and the great mass of outsiders – had something to do with this transformation in the code of behaviour.

Let it be noted in passing that the synchronic formality-informality gradient can also have a quite different structure in different nations in a particular period. There is, for instance, a distinct difference between Britain and Germany in this regard. In Germany, the span between formality and informality is apparently wider, formal behaviour in Germany being far more ostentatious than in Britain. However, the chance of informally letting oneself go is also comparatively greater – as long as like is being compared with like, and in particular class with class. The formal handshaking with the entire group present which is customary in Germany on both arriving at and leaving a party, has been replaced in Britain by a more casual and rather unobtrusive, though none the less well established, ritual of nodding the head and disappearing with relatively little leave-taking. This is just an illustration.

It should thus be noted that the framework of norms and controls, the code or canon of behaviour and feeling in our societies (and perhaps in all societies), is not a unified whole. In every society there is a specific gradient between relative formality and relative informality which can be ascertained with great accuracy and which can become steeper or less steep. The structure of this gradient changes in the course of the development of a state-society. Its development in a specific direction is an aspect of the civilizing process.

3

I shall avoid going into more detail at this point on the nature and general direction of civilizing processes. A few brief notes and comments should be enough to pave the way for the discussion of the peculiar spurt of informalization, a smaller wave of which could be observed after the First World War, and a larger and stronger wave after the Second. These comments seem to me to be particularly necessary in order to remove a difficulty standing in the way of explaining this process. From time to time, it has been claimed that the key to my theory of civilization can be found in a single sentence from a late medieval book of etiquette: loosely paraphrased, it runs 'Things that were once permitted are now forbidden.'[7] The question then understandably arises immediately of whether the direction of change has not been reversed since the 1930s, and whether we should not rather say nowadays, 'Things that were once forbidden are now permitted.' And if that were so, would that not mean that we were living in a time of regression in civilization, or rebarbarization?[8] This question, however, is I think based on an inadequate understanding of the theory of civilizing processes.

If one wanted to try to reduce the key problem of any civilizing process to its simplest formula, then it could be said to be the problem of how people can manage to satisfy their elementary animalic needs in their life together, without reciprocally destroying, frustrating, demeaning or in other ways harming each other time and time again in their search for this satisfaction – in other words, without fulfilment of the elementary needs of one person or group of people being achieved at the cost of those of another person or group. At earlier levels of social development, people took their own way of life, their own social conventions, entirely for granted. Only very late in the development of humanity, and particularly in our own times when people became increasingly conscious that patterns of human life are highly diverse and changeable, did this become a problem. Only then, moreover, could people attempt to explain and examine at a higher level of reflection the unplanned changes in these social patterns and to try to plan future long-term changes.

Central to my approach to the problems of humanity, and accordingly to the problem of civilization, is an examination of the constraints to which people are exposed. Roughly speaking, four types can be distinguished:

1   The constraints imposed on people by the characteristics of their animal nature. The imperatives of hunger or the sexual drive are the most obvious examples of this sort of constraint. But the constraints of ageing, being old and dying, of longing for affection and love, or even the constraints of hatred and enmity, and many more that arise in people spontaneously, equally belong to this category.

2   The constraints arising from dependence upon non-human natural circumstances, especially the constraint imposed by the need to seek food, or the need for protection from the harshness of the weather, to name only two.

3   The constraints which people exercise over each other in the course of their social lives. These are often conceptualized as 'social constraints'. But it is useful to be clear that everything we describe as social constraints, or possibly as economic constraints, are constraints which people exercise over each other because of their interdependence. I will call them 'external constraints' for the moment, but they are literally 'constraints by other people' [*Fremdzwänge*]. Such external constraints are to be found in every two- or three-person relationship. Every person who lives together with others, who is dependent on others – and we all are – is subject to these constraints because of this very dependence. But we are also subjected to external constraints when we live with 50 million people; for example, we have to pay taxes.

4   From those constraints based on the animal nature of humans, and in particular on the nature of their drives, a second type of individual constraint is to be distinguished, which we denote by such concepts as 'self-control' [*Selbstzwänge*]. Even what we call 'reason' is, among other things, an apparatus for self-control, as is 'conscience'. I term this type of constraint 'self-constraints'. It differs from the first category of constraints derived from natural drives, because we are endowed bio-logically with only a potential for the acquisition of self-constraint. When this potential is not actualized through learning and experience, then it remains latent. The degree and pattern of its activation depend on the society in which a person grows up, and they change in specific ways in the continuing process of human development.

The theory of civilizing processes fits in at this point. The constellation of constraints, that is the interplay between the four types, changes. The elementary constraints of human nature – the first category – are the same with relatively few variations at all phases of human development, and are thus the same for all branches of our species *Homo sapiens.* However, the patterns of self-constraints which develop as a result of differing experiences are highly dissimilar. This holds in particular for the relationship between external and self-constraints in societies at different stages of development, and to a lesser extent also in different societies at the same stage.

As far as I know, there is no human society in which the restraint of people's elementary animal impulses rests only on external constraint – that is, on the fear of others or on the pressure of others. In all the human societies that we know, a pattern of self-constraints is formed through external constraints in early childhood upbringing. But in simpler societies, and in fact in agrarian societies throughout the world, the apparatus of self-control is relatively weak and, if I may for once so phrase it, full of holes compared with that developed in highly differentiated, and especially in multi-party, industrial states. This means that for self-restraint, members of the former kinds of society require a very great deal of reinforcement through the fear created and pressure exerted by others. The pressure can come from other people, such as a chief, or from imaginary figures such as ancestors, ghosts or deities. Whatever the form, in this case a very considerable external constraint is required to strengthen the framework of people's self-constraint which is necessary for their own integrity and indeed for their survival as persons – and for the integrity and survival of the people with whom they have to live.

The hallmark of civilizing processes, as my researches have revealed, is a change in the relation between external social constraints and individual self-constraints. Although this is just one of several criteria, I shall concentrate on it here since it permits relatively simple access to the far from simple problems of the contemporary trend towards informalization.

Let us consider a child who is often hit by its angry father whenever, in his view, it has been naughty. Such a child will learn to avoid disapproved behaviour out of fear of its father. But its self-constraint apparatus will in this respect develop only partially. In order to be able to restrain itself, it remains dependent on others' threats. Its capacity to restrain itself could develop more strongly if the father were to make the child avoid the disapproved behaviour of its own accord, through persuasion, reasoning and signs of caring. But the child who is often hit does not learn to restrain itself independently of an external constraint, without the threat of paternal punishment, and is accordingly also to a great extent at the mercy of its own impulses of hatred and hostility. It is highly probable that such a child will in turn become a beater, taking the father as a model without knowing it.

This example can be carried over to political systems without difficulty. Members of a state-society which has long been absolutist – ruled from above in the form of what we would call a police state – develop quite analogous personality structures, in which their ability to exercise self-constraint remains dependent on an external constraint, on a strong force which threatens them with punishment from outside. A non-absolutist, multi-party regime requires a far stronger and firmer apparatus of self-constraint. It corresponds to the model of upbringing which builds up such an apparatus in individual people, not through the use of the stick nor through the threat of punishment but rather through persuasion and conviction. This is one of the reasons why – even though participation and opinion-formation by the ruled is still quite severely limited in today's type of multi-party rule – the transition from an absolutist, dictatorial regime (or from a regime of chiefs) to a multi-party regime is so arduous. In terms of personality structure, even this small claim on opinion-formation and self-control by each voter is enormously difficult for people who have lived under a system of chiefs or despots; this holds especially for the emotionally controlled election campaign and the curbing of passions it demands. These difficulties are so great that it usually takes three, four or even five generations for personality structures to adapt successfully to the non-violent form of party contest.

Put briefly, in the course of a civilizing process the self-constraint apparatus becomes stronger relative to external constraints. In addition, it becomes more even and all-embracing. An example of the latter is that in societies with very unequal power ratios a self-control apparatus develops for the establishment – those in power, those higher in rank – mostly with regard to their equals. In dealing with those lower down the social scale, they do not need to restrain themselves, they can 'let themselves go'. Andreas Capellanus, who wrote about the rules of behaviour between men and women in the twelfth century, described in detail how a nobleman should conduct himself with a woman of higher rank, one of equal rank and also with a 'plebeian' woman. When he comes to speak of behaviour towards a peasant girl, he as good as says,

'You can do what you want.'[9] A lady of the court in the eighteenth century allows her footman to wait on her while she is bathing: for her, he is not a man, not a person in front of whom she needs feel shame in her nakedness.[10] Compared with these earlier societies, in ours an all-embracing feeling of shame is cultivated. Social differences are certainly still fairly great, but in the course of the process of democratization, the power differentials have lessened. Correspondingly, we have had to develop a relatively high degree of self-restraint in dealings with *all* people, including social subordinates.

4

Now let me turn to the current spurt of informalization which is central to these reflections. I would like to limit myself to two areas of relationships in which it can be observed particularly clearly: the relationship between men and women, and between older and younger generations.

How the thrust towards informalization is manifested in the relationship between men and women can perhaps best be demonstrated by comparing the code governing relations between the sexes which was prevalent amongst students in Germany before the First World War with that which is developing today. Before the First World War the majority of German students came from the well-to-do middle classes. They generally belonged to a student society, often a fighting fraternity, were entitled to give and demand satisfaction and thus trained to duel. For them, there was a clear distinction between two types of women. On the one hand, there were women from the same social class – women one could marry. They were absolutely untouchable. The conventions of good society applied to them: one bowed, kissed their hand, danced with them in the prescribed way, kissed them when they allowed it, called, when necessary, on the parents – in short, contact with them was ruled by a quite well-established, strictly formalized code of behaviour. On the other hand, there were girls of another social class, either prostitutes in a brothel or girls from the lower middle or working class, with whom one could have an affair.

It can be seen how very much things have changed in this field. Prostitution and affairs with lower-class girls have, as far as I know, as good as disappeared completely from the horizons of the students. Rituals such as addressing a young woman as '*Gnädiges Fräulein*' ['gracious young lady'], and even the distancing use of '*Sie*' [the formal 'you'] have become obsolete in relations between the sexes at universities, and certainly not just there. Men and women students, like other members of the same age group, use '*du*' [the informal form of 'you'] to each other as a matter of course, even from the very beginning when they are not previously acquainted with each other at all.

This provides a simple example of an informalizing trend; but it poses obvious problems. In the generations of the early twentieth century about which we were speaking, there were pretty precisely fixed court-ship rituals between young men and women. The young student frater-nity member, the 'crass fox',[11] in the unlikely event of not having been taught these rules at home, would very soon have been taught the rules of good behaviour towards the young ladies of the social circle in which the fraternity moved and towards other marriageable young girls by his older fraternity 'patron', just as he would have been taught the ceremon-ials of the pub or of duelling. All this, although it is certainly part of German history, is apparently not considered worth studying by the writers of conventional history. For sociologists, by contrast, it is of the greatest significance, but not to denigrate or praise the past, nor to set up a 'cultural history' approach in opposition to 'political history' – such categories are no longer useful. How could one separate social changes in universities from changes in the state-societies of which they form part? The task at hand is first to make the broad outline of behavioural changes comprehensible, and, through comparison with the structures of an earlier phase, to shed new light on what is problematic about the current phase.

Clearly the emancipation of a previously less powerful group, women, opened the universities to girls as people with approximately the same rights. In this situation, the very peculiar conventional ritual which regulated relationships between men and women in European societies lost a great deal of its function. It is now observed only in very rudimentary form. But this ritual did give men and women a certain amount of support in their relationships with each other. It served as an external constraint, on to which a person with a relatively weak apparatus of self-constraint could cling. The ceremonial of student associations in many ways had the same function. Through it, members grew accustomed to an externally controlled discipline, exactly as in the military.

Emancipation from this socially inherited apparatus of external con-straint, which in some but not all cases took the form of a deliberate revolt, means that young people at university (and of course outside) find themselves faced with a predicament in which society now offers little guidance. In the process of attracting a sexual partner, the entire process of forming pairs which characteristically used to be described from the man's point of view as 'courting', the participants are forced to rely on themselves more than ever before. In other words, dating and pair-formation are individualized to a greater extent. At first glance it may perhaps appear to be paradoxical that this informalization process, this emancipation from the external constraint of a preordained social ritual, makes higher demands on the self-constraint apparatus of each individual participant. It requires the partners to test themselves and each other in their dealings with each other, and in so doing they can rely on nothing and nobody except themselves, their own judgement and their own feelings.

Naturally, the beginnings of the formation of new codes of behaviour, even the beginnings of a form of group control, can also be observed in all this. It sometimes happens that friends in a circle of acquaintances will become involved when a partnership is going through problems, when one of the pair is behaving too badly towards the other according to the opinion of the group. But the main burden of shaping life together at any rate now lies on the shoulders of the individuals concerned. Thus informalization brings with it stronger demands on apparatuses of self-constraint, and, at the same time, frequent experimentation and structural insecurity; one cannot really follow existing models, one has to work out for oneself a dating strategy as well as a strategy for living together through a variety of ongoing experiments.

What I have attempted to illustrate with the example of relations between the sexes at universities also holds for the development of the relationship between men and women more broadly. The American magazine *Time* has occasionally reported on the insecurity experienced by men in whom the old customs are still deeply engrained:

A man seated on the downtown bus might endure agonies of self-examination before offering his seat to a woman. The male has to learn to size up the female by age, education and possibly ferocity of feminism before opening a door for her: would the courtesy offend her? It makes for ambiguity: if a man studiously refuses to open a door for a woman, is he sexually liberated? Or just an ill-bred slob?[12]

And a recent American book of etiquette lays down the rule that 'Whoever happens to be in the lead, opens the door and holds it for the other.'[13] All of this points towards what is particularly relevant sociologically in this context: first the distinctive features of, and then an explanation for, the informalizing spurt which has occurred in the twentieth century. Only when the structure of this trend has been recognized and understood can one then go on to answer the question of whether or not this is the beginning of a process of rebarbarization. Is it the beginning of the end of the European civilizing movement, or is it not rather its continuation on a new level? The example of relations between the sexes shows how closely the breakdown of a traditional, older code of behaviour and feeling is connected with a change in the balance of power between the social groups whose relations were socially regulated by the code. I cannot here go into the sociogenesis of the code which regulated the conduct of men and women of the upper and middle classes to each other in European societies. It must be enough to point out that in this code features of the social elevation of women were connected in a remarkable way with those of their subordination to men. Briefly, forms of conduct which were unambiguously characteristic of behaviour towards higher-ranking people, such as bowing or kissing the hand, were adopted towards women and integrated into a code of behaviour which was otherwise quite andrarchic.[14] The transformation of this entire, ambivalent framework of power in the direction of greater equality is illustrated in the changing standards of behaviour between the sexes.

5

Without a clear sociological idea of the past, one unavoidably arrives at a distorted view of social relations in the present. Just as this is true of relations between the sexes, so too is it of relations between the pre- and post-war generations. In this case, too, for the sake of brevity, I can best bring out the changes in the code of behaviour and feeling by limiting myself at first to comparing university generations, in particular students.

In comparing student life in my own youth with that of today's students, the first thing which strikes me is the emphatically hierarchical form of behaviour under the Kaiser, and the no less emphatically egalitarian behaviour of the generations after the Second World War. The difference is most obvious when one remembers that in the period before the First World War fraternity members comprised the majority of students; moreover, the student fraternities inculcated attitudes in which dominance and subordination were sharply stamped – perhaps they still do so today. The 'young fox' was required to run all sorts of errands for his older fraternal 'patron', if not to polish his shoes daily as in the corresponding relationship at British public schools. The fraternity rules for drinking in pubs – known in German as the *Bierkomment* – demanded that the younger person had to empty his glass every time the elder toasted him or raised his glass to him. And when he eventually felt ill, he was allowed to disappear to the toilet. Since German universities traditionally had no facilities whatsoever for the social life of their students, concentrating on their minds and hardly giving the rest of the human being a thought, the student fraternities played a complementary role which should not be underestimated.

Furthermore, as far as I know, until the First World War the large majority of students had their fees paid by their fathers. This consequently led to a quite specific pattern of social selection. Even without statistical records it can be estimated that before the First World War 90 per cent of students at German universities came from the affluent middle classes. In contrast, consider the breakdown by father's occupation of students at a West German university in 1978:[15]

worker	18.1%
white-collar worker	34.6%
civil servant	19.5%
self-employed	20.5%
other	7.2%

Although this does not in fact tally with the proportions of parents' occupations in the total population, compared with 1910 it does show the trend of change in the distribution of power.

Closer examination reveals that amongst students there are certain traits which are less class-specific than generation-specific. It may be that changes are in the offing. But for the time being, there is a widespread generation-specific mistrust amongst German students towards the older generations – that is, those generations who went through the war. Without it being articulated precisely, they are blamed for all those events of the war and the Nazi era which one would really prefer to forget, and with which the younger generation cannot identify itself. The feeling that 'We didn't have anything to do with it' separates the younger generations from the older generations, and separates them more and more from those who 'did have something to do with it'. Although the latter do in fact occupy positions of authority in West Germany, my observations indicate that their authority is not acknowledged by the students.

The strongly egalitarian tendency among the up and coming generations is also expressed by the students' use of the informal 'you' ['*du*']. To a certain extent, it also extends to younger lecturers and professors. For a while, it was apparently a matter of course to address even full professors without their title, simply as 'Mr . . .' – clear signs of an informalizing tendency, and at the same time of a greater claim to power on the part of the students in relation to the professors. I do not dare prophesy how this trend will develop further. In the end, the development at the universities depends on the overall development of the Federal Republic. If authoritarian tendencies in the latter are strengthened, they will also grow stronger at the universities.

Cas Wouters, in an essay which concentrates in particular on the Netherlands, emphasizes how strongly many people of the younger generation, very conscious of the negative example of regimentation by the state, wish to 'free the individual personality totally from social constraints'. But in contrast to earlier periods, when young people strove to find a meaningful responsibility for themselves as individuals, there exists

> a greater tendency among these emancipatory generations to seek individual self-fulfilment and self-realization in groups or in social movements. In that respect the strongly individualistic tendencies which one encounters here have a very different character from that presented by political or cultural liberalism. [And therefore] . . . the restraints which life in groups or movements inevitably imposes on the individual are apt to thwart again and again the imaginary hopes for individual freedom . . . [16]

With all due caution regarding generalizations, this raises a problem very closely related to informalization. The highly formalized organizations of the early student corporations – the duelling corps, the nationalist fraternities, the gymnastic societies – and their strictly hierarchical and authoritarian structure just need to be compared with the endeavours of present-day students towards more egalitarian forms of organization. Then the difference becomes apparent; but so also do the special difficulties facing these aspirations of present-day students. The outcome of younger people joining together today to form an egalitarian group is in many cases the renewal of hierarchy. Because people living together always impose constraints on each other, any group which does not recognize this fact and attempts to realize a life free from constraints (which does not exist) inevitably (if one can so put it) leads to disappointments.

The comparison of the German student associations at the turn of the century and at the present day reveals a few other important points of difference between then and now, especially with respect to the relationships between generations. Two points are particularly striking. First, the fraternities have declined; the shift of power in favour of students who are not members of fraternities means *ipso facto* a massive impetus towards individualization, an emancipation from a formal group discipline which did not relax its hold on group members even in the easygoing atmosphere of the pub. And the more highly individualized younger generations, who also did not feel the need for the patronage of the alumnus Old Boys [*alte Herren*] in their careers, demanded instead more equality with the older generations. A whole series of interwoven factors contributed to shifting the balance of power between the generations in favour of the younger. The advent of state grants for students has played an important role in this context; so did the discrediting of many of the members of the older generations through their association with National Socialism, and, more generally, with the lost war. But those are only examples. In the conflict between the generations which never totally disappears, a whole complex of factors dealt better cards into the hands of the younger generations of the post-war period.

As is often the case in such a situation, many of the members of the younger generations felt the wind in their sails, and at the same time overestimated their own strength. In a sometimes grandiose misjudgement of their actual power resources, they concluded that they could now achieve everything they wanted. If the older generations had formerly expressed their superior power *vis-à-vis* the younger via formal rituals of behaviour, then for a while members of the latter fought for the destruction of all these formalities – not just those used between the generations, but those used between people in general. Thinking back on this time in the 1960s and 1970s, one remembers perhaps only the excessive expectations and the bitter taste of disappointment left in the mouths of many people by the actual course of events when these expectations were not fulfilled. The futility of power struggles with over-high hopes sometimes obscures the simple fact that, once the froth and turmoil of the conflicts subsided, social development did not just fall back to the earlier stage of formalization. The dreams were not fulfilled, but the distribution of power between the generations remained most definitely less unequal than it had been before the conflict between the generations openly broke out.

One area in which this is especially evident is in the relationship between unmarried daughters and their parents, and between young women and members of the older generations in general. Of all the changes in the patterns of formalization or informalization and in the balance of power between the generations which have occurred in the course of this century, one of the most marked and significant is the growth in the power of young, unmarried women. Right up to the early part of the twentieth century, the life of such women in large parts of the middle class and the aristocracy was predominantly regulated by their family. The individual scope for self-regulation which was open to the young girls of these strata was very limited. Control by older people tightly encompassed all aspects of their lives. To remain alone in a room with a young man not of the family, or even to cross the street unaccompanied, was totally outrageous. Sex before marriage damned a woman who had any self-esteem to life-long shame. Gerhart Hauptmann's tragedy *Rose Bernd* portrays fairly realistically the story of a farmer's beautiful and honest daughter, pursued by men as if she were fair game, who eventually succumbed to the seductive talents of one of them, and who then broke under the shame she thus caused both herself and her family. One should not forget that this regulation of young women's behaviour and feeling by parents, church, state and the entire circle of acquaintances was a type of formalization which corresponded to the then-prevalent balance of power between the generations and the sexes.

In less than one hundred years, as can be seen, a really radical change has been accomplished. If now at the end of this century a young woman gets together with a young man and becomes pregnant, then in many cases neither the parents nor the young people themselves regard this as a scandal. The informalizing spurt is evident in this attitude, even though it has certainly not been adopted to an equal extent by all strata and all sectors in the more developed societies. But what has actually changed, the structure of the change, often still remains unclear in public discussions. People can frequently see nothing in these changes other than degeneration into disorder. It appears merely as an expression of a loosening of the code of behaviour and feeling, without which a society must fall into destruction. But such a view does not do justice to the facts. The change in the social code regulating the life of young unmarried women shows quite unambiguously that the burden of decision-making and regulation has now shifted to a large extent from the parents and family to the girls themselves. In the relationship between the generations, too, there is increased social pressure towards self-regulation, or, in other words, a thrust towards individualization. If such a change is regarded as decivilizing, then this is because the theory of civilizing processes has been misunderstood.

B Duelling and Membership of the Imperial Ruling Class: Demanding and Giving Satisfaction

1

There are certain aspects of social stratification in Germany around 1900 (as in other times and places) with which people are quite familar without thinking much about it, but which may well be overlooked in a systematic social scientific investigation. This becomes apparent when one thinks of two prominent sociological ways of dealing with problems of social stratification: categorizing strata according to occupation and according to class. Both criteria of stratification are essential but neither is sufficient in itself to account for the actually observable ordering of people into higher- or lower-ranking strata. For this purpose, it is also necessary to know how the members of a society who are endowed with unequal power and status opportunities classify themselves and each other. Stratification criteria which show how people in a society are grouped when viewed solely from the investigator's third-person plural perspective, as 'they' and 'them', are inadequate. Such criteria need to be used in conjunction with others derived from the perspectives of the people under investigation. For the people being studied also have their own perspectives on how they are grouped and stratified, viewing themselves and each other from the perspectives of the first and third person plural, as 'we' and 'they', as 'us' and 'them'.[1]

The image which people living together in a specific society have of their own position and that of others in the social pyramid must be conjoined with stratification criteria from the researcher's perspective, in order to form a comprehensive model which will stand a chance of being fruitful in further work; for the experience of stratification by the participants is one of the constituting elements of the structure of stratification. Only by taking into account the structure of the experience of stratification – including its perspectival distortion or blockage – and by setting more objective and more subjective models against each other, can the researcher avoid the academic desiccation of reality, and bring conceptual symbols into better congruence with observable connections.

A one-sided concentration on the image of stratification in terms of economic classes – as first worked out mainly by the Physiocrats and then later fixed programmatically by Marx – can easily make it seem that the social stratification of Germany under the Kaiser was determined solely by the ownership or non-ownership of the means of production. If the inequalities in the distribution of power and the social relationships of dominance and subordination in this period are understood primarily in terms of the relationships between the classes of 'economic' specialists who produced and distributed goods – the industrialists and the workers – then one must view the entrepreneurs, with their abundance of capital, as the socially most powerful and highest-ranking stratum of the *Kaiserreich*. But that is hardly an accurate picture of German society between 1871 and 1918.

When one examines how the people of this society themselves ranked the different social strata, it becomes evident that entrepreneurs and related groups, such as large-scale merchants or bankers, certainly did not rank highest. Top civil servants and military personnel most definitely had a higher social status than rich merchants. And even a relatively well-to-do university graduate, such as a lawyer or a doctor, occupied a higher social status than perhaps a much wealthier non-graduate merchant or industrialist. One might have the impression that a financially strong capitalist, even without a degree, was socially more powerful than a graduate with less capital; but such an impression should be treated with great circumspection. It is rarely the case that the way in which social strata in mutual contact rank each other – that is, their image of the social hierarchy – is independent of the actual power gradient between them. Historically, there are certainly transitional phases, when the popular image of the ranking of the strata no longer corresponds, or does not yet correspond, to their ordering in terms of power. But with the exception of such transitional discrepancies, the image which the participant classes form of the status hierarchy is usually a fairly reliable symptom of the actual distribution of power between them.

One of the criteria for defining the social rank of a person in the 'good society' of Germany under the Kaisers, to a far greater extent than nowadays, was ancestry – that is, the social rank of parents or grandparents. In the civil service and the military, that factor was present from the outset. In the case of university graduates, ancestry was more likely to be overlooked; it was perhaps assumed as a matter of course that only an appropriately well-off family could afford to send its sons to university. And if the father himself did not belong to the upper circles, then the fact that someone had overcome the barriers of fighting fraternity initiation rites and, later on, obtained a doctorate was enough to erase the memory of a not particularly distinguished ancestry. But *nouveaux riches* merchants and industrialists who had not undergone the bloody *rites de passage* demanded of students and the military were looked down upon by the 'good society' of the *Kaiserzeit* as bearing the indelible stigma of lowly origins, of being social climbers and parvenus.

It was not at all the case, as the rather loose use of the expression 'capitalist society' implies, that in the period after 1871 financially powerful capitalists already formed the socially most powerful and correspondingly highest-ranking stratum of German society. Germany was a country in which, in keeping with its late development as a nation-state, the great bourgeois wealth of modern times developed relatively late. Given the current state of knowledge, it is not easy to say how many of the rich merchants and industrialists in the second half of the nineteenth century were 'social climbers', that is, first-generation members of the upper class, but the assumption that they formed a considerable percentage is not all that far-fetched. In any case, in the social structure of the *Kaiserreich* until 1918, the members of 'old' families, who more or less had a monopoly of positions in the high civil service, officer corps and diplomatic service, were unambiguously superior to the 'capitalists' in social power as well as in social status. In his novel *Man of Straw*,[2] Heinrich Mann caricatured the relationship of the industrialist to the noble state official. But his portrayal of the power gradient, showing the noble state official – a chief regional administrator, for instance – as by far the superior, and the industrialist as the less powerful underling, is real enough.

Let us look at an example of how the participants themselves saw the power and status hierarchy in Germany in the late nineteenth or early twentieth century. It comes from Walter Bloem's novel about student life, *Der krasse Fuchs* [The Crass Fox].

> Marburg's citizens were divided into two castes: society, and those who did not belong to society. Whether a particular person or family was to be counted as belonging to the one or other class was decided by a very simple distinguishing mark: the members of the 'Museum Association' formed society; anyone who did not belong to this circle was an inferior form of life. Members of the civil service, of the university, the municipal corporation, the officer corps of the rifle battalion, as well as all members of the graduate professions and the wealthy merchants belonged to the association. For a modest amount, the students could acquire associate membership, and thus all members of the corps, the fraternities, the associations of students from the various regions of Germany, and the university gymnastic clubs were without exception eligible for museum membership.
>
> Within this society, however, there were numerous more exclusive circles, which, even if they were rivals in certain particulars, nevertheless by and large formed another inner social hierarchy with rungs which were at first very wide apart and then slowly narrowing.
>
> That the young corps students had to stick only to certain precisely defined topmost rungs of this hierarchy was impressed on them at every initiation ceremony for junior members by the 'fox major'. Werner thus already knew very well when he went to his first Museum Ball that he could by no means dance with every girl he might take a fancy to; that instead, before he let himself be introduced, he had to inquire every time from a senior corps member whether the particular lady belonged to the circle in which the corps moved.
>
> But he knew too little of life to feel particularly hemmed in by the narrow limits within which he was allowed to seek pleasure and stimulation. Bit by bit, he had become so much a Cimber[3] that he found it quite natural to dance only with 'Cimber ladies'. For his blue–red–white[4] feelings, the other ladies came as little into question as the women of those foreign peoples with whom there was no *commercium et connubium* would have been regarded by a citizen of ancient Rome.[5]

The social divisions of a small German university town around 1900, seen from the perspective of the upper class, are vividly evident in this description. If used critically, novels can help to reconstruct a past society and its power structure for us. As in probably every German town, large or small, in Marburg there was a group, 'good society', which stood out from the rest of the city's population. Its members formed a network of people who, despite all internal rivalry and enmity, nevertheless felt they belonged together, and who together exercised enough power to be able to form a self-contained group and exclude others from their circle of acquaintance. This exclusivity, belonging to 'good society', was made visible by membership in a local association, the 'Museum Association'. The right to attend its functions, in particular its Grand Ball, was the visible and institutionalized sign of the far less visible, non-institutionalized line of division between people who were considered by the members of the 'good society' itself to belong, and those considered not to belong to it. Admission to the Museum Association was thus the manifest expression of 'belonging', but it neither created nor justified this status. Rather, internal criteria were invoked – such as ancestry, title, profession, education, reputation and level of income – in a comparatively discreet exchange of opinions in the gossip channels of the network of the local 'good families' with which the local student corps and fraternities were linked.

As can be seen, the first rank of the Marburg Museum Association comprised members of the civil service, the university, the town council, and the officers and their families stationed in the town; the next rank included graduate professionals of the town and members of the local student societies traditionally entitled to bear heraldic colours. As a local extension, there were also some of the wealthier merchants. In accordance with the distribution of power in the *Kaiserreich*, here, too, representatives of the state held the top position. The merchants, representing the economy, still had a great deal less power and status than they did. A young corps student would have had to break through a number of barriers and probably face the full force of his comrades' anger if he had preferred a pretty little merchant's daughter to a lady from the circle 'in which the corps moved'.

There was therefore, as Bloem explicitly states, a series of gradations within this circle. But on the whole, membership of the Museum Association determined with whom one could associate without endangering one's prominent status. Membership identified a person as a member of 'good society', and thus, in the broader sense, of the German establishment. Non-membership branded a person as an outsider, as someone who was denied access to the positions of power as well as to the social circles of the upper classes.

2

'Good societies' are a specific type of social formation. They form everywhere as correlates of establishments which are capable of maintaining their monopoly position longer than a single generation, as circles of social acquaintance among people or families who belong to these establishments. Court society is a particular type of 'good society'.[6] Most dictatorships are too young and unstable to allow the formation of 'good societies'. But the beginnings of such a social formation can be found in National Socialist Germany as well as in the more stable Soviet Union. In Britain there is a 'high society' with a long tradition, where, until recently, the court was the pinnacle of the hierarchy and at the same time the centrepiece which integrated it (and the court page of *The Times* served as its notice board). When the integration of a country is incomplete or belated, as was the case in Germany, many local 'good societies' develop; none, however, gains undisputed precedence over all the others and becomes the authoritative source for the behavioural code or the criteria of membership for all the others. Whereas in Britain and France the 'good society' of the capital city quite definitely took precedence over all local ones, and Washington 'society' is possibly just beginning to draw such functions to itself in the United States, in the short period of the united *Kaiserreich*, the court society in Berlin succeeded only partially in playing this centralizing and integrating role.

Instead, in Germany older institutions – firstly the army, followed closely by the student fighting fraternities – developed such integrative functions. With acceptance into one of the renowned student fraternities, a young man gained access to the establishment, not just that of the single town, let alone that of the university town. Membership of such a student association identified him throughout the entire empire [*Reich*] to members of a local establishment as one of 'us', someone whose behaviour and feelings followed a specific code characteristic of the German upper classes of that time. That was the deciding factor. The inculcation of a specific code of behaviour and feeling, which despite local variations actually extended fairly evenly throughout all the different branches of good society in the period between 1871 and 1918, was one of the main functions of the student fighting fraternities. Together with the related but somewhat differently accentuated code in which officers were trained, the common code of these fraternities contributed not a little to standardizing the behaviour and feelings of the German upper classes, which, in the *Kaiserzeit*, were still far from uniform. A central element linking both these systems of rules was the compulsion to private single combat, to duelling.

The code of the students and officers was the German equivalent of the code of the 'English gentleman', in function if not in substance. But in the course of centuries, the latter had been gradually transmitted with recognizable shadings and variations from landowning, aristocratic groups to other classes; this migration and modification of what was originally an upper-class code through its absorption by wide sections of the population is indicative of the relatively high permeability of the boundaries between social strata typical of the development of British society. Compared with Germany, the different formality-informality gradient of the code of the 'English gentleman' leaps to the eye. In the nineteenth century, this gradient was not as steep as that of the corresponding German code. To put it briefly, in the course of time British formality became in general more informal and British informality more formal than their German counterparts. This was partly because the land army, and the warrior code of its officers, played a far smaller role in Britain's development of a national code than in Germany's. By the mid-nineteenth century, the obligation to duel had already disappeared even from the army officers' code in Britain; Prince Albert was partly responsible for this. But perhaps the single most important reason for this change was the primacy ever since the seventeenth century of the navy over the army as Britain's chief means of defence and attack.[7]

In Germany, as in almost all continental nations, development followed another course, not least because of its political fragmentation and its repeated role as Europe's arena of war. Here, particularly in Prussia and Austria, the warriors' code of honour – the obligation to risk private duelling to prove oneself worthy of belonging to the established strata, those who possessed 'honour' – retained its crucial role into the twentieth century. As in other continental countries, for example also in France, the noble custom of duelling as a means within the higher strata through which the impugned honour of an individual man was physically defended, circumventing state laws and the courts, spread to higher circles of the middle class. As it spread, its function was transformed: the code of honour and duelling became a means of discipline and at the same time – made visible by duelling scars – also a symbol of membership, proclaiming a student's candidature for admission to the establishment, and to a superior position in German society in the *Kaiserzeit*.

The student duelling corps and nationalist fraternities[8] had a strongly standardizing function in the *Kaiserreich* which, after 1871, remained rather disparate and loosely integrated. They gave a relatively uniform stamp to people from the most diverse regions of Germany, despite all the hierarchical gradations even amongst the student members of heraldic colour-bearing societies. In the belatedly united country and in the absence of both a model-setting 'good society' in its capital city and unifying educational institutions like the British public schools, it was the student fighting fraternities (together with the officers' messes) which gained the function of minting a common code of behaviour and feeling for the German upper classes. But it was a peculiar pattern of behaviour which they attempted to imprint. It can be said that these upper classes, different as they were in the many states and cities of Germany, in fact formed a single large society of men who were *satisfaktionsfähig* – able to demand and give satisfaction in a duel. In their social circle, those who enjoyed the privilege of demanding satisfaction with weapon in hand from any other member by whom they felt insulted were obliged in turn to accept the challenge to single combat from fellow members who felt their honour impugned.

In this way, types of relationships which have always been characteristic of warrior societies – but which were slowly and often hesitantly suppressed in many areas of social life with the increasing monopolization of violence – persisted into the twentieth century in Germany and some other societies as a sign of membership of the establishment. In the form of the duel, this warrior code was maintained up to our grandparents' generation, enabling the man who was physically stronger or more skilful in the use of the means of violence to impose his will on the less strong, less competent with arms, and to carry away the highest honours. Since then, physical strength or skill in handling weapons have largely lost their previous significance in determining someone's status or reputation in social life, especially in the highly industrialized countries. The ruffian who uses his superior fighting skills with or without weapons in order to subject others to his will normally no longer enjoys any special respect. Formerly, things were different. In all warrior societies (including, for example, ancient Athens), proving oneself in physical combat against other people, being victorious over them, and if necessary murdering them, played an integral part in establishing a man's standing. The present-day military tradition seeks to limit training in the use of physical violence as far as possible to violence against people who do not belong to one's own state-society. The duel was a remnant of the time when, even within one's own society, the use of violence in disagreements was the rule, when the weaker or less skilful person was totally at the mercy of those who were stronger.

The tradition of single combat as a means of solving disputes goes back to the time when the central rulers of the state were endeavouring to pacify the area over which they ruled, and to restrict the right to use physical force within this area to themselves and their appointees. It goes back, in other words, to the time when they were proclaiming their own monopoly of the use of violence. In this way, they robbed the warrior nobles in their lands of their foremost means of power in conflicts with their peers as well as in dealing with people who were socially weaker and therefore lower-ranking than themselves. As a gesture of resistance and defiance against the increasingly powerful central ruler, the custom spread among the gradually tamed warrior stratum of the nobility of fighting out quarrels among themselves, at least regarding questions of personal honour, by duelling – instead of upholding the legal authority of the central ruler as required by the law of the centralized principality which now forbade the private use of physical violence. The custom of single combat between peers enshrined for the last time a kind of feeling and behaviour which the warrior nobles, increasingly integrated into the state apparatus, shared with many other upper strata in a similar situation. 'The apparatus of coercion and the laws of the state are useful in maintaining order among the unruly masses' – that was the feeling – 'but we, the warriors and the rulers, are people who uphold order in the state. We are the lords of the state. We live according to our own rules, which we impose upon ourselves. The laws of the state do not apply to us.'

In the *Kaiserreich* as elsewhere, the use of weapons by private persons was forbidden by law. Accordingly so was single combat in which, whether in earnest or in play, people often did each other quite serious physical harm. It represented an open infringement of the state monopoly of violence, the last bastion of an upper stratum which conducted personal affairs among themselves according to self-imposed rules which were valid only for their own stratum, the privileged. But since in Germany between 1871 and 1918 the crucial positions of state power were occupied or controlled by members of the *satisfaktionsfähige Gesellschaft*, and since the custodians of the very laws which threatened to punish any private person breaking the state monopoly of physical violence belonged to the law-breaking privileged society of those entitled to demand satisfaction, the executive organs of state power such as the police were not mobilized against such law-breakers. To make it easier for the authorities to turn a blind eye to the infringement of state laws by duellists, and probably also to enable these tolerated uses of violence to elude the attention of the masses, these events were held in places difficult of access to non-participants, such as a specially prepared village barn, or, for pistol duels, a woodland clearing. But, of course, almost everyone knew what was happening.

3

In the earlier discussion of changing standards of behaviour in the present century (pp. 23–43 above), it was shown that the structure of the formality-informality gradient is very closely related to the power gradient of a society. Compared with the Federal Republic of Germany of the 1970s, the formality-informality gradient of the *Kaiserreich* between 1871 and 1918 was very steep. But the past is never simply the past. It works on – with greater or lesser force according to circumstances – as an influence in the present. It does so not only because of the inertia of traditions which roll blindly on, but also because an image of past phases of one's own society, distorted and deformed though it may be, continues to live on in the consciousness of subsequent generations, serving involuntarily as a mirror in which one can see oneself. It is therefore useful to point out some structural peculiarities of German development between 1871 and 1918 which are relevant to the development of the German code of behaviour and feeling, and thus also to the development of its formality-informality span.

The political unification of the German states, the elevation of the King of Prussia to Emperor of Germany [*Kaiser*], and the promotion of Berlin, the capital of Prussia, to capital of the *Kaiserreich* certainly did not achieve in one fell swoop the integration of the many local and regional 'good societies' and the standardization of their code of behaviour and feeling. But it created an institutional framework for this integration; it gave a strong boost to the formation of a more uniform German upper class.

On account of their own feelings of belonging, the traditional German upper class were particularistic; their loyalty was to their land in every sense of the word,[9] not the empire. In the beginning, even Bismarck's loyalty was primarily to the King of Prussia. It was urban middle-class groups who had taken up the cause of the unification of Germany. But their striving towards this goal automatically became bound up with the centuries-old conflict for supremacy between middle-class and aristo-

cratic strata. In the eyes of its middle-class champions, the unification of
Germany was a step towards ending the dominance of the aristocracy –
towards democratization – but the German middle classes did not have
the necessary power resources for this, partly due to the very fact that
they were split up between the many sovereign German states. In this
way, a highly paradoxical situation emerged in the development of
German society. The middle-class pioneers of German unification failed
in their fight for this goal, firstly because the princes and their
particularistic[10] nobility saw it, not without reason, as a goal of the
middle classes in the class struggle; and, secondly, because the power
potential of the traditional upper class was still far greater than that of
the middle classes, again precisely on account of the multi-state character
of the country. Ironically, it was the noble representatives of particularism who brought an end to German particularism. This came about
above all in conjunction with the dynamics of inter-state relationships,
that is, the rivalry tensions between Germany and other states.

In this way, the traditional ruling class of Germany, the princes and
aristocracy, retained supremacy within the newly unified *Kaiserreich*.
And unification was handed to the middle-class pioneers on a plate,
without them being able thereby to reach the goal of their social struggle,
their class goal – depriving the aristocracy of power, and democratizing
German society. This paradoxical situation had severe consequences for
the entire development of Germany. The old ruling classes transferred,
unbroken and unchanged, their traditional conception of their own role
in the German principalities on to their role in the newly unified empire.
They continued to regard themselves as the actual power-holders in
Germany, even as its embodiment, just as they had taken it for granted
before in the individual German states. They continued in their tradition
as born rulers in the German regions, without realizing that the
unification of Germany, and with it the greater chances of unification it
gave to the bourgeoisie and the workers, must in the long term adversely
affect their own conventional position in the social framework.

With unification, Germany found itself almost automatically involved
in a rapid process of making up for lost time, catching up, and attempting
to overtake the older European great powers; under the pressure of this
rivalry, it found itself in the maelstrom of an accelerated modernization
process which gave a boost especially to the economic specialist groups,
the industrial and commercial middle classes and the industrial workforce. It is understandable that, under these circumstances, the long-
standing and intense feeling of Germany's weakness swung over into a

perhaps even more intense feeling of strength. The Kaiser and the nobility consciously saw themselves as the natural rulers of Germany, confirmed by the decisive role played by their compeers in the unification of the country. That the unification had been achieved through a victorious war brought even higher prestige to the noble officers and the military in general.

The fact that the power chances of the middle class had been strengthened in this new German society was not completely overlooked. But the traditional conviction amongst the warrior nobility that mercantile activity was not quite honourable remained very much alive in the court society of the empire, and in aristocratic circles in general. Even at the beginning of this century, the *Deutsche Adelsblatt* [German Noblemen's Newspaper] was carrying on a small offensive against the shopkeeper mentality. Although among the higher nobility in particular there were cross-cutting connections between large landowners and industry, the view persisted in full force that gainful employment did not befit one's rank as a nobleman. And this stigma remained attached to the middle-class practitioners of such occupations. The court society of the *Kaiserzeit* most certainly opened its doors to commoners more widely than ever before, but it was primarily high civil servants, including university professors and in particular famous scholars, who were drawn into it. It was primarily university graduates who were considered socially acceptable, thanks to the significance of the student fighting fraternities in spreading the aristocratic code of honour.

During the relatively short existence of the newly unified *Kaiserreich*, the peculiarly structured upper class discussed above was gradually formed. Because of Germany's specific pattern of development, all the different rural areas and cities had their own 'good society'. But the criteria for belonging to them became standardized. They encompassed to an increasing extent middle-class as well as aristocratic elements, although keeping intact the conventional status ranking which gave aristocrats precedence over commoners. The prerequisite was the commoner's qualification to demand or give satisfaction, that is, his readiness and competence in the case of an insult to give or demand satisfaction with a weapon in his hand. On the whole, this was only possible when the commoner was an officer, even a reserve officer, or a member of a student duelling fraternity. The uniform criterion of membership represented by the right to demand or give satisfaction – the recognition of the same code of honour and of single combat – was certainly not the only sign, but it was the most striking sign, of the formation in German society of a relatively integrated upper class extended by the incorporation of commoners and which was gradually standardized in the wake of the political unification of the *Kaiserreich*.[11]

The court society grouped around the imperial court formed the highest-ranking centre of integration for this *satisfaktionsfähige Gesellschaft*.[12] Considering the major role played by the military in court society, it goes without saying that males who belonged to it felt bound by the common code of honour and behaved accordingly in their relations with each other. The members of this broad court circle usually knew of each other at least by name and reputation.

The same held for all the German nobility. Even when they were not personally acquainted with each other, nobles from all over Germany could nevertheless place each other precisely. Officers, including reserve officers, legitimated their claim to membership through their regiments. Graduates, when not already distinguished by office and title, legitimated themselves through their fraternities. Moreover, duelling scars proved their membership at first glance. All these people, from the high aristocrats to the reserve officers and provincial graduates, were considered to be entitled to demand and render satisfaction. Merchants, however rich they might be, were not, unless they had other qualifications. Those groups considered not entitled to demand satisfaction included as before shopkeepers, craftsmen, workers, farmers and Jews. During the nineteenth century, some of the latter won access to fraternities, but by the end of the century they were formally excluded.

The social position of the Kaiser certainly gave to its incumbent greater power-chances than a mere ceremonial figure, a symbol of national unity, a father figure for the masses. As commander-in-chief of the armed forces he had at his disposal a major part of the state monopoly of force. In his lofty position he could hardly be aware that armies formed on the basis of general conscription, and wars necessitating mobilization of the entire populace, actually meant an immense strengthening of the power potential of the masses and a weakening of the power of central rulers. Like the Emperors of Austria and Russia, his allies and opponents, he relied on the loyalty of his mainly (at least in the higher ranks) aristocratic officer corps, whose interests on the whole coincided with his own. The Kaiser and his generals may or may not have been aware of the difference between war waged, as in the past, with poor, hired sons of farmers and craftsmen, and war in the present utilizing armies composed of men conscripted from all classes; but the consequences of this structural change with respect to their power of command and their scope for power in war and peace certainly escaped them – and at first it seemed to escape the mass of the people too. Thus it came about that the impression of absolute power which the Kaiser and his generals traditionally maintained until the 1914–18 war (which gradually broke down this impression) far exceeded their actual power-chances.

All the same, these power-chances were much greater for European princes at the beginning of the twentieth century than they were three-quarters of a century later. All foreign policy largely depended on the personal decisions, sympathies and antipathies of the Kaiser. Decisions regarding war and peace rested in the end with him. His opportunities for influencing internal politics were also huge. In the empire, as in Prussia, he personally selected the ministers – including the Minister of the Interior, who controlled the police – although in the empire the parties could topple a cabinet selected by him. The Kaiser was also entitled to name or confirm the appointment of high civil servants. In this way, he could count on the support of the two pillars of state, civil administration and the armed forces. In both cases, following Prussian tradition, he reserved – with one or two exceptions – the top positions and a whole series of middle positions for the nobles. With the diffuse but perceptibly growing pressure from below, the high aristocracy on their country estates, whose members had sometimes looked askance at the Hohenzollerns, generally supported the Kaiser; and the same held for most of the German aristocracy. Up to 1918, the nobility as a social formation were – despite all internal tensions – able to buttress their claim to the highest social status because they had firm positions of power at their disposal and thus still possessed a considerable measure of solidarity.[13]

Directly below the members of the aristocracy in terms of social rank came the higher middle-class civil servants, who were normally trained as lawyers. Here, in the high civil service, there was often close contact between noblemen and commoners, who in many cases occupied offices of the same rank. Even in Prussia, the gradual power-shift in the relations between nobility and middle class, one of the unplanned consequences of ongoing urbanization and industrialization, was evident in a constant increase in the number of middle-class officials compared to nobles.[14] University professors of all faculties also continued to be regarded with middle-class civil servants as directly below members of the aristocracy in rank. The high Protestant clergy, and with some restrictions also those of the Catholic church, were on about the same social level. Below them came all civil servants who were commoners and whose academic qualifications carried the title of doctor, including not only court and state civil service officials, but also heads of department in grammar schools, as well as successful non-civil service graduates of all descriptions.[15]

In this way, the student duelling fraternities, especially the corps and nationalist fraternities, represented in the minds of both the contemporary upper class and the fraternity members themselves preparatory training centres for the development of those character traits in young people which would be needed later on in the exercise of graduate professions like those described, especially graduate positions in the civil service, rounding off the purely specialist and subject-orientated education of the universities. It was an education to fit them for membership of the upper stratum of German society. And the code of behaviour and feeling which gave the life of young people in the duelling fraternities of this period its distinctive imprint is in many respects characteristic of the upper stratum of imperial German society itself.[16]

In understanding the structure of this upper stratum and its code, it may be useful to know that the power relations expressed in this structure also influenced the ideas prevalent in the ruling circles about the purpose of a university and the goals of academic study. At the present time, certain movements are pressing for schools and universities to train young people to a greater extent for the tasks that await them in the economy, in trade and industry. In the *Kaiserzeit*, it was still generally accepted, according to old tradition, that the primary task of a university was to prepare students for the civil service. Students belonging to heraldic colour-bearing societies regarded themselves accordingly as candidates for a career which would raise them above the general mass of people and into the upper realms of society, especially into the higher civil service or into one of the liberal professions open to graduates. Only relatively seldom did members of the fraternities see their goal as a career in business, trade or industry; this was usually the goal of students who, because of their background, were certain of a post in the management of a successful family enterprise. In keeping with the spirit of the *satisfaktionsfähig* establishment with its warrior traditions, even middle-class students entitled to wear society colours tended to regard careers in business as second class, and people who followed them as persons who fell beneath them in social rank.[17]

The *satisfaktionsfähige Gesellschaft*, in which nobles and commoners, hierarchically graded, were bound together through the same forms of conduct, through the same code of self-regulation, was divided, as can be seen, into military and civilian sectors. In the former, the path led via cadet schools, military training schools and similar institutions to an officer's career, and it could carry middle-class recruits in less selective regiments up to the rank of major, or, under favourable circumstances, perhaps to higher positions. All the very top positions and many of the middle ones, especially in the better regiments, belonged to the nobility. In the second, civilian, sector, the path led via university and duelling fraternity – with some variation in non-Prussian regions – to the upper and eventually the topmost ranks of the state administration with its various branches (administration, education, judiciary, etc.). Both pillars were connected with each other through many cross-links; they met at the top of the pyramid in the German government, in the court society, and finally in the person of the Kaiser himself.

4

Superficially the court society of the last Hohenzollerns, especially that of Kaiser William II, might not seem fundamentally different from the court society of, let us say, Louis XIV.[18] The strictness of the ceremonial, the ritual character of festive occasions – a ball, a ruler's visit to the opera, a prince's wedding – were hardly less pronounced than at the French court two hundred years previously. And the same went for the glitter and richness of female dress, and for the splendour of the military and civilian court dress of the men. Yet there were some considerable differences, of which two have special significance in this context.

The relatively continuous line of French state-formation meant that Louis XIV could build on a tradition of ceremonial and court organization, which he extended with the aim of increasing his own power-potential and which he understood how to use for his own ends. The Hohenzollern Kaisers had only the rather austere tradition of the Prussian court behind them. Their rise to the position of Kaiser and the new influx of wealth it brought them, in conjunction with new commitments, presented them and their counsellors with many new kinds of problem in working out ceremonial.

Perhaps even more significant is the difference in the security of the regime. From about the middle of the seventeenth century until the second half of the eighteenth century, the monarchical establishment in France was hardly seriously threatened, either from within or from without. This relatively high degree of security consolidated the courtization [*Verhöflichung*] of a leading part of the French aristocracy; it was one of the conditions for the development of the court-aristocratic code of behaviour and feeling in that period, and eventually also for its stagnation. The developing establishment of the *Kaiserreich* was, comparatively, far less secure. It was new; the organization and ceremonial of the Prussian royal court had relatively quickly to develop forms appropriate to the new role as imperial court. Imperial Germany, unified by war, was threatening for its neighbours; those who felt threatened were in turn threatening for the empire. Internally, the unification of Germany encouraged economic growth. In a long-term perspective, this in turn can be seen to have strengthened the power-chances of the rising strata, the commercial and manufacturing bourgeoisie and the industrial workforce, in relation to the conventional monarchic-aristocratic establishment.

Admittedly, in the short term the latter was strengthened by its victory over France and the new 'great power' status of the empire unified under the Kaiser. Furthermore, the rising power potential of the industrial workforce, along with the accompanying demands for power by those who represented it, gradually drove a significant portion of the German middle class on to the side of the aristocrats. Between 1871 and 1914, the majority of the German middle classes made peace with the privileged high-status group. The spokesmen of trade and industry, as they were called, no doubt suffered from the traditional contempt of an establishment whose members regarded only wealth acquired through inheritance or marriage as of high quality, while wealth achieved by the sweat of one's brow was inferior. Trade and industry, merchants and manufacturers certainly grumbled, and from time to time the newspaper *Vossische Zeitung* thundered against the privileges of the nobles. But wide sections of the upper middle class, with higher civil servants and graduates in the lead, submitted happily and often enthusiastically to the political and military leadership of court and nobility. They sunned themselves in the glow of the new empire, and were contented with the position of second-rank junior partner. A middle class which had, as the name implies, two fronts, one above and one below, became *de facto* a one-front stratum. Their top group towered up into the lower regions of the upper stratum. Here, the front disappeared from view. All energies were then concentrated even more on the struggle in the other direction, and in this the interests of the middle and upper classes met. This meant a strengthening of court and nobility.

At the same time, it meant that the middle-class code, which had once been anti-court and orientated towards social equality, was penetrated more strongly than ever before by elements of the monarchic-aristocratic code, which, in keeping with the social situation and tradition of its proponent stratum, was geared to a warrior ethos, to maintaining inequality among people, to judging the stronger as the better, and thus to the unalterable harshness of life. Until the Napoleonic Wars (and probably for considerably longer still), as a result of the relatively strong and emphatic social exclusion of urban middle-class groups by the court and provincial nobility, German middle-class culture and German court culture mixed relatively little. The former therefore had a specifically middle-class character to a much greater extent than did middle-class culture in Britain or France.[19] How far this peculiarity of the German path of development changed before 1871 remains an open question. After 1871 at any rate a noticeable convergence can be observed in Germany between sectors of the middle class and the nobility, and a corresponding infiltration of the middle-class code of behaviour and feeling by values and attitudes which originated in the aristocratic code of this period.[20] The standardization of the German student code of honour and duelling is evidence of this.

In many European societies, elements of the aristocratic code of behaviour and feeling have penetrated the codes of the middle and working classes in the course of their social ascent, and, 'bourgeoisified' in this way, have become aspects of what is rather awkwardly called the 'national character' of a state-society. The particular charm of women, and the easy elegance of language in the successor territories of what were the two most powerful courts in the eighteenth and even in the nineteenth centuries, the Parisian court and the imperial court in Vienna, testify equally well to these transformations of originally aristocratic patterns of conduct and feeling into national ones. So too does the extension of the code of the 'English gentleman', which was originally limited to the upper classes, but became a bourgeoisified aspect of the British national code. Aristocratic German, especially Prussian, patterns of behaviour and feeling also underwent bourgeoisification, and became elements in the German national character. Such traits had certainly already penetrated wide sectors of the population before the establishment of the empire, but the very pronounced tendency of the German aristocracy to distance themselves from the middle classes made it difficult if not impossible for patterns of behaviour and feeling to be transported from one stratum to another. Only with the unification of the empire and with the increasing incorporation of middle-class groups into the lower ranks of the court-aristocratic establishment, through titles and honours for example, did fewer obstacles come to stand in the way of the flow of aristocratic patterns into middle-class circles and their transformation into national patterns.

The code of behaviour and feeling of the Prussian nobility – and of the German nobility, insofar as it is possible to speak of one before unification – had its idiosyncrasies. In the seventeenth and eighteenth centuries, there was certainly a type of court-aristocratic culture, whose pattern of behaviour and feeling spread out, with variations, from Versailles to all the courts of Europe, and quite often became accepted in middle-class circles too. But Prussia was a relatively poor country, war-torn, and, all in all, on the periphery of the French-centred court culture of the time. The occasional endeavours of King Frederick II to create a court society in Berlin on the French pattern did not have a particularly lasting effect. The frequent turmoils of war, in which Prussia grew large, ensured that time and again the values of the warrior won priority over those of the courtier in the behaviour and feeling of the aristocracy.

But there was also something else. In France until late into the eighteenth century, the fate of the warrior nobility was determined to a large degree by the fact that, while the tension between the two estates was relatively great (for reasons which we do not need to go into here), they and the bourgeoisie had very nearly equal power-chances. Under Louis XIV this constellation was deliberately encouraged and to some extent firmly institutionalized, since it was one of the most important conditions for the especially large scope of the French kings' power.[21] It enabled a king and his representatives to play off the various castes and ranks against each other. In this way, without ever denying his own membership of the aristocracy, he could at the same time distance himself from them; and he could force the high nobility, which posed a particular danger to him (and who complained that the king degraded them into subservience like all his other subjects), to submit to the king's laws and so tame them. In Britain, the tension between parts of the nobility and parts of the middle class had already diminished in the course of the seventeenth century. Together, they were able to curtail the kings' claims to power. Accordingly, in eighteenth-century Britain there developed a complex field of tensions within which the king and court formed one centre of power – possibly not the strongest – while aristocratic and non-noble groups ('gentry') combined to form another which was just as important and perhaps even stronger.[22]

In Prussia, by contrast, poor as it was, the warrior nobility were, as in other countries, first of all tamed by the central rulers. That is, with the transition to standing armies (both a condition and a symptom of the monarchs' growing monopoly of violence), the relatively free, landowning knightly warriors were transformed into officers in the service of the central ruler in this country too. But in Prussia, with its comparatively poor cities, the power-ratio between nobility and the middle classes was relatively unequal and in the aristocracy's favour, while the social tension between the two estates remained, as in most of Germany, particularly high. Accordingly, the balance of tensions between the three central concentrations of power – king/nobility/middle classes – settled into a figuration which came close to a tacit compromise between nobility and king. On the one hand, the aristocracy needed the hereditary ruling house in clashes with other more or less centralized states; it needed the kings as commanders-in-chief of the army, as highest coordinators of the military and civil service organizations, as arbitrators in resolving squabbles between nobility and middle class, and for other integrating functions. The Polish republic of nobles with its elected king showed only too clearly the weakness of rule purely by nobles in conflicts with the highly centralized monarchical states surrounding it. On the other hand, however, if the nobility were already dependent on the king solely for these reasons, the relative weakness of the middle class strengthened their position *vis-à-vis* the monarch. In this way a constellation emerged in which the nobility submitted to the king; they served him as officers, court officials and administrators. But at the same time, the king also submitted to the aristocracy; he undertook to guarantee their position as the highest estate in the land. This tacit pact made him the protector of aristocratic privileges. These included the right to all top positions at court, in the military, in administration, and the maximum possible number of middle positions to provide for younger sons.

Moreover, Prussia's location, endangered as it was on all sides with borders difficult to defend, always making possible renewed war and its accompanying devastation within the country, basically allowed only a moderate civilizing of the warriors.[23] To be sure, here too the warrior nobility was transformed with the increasing monopolization of violence by the kings and the closely associated commercialization and monetarization of society; but this transformation in the code of the Prussian aristocracy still left military patterns predominant by far over court-civilian patterns.

The peculiarities of the code of behaviour and feeling which gradually became a dominant German national code in the course of the growing convergence between agrarian-military noble groups and urban middle-class groups can only be fully understood if it is realized that the 'good society' of the *Kaiserreich*, even though it united in itself elements of the Prussian, Bavarian and Saxon past, had no special wealth of tradition and was basically an uncertain and endangered social elite. Behind it lay a period when the German territories had been relatively powerless, compared with the tradition-rich power of the older great states of Europe. With the founding of the empire, the feelings of humiliation turned into the opposite within a few decades. In particular, the establishment in Wilhelmine Germany was not only under threat from within and without, but, as is the case with *nouveaux riches*, was an establishment not quite sure of itself. Without this cursory review of the situation and structure of the model-setting imperial upper class, the conspicuous and pointed formality of the Germans, for instance, would remain incomprehensible, as would the peculiarity of the formality-informality span of which it is part. Models of behaviour from a military aristocracy which had really only undergone courtly taming to a modest extent were absorbed by wide sections of the middle class in the period after 1871, and in consequence they also then had a considerable influence on what is usually called German national character, or, to put it more precisely, the specifically German tradition in the code of behaviour and feeling.

5

The role of the duel in the social relations of the nobility, and accordingly among the lower ranks of the officer hierarchy too, was symptomatic of how the balance of power between the central rulers and the warrior nobility developed, especially in Prussia. The aristocracy's determination not to submit personal quarrels between men of their own group to the authoritative verdict of the king and his courts of justice, claiming instead the right to deal with them independently – thus breaking the royal monopoly of violence by fighting each other with a weapon in hand according to the rules of their own code of honour – was, as already suggested, a symbolic expression of the nobility's self-conception not only as the highest-ranking stratum but also as the real embodiment of the state. As such, members of the establishment followed their own rules, patterns of behaviour and life strategies; in certain respects they felt justified in transgressing the laws of the land, which were there to keep the mass of the people, the king's subjects, in order. Members of the high aristocracy were especially recalcitrant; so long as they retained their inherited property, they never really defined themselves as subjects of the ruling prince.[24]

Until the early twentieth century, the upper classes of other European countries also probably regarded the rules of an aristocratic code of honour as binding, even if they contravened the laws of the land. However, in hardly any other country did duelling play so central a role, right up to 1918, as in Germany, Austria included; there it remained the centrepiece of the code of honour not only of the upper strata, but also of the upper middle classes, not only of the nobility and the entire officer corps, but also of the middle-class fraternity students and graduates. Duelling played this role, furthermore, not as a stray relic of earlier days which can be looked at in isolation. Its importance was not restricted to the domain of the pairs actually involved in violent armed combat; over and above this it represented the ever-present *possibility* of single combat, a ubiquitous threat which could at any time give the stronger man power over the weaker, the better shot over the worse. The former, in the knowledge of his superiority, could reject any formal attempt at a reconciliation or an apology.

In other words, the duel was characteristic of a socially strategic type of behaviour which was widespread in the less pacified societies of earlier times, and now, hemmed around with formalized ritual, still remained alive in later, more strongly pacified societies, even though it breached the central ruler's and the state's monopoly of violence. It raised above the masses those who belonged to certain social strata; in the first place the nobles and the officer corps, and then the fighting fraternities of middle-class students and their Old Boys – in short, the stratum of those entitled to demand satisfaction. Through it, they submitted to the constraint of a special norm which made the formalized use of violence, possibly with lethal consequences, a duty for individual people under certain circumstances. In this form was preserved the typical social strategy of warrior castes: a scale of values in which physical strength, skill and readiness personally to do battle were ranked particularly high, if not highest of all. Alternative, more peaceful forms of competition and social strategy, especially the art of verbal debate through argument and persuasion, were accordingly regarded as of lesser value or virtually contemptible.[25]

An episode from the mid-nineteenth century shows in miniature how helpless conventional Prussian power relations rendered even a king and his executive organs, the police, in the face of the strength of the aristocratic code of honour, and how they were forced to accept unlawful, albeit formalized acts of violence.

In 1848, a certain Herr von Hinckeldey, who had married an hereditary Baroness von Grundherr, was chief of police in Berlin. He was a staunch, upright man, who followed his kind in not having much sympathy with the democratic agitation of the times, and who let the agitators feel the full strictness of the law. But as a representative of the law, he also saw it as his duty to uphold justice when aristocrats broke the law. It was one of the customs of the aristocratic smart set to seek amusement in gaming clubs, which, although illegal, had up till then been tacitly tolerated by the police when they were frequented by men of very high rank. Von Hinckeldey, however, decided to take action. One evening, he personally participated in the closing of an aristocratic gaming club, in the course of which he came into conflict with a gentleman by the name of von Rochow-Plessow, who felt insulted by von Hinckeldey, and challenged him to a duel using pistols. A leaflet, written 'by an eyewitness', described what then happened. The eyewitness was the physician Dr Ludwig Hassel, who had often treated von Hinckeldey.

On 9 March, 1856, Hassel was requested through the then Superintendent of Police Patzke to attend 'in the capacity of doctor an affair of honour' and to present himself at the residence of the Privy Councillor Baron von Münchhausen, bringing bandages with him. From there, they drove in two coaches to Charlottenburg. In the first sat Hinckeldey and Münchhausen, in the second Dr Hassel alone. Near Charlottenburg Chausseehaus, the coaches halted; there they met the old chief of police Dr Maaß, with whom Hinckeldey exchanged a few words before the coaches could continue. The journey continued at a brisk trot past the Königsdamm forester's lodge to the wood, the so-called Charlottenburg Jungfernheide. They went on foot through the wood to the rendezvous, where Herr von Rochow was already waiting with his second. The referee, Herr von Marwitz, a member of the upper house of the Prussian parliament, was still not there; he arrived a quarter of an hour later – a drawbridge raised to let barges pass had held him up.

The duel began in the usual way. Marwitz once again attempted a reconciliation – to no avail! According to Hassel's report, Hinckeldey's mental and physical state must have been terrible; the unfortunate man suffered from premonitions and kept thinking of his poor wife and seven children. At the beginning of the duel, Hinckeldey's pistol failed; he asked for a second one. Then followed the shots. 'Rochow remained standing, unhurt; Hinckeldey, on the other hand, made a half-circular sort of movement and sank into the arms of Hassel and Münchhausen, who let him slide gently to the ground. Hassel saw immediately that the wound was fatal; arterial blood streamed from the wounded man's mouth, the bullet had penetrated the lungs. With the help of both coachmen and the servant, Hinckeldey was placed in the coach. So that Rochow would not run the risk of being arrested, they decided not to return to Berlin, but instead to take Hinckeldey to the house of Dr Maaß.

Then Hassel and Münchhausen wanted to report to the king, who at that time was in residence at Charlottenburg Palace. . . . The king received the gentlemen much moved, paced up and down in tears and seemed in the depths of despair. The only thing which now remained to be done was to take the sad news to Hinckeldey's family. . . . On the day of the funeral the king, in the company of the princes, appeared at the Hinckeldey residence and comforted the fainting widow.'[26]

This shows most graphically how impossible it is to understand and explain the social life of people if one relies solely on official sources such as written laws. For understanding the code which shapes the pattern of observable behaviour and feeling among people who have been socialized into it, the largely unwritten social rules are indispensable and at least as informative as the official laws which are one of the formal manifestations of the state monopoly of violence. Currently, it is common practice to use the concept of the 'everyday life-world' in observing and investigating such more or less private forms of behaviour and experience.[27] Unfortunately, as used today by some philosophical-sociological sects, it is a rather useless research tool. That can be seen here. Duelling by the upper classes, like brawling among the lower, can be assigned to the 'everyday life-world' of phenomenology, ethnomethodology and other philosophoidal branches of the fragmented sociology of our day. But the spineless use of this concept paralyses any understanding of structures in human beings' lives together, especially power structures. It leads to single situations being analysed in isolation, as if they existed in a social vacuum, and to losing oneself in endless arbitrary interpretations. One is then drifting without a compass in an episodic sea. How can one hope as a social scientist to bring to life such everyday experiences as duelling by the upper classes or brawls among the lower without attempting at the same time to find theoretical models of the social structures which embrace them both?

The comparison between the duel and brawling presents both in a clearer light; in addition, it illuminates the distribution of power-chances in this society. Both duels and brawls are private wars, outcomes of conflicts.[28] But the duel was a highly formalized type of violence, infringing the state monopoly of violence, and reserved in the first place for the nobility and especially the officers, and then also middle-class civilians of sufficiently high status. People of lower rank could beat each other up quite informally when they came into conflict with each other. As long as they did not injure themselves too badly, the state hardly bothered. But if such people went for each other armed with weapons, they would if possible be locked up. If one of them shot the other dead in a fight, then perhaps he himself would be executed in the name of the state. With duelling, by contrast, the state authorities tacitly recognized that such offences were mere peccadilloes which could not be punished in the same way as the violent actions of other social classes. Accordingly, duellists were not sentenced to imprisonment but were confined to barracks or placed under a not dishonourable house-arrest for a length of time which varied according to the severity of the bodily harm inflicted. When the outcome was fatal, the survivor often disappeared abroad for a while.

Episodes such as the one just discussed are representative of a particular society. They reveal its structure, especially its power structure – in this case primarily the distribution of power between the top cadres of society under the Prussian monarchy and its heir, imperial Germany. It is impressive to see how as a matter of course the social code of the upper classes activated the solidarity of its members in the face of state power, even when they had met as deadly enemies just beforehand. The aristocrats' code of honour took priority over state laws. Even the king had to bow to it. Even the custodians of the laws of the state automatically tried to protect the high-ranking killer from the punishment by the courts which would have immediately befallen one who was less high-ranking.

The unanimity with which, in this case, all participants closed ranks – as they did later in the case of student fencing contests and duelling, in order to avoid involving the state courts and laws in their use of weapons and its consequences – expresses a conviction which, to be sure, was not held only by the German upper classes. It was, however, one which had particularly lasting effects on the subsequent development of Germany and is perceptible almost up to the present day. One such effect is the upper-class conviction, which received another strong boost after 1871, that the relatively more powerful groups – the Kaiser, the court society and the nobility, followed by the civil and military pillars of the state – formed the real Germany. In relation to them, the other classes of society seemed to be, if not quite inconsequential, then at least inferiors, subordinates and outsiders. Identification of this establishment with 'the people' or 'nation' was formed in the same way. At least in peace-time it encompassed the entire people simply in the abstract, as a symbolic fantasy loaded with strong positive affects, but in practice it was restricted only to the establishment's own class.

This idea was complementary with the traditional image of the state held by the mass of the German people. Their representatives experienced the state not as something they all formed together, but as something external to themselves, as the authorities, the ruling high-ups, the established, those in command. Given the factually observable distribution of power between rulers and ruled, dominant establishment and dominated outsiders, this idea was already much less true to reality during the *Kaiserzeit* than it had been beforehand under the monarchy in Prussia. But because of the particularly long period of more or less absolute and autocratic regimes, together with the conventional code of command and obedience, the personality structure of people in the German states was largely attuned to a strictly autocratic and hierarchical social order. The anchoring of an autocratic form of rule in the habitus of individual people kept on creating a strong desire for a social structure corresponding to this personality structure: that is, for a stable hierarchy of dominance and subordination, expressed not least in strictly formalized rituals of social distance. To people with such a personality structure, the social formalization of distinctions between those whose duty was to command and those whose duty was to obey gave clear bearings in social relations and made it easier to cope with the problems which arose. It drew precise boundaries around the scope for decision-making of each individual, or, in other words, offered the individual person a firm foothold in making his or her own decisions by allocating restricted areas of responsibility. It thus permitted relatively simple control over personal tensions, which would immediately have increased if this hierarchical social framework had become weaker or even started to totter.

6

The episode just recounted is a useful starting point in continuing the discussion of the problem of formalization. After all, it was not just any act of violence which the Prussian upper class both allowed and commended to its members – it was a most precisely formalized type of violence. Passions and fears were certainly involved in it, but they were brought under tight control through a social ritual worked out in minute detail. The duel between Hinckeldey and von Rochow conveys some impression of this. It was quite obvious that the Berlin chief of police feared his opponent. It is not at all unusual for fear on the part of participants to contribute to technical malfunctioning of the weapons. Without doubt, Hinckeldey knew that his opponent was an excellent shot, and suspected that the latter intended to kill him. But the social pressure exerted on him, the external constraint to self-constraint, left him no choice. To give up and go away would not only have meant losing his position, but also losing everything which gave his life meaning and fulfilment.[29] Von Rochow, for his part, may have been aware that he was a better shot. Perhaps it gave him pleasure – grim pleasure – to put in his place the policeman who had disturbed his enjoyment in gaming. He shot him in the lungs. Obviously he really was intent on killing the other man, well knowing that nothing much could happen to him.

On the one hand, the force of the models of conduct to which the upper class submitted themselves can be seen here very clearly. The term 'formality-informality span' does not just refer to what could be called manners in the narrower sense of the word. It does not refer only to whether one shakes hands with everyone present on a social occasion or merely glances around and says 'hello', or whether a guest brings the lady of the house flowers or not. What is actually meant is rather the extent and strictness of the social rituals which bind the behaviour of people in their dealings with each other – even down to surrendering one's own life.

Furthermore, one encounters in this story once again the relation between social structure and personality structure. Societies in which the use of physical force – even of a highly formalized kind – is tolerated or, as in this case, virtually demanded in people's dealings with each other encourage ways of feeling and behaving which enable the physically stronger person to enjoy playing the bully with another person as soon as he senses a weakness. The immanent dynamics of human groups in which the use of physical violence, even in the formalized shape of duelling and fencing contests, is accorded a central place in social life lead again and again to the same outcome. Types of people rise within such groups who are distinguished not only by their physical strength or skill, but also by the pleasure and enjoyment they take in smashing down other people with weapons or with words whenever the opportunity arises. As in simpler, less pacified societies, there are even in more pacified societies enclaves of ritualized violence which give the physically stronger or more skilful, the more aggressive person, the bully and the ruffian the chance to tyrannize others, and to win great social respect by doing so. The duel as a formalized act of violence was not, as already remarked, an isolated social fact. It was symptomatic of particular social structures, and had specific functions for the social strata to whose behavioural strategies it belonged; it was characteristic of a specific type of social strategy prevalent in these circles, and of a particular way of evaluating people.

When discussing the functions of duelling for the social strata in which it was practised, it should not be thought that for the people who made up these groups these were clearly and unambiguously recognized and explained as the purpose of the practice. One characteristic of such functions deserves to be examined in more detail, but we cannot do so here. It is illustrated by the fact that members of this stratum were probably aware, but only in a rather vague way, that distinguishing institutions such as the duel performed a specific function in their social existence as a class. But their awareness of this function was not explicitly articulated in communication either with each other or with other groups, even if it found expression in indirect ways. In addition, however, there were direct legitimations of the duel which usually served more to obscure than to clarify its actual social functions. Thus, for instance, it used to be said that it was a necessity for an officer to prove his courage at every opportunity, and for him always to be ready with weapon in hand to defend his own name and his family's from being sullied by any aspersions cast by others. It was also said that duelling had great educational value for civilians too, as preparation for responsibilities in service to the nation.

The social functions which were hidden behind these and other explicit legitimations were of a different kind. Perhaps this can be seen most clearly by once again comparing the duel as a means of dealing with conflicts between people of the same rank in the upper classes with brawling as a means of dealing with personal conflicts among the lower classes. Take brawling. Whatever the long-term reasons may be for the antagonism between two people who are beating each other up, in this case argument is usually quickly followed by violence. Spontaneity of feelings – anger, rage and hate – the full force of the passions comes into play. It is only muted to a small extent through a social training which prescribes a particular pattern of physical fighting in unarmed violent clashes between people. Compared with the duel, the spontaneous scuffle of a brawl is highly informal, even if it is partly shaped by patterns of competitive fighting such as boxing or wrestling. The duel, in contrast, is an example of a relatively highly formalized type of physical confrontation. The opponents in this case do not spontaneously throw themselves at each other under the pressure of their anger and hate. Here, the prescribed ritual demands first of all a strict control of all hostile feelings, shutting off aggressive impulses from the executive organs, the muscles, thus preventing any action being carried out. Here the external constraint of the social code requires a most intensive self-constraint. This is not untypical of the formalization of strategies of feeling and behaviour.

The example of the duel reveals one of the central social functions of formalization. As can be seen, it is a distinguishing mark of higher-standing groups, a symbol of the differentiation between the people of a higher and a lower stratum. The ritual of the duel, like other upper-class rituals, raised the members of the groups which upheld it above the masses of people lower in rank than themselves. It was thus a means of distancing themselves. The difference between the kind of act of violence minutely formalized in a duel and the comparatively informal brawling between people of the simpler strata, and the extent of the formality –informality gradient which it demonstrates, can serve as a criterion of the social distance between the respective strata.

However, the duel also combined the function of differentiating and distancing the higher and lower strata with that of promoting the integration of the higher group itself. Together with their feeling of separation from the lower groups, it reinforced their feeling of belonging to the higher groups and their pride in their membership. This is a recurrent double function of the formalization of behavioural strategies in established groups. They impose upon their members patterns of self-constraint, which vary according to the situation and stage of social development; they impose forms of self-denial which also serve as signs of distancing, marks of distinction and symbols of superiority. As reward and compensation for this self-denial, members are offered an increased sense of personal worth, the deep satisfaction to be repeatedly drawn from the awareness of belonging to the higher-ranking group, and the self-conception of being one of 'the better sort of people' which usually goes along with that. Mastery of 'good society's' subtle strategies for dealing with people, which members begin to learn from childhood onwards, is among other things a symbol of the membership of an especially prestigious group, and through the practice of these strategies the need for continual reaffirmation of individual self-esteem is met. It strengthens solidarity with their own group, and the feeling of being better people, superior to others.

The connection between the group-specific self-denials and frustrations imposed by the upper-class code on each member, and the simultaneous pleasure which they draw as compensation for the frustrating self-constraints, from the consciousness of belonging to the more powerful, higher-ranking and socially more highly valued group, is seen more vividly when the power of such an establishment starts to crumble. Then, especially in the understanding of younger members and succeeding generations, the value of their own group is quite often called in question, and thus also the value of the self-discipline and the sacrifices required of every member – whether as a means of ruling, as an indispensable tool in dominating the less disciplined, or simply as a symbol of belonging to the elect. The gain in pleasure, the heightened feeling of self-esteem, the narcissistic premium, which together balance out the costs of obeying the prescriptions and proscriptions specific to the stratum, are diminished and weakened. And, thus, the capacity for following the class-specific code and for bearing the frustrating constraint it imposes upon each person becomes correspondingly weaker.

In such cases, an informalizing spurt of a very particular kind can be observed. A mode of behaviour characterized by a specific pattern of self-constraints becomes brittle and crumbles, without there being another in sight to put in its place. The meaning and value of conventional self-denials, which perhaps previously functioned as conditions for maintaining dominance, are lost in the disintegration; and with the loss of power, even its own members doubt the meaning and value of the group. In such a situation, it is almost impossible for the members of the falling group to form or even to borrow another code which would enable them to regulate their lives in a way they would find equally meaningful and valuable.

One of the most radical informalization processes of this type was the destruction, in the process of colonization and missionary work by Europeans, of the rituals which gave meaning to life and upheld patterns of communal life among simpler peoples. Perhaps it would be useful to discuss this briefly. One of the most extreme examples of the devaluation of a meaning- and orientation-providing group code in connection with the disempowerment of its carrier-group is the elimination of the upper

classes in Central and South America in the course of colonization and
the imposition of Christianity by the Spanish and Portuguese. It is true
that in these cases the old establishment was replaced by a new one, but
the code of rules by which the new establishment ran its life was at first
incomprehensible to the conquered peoples. It could hardly make up for
the loss of meaning. The human side of this process is, as far as can be
seen, still little researched. What it means to the people involved to
experience the relatively rapid destruction of the ways of life which gave
them meaning and value, and to have new ways and a different code
violently grafted on to them by a new establishment, deserves more
careful examination. Expressions such as 'conversion to Christianity' are
of little help: they represent the viewpoint of the conquerors, not of the
conquered.

In the case of the Incas and the Aztecs, there was an almost total
breakdown of an older social organization and its means of orientation.
The old establishment was far more radically destroyed than was the
case in the French Revolution, for instance, and the new establishment
which replaced it was incomparably more strange. One has the
impression that even after centuries the bulk of the indigenous agrarian
population has not quite recovered from these traumatic blows by the
Spaniards and Portuguese. The old language of their nations has survived
in some parts of Latin America amongst the rural population, but the
people there have been so downtrodden by their masters over the
centuries that to all intents and purposes an as yet incurable apathy still
persists. The British anthropologist Rivers reports in greater detail the
similar effect of Protestant missionaries on the inhabitants of the
Melanesian islands. In this case, and perhaps in many others, the
devaluation of the old ways of life by a more powerful group led to a
phase of deep mourning, and to symptoms of what in clinical language
is called depression. Only here it was not an individual depression, but a
group depression.[30]

There is no shortage of structurally similar processes in the history of
European societies, although here the break in the succession of establishments was probably usually less radical. But we cannot yet be certain
of that. For what we call the history of Europe is to this day still written
to such a great extent from the viewpoint of the victors that the
viewpoint of the defeated seldom enters into the current picture of
history; and the polyphony of ways of life, the absorption of typically
upper-class patterns by middle and lower classes, the rise of lower-
and middle-class patterns of behaviour and feeling to the top, and the

transformation of social structures, the framework within which these changing patterns occur, remain largely unexplored.

7

Effects of this kind which arise in the course of specific shifts in social power are what is meant by a formalizing or informalizing spurt. One such process in particular has been much discussed recently. It is referred to by such expressions as 'the permissive society'. But terms of that kind are hardly suitable for the process under discussion. To be sure, its kernel is the partial breakdown of customary formalization. Accordingly, the extent and character of the *informalizing* process which has been taking place – with many advances and retreats – in the course of the twentieth century only becomes clear in one's mind when seen in relation to the extent and character of the *formalization* which was typical of the upper and upper-middle classes, and associated with their relative power-potential. Only then can the problem posed by the relaxation or even the disappearance of many previously encodified rules of social life be formulated precisely. An answer to the question of what are the reasons for and what is the structure of the contemporary informalizing spurt depends, in short, on examining the formalizing spurt of the previous phase – the formalizing process which occurred in Germany in the context of the unification of territories under German rule through the imperial court establishment. Only from this rather broader point of view can one begin to say whether the informalizing process of today is a breakdown *per se* of civilizing self-controls, or rather a disintegration of formalizations which have lost their function – totally or partially – in the course of social change.

A certain tightening up of manners and an accentuation of etiquette and ceremonial can be observed in the development of the behavioural code of the German upper and upper-middle classes, firstly in courtly circles under the Prussian monarchy and then in the court society of the *Kaiserreich*. This was not an abrupt process. Change in this direction was, relatively speaking, still barely perceptible as long as the old Kaiser was alive; but it became stronger in the reign of Wilhelm II. For example, when he appeared at balls, the old Kaiser sometimes enjoyed being introduced to unknown people and chatting with them. Wilhelm II kept his distance. During his reign, ceremonies became much more precise and ostentatious, people's movements more dashing, the toilette of the ladies more elegant, their jewellery richer. At the same time, status competition in the broader 'good society' became more hectic, with participants endeavouring to outdo each other in the furnishing of their houses, the sumptuousness of the tables they kept, or even in the high bids they made in gaming or horse racing. Like Louis XIV, Wilhelm II loved the self-portrayal of his own greatness and dignity through ceremonials. In both cases, this type of self-presentation served as a visible symbol of power and social distance – it was an instrument of rule.

Today it is often forgotten that in Germany during the first two decades of the twentieth century a powerful court society still formed the upper segment of a *satisfaktionsfähige Gesellschaft* which reached deep into the topmost middle-class groups. An example may jog the memory; it is taken from a collection of old newspaper reports, written by Fedor von Zobeltitz and published under the title *Chronik der Gesellschaft unter dem letzten Kaiserreich* [Chronicle of Society under the Last Kaiser]:

23 January 1897

The great *celebrations at court* have begun. The full pomp of the ceremonial unfolded on the 18th at the assembly of full Knights of the Black Eagle. One might occasionally believe oneself transported back to the times of the first Prussian king, when one reads the speech given there by Count Eulenburg. But it cannot be denied that the splendour and magnificence are impressive. This year, the ceremonial involved the investiture of six new knights: three royal personages, the Grand Duke of Saxony, the Prince zu Schwarzburg-Rudolstadt and the Prince zu Wied, the Generals von Hänisch and von Seeckt, and Minister of State von Delbrück. The solemn procession started from the so-called panelled gallery, next to the royal apartments. It was headed by two heralds in old German costume, followed by the personal pages of the Kaiser, von Trotha and Baron von Rechenberg, and the court pages in their red jackets trimmed with gold, carrying on velvet cushions the insignia of the new knights-to-be; the Treasurer of the Order, Privy Councillor Borck, and its Secretary, Count Kanitz, with the statutes; the Master of Ceremonies Count Eulenburg; the full members of the order in dress uniform with ribbon, chain and cloak; the Princes and Royal Knights of the Order; and finally the Kaiser himself. When the procession reached the Knights' Hall, the corps of trumpeters in the Silver Gallery sounded . . . a blaring fanfare. The Life Guards and Cuirassiers usually supply these trumpeters; the trumpets are long and old-fashioned, decorated with banderols, and are used only at court ceremonies. The number of invited guests was particularly large this time. The total number of male court officials alone represents an imposing entourage; their uniforms are graded from gold-encrusted court dress to the simple, dark-blue chamberlains' tailcoat. In addition, there are the ministers and the giant swarm of generals and admirals. Between them, the First Class Privy Councillors, also in uniform and all in knee breeches – a veritable parade of calves – almost disappear. The fanfares, taken up by trumpeters further away, continue until the Kaiser has mounted the throne and the royal household has assembled around him in the prescribed ceremonial way. Only then does the act of investiture begin. Royal personages, in this case the Duke Johann von Mecklenburg and the Crown Prince of Saxe-Coburg, escort those who are to be admitted to the Order – the princes, the two generals and the remaining new knights – to the throne, where the Kaiser as Grand Master hangs the chain around their necks, bestows the accolade and, after their vows of homage, gives them his hand. . . .

Less stiff and full of dignity, therefore livelier but no less colourful, was the *grand présentation* [*die große Cour*] on Wednesday. For the young officer who enters court circles for the first time on this occasion, this is a day of especial pleasure. Since the throng of guests in the palace tends to be colossal on such days, the office of the Master of Ceremonies has its work cut out to regulate the various contingents. Even the Archivist's Office on the ground floor had to be pressed into service. This time, the procession formed from the imperial apartments. The *grande entrée*, as it is called, was led by all the highest officials of the court, with the Lord High Chamberlain, the Crown Prince zu Hohenlohe-Oehringen, foremost among them; then followed the imperial couple, the princesses and princes. The entire corps of pages was present. The personal pages of the Empress and the princesses carried their ladies' trains – which, by the way, looks easier than it really is, since it requires a great deal of dexterity and constant attention to follow each movement of the ladies. In earlier days, cadets seconded to service as pages usually practised carrying trains with large bed sheets, which the '*Schnappsäcke*', the younger cadets, had to tie around their hips. After their Imperial Majesties had taken their place on the throne in the Knights' Hall, with the princes and princesses to their right and left, and when the royal household and the foreign guests were in position, the ceremonial march past began to musical accompaniment.[31]

One of the most important celebrations in the *Kaiserreich*, the second German empire, was the Kaiser's birthday. Under Wilhelm II, 29 January became a holiday, marked by many ceremonies, for the entire German people. Officers and students celebrated it in their messes and fraternity houses, schools were closed, flags fluttered in German towns, and in Berlin there was the drive to the Emperor's Birthday reception. The streets to the flag-bedecked palace were cordoned off to keep the throngs of people at bay. They certainly did come – in 'grey masses' – to watch the lumbering state coaches and the persons of high standing in them drive by. After the reception in the palace, there was a military display, the great changing of the password ceremony. It often snowed during it, but people used to talk a great deal about 'Hohenzollern weather'. The skies were expected to clear for the Kaiser at outdoor ceremonies. The following is a report of the changing of the password ceremony on the Kaiser's birthday, also in the year 1897:

> Suddenly muffled shots echo out from the pleasure garden: the salute of the artillery – the signal that the Emperor's Birthday Reception has begun in the palace. At the same time, a company of Kaiser Franz's Grenadier Guards approaches to the sound of marching feet, and takes up position in front of the arsenal. The public become restless; the hour of the great changing of the password ceremony is nearing. The throng jostles; the police, courteous as ever, can hardly keep back the shoving people . . . . Now distant cheering, gradually rising to a thunderous roar. A glittering group approaches the armoury from the palace. In the forefront marches the hero of the day, the Kaiser, in a grey coat with broad fur collar, over which is the orange sash of the Order of the Black Eagle, and wearing an ostrich-feather hat. The slightly flushed countenance is blooming with glowing good health. Next to him stands the general commanding the Guards brigade, Herr von Winterfeld, with whom the Kaiser is chatting warmly; behind him the gentlemen from headquarters, the generals and adjutants, a multitude of higher officers. The Kaiser inspects the front row of the company and then greets the commander of the arsenal. During the changing of the password ceremony – as always, it runs 'Long live the Kaiser and King' on this occasion – the band of the Alexander regiment bursts into a cheerful marching tune. Then the drums roll, bugles and fifes come in – the march past begins . . . . Renewed hurrahs and calls of 'Three cheers for the Kaiser'; the ceremony has ended, and the General Staff accompany his Majesty back to the palace . . . .[32]

It was an official policy of Kaiser Wilhelm and his government to do everything in their power to foster trade and industry. So the opening day of each Berlin Trade Fair also became a highly ceremonial affair. Zobeltitz's report of the opening of the second Berlin Trade Fair in May 1896 gives a vivid picture of the formalities. Those who could not appear in uniform appeared in tails, and it went without saying that one wore all one's decorations. Zobeltitz sneered a bit at a particularly Jewish-looking gentleman who wore the cross of the Order of Christ around his neck, and that of the Greek Order of the Redeemer on his breast:

A wicked individual reckoned that they were the crosses on which the gentleman had forgotten to nail his vanity. That we are living in the age of uniforms was further proven by the masses of senior civil servants – Permanent Secretaries, Deputy Secretaries, Under Secretaries and Assistant Secretaries – who appeared in their gold-embroidered court dress and gold-braided trousers. Previously, no senior civil servant at all would have had a uniform; tails sufficed. But times change, and the senior civil servants with them.

The Organizing Committee seemed to have expected a rather heartier reception on the part of the highest of all. All sorts of mishaps arose. For example, one of the three gentlemen, it was said, otherwise the most adroit and assiduous of individuals, forgot to remove his pince-nez from his nose when he spoke with the Kaiser. That was apparently noted with disapproval. It was also very much commented upon that the Kaiser did not invite the Organizing Committee to breakfast, which he took with his entourage on board the *Bremen*. It would have been more correct, however, if the Organizing Committee had sent an enquiry as to whether the Kaiser would be inclined to 'accept' a breakfast. And the most proper form would have been to have enquired beforehand from some influential person, for example Herr von Mirbach, how one ought to behave in the presence of the Kaiser. Then *faux pas* and unpleasantnesses could have been avoided, and there would have been no need to bewail this or that unfulfilled wish and to scream blue murder on the Berlin Stock Market. Whether we like it or not, we are living in times in which the outward form counts a great deal; whether it would be better or not to trim the court pigtail a little is another matter – for the time being, one must take it into account, however long it is.[33]

It can be seen that at court a formalization process was taking place and that the commercial and industrial bourgeoisie, especially, did not always quite keep pace. Perhaps it was not yet common knowledge even amongst the most obsequious and adroit representatives of bourgeois industrial enterprise that His Imperial Majesty required that, on meeting him, as well as making the ceremonial bow one had at the same time to remove one's pince-nez as a sign of the respect due to him. As a sign of his disfavour, he then did not invite the obviously deeply distressed Organizing Committee to breakfast on board his yacht. Taking off one's pince-nez when greeting someone higher in rank than oneself, as an expression of respect and good manners is, in miniature, the symptom of a formalizing spurt. The trial of strength which lay behind it can be seen here on a small scale. The Kaiser had the power to grant or withhold signs of his favour. For a bourgeoisie made up of merchants and entrepreneurs, who formed a subordinate stratum, ranking second in power and status to the imperial court society, this disfavour meant a great deal. Zobeltitz recommended that they should have asked for advice beforehand from one of the leading personages, that is, from a man of the court.

Another sign of the formalizing process afoot during the Wilhelmine era is that on ceremonial occasions all the senior civil servants, the Permanent Secretaries, Deputy Secretaries, Under-Secretaries and Assistant Secretaries, now also appeared in gold-embroidered court uniform. In the court-aristocratic society of the second German empire under Wilhelm II, uniforms achieved particularly high prestige. The gentlemen in tails, the civilians, gave themselves away as second-rank people by their lack of a uniform alone. As a sign of his favour, the Kaiser, like other ruling princes, therefore granted high officials of the civil administration, who had no right to a military uniform, at least the right to wear a court uniform corresponding to their respective positions. Zobeltitz, who possessed quite a critical eye in this respect, notes that these expensive, gold-encrusted uniforms of the court bureaucracy were becoming ever more tasteless. Some persons thus dressed up, he comments on one occasion, resemble the porters at one of the great Parisian hotels.

The 'court pigtail' of which Zobeltitz writes, and his observation that he was 'living in times in which the outward form counts a great deal', are also signs of the formalizing trend of a regime which could perhaps have been transformed into a constitutional monarchy in response to the growing pressure of the industrial classes, had there been more moderation and greater skill on the part of the leading men. But the code of the ruling groups was shaped to a very large degree by the highly inflexible military tradition of command and obedience. In the Kaiser's self-conception, he himself and his courtly circle formed the real Germany. He was already much too subject to public criticism to be able to say openly what even Louis XIV possibly never said explicitly: '*L'état, c'est moi*.' But tradition and the still semi-autocratic apparatus of government which he had at his disposal permitted him to feel that opposition to its rulers was the same as treason against the country itself, something which many contemporary dictators also seem sincerely to believe. Neither the peculiar desperation of the imperial strategy, nor the formalizing spurt in the Wilhelmine era can really be understood without taking into account that this was a regime which felt threatened and was correspondingly insecure. The catch-up industrialization in Germany, which accelerated and became more general from 1871 onwards, weakened the supremacy of the traditional privileged strata who rallied around the Kaiser at court, in the army and throughout the country. National unification, which had been brought about by the imperial dynasty and of which the Kaiser, the army and the court had thus become the symbol, strengthened the regime.

The picture of this formalizing trend would be unbalanced without at least briefly mentioning the smouldering opposition, and the total incomprehension which it met with in the higher circles. It is hard to resist the opportunity of quoting yet another excerpt from Zobeltitz's *Chronik*, which illustrates in one small example both the attitude of the privileged towards the 'unpatriotic rabble' and the comic element in the formalities:

> 8 September 1895
> The *jubilee celebrations* commemorating the battle of Sedan have faded away, but the nasty episode organized by the Social Democrats to disrupt the great celebrations is still continuing. If one goes for a stroll through the main streets of Berlin in the late evening at the present, one is constantly harassed by a gang of lads who prowl up and down the pavements with parcels of newspapers under their arms and annoy passers-by with the shrill cry, '*Vorwärts* [Forward] sir! . . . *Vorwärts* of September 2nd!' The proprietors of the Social Democrats' central mouthpiece have attempted to make business out of their lack of patriotism. The infamous issues of *Vorwärts*, with their abuse of the great old Kaiser, of the army and the festive mood of the people, and including the publication of someone else's private letters, are being bought by the thousand at 20 pfennigs each by inquisitive people. Business above everything else! Only yesterday did the police put a stop to their games and forbid the sale of the issues which in the meantime have been confiscated. The conduct of the police over the last few days, by the way, deserves boundless praise. Mind you, the measures taken to control the crowds during the consecration of the Memorial Church were quite extensive; the people were crowded into densely wedged masses where Kurfürstenstraße meets the Kurfürstendamm, and it is really a wonder no accident occurred.
> A curious little incident at the consecration of the Kaiser Wilhelm Memorial Church has not been mentioned, as far as I have seen, in any of the newspaper reports. A friend had offered me a place on a balcony on the Kurfürstendamm, from where I could comfortably view the arrival of

all the most important personages. Exactly opposite, on the other side of the Kurfürstendamm, stretches the wall of the Zoological Gardens. As the bells began to ring and His Imperial Majesty was expected at any moment, an unpleasant noise suddenly sounded out against the rhythm of ringing metal and the first distant cheers and hurrahs of the people. The beasts of prey in the Zoological Gardens, especially the wolves, began to get restless; there was also excitement in the dogs' kennels. Long echoing howls, the yapping of the curs and the hoarse barking of the wolves mixed with the pealing of the bells to peace and accompanied the cheering of the public. That, however, was not on the programme. A mounted policeman galloped like mad to the Zoological Gardens; a couple of constables stormed in to forbid the howling beasts their singing, on the strength of their office and their authority – but the rebellious animals had little respect for blue uniforms: they continued to howl, yap and bark unmoved. At last a keeper was run to earth. How he made the beasts quiet, I do not know; perhaps he gave them their breakfast an hour earlier than usual. In any case, they were silent – but they had brought an amusing episode into the serious celebration.[34]

8

In the foreword to his collected reports and sketches of the *Kaiserzeit*, which were originally written as descriptions of daily events for the newspaper *Hamburger Nachrichten*, Zobeltitz speaks of his feelings on re-reading these writings, 'from days which seem to be infinitely long ago', as a citizen of the first German Republic at the beginning of the 1920s. He regards them, as he says, 'with some wonderment . . . with a resigned smile . . . and a feeling of astonishment':

> So *that* was what it was like *yesterday*, and between this yesterday and today lay that immense upheaval which transformed a 500-year old monarchy into a republic overnight, and in so doing completely reshaped the old society in all its parts.[35]

Then he points out something which was still clearly evident to him but is becoming increasingly difficult for later generations to see – or to conceive of – namely the fact that this society formed a kind of co-operative, 'like workers in the various trade unions do today'; 'what was called "society" was in those days also a group conscious of and pursuing its own interests'.

For a contemporary observer who himself belonged to this 'society', it was thus totally clear that it was a relatively closed social formation. The comparison with trade unions does not quite hold, insofar as the unity of the people of this 'society' was not overtly represented by a single organization created for specific purposes, and was not institutionalized through a deliberately planned and maintained organization. But the cohesion of the people who formed what Zobeltitz just calls 'society' (and which in broader perspective proves to be one instance of the 'good society' as a type) was certainly no less than that of people who band together in organizations with explicit and mostly written codified rules. The people who form a 'good society', like the hierarchically graded establishment of the second empire about which Zobeltitz is speaking, are actually joined together to a large extent by unwritten criteria and implicit symbols of membership which are generally self-evident only to the initiated and never quite understood by outsiders; this helps explain why historians as well as sociologists have paid relatively little attention to such social patterns, although in many cases they count among the most powerful social formations of their times. In particular, modern historians since Ranke have been so trained to focus on explicit documentation that they really have no eye for forms of social life where cohesion is based largely on knowledge of scarcely articulated symbols.

In the circles in question, an intimate feeling of common membership prevailed among all the people belonging to it, even binding together the greatest enemies. And it was expressed not least through the strict observance of shared rituals such as duelling. It was certainly one of the factors which, in favourable times, and despite the lack of any explicit organization, gave the apparently loosely connected social formation of a good society very strong unity and cohesion. Their members' annual round of appearances at balls, charity bazaars, the opera, at military and court ceremonies, and on many other occasions functioned constantly to strengthen the solidarity, the sense of group membership and identity, and the feeling of superiority over all the outsiders, the masses of the people; for their part, the masses as cheering spectators, or at any rate as approving onlookers, could from time to time catch a glimpse of the upper strata ceremonially assembling, and in this way serve to strengthen further the elite's conviction of its own superior worth.

The implicit symbols of belonging to the 'good society' were familiar from early childhood on to members of the relevant groups, especially people growing up within the tight bonds of the Prussian and subsequently German nobility. The symbols served as a yardstick, not only for themselves but also for other people, which they used without really being conscious of it to judge and evaluate people according to the standards of a specific class – their own. In their own circles, everyone judged people in this way, and so they took their way of judging to be quite natural. There was no cause for them to think about this.

In Zobeltitz's *Chronik*, there are plenty of examples of this unreflecting use of a class-specific model as a yardstick for evaluating people in general. Nevertheless, even if the events of the aristocratic world were certainly his central interest, he also had contact with people of other circles and possessed a good-natured tolerance of them. Precisely because during the second empire elements of the aristocratic code were being absorbed to an exceptional extent into certain parts of the middle classes, and then becoming part of the national German code, it is illuminating to look *en passant* at an example of his judgement of people. On 18 May 1913, he published an obituary of Erich Schmidt, the discoverer of the original *Faust*, professor of German literature and sometime Rector of the University of Berlin. This is an excerpt:

> He had a splendid appearance, so women idolized him. He was a person full of overwhelming strength, therefore the men loved him. Nothing of the old kind of professor clung to him; he had in truth created a new type. Anyone seeing him for the first time could have mistaken him for an officer in civilian dress. A dashing Aryan spirit shaped his every movement; there was also always something sunny about him, and his glance had a stirring warmth.[36]

As can be seen here, in this scale of values for judging people, it rates particularly highly if a civilian looks like 'an officer in civilian dress'. That he was purported to have, as highest praise, 'something sunny', 'a stirring warmth' and 'dashing Aryan spirit' should not be blamed on Erich Schmidt himself, who had received many decorations and never wore them. 'Dashing Aryan spirit' – Wilhelm II displayed it, and Hitler imitated it. A concept, a characteristic, which was coarsened by the Nazis and continues to play a role as a rejected counter-image among Germans of the younger generation can be seen here by anyone looking back at its original context as part of the human ideal of an aristocratic officer. It would be worth investigating how much of the National Socialist way of evaluating people was a degenerate and coarsened version of old German noble virtues.

'Sunny' is a term of praise along the same lines, just like the posturing to which Zobeltitz awards high marks elsewhere in his obituary: 'A little bit of posture is also quite nice . . .'. Zobeltitz also mentions that Schmidt called himself a liberal, but, 'God knows', he added by way of excuse, 'not in the same sense as people on the left', and he praised him as 'a man of the world from head to toe: probably the only "professor of literature" who could combine profound knowledge with an urbane personality'.[37] The picture is taking shape. Among the positive traits emphasized by Zobeltitz belong – in addition to a comely appearance – refinement, elegance, kindness, dashingness, and a little posturing, showing oneself off. All in all, these were the criteria by which a military-aristocratic class judged people. Elements of this upper-class code were then absorbed through a specific selection process by middle-class strata and, according to their own needs, selectively built into their behavioural code.

Incidentally, the attraction felt by middle-class strata for upper-class models gradually decreased after the turn of the century, as the weakness of the nobility and its inability to protect the middle classes from the rise of the working classes became ever clearer. Advancing industrialization and especially urbanization contributed decisively to this development. They lessened the political clout of the rural and agricultural population in relation to the urban population. At nearly every general election, the Social Democratic Party increased its votes and its number of members of parliament. It is difficult to visualize the reaction of the *satisfaktions-fähig* upper class when the Social Democrats emerged from the 1912 general elections for the first time as the strongest party. Like every old establishment, the German and in particular the Prussian aristocrats and the middle-class stratum which made common cause with them – the people of the *satisfaktionsfähige Gesellschaft* – took it for granted that they and only they were intended to rule in Germany. As they saw it, it was quite clear that these people from below, these workers and their representatives, did not have what it took to govern a realm as great as the German empire. And now they saw, in the increasing number of votes for the Social Democrats, the unstoppable avalanche of what they called the 'masses' rolling towards them.

Certainly, the tension between urban commercial, industrial and agrarian groups increased in the course of this process, which was one of the standing features of the second empire. And the urban commercial classes, represented in the Reichstag by the Liberals for instance, also formed part of the opposition bloc that even before the beginning of the 1914–18 war no longer always obeyed the rules of the court-aristocratic good society. In their camp, by the end of the imperial era, there were already tendencies towards informalization, infringing the strict, highly formalized upper-class code.

One example is in the development of women's clothing at about the end of the imperial era. Zobeltitz noted in June 1914 with considerable outrage that the dress even of good middle-class families was no longer guided by the more stringent code of the upper classes. This is an early sign of an informalizing process which was to gain strength after the war in the context of the defeat of the imperial upper classes:

> The protectors of morality have very often railed against modern women's clothing; it has been inveighed against from the pulpits; a bishop has had sharp words to say against the sinfulness of slit skirts and blouses with deeply cut necklines. Now I am not a zealot and do not regard everything that is saucy as sinful; I have even recently spoken out against the general condemnation of our ladies' fashions. However, I admit that my view has changed, that the customs of our ladies have become not only saucy but here and there decidedly distasteful. For girls from so-called good society to show their legs to the knee at every movement requires a disconcerting lack of modesty. Toilettes as we see them today would have been impossible twenty years ago; under the Directory the nymphs of the *Palais Royal* may have worn similar garb. In those days, the revolution from above gave the push for upheaval; nowadays the impetus comes from the midst of the good-as-gold middle class. The ladies in slit skirts and with deep *décolletage* are, for heaven's sake, no women from the night clubs, but belong to good families. And that is exactly what is so scandalous. . . .
>
> But gentlemen's modes of dress in summer have also become quite negligent. To carry one's hat in one's hand may be just about acceptable. But to go for a walk with one's jacket over one's arm is really more like the manners of a travelling workman. And even if one's shirt is spotlessly clean, it is unseemly and *equally* signifies a lack of modesty to show oneself publicly in a get-up that does not meet the usual conventions of society.[38]

Here we catch a passing glimpse of the beginnings of a long process of informalization in clothing which has occurred in the twentieth century. In the course of it, women's legs and busts gradually emerge from the hiding into which they were driven as a mark of unperturbed male dominance. For men, too, it became possible in the course of this process to show themselves in public without headgear, and not to lose the respect of their neighbours, or their status as respectable citizens. They can venture to go for a walk or even appear at the office in shirt-sleeves without being looked at askance. The extent of this informalization of dress is not, however, the same in all countries. In Germany, more value is still placed, for example, on smart men's clothing, on formal, well-cut, fitted suits; and even now, people are less ready to take off their jackets and to go about in shirt-sleeves in Germany than, for instance, in America. A remnant of the rule that a man should look spruce has survived in Germany. It is part of that country's somewhat assertive social forms. In comparison, in the British code of dress, unobtrusive hallmarks rank especially high, such as the quality of the material or a discreetly good cut. That a Cambridge don gave a pair of new trousers to one of his students to wear first so that they would look worn is probably only a myth, but a myth not quite without significance.

Whatever national differences there may be in the development of the dress code, the fact that during the twentieth century an informalization of both men's and women's dress has taken place in the more advanced industrial countries can hardly be denied once it is viewed in the context of long-term processes. It is tempting to explain the change simply as a process of rationalization. It could be said that it is simply more rational for men to go around bare-headed and in shirt-sleeves when it is warm enough. But how closely an informalizing spurt is intertwined with changes in power relations becomes very clear in this context. A person's clothing gives out a whole range of signals to others; above all, it signals how the person sees him- or herself, and how, within the limits of what he or she can afford, he or she would like to be seen by others. But how a person sees him- or herself and would like to be seen also depends on the total power structure of a society and his or her position within it. For court-aristocratic upper classes, conspicuous differences between groups, ceremonies and rituals, and also people's appearance as symbols of social membership and social distance, played a far greater role – among other things as means of ruling – than for commercial and manufacturing upper classes. The abandonment of formalities, and along with them types of clothing whose exclusive or primary function had been the visible symbolization of social differences, distances, superiority and subordination, was therefore easier in the more developed industrial states where the main power struggle was between the middle-class and working-class groups than it had been in the industrial nation-states of the early twentieth century in which the establishments still had to a large extent a court-aristocratic and military character.

9

Zobeltitz, himself a nobleman (and Prussian officer before circumstances forced him to turn to writing light novels and weekly reports about Berlin society for the avid Hamburg public), describes the court society as if it were a single social estate or status-group. The aristocracy did indeed form the core unit of the establishment under the *Kaiserreich*. But it is not really possible to do justice to the peculiarities of the upper class of this period without taking into account the categorization of top middle-class groups and their hierarchically graded amalgamation with the nobility to form a broader 'good society'. Since this more extended good society of the *Kaiserreich*, taken as a whole social formation, had no explicit constitution, and because its members themselves employed unwritten criteria in recognizing each other as members, I have chosen one of the most prominent of these unwritten criteria as a technical term to denote them conceptually: that of being entitled to demand and give satisfaction in a duel. It draws attention to the fact that the imperial German upper class was not solely a class made up of one estate, the courtly, military and official aristocracy, but was a hierarchical fusing together and integration of these aristocratic status groups with middle-class groups. Merchants, capitalists, entrepreneurs, were not included, but senior civil servants and university professors, and all sorts of graduate professionals, were. In line with its continuing position of power, the warrior nobility's traditional contempt for businessmen was still fairly acute; and the stigmatizing upper-class term *Koofmich*[39] ('tradesman'), just like the negatively loaded expression *Verstädterung* (which literally means 'urbanization', but became a rural-aristocratic term of contempt) has entered into national colloquial German, together with other elements of the aristocratic cultural baggage.

The bourgeoisification of the nobles' code of honour has quite a complicated history, which we do not need to go into any further here. In any case, the shared code of honour was one of the clamps which attached student fraternities and graduates to the noble apex of society within one great society of *satisfaktionsfähig* men. Perhaps it would help bring the concept to life if I sketch an example of this society's own conception of itself.

At the beginning of March 1895, the students of the Berlin universities organized a Bismarck Evening in honour of the great old man from Friedrichsruh. Taking part in this celebration were not only the fraternities with their sworn members and banners, but also the Imperial Chancellor, Prince Hohenlohe, and several of his ministers, as well as a whole lot of generals, members of the federal parliament, including the leader of the German Conservative Party, privy councillors, professors and some princes and diplomats. Some of the students had composed a new song about Bismarck, to a bracing tune which was sung with fervour by those present. It began:

> Now rises the flame of enthusiasm
> Blazing in our song,
> For the man from the German tribe,
> For the hero who slew the dragon,
> Who on the Rhine's wine banks
> Planted the empire's mighty tree,
> For the man through whom the dreams
> Of our fathers came true.[40]

There had been times when the mass of German students were in more or less pronounced opposition to the establishment, and perhaps to the older generation, of their day. At the beginning of the nineteenth century, the nationalist fraternities in particular were at the forefront fighting for greater equality between people. They were thus also representative of an informalizing movement which attempted to relax the inherited rituals of inequality, such as the relative lack of rights of students in their early semesters compared with more senior students. The nationalist fraternities' goal of German unification was in some cases combined with striving to push through democratic constitutions in the individual German states, as a preliminary step towards a German parliament.[41] The enthusiasm of the early nationalist fraternity members for the type of gymnastics introduced by Jahn[42] also shows this longing for freedom and equality. For what Jahn understood by gymnastics was not the formalized gymnastics with elaborate apparatus, which at a later period became an instrument of political education. Jahn himself rejected every form of discipline and drill.[43] Nor should gymnastics be a duty; every participant should be able to structure the session himself, everyone should be able to exercise just as he felt like. Even team gymnastics was considered to be restrictive in his circle. Only voluntary exercises and games which met the needs of the individual participants complied with the ideals of that time. Accordingly, Jahn's gymnastic games and exercises were anything but tame. Many of the early nationalist fraternity members liked this sort of gymnastics precisely because it did not force them into hard and fast forms and gave individual freedom wide scope within a framework of equality for all.

But now at the end of the nineteenth century, the long-desired goal of the unification of Germany, which, like a beautiful dream, had seemed very distant at the beginning of the century, had become an accomplished fact. The mostly middle-class nationalist fraternities were ranked below the duelling corps in the status hierarchy – Wilhelm II had belonged to the Bonn corps *Borussia* for a short period in his youth – but they, too, now accepted their place in the hierarchical order of the German upper strata, just as did the top cadre of university graduates in the German middle class in general. Quite a number of earlier nationalist fraternity members had been persecuted as demagogues by the state authorities because of their liberal and democratic opinions. Later members of the fraternities abandoned the attempt to achieve their former social goals once their national goals had been fulfilled. They accepted the inequality, their own second-rank social existence as commoners, and accepted the noble stratum's privileged supremacy under the second empire, as the price for their own unwritten privileges and elevation over the masses being protected against the growing pressure from below.

This was because hand in hand with national unification went the unification of the workers' party organizations and their increasing political potency. Fear of revolution was already making the German upper classes, the aristocratic as well as the middle-class parts of the *satisfaktionsfähige Gesellschaft*, nervous in the nineteenth century, long before the successful revolution in Russia. Zobeltitz expressed it clearly and openly. On 19 October 1894, he wrote:

> Only the Philistine who can be shaken out of his comfortable peace by nothing until the roof over his head is set alight can shut out the rumbling of the socialist volcano which is forming under the surface of today's society; and only the Philistine whose income is reduced by taxes can oppose the view that a strong army is the only protection and the strongest barrier to the growth of elements threatening the state. Yesterday's consecration of the flag forms a new milestone in the defence of the government against revolution. The Kaiser's words, which a blind press carried away by party passion has already begun to criticize again, voiced this too.[44]

The integration of predominantly middle-class student fraternities, in which originally democratic tendencies critical of state and society had quite often been prevalent, into the core 'good society' of the empire with its court-aristocratic peak had several consequences for the structure and the behavioural codes of these fraternities. In rebelling against the ruling order, they had also been protagonists of a conflict of generations; their earlier opposition to the social and especially state establishment of the day went hand in hand with opposition to the values, attitudes and whole code of the older generations. Now, as junior partners of the social and governing establishment, the student nationalist fraternities made the values and attitudes of the older generations more and more their own.

Until the Franco-Prussian War, the nationalist fraternities, which by tradition were predominantly middle class, differed from the more aristocratic corps mainly in their social and national goals. The outcome of the 1870–1 war did not fulfil all the political hopes and wishes of the nationalist fraternities, since some of their members were disappointed that the unification of Germany excluded Austria. But even if not all dreams were realized, unification itself was now achieved. The realization of a group's political goals, however, has consequences for its further development which are scarcely less important than the total destruction of a group dream. In this case, moreover, the group's social goals had been realized in a manner scarcely in accord with the expectations of the nationalist fraternities or the German upper middle class in general. The hope of German unification was not achieved through their own victory over the aristocratic groups which, with the princes at their head, had previously been largely geared towards maintaining the existing multi-state structure of Germany; the middle-class groups, especially the nationalist fraternities, who had been endeavouring to obtain national unity, received the fulfilment of their wishes and hopes as a present, so to speak, from the hands of their social opponents.

This fulfilment of the hopes and dreams of the middle class and the fraternities, coupled with the strengthening of the social groups who had brought this about – in the first place, the Kaiser and his generals, then the aristocracy in general – required a rather radical reorientation for the students who formed the nationalist fraternities. Their national goals had been achieved, and, as for their social ones, these now retreated into the background – as payment for being incorporated into the new German establishment.[45] This whole readjustment did not occur in one fell swoop, but it was symptomatic of the process of change in large parts of the German middle class. It involved the merging of its top strata into those of the German aristocratic hierarchy grouped around the Kaiser and his court – as the latter's lowest rank, in effect. They became part of an upper-class network, central to whose membership criteria were the entitlement to demand satisfaction and the obligation to uphold a common code of honour. If, before 1870, the nationalist fraternities and the duelling corps had differed in many respects both in their behavioural codes and in their political objectives, afterwards the former gradually aligned their code and their goals with those of the latter. Future objectives disappeared more and more from their agendas; maintenance and consolidation of the existing social and political order moved noticeably into the centre of their attention. The more idealistic aspects of their programme disappeared. Those nationalist fraternities which had beforehand insisted on celibacy for their members now renounced it. Like the duelling corps, so now did the nationalist fraternities also firmly establish the principle of unconditional satisfaction, the obligation to duel, on which they had previously not insisted for their members. All members were obliged to participate in a certain number of fencing matches by appointment [*Bestimmungsmensur*] each semester. The rules under which these engagements were conducted, like those for duelling with heavier swords or pistols, became stricter and – in the course of time – more standardized for all the student fighting fraternities.

With the disappearance of shared goals for the future, contemporary formalities took on heightened meaning in student life. They served as status symbols, as a sign of being raised above the masses, as weapons in status competition between students within the same association as well as between different associations. As a counterpart to the distribution of power and the status hierarchy in the macrocosm of the German upper classes, a more set and more unambiguous status hierarchy gradually became established in the microcosm of the student fighting fraternities. Within it the corps, with the exclusive *Borussia* of Bonn at the top, were accorded the highest place. The nationalist fraternities were content with second place, but, through the strictness of their fencing customs, constantly endeavoured to prove that they were second to none in courage and honour. Below them in the status order came the other duelling fraternities.

Let us now take a closer look at the life of these corporations.

10

One of the unplanned functions of the student fighting fraternities, as already explained, was the broader upbringing of young men – at that time, women students were few and far between – in the sense of inculcating a standardized upper-class code. In particular, the baptism by blood through the fencing competitions contributed to bringing the scions of honourable but not very distinguished houses more into line in behaviour and attitudes with the customs and cast of mind of the 'old' families.[46]

The peculiar training which these corporations bestowed upon their members matched a need created by the character of German – and not just German – universities. Their entire set-up made the universities primarily places of teaching. No doubt some university teachers, along with their function as producers and transmitters of knowledge, also fulfilled tasks relating to more general upbringing. In such cases they had a certain influence on the personal life of students, taking part in their social life. But that was not the rule. Then, as now, the universities left their young charges to themselves in this respect.

The student fraternities at German universities thus filled a gap. Students in their first semester were living away from home possibly for the first time in their lives, perhaps in a town where they knew hardly anybody. Certainly, some of them had already been recommended to a particular fraternity from home; but it also happened again and again that the fraternities themselves cast an eye over the new arrivals for suitable new members, and attempted to 'rope in' some of them. Joining a fraternity made the life of a new arrival easier in various ways. It made contact with other students easier; it helped him to escape quickly from the loneliness and, perhaps, the insecurity of his new situation. In the fraternity, a full programme of social events awaited him; to begin with it often left little time for study – morning drinking sessions, early morning walks, fencing, beer evenings, bowls, cards or ceremonial drinking evenings took precedence. Fraternity life definitely demanded obedience and subordination to the older members, but newcomers were treated a bit more leniently at first; there was a certain honeymoon period for 'foxes'. Perhaps the novices felt it beneficial that everything had a precisely regulated form. They were among their own, and needed merely to let themselves be carried by the current, following the fraternity rules and the older students who propounded them, and everything would be fine. The universities taught formal knowledge, the fraternities good breeding. They offered company and conviviality to the individual, a wealth of things to do, and, in the shape of the Old Boys, the promise of a network of connections in later life, very helpful in their career.

But for the moment, the formalization of social life in the framework of a student fraternity still had a great deal of the wildness of youth about it. It was basic to this character training that it not only allowed but actually compelled the acting out of comparatively infantile and barbaric impulses which, for many novices, had probably long since been repressed by the controls of conscience. This acting out of forbidden impulses was at the same time strictly hemmed in by a mesh of rituals which had to be followed exactly. For the newcomers, the 'crass foxes', it can hardly have been easy to adapt to the obligations of this paradoxical student code which encouraged the acting out of wild impulses previously beset with strict taboos – such as deliberately having bloody fights with other people – and which at the same time also encouraged the ceremonial enchainment of this acting out through strict compliance with a tightly constructed framework of rules of conduct.

The power structure of the fraternities enabled new recruits to become accustomed to this compulsion to act out the forbidden, and simultaneously to control this acting out through a rigid formalization. Every fraternity was an association between age groups, within which the seniors had precisely graded powers of command and decision-making over the juniors. In this relationship between age groups there was no lack of comradeship, affection and friendliness – each newcomer had to choose a patron from amongst the older members, who to the best of his ability stood by him in his difficult transition, despite the gap in years. But for all the support the newcomers might be given, the power structure of the fraternities was at the same time rigid and unrelenting. Seniors just as much as juniors were its prisoners. It formed that very apparatus of external constraint which was necessary to give the younger ones the strength to cope with the explosive student code of behaviour – in other words, to keep them under control while they were getting used to it. Older members too, those who had already succeeded in identifying completely with their fraternity, were helped, amid this competitive life with its high pressure to compete, its drinking wagers, its minor and more serious duels, its hither and thither of release and ritual enchaining, to avoid all dangers and to keep themselves constantly under control.

The greatest danger was, of course, permanent expulsion from the fraternity. This threat hung over all members. It strengthened the seniors' power over the younger members, and the power of the fraternity as a whole over any single person, since anyone who had been 'thrown out' of his fraternity was marked for life. With the knitting together of a *satisfaktionsfähige Gesellschaft* which stretched over the whole of Germany, there was no escape in a case like that. The stigma of having lost membership of a fraternity did not burden a student only in his university town. If he moved to another town, the news soon caught up with him, and followed him across the entire country whenever he sought admission to the circles of the *satisfaktionsfähige Gesellschaft*.

Other groups might be open to him. But quite often, his self-conception and sense of social status – his whole personal identity – were geared up with belonging to just those circles. The threat of losing fraternity membership was thus a very serious disciplinary measure, which contributed to holding on to even reluctant students or, if need be, overcoming their resistance to fraternity rituals.

On the other hand, the fraternity offered a large number of pleasures in compensation for the never-ending fear of the constraints – of failing at fencing matches, of being at the mercy of a stronger and more skilful duelling opponent, of failings in observance of the drinking code, of any slip in doing the right thing before it became second nature – a slip which could have such dangerous consequences. The compensations included being embedded in a group, taking part together in the drinking evenings and in singing the old songs in the course of growing beer-induced conviviality, the procession in full regalia with colourful banners on ceremonial occasions, the sense of being superior to the masses, and the pride in passing the difficult tests which took one upwards, and so to belonging to those at the top.

The power structure of these student fraternities, with its hierarchical apparatus of constraint, throws some light on the characteristics of the personality structure which was developed within them. It was not like what Max Weber, correctly or incorrectly, termed a 'Protestant conscience-formation': the construction of a mechanism of self-control, with the help of which a single person, completely alone, was enabled to steer his own actions whatever other people said, deciding for himself and responsible only to his conscience and his God. The training of the corps and the nationalist fraternities was unintentionally much more directed towards the formation of a personality dependent for the taming of its own impulses to a large extent on social support, or control by other people. In order to tame his socially strengthened fighting impulses, the person who went through the training of fencing bouts needed a supporting society with a clear structure of dominance and subordination, a hierarchy of command and obedience. He developed a personality structure in which his self-constraints, that is, his own conscience, required support from the external constraint of a strong power in order to be able to function. The autonomy of the individual conscience was limited. It was bound by an invisible umbilical cord to a social structure which included a strictly formalized hierarchy of levels of command. Left to themselves, the self-controls which the typical fraternal life of students was geared to fostering were too weak to resist the impulses which were brought to the surface partly by this very way of life. In short, the society was so structured that, in each person brought up within it, there was produced a need for a society of that kind. The authority of the individual conscience was dependent on its directives. On its own too weak to keep the elementary drive-impulses in check, it required either commands from others or command over others to become fully effective. The conscience-formation stamped in people by character training in the fraternities therefore shows a close affinity with that of officers, who were also yoked into a hierarchy of command and obedience from the beginning.

Now the idea of groups which are so structured that member individuals develop a totally independent, fully autonomously function-ing conscience is undoubtedly an ideal-typical exaggeration. In reality, unless sick, no one in his or her decisions – his or her self-steering – ever undertakes a plan of action without taking any account of what it may mean for others as well as for him- or herself. All that can actually be observed is greater or lesser *relative* autonomy in individual consciences according to whether self-constraints or external constraints have the bigger share in steering the conduct of particular persons. What was said earlier, therefore, can only mean that the individual character structure produced by being brought up in accordance with the student and military code of honour included a conscience which was *relatively* highly dependent on the opinion of other people, and thus also *relatively* heavily reliant, in coping with short-term drive-impulses, on self-controls being reinforced by external constraints. The very concept of 'honour' itself points to this structure. For however much an awareness of one's honour guided one's conduct, fear of losing honour in the eyes of one's we-group always played a central part in reinforcing the self-constraint which was necessary to behave as the code of honour demanded.

This is in keeping with the fact that the concept of honour, viewed as an observable social fact and not as a philosophical idea, plays a central role in closely knit human groups, and especially in warrior groups and their derivatives. Originally, it was above all warrior strata who legiti-mated themselves through a code of honour, that is, through the pairing of violence with courage. Pacified middle strata legitimated themselves far more through the conceptual symbol of being honourable in the sense of moral and honest. For those who have *honour*, the concept of honour is a means and sign of social distinction. By means of it, noble ruling groups raise themselves as a class above the other groups of their society, especially over those middle classes who legitimate themselves primarily through a *moral* code. The comparison illustrates the difference. The moral code of the middle classes requires and represents a higher degree of individualization, and greater relative autonomy of individual self-controls, than does the code of honour – even if, as an observable social fact, it never entirely possesses the absolute autonomy usually attributed to it in philosophical discussions of what morality ought to be like.

Whatever the case in this regard may be, the comparison of the code of honour of warrior strata with the moral code of middle strata makes it clear why the former is so closely associated with a power structure which rests on a strict hierarchization of human relationships, a clear order of command and obedience, whereas the latter, the middle-class code of morality, seems explicitly to advance a claim to be valid universally, and thus implicitly to express the postulate of the equality of all people. One of the peculiarities of the German student fraternities is that the middle-class moral code, the most grandiose philosophical expression of which is Kant's *Critique of Practical Reason*, really played a role only in the early days of one group of them, the nationalist fraternities. Even in their case it became blended in a specific way with the code of honour of the upper stratum. After 1871, as a considerable part of the middle classes merged more and more with the aristocratic upper classes in the framework of the Kaiser's new German empire, even the predominantly middle-class nationalist fraternities more and more lost all earlier elements of the moral code. The goals of upbringing and social life they provided were from now on, no differently from those of the corps and the other fighting fraternities, orientated towards the pure code of honour, without moral admixtures.

The same goes for hierarchization. In the early days of the nationalist fraternities, as already mentioned, some of their members attempted – in accordance with the egalitarian tendencies of middle-class strata in a period of aristocratic dominance – to abolish or at least to mitigate the sometimes brutal regime of the older over the younger members. Now, by the end of the century, the rituals of rule by the seniors had also become – in a more regulated form – firmly established customs in the nationalist fraternities. Perhaps rule by the seniors was easier to bear in these student associations than in adult society because in the former it was shorter lived. Student age groups turned over relatively quickly. If the younger members had now to suffer under the rule of the seniors, they still knew that in one or two years they themselves would be the seniors. The officers' maxim of instilling into youngsters strict obedience so that they themselves could one day issue commands as seniors was also a central element in the code of the student associations. Only the means were somewhat different.

One of the most peculiar formalities of the student associations was the strictly ritualized bouts of drinking. These had a long history. The drinking rules – the *Bierkomment* – of the student associations were the late offshoot of a German tradition which can be traced back to at least the sixteenth or seventeenth century. In those days, in an epoch of never-ending wars when Germany eventually became the central arena for the violent fighting-out of all the larger European conflicts, a type of drinking epidemic developed throughout the German territories. It did not take the form of the individualized alcoholism of today, but rather that of group boozing. At that time, perhaps as compensation for the afflictions of never-ending war, rituals of toasting and drinking for wagers took hold even at the courts, giving the drinking sessions something of the character of competitive games.

In its later form, this German code of toasting and drinking for wagers became for the student corporations both a formalized type of conviviality and a means of training, an instrument of the power of the seniors over the juniors. For the juniors were compelled to drink at these bouts – they had to learn to 'keep up' if a senior raised his glass to them, whether they wanted to or not; they had to learn to keep themselves under control to some extent even when they were more or less drunk, and when they felt sick they had to follow the measures intended for this. They raised their glasses to each other, they 'rubbed salamanders',[47] they sang the old songs, 'Free, free, free is the lad.' In the course of the bout they became merrier, freer, more boisterous even; but it was a merriment ritualized to the highest degree, hemmed in by an edifice of constraints. It fostered the competitive spirit: 'Let's see how much the newcomers can take' – they toasted them more and more, they drank for wagers with and against each other. Whoever could take the most was the winner. The merriment strengthened the feeling of belonging together, one with another. In singing, the voices blended together, the chorus represented the group itself, and the individual merged into it, the barriers disappeared. And by daylight they were there again.

At the turn of the century, the Old Boys started a movement against the compulsion to drink. They pointed out the harmful effects of excessive drinking, pleaded for the relaxation of the compulsions of the *Bierkomment*, and even advocated the toleration of teetotal members – with what success it is difficult to say.

It was similar with the fencing matches. Up to the 1860s, student fencing competitions were still like actual duels. Real quarrels between students, like officers, were resolved with naked weapons. Single combat was comparatively little ritualized. The opponents had considerable freedom of movement: they could move sideways, dodge with their heads and bend the body forwards a little in order to get in a better thrust. When, with the unification of the German empire in 1871, even the formerly oppositional nationalist fraternities began, like the corps and other fighting fraternities, increasingly to see themselves as representatives of the new Germany and assistants of the imperial government, the student duelling rites began to differentiate in a characteristic way. That is, the rites of single combat bifurcated. One part persisted in the form of the duel; through this, upper-class people, who regarded it as beneath their dignity to beat each other up like commoners, could act out their anger and hate for each other in a somewhat more regulated way more appropriate to their station. In this form of single combat, people could severely wound or even kill each other.

At the same time, however, in accord with the function of student corporations in minting members of the new German upper strata, a particular form of single combat developed into a peculiar means of training. It was demanded of members of the fraternities that they learn to inflict bloody wounds on each other with their weapons, but these were to be solely on the face, on the skull or on the ears, and were to leave behind no greater damage than a few deep scars on the head. This type of single combat, which served purely as a means of discipline, was called a fencing match by appointment [*Bestimmungsmensur*]. Those in charge of two fighting fraternities would decide which of their young members were to fence against each other. The seniors also fought by appointment. This was thus no longer a case of avenging an insult or slur on one's honour in single combat, or giving vent in a passage at arms to the anger and rage one felt towards another person with whom one had had some argument or whom one could not stand. In these single combats by appointment, in most cases one fought against someone not personally selected by oneself, one fought against him at best for the honour of one's fraternity, and otherwise quite simply as a compulsory exercise. Not only was every member of a fighting fraternity duty-bound to fight a certain number of fencing competitions by appointment per semester, but he was watched to see if he carried himself well during them. Anyone who did not satisfy these strict rules was thrown out – with all the consequences of being excluded from the *satisfaktionsfähige Gesellschaft* of unified Germany.

11

The push towards the unification of Germany on the political level had its counterpart on the level of the fighting fraternities in the standardization of the code of honour and the rules of the duel. From this point onwards, they developed against the background of strong status competition within and between the fighting fraternities, and through this pressure they acquired a dynamic of their own; their development could only be steered to a minimal extent by the people bonded to each other in this way, since in the end it depended on the overall situation of the social groups involved and their development.

In the case of the fencing matches by appointment, this dynamic resulted in constantly rising demands on the behaviour of opponents. The caps which had protected the head were done away with, stances which would help to parry the opponent's thrusts were restricted. Students selected by their fraternities to participate in a fencing match by appointment had to return every thrust, but were allowed to move only hand and arm in doing so. In this way, the rounds became shorter since most of the young students could keep up these demands on themselves for only a very few thrusts. The fencers themselves became ever more dependent on their usually older seconds, who kept an eye on the strict observance of the rules.

Georg Heer points out in his *Geschichte der deutschen Burschenschaft* [History of the German Student Duelling Associations] that the 1870–1 war was a decisive turning point in the development of the fighting fraternities. He says among other things, that, since then,

> life within most nationalist fraternities has become flat, and the students'
> preoccupation solely with arms leads to the neglect of patriotic political
> training, academic and moral education, and physical toughening, and it
> gives rise to a tendency towards triviality.[48]

He reports that fraternity members increasingly kept an eye open for any weakness or mistake on the part of their own fraternity brother during a fencing competition, in order to force him afterwards, by general resolution, to participate in a remedial match, and that if they were still not satisfied, he would be thrown out of the fraternity.[49] The seconds on each side were more and more concerned with finding fault with the fencer on the opposite side. The opposition seconds, caught up in the same dynamic, were in turn geared to denying these accusations. It could happen that the seconds themselves got into an argument with each other, and then on their part challenged each other to a duel – to a challenge between seconds which had to be fought immediately; and then the students who functioned as seconds in this bout between seconds sometimes fell into dispute in their turn. The result, as Heer noted,[50] was that 'most people who attended as seconds were those who enjoyed stirring things up and having a scrap'.

All in all, after 1871 single combat, whether in the form of the fencing match by appointment, or a duel with heavier weapons, sometimes even with pistols, gradually came more and more into the centre of student life in the fighting fraternities. Just as, under other determinable circumstances, one encounters a dynamic of increasing refinement, so what we encounter here is a dynamic of coarsening. Its connection with a formalization of violence is easily recognized.

The whole complex of person-to-person social relationships governed by the code of honour – in the first place, the obligation to duel, but also the compulsion to drink according to the rules of wagers and toasting, and other student derivatives of the warrior code – had a double function: it was both a training process for inculcating quite specific values, and a selection process for choosing quite specific personality structures. The selection process favoured the physically strongest, the most agile ruffians and fighting cocks, as is always the case in societies with a warrior ethos. The education attuned people towards a society with pronounced hierarchical inequalities where the person who was higher at any one time ostentatiously behaved as though he were a superior and better person, and expressly made all those lower than himself feel that they were lower, weaker and worse than he was.

In the *Kaiserzeit*, the fighting code of the fraternities developed on the whole in the direction of increased, more accentuated and formalized ritual violence. To many members of the *satisfaktionsfähige Gesellschaft* at the time, the dynamics of the ritual exercise of violence, whether in the form of fencing matches or settling a matter of honour with weapon in hand, seemed an accidental morbid growth or defect in what was otherwise a basically positive and good institution. However, the extent to which these so-called defects were actually aspects of the immanent dynamics of the student fraternities – trends closely bound up with the very character of the human relations fostered by their code – points to the futility of the repeated attempts to reform them. Heer describes some of these reforming efforts to remove the 'cancerous growth of degenerated fencing customs'. They recurred from the late nineteenth century up to 1914. The 1912 convention of nationalist fraternities formulated another series of recommendations to remedy the defects; at a further convention in 1914 its fencing committee declared 'that in view of the resistance of the fraternities to any reform, they had no suggestions to make'.[51] The great significance which the ritual use of violence had gained among the German upper classes, more than anywhere else in Europe, as a symbol of the power and superior status of their members, together with the strong competitive pressure which the hierarchically ordered student associations exercised upon each other, and the basically precarious situation of the Wilhelmine establishment, despite its external brilliance – all this together contributed not insignificantly to increasing the momentum of duelling amongst students. Also operating in the same direction was the tacit selection process favouring people with the traits of an aggressive and skilful swordsman.

Closely connected with the high value placed on duelling as a symbol of distinction and a mode of behaviour which, in the eyes of every member of a fighting fraternity, raised him and his group above the masses of Germans was the entire orientation of the training which the older members of the fraternities sought to give each new generation. It was expressly designed to show off one's own rank in the hierarchy of the social gradations of rank. From this point of view, the student symbolization of relations of power and rank through a person's whole deportment in social relations with others resembled the ceremonial customs of a court society, with which the customs of the fraternities under the second empire were indeed connected. The dissimilarities, however, are no less clear.[52] Whereas, at court, differences in rank between adults were already fixed simply through courtly etiquette and therefore hardly required emphasis through gestures on the part of individual bearers of rank and title, the ceremonious manner of a young student was often combined with gestures ostentatiously asserting his own higher position in accordance with the rank of his fraternity. Here is an example of the strategy of the ritualized sneering behaviour between students:

With regally uplifted nose, Werner strode past the tables of the gymnasts and nationalist fraternities, with solemnly doffed cap past the Hessian and Westphalian groups, smiling but also with a ceremonial bow he came up to the table of the Cimbers, where he was made welcome, but not with loud youthful hallos, but instead with the studied cheerfulness which the corps students always affected when they knew they were being watched.[53]

In its context, this quotation once again illustrates the formality-informality gradient which prevailed in the social lives of fraternity students, as in the *satisfaktionsfähige Gesellschaft* of Wilhelmine Germany in general. This scene takes place during the Marburg Museum Association Ball, mentioned earlier – a dance where the high-ranking student fraternities appeared together as groups, and where their members could – under supervision – meet and dance with young girls from the best of local society or from the accredited boarding schools. On this occasion, extremely formal conduct was what mattered, and it had to be precisely graded and varied according to the higher or lower rank of the persons one encountered. In this case, the ostentatious and meticulous adjustment of individual behaviour to the hierarchical ranking of the various student associations, as well as towards all persons present, therefore meant that the formality gradient was very steep. It required a strict self-discipline under the eyes of other people, a self-constraint which each person learned to exercise whenever he knew he was being observed by members of other fraternities or, if applicable, by the girls and their mothers.

The training to be self-constrained in the presence of one's own fraternity brothers was, according to circumstances and position in the hierarchy, not always quite as strict as it was during official collective appearances in public. Nevertheless, even in relations within the fraternities, there were very precise rituals of superiority and subordination. Even at the height of a drinking evening, fraternity members were never in the least allowed to forget that non-observance of distances always remained dangerous for lower-ranking, younger members. The reins could be relaxed to a certain extent only in the company of those of the same age and rank, but even this was limited. Thus, even in moments of the greatest boisterousness, a fraternity student still had to know exactly how far he could go. In social contact between members of the *satisfaktionsfähige Gesellschaft* in general, the formality-informality span was relatively narrow. Only in dealings with non-members, people of lower status, could one, if need be, let oneself go a bit more.

This is a characteristic of pretty well all upper classes in societies with relatively long and highly differentiated chains of interdependence. The web of prescriptions and proscriptions which such strata oblige their members to observe, as it applies to relationships between members, is quite tightly meshed and rigid. Behaviour even at amusements befitting their rank – for example, hunting, gambling, balls – is very precisely formalized. The code demands – and produces – a type of behaviour which even at these times of relaxation follows quite specific, preordained rules; it requires and leads individuals always ostentatiously to portray themselves as members of the upper class. They thus pay a price for sharing in the privileges of status and power of 'good society': in the presence of social equals or superiors, they always have to represent and legitimate themselves as members. They can often let themselves go more if they are not with their social peers. But whether or to what extent that is the case depends on the power gradient in the particular society.

The difference in the formality-informality gradient between upper-class people's dealings with each other and their dealings with non-members can be most simply illustrated through the example of the student fraternity code regarding conduct between the sexes. In their relations with girls of their own class, members of the fighting fraternities had to keep to very exact, unbendable rules. In contacts with girls from lower strata, as far as the prescriptive rules of their code were concerned, they were fairly free to do as they chose. Here, only the laws of the state applied.

What this well-known code of double morality for males meant for the young people who were subject to it is very vividly described in the novel by Bloem which I have cited several times before. A student who came fresh from school to a university town and joined a fighting fraternity came upon things there about which he previously perhaps had hardly any idea, and which at first severely shook him. He was the product of that curious upbringing in which, both at home and at school, problems of sexuality were, if at all possible, kept entirely outside the realm of the adolescent's learning and experience. However much other knowledge was imparted to boys and girls, giving them any knowledge at all of the relations between men and women was carefully avoided. What they learned about this came from their own contemporaries, or from the Bible and other books from which they secretly attempted to pick up just that knowledge – knowledge relevant to themselves – which the adults close to them did not want to impart, or perhaps were unable to impart because they themselves were too bashful and had too much internal resistance to overcome for them to be able to speak openly about the socially tabooed subject of sexuality. A young middle-class student therefore often came up to university without any sexual experience, without any clear understanding of his own desires, with a lot of more or less vague wishful notions and a conscience-formation orientated towards the moral precepts of his parents. Since his desires and his conscience were not really compatible, he suffered. Adults regarded this suffering as a natural characteristic of adolescence, as a sign of so-called puberty, and Bloem depicts his main character accordingly.

The 'crass fox' is rather abruptly shaken out of this situation through meeting his fraternity brothers. Even the songs they sing make it clear that there are two types of girls:

> Girls who love
> And practise kissing[54]

– of these, the song says that there were 'always heaps of them'. In contrast to them were girls

> . . . who yearn
> And strive to be platonic.

At the same time, Werner hears that the head of his fraternity, who has the reputation of being the greatest tough-guy in the university, already has three illegitimate children running around town.[55] Perhaps it is not quite realistic for Bloem to convey the impression that these are the very first occasions on which the young fox finds out that there are girls 'who love and practise kissing', and that not all girls only 'strive to be platonic'. But whatever fictional exaggeration or distortion there may be, he gives quite a good picture of the basic structure of the social scenario of the double morality.

In other words, at the beginning of this century in Germany, as in many other countries at the time, the middle-class code of relations between the sexes was, on the one hand, based on what is conventionally called morality – meaning that it laid down apparently eternal prescriptions valid for people at all times and places. Central to it was the precept restricting sexual relations between men and women to those within marriage. For young people, especially students, this code accordingly demanded total sexual abstinence, as long as they were not married. Since students were often not in a position to marry until their mid- or late twenties, consistent observance of this precept of their society meant a long, monkish life. But, on the other hand, the society of this period was selectively tolerant or 'permissive', to use a current expression, with respect to the observation of the moral code which it itself set. It demanded a strict observance of the rule of celibacy until marriage only from young women, while it allowed young men informal infringements.

In practice, for young middle-class men, including many students, this moral commandment of sexual abstinence until marriage was limited merely to relations with girls from their own social class. Since abstinence was indeed demanded from these young women until their marriage, and in their case transgressions of the rule were most heavily punished, for instance with social disgrace or banishment, young men of the higher classes were absolutely forbidden to push erotic relations with girls of the same rank to the point of sexual intercourse.

What appears to be a contrast between a general moral prescript and selective practice was thus *de facto* an expression of the social power gradient: for upper-class young men, contact with girls within the same class was either at a strict distance or in marriage, whereas in contacts with girls from outside the class sexual intercourse was allowed in the context of affairs or prostitution. At the same time, this is a striking example of the gulf between an ostentatious formality of behaviour, the maintenance of which presupposed the existence of strong external social pressure, and, at the opposite pole, fairly extreme informality, letting oneself go, acting out of emotions in realms where no external constraint reinforced the relatively weak capacity for self-constraint.

12

Becoming accustomed to the curious mixture of rigid formality and precisely delimited informality typical of the code of conduct of the student duelling corps and the nationalist fraternities was, as already remarked, seldom totally easy for the young students. In particular, being introduced to the rituals of the fencing match by appointment, and duelling in general, confronted them with a difficult problem.

Although duels by appointment were so structured that normally no really serious bodily harm was done to the participants, they were nevertheless, all in all, fairly bloody events. The older fraternity brothers were prepared for the fact that the beginners who were taken to the fencing ground for the first time often felt rather uneasy. They came from a society in which it was most strictly forbidden to get into bloody fights with anyone. Any wild childhood dreams of blood and murder which they might have had were long since banished from their consciousness. That some of the beginners shuddered was a sign that their consciences, which forbade such bloody deeds, were rebelling. But if they showed even the slightest sign that they were uneasy about this, they earned nothing but good-natured ridicule from the older members.

It was a popular joke to get one of the beginners to bring a live chicken to the fencing ground. It was needed, he was told, so that its flesh could be used to replace the cut-off tips of noses. The rapiers with which the duels by appointment were fought were essentially designed to cut through the skin of the face and skull and the blood vessels lying below the surface. Only the eyes were protected. One could injure one's opponent with a single blow so that the skin of the head hung down in great shreds. One could split one's nose and lips so that, for the time being, one could no longer speak; cut ears might hang down, and blood flow in streams from the veins in the temples.

Usually the beginner required a certain period of toughening up before his fraternity confronted him with a suitable opponent from another fraternity to fight. But when the test had been passed, the feeling of pride was increased. The procedure was certainly no worse than the initiation ceremonies of some simpler societies in which the bearing of pain as a proof of manliness and scarification as a sign of group membership also play a role. No doubt fighting for one's own fraternity against a representative of another served to reinforce the feeling of solidarity with one's own association. But it also strengthened the internal pressure of rivalry, the remorselessness with which the individual members of these fraternities judged the bearing of every other member during the fencing match, and helped to validate their – deeply group-orientated – code of honour. One of the consequences was that, in a milieu of groups of young men where (in contrast with the officers' milieu) this code did not have a direct link with any clearly defined duties or professional responsibilities, competition for higher status in the public opinion of one's own group – something seen in local groups in general – automatically intensified the fighting ritual. In this way, the members of student fraternities were prisoners of that very social structure which had made duelling a central, perhaps the most central, means of legitimating their claim to status.

With all this, one gains a further insight into the attitudes, or, more generally, the personality structure which this sort of communal student life and character training of young men were directed towards producing. It was a pitiless human habitus. Anyone who revealed himself as weak counted for nothing. Basically, people were brought up here to lash out hard whenever they realized they were confronted with a weaker person, making him immediately and unambiguously aware of their own superiority and his own inferiority. Not to do so was weakness, and weakness was contemptible.

Naturally the fraternities had systems of legitimating arguments designed to make clear to both members and outsiders the meaning and purpose of the student way of life, especially duelling. In his novel about student life, Walter Bloem sometimes put the classic justifications into the mouth of one or another of his characters.

After a short time, the hero of the book, Werner Achenbach, is not a little horrified at his experiences in the corps. He asks an older fraternity brother what this 'honour' of a student corps really is. How could he uphold it if he did not know what it was? The older member explained:

> Mmm, my dear chap, honour! Student-corps honour! If one could only put it in words! ... Look, I think that honour, it's just like ... like with fencing matches. You see, isn't it all really nonsense, the whole fencing business? Two young fellows, who have never done any harm in their lives, are set up against each other by the leaders and must then smash each other's noses and heads in two. It's total nonsense! But ... *one becomes a real man by doing it!* You get some spunk put into you ... and that is what really counts in life. ... I know perfectly well that this is all just touching on it, and that under the smooth, hard shell of the student corps there are also sometimes some dead losses and sometimes some rotten ones, too. But, you know, if the kernel is healthy, afterwards you should see how much good it does them, when the shell is so firm and so smooth![56]

Here, in a somewhat different version, there recurs the image of the kind of person of whom we have already seen Zobeltitz approving: a hard, smooth person. This image of people is intimately connected with a specific image of society. Adult life is a constant war of all against all. One has to be a tough customer to win through in this struggle. The untamed warrior ethos comes to life here once again in a bourgeoisified version. And indeed, in a society where a tradition of conduct in which life is seen as a struggle of all against all has gained dominance, and where there are institutions directed towards bringing up people with an appropriate personality structure, this type of social life may have such deep roots that, without far-reaching upheavals in the entire social structure, it will continue to reproduce itself. Even this late form of the warrior code thus shows one of the characteristic traits of societies in which people's physical fighting against each other, in however formalized a way, plays a central role. The harshness of human relationships which finds expression in the use of physical violence, in people being wounded or if need be killed by other people, spreads like an infection even to those areas of relationships in which physical fights do not occur at all.

One of the oddities of this code is that a whole range of aspects of human social life are not comprehended in it. They may develop as personal traits of individual persons in the interstices, so to speak, of the web of rules in such a society, but they are not incorporated into the code. This can be seen if one considers what could be described as one of the central criteria of a civilizing process: the extent and depth of people's mutual identification with each other and, accordingly, the depth and extent of their ability to empathize and capacity to feel for and sympathize with other people in their relationships with them. From the evidence presented here, this aspect of human relationships and everything which is derived from it is almost completely absent from the student code of honour. The upbringing provided by the student corporations during the *Kaiserzeit* certainly instilled a feeling of solidarity with other members of the same association. But it was narrow, relatively shallow and probably finer in nostalgic recollection than in the actual life of students at the time, when a moment's weakness on the part of a fraternity member was often enough to encourage the others to smash him down, even if only metaphorically.

Bloem sketches a scene which illustrates rather vividly this tendency to strike out mercilessly whenever another person showed a sign of weakness. One of the young men, called Klauser, had not satisfied the standards of his fraternity brothers in a fencing match: he had become engaged on the previous evening, and his thoughts were with the girl. Consequently, he was expelled by his corps and had to wait for the not very easy remedial rematch to clear himself, which would give him a chance, with some luck, to be taken back into the fraternity. In the meantime, he sat alone in his room, his head covered with a thick bandage, like a turban hiding his wounds. He could not go out, because every second person on the street would have pointed at him. Werner Achenbach visited him, and because as a first-semester 'crass fox' he still did not quite understand what had happened, he asked Klauser, who replied:

'Well, look here, for us corps students, fencing is not a simple sport, a game with weapons, but a . . . a means of upbringing. That is, the corps student is supposed to prove in fencing that bodily pain, disfigurement, even severe wounds and death . . . that all that is a matter of indifference to him. . . . When you have been in the corps longer, you will learn to

understand all this better. In the corps over the last few years the –
standards of fencing competitions ... have become a bit exaggerated.
Things ... are demanded, which ... well, which not everyone can
perform. And some can achieve them today, but then not again tomorrow.
Mood plays a big part ... health ... one's nervous condition.'

'Well really, my God – so you are being punished in this way because
you ... you got engaged the previous evening – ?!'

'Yes – to speak bluntly – that's right.'

'That is crazy. It's crazy.'

'Mmm, look – you really shouldn't ever forget ... those are people who
are judging us ... young devils like you and me ... naturally they are not
perfect. The C.C. thought that my fencing was poor, and so it was poor.
It is just like being in front of a jury. Sometimes even an innocent person
takes the rap. That is just tough luck.'

'Tough luck?! I think that is terribly severe, a horrible shortcoming of
the corps! – Oh, Klauser. ... The whole thing with the corps!! – ... I'm
really almost at my wit's end!! – And what about you? You must be in a
similar state! You are really and truly feeling the blessings of this wonderful
institution with your own flesh and your own blood ... at this very
moment!'

'With my own flesh and my own blood! Yes, I am. ... As I sit here, the
corps has debarred me from my fifteenth fencing match, has taken my
office away from me, and I don't even know if I'll be readmitted Saturday
week or whether I'll be thrown out permanently. Yes, believe you me, I'm
not really in the mood to paint a rosy picture and hush things up. Yes, a
great deal is not very nice in the corps. A lot could be different – gentler,
more humane, less in the same old way. But ... if I were a 'crass fox'
again ... I would nevertheless still be a corps student!!'

'Really, again? In spite of all this?'

'Yes – in spite of all this! I don't know: my feelings tell me that things
must be so. That it is all just so, so that we shall become useful for what is
to come later. ... So that we learn to grit our teeth – so that we become
men!'[57]

The *satisfaktionsfähige Gesellschaft*, which from 1871 to 1918 formed
the strictly hierarchically organized establishment of Germany, forced its
youth into a finely meshed net of rules; it encompassed the whole of
social life, as is the case with many upper-class associations. Now if –
particularly in their youth, but even later in life as well – people are
subjected to a highly formalized apparatus of social constraint, which
imposes severe privations on them and yet at the same time promises a
commensurate bonus of pleasure, for instance gaining or maintaining

high status, then they very easily persuade themselves to believe that the sacrifices they are making and the frustrations they are expected to endure have some point. Quite often, they do not know or understand the point of it themselves at all, but they are convinced it all makes sense even if they do not know what that sense is. This is because it would perhaps be disillusioning to have to admit that the privations one has borne actually have no point, no function, other than to maintain or increase the power of one's particular group and serve as a symbol of one's own higher status *vis-à-vis* other people. If one has expended a great deal of personal effort in obtaining skills such as those demanded by the student fraternity rules of that time, then it seems reasonable to suppose that one's own sacrifices and frustrations are meaningful and necessary. And if one basically cannot see their point, one at least becomes convinced that these privations are actually necessary because the common opinion of everyone in one's own social circle holds them to be necessary.[58] Bloem illustrates this attitude rather impressively.

The anchoring of the framework of rules of the *satisfaktionsfähige Gesellschaft* deep in the individual personality of its members, as a code which has become second nature to them, identifies each individual as belonging to this establishment. His entire habitus – his attitudes, ways of expressing himself, fundamental ideas about human beings, dis- tinguish him as such. That is his reward. In this society, of which the top court-aristocratic groups owed the continuance of their supremacy to victory in war, military forms of behaviour and feeling played a leading role. There was usually no further reflection upon the conceptions of the relations between human beings incorporated into the framework of rules of these strata and into the way that people accordingly behaved towards each other. These conceptions were hardly ever expressed in thinking at a higher level of synthesis; most members of this *satisfak- tionsfähige Gesellschaft* would probably have had little interest in or understanding of philosophical books anyway. At most, they were articulated by them in current sayings like the one the author puts in the mouth of a young student in a perilous situation: 'Grit our teeth, so that we become men.' He knows and says that in his society there is little kindness or compassion. Society demands unconditional submission to the rules of the code. Transgressions are punished, inexorably and without compassion.

Even though they lack forms of organization specifically intended for this purpose, relatively tightly closed upper classes have at their disposal severe and highly effective sanctions against people who break their code. They are of a kind which resembles those purposefully developed (especially in more recent times) by lower strata combining in organizations. Through such organizations, strike-breakers, for example, can be expelled from trade unions and may lose their jobs. The numerically far more restricted upper classes, too, threaten those who transgress against the code with punishments in the form of stigmatization and expulsion. And fear of these sanctions is so much more effective in this case, since it threatens to destroy not just the career but also the identity of the person in question. For if a person whose personal pride, self-esteem and sense of superiority are legitimated through membership of the upper class comes to lose his membership of the highest-ranking and most powerful stratum of his society by breaking its code, this involves a loss of identity and self-esteem which is frequently irreparable; it is difficult to make up for it and get over it.

Besides, in this case breaking the rules of the code is often not a decision of the person concerned in the way that a strike-breaker, for instance, goes against the group precepts fully aware of the probable consequences. The transgression can come about completely unexpectedly like a bolt from the blue. The episode from the novel quoted above is an example.

Underlying both the training provided within the student fighting fraternities and the life as a member of the imperial upper classes at which it was aimed is an implicit picture of human social life as a struggle of all against all which was almost Hobbesian in character. But as it developed in Germany, it was not a logically thought-out philosophy, but rather an unplanned tradition of behaviour and feeling produced by the blind fate of history. Precisely because it was not intellectualized, it appeared to be all the more self-evident and inescapable. To reiterate the quintessence of this tradition, in order in life to be a man, one had to be tough. As soon as one showed any weakness, one was lost. Therefore it was a good thing to display one's strength. Anyone who showed weakness deserved to be expelled; anyone who was vulnerable deserved to have salt rubbed into his wounds – and *Schadenfreude*, that untranslatable German word. (It is noteworthy in this connection that, although the emotion probably exists in many societies, there is a concept and hence unintentional canonization of it as a quasi-normal human characteristic in only a few.)

Like the duel and the code of honour, the associated image of social life, too, becomes understandable when seen as the manifestation of an upper class which, after many defeats and humiliations, caught up with its neighbours relatively late by virtue of a short series of victorious wars, but which at the same time knew itself to be most seriously threatened from within. In the face of the unstoppable election successes of the Social Democrats, who eventually forced their way into the Prussian Chamber of Deputies despite the three-tiered system of voting rights, the then leader of the conservative faction among the members, von Heydebrand, declared:

> The future does indeed belong to them; the masses will assert themselves and deprive us aristocrats of our influence. This current can only be temporarily held back by a strong statesman. We shall not, however, sacrifice our position voluntarily.[59]

Other countries, especially Britain, had a more flexible upper class. With very few exceptions, the strategy of compromise had a bad name amongst the German upper classes and from there it spread to the broader German tradition. To fight to the last man, to fight a losing battle to the bitter end, is an old European warrior tradition.[60] In Germany, with the co-option of important middle-class groups into the court-aristocratic establishment, it became a national tradition.

13

If the German middle class of the second half of the eighteenth century is compared with the German middle class of the second half of the nineteenth, a striking change is apparent. The changed ranking of culture [*Kultur*] in the scale of values of the more prestigious middle-class circles is enough to illustrate this. In the latter half of the eighteenth century, cultural achievements, especially in the areas of literature, philosophy and science, had a very high rating in the German upper middle-class scale of values. The economic power of urban middle-class circles and their world consciousness began to grow once more at this time. But, with few exceptions, the middle class had hardly any access to those government positions where decisions were made regarding the political, military, economic and many other affairs of the various states. These were almost exclusively in the hands of the princes and their court-civilized public servants. In court circles, aristocrats took precedence. Commoners who had gained access to the higher ranks of state administration and the judiciary broadly adopted the modes of behaviour of the court-aristocratic tradition. At that time, these circles were largely orientated to French patterns of behaviour and feeling, and indeed spoke French. Court people of middle-class background did the same; in short, they civilized themselves.[61]

Those sections of the rising middle class who remained largely excluded from access to the court societies and their power-chances developed a code of behaviour and feeling of their own. In this code, questions of morality played the same role that questions of courtesy, manners and good form played in convivial social life in the other. As in the codes of other upwardly mobile groups, the ideals of equality and humanity were also central to the code of the upwardly mobile German middle classes – Schiller wrote 'You millions I embrace you' and Beethoven took up the theme – whereas the idea of human *in*equality was embedded at least implicitly in the court-aristocratic code. The concept of culture, which in this period became a symbol of middle-class self-awareness and self-esteem, had a correspondingly strong humanitarian and moral element. The pattern of morality it embodied was taken by its proponents to be valid for people of all times and places, although in fact it mirrored the limited class-specific morality of these middle-class circles.

The changed part which the concept of culture and everything to which it referred played among the top middle-class strata in Germany after 1871, compared with its role in the second half of the eighteenth century, brings sharply into focus on a small scale the much larger changes in the character of the German middle class in this period. Certainly there were still sections of the German middle class who continued after 1871 to justify themselves in terms of the concept of culture, and in whose code of behaviour and feeling humanitarian ideals and problems of morality still occupied a central position. But large parts of the middle class – those in fact who had been integrated into the *satisfaktionsfähige Gesellschaft*, or who sought to be accepted by it – adopted the upper-class code of honour as their own. And in the rank-order of values represented by this code, especially in its Prussian version, cultural achievements and everything the German middle class had held dear in the second half of the eighteenth century, including humanity and a generalized morality, were ranked lower, if not positively despised. The musical interests of the court-aristocratic society itself were minimal, and the same was true of the model-setting circle of officers in the *Kaiserreich*. It goes without saying that, in these circles, the traditional warrior code of honour and not the middle-class code of culture and morality continued to be upheld. It is just as self-evident that this tradition was bound up with a convention of hierarchical inequality between people, of unconditional dominance and subordination.

The inclusion of a growing number of middle-class students in the *satisfaktionsfähige Gesellschaft*, as members of nationalist fraternities or of duelling corps, shows in a nutshell the difference between the educated middle class [*Bildungsbürgertum*] of the eighteenth century, which was largely excluded from the establishment and good society of the day, and the *satisfaktionsfähig* middle class of the late nineteenth and early twentieth centuries, which was part of the establishment and of good society. Compared with the interest in fencing, drinking sessions, pubs and convivial social events, in the fighting fraternities cultural and educational interests played a relatively small role. Questions of honour ranked high, moral questions low. Problems of humanity and mutual identification between people disappeared from view, and these earlier ideals were by and large despised as weaknesses of socially lower classes.

To express their own code of behaviour and feeling in more general intellectual or literary form fell neither in the area of responsibility nor the field of interest of people bound by the code of honour; but one man, who may well have seemed an outsider to them, did from time to time do just that in his own way. If one is looking for a clearly articulated version of the principles on which the training and social customs of the fighting fraternities were based, it can be found in the writings of a man of the Wilhelmine era – Friedrich Nietzsche, who, despite his occasional hatred of Germans, formulated some of the implicit articles of faith of the *satisfaktionsfähige Gesellschaft* of the *Kaiserzeit* better and more sharply than anyone else. What has previously been demonstrated in cameo by the fate of a young student is expressed in his work in more powerful language and greater generality. For example:

> What is good? – Everything that heightens the feeling of power in man, the will to power, power itself.
> What is bad? – Everything that is born from weakness.
> What is happiness? – The feeling that power is *growing*, that resistance is overcome.
> *Not* contentedness but more power; *not* peace at any price but war; *not* virtue, but fitness (Renaissance virtue, *virtù*, virtue free of moral self-righteousness).
> The weak and the failures shall perish; first principle of *our* love of man. And they should be given every possible assistance.
> What is more harmful than any vice? Active pity for all the failures and all the weak; Christianity . . . .[62]

Nietzsche's occasional hatred of Germans was probably partly a type of self-loathing. Even when he was at odds with the Germans because of their 'inner cowardice in the face of reality', their 'insincerity that has become instinctive', or because of their 'idealism', he was also basically at odds with himself. After all, he hid from himself that he himself was the weakling, desiring a war-like strength of which he was not capable.

What Nietzsche preached so angrily and with such a loud voice as something new and unusual was merely the well-considered verbaliz-ation of a very old social strategy. Despising the weak and feeble, upholding war and strength over peace and civil contentment – all these are hallmarks of the code discussed here, which had developed from the social practices of warrior groups of long ago. It may be restricted according to situation and experience by obligations of honour and knightly ritual, but warrior classes follow it without pondering overly much about it. In Europe, it was during the Renaissance that people first began to think about this warriors' code of behaviour at a higher level of generality. Machiavelli is the best known and perhaps the greatest, but certainly not the only, exponent of the first great wave of reflection, which raised the age-old social customs of warrior groups to a higher level of synthesis, recasting them more or less explicitly as a set of prescriptions. Nietzsche went only one step farther, insofar as he raised the warrior code in his thinking to an even higher level of generalization, and transformed it into an even more general prescription.

In doing so, he referred to the Renaissance as the last period in history before the Europeans followed the erroneous path, as he saw it, of the Christian religion with the high place it accords to compassion and weakness. Like many other people before and after him whose learning is based on books, he could not differentiate between reflections on social practices and these practices themselves, of which, needless to say, reflections on a lower level of synthesis also form part. He was not aware that, while his praise of the Renaissance was based primarily on books which innovatively and at a higher level than before considered the strategies of coercion observable in society, these strategies in themselves were prevalent in social usage long before they found higher-level intellectual expression; and despite all book censorship, they continued to play – with increasing restrictions – a quite considerable role in social usage. People whose knowledge is based on books tend to obscure the difference between reflections of higher generality on social usage set out in books and the relatively unreflected or less highly reflected usage itself. And Nietzsche was no exception. He barely took into account how deeply his praise of strength and the will to power was connected with then-contemporary events, and the practical conclusions which they suggested to thinking people.

The structural change which the German territories underwent in the course of the nineteenth century was one of these events. At the beginning of the nineteenth century, the German states were weak; even war-like Prussia was overrun by Napoleon's revolutionary armies without much difficulty. That contributed directly or indirectly to relaxing the grip of unenlightened, absolutist forms of rule in these areas, and shook some young men into a not very efficient and often rather pitiful resistance movement; but the German states were hardly strong enough to win wars of liberation on their own, only as allies of the great powers of the time. In middle-class circles, the memory of humiliation and the feeling of present weakness were not lost after the victory over the French. However, in the second half of the century, Germany rose relatively quickly to become a great power itself: indeed, Germany, which was still considered to be a weak giant in the balance of power in Europe at mid-century, became the leading power in continental Europe within a few decades.

If people living through these events sought to visualize how this rapid change had come about, then it was easy to find a clear and unambiguous answer. It came about through a short series of military victories – over Austria, Denmark, France. It is not surprising that for many German people the experience of this astonishing, scarcely foreseeable swing from the depths to the heights, from weakness to strength, also then led to a glorification of strength, and to the idea that upholding consideration towards others, love and readiness to help others were mere hypocrisy. The events themselves, the series of victorious wars, are surely quite well known. But perhaps close enough attention is not always paid to what these familiar foreign policy events – together with their domestic political consequences for the distribution of social power – meant for the feelings of the people. Is it surprising that experiences such as the rise of Prussia and Germany through one victorious war after another allowed the idea to become dominant that in human social life weakness was bad, and strength was good?

The rise of such views was undoubtedly connected with the pre-eminence accorded to the military – particularly as a result of the decisive part played by success in war in the rise of Germany – within the court society and more broadly good society in Germany as a whole. But this pre-eminence of the military in the time of the *Kaiserreich* was linked extremely closely with a scale of values built deep into the new German self-consciousness and which granted a very high if not the highest place in social life to power, and the lowest place to social weakness, from which Germany had escaped only shortly beforehand. There was certainly no lack of voices in Germany after 1871 which bemoaned the supremacy of the military and uniforms in the social life of their times. Many contemporaries saw quite clearly that the elevation of warlike values, in particular those of the code of honour of the *satisfaktions-fähige Gesellschaft*, went hand in hand with a denigration of those achievements and attitudes which had been particularly highly esteemed primarily in middle-class circles in the later eighteenth and into the first half of the nineteenth century, a denigration of what in short was called culture, including the middle-class moral code. The development of a branch of history writing which focused principally on culture, thus seeking to distinguish itself from the kind of history writing which concentrated on affairs of state and political issues, was just one of many manifestations of these opposing opinions. But after 1871 the impetus given to the supporters of the code of honour was too great for those who upheld the alternative code of culture to be able to gain more than a subordinate place in the framework of imperial German society.

Nietzsche was certainly not aware that, with his elevation of power in the scale of human values, with his belittling of the socially weak and of the middle-class code of morality, he was giving intellectual expression on the level of highest philosophical universality to developmental tendencies which, unintentionally and with little discussion, were becoming dominant in the German society of the *Kaiserzeit* which he so often attacked. He was just as obviously unaware that this aspect of his philosophy was a philosophical paraphrasing of forms of behaviour and values which are among the constitutive elements of the way of life of warrior groups in many human societies. Such societies take it for granted that strength is good and weakness bad; for their members, it is an everyday experience of life.

Thus what Nietzsche's song of praise to war and strength expressed was the adoption by wide sectors of the middle class of his time of a warrior code which had at first belonged to the nobility. In the *Kaiserreich*, these sectors of the middle class had become a stratum within the establishment, although they continued to be overshadowed in power by the first estate, the warrior nobility. So, although they themselves were not particularly warlike, they adopted elements of the higher-ranking stratum's warrior code, and, with the enthusiasm of converts, transformed them in accordance with their own situation into a middle-class nationalist doctrine, or, as in Nietzsche's case, into philosophical teachings on the same level of generality as the classical moral philosophy, only with the sign inverted. The difference between Kant's categorical imperative and Nietzsche's proclamation of 'virtue free of moral self-righteousness' encapsulates the transition of the German middle class from the position of outsiders to a second-rank place within the establishment.

II
A Digression on Nationalism

1

Studying the long-term development of the words 'culture' and 'civiliz-ation' leads to a number of relatively unexpected discoveries. One is that in the eighteenth century both terms to a large extent referred to *processes*, while in the twentieth century they represent something almost entirely static. This declining sense of the dynamics of social processes is by no means confined to the changing meanings of the concepts 'culture' and 'civilization'. The increasing tendency to conceptualize processes as if they were unchanging objects represents a more widespread pattern of conceptual development running conversely to that of society at large, the development and dynamics of which have noticeably quickened from the eighteenth to the twentieth centuries.[1]

The paradox was not confined to Germany, but the way it developed in Germany can serve as an illustration. It also suggests an explanation.

That the term 'culture' once referred to a process of cultivation, to the transformation of nature by human beings, is almost forgotten today – in Germany as elsewhere. Even when it was gradually adopted by the rising German middle-class elites of the eighteenth century as an expression of their self-image and their ideals, it represented their image of themselves as they saw it, namely within the wider context of the development of humanity. The vision of this development of the German middle-class intelligentsia was very similar to that of the French or the British. In fact, the writings of Scottish historians like William Robertson and of Voltaire and his circle in France had a formative influence on the ideas of the rising German intelligentsia. Perhaps their thinking soared higher and their orientation was more idealistic than that of their counterparts in the Western countries because their social situation in a relatively underdeveloped country with a very exclusive upper class of courtiers and nobles was more confined. But their sense of living in an advanced and continually progressing age was for a time almost as

---

The following text originated (in English) as a reworking of the first chapter of *The Civilizing Process* (trans. Edmund Jephcott, Oxford, Blackwell, 1994), 'Sociogenesis of the difference between *Kultur* and *Zivilisation* in German usage', pp. 3–28. [German editor's note]

strong as that of the rising middle-class intelligentsia of other European countries.

When Schiller, in his inaugural lecture 'Was heißt und zu welchem Ende studiert man Universalgeschichte?' [What does universal history mean and why do we study it?], painted on a broad canvas the development of humankind, he gave what was more or less the standard view of the enlightened intellectual avant-garde of his time. The year was 1789. Soon afterwards, fear of revolutionary violence and upheavals began to fall like a shadow over the thinking of Europeans and to cloud their hopes for a better future, just as happened again in the twentieth century under the influence of the violent upheavals of new revolutions. But in Schiller's lecture the hopes were still untarnished by fear. Even if his picture was overly simple, it still remains surprising, despite the immense growth of detailed knowledge, how much could be seen then which today – since the hopes and confidence of people in their ability to produce a better form of living together on earth have been shattered by the fear of revolution and war – is no longer or at best half-heartedly and reluctantly recognized as a fact.

Schiller could still note with confidence the fact that human 'culture' had advanced, that one could see it clearly if one compared one's own ordinary mode of living with that of simpler societies. He spoke of the roughness and cruelty of the life of many simpler societies, of the repulsiveness of some of its aspects which arouses in us, as he said, either disgust or pity. And he could still state as fact with great directness and without circumlocution what, at a later age when nationalistic thinking increasingly demanded the glorification of the national past, might have appeared as a kind of treason:

> This is how *we* were in the past. Caesar and Tacitus encountered us in a state not very different from these primitive people eighteen hundred years ago. What are we now? The same people settled in the same region presents itself as immeasurably different if one looks at it in different periods of time.[2]

He went on to remind his listeners that they were indebted to past ages and distant regions, that all these 'highly dissimilar periods of human-kind' had contributed to *their* culture, just as 'the most distant parts of the world' were contributing at present to their comforts. And he justified the study of universal history with the argument that the concatenation of events which had led to the circumstances of the generations living today could only be understood when it was recognized, to quote his own words, that:

> A long chain of events, interlocking as causes and effects, stretches from the present moment right back to the beginnings of the human race.[3]

Schiller recommended the study of universal history, the history of humanity with comparative studies as one of its principal methods, because the factual interweaving of events and the factual interdependence of all regions of the world are such that one can only understand the present conditions of these regions within the framework of the development of humanity as whole. His grasp of the factual connections, like that of many of his middle-class contemporaries, was not yet disturbed and confused, as is the case today, by the growth of an immensely large and rapidly growing body of detailed knowledge to which the overall picture has to stand up. While twentieth-century historians and other human scientists can often no longer see the wood for the trees, among which they wander as if in a structureless maze, those of the eighteenth century often seemed to perceive only a wood without any trees.

The meaning of terms like 'culture' and 'civilization' was in the eighteenth century attuned to this overall vision. Today the term 'culture' can be applied to less and to more developed societies regardless of their stage of development, and the use of the term 'civilization' appears to be moving in the same direction. People speak of the 'culture' of Australian aborigines as well as of the 'culture' of the Renaissance and of the 'civilization' of neolithic hunters as well as that of nineteenth-century Britain or France.

In Schiller's time things were different. If one spoke in Germany of 'culture' (*Kultur*) – or in France of *civilité* or *civilisation* – one had in mind a general framework which took account of the development of humanity or of particular societies from a less to a more advanced stage. As spokesmen of rising social strata, the middle-class intelligentsia of that period looked with hope and confidence to a better future. And as the future advance of society was important to them, they had the emotional impetus to notice and to single out for attention the advances which had already been made by humanity in the past. Many of their concepts, particularly those which like 'culture' and 'civilization' were related to their 'we-image', reflected this deeply development-orientated and dynamic character of their attitudes and basic beliefs.

No less characteristic was the use made of these and other related concepts as code-words for what was then a new outlook on history conceived by spokesmen of the rising middle classes. Voltaire and others initiated a type of history writing which was intended to correct and to oppose the at that time dominant type of writing, the 'political history' which placed in the centre of attention the deeds of princes and courtiers, the conflicts and alliances of states, the actions of diplomats and of great military leaders, in short, the history of the aristocratic ruling sections of absolutist states.

It was quite decisive for the position and self-image of the German middle-class elites that the tradition of history writing most clearly opposed to 'political history' became known as 'cultural history' [*Kultur-geschichte*]. It brought into focus those areas of the social life of humans which provided the politically excluded German middle classes with the main basis for their self-legitimization and the justification of their pride – areas such as religion, science, architecture, philosophy and poetry as well as the progress of human morality as it can be observed in the customs and conduct of ordinary people. In accordance with the special situation of the German middle classes, the dividing line between 'culture' and 'politics' and the antagonistic undertones of history written as 'history of culture' and as 'political history' in the eighteenth- and nineteenth-century sense was particularly pronounced; it was probably more pronounced than that between 'civilization' and 'politics' in Britain and France. One can say that embedded in the meaning of the German term 'culture' was a non-political and perhaps even an anti-political bias symptomatic of the recurrent feeling among the German middle-class elites that politics and the affairs of state represented the area of their humiliation and lack of freedom, while culture represented the sphere of their freedom and their pride. During the eighteenth and part of the nineteenth centuries, the anti-political bias of the middle-class concept of 'culture' was directed against the politics of autocratic princes. It was directed against the politics of absolutistic courts, and was in that sense a companion piece to its anti-civilizing bias. Both political and civilized behaviour represented the *grand monde*, the 'great world', where people, so it appeared to those living in the 'smaller middle-class world', were full of conceit and pretence, without truthful and genuine feelings. In that respect, the world of civilized courtiers, with their ideals of civility, politeness, good manners and caution with regard to the expression of spontaneous feelings, and the world of politics, with its demands for emotional restraint and diplomatic strategy and, again, tact and good manners, belonged together.

At a later stage, this anti-political bias was turned against the parliamentary politics of a democratic state. It is always astonishing to see the persistence with which specific patterns of thinking, acting and feeling recur, with characteristic adaptations to new developments, in one and the same society over many generations. It is almost certain that the meaning of certain key-words and particularly the emotional undertones embedded in them, which are handed on from one generation to another unexamined and often unchanged, plays a part in the flexible continuity of what one otherwise conceptualizes as 'national character'.

2

The discussion about the nature of a 'history of culture' as distinct from political history continued in Germany intermittently from the eighteenth to the twentieth century. It gained impetus as a number of larger specialist works appeared, among them Burckhardt's *The Civilisation of the Renaissance in Italy*.[4] There was no lack of attempts at defining the demarcation line between 'cultural history' and 'political history'. But the primary impetus for the distinction did not come from any dispassionate inquiry into the nature of history – or of society – itself. It was ideological in character. In a devious way the distinction expressed the continued non-political opposition of German middle-class elites in relation to the politically privileged and socially higher-ranking upper classes of their own society. This opposition helped members of these elites to perceive the one-sidedness and the limitations of the kind of political history written by men who accepted as a matter of course the existing social order of the German states and the scheme of values represented by it. Hence attempts at determining the distinction between 'cultural history and 'political history' without reference to the specific social structure of the society where it originated remained unsatisfactory.

For many members of the educated German middle classes, 'culture' continued to represent a realm of retreat and of freedom from the unsatisfactory pressures of a state which accorded them the position of second-class citizens by comparison with the privileged nobility and denied them access to most of the leading positions in the state and to the responsibilities, power and prestige associated with these positions. Withdrawal into the non-political realm of culture made it possible for them to maintain an attitude of reserve, often highly critical reserve, towards the existing social order without embarking on any active opposition to the regime itself and without any overt conflict with its representatives.

This was one of the possible solutions which could be chosen in order to cope with the cardinal dilemma of many middle classes, of which that of the modernizing, but still feudaloid and semi-autocratic Germany of the nineteenth and early twentieth centuries was only one variant. Any determined and active opposition against this regime and its princely and aristocratic ruling groups on the part of middle-class groups was made difficult – and often paralysed – by the fear that they might endanger their own elevated position in relation to the lower orders by upsetting the existing regime through a fight against the elevated position of the higher orders. There were two main avenues along which they could seek relief from the pressures of this dilemma. They could identify with the regime in spite of its oppressive and humiliating aspects. That was the road which sections of the German middle classes took in increasing numbers after 1870. Or they could, as before, retreat into the non-political area of 'culture' which provided compensatory chances of creativeness, interest and enjoyment and which enabled them to keep intact their 'inner freedom', the integrity of their own person and their pride. This was the road usually chosen by historians and other representatives of the educated German middle classes whose temper and conviction was what one might call 'liberal', though this term comprised beliefs of a variety of different shades. Their often quite considerable distaste for the political regime in which they lived was eased and their political willpower sank into passive resignation, because no reasonably safe way of altering the regime was in sight.

One need not follow here in detail the fortunes of the long-drawn-out discussion between the representatives of 'cultural history' and 'political history' in Germany. In France the opposition of representatives of the rising middle-class intelligentsia against the traditional type of political history characteristic of the *ancien régime* led after the Revolution to a general broadening of the historians' interest and field of vision, while the debate between the historians of civilization and the political historians lost much of its earlier sharpness. It was symptomatic of German development, of the dogged persistence of a social order which, in spite of a rapid and hectic industrialization, from a political standpoint retained many characteristics of the *ancien régime*, that the tug-of-war between cultural historians and political historians continued in Germany intermittently during the nineteenth century. At the turn of the twentieth century the controversy between representatives of the two types of history flared up once more. It showed very clearly the continuity of the role of 'culture' in the development of German society as a protective and often productive sanctuary of middle-class people who, without active opposition, remained critical of the regime, while their opponents were historians representative of the other road open to the educated German middle classes; they had not only come to terms with the state in which they lived; they identified themselves with it and found in it their ideal.

3

It may be enough to give two short extracts as illustrations of the struggle over the peculiar character of 'cultural history' as distinct from 'political history' centred on the affairs of states, which flared up in Germany around 1900.

The first excerpt comes from a short book by one of Max Weber's close acquaintances and friends, the Heidelberg Professor Eberhard Gothein, *Die Aufgaben der Kulturgeschichte* [The Tasks of Cultural History] (1889). The continuity which leads from Schiller's approach in 1789 to that of Gothein exactly one hundred years later is clearly visible. One can still see the non-political, if not anti-political and humanist, implications of the concept of culture. A personal note appears in this context, the idea that history, in the form of the history of culture, might be able to take the place which philosophy held in former centuries:

> If in the present stage of the intellectual development of humanity, history is to occupy this place (the place of philosophy), it can only do so as a history of culture. It must be the historian's aim in that case to let emerge before our eyes the culture of man [*die menschliche Gesittung*]. A type of history which is exclusively concerned with the affairs of states, an exclusively political history, cannot do justice to that task. For although religion, science and the arts take place within the framework of a social order and their progress can be impeded or fostered by it, who would like to assert that they receive from the state their main impulse?
>
> Political history continues to fulfil a necessary task; it retains its value. But universal history, the history of culture, must demand that political history adapts and subordinates itself to it. Cultural history can regard the state itself only as part of culture – perhaps its most important part (who can measure importance with precision as all parts are equally indispensable?) – but certainly only a part related to all other parts which in turn

are related to it. Far from assessing the value of other areas of culture according to their value for the state, the history of culture rather tends to assess the value of individual states according to their contribution to the overall development of humanity in cultural fields such as religion, sciences, arts, economics or law. It is only to be expected that this concept of history arouses a good deal of opposition, especially among political historians.[5]

One can see very clearly that this is an argument about different scales of values in the guise of an argument about different conceptions of history. It would be paradoxical to call it a political argument. Languages are still too clumsy to provide a clear term expressing the political implications of a non-political or anti-political belief and value system. But whatever word one may choose, the views expressed in this quotation indicate briefly the way in which men of the German middle-class intelligentsia maintained with the help of a broadly humanist concept of culture their self-respect, their personal integrity and the sense of their own value in the face of a rising nationalist belief system which with renewed vigour placed the state and the nation above all other values in the writing of history as elsewhere.

The basic position represented by the views which have been quoted was still almost identical with that taken up by men of the educated German middle classes for more than a century. Yet compared with earlier, the antithesis had broadened. It now no longer lay between 'culture' [*Kultur*] as a representative symbol for fields in which educated middle-class people could find their own sense of achievement and fulfilment, and 'civilization' [*Zivilisation*] as a symbol of the world of princes, courts and the ruling upper classes. It was rather between 'culture', still the preserve of educated middle classes with humanist ideals, and the state, which, in its highest regions, remained the preserve of aristocratic upper classes skilled in political strategy, diplomacy and good manners and who, in the eyes of men from the humanist middle-class elites, often lacked true 'culture'.

Even at the turn of the twentieth century, the newly united German empire [*Reich*] was divided not only along class lines, but also along lines derived from the traditional estate order which gave men of noble descent distinct legal or customary privileges by virtue of their birth. As access to many leading state offices was among these traditional privileges, the state itself remained for a section of the middle-class intelligentsia an institution with which they could not wholly identify.

Gothein's argument about the priority of the history of culture over political history is a small ideological example of the continued tension in German society between members of different estates. It is characteristic of the differences between the British development, on the one hand (to mention only one example), and the German development on the other, that, in English the term 'estate' as the expression for a particular type of social stratification sounds old-fashioned and is difficult to handle because other meanings of the word (property, land ownership, etc.) have gained prominence in preference to its use with reference to a specific social stratum. In Germany the corresponding term *Stand* has remained in common usage. In fact, for a long time people preferred to speak of 'middle-estate' [*Mittelstand*] rather than of 'middle class' [*Mittelklasse*]. The former sounds unfamiliar in English, the latter unfamiliar in German. In this respect, too, conceptual differences reflect differences in social development and structure: together they help to explain why German conservative and nationalist circles were much more apt than their British counterparts to seek salvation for their country's difficulties in the re-establishment of an estate order [*ständische Ordnung*]. There are many ways of shedding better light than has been possible so far on the apparent mysteries of differences in the conduct of different nations. As can be seen, the sociological analysis of concepts is one of them.

The humanist middle-class scholars' advocacy of 'cultural history' in preference to political history, moreover, indicated – in a small way – the manner in which constructive withdrawal into the non-political realm of culture, like many other positions hemmed in by social stratification of a comparatively rigid kind, selectively opened and selectively blocked the outlook of the people concerned. The prioritization of humanist values as opposed to national values was still stressed, though more hesitantly than a hundred years before – 'the state is only a part of human culture, *the most important aspect perhaps*' – and the awareness of the narrowness of a type of history writing which selected for attention above all the activities of princes, state legislation and diplomacy, wars, power politics and related topics was quite unambiguous. But the blockages were equally clear. In discussing the relationship between 'cultural history' and 'political history', the scholar was not concerned with the factual connections between arts, sciences, economics, religion and other phenomena classified as 'cultural', on the one hand, and political or military phenomena, on the other. What he considered was only the *value* to be attributed to these different fields.

The whole statement belonged to the twilight area where factual and ideological considerations, autonomous and heteronomous evaluations intermingle and fuse in such a way that it is difficult to disentangle them.

4

It is worth considering briefly one of the statements from the opposite camp, from the camp of the middle-class historians, who had not only come to terms with the existing division of power in the *Kaiserreich* and with the secondary role of their class (or 'estate') in the affairs of state, but who wholeheartedly identified themselves with the Reich and its order. In contrast to the declining liberal and humanist trends, they represented the rising nationalist trend. Dietrich Schäfer, the author of the following words, gave his inaugural lecture in 1884 in the same place, Jena, where Schiller had spoken about universal history nearly a century before:

> I may be permitted to remind you of the fact that from this place, not quite a hundred years ago, Friedrich Schiller tried on a similar occasion to answer the question: what does universal history mean and why do we study it? At that time the enthusiasm for human rights was spreading from Paris through Europe. According to Schiller, history speaks above all to the human being. He thought that in order to collect material for the writing of history, one should regard as the frame of reference of an historical phenomenon the present state of humankind – 'our humane century', as Schiller calls it. ... However, the events of the following decade threw a very peculiar light on Schiller's concept of history. The excesses of the French Revolution and of Napoleon fanned the incipient national sentiments of peoples and made them burst into flame. Nationality took the place of humanity. The striving for universal human culture was followed by that for national culture. ... And the science of history itself now swims smartly in the national current. Its representatives, very rightly, regard it as their most important, and frequently with a one-sided exaggeration, as their only task to cultivate and to revive the national sentiment. One can hardly deny that the science of history actually learned to swim only in the slipstream of nationalism.[6]

There is much in this statement which can be regarded as characteristic of both the continuity and the new turn in the situation and beliefs of German middle-class elites after 1871 – in the new empire of the Kaiser.

While sections of these elites still remained aloof from the state and continued to hold humanistic ideals such as 'culture' in the direct line of succession of the classical thinkers and poets of Germany with strong, though strictly inactive, undercurrents of criticism of Germany's ruling classes, others, gradually increasing in power, became reconciled to the secondary role allotted to the leading sections of the middle classes in the newly unified empire as junior partners of the still highly exclusive and highly class-conscious ruling nobility. The frustration and resentment inherent in such a position found expression in their case not in relation to their social superiors, with whom as representatives of nation and empire they came, in a general way, to identify themselves, but rather in relation to all those social formations which were inferior to them in status or power; among the latter were the humanist or liberal sections of the German middle classes, particularly the humanist intelligentsia.

The controversy over the respective merits of 'cultural history' and 'political history' was one of many symptoms of the antagonism between the two rival groups in the middle-class intelligentsia. It also marked the turning point in their fortunes. Gradually, the nationalist sections became stronger, the humanist sections weaker; the latter in turn became more nationalistic; that is to say, they, too, gave a higher place to an ideal image of state and nation in their self-image and their scale of values, though they still tried to reconcile it with wider humanist and moral ideals. The other more radical sections of the German nationalist intelligentsia made no such attempt. The passages which have been quoted are in one way quite representative of their credo: they indicate the peculiar scorn and contempt with which intellectual representatives of the nationalist sections in the German middle class came to speak of the humanist and moral ideals, among them the belief in a better future, in 'progress', which had sustained the German and the other European middle classes in the early period of their social rise. The conservative-nationalist sections of the middle classes in other countries often attempted to fuse humanist and moralist with nationalist ideals. The comparable sections of the German middle classes rejected the compromise. They turned, often with an air of triumph, against the humanist and moral ideals of the rising middle classes as ideals whose falsehood had been unmasked.

A question which deserves more attention than it can be given here is why the rejection of the humanist and moral ideals of an earlier period by the rising nationalist middle-class intelligentsia in Germany from about 1870 on was particularly radical and contemptuous. But it has some bearing on the main problem under discussion. One cannot entirely neglect it.

From Humanist to Nationalist Middle-Class Elites

5

The general trend, a shift in priority from humanist and moral ideals and values applicable to people in general to nationalist ideals which placed an ideal image of country and nation above general human and moral ideals in one's scale of values, can be observed in the outlook of the middle classes of most European countries between the eighteenth and twentieth centuries. Almost everywhere in Europe, the intellectual elites of the rising eighteenth-century middle classes shared a general belief in moral principles, in the rights of human beings as such and in the natural progress of humanity. They were forward-looking. Even if they were to some extent assimilated in outlook and manners by the ruling court aristocracy – as they were in France – and, up to a point, accepted the established belief of the ruling groups that their own age surpassed in civility and civilization all previous ages of humans, they – the middle-class intelligentsia – at the same time took it for granted that the conditions of humanity would further improve in the future. And the better future, symbolized by the concept of 'progress', assumed in their beliefs the character of an ideal towards which one could strive and for which one could struggle with complete confidence in its eventual realization. The barbarities and inhumanities, the illnesses and humiliations, the poverty and, generally, the sufferings which they witnessed and often enough experienced in their own societies were worse than almost anything which middle-class elites of the twentieth century lived through in the highly industrialized societies of their time; but these experiences, including the recurrent catastrophes of war and epidemics, did not diminish but rather strengthened their trust in the better future, their confidence in the steady progress of the human lot.

When, in one European country after another, men of middle-class descent rose to power and increasingly shared with, or altogether took over from, the traditional aristocratic ruling classes the reins of government in their societies, and when the leading middle-class sections established themselves more and more as their societies' most powerful groups, forward-looking beliefs and ideals – the hope for a better future – lost their former significance for them. While factual scientific knowledge about the long-term advances of humankind greatly increased, this knowledge ceased to have any relevance as emotionally satisfying evidence for the belief that human conditions would advance still further and improve in the future. The actual progress made in the twentieth century in the mastery of physical and biological and, indeed, even of economic and social problems, by and large, was greater and certainly more rapid than in the eighteenth century. Intentionally or not, the work of industrial, commercial and graduate-professional middle classes of the twentieth century produced advances in numerous specific areas. But as the symbol of an overall aim, as an ideal, the concept of 'progress' lost status and prestige among the middle-class intelligentsia of the countries where middle-class groups joined or replaced aristocratic groups as the ruling groups of their countries. It was no longer the auspicious symbol of a better future suffused by the glow of strong positive feelings.

Instead, an idealized image of their nation moved into the centre of their self-image, their social beliefs and their scale of values. During the period of their ascent, the middle classes of European countries, like other rising classes, had been forward-looking. Once they had risen to the position of ruling classes, their leading sections and their intellectual elites, like those of other ruling groups, increasingly founded their ideal image of themselves on the past rather than on the future. The emotional satisfactions derived from looking forward gave way to emotional satisfactions derived from looking back. The core of their we-image and their we-ideal was formed by an image of their national tradition and heritage. Just as aristocratic groups had based their pride and their claim to a special value on their family's ancestry, so, as their successors. the leading sections of the industrial middle classes – gradually in conjunction with those of the industrial working classes wherever the latter, too, had reached a ruling position – increasingly based their pride and their claim to a special value either on their nation's ancestry or on seemingly unchanging national achievements, characteristics and values. An ideal image of themselves as the nation moved to the highest place in their public scale of values; it won precedence over the older humanistic and moralistic ideals, triumphing over them in case of conflict, and, pervaded by strong positive feelings, became the centrepiece of their system of social beliefs.

6

It was in connection with this change in outlook, with this shift in emotional emphasis from the future to the past and the present, from the belief in change for the better to the belief in the unchanging value of national characteristics and traditions and with the corresponding change in the whole climate of opinion of middle-class intelligentsias that took place in the highly developed European societies between the eighteenth and the early twentieth centuries, that concepts such as 'civilization' and 'culture' changed from concepts referring to processes – to progressive developments – into concepts referring to unchanging states. While serving initially, each in its own way, as symbols of the we-image of forward-looking groups who found the emotionally most satisfying justification for their self-image and their pride in general humanist and moral values and in their contribution to the continued progress of humanity, they now came more and more to serve as symbols of the we-image of groups who found the emotionally most satisfying justification for their self-image and their pride in the past achievements of their collective ancestors, in their nation's immutable heritage and tradition.

The conceptual symbols which reflected this shift of emphasis in the we-images and we-ideals of middle-class elites from the future to the past and from changing to unchanging conditions as a high value, were different in different nations. Nevertheless, expressions such as '*la civilisation française*' or '*die deutsche Kultur*' had unmistakably similar characteristics insofar as they referred to what seemed to be unchanging and eternal attributes of a nation. The difference was that the term 'civilization' retained, as the German term *Kultur* did not, even as middle-class symbol of the we-image of a particular nation, some of its associations with general human and moral values. Thus the claim '*la civilisation française est la civilisation humaine*' was, on the one hand, undoubtedly an expression of French nationalism and expansionism. But it expressed at the same time the belief that the French national tradition embodied and represented moral and other values and attainments valid for humanity as a whole.

Similar beliefs were initially associated with the German term *Kultur*, for instance when it was used in the sense of the cultivation or education of human beings to their fullest potential. But in the late nineteenth and early twentieth centuries when the term 'culture' was increasingly used in the sense of 'national culture', the humanist and moral connotations associated with it at an earlier stage in its career faded into the background and finally disappeared.

It is possible that it was precisely this complete fading of humanist or moral connotations, together with the emphasis on the past – on that which is handed on in a particular group from one generation to another regardless of its positive or negative value for other groups or for human beings generally – which helped in the diffusion of the term 'culture', more or less in the sense which it had acquired as symbol of the we-image of strongly national-minded and conservative sections of the German middle classes, to social sciences such as social anthropology and sociology. If one were looking for a term which represented the distinguishing properties of a particular society as essentially unchanging and at the same time as a tradition handed on from the past, the term *Kultur* in the sense which it had gradually acquired in the course of its German development undoubtedly served this purpose very well. In a scientific context, the absence of any absolute moral or humanist evaluations and the absence of any developmental connotations, of any references to the processes of becoming, could well be regarded for a time as an advantage.

7

In connection with a national self-image, this reduction meant something different. It indicated the subordination of moral or humanist values under national ones. A systematic inquiry into the processes of social change in the course of which an ideal image of one's own nation rose to a very high, if not to the highest, place in the we-ideal and the value system of the leading sections of the middle classes, and gradually, perhaps more hesitantly, also of those of the working classes, has not yet been undertaken. And this is not the occasion to do it. But it may be useful for future consideration – and also for the clarification of the immediate topics under discussion here – to state briefly the unexplored problem itself.

Mutual distrust between human groups, the unbridled use of violence in their relations with each other so long as they expected an advantage and were not afraid of retaliation, has been very general, one might almost say normal, throughout the ages. The vicious circle was sometimes tempered by fear of retaliation by superhuman agencies, but only on the rarest occasions, if at all, by the simple insight that people must keep their own house in order, that if they want to live without fear of each other as groups no less than as individuals in groups, they can only do so by imposing certain common rules of conduct and the corresponding restraints upon themselves. It has sometimes been claimed that a belief in supernatural retribution could act as an instrument of restraint which might prevent human groups from having to live in constant fear of each other and from using physical force in relation to each other whenever they believe they can do so unpunished. But in fact there are many forms of belief in superhuman agencies. The special religious groups which have developed in connection with them are no less plagued than any others by mutual suspicions and fears; they have fought and still fight each other on many occasions as fiercely and violently as other human groups.

Still, it was probably not entirely accidental that, in Europe, at the same time when the most powerful organization of superhuman beliefs, the medieval church, with its pinnacle in Rome, was losing a considerable part of its dominions, and with it the monopoly of thought-control in Western European societies, understanding of the manner in which the ruling groups of different territories related to each other became secularized. The traditional practice of power politics which dominated the relations between the ruling groups of different territories had always been that of pursuing what one believed to be one's self-interest ruthlessly with no holds barred in accordance with the relative power resources at one's disposal. Now the traditional practice became a matter of explicit reflection. Machiavelli's treatise on the subject of power politics is the best-known example. He transformed the traditional practice of ruling groups, the practice of unrestrained pursuit of self-interest in inter-state relations under the pressure of mutual fears and suspicions, with deception and killing as normal means to one's ends, into a kind of set of general principles of action. He did this not in order to discover how the uncontrollable mechanisms of inter-state rivalries and suspicions might be brought under better human control; the facts of power politics themselves appeared to him as unalterable. He used his inquiry into the unintended mechanisms of the power game mainly in order to draw lessons from it for the more skilful and deliberate playing of the game.

However, whether elevated to the level of explicit reflection or not, the practice of unrestrained pursuit of competitive self-interest in inter-state relations remained from the sixteenth to the nineteenth and early twentieth centuries, in varying degrees, largely the practice of princes and aristocratic ruling groups. Even within one and the same country, the rules and restraints which governed the relations of these ruling strata with each other did not have the character of humanist or moral norms. The aristocratic code was a code of honour, of civility and good manners, of expediency and diplomacy, which, even in its application to members of one and the same society, included the use of violence provided it was used in a gentlemanly fashion, for instance in the form of duelling. To some extent, the code of honour and civility which ruled relations among noblemen and gentlemen within the dynastic states also ruled the relations between members of the upper classes of different states. It even tempered to a certain degree the traditional conduct of inter-state relations where princes and their aristocratic helpers – forming with each other a balance of power figuration which for them was uncontrollable as well as inescapable – used deception, violence or any other device which they thought might help them to get the better of others in a 'Machiavellian' manner, without moral scruples and restraints and as a matter of course, as long as they were not afraid of defeat and humiliation from the hands of a more powerful prince. In their case, in the case of dynastic states with ruling elites dominated by nobles, few if any contradictions existed between the code of rules they observed among themselves within one and the same state and the code they observed in inter-state relations.

8

The situation changed considerably when social classes which normally worked for their living or lived largely on earned income moved from the position of subordinates into that of ruling classes. The first of these classes to rise in status and power – the multiply differentiated 'middle class' – had developed among themselves a code of conduct which was very different from the aristocratic code of honour and civility. The specific type of self-imposed regulation of human conduct and human relations to which we refer as 'morality' had its primary social locus among people of this type, among people who normally worked for their living – in middle-class circles.

Their code was a code of virtue rather than of honour. One of its characteristics was its lesser dependence on the fear of other persons and its greater dependence on the automatisms of one's own conscience. Its norms were to a higher extent, as we often say, 'internalized'; they were, therefore, also to a higher extent inescapable. They appeared as absolute. They were humanist in the sense that they applied in principle to all human beings regardless of class and of country. In fact, a moral and humanist code of human conduct developed first, in connection with selective themes from the Judaeo-Christian tradition, in middle-class groups of European societies at that stage in their development when upper sections of the classes which earned their living by work, although rising, were still unequivocally inferior in social rank to the ruling hierarchy of nobles. In fact, a code of rules in the form of a morality regarded as valid for all people was often used as a weapon by the middle classes in the standing tensions with the aristocratic upper classes. They used their code stressing goodness and virtue as a counter to the exclusive code of honour and good manners which those obeying it did not expect to apply to human beings who did not belong – to human beings of the lower orders.

In the course of time, the standards which had thus developed among sections of the 'third estate', among people who worked for their living, the absolute and egalitarian moral code claiming validity for all human beings, was *a posteriori* systematized in reflection and elevated into philosophical propositions by members of the middle-class intelligentsia, such as Kant. It was symptomatic of the higher degree of 'internationalization' of the egalitarian, humanist, middle-class code of norms which we call 'morality', compared with the exclusive upperclass code of honour, that the demands of the former often appeared in philosophical discourse simply as general laws of almost the same kind as natural laws. Middle-class thinkers, in other words, conceptualized these rules of behaviour not as *made* by people but as *given* to them by some kind of metaphysical *a priori* which was experienced as an eternal absolute, whether nature, heaven, reason, instinct or an inner voice.

9

One may find this excursion far-fetched in the present context. But without a flashback to the sociogenesis of this particular type of human norm, it is difficult to see in perspective the transformation which the beliefs and ideals of European middle-class elites underwent between the eighteenth and twentieth centuries. One may find it difficult to empathize with the experiences which confronted groups of people when they or their representatives moved from the position of 'middle classes' in dynastic states and, brought up in the traditions of their class, rose to the position of ruling classes of national states in connection with industrialization, urbanization and other facets of the overall process of modernization of that period.

The question of what happens to the traditions – or, one might say, to the 'culture' – of a class in such a case has perhaps not been sufficiently considered. As long as one fails to take the wider problem into account, as long as one does not consider as a basic feature of *all* European societies the changes which occur in the traditions and attitudes of lower-class elites when – whether gradually or suddenly – they move up into the position of a ruling class, one will not be able clearly to determine the distinguishing features of this development in particular societies.

Individually, men of middle-class descent had risen to high positions frequently enough prior to the nineteenth and twentieth centuries. But, in accordance with the structure of dynastic state-societies, they were more or less absorbed into the traditions of the ruling classes of their societies. In most cases they rose to high positions in the service of a prince. Rising in his service they became courtiers; they dressed like courtiers; they adopted the manners and outlook of courtiers. Rising individually they left, as it were, the traditions of their own class; they became more or less assimilated to the traditions of the ruling classes and their elites, and the dividing line between them and the middle class became almost as marked as that between this class and courtiers of aristocratic descent.

But from the late eighteenth and nineteenth centuries onwards the problem which rising middle-class elites had to face was different. In these centuries, the rise of middle-class men into high positions in the state was no longer a matter of the rise of individual people or of families which in one or two generations left their class and became assimilated into another. In these centuries the former middle classes themselves were rising in status and in power. If people in that phase of the development of society moved into the highest positions of the state, it no longer meant that they moved into a different class, that they sooner or later abandoned the tradition, the outlook, the code of conduct of their own class and assimilated themselves to those of a higher class. It meant that they occupied the highest positions in the state without abandoning their status, their outlook, their code of conduct, in short their 'culture' as persons of the middle classes.

Thus when elite groups from the former 'middle classes' in that phase of the development of societies moved into the position of ruling elites, two traditions or 'cultures' which had before developed in relatively separate social compartments, in social strata whose contacts and communications with each other were not very close (although the degree of separation varied greatly from society to society), were brought into very much closer contact; they merged, or, rather, since they were in a number of aspects hardly compatible, they collided often enough within one and the same person.

Men of middle-class descent brought up in the specific traditions of an egalitarian and humanist code of morality had to adapt themselves to duties and responsibilities, and became exposed to experiences and a manner of life which previously had not been, or had not been directly, accessible to people brought up with middle-class traditions – except, of course, in cases of individual rise when the upwardly mobile persons and their families sooner or later switched over into an alien 'culture'.

When the former middle classes rose as such into the position of ruling classes, their representatives who entered the commanding positions of the state were exposed to experiences, particularly in the field of inter-state relations, which had formerly been accessible mainly to people in the tradition of the nobility and court. They were exposed to these experiences without abandoning their middle-class traditions and their middle-class code of conduct. It was difficult to apply this code, which had originated in the more limited world of pre-industrial artisan and trading communities and of the elites descended from them, to some of the new experiences as ruling elites of a state. Especially in inter-state relations they were faced with types of conduct to which it was difficult to apply their own code of morality. It was in this field above all – though by no means only – that they drew, in their capacity as ruling groups, on the models provided by the 'culture' of the former ruling groups, on a code which, for want of a better label, one might call 'Machiavellian'. For in this sphere the belief in the pursuit of unrestrained self-interest as the leading principle of conduct, checked only by the fear of the greater power or the greater skill of potential opponents, which had dominated the politics of the leading dynasties and the leading aristocratic groups of different states in their relations with each other, had left a heritage of mutual fears and suspicions in inter-state relations.

The aristocratic tradition of inter-state relations – the tradition which had its origins among the warrior classes of Europe and which was perpetuated by nobles whose beliefs and values were those of military men – certainly did not fit the traditions, beliefs and values of the pre-industrial and early industrial middle classes. And before the latter fully moved into the position of ruling groups some of their intellectual spokesmen, for example Herbert Spencer, expressed the firm conviction that the rise of the 'industrial' classes would almost automatically bring to an end the dominance of the military inheritance in inter-state relations.

What happened in fact was that the leading groups of the industrial classes to some extent absorbed the dynastic and aristocratic traditions in this field. They tried to combine the belief in their traditional egalitarian and humanist code of norms – in the moral code which excluded violence and implied a fundamental identification with all human beings – with the belief that in the relations between states unrestrained self-interest must prevail. Thus they entered into, and perpetuated, the vicious circle of mutual fears and suspicions which in inter-state relations had existed before and which must exist in human relations everywhere as long as those forming a particular figuration with each other do not agree on, and do not maintain effectively among themselves, a common code of norms.

10

However, when the middle classes moved into the position of ruling classes and middle-class elites came to occupy the commanding positions of society, they did not simply take over the aristocratic heritage. They did not simply make the tradition of unrestrained pursuit of self-interest, backed by military means and of mutual fears and suspicions in inter-state relations, their own without changing it to a considerable extent in the process. By assimilating it they altered the dynastic tradition. The aristocratic code of valour and honour was up to the eighteenth century the common code of the ruling classes in most European states. As in the case of duelling, noblemen and gentlemen who encountered each other as opponents in the case of war might do their utmost to defeat and even to kill the men on the other side; but even the use of physical force, even violence and killing, were, within limits, subject to a code of honour and valour which military officers on both sides shared with each other. Wars, like duels, were the affairs of gentlemen; they did not destroy the fairly highly developed *esprit de corps*, the 'we-feeling' of military officers on opposite sides in their capacity as gentlemen or noblemen, as members of the same 'estate'. On balance this 'we-feeling' of the pre-revolutionary upper classes of Europe, which surpassed the frontiers of states, was probably stronger than any 'we-feeling' – any feeling of identity – which men of these upper classes had with the lower classes of their own country. Their attachment to their own state did not yet have the character of an attachment to their nation. With few exceptions national sentiments were alien to the noblemen of Europe prior to the French Revolution and in some countries for a long time after it. They were, of course, conscious of being French, English, German or Russian noblemen and gentlemen. But before the rise of commercial or industrial middle classes and their elites, the 'we-feelings' of local groups in relation to their locality, region or country were, in societies whose stratification had the character of a hierarchy of estates rather than of classes, in no way equivalent to national solidarity feelings. One cannot quite understand the specific characteristics of nationalist values and belief systems as sociological data unless one has a clear understanding of their connection with a specific stage of social development and, therefore, with a specific type of social structure. It was only in class-societies, not in estate-societies, that the identity feelings of the ruling elites, and in course of time those of wider strata, too, acquired the specific stamp of national feelings.

It can be seen very clearly in what way identity feelings changed in European states when, whether gradually or abruptly, ruling elites descended from the middle classes replaced those descended from the traditional aristocratic upper classes.[7] On balance, their identification with their own compatriots became stronger, that with men of the same class and standing in other countries weaker. This change in the pattern of people's 'we-and-they-feelings', of identification and exclusion, was one of the principal conditions of the development of nationalist sentiments, values and beliefs. As Sieyès's treatise and other revolutionary pronouncements indicated, sentiments, values and beliefs centred on the image of the nation were from early on associated with the self-image of middle classes – and somewhat later also of working classes – which were on the point of claiming, or actually ascending into, the commanding positions of a state.

11

That the middle-class elites saw themselves, when they came to occupy the ruling positions of the state, as leading groups not only of a country or a state but also of a nation influenced their conduct in inter-state relations. In one sense they simply took over the code of princes, the Machiavellian code of power politics. The continuity is unmistakable. However, in the course of becoming a middle-class code, the Machiavellian code was also significantly transformed. In its original form it was a code of conduct primarily tailored for a prince in his relations with other princes. Now it became a code primarily applied to the conduct of the affairs of a nation-state in its relations with other nation-states. The development implied change as well as continuity.

One can get a glimpse of both if one compares the manner in which Machiavelli presented the policy of unrestrained self-interest as the principle for the rulers of states in inter-state relations and the manner in which essentially the same policy was centuries later, in the twentieth century, usually presented by national elites. Machiavelli's policy prescriptions[8] were of a highly practical nature. He explained what he believed was the best way in which a prince could hold his own in the jungle of inter-state relations. As an experienced servant of rulers he gave the rulers of states, some of whom he knew personally, practical advice.

When power politics came to be pursued in the name of a nation, certain basic aspects of the figuration which states formed with each other remained unaltered. In that case, too, the ruling groups of interdependent and yet sovereign state organizations pursued in relation to each other policies of uncontrolled and apparently uncontrollable self-interest which induced, and were in turn induced by, mutual fears and suspicions; these were at the same time the main checks to the unlimited pursuit of self-interest by any individual state. But power politics, pursued in the name of a nation and not of a prince, could no longer be conceived of and represented as the policy of or for a person. They were politics in the name of a collectivity which was so large that the majority of its members did not and could not know each other.

Power politics remained largely unchanged, but the shift from thinking about them in terms of a sovereign person to thinking about them in terms of a sovereign collectivity had curious consequences. It was easier to speak about matters of policy unemotionally in practical and realistic terms to and about princes than it was to do the same in relation to a sovereign collectivity. Both the sovereign prince and the sovereign people required for the execution of any policy undertaken for them or in their name a measure of emotional attachment on the part of those helping to execute the policy or acting in their name. But in the first case the feelings of loyalty and attachment were still feelings from person to person. In the second case the emotional bonds had to some extent a different character. They were to a much higher degree symbolic attachments – attachments to symbols of the collectivity. These symbols could be of many types. But among them verbal symbols played a special role. Whatever form they took, these symbols for a collectivity and its various aspects became focal points for the emotional bonding of persons to the collectivity, and appeared to endow the collectivity itself with a peculiar quality; they endowed it, one might say, with a numinous existence of its own outside and above the individuals who formed it – with a kind of holiness formerly associated mainly with superhuman beings.

It is a mark of democratization processes which has perhaps not found the attention it deserves that, in the course of these processes, whether they result in a multi-party or a one-party state, a parliamentary or a dictatorial regime, these numinous qualities and the corresponding emotions are attached by people to the societies they themselves form with each other. In simpler societies, according to Durkheim's suggestion, these emotional bonds of individuals with the collectivity they form crystallize and organize themselves around figures or images of gods or ancestors – of beings of more or less superhuman stature; whatever other functions they may have, they also have that of emotion-laden symbols of a we-group. Compared with simpler societies, the nation-states of the nineteenth and twentieth centuries are large and extremely populous. Moreover, the factual bonds of millions of individuals belonging to the same society, their interlinking through the occupational division of labour, through integration within the same framework of governmental and administrative organizations and in many other ways, are much more complex, much more elusive from the point of view of most of the individuals who form these gigantic social organizations, than the interlinking of people in simpler societies. Unless educational levels are very advanced, the factual interdependencies of the individuals living in highly differentiated industrial nation-states remain at the most half-understood – they are often obscure and incomprehensible for most of their members. So, the emotional bonds of individuals with the collectivity which they form with each other crystallize and organize themselves around common symbols which do not require any factual explanations, which can and must be regarded as absolute values which are not to be questioned and which form focal points of a common belief system. To call them into question – to cast doubt on the common belief in one's own sovereign collectivity as a high, if not the highest possible, value – means deviancy, a breach of trust; it can lead one to become an ostracized outsider, if nothing worse.

Of course, in contrast to less differentiated societies, the symbols of the collectivity which attract and integrate the feelings of individual members in highly differentiated nineteenth- and twentieth-century societies have a much more impersonal character. The verbal symbols which play this role are an example. To some extent they vary from one nation-state to another. But they all possess emotional radiance and strength, and endow the collectivity which they represent with the numinous qualities which have been mentioned. For the most part, the names of the nation-states and their derivatives are used by their members in appropriate situations with overtones of sanctity and awe. Thus the term '*La France*' is often used by Frenchmen, the term '*Deutschland*' by Germans, and the term 'America' by Americans as verbal symbols of a collective entity with numinous qualities, and the same use of national names can be found in almost all relatively highly developed nation-states, while the corresponding name is probably used at the same time in other languages with quite different and often enough negative connotations in accordance with the paradoxical character of inter-state relations.

But it is not only the name of a country which can have functions of this kind – a whole range of verbal symbols, among them terms such as 'Fatherland', 'Motherland' or '*Volk*', can have them too. As far as one can see, the terms 'nation' and 'national' have become the most general, most widely used symbols of this kind. One need only ask what distinguishes the term 'nation' from others such as 'country', 'state', 'people', in order to recognize the difference. The social data themselves to which these terms refer are largely identical. So far as the facts are concerned, allowing for local developments, expressions such as 'a nation', 'a people' or 'the people of a country', 'the members of a state' are largely synonymous. But in communications among the members of the same country, the term 'nation' tends to convey a different range and a different depth of emotions. The collectivity to which it refers is clothed by its use with a highly specific emotional aura and thus made to appear as something highly valuable and sacrosanct which deserves to be admired and venerated. And this feeling usually extends to everything which can be said to belong to the nation or to be in the national interest, including the use of force, of fraud, deception or, if it comes to that, of torture and of killing.

12

One can understand better the confluence of change and continuity in the development which led from the original Machiavellian code to its sublimation as part of a nationalist belief system if one considers the change in the focus of emotional attachments from living princes to impersonal symbols of a hallowed collectivity. In a world of dynastic states, particularly of monarchical states ruled more or less autocratically, a policy of unrestrained self-interest in inter-state relations was a personal policy of rulers who, either by birth or by their own military and political achievements, stood in the line of succession of a warrior tradition. The code they followed in inter-state relations was largely an extension of the code which they followed in personal relations. There was no high barrier, no sharp dividing line between the two – no basic contradiction between personal or private and public or state morality. What had once been the principle of a practical and, one might say, reasonably realistic strategy for the conduct of princes in inter-state affairs changed its emotional colour when it became a strategy of nations or, more specifically, of their ruling elites. The realistic aspects of the traditional warrior code which sowed mistrust and fear between ruling groups, just as, conversely, it grew out of mistrust and fear between them, fused with the mystique of a nationalist creed which thousands could believe in as something absolute without asking questions.

It is easy to see why this belief in the 'nation' as a sacrosanct we-ideal arose in an age of highly differentiated mass societies with conscript armies and an increasing involvement of the total population in conflicts with other mass societies. In that situation simple drill and obedience to a prince or a military commander were not enough to ensure a country's success in a power struggle with others. Under these conditions it was necessary that all citizens were, in addition to any external compulsion, also compelled by their own conscience and their own ideals, by a fervently held belief, or in other words by a compulsion they exercised upon themselves individually, to subordinate their individual needs to those of the collectivity, the country or the nation, and if necessary to lay down their lives. It was necessary that the individual members of all these relatively highly differentiated mass societies of the twentieth century should be motivated by an unquestionable belief in the value of the society they formed with each other, of the 'nation'; for it was not always possible to explain in factual terms the merits of the society for those whose services or whose lives were demanded.

Although the primary impulse for the formation of nationalism as a belief system came from the inter-state sphere, whether from common fear for the integrity and survival of one's own society or the common wish for an increase in its power, status and prestige in relation to other sovereign societies, a nationalist creed could also serve as an instrument of rule and domination, or attempted domination, by a small group over others. One of the basic characteristics of industrial state-societies at the stage of development reached in the nineteenth and twentieth centuries is the simultaneity of, on the one hand, a growing interdependence of all social classes and, on the other, standing tensions between the leading working-class and middle-class groups. Many subsidiary tensions between different occupational groups cluster around this main axis of tension usually represented by that between employers' federations and trade unions. In this situation the appeal to national sentiments and loyalties, which, for a variety of reasons particularly connected with wars and the advancement of education through state-controlled schools and armies, had taken firm roots in all classes and could be used within a society as a lever for fostering sectional interests by one or another of the leading groups. As is well known, they were used in this manner in a number of countries, Germany among them, mainly by discontented middle-class groups.

Nationalist belief and value systems in highly developed countries with relatively high standards of living are usually backward-looking creeds. They are used in societies of this type with the aim of preserving the established order, even if the social movement rallied in the name of the national heritage and its virtues in fact aims at overthrowing the existing order. If that is done, it is usually in the name of the restoration of the past, of the unchanging heritage of the nation. In short, the character of nationalist ideas can hardly be understood if it is deduced from the study of these ideas alone as they may appear in books by philosophers or other prominent writers, in other words if they are studied in accordance with the traditions of the 'history of ideas'.

Nationalist ideas and ideals do not form an autonomous sequence of the type which is often attributed to sequences of philosophical ideas. Their succession in time is not simply due to the fact that authors of one generation read, as a matter of course, books written by authors of previous generations and develop further, approvingly or critically, the ideas of previous authors without reference to the development and to the structural peculiarities of the societies where these books are written and read. Nor are the nationalist ideas of prominent writers the 'cause' of 'nationalism'. In a latent or manifest form, nationalism constitutes one of the most powerful, perhaps *the* most powerful, social beliefs of the nineteenth and twentieth centuries. Book ideas constitute, to use an apt if well-worn simile, only the tip of an iceberg. They are the most articulate manifestations of a process during which national sentiments and a national ethos spread sooner or later through the whole of a society. Unless one asks what changes in the structure of state-societies account for the change from an expression of loyalties and of feelings of solidarity in terms of an attachment to kings and princes – 'Vive le roi!' – to an expression of loyalties and feelings of solidarity in terms of a nation – 'Vive la France!' – in society at large, one cannot assess the role which publications of a nationalist intelligentsia have in the nationalization of ethos and sentiment of the great mass of individuals who form these societies.

Sociological research into the development of nationalist ideals which places beliefs, concepts or ideas as found in books firmly into the context of the development of societies and shows their functions for the various subsections of these societies is only just beginning. In this context it must be enough to indicate briefly how and why beliefs and ideals of this type are common to all societies at a specific stage of development – with a reminder that their development depends on both inter-state and intra-state relations.

It would be a rewarding task to work out at greater length a theoretical model showing the constant interweaving of social developments on the inter-state and intra-state levels in this as in other respects. One could show better with the help of such a wider theoretical framework that even the exploitation of the latent nationalist propensities of members of highly differentiated and integrated industrial nation-states by sectional interests is rarely undertaken by their representatives in full awareness of the nature of their own undertaking, that is to say, simply as a cold-blooded and premeditated ideological deception. Traditional theories which sometimes represent ideologies in that sense oversimplify matters. Nationalist beliefs, like others, tend in specific situations to gain power over the believers themselves through a self-escalating process of mutual reinforcement. Since the creed affirms the loyalty to one's own group as well as placing it on a pedestal, since no one can publicly deny approval to those who most strongly affirm their belief in the supreme virtue of the group, the tendency of people or groups of people to outbid each other in their affirmation of such a belief becomes in certain social situations very strong. It is not difficult to see how self-praising belief systems, particularly if the collectivities who carry them are very large, can gain through mechanisms such as this a momentum of their own which no single person or group is able to control.

13

Nationalism, even in a preliminary sociological analysis, is thus revealed as a specific social phenomenon characteristic of large industrial state-societies at the level of development reached by the nineteenth and twentieth centuries. It is related to, and yet clearly distinct from, group beliefs representing the attachment and solidarity of individuals in relation to collectivities such as villages, towns, principalities or kingdoms in earlier stages of social development. It is a question of a belief of a characteristically secular kind. That is, it can be sustained without justification through superhuman agencies; it approximates to the types of belief and ethos which Max Weber called 'inner worldly'. It presupposes a high degree of democratization of societies in the sociological, not in the political, sense of the word: if social barriers between groups of different social power and rank are too high – as they are, for instance, in estate societies with a hereditary nobility or in dynastic states with a very steep power gradient between princes and subjects – individual feelings of attachment, of solidarity and obligation in relation to a state-society have a different character from that expressed in the form of a nationalist ethos.

A nationalist ethos implies a sense of solidarity and obligation, not simply with regard to particular persons or a single person in a ruling position as such, but with regard to a sovereign collectivity which the individual concerned him- or herself forms with thousands or millions of others, which, here and now, is organized as a state – or which according to the beliefs of the people concerned will be so in the future – and the attachment to which is mediated through special symbols, some of which can be persons. These symbols and the collectivity for which they stand attract to themselves strong positive emotions of the type usually called love. The collectivity is experienced and the symbols are represented as something apart from, something holier and higher than, the individuals concerned. Collectivities which generate a nationalist ethos are structured in such a way that the individuals who form them can experience them – more specifically their emotion-laden symbols – as representatives of themselves. The love for one's nation is never only a love for persons or groups of whom one says 'you'; it is always also the love of a collectivity to which one can refer as 'we'. Whatever else it may be, it is also a form of self-love.

The image of a nation experienced by an individual who forms part of that nation, therefore, is also a constituent of that person's self-image.

The virtue, the value, the meaningfulness of the nation are also his or her own. Current sociological and social psychological theories, insofar as they are concerned with such problems at all, offer for reflections on phenomena of this kind the concept of identification. However, it is a concept which is not wholly appropriate to what one actually observes in this case. The concept of identification makes it appear that the individual is here and the nation is there; it implies that 'individual' and 'nation' are two different entities separated in space. Since nations consist of individuals, and individuals who live in the more developed twentieth-century state-societies belong, in the majority of cases, unambiguously to a nation, a conceptualization which evokes the picture of two different entities separated in space, like mother and child, does not fit the facts.

Relationships of this type can be adequately expressed only in terms of personal pronouns. An individual does not only have an ego-image and an ego-ideal, but also a we-image and a we-ideal. It is a central aspect of the nationalization of individual ethos and sentiment, which can be observed empirically in nineteenth- and twentieth-century industrial state-societies, that the image of these state-societies, represented, among others, by verbal symbols such as 'nation', form an integral part of the we-images and the we-ideals of most of the individuals who form with each other societies of this type. This, in short, is one of the many instances of correspondence between specific types of social structure and specific types of personality structure. A member of a differentiated twentieth-century industrial nation-state who makes statements in which he or she uses an adjectival form of the name of his or her country as an attribute of him- or herself – 'I am French', 'I am American', 'I am Russian' – expresses in most cases much more than: 'I have been born in this particular country' or 'I have a passport of this particular country'. For the bulk of the individuals reared in a state-society of this type such a statement carries with it a reference to their nation and to personal characteristics and values at the same time. It is a statement about both himself/herself perceived as an 'I' *vis-à-vis* others to whom he or she refers in communications as 'you', 'he' or 'she', and himself/herself perceived as a constituent of one of the collectivities to which he or she refers in thought and sentiment as 'we' *vis-à-vis* others which are to him/her 'you' or 'they'. To say 'I am Russian, American, French', or whatever, usually implies 'I and we believe in specific values and ideas', 'I and we are suspicious and feel more or less antagonistic in relation to members of this or that other nation-state', 'I as well as we have attachments and obligations in relation to these symbols and the collectivity for which they stand'. Moreover, the image of this 'we' forms an integral part of the personality organization of the individual who in these cases uses the pronouns 'I' and 'we' with reference to him- or herself.[9]

14

The term 'nationalism', as one can see, is not being used in this inquiry entirely in the same sense in which it is used in everyday life. In ordinary usage the term 'nationalist' is often loosely distinguished from others such as 'national' or 'patriotic' in order to express disapproval with the help of the former and approval with the help of the latter. But in many cases what one calls 'nationalism' is simply the 'patriotism' of others, what one calls 'patriotism' one's own brand of 'nationalism'.

For the purposes of a sociological inquiry one has to standardize a term which can be used without undertones of either disapproval or approval. One requires a term indicating the specific scale of values, the specific type of sentiments, beliefs and ideals by means of which, in the more industrialized state-societies of the nineteenth and twentieth centuries, individuals attach themselves to the sovereign society which they form with each other. What is needed is a unified term, a clear conceptual instrument for registering the common structural properties of that type of emotional bonding, belief and personality organization which sooner or later appears, not just in one or another but in all industrial nation-states at the developmental level of the nineteenth and twentieth centuries. And since substantives with the suffix '-ism', adjectives with the suffix '-ist' are the accepted linguistic expressions for social belief systems of this kind, and for the personality structures connected with them, the common language offers for sociological standardization as a unified concept mainly the choice between the two terms 'patriotism' and 'nationalism'. On balance, the latter seems preferable as a standard sociological term; it is more flexible; one can form with its help easily understandable derivatives with a process character such as 'nationalization of sentiments and thoughts'. It is in that sense, cleansed of undertones of approval or disapproval, that it is being used here. It is simply intended to refer to one aspect of an overall transformation which specific state-societies in conjunction with the balance of power within a specific figuration of interdependent societies underwent during a specific period of time. It refers to a social belief system which, latently or acutely, raises the state-society, the sovereign collectivity to which its members belong, to the position of a supreme value to which all other values can and sometimes must be subordinated.

As one of the great secular social beliefs of nineteenth- and twentieth-century societies, nationalism distinguishes itself in certain respects from the other great social beliefs of the time, such as conservatism and communism, liberalism and socialism. The latter gain their primary impetus from the changing balance of power within particular state-societies and irradiate inter-state relations only secondarily. Nationalism gains its primary impetus from the changing balance of power among different state-societies and irradiates only secondarily the tensions and conflicts among different social strata within them. And although the ideals and beliefs associated with the polarization of interdependent classes within one and the same state-society blend in a variety of ways with the nationalist beliefs which arise primarily from the polarization of interdependent states within their balance of power-figuration, in the long run the impact of the latter on the direction of politics is more decisive and continuous. Societies may differ with regard to the beliefs and ideals which guide their ruling elites in their intra-state politics; but they all have in common the nationalization of ethos and sentiment, of we-attachment and we-image of most of the individuals who form them. As is easy to see, this nationalization of ethos and sentiment takes place sooner or later in all modernizing countries at the nineteenth- and twentieth-century level regardless of the social complexion of their ruling elites. Although at first mainly characteristic of nation-states dominated by ruling elites whose outlook, ideals and values stand in the tradition of the former middle classes (former since, by rising into the ruling position, they gradually lose their position in the middle) it becomes no less pronounced in nation-states dominated by ruling elites whose outlook and values stand in the tradition of the former working classes (former since, by rising into the ruling position, they gradually lose their character, if not as a social stratum, at least as a social class).

The Duality of Nation-States' Normative Codes

15

However they may be organized, most of the sovereign interdependent nation-states which together form the balance of power figuration in the twentieth century produce a two-fold code of norms whose demands are inherently contradictory: a moral code descended from that of rising sections of the *tiers état*, egalitarian in character, and whose highest value is 'man' – the human individual as such; and a nationalist code descended from the Machiavellian code of princes and ruling aristocracies, inegalitarian in character, and whose highest value is a collectivity – the state, the country, the nation to which an individual belongs.

Henri Bergson, one of the few philosophers who posed the fact of this double code, at least stated the problem;[10] it was not his aim, and lay outside the scope of his considerations, to explore the specific development of inter-state and intra-state relations responsible for this peculiar duality. His proposals for a solution of the problem, therefore, remain speculative and vague. But it was already an important step to perceive and to state clearly the problem as such. He asked: To which society do we refer if we speak of moral obligations? Is it humanity as a whole? Or do we only speak of moral obligations towards our compatriots, our fellow citizens, the members of the same state? He wrote:

> A moral philosophy which does not emphasize this distinction misses the truth; its investigations will thereby be inevitably distorted. In fact when we lay down that the duty to respect the life and property of others is a fundamental demand of social life, what society do we mean? To find an answer we need only think what happens in time of war. Murder and pillage, perfidy, lying and cheating become not only lawful, they are actually praiseworthy. The warring nations can say with the witches in *Macbeth*: 'Fair is foul and foul is fair.'[11]

One sees here once again the line of continuity which leads from the absolutist or, as the case may be, from the aristocratic to the nationalist ethos in state affairs. The latter stands in a direct line of succession to the former. Once more the voice of Machiavelli can help to clarify differences and similarities, change and continuity along that line:

> ... it is necessary that the prince should know how to colour ... [malice] well, and how to be a great hypocrite and dissembler. For men are so simple, and yield so much to immediate necessity, that the deceiver will never lack dupes. I will even venture to say that to have and to practise the above-mentioned quality constantly is pernicious, but to seem to have them is useful. For instance, a prince should seem to be merciful, faithful, humane, religious and upright, and should even be so in reality; but he should have his mind so trained that, when occasion requires it, he may know how to change to the opposite. And it must be understood that a prince, and especially one who has but recently acquired his state, cannot

perform all those things which cause men to be esteemed as good; he being often obliged, for the sake of maintaining his state, to act contrary to humanity, charity and religion. And therefore it is necessary that he should have a versatile mind, capable of changing readily, according as the winds and changes of fortune bid him; and, as has been said above, not to swerve from the good if possible, but to know how to resort to evil if necessity demands it ... A prince then should look mainly to the successful maintenance of his state. The means which he employs for this will always be accounted honourable, and will be praised by everybody.[12]

In later times – and occasionally already in his own time – Machiavelli was sometimes remembered as the advocate of an amoral, devilish doctrine about the conduct of state affairs. In fact, he merely formulated more clearly and in more general terms than is usually done rules for the conduct of inter-state relations. In practice and without any theoretical formulation, both before and after Machiavelli's time, indeed right up to the present day, it has been the standard practice of ruling elites in charge of what has come to be called their countries' foreign policy to follow such rules. One can say that the belief in the rightness and inevitability of conduct in inter-state relations along Machiavellian lines is itself one of the major factors in the perpetuation of this type of conduct. Social strategies determined by fear and suspicion of others, and not subject to an agreed and effectively maintained common code, reproduce the fear and suspicion and give rise again and again to a self-perpetuating dynamic. That is the case whether they are strategies adopted by individuals in relation to other individuals or by groups in relation to other groups. Thus the continuity of a Machiavellian ethos in inter-state relations is simply understandable, almost irrespective of the social characteristics and traditions of the ruling elites, in terms of the fact that these relations themselves continue to remain a sphere of social life in which none of the interdependent social units can be sure that others will not ultimately resort to the use of physical force in order to pursue their supposed interests.

However, the continuity in the self-perpetuating beliefs and code of conduct linking the strategy of princes and aristocratic ruling elites in inter-state affairs to that of the middle- or working-class elites of twentieth-century nation-states was not absolute. It left room for specific changes. Of these perhaps the most noticeable was the change in the character of the postulate that in inter-state relations the interests of one's own state ought to be regarded as the decisive consideration overruling all others. This originated as a simple practical maxim of princes and their ministers or of aristocratic ruling elites with a privileged position who regarded their state and the mass of its subjects as a kind of possession and themselves as the hub of the state. However, with the increasing democratization of state-societies and with the corresponding nationalization of the outlook and sentiments of most of the individuals who formed them, this practical maxim became a categorical imperative with deep roots not only in the feelings of these individuals, but also in their conscience, their I-and-we image, their I-and-we-ideal.

The majority of people who form with each other differentiated industrial nation-states have no direct experience, no specialized knowledge and, indeed, no opportunities for gaining any specialized knowledge about problems of inter-state relations and politics, except the knowledge communicated to them indirectly, often in a highly selective or muddled and biased form, by public media. A deeply felt belief, an individual conscience-formation embodying in one of its layers one's own state as the highest value, thus performs in the large and populous nation-states of the twentieth century, *mutatis mutandis*, a function similar to what could be achieved in dynastic state-societies by practical and comparatively rational considerations of self-interest on the part of small ruling elites. Such a national belief creates in the mass of the members of a nation-state personality dispositions which make them inclined to exert all their strength, to fight and if necessary to die in situations where they see the interests or the survival of their society threatened. In this way, dispositions are created to which actual or potential ruling elites of these large sovereign collectivities can appeal by the use of appropriate releaser symbols when they judge the integrity of their collectivity to be in danger. Or else they may be activated by reciprocal pressures of different sections of the state population. And being all-pervasive, such dispositions colour thinking; they create blockages and biases. The difficulty is that they work automatically to a large extent. In many cases they can only be partly tempered and modified by informed knowledge and realistic judgement. They can be triggered by releaser situations almost automatically without anyone's intention.

In nineteenth- and twentieth-century state-societies, people are thus brought up with dispositions to act in accordance with at least two major codes of norms which are in some respects incompatible with each other. The preservation, integrity and interests of the state-society, of their own sovereign collectivity and all it stands for, are assimilated by each individual as part of his or her habitus, as a guiding principle of action which in certain situations can and must override all others. At the same time, however, they are brought up with a humanist, egalitarian or moral code, whose supreme value overriding all others is the individual human being as such. Both become, in the usual language, 'internalized', or perhaps one should simply say 'individualized'. They become facets of the individual's own conscience. To break either of these two codes can expose an individual in appropriate situations to punishment not only from others, but also from him- or herself in the form of guilt feelings, of a 'bad conscience'.

16

Social norms are often discussed in a manner which suggests that the norms of one and the same society are all of a piece. The facts, as one can see, are different. In societies above a specific level of differentiation, inherently contradictory codes of norms can co-exist in varying degrees of amalgamation and separation. Each may be activated in different situations and at different times. Private affairs may call into action a moral code, public events a nationalist one; in times of peace the former may predominate, in times of war the latter. However, many situations activate both at the same time. The inter-state tensions and conflicts of the twentieth century appear in most cases, though perhaps not in all, to be of this type. They lead easily to struggles for dominance, tensions and conflicts between the two codes and can express themselves in tensions and struggles between different sections of a state population or in struggles of the same individuals with themselves.

Different groups or individuals may resolve these struggles in different ways. In fact, the representative self-images and self-ideals of the members of different nations often embody different forms of coping with the problem of these contradictions; and such differences are apt repeatedly to create blockages of communication between members of different state-societies and to aggravate inter-state tensions. But a clear perception of the basic problem which all twentieth-century nation-states share with each other is usually lacking.

As a rule, the dispassionate exploration of nationalist or patriotic articles of faith is still today subject to a very strong intellectual prohibition. It is socially tabooed. One of the manifestations of such taboos is the widespread use of the term 'norm' as if norms were always benevolent, socially wholesome and integrating facts. Particularly in sociological textbooks it is customary to consider the role and function of social norms by separating, as it were, form and content: one does not consider that different norms can have different social functions, nor that most types of norms have integrating as well as dividing and separating functions. In many cases norms are conceptualized in a highly idealized manner which allows the user to see those functions of norms which he or she wishes them to have and blocks the perception of those functions which he or she does not wish to perceive. There is often in the most intelligent presentations of the fundamentals of sociology a clear description of the functions of norms on what one might call the 'empirical level', that is, in studies of specific details, together with a blockage of the perception of these functions on the theoretical level.

Here is an example from one of the best and most widely used textbooks of sociology in the 1950s and 1960s:

> A social system is always normative. Its integration rests upon the fact that its members carry in their heads, as part of the cultural heritage, the notion that they *ought* or *ought not* to do certain things, that some actions are *good* and others are *wrong* or *bad*. Each person judges himself and his fellows according to these subtle and ubiquitous rules; and any violation is punished by some negative reaction, be it slight or great. An evaluative attitude, an attitude of praise or blame, of accusation and justification thus pervades every human society. To question the rules or, worse yet, to question the sentiments lying behind them, is to incur certain penalties, the least of which is controversy. The person who tries in his own thinking to escape entirely the moralistic system in order to study behavior objectively . . . is quickly branded as an agnostic, cynic, traitor, or worse. Instead of public support for his work, he must count on public hostility. . . .
>
> In any society there are sentiments not to be questioned. They are not even to be studied dispassionately because the mere mention of their violation in anything but a horrified tone may be taboo. More than one professor has been dismissed from an American university for inquiring about the sex life of the unmarried, for taking an open-minded attitude towards religious dogma, for teaching a course about socialism or for adopting an unpatriotic attitude. Such subjects, if touched at all, must always be handled circumspectly with the professor reiterating his devotion to the supreme values.[13]

Thus an eminent sociologist who, when he is concerned with problems of detail, perceives some of the conflicts which result from the manifold and contradictory character of social norms, circumspectly ascribes to the norms of his society only an integrating and not at the same time a dividing and excluding character when he considers them in their role as 'supreme values'. He cannot bring himself to draw the reader's attention unambiguously to the inherently double-edged character of social norms, to the fact that they bind people to each other and at the same time turn people so bound against others. Their integrating tendency is, one might say, also a disintegrating tendency, at least as long as humanity as a whole is not their effective frame of reference. Moreover, no account is taken here of the fact that the supreme values of a particular society may themselves be inherently contradictory. In contemporary nation-states the supreme code of one and the same society may impress upon its members that the single human being, the individual, is the supreme value and at the same time that the sovereign collectivity, the nation-state, is the supreme value to which all individual aims and interests – even the physical survival of individuals – are to be subordinated.

As has already been said, conflicts as a result of an inherently split and contradictory code of norms and a correspondingly contradictory con-science-formation of individuals may be latent only for certain periods of time and become acute only in specific situations. Nevertheless, the fact itself that contradictions of this type exist is of significance not only for the understanding of these societies, but also for that of society as such. One cannot fail to take account in any theory of society of the fact that in the past and present stages of social development the survival of a group of individuals as such was and is regarded as a higher value than the survival of these individuals considered singly.

A theoretical approach which uses as an instrument of sociological analysis an idealized concept of 'norms' cannot serve as an adequate instrument of sociological research. It may well be that problems such as that of the inherently contradictory normative code characteristic of the more developed industrial nation-states are subject in these societies to a social taboo and that it is for that reason difficult to conceptualize and to discuss them. However, it is probably the case that nation-states have so far been unable to escape from the vicious circle of their mutual suspicions, threats and fears precisely because problems such as these cannot be studied and discussed openly and dispassionately. Whatever the reasons, the basic contradictions are simple enough; they can be summed up very briefly.

17

People in societies whose ruling elites stand in the traditions of the industrial middle and working classes are generally brought up to believe in a moral code of norms according to which it is under all circumstances wrong to kill, maim or attack human beings physically, or to defraud, lie, steal and cheat. They are at the same time taught to believe that it is right to do all these things, and to sacrifice their own lives, if that is found necessary in the interests of the sovereign society they form with each other.

Some of the reasons for the dual and contradictory character of this code of 'norms', though by no means all, have been shown. In the field of inter-state relations, representatives of the former middle and working classes encountered conditions as members of ruling elites and were exposed to experiences to which they had no direct access as long as non-aristocratic strata remained socially subordinate. In that field, therefore, they continued the traditions handed on to them from the former ruling classes whose code of norms, in spite of all refinements, had retained the characteristics of a warrior code. In all European countries, even in Britain where the aristocratic ruling groups were joined in that capacity by a middle-class group – a group of middle-class landowners – earlier than in most other European countries, the professions most concerned with inter-state relations were usually a preserve of people who stood in the traditions of a nobility. In many cases their representatives continued this tradition after the rise to power of industrial classes. However, democratization, as suggested, gave a different complexion to this tradition. The warrior code assumed the characteristics of another morality; and this parochial, inegalitarian, nationalist morality was no less demanding, no less unconditional and unquestionable than the universal, egalitarian, humanist morality.

The development of a dual and inherently contradictory code of norms is one of the common features of all countries which have undergone the transformation from an aristocratic–dynastic into a more democratic national state. The contradictions, conflicts and tensions inherent in this development may come into the open and become very acute only in specific situations, above all in national emergencies such as wars. But even as a latent determinant of action, even in times of peace, a dual code of norms of this type has very considerable influence on the attitudes of individuals and on the conduct of affairs. It accounts for a specific polarization of political ideals. It enables some groups to lay greater stress in their programmes on the values of the nationalist creed and of the warrior tradition without necessarily completely abandoning those of the humanist, egalitarian moral tradition. The stress of others is the reverse, in a great variety of combinations. It makes it possible for different individuals, in accordance with their social position, to link their attitudes, their personality structure, with a group, whether it stands more towards the centre or towards one or other pole of the spectrum. The whole figuration itself, the alignment of groups of people somewhere between these two poles, is a common feature of all societies of this type.

18

Many problems connected with this polarity, above all that of the recurrent stress on a nationalist creed by the more prosperous conservative groups of a country and the appeal which a more militant, more ·extreme nationalist creed has for less prosperous middle-class groups, must be left aside here. But a word has to be said about the way in which the common problem – the contradictions of conduct which spring from the co-existence of two in many respects inconsistent codes of norms – are handled in different countries. For this is the immediate reason for this digression into the sociology of nationalism: German nationalism is often treated in isolation as if the nationalization of sentiment, conscience and ideals had occurred in Germany alone.

In fact, if one touches upon problems of the German nationalist creed – and one cannot neglect it if one is concerned with the sociological aspects of the development of the concept of 'culture' – it very soon becomes clear that it is difficult to determine what is peculiarly German in the German variety of a nationalist creed without an outline model of the common developmental trends which have made for varieties of nationalism in all industrializing state-societies of the nineteenth and twentieth centuries. The presence of a dual code centred on and stressing as the highest value, on the one hand, the human individual and, on the other, the nation-state is one central moment of development common to all these societies.

Perhaps one can best illuminate the distinguishing characteristics of the German manner of dealing with this problem by means of a brief glance at least at *one* other national way of dealing with it which is sufficiently different from the German to indicate the broad spectrum of possible variations – the British way. A fundamental and recurrent difference between the British and the German traditions surfaces in this connection once more. In Britain, the tendency to amalgamate the two codes prevailed. Attempts were made to find compromise solutions for their contradictory demands and – so it seems, with success – to forget that the problem existed at all. The German tendency was to stress the incompatibility of the two codes. It was a question only of an either–or. Compromise between different codes, according to the whole tenor of German thinking, was untidy; it was muddled thinking, if not outright dishonest. And as strategies of inter-state relations were usually devised in accordance with each state's own traditions of thinking, these differences in the approach to the duality of norms quite often created serious difficulties of communication. In communications among themselves, members of each state took their own way of dealing with the Janus-faced code for granted; it simply appeared as right, as the only possible way of thinking and acting. Any other way appeared as wrong, if not as reprehensible.

In 'extramural' encounters – in communications between members of the two nations – the different ways of dealing with the basic duality of norms therefore created blockages of mutual understanding. Germans, who thought that the contradictory aspects of a moralist and a nationalist code of norms were not amenable to any compromise solution, implicitly assumed that British people, while perceiving, as they themselves did, the amoral aspects of a nationalist power policy, intentionally concealed these aspects behind a cloak of morality. In their own terms, they had no other way of comprehending the British attempts at compromise solutions to the dilemma than that of explaining them as a piece of deliberate deception – of hypocrisy. By contrast, British people, who had learned that their compromise solution to the dilemma was natural, that is, equally sensible and practical – which in fact it was – found the uncompromising stress of the nationalist sections of the German people on the idea that amoral power politics in the interests of one's own state are the common policy of all states to be reprehensible and dangerous. In both cases the 'intramural' tradition of thinking and acting was automatically used as yardstick for comprehending and for judging the other side.

It would be a worthwhile task to show in detail how the gradual nationalization of sentiments, conscience and ideals of all classes and the corresponding moralization of the image of nation and state took place in Britain during the nineteenth and twentieth centuries. One could show how closely the interpenetration of the two codes of norms was linked to the fact that the permeability of stratum barriers between different estates, particularly after the virtual unification of England, Scotland and Wales in the seventeenth and early eighteenth centuries, was high compared with that of the corresponding barriers in continental European societies. The basic sociological explanation in this as in many other cases is very simple – the safety of the island population in inter-state conflicts did not primarily depend on a standing army officered by men who stood in the traditions of the old warrior estate, of the landed nobility, but on a military formation specialized for warfare at sea, on a navy.

A corps of naval officers, quite apart from the special character of its fighting techniques and from its social composition, could not, by the very nature of the military establishment which it served, play in inter-state relations the same role which the officer corps of a standing army played in the absolutist autocracies of the continent and in Germany up to the end of its dynastic phase in 1918. It could not serve rulers, whose power depended on the separation and differences between the principal social cadres in their realm and on a fluctuating tension-balance between them as an instrument for maintaining and often reinforcing a low permeability of barriers between strata. As a result the flow of middle-class models upwards and of aristocratic models downwards became in Britain, after a slow and intermittent phase in the seventeenth century, relatively continuous in the eighteenth century. A first spurt in the direction towards the moralization of the image of the state and a nationalization of morals, still in their religious form, can be observed in the short period of Cromwell's commonwealth. In the nineteenth century the moralization of the image of Britain as a state and as a nation was beginning to be recognizable, as a corollary, first, of the rise in power of sections of the industrial middle classes and, a little later, of their rise into the position of a ruling class. And in the twentieth century, particularly after the First World War when their rise into the position of the dominant ruling class was almost completed and sections of the working classes moved into the position of a secondary ruling class, the moralization of the guiding image of state and nation and the nationali-zation of the self-image of the middle and, with a certain time lag, of the working classes became firmly established.

This blending of codes in Britain was no more an expression of the mysterious workings of an 'ethnic spirit' which made the British people inclined towards compromise than the contrary tendency of Germans was the manifestation of mysterious ethnic or racial properties. When it comes to problems such as these the temptation is to turn to some metaphysical racial theory as an explanation. The sociological answer, which has already been touched on, is very simple. It revolves around the problem of why in Britain in contrast to Prussia the attempt of the ruling dynasty of the seventeenth century at establishing an autocratic regime in the teeth of the opposition of the estate assemblies failed. The inability of the British kings to lay their hands on sufficient money for the maintenance of a standing army and to get together sufficient troops to enforce the collection of taxes played a central part in their inability to win their battles with the estates. And this inability rested precisely on the fact that the safety of Britain did not depend on a standing army on land, but on a navy.

In order to understand the connection between the victory of the estate assemblies, of the two houses of parliament, over the British kings and the greater permeability of stratum barriers in Britain, it is useful to bear in mind the consistency with which absolute princes in France, Prussia and many other continental countries strengthened the barriers between the estates and treated any weakening of these barriers as injurious to their interests. This in turn accounts for the greater blending there of the 'cultures', of the different traditions of different estates and later of different classes. The greater interpenetration of aristocratic and middle-class traditions from the eighteenth century on – greater by comparison with the corresponding German development – and, as part of it, the attempt of sections of the British middle class to combine the aristocratic code of norms in inter-state relations with the moralist and humanist code with which they had risen to the top, is only one of several instances of this basic sociological fact. In this case, that is, the greater interpenetration of neighbouring social strata facilitated a specific fusion of their codes of norms and a general inclination towards pragmatic compromises.

Such a conceptualization may help one to place in better perspective a number of facts which, though readily observable, usually remain unconnected and unexplained. Take the change in the role of the royal family in British society. In the eighteenth century, the king's court was one power centre in a party game in which nobles set the tone. The code of norms ruling the conduct of the royal family was an aristocratic code. In accordance with the distribution of power in British society, middle-class morality had little chance to assert itself at court. Kings and queens were still primarily seen as living persons and only secondarily as symbols of the realm. With increasing democratization, the symbolic function of royalty as a living representation of a national ideal steadily – though with a number of fluctuations – increased. When the large industrial classes, one after the other, rose into the position of ruling classes, the British people's image of themselves as a sovereign collectivity, as a nation, was formed, as a matter of course, in accordance with the demands of a moral code. The mass of the people expected that even Britain's foreign policy would be conducted in accordance with these demands, with the principles of justice, human rights and help for the oppressed, including oppressed nations. Individuals might fall short of the moral code of norms, but the nation, which presented itself in the eyes of the mass of the people as an ideal 'we', could only justify the restraints and sacrifices demanded of its members if it appeared to live up to the demands of a moral code. Royalty too, as the living symbol of how Britons ought to behave, of the national we-ideal, had to comply, therefore, with the demands of middle-class and later of working-class morality. The royal dynasty retained a limited place in the multipolar power equilibrium of British society and a larger place in the affections of the people as the embodiment of the ideal 'we', the collective self of the nation, provided the members of the royal house fitted into the role of a living ideal and complied, or appeared to comply, with the demands of middle- and working-class morality.

The function as symbol of the state-society certainly always formed an ingredient of the complex of functions of the monarchy. But as long as the power at the disposal of the social position of kings and queens was large by comparison with that of the mass of the people, the need to represent in their persons the people's ideals was smaller. The steady shift in the distribution of power conceptualized here as 'democratization' made the holders of the royal position more dependent on the mass of subjects. From being rulers of the state they became symbols of the nation. The moral demands made on royalty in Britain are thus an example – one of many – showing the processes of democratization, moralization and nationalization of sentiments, conscience and ideals at work as strands of one and the same overall transformation of society.

In practice, the confluence and fusion in Britain of the Machiavellian dynastic and warrior tradition in its nationalist guise (a process which obtained its impetus from the unmanageable character of *inter* state relations) with the humanist moral tradition of former subject classes (a process which obtained its impetus from the relatively high control of violence in *intra*-state relations) did not remove or lessen the contradictions between the two traditions. But the fact that those responsible for British foreign policy had to account for their own directives as well as for the actions of their subordinates to a public which was sensitive with regard to the moral issues involved and whose loyalty to the nation was to some extent bound up with the preservation of the belief in the nation's superior value acquired in course of time a specific limiting and restraining function.

This belief itself – the conviction of the higher value of one's own country over all or most others – is one of the common denominators of all nationalist belief systems. But the particular national ideology, the specific basis of the claim to a superior value, is to some extent different from country to country in accordance with its specific fortunes past and present. These differences are of considerable significance. They make themselves apparent, among other ways, in the strategy of a country's ruling elites in inter-state relations. In fact without knowledge of the dominant nationalist credo of a society, without a reasonably clear picture of the national 'we and they' image and its social development, it is difficult to understand and to foresee how, in practice, its ruling elites seek to secure its interests in relation to other nations.

19

Yet another factor has to be taken into account. While the general direction of this development was the same in all industrializing states, the time at which each of the interdependent states of the European power-balance figuration entered a particular phase differed considerably. The figuration was formed by societies at different stages of development, the less developed, less civilized and less humanized drawing the more developed towards their own level and vice versa.

The period up to the end of the so-called First World War showed the effects of this interdependence of states at different stages of development very clearly. In some of the more advanced states, the high bourgeoisie had already moved into a ruling position though, as yet, only as partner of the ruling aristocracy whose social pre-eminence was still almost as great as it had been in previous periods and only a little less than it was in the less developed European countries of the same period. Up until 1914, it was still a common characteristic of the leading powers in the European state system that their military establishments, their inter-state diplomacy and the whole outlook of governments on inter-state relations were – to put it at its mildest – determined by aristocratic traditions even if the actual promoters of policy were of middle-class origin. In a number of powerful European countries, such as Russia or Austria, the traditional dynastic and aristocratic elites still ruled more or less autocratically; they still held the commanding positions of the state almost alone

– at the most with smaller or greater concessions to urban industrial classes insofar as they existed.

One cannot understand the development and structure of a network of inter-state relations of that type, that is, of the balance of power system as such, in terms of the development and structure of any of the component states seen singly; one can understand it only as a figurational level *sui generis* interdependent with others but not reducible to them. On the inter-state level dynastic and aristocratic traditions and norms dominated the scene in the nineteenth century and beyond, even though the technical, scientific and industrial developments of the time gave an impetus and expansionary momentum to the power rivalries of European states which was stronger than in preceding centuries.

The nineteenth century is sometimes represented as the bourgeois century *par excellence*. But this is a one-sided view.[14] The decline of dynastic and aristocratic groups as the ruling groups of European societies and their replacement by industrial middle and working classes was a gradual process. So far as the middle classes were concerned it was hardly complete prior to 1918. The full weight of the older ruling groups before the end of the first great war in the twentieth century is easily obscured if one perceives as structured only the internal, and particularly the internal economic, development of European states and sees as unstructured and accidental the development of inter-state relations. The latter, including the conflicts, the rivalries and wars, are inseparable from the internal development of states. If both are taken into account it appears less paradoxical and accidental that, even in the more advanced countries of the nineteenth century, aristocratic groups with a strong military and diplomatic tradition still played a leading part. So it was in no way a contradiction of the then-existing social structure that an aristocrat of the purest 'blood' such as Lord Palmerston, whose norms and standards of behaviour in both public and private life would have fitted very well into the eighteenth century, was for a while the idol of the British industrial classes, or that Bismarck, the quintessential Prussian noble, was the man who translated into fact the middle-class dream of German national unity – what the German middle classes were not able to achieve on their own.

The pre-eminence of dynastic and aristocratic ruling elites in nearly all member states of the European state system during the nineteenth century was a structural characteristic of the system in this transitional phase. Even in the more advanced industrial countries, the power of the industrial middle classes was, at most, just great enough to make it possible for them to rise into the commanding positions of their society as allies of the old ruling groups. The time-honoured 'culture' of the latter gave people who grew up in it or who became assimilated into it, a clear superiority in the skills of traditional statecraft which, with all its built-in deficiencies and blockages, still dominated the views and attitudes of most leading statesmen. That held above all in inter-state relations, which had contributed only marginally to the experiences of the middle classes and hence to the making of their traditions. In Britain, Gladstone's peculiar mixture of absolute and unswerving righteousness in principle with expediency, opportunism and compromise in practice indicates the problems which middle-class men had to face when they ascended to a position of power. This split was not simply the expression of a unique personal disposition but rather showed in an individual form the problems arising from the encounter of the cultures of two different strata, and particularly of two different and in many respects contradictory codes of norms which had developed in connection with very different types of social experiences.

Perhaps one can see the problem in better perspective if one remembers by way of conclusion what another Anglican, one who developed nonconformist sympathies, wrote about Machiavelli in an earlier age when urban middle classes were still largely excluded from the commanding positions of the state and were not exposed to the temptation of besmirching the purity of their belief through compromises. Here are some of the words with which John Wesley denounced Machiavelli, probably not without reference to the possibility that his own country's affairs might be conducted according to Machiavelli's prescriptions:

> ... I weighed the sentiments that were less common; transcribed the passages wherein they were contained; compared one passage with another, and endeavoured to form a cool, impartial judgment. And my cool judgment is, that if all the other doctrines of devils which have been committed to writing since letters were in the world, were collected together in one volume, it would fall short of this; and that should a Prince form himself by this book so calmly recommending hypocrisy, treachery, lying, robbery, oppression, adultery, whoredom and murder of all kinds, Domitian or Nero would be an angel of light compared to that man.[15]

The rapprochement and attempted reconciliation between the moral–middle-class code of norms and its Machiavellian–dynastic counterpart was no easy matter. It is not surprising that, like the rise to power of the industrial middle classes generally, it took the form of a gradual process, even if the long-drawn-out social tensions and conflicts which were associated with it erupted during a specific phase and in various places in violent, revolutionary struggles.[16]

III

Civilization and Violence

On the State Monopoly of Physical
Violence and its Transgression

III

1

The civilization of which I speak is never completed and always endangered. It is endangered because the safeguarding of more civilized standards of behaviour and feeling in society depends on specific conditions. One of these is the exercise of relatively stable self-discipline by the individual person. This, in turn, is linked to specific social structures. These include the supply of goods – that is, the maintenance of the accustomed standard of living. They also include above all the peaceful solving of intra-state conflicts – that is, social pacification. But the internal pacification of a society, too, is always endangered. It is endangered by social as well as personal conflicts, which are normal attributes of human communal living – the very conflicts which the pacifying institutions are concerned with mastering. It is with this side of a civilizing process, with the tension between pacification and violence, that this essay is concerned. It treats these conflicts with special reference to specific German problems.[1]

In striving to examine the problem of physical violence in the social life of human beings, people often ask the wrong sort of questions.[2] It is usual to ask how is it possible that people within a society can physically strike or kill others – how, for example, can they become terrorists? It would better fit the facts and thus be more fruitful if the question were differently phrased. It should rather read, how is it possible that so many people can normally live together peacefully, without fear of being attacked or killed by people stronger than themselves, as is nowadays largely the case in the great state-societies of Europe, America, China or Russia? It is all too easy today to overlook the fact that never before in the development of humankind have so many millions of people lived relatively peacefully with each other, with physical attacks mostly eliminated, as they do in the large states and cities of our time. Perhaps this fact first becomes evident when one realizes how much higher the level of violence was in the relations between people in earlier epochs of human development.

It is certainly the primary attitude that, when they come into conflict, get angry with others or hate them, people let fly and attack and beat each other and in some circumstances even commit murder. This is exactly the problem that I mean, since all this – anger, hate, enmity, rivalry – is still with us, but physical attacks and even murder have retreated comparatively speaking into the background. As one can see, I am focusing the lens differently. It is a question of reawakening people's feeling for a fact which is astonishing and unique: the relatively high degree of non-violence that is characteristic of the social organizations of today. Only from such a standpoint can it really be explained and understood why certain people do not submit to the code of civilization of our time.

The question of how such a pacification came about is – at least at first glance – not difficult to answer. The creation of durably pacified social spaces is connected with the organization of social life in the form of states. One aspect of this problem was first looked at by Max Weber. He pointed out that states are characterized by the people who are their rulers at any given time laying claim to a monopoly of physical force for themselves. This means that we live in a form of social organization where rulers have at their disposal groups of specialists who are authorized to use physical force in emergencies and also to prevent other citizens from doing the same.[3] This monopolization of force can be described as a socio-technical invention of the human species.[4] There are inventions not only on the natural level, but also on the social level. However, the latter are seldom thought up by single persons alone, but mostly develop unplanned as collective achievements. The monopolization of physical force is one of these unplanned social inventions; it has emerged very gradually over the course of hundreds of years as part of a long-term social process until it has reached the level of today. And this is definitely not the last stage. It would be quite unrealistic to say that the intra-state monopoly of force functions in an entirely problem-free way. People will have to continue working at it, and the formation of sociological concepts can contribute a little by helping them do it with greater awareness.

Such monopolies of physical force, which nowadays are usually controlled and directed by state governments and represented by the military and police as executive organs, are, like so many human inventions, achievements that cut two ways – they are Janus-faced. Just as the discovery of fire-making enabled food to be cooked as well as the destructive burning down of huts and houses, just as the invention of iron-working brought with it great progress in both agriculture and warfare, just as atomic power can be a source of energy as well as a terrible weapon, so, too, can social inventions be two-faced. The emergence of monopolies of physical force is an example. I am obliged to leave this aspect of the problem to one side here. But this much is clear: one property of such a state monopoly of physical force is that it can serve people as a dangerous weapon. From the pharaohs to the dictatorships of the present, control over the monopoly of force has been used by small established groups as a decisive power-source to secure their own interests. Its function for those who control it, however, is not the only function of the state monopoly of force. It also performs an important function for people bound together in the form of states. This control has been, up till now, an essential condition of the internal pacification of larger social units, in particular of the peaceful communal life of larger masses of people in the more developed industrial states – a condition which in turn is closely linked with the monopoly of taxation, since, without taxation, there can be no weapon-bearers, whether armed forces or police, and without armed forces and police, no taxation.

The crucial point is the balance between the two functions of the violence-monopoly: between the function for its controllers, and the function (or functions) for the entire population of a state, for example with respect to internal pacification. In earlier times, the balance of power in this respect was so unevenly distributed that the controllers – one could almost say the owners – of the monopoly of force were in a position where, in exercising it, they were able unrestrictedly to place its function for themselves above its function for their subjects. It is reported of Louis XIV that he said '*l'état c'est moi*'. He felt himself in fact to be the state's owner. Since then in some countries the balance of power has shifted somewhat in favour of the other function, the function for the total state-society. At the highest level reached so far, the commanders and controllers of the violence-monopoly are themselves under the control of other representatives of the society in question. The latter keep watch to see that the former do not use the means of violence they command only in their own interests, or only in the interests of particular strata of the population organized as a state.

The pacification of people as individuals, the fact that in conflicts most of us only seldom contemplate attacking an opponent and starting a fight, however angry we may be, testifies to a deeply rooted civilizing transformation of the entire personality structure. Babies, irrespective of the society to which they belong, defend themselves spontaneously with hands and feet. Children scrap with and hit each other willingly and often. That the taboo against violent acts is imprinted so deeply into the youth of the more developed state-societies is linked to a large extent to the growing effectiveness of the state monopoly of force. In the course of time, the personality structures of individual persons become geared up to this. They develop a certain reluctance or even a deep aversion, a type of disgust, towards the use of physical violence. The development of this process can be followed. In earlier times, even as late as the nineteenth century, it was still taken quite for granted in many strata that men beat women in order to impose their will. Nowadays, the precept that under no circumstances should men hit women – not even each other, even when they are stronger – that not even children should be hit, is far more deeply anchored in the feelings of individuals than it ever was in previous centuries. The pacification of the state, the constraint from others, has been transformed into a self-constraint. Only when one becomes aware of this far-reaching self-activated taming of spontaneous violent impulses in relatively civilized state-societies is the problem of deliberate and premeditated acts of violence placed in the proper light.

Within states there are thus legal and illegal violent groups. The situation is further complicated by the fact that there is no monopoly of force on the international level. On this level, we are basically still living exactly as our forefathers did in the period of their so-called 'barbarism'. Just as formerly each tribe was a constant danger for the other tribes, so nowadays each state represents a constant danger for other states. Their representatives and members must always be on guard against and must constantly reckon with the possibility of being attacked by a stronger state, and being made dependent on it or even brought under its rule. A mechanism of reciprocal threat and fear – I call this a double-bind process – drives states to become stronger and more powerful than others, in order not to fall behind them.[5] In particular, it is a normal state of affairs in inter-state relations that the strongest states at any time are embroiled in hegemonial struggles with each other – partly just because they live in constant fear of each other. On this level, no dominant power restrains any of the participants from acts of violence when they deem themselves stronger and see advantages from them. In earlier times, this was the case everywhere, often even within states themselves. The stronger neighbour had to be feared. The physically stronger could use their strength to threaten, to extort, to rob and to enslave other people.

In contrast, the pacification and civilization of people within states is comparatively advanced. A consequence is that, in this respect, a curious split runs through our civilization – our civilization understood as now being that of humanity as a whole. In intra-state affairs, violence between people is tabooed, and, when possible, punished; in inter-state relations another code holds good. Every larger state is in constant preparation for violence with other states, and when it comes to such violence, those who perpetrate it are extremely highly valued, and in many cases praised and rewarded. If one accepts the reduction of the physical dangers which people represent for each other as one of the decisive criteria in the sequential ordering of the stages of civilization, that is, the extent of reciprocal threat, or conversely, of pacification, then one can say that in intra-state relations people have reached a higher level of civilization than in the relationships between states. In the case of the more developed industrial states, which are often fairly effectively pacified internally, the gradient between pacification within the state and the threat between states is often especially steep. In inter-state relations, people today do not find themselves on a lower rung of the civilizing process because they are naturally evil or because they have inborn aggressive urges, but rather because specific social institutions have been formed which can more or less effectively impose a check on every state-authorized act of violence in relations within the state, while such institutions are completely lacking in relations between states. Thus, all larger and many smaller states keep violence-specialists in a state of constant readiness so they can be deployed in the case of a threat of violent invasion by another state, or, alternatively, if their own state should itself threaten another.[6]

On an inter-state level the formation of a monopoly of physical violence, and thus also the process of state-formation, remains quite rudimentary – for reasons and with consequences which I do not need to go into here. The development of such a monopoly on an intra-state level has certainly progressed further, though not everywhere to the same extent. Even where it is comparatively effective, it remains vulnerable. In the crisis-situations of society, the state-authorized specialists in violence – the representatives of the state monopoly of force – can become embroiled in a violent struggle with groups not authorized by the state. In what follows, two such cases from recent German history will be discussed.

2

It would, I think, be a rather nice task to write the 'biography' of a state-society, for instance Germany. For just as in the development of an individual person the experiences of earlier times continue to have an effect in the present, so, too, do earlier experiences in the development of a nation.

The experience that the German empire was for a long time a weak state and occupied a relatively low position in the hierarchy of European states still lives on in Germany's development. The self-esteem of the people involved suffered as a result; they felt humiliated. One can read from many witnesses of Germany in the seventeenth and eighteenth centuries how often people felt and experienced through their own bodies that Germany was weak, for example in relation to France, Britain, Sweden or Russia, because it was fragmented.

In a biography of Germany one would then have to describe how this feeling of weakness and power inferiority changed suddenly into the opposite, when the one-time loosely integrated state late in its history became unified in the context of a victorious war. In place of the often deep-rooted feelings of national inferiority, strongly emphasized feelings of national greatness and power now appeared. The way to great power status was open to the unified Germany, and as is usually the case in power and prestige struggles between states, the determination to fight for supremacy arose very rapidly out of this. The pendulum swung from the extreme of abasement to the extreme of exultation, and accordingly more and more members of Germany's leading strata felt that their country ought to prepare for the fight for hegemony in Europe, if not the world. As in other cases, here too a previously humiliated and oppressed group transformed itself with a change in its situation into one that was arrogant and repressive, or, to use the contemporary language, into a master-race [*Herrenvolk*]. And since the stage of national integration in the German territories and the corresponding rise of Germany into the upper rank of European great powers took place so late, people were in a hurry. The representatives of Germany had to acquire as quickly as possible all the trappings of a great power – everything that was needed in the competitive struggle between states, especially colonies and a navy.

One cannot fully understand the development of Germany, nor the current attitude to the use of force within the Federal Republic, without bearing in mind this line of development of Germany's position in the inter-state framework and correspondingly in the power and status hierarchies of states. It is impossible here to separate inter-state and intra-state lines of development; from a sociological standpoint, intra-state and inter-state structures are inseparable even though the sociological tradition up till now has involved a concentration mainly, and quite often exclusively, on the former. The development of Germany shows particularly clearly how processes within and between states are indissolubly interwoven.

The rise of Germany after 1871 into the ranks of European great powers – into the dangerous magic circle of states fighting for hegemony – had great significance for internal politics. The unification of Germany had been achieved through military victories over rival states. The leadership in these struggles lay in the hands of the nobility. Compared with them, the German middle class had played a second-rank political role. Middle-class people were largely excluded from the highest positions of command in the German states. The great political and military decisions were still taken at the princely courts. In Prussia especially, with a few exceptions, all top positions were reserved for aristocrats. It is true that many middle-class people had not been satisfied with their outsider role, and had fought in some way or another against the supremacy of the courts and aristocracy. It was a sign first and foremost of the failure of this struggle that the middle-class dream of a unified Germany was reached through the efforts of more powerful and higher-status strata – through the achievement of a prince and his noble ministers and generals – on the basis of a successful war.

That the national victory under the leadership of a court and military aristocracy implied at the same time a social defeat of the German middle class in the domestic social struggle against the supremacy of the nobility had far-reaching consequences for the political and social attitudes of the German middle strata. Many, although certainly not all, members of the German middle class now gave up the domestic struggle against the hegemony of the nobility. They acquiesced in their position as a social stratum of the second rank. The increase in self-esteem which they experienced as Germans, as members of the new *Kaiserreich*, compensated for the relative degradation they felt in having to accept their second-rank standing below the aristocracy in power and status.

In conjunction with this self-acquiescence, a remarkable change occurred in the attitudes and codes of behaviour of substantial segments of the German upper middle class, which is of significance for every theoretician of civilization. The idealistic component of the German middle-class cultural tradition which was still dominant at the end of the eighteenth century, and which often went hand in hand with an anti-court, anti-aristocratic attitude, began to ebb. At least, it continued to be upheld only in limited circles. In its place, there occurred in other segments of the middle class, especially the high civil service and the entire academic world, an adoption of aristocratic values, namely the values of a class with a strongly warlike tradition and which was orientated to the politics of international relations. In other words, parts of the German middle class were assimilated into the higher-ranking stratum and made its warrior ethos their own.

But in the course of being adapted, this aristocratic code was transformed. To put it briefly, it became 'bourgeoisified'. In aristocratic circles, military values embodied in conceptual symbols such as courage, obedience, honour and discipline, responsibility and loyalty were usually part of a long family tradition.[7] In accordance with their different social situation, middle-class circles adopted the aristocratic code only in a certain version. In this way, it underwent a class-specific change in function: it lost the character of a tradition-bound and correspondingly little reflected upon pattern of behaviour, and became expressed in an explicitly formulated doctrine hardened by reflection. What was for the aristocracy a more or less unquestioned tradition – a largely naïve high estimation of warlike values, a socially inherited understanding of the meaning of power-potentials in the inter-state play of strength – was now cultivated very much more consciously by the upper sectors of the middle classes as something newly obtained. Seldom before had so much been said and written in praise of power, even of the violent sort.

Since the longed for unification had been achieved through victorious wars under the military leadership of the aristocracy, the conclusion was drawn that war and violence were also good and splendid as political instruments.[8] Not the whole, but certainly very important sections of the German middle class developed this strain of thinking into the kernel of their ideology. Whereas for many nobles war and diplomatic intrigues were a customary craft, a speciality in which they were experts, among those parts of the peaceable middle class which had assimilated the warrior code can be seen a romanticization of power, a literature in which power won by force appeared in embellished form, as a highly held value. Nietzsche, who had participated for a time in the 1870 war between Germany and France as a volunteer nurse, gave philosophical form to this ideology of the Wilhelmine middle class, almost certainly without being aware of it, in his book *The Will to Power*. [See appendix 1 to this part, pp. 204–6.] When one considers the books of that time, especially novels of the Wilhelmine period, when one considers the duelling of middle-class students according to the unifying codes of honour of primarily middle-class or primarily aristocratic student associations, or when one considers the special status of middle-class reserve officers or of the middle-class privy councillors in court uniform, then one can easily recognize the process of incorporation of the upper middle classes into the aristocracy and the court. At the same time, one sees the peculiar paradox represented by the social and psychological structure of broad circles of the official and graduate middle class of that time. In their efforts to assimilate to the warlike and often Machiavellian values of the more powerful nobility, despite their own predominantly peaceful professional and less military cultural tradition, a hidden yearning of these middle-class people is reflected – the yearning to be something they could never become, at least never in a single generation, namely aristocrats.

An example may help somewhat to clarify this pronounced affirmation of violence. In 1912, a popular middle-class writer, Walter Bloem, published a novel under the title of *Volk wider Volk* [Nation against Nation], in which he once again recounts for his readers the wonderful experience of the victorious war of 1870–1. I quote from it an episode, the encounter of German troops with French *francs-tireurs*, meaning irregulars or partisans:

The *francs-tireurs* ran for their lives. ... One of them stumbled ... a second later, George's bullet missed him narrowly – a thrust of his dagger met the outstretched arm behind which was hidden a staring face full of panic and fear of death ... it was a woman.

Now all three were tied together, the wench and the two peasants. Then

they continued at a brisk trot. If they wanted to avoid being put to death,
the captives had to run until their tongues hung out. . . . The lancers did
not spare them from thumps, kicks, blows to the neck with the shafts of
their lances . . . even the woman got her share. . . . They had long since
forgotten to distinguish between humans and cattle. . . . An enemy prisoner
was nothing other than a wild, malicious beast.[9]

Feelings such as these are spontaneous, and the corresponding actions
are certainly routine in the tumult of war. What can be regarded as
characteristic of the situation of the German middle classes in 1912 is
the fact that this type of brutality in a light novel is presented quite
expressly as a sign of an accepted and praiseworthy code of behaviour.

When one reads such testimony, and there is plenty of it, one sees in a
trice that a fundamental transformation in the attitudes of broad sections
of the middle class had taken place since Schiller's 'You millions I
embrace you', and since the time of the great German classical idealists
whose books found considerable resonance amongst the educated
German middle class [*Bildungsbürgertum*] as models of thought and
reading. The ultimate identification of humans with each other, which
was perhaps a bit idealistically exaggerated in the classical authors, was
emphatically negated in these later middle-class groups in favour of an
exclusively national identification. In war, the ordinary people of the
enemy no longer needed to be treated as human beings. These people are
nothing more than 'wild, malicious beasts'. The popular author
obviously expected his readers to share and condone this attitude.

3

Many young Germans went to the battlefield in 1914 with the idea that
war was something wonderful, great, glorious. They were filled with a
feeling of certain victory,[10] in which the strength of their dreams about
the future Great Germany was reflected. 'Hurrah', wrote home a law
student, who would be fatally wounded one and a half months later on
the Marne,

at last I have my battle orders. . . . We shall win! With such strong
determination to be victorious, absolutely nothing else is possible. My
dear ones, be proud that you live in such times and belong to such a
people, and also that you may send more of your loved ones to this proud
battle.[11]

As it actually developed, the war was dreadful. The unplanned military process ran counter to the preconceived plans of the generals. The leading military men on both sides had planned for a vigorous offensive war which would be as brief as possible. The French generals, yesterday's vanquished, gambled on an *offensive à l'outrance*, with battles *aux allures dechainées*; the Germans followed the modified Schlieffen plan, which foresaw a decisive blow against the French enemy by the unexpected invasion of Belgium and from there to France, so that German troops in the West would be freed for the war in the East. The planned offensives of both sides annulled each other. After heavy losses, they seeped away in a grey trench war. This had been predicted by those few outsiders who had recognized that developments in weapons technology at that time favoured the defensive *vis-à-vis* the offensive. H. G. Wells and others had foreseen the coming of the war of attrition [*Stellungskrieg*].

When the United States, which like Britain feared a continent ruled by Germany, entered the war, Germany's chance of winning disappeared completely and utterly. The inconceivable became fact. Germany exhausted its strength and was defeated. Kaiser and princes lost their thrones. The courts, centres of the 'good society' of Germany, disappeared. This 'good society' itself, the society of those entitled to give and demand satisfaction, from the high nobility to members of the middle-class nationalist fraternities [*Burschenschaften*], from the field marshal to the middle-class reserve officer, united by a code of honour binding for all and which raised them all above non-members, was, like a runner colliding at full pace with a wall, halted in its race for the supremacy of Europe at a single blow. A traumatic shock was the consequence. [See appendix 2 to this part, pp. 207–13.]

Furthermore, the downfall of the Wilhelmine establishment in the struggle between states went hand in hand with an – at least partial – defeat in the intra-state struggles. The end of the old regime and the destruction of the country after the lost war increased the power-chances of previously outsider groups, first and foremost those of organized labour. For the first time in the history of Germany, their representatives took over the government of the Reich.[12] As always in such cases the rise of outsider groups which used to be lower in social standing – a former master saddler was the successor to the Kaiser – was felt by many members of the German 'good society' to be an unbearable wound to their feelings of self-esteem.

The development of Germany shows here in paradigmatic form the reaction of a ruling establishment and its supporters to a change in social structure which contributed to a shift in the power-ratio to their disadvantage. Not only revolutions but also wars bring to light structural changes in power relations already under way within the traditional institutional fabric but previously hidden by this very fabric. A victorious war would probably have guaranteed once more the subordination of the mass of the people to the victorious leadership classes. The lost war brought into effect the redistribution of power which had been quietly occurring beneath the surface of the imperial state in the course of Germany's rapid industrialization. Soldiers and workers *en masse* withdrew their obedience from their unsuccessful leadership class.

A better understanding of the development both of Germany and of terrorism in the period of the first German republic will be possible if one bears in mind a clear outline of the intra- and inter-state power structures of the time and how they were experienced. The Wilhelmine establishment, the *satisfaktionsfähige Gesellschaft*, now expanded by the previously excluded merchant and entrepreneurial strata, had suffered both an internal and an external defeat. It was not prepared simply to accept the situation thus created. At first, it did not know precisely how it would be possible to make good both defeats, that is, on the one hand to re-establish Germany as a major power based on a strong army, and, on the other, to maintain their privileges as the ruling elite of Germany in the face of the power claims of the organized working class. But the objectives themselves very soon became clear again to the losers.[13]

There have been many such situations in the development of human societies. Such cases of loss of power by former establishments in relation to rising outsider groups trigger bitter resistance – a scarcely realistic longing for the restoration of the old order – not only for economic reasons, but also because through such a loss of power the old ruling strata find themselves on the same level in the hierarchy of power and status as groups they had previously despised: groups of low standing, of lesser human value, rabble. As a result, they feel themselves lowered in their own self-esteem.

There is written testimony from as early as antiquity which shows clearly that established groups understand their superior power relative to outsider groups as proof of their higher human value. Even the unknown writer of a letter attributed to Xenophon, probably from the late fifth century BC, who is nowadays usually called 'the old oligarch', shows this evaluation of less powerful groups as of lesser human worth.[14] The author of this letter was probably an Athenian aristocrat who, with others of the same estate, was driven out of Athens by the revolt of broad sectors of the population and the introduction of a democratic constitution. He speaks with considerable contempt of the democratic mob. Everyone knows, he wrote, that such elements are comprised of undisciplined people of bad character. An analogous attitude can be found in a letter dated 2 January 1920 from a Lieutenant Mayer reporting to his superior, Captain Berchtold. He had been sent to Würzburg as the recruiting officer of a *Freikorps*:

> After not having missed a single day . . . in directing my attention to observing the current mood of the people, my view is confirmed that everything above the rabble yearns to be freed from the current pigsty, in particular from the Jewish yoke that burdens the people, and, what is of the utmost progressive meaning compared with earlier, they are especially willing to participate personally in the coming work of liberation! The call 'Down with the Jews!', 'Down with the betrayers of our people!' rings out from every pub bench; posters and inscriptions everywhere say the same. Erzberger is hanged every evening umpteen times. . . .
>
> Two gentlemen together with their men from the army stationed locally have joined us. I hope to win two or more to our cause.[15]

Even if not everyone expressed it so drastically, in those days there was a widespread idea among members of the circles who followed the tradition of the old Wilhelmine establishment that the participation in ruling by groups considered to be of lower social standing implied a denigration of themselves and thus also of Germany. They called themselves, and felt themselves to be, 'national' since they fundamentally regarded themselves as the real representatives of the nation; and all outsiders, especially workers with their organizations and the minority groups constituted by the German Jews, were regarded as belonging neither to their own society nor to the German nation.

4

The excerpt from Lieutenant Mayer's letter gives a very vivid picture of the mood in the 'better' circles of Würzburg at the beginning of the year 1920. At the same time, it conveys an impression of the mentality of the *Freikorps* who at this time were the main actors in extra-state political violence. Their propaganda among wide sectors of the population served as preparation for a putsch against the hated parliamentary republic.

The first such attempt, the Kapp putsch, failed owing to well-known reasons which I do not need to go into here. One of the *Freikorps*, the Ehrhardt Marine Brigade, was directly involved in it. Later, the undercover terrorist organization 'Consul' arose from it, one of whose goals was the systematic murder of prominent politicians whom they regarded as 'undesirable'. The murderers of Erzberger, a member of parliament, belonged to this organization; they attacked and shot him on 26 August 1920 while he was walking in the Black Forest. His companion and fellow member of parliament, Dietz, escaped with a bullet wound. The murderers – Heinrich Schulz and Heinrich Tillessen – were former officers who then belonged to the staff of the Ehrhardt Marine Brigade, and were eventually employed by a leading Bavarian politician, the Privy Councillor Heim. They were members of the German nationalist *Schutz und Trutz* [Protection and Resistance] Association and of other nationalist organizations. After the deed was committed, both men travelled to Munich, where the assassination had been planned. From there, they fled with forged passports, presumably issued by the Bavarian police, to Hungary, where they were temporarily arrested but were let free after a telephone call to some Bavarian authority. Their superior in the secret organization 'Consul', Lieutenant Commander von Killinger, also a former army officer who had fought against the Bavarian Soviet Republic and then taken part in the Kapp putsch, was charged with being an accomplice in the murder of Erzberger, but was acquitted by the jury in Offenburg.[16]

It is difficult to estimate how many people were murdered as politically undesirable by members of the *Freikorps* and the student associations close to them in the early years of the Weimar Republic. It was probably several hundred, possibly more than a thousand. Their victims included prominent communists such as Rosa Luxemburg and Karl Liebknecht, who were dragged from a besieged house after an unsuccessful workers' uprising, and, as far as can be ascertained today, were beaten to death one after the other with truncheons on their way to prison. There were also less well-known victims. One of them was my schoolfellow, Bernhard Schottländer, a completely unathletic, highly intelligent person, who, with his thick spectacles, looked like a young scholar even as a first former, and who tended to communism after reading Marx, and whose corpse, if I remember rightly, was found in the Breslau city moat, tied up with barbed wire. Liberal politicians such as Rathenau[17] were also among them, and many others whose names are forgotten.

Just like the majority of terrorists in the Federal Republic, those of

Weimar Germany also came predominantly from middle-class families. They were mostly young people and a minority were nobles. The younger cadres of Wilhelmine 'good society' were either officers or students. They were precisely the groups from which the terrorists of the Weimar Republic were recruited. Accordingly, one finds, for example, in a Bavarian memorandum in preparation for the dictatorship, a special paragraph: 'Mobilization of the Reich's armed forces and student body'.[18] In another memorandum, also from the time before the Kapp putsch, the entry under 'student body' reads:

> Feelers must at once be put out by the mobilizing committee among allies in the student body regarding the extent to which students are organized and which sections still stand on the sidelines. Here it is particularly important whether any sections will eventually be our enemies, since these are fanatics and will have to be rendered harmless. The principle must be upheld that the student body will be organized in its own squads, and be used as the main supply of reserves. This is because our main strength rests with the student body.[19]

One sees the problem. At that time, the majority of students were on the side of those who, together with the *Freikorps* and other military organizations, sought, if necessary with violence, to overthrow the young parliamentary republic and replace it with a strong military dictatorship. There were certainly exceptions, for example students who were not strongly for a patriotic revolt against the republic, or for a military-bourgeois dictatorship. But, as the terrorists of those times saw it, those were the 'fanatics' who had to be murdered. The idea that murdering political opponents was right and proper seemed to be taken for granted.

But it was also certain that this idea was not confined to one side. The war had left behind in working-class circles quite considerable unrest and a great deal of bitterness. Perhaps they would have borne the ruling elite's often rather overbearing claim to rule if the Kaiser and his generals had been victorious. The defeat, however, proved that the officers, the ruling classes up above, had led them falsely, that their promises were empty words, that the privations and misery of the war had all been in vain. The unsuccessful Kapp putsch fanned the bitterness of the workers. The hatred was mutual. When the Ehrhardt Brigade withdrew from Berlin after the failed putsch, crowds at the Brandenburg Gate shouted abuse at them. Some of the retreating troops turned abruptly around and shot into the masses. About a dozen dead and many wounded were left on Pariser Platz.[20]

As always, the hatred and violence on both sides spiralled reciprocally upwards. At the time of the Kapp putsch, officers in uniform could not let themselves be seen in the north and east of Berlin, and also in some suburbs, without running the risk of being attacked and abused by residents. To be sure, the military leaders of the putsch did organize troops, mostly consisting of former officers, to maintain order. But after the enterprise failed, these troops, who went on patrol in relatively small groups, found themselves in a highly threatening situation facing the mass of local residents. The officers stationed in Schöneberg received orders to withdraw without weapons in order not to provoke the population. They were to be taken to Lichterfelde in two lorries supplied for them. But the lorries had driven only about 100 metres when they were held up by the pushing crowds. The excited crowd threw stones and beer bottles at the officers. In the hand-to-hand fighting which followed, nine officers were trampled to the ground and killed. The police were notified and the rest, beaten and wounded, were taken to safety.[21] Similar scenes occurred in conjunction with the workers' uprising in the Ruhr district.

Such examples allow one to follow very clearly the course of a violent double-bind process. The Russian Revolution played a large role in this regard both as a model and a horrifying warning. Comparison with the course of events there – especially with the organization of Russia's still predominantly agrarian masses for violent uprising – shows, of course, that the German industrial workforce was in certain respects at a disadvantage in mobilizing for violence. The Communist Party evidently attempted to transform the spontaneous excitement of the workers and the many local skirmishes and fights with the *Freikorps* or the army into organized military action. But the appointment of a high command in Mülheim (in the Ruhr district) through a proclamation of the Party's military leadership on 28 March 1920 did not have the desired effect. The placing of local workers' fighting units under central command was not successful. Again and again, local leaders acted off their own bat. One might imagine that, corresponding to the then-existing level of technology, it would have been easier to transform peasants used to obedience into battle-ready troops than independent and self-confident industrial workers. In any case, that appears to have been one of the experiences of the Ruhr uprising.

But at the same time, this experience highlights the peculiar course of the double-bind process between the young middle-class officer groups and their student allies, on the one hand, and the groups of workers, on the other. Both sought to realize political goals through the use of military force. It is an open question to what extent the Russian officer corps remained intact as legatee of the traditional order after the abdication of the tsar. The German officer corps remained fully operational as a united cadre after the abdication of the Kaiser. Their *esprit de corps* remained intact, too. The supreme military command felt responsible for the integrity of the state, and actually was to some extent. Of course, the Allies had imposed severe restrictions on the German armed forces. They had had enough of German militarism, but they feared just as much that Russian communism would find adherents in Germany. As a compromise, they allowed Germany an army of 100,000 men instead of 400,000. This meant at the same time a radical numerical reduction of the officer corps. Many of the officers returning home from active service were still relatively young; most had no ambition other than to remain as officers. Military service was for them the only meaningful job, the profession they understood and which gave them pleasure. Where else should they go? The volunteer associations of the *Freikorps* were the answer.

There were many *Freikorps*, each formed round former officers with specific leadership qualities. These predominantly young middle-class groups had, in line with their social situation, a whole range of decided enemies whom they sought to fight with all means whenever the opportunity arose. These enemies included, first, all the groups they lumped together under the name of Bolsheviks, especially sections of the working class which had participated in uprisings, whether under the influence of the communist leadership cadres or quite spontaneously, and which, purposefully or not, strove to topple the parliamentary republic in favour of a soviet republic along the lines of the Russian model. The enemies, furthermore, included this parliamentary republic itself, particularly in the form of those members of the government and parliament who were committed to the signing of the peace treaty – the 'ignominious peace' – and the fulfilment of its conditions. The aversion of the guerrillas to the republic (the pigsty), to the parliament (the talking shop), and especially to the representatives of social democracy (the big shots), who now occupied influential positions in many government offices, was only a little bit less than that against the Bolsheviks (the workers stirred up by the communists).[22]

The power balance between the two violence-orientated groups in the

Weimar Republic, between the workers' groups orientated towards the Russian model and the middle-class and noble officers organized in the *Freikorps*, was, admittedly, very uneven. Despite their barbarization, and despite their often mercenary-like behaviour and mentality, the *Freikorps* were disciplined fighting troops whose members were steeped to the core in military tradition, as long as the sometimes somewhat charismatic leaders kept their trust. Against them stood the comparatively undisciplined groups who, although they were often highly capable of immediate and spontaneous fighting, did not relish the long-term military discipline necessary for the execution of strategic battle plans. With the mutual restriction of the groups who renounced physical violence to the two wings of the non-violent parliamentary party spectrum, the *Freikorps* usually easily won the upper hand in their violent encounters with the radical workers' groups, especially since they also often received the support of the army as well. They were not only better drilled, but also mostly better armed than the workers' fighting groups.

The factual chances of success of the workers' uprising in the first years of the Weimar Republic were thus very small, because the old officer corps remained intact and was quickly reorganized, and because of the hostility of the Allies to any spread of the Russian Revolution. But for the legitimation of their own existence, the danger of Bolshevism was for the *Freikorps* and the army of the greatest significance. By alluding to the Russian Revolution and the danger of its spreading, not only the *Freikorps* and the army but also many other nationalist associations that were formed at this time, not least the terrorist organizations, could win the support of countless middle-class and noble sympathizers. The subsequent success of Hitler, and especially the inaction of the Allies regarding the rearmament of Germany, can only be fully understood as a consequence of the Russian Revolution; it was an expression of the universal aversion of wide sectors of the middle class, and even of considerable parts of the working class, to the spectre of Bolshevism and to the Russian Revolution's spreading as a model to other countries. [See appendix 3 to this part, pp. 214–23.]

5

Most of the people who streamed in to join the *Freikorps* had been thrown off-track. Thousands of officers found themselves at the end of their career owing to the defeat and the conditions of the armistice.

Often, they had fought for years at the front. It was seldom possible for them to find a civilian position appropriate to their knowledge and status expectations. Many hoped to be able to continue their career as an officer in the regular army once Germany was able to set up larger armed forces. For this reason they already hated this republic, whose 'policy of compliance' seemed to block this ambition. Others saw a new future in the Baltic provinces, where a German upper class had lived for a long time. German-Baltic landowners and some leaders of the Latvian nationalist movement promised German guerrillas land for settlement in return for help in freeing them from Russian control. In this way, a large number of *Freikorps* went to the Baltic. There they could fight against the most hated enemy, the Bolsheviks. They also hoped to be able to make good the expected loss of Alsace-Lorraine by the annexation to Germany of the Baltic provinces. At the same time, by the acquisition of land, they would be able to start up a new existence befitting their rank.

Calling to mind the campaign in the Baltic may help in comprehending the development of some of these groups into political terrorism directed against the new German state. Once again some excerpts from a novel, this time from the more or less autobiographical novel by Ernst von Salomon *Die Geächteten* [The Outlaws],[23] can clarify the process which led people to terrorism, to the systematic organization of murder and other acts of violence as a means of shaking and, if possible, of destroying a hated regime.

Ernst von Salomon, who belonged to the inner circle of the Rathenau murderers, already indicates the direction of this development in the chapter titles of his novel. They read:

1 The Dispersed
2 The Conspirators
3 The Criminals

The stages each individual passed on this path in the 1920s were roughly the following:

1 Officer in the Wilhelmine army (or, if too young, perhaps a cadet in the Prussian cadet corps).
2 Member of a *Freikorps*, often participating in their unsuccessful Baltic campaign.
3 Member of a conspiratorial secret association of a terrorist character.

The fourth stage, which need not be considered further here, would have been joining the National Socialist Party. This meant, for many of the former members of the *Freikorps* constantly threatened by the danger of social degradation, the chance at last of climbing securely back up, and the – in the end deluded – fulfilment of their political hopes. It has indeed been said, not without justification, that Hitler's domestic rise to power would hardly have been possible without the organizational and military contribution of former members of the *Freikorps*.

As a young man, Salomon went straight from the cadet corps into a Hamburg *Freikorps* led by a Lieutenant Wuth. Here he found himself in the company of rather wild but also rather romantic adventurers with mercenary-like habits. He recollected the advance in these terms:

> The word 'advance', for those of us who went to the Baltic, had a mysterious, joyfully dangerous meaning ... the meaning of a tough fellowship ... the dissolution of all ties to a sinking, rotting world, with which the real warrior can no longer have anything more in common.[24]

A characteristic stage of the process by which people become terrorists is illustrated here very clearly. They feel like detached outsiders in relation to a society which seems to be rotten to the core. They are convinced that the society is going under, and wish for this to happen, although it is not perhaps particularly clear what will happen when it has done so. Ironically, at least in the case of the young Salomon, for whom the young and fragile German republic seemed as he remembered it to be like a 'sinking, rotting world', it was precisely the old society in whose tradition he himself and many of his comrades had grown up which had been defeated and was definitely sinking. Gone was the empire, but countless of its representatives had survived. With the passing of the empire, the life tasks which seemed meaningful to these people disappeared as well. Training in the cadet school had prepared Ernst von Salomon for an officer's career in the Prussian army. The old army had disintegrated, a new one, far smaller, was just being formed. The supreme commander-in-chief had defected to Holland. Where in this republic which had arisen from defeat was there still a place, a meaningful future purpose for people like him?

The campaign in the Baltic, which promised to compensate for the German loss of territory in the West and promised the participants a new position befitting their rank – perhaps even an estate – gave new hope. They did not ask themselves what the victorious enemies of Germany or the government in Berlin would say to an occupation of the

Russian Baltic provinces. World politics were far away and the dream was beautiful. But however much this dream represented the new, better future in the feelings of its adherents, however much it contrasted with the shabby republican Germany which they hated because of its peace policies, what these people were fundamentally dreaming of was the restoration of the old world, namely the restoration of a German empire with a mighty army and in whose status hierarchy officers and military values would once again take the high place befitting them. Military discipline, firmness and courage would then be highly valued again, as they deserved; spinelessness and moral scruples of a bourgeois kind would attract the contempt they deserved and so would the unmilitary civilians who now governed in Berlin, as well as members of parliament who talked a great deal but did little.[25]

For the guerrillas in the Baltic, this parliamentary state was an alien world. Its cohesion was no longer, as in the old army, determined through state-sanctioned, bureaucratically worked-out military regulations, through an officers' hierarchy whose symbolic apex was the supreme figure of the Kaiser. The men of the *Freikorps* did not feel they were really duty-bound to anyone except their own group. Almost every *Freikorps* had its own charismatic leader, whose personal authority, physical participation in fighting, tacit promise of victory, booty and a better future bound them together, and was decisive for the solidarity and fighting strength of these guerrilla troops.

Lieutenant Wuth, of the Hamburg *Freikorps*, was one such leader. He was, according to Salomon's description, a large, tanned, angular man. He had the habit of whetting a boar's tooth that stuck out of his mouth on the bristly hairs of his small beard and before each battle exchanged his field cap for a velvet beret like those worn by the original *Pachants* and the *Wandervögel*.[26] The battles in the Baltic were heavy, the losses high, but hope persisted. And life was unfettered and free, an alternative to the stiff and routinized middle-class life with all its constraints. Here in the Baltic there was still action and the possibility of new victories to help one forget the defeats in the West.

Then came the blow which destroyed all hopes. The unthinkable happened. Those authorized by the government signed the terrible peace treaty which sealed the humiliating defeat. Salomon described this traumatic experience:

> One day towards the beginning of the armistice we were sitting in Lieutenant Wuth's cabin. Schlageter was there visiting, we were speaking

about the possibilities of settling in this country. Wuth wanted to buy a
farm and saw-mill. ... Then Lieutenant Kay entered the room and
speaking hastily into the tobacco smoke said 'Germany has signed the
peace treaty!'
    For a moment, all was quiet, so quiet that the room almost shook as
Schlageter stood up ... he paused, stared straight in front of him, and
suddenly with an ugly tone in his voice said, 'I think, in the end – is this
any of our business?' And slammed the door. ... We were alarmed. We
listened to this and were shocked at how little in actual fact all this really
affected us.[27]

For a moment they could perhaps really believe that this far-off event
need not concern them. But the invisible threads connecting them with
their distant home were soon perceptible. They were really nothing more
than scattered German troops in the vast Russian countryside. The
conclusion of the peace treaty by these *parvenus* who now represented
Germany sealed their fate. They felt they had been betrayed:

We looked at each other, shivering. Suddenly we felt the coldness of
unutterable abandonment. We had believed that our country would never
discharge us, that it bound us with an indestructible current, that it fed
our secret wishes and justified our deeds. Now all that was ended. The
signing released us.[28]

This example clearly shows the far-reaching emotional significance of
the Berlin government's failure to state loudly and clearly in public: 'On
the advice of the army's supreme command, our appointees have signed
the peace treaty in the form in which it was submitted to us.' Hindenburg's often extolled native cunning had managed to pass the odium of
the signing of the peace treaty and therefore of the military defeat on to
the representatives of the parliamentary republic. This allowed all those
who felt themselves to be disadvantaged by this republic to renounce it.
In the case of other individuals, the shock of the signing of such a
humiliating and burdensome treaty may have been evident in other
ways. But the traumatic effect on the guerrillas, as it is described here,
had in certain respects an exemplary significance. They knew nothing of
the compelling circumstances which had caused the government to
decide to sign. Perhaps they might have accepted it if the Kaiser, or
Hindenburg and Ludendorff, had signed the treaty. But now it appeared
that the sole responsibility for the signing of this peace treaty was borne
by people who, according to the tradition of the old *satisfaktionsfähige*

Gesellschaft, and especially that of the officer corps, were considered to be *arrivistes* or *parvenus*.[29]

Under the pressure of the entente and in accordance with the terms of the peace treaty, the Berlin government eventually ordered the withdrawal of the *Freikorps* from the Baltic. At that, many of the guerrillas withdrew their allegiance from the German government. They remained and continued to fight – not against the Red Army, which had already withdrawn, but against the newly organizing Latvian and Estonian troops which were supported by British warships. Step by step, the guerrillas were forced back. That was a second traumatic experience for them. People who could not admit that Germany had been defeated in the West were now experiencing defeat at first hand in the East.

Little by little, the situation of the guerrillas in the Baltic became increasingly untenable. When the first sharp frosts of the Russian autumn came, the dearth of clothing supplies from home gradually made itself felt. Many did not have coats. Tunics and trousers were in shreds. Their boots had holes in them. And the local people pressed down remorselessly on the withdrawing troops, just as the Russians had done once before to Napoleon's retreating army. In the end, the desperate guerrillas with their hopes destroyed became angry. Salomon, among others,[30] described what happened then. Once again they hit back – in anger and desperation – the last remnants of their humanity gone:

We made the last push. Yes, we rose up once more and stormed forwards. Yet again we pulled the last man out of cover and plunged into the woods. We ran across the snowy fields and broke into the wood. We burst into surprised crowds and stormed and shot and lashed out and hunted down. We drove the Latvians like hares across the fields and set fire to every house and pulverized every bridge to dust and broke every telegraph pole. We threw the corpses into wells and threw hand grenades in after them. We killed everything that came into our hands, we burnt everything that would burn. We saw red, we no longer had any human feelings in our hearts. There where we had wreaked havoc, the earth groaned under our destruction. There where we had raged and where before had been houses, lay rubble, ashes and glowing beams, like festering sores in a bare field. A huge plume of smoke marked our path. We had lit a funeral pyre, where more than dead material was burning; there our hopes were burnt, our longings; there burnt the bourgeois tablet, the laws and values of the civilized world; there burnt everything that we still dragged with us like dusty junk of the vocabulary and beliefs in the things and ideas of the time that now dismissed us.

We withdrew, boasting, intoxicated, laden with booty. Nowhere had the Latvian stood his ground. But the next day, he was there again.[31]

If one inquires into the conditions in a society under which civilized forms of behaviour and conscience begin to dissolve, one sees once again some of the stations on this path. It is a process of brutalization and dehumanization which in relatively civilized societies always requires considerable time. In such societies, terror and horror hardly ever manifest themselves without a fairly long social process in which conscience decomposes. In attempting to understand the appearance of naked violence as a group goal, with or without state legitimation, people all too often use short-term static diagnoses and methods of explanation. There may be some point in that when one is not really concerned with finding explanations, but rather with questions of guilt. Then it is easy enough to depict the barbarization, the decivilization, and also one's own reserve and civilized behaviour, as an expression of a freely chosen personal decision. But such a voluntarist diagnosis and explanation does not lead far.

If one recognizes the developmental course of the *Freikorps* as one of the routes which led to extra-state acts of terrorist violence during the Weimar Republic, as well as to the acts of state violence in the Hitler era, then one gains a degree of understanding of the long build-up period which preceded the great acts of barbarism which were at first hardly visible, then became more obvious as though they had sprung from nowhere.

The people who in anger and despair took part in an orgy of annihilation and destruction in the Baltic, and some of whom later, like Salomon himself, sought to destroy the hated republic by acts of terror, had marched off with great expectations. The adventure lured them. They dreamed of great successes for their cause as well as for themselves. As the signs of failure and defeat increased, they at first refused to accept the writing on the wall. They wrapped themselves up in their dream as in a warm and protective cloak. When the grim reality finally dawned on them through their crumbling hopes, they went completely wild. Under the ever-stronger pressure of frustrating reality, their dream was shattered and with it their conscience. In anger and desperation, they killed everything which crossed their path. They followed a course which some of them sought to continue with greater circumspection in secret organizations after their return home. They busied themselves with destroying a world which denied them meaningfulness and therefore appeared to them to be meaningless itself – to be worthy only of being destroyed.

Once again their hopes were revived – in preparations to topple the Weimar regime and set up a dictatorship. As this hope, too, was shattered with the failure of the Kapp putsch, some determined members of the many *Freikorps* saw no other way than the use of terror to unsettle and finally topple the hated regime. During this period, correspondingly, a number of former officers, mostly members of the Ehrhardt Brigade, formed their secret organization. The murder of prominent politicians was supposed to sound a trumpet-call. With the aid of such actions, the rotten regime was to be so shaken that it would collapse. [See appendix 4 to this part, pp. 224–8.]

Hitler succeeded where the *Freikorps* leaders did not: in actually destroying the Weimar parliamentary regime.[32] He was successful largely because he made the effort to mobilize wide sections of the masses through the use of extra-parliamentary propaganda. The *Freikorps* were among his most important precursors, paving his way. Their goals were in many respects identical to his. But despite all the barbarization process their attitudes and mentality had undergone, they remained rooted in the elite officers' tradition – the tradition of the old, noble and middle-class *satisfaktionsfähige Gesellschaft*. Hitler, the lance-corporal, broke through the elite barriers of the officer and student movement and transformed it into a broad populist movement without the elitist restrictions which stood in the way of its spreading to the masses. Being a member of the 'German race' opened the door for many more people than membership of the 'good' noble and middle-class society, and, in their youth, of the officer corps or the student associations.

6

In a way similar to what happened in the Weimar Republic, an illegal organization was formed among young people in the Bonn Republic to carry out political assassinations as a means of contributing to change, and possibly to the fall of the existing state and social order, and to open up for the parties concerned new prospects for the future which for the time being were closed to them.[33] In both cases, these organizations at first developed gradually, after a series of severe disappointments and failures. In terms of class membership, most of the terrorists in the Bonn as well as the Weimar Republic came from middle-class homes. There were also many students or former students among them. But there were almost no officers at all. Instead, they had women members, who had been completely missing among the Weimar terrorists.[34]

One sees the problem. In the Weimar period, young middle-class groups, who felt that the existing regime blocked their chances for a meaningful life, regarded the workers as opponents, the communists as their worst enemy and even the liberal middle class as hateful. In the Bonn Republic, the extra-parliamentary opposition, which also consisted primarily of young middle-class people, from whose ranks members of the secret terrorist associations were mainly recruited, had the opposite outlook. They sympathized with the workers, sometimes also with one or another form of communism.[35] Their enmity was directed against the established middle-class society – a society which in their eyes was built solely on selfishness and on the pursuit of individual interests. They, too, felt that the existing social circumstances and the constraints which were thereby imposed on them were unbearable. And if one looks more closely, then one also discovers here at the root a younger generation searching for a meaningful life for itself and which finds the channels to such a life restricted or blocked. *What* was valued as meaningful was highly different in the two cases. But the basic motivation was the same: the feeling of being trapped in a social system which made it very hard for the younger generations to find chances for a meaningful future.

This fundamental motivation has been discernible again and again in the testimony of the extra-parliamentary movements from the 1960s up to the present. But usually it remains more peripheral. It often disappears behind a veil of Marxism or its derivatives. In my view, however, it is central. One obstructs the view of a very serious social problem of our time if one does not recognize this.

There is a tacit assumption in the multi-party industrial societies of today which hinders awareness of this problem. According to this assumption, the societies in question are so constructed that each and every person growing up in them can find a meaningful and satisfying task in life, if only he or she tries. That is misleading. There are distinct phases in these societies in which the channels for upward mobility for the up and coming generations are relatively numerous and open, and others in which they are limited and restricted. I am not speaking here simply of career opportunities. What I have said holds just as much for non-career opportunities for meaningfulness, including above all oppor-tunities in the sphere of political struggle. Political conflicts today have in many respects taken over functions of meaning-creation which in an earlier epoch were performed by religious struggles. The orientation within the political spectrum which today – but certainly not for all time – stretches between the two opposite poles of communism and fascism, which are, in the end, both geared to the use of violence, has perhaps more than ever become for broad circles the centre of world-orientation.

But it is exactly in this direction which young people nowadays find that the practical work of the political parties, as they experience it, frequently closes the door to meaningful activity. Many of them are alert and intelligent enough to recognize clearly the weaknesses and shortcomings of existing societies. People of older generations, with experience in power struggles, often recognize the need to compromise. Younger people are often more unbending regarding half-measures. Here can be seen an aspect of the generational conflict which runs only half-recognized through Western industrial societies. Many of the most alert people of the younger generations do not want to make do with compromises. So when they seek to express and put into practice their political desires through the institutional channels of the party organization, they often see the path as obstructed, their need for meaningfulness blocked.

The formation of an extra-parliamentary opposition in the 1960s provides a graphic example of this situation. This holds similarly for the student movement connected with it, which to a large extent shared the same members. At first, younger people found here something they no longer found within the framework of established political institutions, especially the firmly organized parties. Communal activities, communal living and mass demonstrations all gave the participants not only a feeling of belonging together, but also the feeling of having a meaningful goal, a feeling of power, and a pleasurable and happy excitement. Here were purposes; here was meaning.

The relatively long path along which the initially peaceful actions gradually became more violent – for example through arson attacks against shops or repeated attacks against American installations planned as protests against the Vietnam War – need not be described here. But it is perhaps not unimportant to say with hindsight that it was a question again of a typical double-bind process with a strong tendency to self-escalation. From the outset, the actions and demonstrations of the extra-parliamentary movement were directed against existing institutions, among them the existing authority structure in the universities. No wonder that the established authorities struck back, or that mistakes thereby arose, of which the shooting of Benne Ohnesorg, a student, probably had the most far-reaching consequences. In such a situation, an error like that is like a beacon: there was a widespread feeling that if the state uses violence we must use it too. Such double-bind processes have no real beginning. The police certainly must have felt provoked and perhaps threatened by the demonstrators. But that is a well-nigh universal regularity of a double-bind: violence engenders counter-violence, counter-violence heightens the violence on the other side, and so on.[36]

If one looks at the power relations involved, one quickly reaches the conclusion that the balance between the violence-potential of the state and that of the extra-parliamentary movements – and, later, of the terrorists – was too uneven for the latter to stand any serious chance of success. But most certainly, many leaders of the student movement and the extra-parliamentary opposition in those days felt that they could contribute to the downfall of this social order of self-interest, and open the way for themselves and the working class towards a less selfish, less repressive, more meaningful order. Then, after the successes of 1968, many of the participants were faced anew with the question of a blocked future – with the question, where are we going, what shall we do? The recognition dawned that they were really not getting any further; after the elation of success, disappointment gradually set in; after the dream came the awakening, with the insight that the hated social structure, although it had been scratched here and there, was still fully intact. Furthermore, besides the disappointment over their own undertakings, some of them experienced a second disappointment in the same year, when Russia sent troops into Czechoslovakia.

Disregarding various intermediate steps, such as the liberation of a leader from prison, the conviction started to develop in certain circles of the extra-parliamentary movement that the superior strength of the state organization of violence could not be broken by legal means. In a similar way to some of the embittered and disappointed young middle-class people from the groups who rejected the state in the Weimar period, so now some embittered and disappointed middle-class young people in the Bonn Republic drew from their experiences the conclusion that this social structure could be shaken only through conspiracy. It could be done only through the formation of secret associations and systematic terrorist action against its prominent representatives, in that way perhaps rousing the lethargic population.[37]

One of the central fears of those who seized the opportunity to form urban guerrilla units, as well as of those who took over their leadership, was that there could be a return in Germany to a party dictatorship. Perhaps they already regarded the Federal Republic as a semi-fascist regime. Some members of the terrorist organizations were of the opinion that it would be better to bring the hidden fascism which appeared to be manifested in state acts of violence out into the open through counter-violence, ripping away its mask. Undoubtedly, the coercive measures of the Federal Republic were in some ways reinforced by the pressure of terrorist acts.

If one looks back today and draws up the balance sheet, one can hardly refrain from feeling sorry for the victims which this struggle claimed, for the suffering it caused, and for the futility of all the sacrifice and suffering. The task is therefore all the more pressing to become aware of the social problems which gave rise to these conflicts. They are to a large extent unsolved; they still exist. I shall attempt to summarize what seems to me to be the core of the issue.

Perhaps I can best do this by expanding on an expression I have already used from time to time. I have said that the people who played a leading role in the non-violent as well as the violent extra-parliamentary organizations were predominantly 'young bourgeois'. In many ways, they used an ideological orientation centred on problems of the working class, but it has been written of such groups with some justification that: 'The mythical working class is a club which is meant to shatter the world of the father.'[38] Here, in fact, as in other cases, behind the ideological use of class conflict stands the reality of a generational conflict as a driving force. There were certainly people in the terrorist organizations in the Federal Republic who came from the working class, and who to some extent continued to earn their living as workers. But they were in the minority. The difference between them and the terrorists of middle-class origin regarding their attitude towards and preparedness to use physical violence as a vehicle of political struggle was astounding. But that is another matter.

One member of the working classes who played an active although apparently never a leading role in a terrorist organization was Michael Baumann. His book, *Wie alles anfing* [How it all Began] (1975), in many respects helps in understanding the human side of terrorists. Just like Hans-Joachim Klein – another one-time worker-terrorist who has written an autobiography[39] – Baumann was a person who, through his contact with the student movement and above all through self-education, became an intellectual. Both young men never lost what was typical of their origins. But, different as they were, they remained loners. Baumann in particular was more anarchist than Marxist. He quite deliberately rejected the career that his origins seemed to suggest for him, just as he later rejected the terrorist movement. He was, to use his own words, a 'freaked-out worker'.

It is revealing that he asked himself relatively early on in life what sort of meaning his work had for him:

> In the work you do, you can see no sense, let's say running errands or some such rubbish. Then you just don't feel like learning a manual trade. It only causes aversion in you, it's just another thing you rip down.[40]

It became clear to him that what he was learning then he would have to do for the next fifty years. He was physically shocked and eventually succeeded in opting out. He describes it very vividly:

> For example, on the first day when all the apprentices had gone to the office and then were driven off in some car to the building site, it suddenly struck me, you're going to be doing this for the next 50 years. There is no escape. I was pretty horrified, so I always looked for a way to get out of it.[41]

If one asks oneself why extra-parliamentary opposition movements in the 1960s and 1970s and certainly later as well were formed primarily by people of middle-class origins, then it seems useful to start at this point. For young workers, the experience described by Baumann is probably rather rare. As a working hypothesis, one can assume that the transition from school to an apprenticeship and from there to the workplace still occurs today in the traditional and relatively unreflected way: everyone one knows does this, so do I. One submits to the constraints, but apparently with growing lethargy. People like Baumann, who do not do it and suddenly see their future in front of them and say to themselves with horror, 'And that's supposed to be my whole life?', are apparently still an exception amongst young workers.

For young people of middle-class origins, especially young students, the question of the future, 'What shall I become? How should I shape my life?', is usually a very pressing and central issue. The desire for a future which is meaningful for oneself, which is felt to be satisfying, is stronger, the quest for meaning accordingly more conscious.

Whatever the rebellious young middle-class groups of the 1960s and 1970s themselves saw as the goal of their demonstrations, squats and standing up for the oppressed and defeated, this issue of meaning stood in the background as a powerful driving force. If a considerable number of younger people have their opportunities for meaningfulness strangled, as often happens today, then there is an emergency in society, an explosive potential which under favourable conditions will again and again find expression in movements which set themselves up in pronounced opposition to established political institutions. I have referred above to the terrorists of the Weimar Republic because it seemed to me to be useful to point out that extra-parliamentary movements, whether peaceful or violent, are not an isolated phenomenon, but under certain conditions are part, so to speak, of the structure of non-dictatorial and perhaps also of dictatorial industrial societies.

Furthermore, especially in the Federal Republic, the difference between the moral ideas of the older and the ethos of the younger generations is particularly striking. As a reaction to the traumatic memory of the inhumanity of the Hitler period, a very accentuated ethos of standing up against inequality, oppression, exploitation and war and for a new type of decency between humans has become accepted among younger people. We still have to wait and see if this often utopian ethos still survives as these people grow older. But whether or not that is the case, one can assume with some certainty that the problem of meaning for the younger generations, which was expressed in the terrorist movement among others, will make itself felt again and again, even in acts of violence, as long as people do not strive for improvement much more conscientiously and intensively. It is actually not difficult to see that this barrier to meaningfulness for a not inconsiderable part of the younger generation, whether created through laws, unemployment or whatever, generates a broad recruiting field not only for the drug-dealers of the present, but also for future urban guerrillas and for future radical movements in general, whether right- or left-wing. No one can say what is in store for the Federal Republic of Germany if this seed once germinates. [See appendix 5 to this part, pp. 229–97.]

Appendices to Part III

1 On the Ethos of the Wilhelmine Bourgeoisie

Although there were exceptions like the writings of Nietzsche, the bourgeoisified warrior ethos of Wilhelmine society found its expression less in learned books than in the everyday thinking and actions of the people concerned. Evidence for it appears, for instance, in changes in word usage or in the popular novels of the time.

Rudolf Herzog, a respected exponent of high-level middle-class light literature, used contemporary entrepreneurs as central characters in several works. One of his novels, first published in 1909, was *Hanseaten* [Hanseatic Merchants], in which the main character is Karl Twersten, owner and manager of a Hamburg shipyard inherited from his grandfather. At the beginning, Herzog describes, among other things, how the workers stand to attention when the owner of the shipyard goes on board a newly built ship. Then, when on one occasion they are prevented from arriving at their workplaces in the harbour because of a storm and bad weather and send a deputation to the boss because the day's lost labour will be subtracted from their wages, the discussion with Twersten takes the following form:

'Listen,' he began, and eyed them sharply, 'you've all been soldiers, haven't you? Or sailors? Even better. Then in that case you should know full well what discipline means. And you old hands know as well as I do that in a shipyard there must be discipline just like on board a ship. Because here business and political affairs meet. Therefore all I need to do is give in to your demands, and I'll be opening the door to lack of discipline. Why? Now I'm not saying anything about you three. You've got honour in you, and I've known you long enough. But it could occur to hundreds of shirkers every day to use wind and rain as an excuse when they want to come to the shipyard a few hours late. It only has to become known today that it's a good excuse and it works – we're still going to get paid! – and you hard workers who are decent, you'd be the ones taken for a ride. . . . No, you people, I don't need to say anything more to you. You're not green and know that there must be discipline. Whether it hurts or not. It must be so!'

'That's right,' the smith said, and put on his cap with a jerk.

'In that case, you can make up the time in overtime. That's agreed.'

'Agreed, Mr Twersten. An' please excuse us disturbing you like this, Sir.'[42]

This partial shaping of the relationship between employers and workers in the early period of industrialization by military tradition did not occur only in Wilhelmine Germany. Such a transfer of military patterns of social behaviour on to industrial ones can also be observed in Japan. The novel does not necessarily present this relationship as it actually was. But it does express very clearly and reliably how, in the opinion of the author and his expected readership, it ought to be. In that sense, the role military models played in the construction of industrial work relationships can be seen here fairly clearly. That the military ethos to a certain extent defined the ethos of work for workers themselves, and ultimately also the national work ethos and the consciences of individuals, was also in keeping with the social power ratios of the time.

The vocabulary, too, has a military ring. Key words such as 'discipline' and 'honour' which played a role in the military code are also to be found in the code governing the entrepreneur–worker relationship. But in the course of their transformation in class and function, such symbols of a taken-for-granted tradition became symbols of reflected principles, means of explicit ideological argumentation.

The same holds for attitudes such as toughness and ruthlessness. These sorts of attitudes are certainly to be found all over the world wherever there are steep power gradients in confrontations between more and less powerful groups, between established and outsiders. It is much less common, however, to find members of more powerful groups who, in relationships with subordinates, not only behave toughly and ruthlessly but, at the same time, present this as an ideal attitude, as something to be highly valued. Such an idealization of human toughness, this cult of human ruthlessness, can be found in the literature and utterances of parts of the Wilhelmine middle class.

Karl Twersten is discussing his son with a very good acquaintance. He expresses doubt about the boy's toughness because he has inherited the blood of his mother, a happy-go-lucky woman from Cuba. His acquaintance advises him to show love to his son. This is Twersten's reply:

> I'd like to do that. And I want to do it, because I love him with all my heart. But he must first turn out like I want him to. I cannot give way on that. His character must show its true colours, one way or the other, and those must be mine. I can't imagine any more terrible thought than that the owner of K.R. Twersten's shipyard could one day be a weakling, or a person who could hesitate to get something done, with an iron will when necessary, because of some soft-hearted impulse.[43]

'Iron' is another key word of this period. To be weak or even just to show weakness is, as can be seen, something quite terrible. The memory of the years of weakness still haunts the middle class of this epoch and thus to an extent demands the over-exaggeration of the opposite attitude. One encounters evidence of this everywhere in the documents of the time. Germany used to be weak; now it is strong, and we must do everything in our power to become stronger, militarily as well as economically.

In war, too, one had to show oneself to be tough. Warriors could not be allowed to identify with the enemy very much, otherwise they could not attack them or kill them, and therefore would be unable to defeat them. In the vocabulary of the time, expressions surfaced which stigmatized sympathy with others. One could simply dismiss such humane feelings as pernicious by defining them as 'mawkishness'. Where 'iron will' prevailed, 'pluck' and 'snappy behaviour' were encouraged, and 'misplaced sentimentality' was inappropriate. Even morality was suspect. Arguments based on morality were rebutted by expressions such as 'sermonizing' and 'priggishness'. In keeping with the change from a weak state to a strong state, the humanist-moralist-civilizing code was correspondingly transformed into a counter-code with strong anti-humanist, anti-moral and anti-civilizing tendencies.

2 The Pro-War Literature of the Weimar Republic (Ernst Jünger)

The literature of the first, still unpartitioned German republic which came into being in 1918 treated the experience of war in a variety of ways. Two diametrically opposed trends can be distinguished in this connection – literature supporting war, and literature which was against war.

Already in the war literature of the Wilhelmine period, one encounters a way of depicting war that was later taken up and developed considerably further in the pro-violence, pro-war literature of the Weimar Republic. Novels such as Bloem's *Volk wider Volk* promote a positive attitude to the use of military force and pride in lack of pity for the enemy. Moreover, in such novels, without hiding the horror of war, an attempt was made to make it acceptable to the reading public and to keep the public's enthusiasm for it alive by romanticizing violence as heroism and representing war as, so to speak, some great cosmic event, an exhilarating experience in which the individual loses his own special identity. In this way, the prosaic hegemonial struggles of states were invested with a mysterious meaning:

> Strange: when Alfred, from his raised standpoint atop the pile of rubble that had been the mortuary, was able to survey the entire arena of the mute, grim resistance and the mist-shrouded foreground – the distant, flat

skyline over which lay the grey steaming clouds of the enemy batteries –
the houses and mills and folding countryside, behind which the infantry of
the aggressor could gather for a renewed onslaught . . . and all around the
wide, jagged expanse of rubble which had been a churchyard an hour and
a half ago . . . and crouched against the last remaining miserable stumps
of the churchyard wall, the little unruffled band, already covered to the
shoulders with rubble in which the churned up bones of those long-since
decayed were mixed . . . as he looked across this whole unbelievable,
incomprehensible scene of human fury and human defiance, every slightest
feeling of personal danger was extinguished in him . . . and nothing
remained except an unnameable feeling of astonishment. . . . For him, it
was as though it were not he himself who was experiencing all this . . . his
own self had sunk deep, deep down . . . and for the first time in the entire
campaign he felt in this hour purely immersed in the idea of all this titanic
struggle. . . . Here it was no longer one person pitted against another . . .
no longer regiments and divisions against regiments and divisions . . . here,
it was nation against nation . . . fatherland against fatherland . . . that in
the struggle of these highest units into which mankind had evolved up to
this point in time, all the highest virtues of mankind were unfolded for a
last blossoming . . . on this side . . . *on both sides*.[44]

After 1918, this tradition of depicting war was continued. One of the
earliest examples, perhaps the best and, in any case, the most representative work of the German pro-war literature of this period is Ernst
Jünger's *In Stahlgewittern* [The Storm of Steel], first published in 1922.
The barbaric nature of war is not in the least disguised in this novel
either. It is even depicted with a certain gusto. For instance, after a hard,
duel-like shoot-out in the enemy trenches when Jünger and his men drag
off a few wounded and dying Indians as prisoners, 'as there was a prize
on the head of every prisoner, dead or alive', he describes the triumphant
return to their own trenches thus:

> Our procession, in which the whining of the prisoners was mixed with our
> cheering and laughter, had something atavistically warlike and barbaric
> about it.[45]

Here, Jünger, like Bloem, raises the barbarity of war to a higher plane
by depicting it as something elemental which seems to break out
spontaneously from warlike people. Elsewhere, he speaks of the profound enigma posed by war and of battle as a person's destiny.[46] In
short, the real events of a power struggle between states and its

murderous character are thus cast in a positive light which, without ignoring its repulsive character, wraps it in a finely spun net of noble and uplifting feelings. The horror of corpses, mangled bodies, people dying in agony, is toned down through tales of bold warriors, exemplary courage by officers and the loyalty of faithful men.

Jünger's edited war diary does not portray the human being but rather the exemplary and often heroic officer who is always composed and has come to terms with the thought that his fate could overtake him at any time. To kill people without hesitation has become second nature to him, and Jünger does not at all conceal that the successful killing of enemies is also pleasurable. He wants to win over his readers to that. One hears nothing of moments of fear, hesitation, anxiety and weakness. Here, too, the Wilhelmine code holds: weakness and frailty are fatal and must be concealed. Only strong and always courageous German officers appear in this book. In this way, there is a glorification of horror, a romanticization of violence which, in conjunction with references to the mythical origins of war, bathes the barbaric in a golden light.

Furthermore, there is the great rapture – war as a drug – which can transport a person in precisely the moments of greatest danger into a condition of joyful excitement and lift him above his isolation. In Jünger's account, as in Bloem's, a decisive battle – viewed in a calm light, the last, futile attempt of the Germans to break through – gains cosmic traits:

> The deployment of the troops presented a strange spectacle. In craters in front of the enemy trenches which were being churned and churned up again by the intense shell-fire, the attacking battalions were waiting massed in companies as far as the eye could see. When I saw this massed might assembled, the breakthrough seemed to me to be assured. But was there strength in us to shatter the enemy's reserves and smash them to smithereens? I was confident of it. The decisive battle, the final advance, had begun. The destiny of the nations was drawing to its irresistible conclusion, and the stake was the domination of the world. I felt conscious of the significance of that hour; and I believe that on this occasion every man felt his individual identity fall away in the face of a crisis in which he had his part to play and by which history would be made. No one who has lived through moments like these can doubt that the history of nations stands and falls with the fortunes of battle.
>
> The atmosphere of high tension was amazing. Officers were standing erect and excitedly shouting jocular remarks to each other.[47]

Then at last came the critical moment when the mass of attacking men had to clamber from the protecting trenches and, after the long preparatory wearing down of the enemy by the artillery, had at the risk of their lives to attempt to break through the enemy's defensive lines. Everywhere in the world warriors have ways and means to overcome their own fear of death and mutilation at such moments and to give more or less free rein to the pleasure in killing. For groups of people among whom violent clashes with other creatures are everyday events of life – for the warlike Indians of earlier stages, or for the mounted and armoured warriors of the Middle Ages – this switch into battle was perhaps not so difficult. For members of powerful industrial state-societies who are imbued with a high degree of civilizing restraint in respect of all personal inclinations towards using physical violence, it is probably rather more difficult. Jünger's description gives some idea of this. He shows how, through mutual encouragement, the use of alcohol and working themselves up into a mood of extreme fury, people sought collectively to overcome the inner barriers and to meet the social obligation to be courageous:

> Three minutes before the attack, my batman, the faithful Vinke, beckoned to me, pointing to a full hip-flask ... I took a long pull. It was like drinking water. Only the cigar which was usual on such occasions was lacking. Three times the match was blown out by gusts of wind. ...
>
> The great moment had come. The bombardment lifted over the first trenches. We advanced ...
>
> With a mixture of feelings compounded from rage, alcohol and the thirst for blood, we stepped out ponderously yet irresistibly for the enemy's lines. ... I was far out in front of the company, followed by Vinke and a one-year volunteer called Haake. In my right hand I gripped my revolver, in my left a bamboo riding cane. I was boiling with a fury now utterly inconceivable to me. The overpowering desire to kill carried me forward. Rage squeezed bitter tears from my eyes.
>
> The dreadful will to destruction that hung over the field of battle was compressed into our brains and immersed them in a red mist. We shouted broken phrases to each other, sobbing and stammering, and an uninvolved spectator might perhaps have believed we were moved by an excess of happiness.[48]

That Jünger, without concealing his fearfulness, succeeded in making war appear something simultaneously enjoyable and inspiring – in short, something of great and positive value – certainly says a lot about his literary talent. But this effort itself stood in a clear social context.

Although Jünger's war novel is based on notes from a diary he kept during the war, the version above is a post-war work. As such, the book belongs to a literary genre of the time which had a specific propaganda and ideological function. It depicted war, despite its horror, as something to be approved of, in pronounced and deliberate contrast to the anti-war literature of the same period. In the framework of the Weimar period, Jünger's *In Stahlgewittern* could be said to be the antithesis to Erich-Maria Remarque's *All Quiet on the Western Front* (1929), which quite unromantically shows the bitterness of everyday life in the war, and was probably intended to spoil even young people's appetite for war. Precisely because they could adversely affect people's willingness to do military service, novels such as Remarque's were regarded in some circles of the German population as a type of treachery. It was mostly from these circles that the pro-war literature came. With its help they hoped to keep alive the joy in the heroic adventure of battle and thus also to maintain people's readiness for it.

The contrast between the two species of war literature is evident in another respect. One was written by and large from the officers' perspective, the other more from the perspective of non-commissioned officers and men. Here, too, Jünger's novel can serve as a prototype.

In Stahlgewittern is really a glorification of the young, middle-class German officer, a member of the generation born in the 1890s. The higher, mostly aristocratic officers appear only in the distance, as superiors. In the limelight stands the lieutenant and company commander of middle-class origin who has fully assimilated the aristocratic code of the German officers and who feels proud to be a member of the German officer caste with its very pronounced and distinctive rituals of behaviour.

Of course, for these young middle-class officers the internalization and nuances of the officer code were somewhat different from those of the nobles in the higher ranks. The former, and Jünger is a prime example, were in many ways rooted in the anti-moral, anti-humanist, anti-civilizing tradition of large groups of the Wilhelmine middle class. That means they saw war not in the way the warrior nobility did, simply as a social fact, as part of the human lot especially for soldiers, but instead regarded it as something imperative and desirable, an ideal of manly behaviour, so that its violence and brutality appeared to be something great and meaningful. This difference played a not insignificant role in the internal power struggles of the Weimar Republic, whose small official elite army permitted by the Treaty of Versailles, the *Reichswehr*, was on the whole led by aristocratic officers, whereas predominantly middle-class officers headed the *Freikorps* and other semi-illegal para-military organizations. The latter were outsiders and the German offi-cer's code of honour sat more loosely on their shoulders.

One of the characteristic traits of the old officer tradition was that officers lived in relatively close proximity to their men, but at the same time a strict social distance between officers and men was maintained. By and large, in Jünger's book the men played a non-speaking role. The many batmen he had in the course of the war have no individuality, appearing as 'the trusty Kettler', the 'good Knigge':

> I should like to put on record, to show what sort of fellows ours were, that nothing I could say would induce my batman, the trusty Knigge, to make his bed in the warm sitting-room. He insisted all the time on sleeping in the cold kitchen. The attitude of reserve which is typical of the Lower Saxon made the relations between officer and men work very smoothly.[49]

In the 1920s, when this book was finished, people had already had the experience of seeing men refusing to obey their officers. The memory of the 'reserve' of the simple soldiers which made 'relations ... very smooth' between commander and men was the memory of a better past and was identical with the hope for a better future.

Behind this pro-war literature, there thus lay a tacit and seldom clearly thought-out ideological and propaganda goal. With respect to foreign policy, this goal was the reinstatement of Germany as a great power, and, if possible, to its position of supremacy, if necessary by means of a new war. With respect to domestic policy, the aim was the return to a clear order of superordination and subordination in the relations between leaders and men, not only in the army, but in the entire nation.

The controversy between pro-war and anti-war literature in the early Weimar Republic reflected one of the most central and far-reaching controversies in the Germany of the period. There were groups which had had enough of war and which believed that Germany could do well even without an extension of its military power – so long as the unity of the state and its existing borders could be maintained and the enormous burden of war debt could be reduced. To this sector of the population belonged the great mass of the industrial working class, parts of the liberal middle class, and many intellectuals. In general, they were groups which were happy that the Kaiser had disappeared from the German scene, and which endorsed the founding of a parliamentary republic.

They may have regretted the military defeat and the financial burden that it brought with it. They were joint losers in the inter-state struggles – but victors in the intra-state ones.

On the other hand, for the former ruling strata and all among the German population who had supported them, the outcome of the 1914–18 war meant a double defeat: internationally, in the decisive struggle for supremacy in Europe and the world dependent on Europe; domestically, in the fight for supremacy within Germany. The groups in question included the German aristocracy with its extension in the officer corps, the senior civil servants in administration and the judiciary from the high middle classes, and a large proportion of the German industrialists, large-scale merchants and bankers. They included, finally, a considerable number of the young men of middle-class origins who had become officers in the war. As officers in the *Freikorps* and other paramilitary organizations, many of them formed a vanguard, specializing in acts of violence, of all those strata and groups of the first German republic which, although with different emphases, pursued a double goal: within the state, of ending the multi-party system and restoring clear, hierarchical and formalized relations of dominance and subordination, as they had existed during the Kaiser's reign, the *Kaiserzeit*; and externally, regaining Germany's position as a great power, with or without a war.

3 The Decay of the State Monopoly of Violence in the Weimar Republic

1

The decrease in the power-ratio of the older Wilhelmine establishment after the defeat of 1918 did not have the same significance for its noble and middle-class strata. The former, whose claim to power and pre-eminence had been legitimized primarily through military successes, and who, as mostly agrarian strata, had already forfeited power through increasing industrialization, lost their privileged position in the state apparatus with the military defeat and the abdication of the Kaiser. There was, however, one exception, and that was that their dominant position in the German armed forces at first remained unshaken. The loss of their privileges, which had been buttressed, for example in Prussia by the Upper House of the Diet and a three-tiered suffrage system, meant a gain for the upper middle classes. The topmost middle-class groups, until then a second-grade elite, saw themselves transported at a stroke to the position of upper strata. What the middle classes of France had achieved through revolutions – liberation from the privileges and political supremacy of the aristocracy – fell of its own accord into the laps of the middle classes of Germany after the First World War, with the uprising of the workers and soldiers and the disappearance of the throne. But this gain was counterbalanced by the simultaneous increase in power achieved by the organized working class through the disintegration of the absolutist regime and the transition to an authentic parliamentary republic, that is, one dependent on majority voting.

Had the industrial working class been organizationally unified, then their party could possibly have won a long-term position of supremacy within the framework of a constitution granting the party with the majority of votes the right to govern. But as an unintended consequence of the Russian Revolution and the coming to power of the Communist Party in Russia, the organized working class in Europe split into two camps which feuded bitterly with each other: the camp of those who sought a way of organizing society which would serve the interests of the workers without violence; and those who sought to achieve this in the end by the use of violence, following the Russian example.

This splitting of the working class and their sympathizers in the middle-class intelligentsia into a nationalist and a Russophile group had far-reaching consequences. One of them is as clear as daylight: organizational unity was for the industrial working class a more important determinant of their power-ratio than it was for middle-class groups. The split into two antagonistic camps therefore had as one unplanned consequence a considerable reduction in the power-potential of the workers. But that was not the only one.

I do not need to go into the question here of whether the unsuccessful and oppressive tsarist regime would have crumbled after its defeat in the First World War even without the use of extra-state violence. In any case, the example of the violent revolution in Russia had an extraordinarily long-lasting, widespread impact, both as model and as nightmare. The fact that in Russia the use of extra-state violence had proved to be an effective means of ousting a ruling group from control over the centralized state monopolies of force and taxation, and in enabling the leaders of the violent groups to take over these monopolies, had such strong and long-lasting effects on the relationship between extra-state and state use of force in other countries that this type of violence, under the name of revolution – as already remarked, either as model or as nightmare – became one of the dominant action models of our century.

Far more even than the nineteenth century had stood in the shadow of the French Revolution, the twentieth century has stood in the shadow of the Russian Revolution. One reason for this difference is that belief in the ideals of the French Revolution was not linked to a belief in the necessity of using violence – revolution – for the realization of these ideals. Nor did it possess any firm theoretical base in a canon of authoritative books. The extraordinarily far-reaching effect of the Russian Revolution acquired its specific character, however, precisely because in this case it was both linked to a belief in the necessity of violence and based on a theory set out in books. Certainly the starting point was the class stratification of industrial (and also of predominantly agrarian) countries with their often firmly institutionalized and unequal distribution of power. But over and above that, there was a small number of books of intellectually high calibre which served to standardize and spread the belief. And in them, in the works of Marx and Engels, realization of the ideals of greater equality and humanity was intimately linked, even theoretically, with the use of extra-state violence. In the French Revolution, the use of violence was by and large spontaneous and unplanned. After the Russian Revolution, it became an integral part of the plans of weaker outsider groups. Moreover, the leaders, who had come to power in Russia through the use of extra-state violence, and their successors, who were now masters of a mighty empire, supported the spreading of their ideals to sympathetic groups in other countries.

And this is where the peculiar dialectical dynamics of the use of violence come into play. The Russophile movements outside Russia which, following this model, sought to realize their ideals in the last instance through extra-state violence, and which relied primarily on sectors of the working class and smaller groups of the middle-class intelligentsia, set themselves against other groups which for their part planned to counter the danger of violence posed by the former with the help of their own extra-state violence. In order to prevent the violent conquest of the state monopolies by the other side, they themselves prepared to conquer these monopolies.

That was the problem. Up to the present, there has been relatively little understanding of how the use of violence by a particular group against another gives rise with a high degree of probability to the use of violence by the other group against the former, as soon as there is the slightest chance to do so. The violence of the second group then in many cases triggers off increased violence from the first group. If such a process, a double-bind process, is once set in motion, then it is exceedingly difficult to halt; it often gains a momentum of its own. It gains a self-perpetuating and very often escalating power over the people, the opposing groups which constitute it, and becomes a trap forcing each of the participating sides, out of fear of the violence of the other side, to fight each other with violence.

Since the Russian Revolution, many countries in the world, perhaps all countries, have found themselves caught up in the vicious circle of such a mechanism. The fact that the use of extra-state violence has proved its value in the struggle against the state's violence has triggered off violent double-bind processes across the world. One of the first countries in which this spread became evident was Germany. Compared with Russia, it had reached a considerably higher level of industrialization, urbanization, national education and all other relevant aspects of a modernization process. Correspondingly, the German industrial working class was organized and politically educated to a far greater extent than the Russian. This meant that in middle-class circles the fear was even greater that, after the Russian Revolution with its violent expropriation of private property and with its very close connection with the military defeat of the tsarist regime, a revolution would also follow in Germany after the defeat of its imperial regime, with a programmatic change of power and property relations. The indubitable growth in power that the German workers had won, partly in the course of the war itself and partly in the wake of the defeat, reinforced this fear.

2

The splitting of the German workers' organizations in the wake of the Russian Revolution into a camp advocating non-violent reform and another advocating violent revolution corresponded to a parallel development on the middle-class side. Here, too, there were groups who fixed their objectives within the framework of the existing state monopoly of force and organized their business with each other through the game-rules which this monopoly safeguarded, and others who advocated the use of extra-state violence especially in the fight against the workers' organizations and the state which gave these organizations legitimacy. But whereas the pro-violence (thus anti-state) and anti-violence (thus pro-state) workers' organizations feuded furiously with each other, between the analogous middle-class organizations there was an open or tacit agreement. Not only defence associations, secret associations and other violent groups, but also wide sections of the middle class who were not prepared personally to use violence in internal struggles were inclined to be hostile towards the republic. As a result, the latter did not hesitate to support the former in every possible way. After 1918 the high value placed on physical force among sectors of the German middle class which had already been encountered in the Wilhelmine era was accordingly strengthened; but now it acquired a new character and tone.

In the Kaiser's Germany, the resort to violence in internal conflicts, such as in the case of a strike, was an affair of state and therefore used for the most part without much thought; it appeared to be a self-evident and legitimate use of the state monopoly of violence. But just as the use of physical violence in the course of the Russian Revolution was in large measure a conscious and deliberate form of the exercise of violence, theoretically supported by Marx's high valuation of revolution, so now, in the middle-class camp as well, the threat and use of violence became consciously manipulated, thought-out weapons in the power struggle between class organizations. Double-bind processes in the course of which the threat of violence by communist groups provoked and reinforced similar threats from 'fascist' groups, and vice versa, were from now on, as has been said, permanent part-aspects of the development of many countries in Europe and elsewhere. The extent to which the state monopoly of force could be broken in particular cases depended on the strength and stability of the central state power, in particular on the efficiency of the monopoly of force itself and on the closely connected security and stability of a state-society's economic development.

It was characteristic of Germany's situation at the end of the 1914–18 war that the new ruling authorities had control only to a quite limited extent over the military and police forces which are necessary for maintaining the monopoly of physical violence and, with it, domestic peace. The German state in the Weimar period was to that extent a rudimentary state. It was this which gave the violent movements and organizations on the side of both the middle class and the working class their chance.

The capacity of the government, in other words, to employ the executive organs of the violence-monopoly, the armed forces and the police, in support of parliamentary and government decisions was very limited. In relation to the republican central government which represented a kind of alliance between the moderate middle class and the moderate working class, the army, still led by the nobility, possessed an independence and a power-potential of its own that its predecessor in the Kaiser's Germany did not have.[50] As is similarly the case in many developing countries of our own times – for example, in some Latin American republics – the top military command in the Weimar Republic followed their own political goals, too. In the power-play of that period, they represented a semi-independent focal point of power. As a result, the national government could at best rely on the police forces of particular provinces [*Länder*] to maintain the peace and to track down and punish the perpetrators of violent acts. By and large, the Prussian police were at its disposal for such tasks, but those of other provinces, such as Bavaria, were not.

Of considerable importance for the struggle between the violent middle-class and workers' organizations, too, was the fact that, on the one hand, the social democratic representatives of workers in the government, men like Ebert, Scheidemann and Noske, wanted strongly to reform the still quasi-autocratic imperial regime into a parliamentary regime unhindered by any privileges whatsoever, but, on the other hand, they simultaneously renounced the use of physical violence for achieving workers' interests with great resolve and an astonishingly strong emotional aversion. They were therefore hardly less hostile towards that part of the working class that was orientated towards the Russian example, towards a violent revolution, than were the middle-class associations and organizations.

That was one of the reasons leading to an alliance – a marriage of convenience – between the people's representatives and the high command of the army (and even with individual *Freikorps*). The alliance contributed, together with the workers' strike, to the failure of the first attempt on the middle-class side to topple the government, the Kapp putsch.[51] At the same time, however, it showed the high dependency of the Weimar government on the semi-autonomous army and with it the essential weakness of the regime. Together with the Social Democratic Party and the trades unions, the officer corps was one of the nuclei of organization which had remained more or less intact despite the incipient disintegration that followed the defeat. These two groups, represented by Ebert and Groener, formed a kind of alliance in the desperate situation and confusion after 1918. What united them was a very realistic awareness of the danger threatening the country of violent attempted *coups d'états* of every colour, whether from the side of middle-class/military circles or by groups of communist workers. It was predictable that all such attempts would bring allied intervention in their train.

3

From the very beginning, therefore, the state structure of the first German republic had two faces. On the one hand, the struggle of class interests and class ideals was carried on in the form of a party struggle on the parliamentary stage, relatively non-violently, according to parliamentary rules and in the full searchlight of the public gaze. On the other hand, this struggle was also fought out by defence associations and secret societies using physical violence in a conspiratorial twilight. In these murky and violent battles, however, the balance of power was far more unevenly distributed than in the parliamentary party struggles. In the parliamentary context, the representatives of workers' organizations concerned with securing non-violent reform now had access to power-chances through the potential or actual take-over of government and other state positions which had previously been closed to them. In the struggle of the violent gangs, on the other hand, the middle-class organizations won the upper hand early on, after the communist-orientated ones had relatively quickly been subdued. They attempted to destroy the republican state and social structure from within by under-mining the state monopoly of violence and by making the people associated with it uneasy through acts of terror of the most diverse types. In this way, they wanted to bring the hated system to the point of collapse. And in the end, aided by economic crisis, they succeeded, when the legitimate state power was taken over by the man who had distinguished himself in the competitive struggle with other paramilitary organizations by the particularly hard and systematic use of non-legal, extra-state means of violence.

I have the impression that this undermining of the German state from within through acts of terror, through the systematic use of violence, has still not as yet been accorded the historiographical significance which it actually deserves. That has obscured insight into the paradigmatic meaning which this threat, and, in the end, the near paralysis of the state monopoly of violence in the Weimar period, has for the understanding of similar processes elsewhere and of the function of state monopolies of violence in human societies in general. It has become customary to examine economic developments largely in isolation from political developments. These, for their part, are generally understood in terms of the development of legal institutions. The difficulty is to show convinc-ingly that the development of the organization of violence, with its integration and disintegration spurts, is no less structured than, for example, the organization of the social production of goods.

I must deny myself the chance of showing here in detail the direction and the transformations of this extra-parliamentary power struggle which was played out between 1918 and 1933 in the half-light of an illegality which the state either tolerated or could no longer prevent and which was also connected with the parliamentary power struggles. It must be enough to establish that a continuous line of development in a subculture and in circles of people led from the terror acts of the guerrillas in the first years of the republic to the brawling at public meetings and street fighting of the early 1930s. My own experiences in this period have certainly contributed to sharpening my understanding of the problematic of the state monopoly of violence and how it is related to collective changes in behaviour, whether in a more civilizing or a more barbarizing direction. It is probably difficult for the crescendo of extra-state acts of violence which prepared the way for Hitler's take-over to reach the ears of the younger generations of our times. But perhaps a brief reference to a personal experience I remember may help.

In 1932, I attended a meeting in the Frankfurt *Gewerkschaftshaus* [Trades Union Headquarters] about a student's scholarship. During a pause in the conversation, I asked, 'What preparations have you made to defend yourselves in the *Gewerkschaftshaus* in the case of an armed attack?' I remember the silence which followed this question. Then began a rather stormy debate which made it clear to me that I had brought out into the open a thought which had for some time lurked in the back of the minds of several of those present. But they had not trusted themselves to express openly in words the possibilities which it raised, because they posed too great a contradiction to the tenor of the life to which they were accustomed, because it was too terrible to look the fact squarely in the eye that their accustomed way of life was now coming to an end. Besides, there were even one or two voices which declared such events to be utterly impossible. The conviction of the speakers that a kind of historical providence would always ensure the victory of what they regarded as 'reason' over forces of darkness was unshakeable.[52]

The question arose as to what one could do. It was obvious that, in the intensifying battles of the violent right- and left-wing extra-state associations, the right were in the process of gaining the upper hand. I wanted to know why that was the case. I still remember most vividly the picture which emerged then and also from further questioning. It points to some of the structural characteristics of Hitler's victory which could easily be overlooked.

Republican defence associations, such as the social democratic orien-tated 'Black–Red–Gold' Ex-Servicemen's Association [*Reichsbanner Schwarz–Rot–Gold*], lacked three things which were essential for victory or even for simply enduring these violent extra-parliamentary power struggles between fighting organizations with 'proletarian' and 'bourgeois' goals.

1   Such organizations were expensive. The money at the disposal of the defence associations of the organized workers for buying weapons, uniforms and other equipment was minimal in comparison with the money available to the other side. Only to a limited extent could they afford to offer their members fully paid posts, or to pay for loss of earnings or transport costs. And they were, on the whole, dependent on the voluntary participation of people who, after work or on their days off, put on their uniforms to take part in exercises, street demonstrations, guard the halls where speakers were appearing, and to take part in the ensuing, often rather dangerous, brawls. The opposing associations, especially Hitler's storm-troopers, had a far higher percentage of full-time mercenaries. They could afford to bring in unemployed people, drill them and ideologically indoctrinate them.

2   Furthermore, the fighting associations of the organized working class suffered from a dearth of officers. The overwhelming majority of German officers were on the other side. The sharp division that had existed in the Wilhelmine empire between officers and other ranks thus affected the efficiency of these extra-state fighting organizations after the war. The 'proletarian' defence associations quite simply lacked a militarily educated leadership and organizers.

3   Finally, there was no adherence to a military tradition in their circles, no predisposition for warlike activities, which was almost a matter of course on the other side.

No wonder, therefore, that the workers' associations in these violent extra-parliamentary power struggles often came off second best, and that their propagandists, not least in election meetings, often had a hard time. No wonder, either, that wide sections of the population, tired of violence and commotion, gave their votes to the leader of the evidently stronger battalions.

It is thus much more than a literary metaphor when, looking back on the Weimar period, one speaks of an increasing 'paralysis' of the state monopoly of violence, or of an increasing 'undermining' of the German state from within. The destruction of the parliamentary-republican regime was one of the political goals of wide sections of the German middle class as early as the immediate post-war years. The other was military rearmament as a step on the path to recovering Germany's position as a great power. But in the early days after the war, this was hardly anything more than wishful thinking. Such goals were unrealistic to start with because, after the signing of the peace treaty, extra-parliamentary defence associations could no longer appear in the open. In the early 1920s, the victorious powers, the Allies, kept watch with undiminished attentiveness to see that Germany's military potential did not exceed the limits imposed by the Treaty of Versailles. This was one of the major reasons why the terrorist acts of violence of those years, through which the perpetrators were already hoping to wear down and if possible bring about the collapse of the parliamentary republic, took a rather different form from those in the late 1920s and early 1930s.

Especially in this early phase, they were far more conspiratorial in character than at the time of the Great Depression and afterwards. In the later period, the Allies' fear of German militarism was being slowly pushed into the background by their fear of Russian militarism. A strengthening of anti-Russian and anti-communist forces in Germany was therefore not in the least displeasing for many Western statesmen. It thus came about that the bourgeois-orientated paramilitary defence associations, which had already been pursuing their foreign policy/national goals and their domestic policy/social goals using the same violent means, gradually emerged from the conspiratorial twilight. They could now show themselves relatively openly in public and, through public threats and acts of violence, contribute to bringing about those very chaotic circumstances which they laid at the door of the parliamentary republic as a sign of its weakness and unfitness. The struggles on the parliamentary and extra-parliamentary levels which had taken place alongside each other in the early days of the republic now affected each other more and more closely, and in the end fused together when parliament legalized the organizations which supported extra-parliamentary violence.

The economic crisis from 1929 onwards most certainly did not affect Germany alone. But in Germany at that time, the economic crisis stood in a double-bind relationship with a political crisis bordering on civil war. Both aspects of the crisis mutually reinforced each other. The economic crisis, deepened by the political crisis, fanned the flames of the violent political clashes, and vice versa. In the end, the republic of the Weimar period foundered on the structural weakness of its monopoly of violence and the purposeful exploitation of this weakness by middle-class organizations which, because of the lack of a parliamentary tradition, felt that the parliamentary-republican regime discriminated against them and therefore sought to destroy it.

4 Lucifer upon the Ruins of the World

1

Whereas the Hitler organization was a mass association which prepared for the attrition and destruction of the multi-party regime with the help of brawls and large-scale demonstrations, the *Freikorps* had sought years earlier to achieve the same goals using more elitist terrorist methods of acts of violence against prominent representatives of the regime – with correspondingly little success. They were forced to accept defeat with these attacks, too.

In Salomon's *Geächteten*, there is a selective description of the preparations for the attack on Rathenau, and his (Salomon's) disappointment over the unsatisfactory response to the deed after it had been done. Salomon reports how he went in search of the assassins, his friends, in order to help them. In the train, hearing of their violent death, he travelled on in complete despair and, already half-feverish, had to bear the trivial comments of his fellow passengers about what had happened. They told each other jokes about how the murdered Erzberger wanted to invite the murdered Rathenau to share a bottle of wine on the latter's arrival in heaven, but St Peter said that the wine bar was still closed.

It thus became clear to him that the hopes they had set on the great murder had not been fulfilled, and that his friends had sacrificed their

lives in vain. In this mood, he voices something which may be characteristic of the structure of terrorist goals and expectations in general. The
murder of the prominent man was supposed to have been a signal to
shake up the citizenry and to shake the rotten structure of the existing
regime to its very foundations. But nothing of the sort happened. The
act of terror did not spark off anything. People certainly got excited.
One part of the press loudly condemned the deed in vehement words,
others in a tone which was softer and more subdued. But the lethargic
course of normal civic life continued. Nothing indicated that the murder
of the Foreign Minister had even in the slightest shaken the regime as
such.

Salomon's despair expressed itself in a remarkable fantasy which,
whether invented or not, illuminates at a stroke the feelings of people in
such a state of deep frustration:

> This stale, abominable world had to be annihilated. . . . There were no
> people any more – only masks. It is indeed already there, the uniformity
> of everything carried by the human face. There was nothing to be done
> but to fire into the middle of the whole pack and destroy them, coldly and
> systematically. The earth does not suffer devils any more. . . . Why not
> sign the infernal contract? My wish would be for invisibility – if only there
> were some means of achieving it – some magic ointment, or a ring which
> one could turn on one's finger – a cloak of invisibility, dedicated not to
> Siegfried but to Hagen – perhaps the philosophers' stone, which one could
> put in one's mouth in order to become invisible! And a beacon should be
> lighted to Kern [one of the murderers], a signal which would shine over
> the heap of ruins – in the cities, fires should be kindled up and down the
> streets and plague bacilli thrown into the wells. The God of Revenge has
> his angels of death – I would enlist in the company. No cross of blood on
> doorposts should be any safeguard. Explosives should be put under this
> decayed, stinking pap, so that the muck splatters on the moon. How
> would the world get on without people? I would wander through the
> smoking places, through the faded, depopulated towns, in which the smell
> of corpses would stifle whatever still breathed. All the junk would then
> hang in sad tatters from the cleft walls, nakedly showing the hollow
> desires. I would set in motion all the machinery in the dead workshops
> and let them roar to destruction. I would stoke up two railway trains, let
> them meet and rear and fall and crash down the embankment; ocean
> liners, giant ships, those marvels of the modern world, I would set at full
> steam ahead and drive them into the harbour walls, so that their shining
> sides should be riven and they should vanish in a boiling maelstrom. The
> earth should be clean shaven so that nothing remained of the work of

human hands. Perhaps a new race will come from the moon or Mars . . . ;
well, let them come – the world should have a meaning once again.[53]

This shows in almost paradigmatic form a fantasy-idea which is characteristic of political terrorism, including its present forms, as it is of many other violent groups in a specific phase of their development. Recognizing this can contribute to making specific traits of such violent groups more understandable.

A central role – evident here, and apparent time and again – is played by a feeling of the total meaninglessness and worthlessness of the society in which one lives. The only hope of a more fulfilling, more meaningful life lies in the destruction of the society. In this situation, destruction can easily become an end in itself. One stops thinking about what should actually happen afterwards; one concerns oneself only very marginally with the question of what another society, promising a higher degree of meaning, should look like. All plotting and scheming revolves around the present, the planning of the next act of violence and the constant need to evade the authorities. The nihilistic component becomes more strongly evident in the agenda as well as in the routine work of the violent group in this situation. They think only of the success of the next assassination attempt, the next fire or murder. Destruction is all that counts. Every other hope has vanished. Nothing other than destruction is meaningful. And the capacity to destroy at the same time conveys a feeling of one's own power. If a society denies members of the rising generations a creative meaningfulness, then, in the end, they will find their fulfilment in destruction. He who destroys is all-powerful. The fantasy just quoted gives voice to this. In the end, the destroyer triumphs – Lucifer upon the ruins of the world.

One encounters this nihilistic component in particularly pronounced form in terrorist groups in a late phase of their development. The desired collapse of the dominant society has not occurred. The death of their victims, the death of the men and women who are their own comrades in arms, or, as the case may be, their lives behind prison walls, are also slowly revealed to be meaningless themselves. The great hope has gone up in smoke. The net of the pursuers is drawn more tightly. But these now unfeeling creatures continue to plan destruction and sow annihilation. The belief in the salvation which was supposed to have been achieved through acts of violence becomes weaker. But planning and executing such acts have become routine. To give them up would be proof and recognition of defeat. The futility of their endeavours is staring them in the face. They would have to admit to themselves that the meaninglessness of the society which they are seeking to unmask has been superseded by the meaninglessness of their own acts. And this realization is unbearable. For people in this situation, too, there is no escape. Where should they go? The belief in the future of each individual may long since have dwindled to a low flame or been extinguished; and in the depths of their hearts, individual terrorists may feel or know it. But in the communal life of the group no one can say so. That would be treachery and perhaps even put one's life at risk. In the close, conspiratorial life of the group, the obligation to profess the once living but now anachronistic belief is preserved as a routine usage of familiar catchphrases. Pleasure in the omnipotence of the destroyer replaces the great hope in a better future for the society. To stop would be an admission of the futility of all earlier endeavours and sacrifices. So, they carry on destroying, with the almost certain expectation – or even the hope – of their own destruction. Perhaps it would sometimes be less costly for a society to build bridges to these people who have no way out.

2

The wrath and will to destroy, a consequence of disappointed dreams, which seized hold of many members of the early *Freikorps*, are also mentioned in a speech which refers to a number of former terrorists under the Weimar Republic (and some of what is said there could also be said about terrorists in the Federal Republic):

> [They are permanent revolutionaries who] were uprooted and [who] thus have lost all inner connection with a regulated human social order. ... [People] who ... have found in nihilism their ultimate creed. Incapable of any real cooperation, determined to take a stand against any kind of order, filled by hatred of every authority, their uneasiness and restlessness can be quelled only by permanent mental and conspiratorial preoccupation with the disintegration of whatever exists at the time. ... As a matter of principle, they are enemies of every authority.[54]

The irony is that these are excerpts from a speech by Hitler – a speech which he, by now having almost attained his goal, made to the Reichstag as a commentary on the events of the bloodbath of the night of 30 June 1934. In this 'night of the long knives' and in the nights that followed, besides the *Freikorps* leader, Roßbach, a large number of other former mercenaries who had joined the National Socialist organization, and who saw in Hitler's rise the fulfilment of all their hopes, were murdered by Hitler's own people.

The violence of the National Socialist movement, with the aid of privately organized defence associations, had brought about the almost complete dissolution of the monopoly of force – without which a state, in the long term, cannot function – and destroyed the Weimar Republic from within; it was, so to speak, the dream of the members of the *Freikorps* and their sympathizers come true. The plan of the nationalist youth of those days, who had often joined together to form fighting groups, had been rather vague and negatively defined. Ernst Jünger wrote that he had nothing to do with monarchy, conservatism, middle-class reaction or with the patriotism of the Wilhelmine period. Through Hitler's seizure of power, this negative purpose was given a positive face. Thus 30 June 1934 was the typical, almost paradigmatic symbol of the watershed in the development of a radical revolutionary movement, which achieves success and whose supporters then turn from being destroyers of the state into representatives of the state.

5 Terrorism in the Federal Republic of Germany – Expression of a Social Conflict between Generations

The Need for Meaning and the Power Struggle between the Generations

1

In the more developed societies of the twentieth century, the need for personal meaning, which is part of the distinguishing cultural tradition of the middle rather than of the working class, is often satisfied by dedication to a political ideal. In the state which succeeded the Third Reich in the West, this need is bound up more than anywhere else with a specific generational problematic of middle-class groups.[55] The unavoidable discord over the stigma which the excesses of almost thirteen years of Hitler's rule stamped on German history and society contributes over and over again to young people of middle-class origin in their search for meaning, seizing on political ideals which stand in opposition to the great catchwords of this polluting past. After a phase of almost boundless over-elevation of the national ideal, the rising generations saw themselves burdened not only with the stigma of defeat, but over and above this – and more difficult to overcome – with the stigma of a nation which had a tendency towards barbaric acts of violence.

One of the strategies for obtaining exoneration from this stigma for many young middle-class people was to turn to a political creed which ran contrary to the dominant middle-class creed of the pre-war and wartime period – that is, the creed they often turned against was the creed of their fathers and grandfathers. With the help of a contrary creed, they hoped both to absolve themselves from the polluting associations of that period, as well as to find a new sense of meaning which could at the same time give expression to the generation conflict which was particularly acute in the then-current situation. Marxism in its various shades fulfilled these functions. It facilitated a decisive distancing from the atrocities of their fathers, and promised entry into a new, just world. The teachings of Marx, in brief, served as an antitoxin to Hitler's teachings. The longing for meaning of the post-war middle-class generations flowed accordingly not only into a mighty political movement which stretched far beyond their own country, but at the same time brought with it a catharsis, a cleansing from the burdensome curse of the national past. For this curse also clung to the heels of the young generations, even though they felt themselves to be personally innocent because, at the time of the decay of their nation's conscience, many of them were not even born.

It is neither necessary nor possible here to discuss in detail the differences and relations between the middle-class and working-class variants of Marxism.[56] It must be enough to emphasize that the working-class variant is concerned primarily with the struggle for the tangible interests of workers, whereas, for the middle-class variant, quasi-moral meaning-conveying functions stand in the foreground. From this standpoint, Marxism appeared to quite a few of those born during or after the war to embody a way out of a society full of meaningless compulsions and the hope of the speedy coming of a society without oppression and inequality. It was the theoretical and moral aspects of Marxist teachings which played a decisive role in the student movement and extra-parliamentary opposition in the Federal Republic in the 1960s and 1970s.

Many young soldiers returning in officer's uniform from the First World War had, in the name of the greatness of Germany which gave their lives meaning, fought very hard against what in their eyes was the lukewarm if not treasonable Weimar Republic; now the new cohorts of young people brought the same intensity to their fight, in the name of their burning ideal of social justice and freedom from oppression and constraint, against what, for them, was the lukewarm Bonn Republic. In both cases, these were predominantly middle-class movements of the rising generations who, by choice or fate, adopted an outsider position in relation to the established middle-class generations of the Germany of the time. The young outsiders of the later period, however, deployed their forces most decisively against what their own fathers and grandfathers had, in the 1920s, when they were young, regarded as being most sacred and most meaning-bestowing, and which had now been absolutely devalued and rendered meaningless by the memory of an orgy of violence and of a catastrophic defeat which had destroyed the nation's unity.

All this was incorporated, for the young middle-class generation of the 1960s and 1970s, in the expression 'fascism'. It became the symbolic counter-image of the meaning-bestowing objectives of their own endeavours. In it, the image of the earlier German ruling generations – not necessarily the personal but rather the national fathers and grandfathers – from whose burdensome articles of belief and acts of violence they were seeking to free themselves, fused with the image of the established, ruling middle-class generation of the present day, to represent all the oppression and all the constraints they felt were being imposed on them, as it were, 'body and soul'.

2

Since Marx is practically the only social scientist to have left behind an edifice of ideas whose kernel is a theory of social inequality and oppression with a built-in promise of the solution to this problem, his work became the central means of orientation for those groups of the upwardly mobile younger middle-class generation who were troubled by the present social situation and their own position in it.

The difficulty with this, though, was that Marxist teachings are restricted to a specific type of social inequality which certainly plays a quite central role in industrial societies, but the theoretical extension of which permitted only a partial view of the social constraints, inequalities and conflicts of the times. At the core of these teachings are conflicts between industrial entrepreneurs, who monopolize control over capital, and industrial workers, who are excluded from control over capital; but many forms of social inequality and oppression cannot be explained adequately in this schema. When, later, the younger generations of the middle class adopted Marxism, this limitation of the theory gave rise to a certain confusion. Their own struggle had to be legitimated again and again by referring to economic constraints to which industrial workers in societies like their own are exposed. Young people of middle-class origin – and sometimes older ones too – whose life experiences were quite different from those of industrial workers, and who, furthermore, were often not very familiar with the workers' problems, thus sought to orientate themselves with the aid of a theoretical apparatus which prophesied the transcendence of social inequality via the detour of a dictatorship of the working class.

Peculiar inconsistencies were thus inherent in bourgeois Marxism and they showed themselves in the mode of action of the groups in question. Because of their legitimating theory they felt obliged time and time again to make contact with industrial workers. But these efforts were seldom simple, and often forced. One can see this particularly in the different attitude of young middle- and young working-class people to the use of physical violence as a means of political struggle. Michael Baumann, the son of a worker, who experienced this contradiction during his time as a terrorist, describes it in the following words:

> An intellectual draws the moment when he uses violence from an abstraction, because he says, I am making a revolution because of imperialism or from other theoretical motives. From this, he deduces the right to use violence against others. Naturally, he also draws it from the experiences of the movement which he has shared, but nevertheless mostly from the abstract situation. That is why he is indeed an intellectual; that distinguishes him, that he can first check things out in his head.
>
> We have lived from childhood with violence which has a material root. On pay day the old man comes home smashed, and the first thing he does is beat up the old woman – it's the same old story. At school, you have a punch up, get your own way using your fists, that's totally normal; you have a punch up at work, you have a punch up in pubs, you have a healthy relation to it. For you, violence is a totally spontaneous thing that you can deal with really easily.[57]

These observations are both close to reality and theoretically relevant. Perhaps it is no coincidence that Baumann attributes his attitude to violent actions to experiences with his father and to the relatively high level of family violence and violence at school. In this way, he relates what he calls his 'anti-attitude' to his early experience of generation conflict. With younger people of middle-class origin, breaking through the civilizing barriers against the use of physical violence is, in correspondence to the different standards of their families of origin, much more difficult. To a much greater extent, it requires justification through reflection, legitimation through a theory. But the theory of constraints and conflicts which justifies such a transgression of state laws and personal norms of conscience does not need to tally at all with the factual nature of the constraints and conflicts that drive people to violence. That derivatives of a theory which makes economic conflicts between workers and entrepreneurs its focal point were actually used not by worker-terrorists but by middle-class intellectuals who had no particularly close contacts with industrial workers and who quite often had communication difficulties in their dealings with them seems to point to a discrepancy of this sort. It is questionable whether, when middle-class terrorists placed their lives at risk, it really was a question of the transcendence of the economic oppression of one industrial class by another. Presumably their own feeling of being burdened with heavy social constraints, and their desire for their own freedom from an unbearable oppression, played a much larger role in their violent struggle against the existing social order than their theory led them to believe.

This supposition gains particular importance when one looks into the differences in the degrees of pacification of families from different strata, mentioned in the above quotation. Baumann's autobiographical comments certainly refer only to a minority of working-class families, but his observations about the difference in the degree of spontaneity in using violence between terrorists from working- and middle-class backgrounds are nevertheless instructive. I want to single out only one point: one can correctly assume that, for young middle-class intellectuals from highly pacified families in which the use of violence in the authority relations between parents and children, in the power struggle between the generations, is tabooed, the transition to acts of violence, bank robbery, arson and murder as means of fighting political battles is far more difficult than it is for people from those working-class families in which physical threats against the weaker by the stronger are the order of the day. Without doubt, in the case of these middle-class people, the use of violence in political struggle is less spontaneous; transgressing the taboos against the use of violence – both the social external-constraint taboo and the personal self-constraint taboo – requires far greater effort. The need for intellectual justification, for legitimation through reflection, is a sign of this.

Only when one is aware of these conditions can one see with any clarity the peculiarity of the problem of such middle-class terrorism. The question is: what leads people, who for the most part have grown up with a heritage of violence-taboos, to risk their own lives and break from this heritage and, perhaps transgressing the constraints of their own conscience, to opt for endangering and killing other people? It must be a feeling of very strong pressure, a feeling of heavily burdensome constraints, which facilitates this transgression and brings about the decision. Indeed, when one reads the statements of intellectual terrorists, one comes across testimony again and again to the feeling of living in an unbearably oppressive and unfree society which must be destroyed in order to allow people a free and just existence that is worthy of human beings.

3

One can hardly doubt that the Federal German terrorists of the first generation, or most of them at least, were completely sincere in their feeling and conviction concerning the highly oppressive and unjust character of the society in which they lived. An explanation of this conviction (which was certainly not restricted to the terrorists) is particularly difficult because, observed from a distance – especially when one focuses on long-term processes – the Federal Republic as a society is probably less oppressive, less unjust and less unequal in the distribution of power-chances than all earlier social forms in Germany.

This is not to say that there is no social inequality, no social injustice and no oppression in it. All these failings and the corresponding social conflicts are among its most obvious problems. It is to a less obvious problem that I am trying to direct attention here: how can one understand that the feeling of living under the constraints of an unbearably prison-like society, and a sense of that society being morally reprehensible because of its social inequalities, became particularly strong precisely in a period of development when the oppression of the less powerful by established groups has decreased in comparison with earlier times? How can one understand why the protest movements and young middle-class people's declaration of war against those injustices became particularly strong precisely when the economic standard of living of the less powerful had reached a higher level than ever before? This superficial paradox can only be explained if one probes in a slightly different way from what is often done: that is, if one takes seriously the feeling of social oppression and constraint which the people in question articulate, and inquires into its bases – without, however, being satisfied with their own explanations of these constraints as being predominantly economic in character.

The most general answer can be quickly put: human groups usually revolt against what they experience as oppression not when the oppression is at its strongest, but precisely when it begins to weaken. All over the world, *younger* groups – with which we are concerned here – are dependent for some time while growing up on more powerful groups of *older* people. The constraints they are thereby exposed to – however essential they may be for those growing up – can in fact be more or less oppressive in character, and at any event can be experienced as frustrating oppression by those who are themselves growing up. And they become even more so if the power gradient between the younger and older generation is *de facto* decreased. That, however, was the case in all the more highly developed industrial societies in the course of the twentieth century and certainly not only in the Federal Republic.

In the aftermath of both great wars this century there have been specific emancipatory spurts or, to put it differently, an increase in the power-chances of previously weaker or oppressed groups.[58] The increase in the power of the working class in relation to entrepreneurs, of women in relation to men, and of overseas colonial peoples in relation to the colonizing countries of Western Europe come most readily to mind. In all these cases it was a question of a diminution of power differences, though not, of course, the achievement of equality of power in the relations of the groups concerned. This also holds for the power-shift between the older, established generations and the younger, rising ones, especially of the middle class. It is reasonable to suppose that the improvement in the economic situation which was especially noticeable from the end of the 1950s onwards contributed its part to the intensified desire for emancipation of young middle-class and above all student groups, and thereby to the sharpening of the conflict between the generations.

This change, too, was not without its paradoxes. Compared with the generations of their fathers and grandfathers, children from middle-class circles in the 1960s left their families earlier and became independent. The establishment of the welfare state and the relative ease with which young people could earn money by short-term work enabled them to become financially independent of their parents more quickly. But the greater independence from their parents of youngsters liberated in this way also exposed them earlier to the anonymous constraints of the state bureaucracy and, in certain respects, of the job market. Here lay one of the decisive bases – certainly only one – of the willingness of young middle-class groups to accept a set of teachings which placed at the centre of attention the problem of the social oppression of specific classes by others, the mastering of anonymous social forces, and beyond this the problems of social inequality and injustice.

Without clarifying this peculiar paradox of their position, one cannot quite comprehend the intensity of the feeling of social oppression which is found in many statements by members of the younger generations of middle-class origins in the 1960s. They were less subject to the power of their parents than previous generations had been in their youth. In their relationship as sons and daughters, if one may express it thus, they were less oppressed and freer than the sons and daughters of middle-class circles in earlier times had been: but as a result of their earlier independence, especially in earning their own living, they were also exposed earlier to the pressure of the relatively impersonal constraints of adult society. In this situation, the Marxist theory of the oppression of the workers by the capitalists could serve as a welcome means of orientation. At the same time it facilitated identification with oppressed groups throughout the world, for instance with the little nation of the Vietnamese, who successfully fought against the superior might of capitalist America.[59]

At the time, the work of Marx and Engels undoubtedly formed not only the most comprehensive and impressive theoretical structure, but also almost the only one usable both as a means of orientation and as an ideological weapon at the disposal of *outsider groups* which, in relation to specific *established groups*, are weaker in power and cut off by them from satisfying their needs. On account of this, it has been used for intellectual orientation by outsider groups of the most diverse types. Its pattern of explanation, however, is only reality-congruent to a limited degree. When the specific worker–entrepreneur model, and the promise of salvation which lies in the transcendence of this contradiction, are adopted as a universal model for each and every established–outsider relationship, the model in many cases acquires an ideological character which makes it useful as a weapon but which, as a means of orientation, can at the same time be highly delusive.

4

The young middle-class movements of protest and rebellion in post-war European societies used the heritage of Marxist ideas as a means of orientation and struggle. But in the very use they made of these ideas there are clear signs that the conflicts and power struggles between the generations under discussion here can only be partially and inadequately understood in terms of the Marxist model of a conflict between entrepreneurs and workers which is determined by the contradiction of their economic interests.[60] If one examines more closely the statements of middle-class terrorists of the first generation, then time and time again one finds very clear indications that the distress and constraints to which they felt themselves and others to be exposed in their society did not stem only from economic class contradictions. It is true in a general sense that, in the investigation of the social constraints which affect people, attention to economic constraints is unavoidable. But that is not enough. Up until now other types of constraints have been less precisely articulated theoretically. In practice, they are playing a growing role in the course of social development, especially on the level of the relatively highly developed industrial societies of our times. One of them is the constraint of the search for meaning, the search for a personally fulfilling purpose which can be experienced as meaningful.

Accordingly, one of the recurring complaints encountered in the terrorist camp – and certainly not only there – is about the emptiness and meaninglessness of existing society. It is often conjoined with the idea that life could only be meaningful in a society where the collective utility of personal acts took precedence over private utility. For instance, Horst Mahler, looking back on his time as a terrorist, says:

> The experience of not being able to realize one's ideas about a meaningful life, everywhere meeting with private interests prevailing – often cynically and ruthlessly – over what is generally recognized as being of value for the community, is just the way things are in our society. Young people's demand for something higher is disregarded. That puts the alienating mechanism into gear: it is so pointless. We simply can't achieve anything. We have to beat everything to a pulp.[61]

This quotation does not stand alone. Michael Baumann, from whose life a relevant episode was cited earlier, writes to his girlfriend from prison: 'Life as it's gone on up to now seems meaningless to us,' and mentions the slogan for which his group has become famous, 'Destroy what destroys you' [*Mach kaputt, was euch kaputt macht*].[62] It expresses a feeling which has become a leitmotif of many terrorists: the feeling that this society threatens to destroy them as persons through the meaninglessness to which it condemns them. Some seek to escape the emptiness by numbing themselves with drugs, others numb themselves with alcohol. But instead of destroying themselves – this is what the slogan means – it is better to destroy the society which drives them to self-destruction.

Statements like these, or so it seems to me, lead rather more closely to the roots of the terrorist problem than explanations on the level of what are politically labelled the left or right. The problems that are being addressed here can lead to either extreme of the political spectrum according to the generation of the groups in question and conditions in the wider society. What has to be explained is the fact that, compared with the problem of hunger for food and the search for a social existence which satisfies this primary need, the problem of the hunger for meaning – and the search for a social existence which stills it – has moved in the course of the twentieth century more strongly into the foreground among members of the rising generations of predominantly middle-class origin.[63] I shall single out two aspects which are of importance in this connection.

One of them is the process of increasing secularization. I do not need to go into the explanation of it here. It is enough to say that, in the course of this transformation, the efforts of people to find a this-worldly – as compared with other-wordly – meaning for their existence come to the fore. In other respects, secularizing tendencies are functionally very closely related to the increased security of human life in state-societies – for example, to the greater protection from being physically attacked by other people which the growing efficiency of the state monopoly of force ensures, or to the greater protection from sickness through advances in social hygiene and medical science. The enormous rise in average life expectancy in the course of the last two to three hundred years is symptomatic of this increase of intra-state security for individual people. One should also keep in mind, for the discussion which follows, that social representations of youth, adulthood and old age have shifted correspondingly.

A second change is no less important: the raising of the prosperity of even the poorer strata of society. Where people are constantly unsure whether they can satisfy their physical hunger and where, accordingly, the 'struggle for daily bread' claims the greater part of their energy, success in this struggle is highly meaningful. In conjunction with the battle against other dangers which threaten mere survival, the desire for help and success on this level overrides all other types of desire for meaning. Even up to the nineteenth and early twentieth century, many people even in the most developed industrial nations of the time accepted as one of the immutable givens of social life that a considerable proportion of the population was constantly in danger of going hungry, if not of starving. It was only in the twentieth century that some state-societies reached a level of productivity which made it possible for them to ensure for practically all their members, young and old, a standard of living which lay considerably above the starvation line. Now, however, people have quickly forgotten how quite extraordinary – measured relative to social development up till now – is a society without hunger; and they have come to take for granted social protection against the danger of starvation, as well as against many illnesses and other threats to physical existence. Being released from the daily pressure of having to search for ways of satisfying one's own and one's family's most elementary needs led consequently to greater significance becoming attached to the search for tasks within society which each individual person could feel to be meaningful and satisfying.

5

Changes in human society like those just mentioned – and others of which I do not need to speak here – form a type of background framework. This must be borne in mind, even though greater attention to it is not possible in the present context. It is a co-determinant of the problem of which the terrorist variant of the middle-class youth protest movement represents the tip of an iceberg. For what in the end this movement expresses is a peculiarly acute and intensified form of a conflict which is actually ever-present but takes place for the most part below the surface of society and, accordingly, all too often eludes observation and reflection: the conflict between the generations.[64]

Conflicts between generations, as they are conceived here, are among the strongest driving forces of social dynamics. Justice cannot be done to them if they are understood primarily as conflicts between parents and their children or children and their parents. From time to time, the terrorist problem has been discussed on this level. For example:

> The social origin of the terrorists and their passionate opposition to their class of origin (the 'bourgeois parental home') indicates an omission, a failing of these parental homes and indeed of the 'adult world' in general. Meaningful reflection about the causes of terrorism has to start with this, among other things. Keys to critical self-questioning could be: have we

provided our children with an example of a meaningful life and shown them the way to more satisfying, life-fulfilling activity? Have we not set ourselves up all too comfortably in the 'affluent society' after 1945, happy 'to have had a lucky escape'? Have we not all been too self-satisfied? Have we not dismissed as a Sunday luxury or postponed till 'later' every thought of a fundamental improvement in the living conditions of members of the wage-dependent classes, the guest-workers, the starving and exploited peoples of the Third World?[65]

This way of posing the problem of conflict between the generations may well be worthy of discussion, but it is not relevant to what I mean here. Here, we are not concerned with the question of whether individual parents have done anything right or wrong in their relationship with their children. Such conflicts, which occur in particular families, form only one level, the individual level, of a far more all-encompassing conflict between the generations. As long as attention is fixed on them, as is still the case for instance in the Freudian theory of the Oedipus complex, it blocks access to understanding of the generational conflicts which take place on the social level. In those, the intentions and plans of individual parents and children play a far smaller role, while unplanned and unintended confrontations – where the participants are often not even aware that these are generation conflicts – play a far greater role.

The generation conflict to which I am referring is a *social* conflict. It is certainly to be seen in the personal conflicts between specific parents and specific daughters and sons; but even these do not quite have the immutable character Freud attributed to them. The *structure* of the tensions and conflicts between individual parents and children also changes in accordance with changes in the parent–children relationship, whether in the wider society or in particular strata. The influence of these tensions and conflicts on the drive- and affect-modelling of children changes correspondingly. There are undoubtedly recurrent basic structures: the parent–children relationship is nearly always an authority relationship with a decidedly unequal balance of power. And certainly there are continuous changes in the balance of power within the individual family group, too. But they do not form the main focus of what I am saying here about the balance of power and transformations in the relations between the generations. In the last analysis, the structure of these processes on the individual level is determined by the structure of the relationship between the generations in the wider society, whether in a tribe or state.

Examples of social conflicts between the generations are not difficult to find. In most societies, the simplest as well as the most complex, the privileges of older generations include occupying positions which give their holders a monopoly over chances for making decisions and issuing orders at the highest levels in matters which concern the whole group. The younger are usually excluded from access to positions of command. The reason often given for excluding them is the need for quite a long period of preparation and learning without which people are not in a position adequately to fulfil the responsibilities associated with ruling in every society. But of course, there can be very different institutional patterns for regulating and managing the power of command which is accorded to the older generations over the younger by the nature of their position. Equally variable is the length of time during which particular older generations retain their occupancy of decision-making positions in the society; there is a corresponding variation in the length of time for which the younger generations have to wait in relatively subordinate positions before access to positions carrying power is opened to them.

The conflicts arising from this near-universal monopolization of social functions by older generations and from the desire of younger generations for access to the relevant positions have been extremely variable in the course of social development; but at each and every stage they are socially specific. They have a structure which can be explained as a function of the whole structure of the society in question. So, in a simpler society, for example, a member of a specific family may occupy the position of king as long as he remains strong and healthy, since according to the notions of those involved, the weal or woe of the whole group depends on the strength and health of their central ruler. If, however, famine, epidemic diseases or defeat in battle against enemies show that the charisma of a king is failing, tradition may dictate that he should be killed and one of his younger descendants, who is still in full possession of his magical strengths, should be put in his place. In the case of a farm, it may be customary for the farmer, when he gets weaker, to hang up his hat in favour of a son. On the other hand, there are also societies in which the old farmers are accustomed to keeping charge of their property until they are 60 or 70 years old, with the consequence that their sons remain without any property of their own until the age of 40 or older and therefore cannot marry.

Already in this latter case, withholding the chance to possess property is at the same time associated with a cutback in chances for meaning. The old farmer runs the risk, through the pressure from the young one, of losing everything which gives his life meaning, not only his power of command but also the independence which he will lose when he eventually steps down. And the young farmer runs the risk of becoming older and older and still remaining unmarried because of the longevity and stubbornness of the old one, without finding the meaningfulness which, according to the code of his society, only control over a farmstead and land and starting a family can give. Even without any special detailed knowledge, it is easy to see that every so often one of these young farmers would fall into despair, become violent and perhaps even assault his father. All this is an illustration that generation conflicts cannot be explained by reference only to the guilt of one side or another, but in many cases quite definitely have to be explained by reference to the specific structure of social institutions.

In societies like the industrial nation-states of the twentieth century, whose structure and manner of functioning are often highly opaque to their individual members, the nature of conflict between the generations is, of course, far less immediately intelligible than in the case of simpler societies to which these examples refer. It is therefore even easier to fail to appreciate that, in these cases, it is not a question of conflicts which arise from individual idiosyncrasies, but rather of institutional conflicts.

6

I have already pointed to the remarkable fact that many members of the young middle-class circles who found themselves together in the extra-parliamentary opposition, and later in terrorist groups, clearly experienced their society as unbearably oppressive, unjust and in this sense highly reprehensible, whereas *de facto* the social inequality and oppressive tendencies which were, of course, present in the Federal Republic were comparatively speaking weaker than in the time of Hitler and most other periods of earlier German history. This paradox, it seems to me, can be explained against the background of just such an encompassing generation conflict.

In the development of more differentiated societies, it is easy to distinguish between periods with comparatively open channels for upward social mobility for the younger generations, and other periods in which these channels become narrower and narrower and perhaps for a while even become completely blocked. The problem I am addressing here is complex; especially in highly differentiated societies, it sometimes happens that a narrowing of the channels for upward mobility in many sectors goes hand in hand with a widening in others, or with the carving out of newer, more wide open channels. With reference to a single social field, the simplest – perhaps far too simple – model for such closure and opening of channels of upward mobility is the traditional military organization of modern states, in particular the officer corps. To bring it down to a succinct formula: in times of war, the career channels of such an organization open up, in times of peace they narrow and can even temporarily close.

It is difficult to obtain an overall view of the degrees of closure and openness of career channels in different phases of the development of a state-society. But here, too, phases of violence, whether in the intra-state or inter-state relations of people – that is, periods of war and civil war or revolution with subsequent restoration of the state monopoly of force – are usually at the same time phases with relatively wide and open channels of upward mobility. By contrast, long periods of peace, in the domestic just as in the inter-state sphere, are periods in which the flow through the channels of upward mobility slows down. The circulation of the generations becomes more sluggish. In most cases, the average age of the established groups at the pinnacle of the career hierarchy is correspondingly raised. For the younger generations, life chances become more limited, especially those chances with which individual feelings of meaningfulness are connected. At the same time, the pressure of established groups on outsider groups increases, one but not the only example being the pressure of the higher-ranking older generations on the younger ones dependent on them. This pressure, and this tendency for the circulation of the generations to slow down, have many consequences or side-effects which are tangible for instance in the literature or in what is rather vaguely called the 'feel of life' [*Lebensgefühl*] in a period.

One certainly cannot understand social power-shifts without taking into account the particular classes or strata whose relationship to each other changes in the course of revolutions or domestic upheavals. But nor, frequently, can one understand and explain such power-shifts without taking into account generation conflicts and the problems of generational change in general. I recall having read somewhere that the established groups of the Hitler regime and the Soviet Union before the war were on average the youngest of their century.

The narrowing and widening of life chances, and opportunities for meaning in general and career chances in particular, for the younger generations of a society at any one time are processes that undoubtedly most strongly affect the balance of power between the generations. One could say that these processes form the kernel of social conflicts between the generations.

From all this, it will perhaps become clearer why it would be erroneous to assume that these conflicts are exclusively about deliberately planned clashes between generation groups with opposing interests. At first glance, it may appear to be so: each of the older groups concerned at any time are *beati possidentes*; they are in possession of power-chances, including chances for meaning, and as long as they are not too old and frail to carry out the associated functions – as long, in other words, as they use these functions as a monopoly of their own generation – access to them remains blocked for the waiting younger generations, or can be regulated by the older generation in their own interests. But although the succession of the generations can be regulated to a certain degree by the established older cohorts, the social processes of narrowing and widening – the closure and opening of career channels and the corresponding life chances and chances for meaning for the rising cohorts – are unplanned processes. War and revolutionary upheaval are not planned with the objective of contributing to an acceleration of circulation between the generations; plans of this kind are all the less likely since, by and large, we lack an articulated theory of how such processes operate. Nevertheless, wars and revolutions, even if their declared aims are completely different, are as a rule accompanied by an acceleration in the circulation of the generations. It would be equally simplistic just to blame the older generations, in possession of the topmost career and establishment positions, for narrowing the access of younger people to desired life chances in long periods of peace. This, too, according to the present level of knowledge, is characteristically an unplanned process. But if such unplanned processes are raised into consciousness, they will gradually become more accessible to conscious control.

It goes without saying that the fate of younger people from strata whose life-expectations are directed towards a career will be most deeply affected by this periodic opening and closing of career channels in their society. The latent generation-tension and the associated conflicts intensify if the channels become narrower, but the forms in which this conflict appears are extraordinarily variable.

Unless one is clear that the problems which arise here are class-specific, one will not be able to put them into perspective. Characteristic of the occupational structure of industrial workers, among other things, is the shortness of the career ladder open to them. In workers' circles, career expectations are correspondingly less sharply defined and also do not have the same significance to occupational consciousness as they do in middle-class circles. It is not rare for young middle-class people to have in mind a fairly precise, chronologically specified career plan showing at what age they should have reached what step of the career ladder. The difference between the career structures normally available to adolescents from working-class and middle-class homes plays a not inconsiderable part in determining their different reactions to congestion of career channels in their field.

Furthermore, for both groups in more complex societies, there are alternative channels through which a small percentage of the people in question can circumvent the narrowing or congestion of career channels. For young workers, a career as a football player or boxer is one such alternative channel; for people of middle-class origin alternatives include for instance a career as writer and poet; and, for both, there is the possibility of a political career.

Among the hallmarks of contemporary societies, indeed, is the fact that the conflict of the generations plays a significant role not solely on the occupational level but on the political level as well. This is connected with the fact that the decisive model of the state in the twentieth century has been the model of a *party* state. That is, a state within which the incumbents of the ruling positions and, according to circumstances, the higher administrative positions, too, legitimate themselves as members of their society's political establishment through membership of a party organization which at the same time incorporates parts of the broader population, usually including members of the younger generation. The organization of society in the form of a party state, whether a dictatorial one-party state or a parliamentary multi-party state, is a relatively new development. One of its consequences is that, besides occupational channels, party states also produce political channels which can open or close, widen or narrow. Therefore there can be open or latent generation conflicts in the network of these channels, too. Access to the command positions in party and government, occupied by people of an older generation, may remain blocked to the younger generations for many years; access may reopen for younger people through competition between the parties or with the death of members of the party and government establishments. Whatever the case, the pressure bearing down on younger generations can originate in the constriction of life chances and chances for meaning on both the career and political levels. Very often, it stems from a combination of restrictions on both levels.

7

In this study, I have presented two examples of the possible effect of such a cutback in life chances and chances for meaning on a rising, predominantly middle-class generation. In the Weimar case, it concerned younger officers, who after the First World War played a decisive role in the formation of *Freikorps* and later of conspiratorial terrorist groups after the First World War. For most of them, the normal career as an officer in the German army appeared to be the only career which accorded with their abilities, satisfied their status-requirements, and so could give fulfilment and meaning to their lives. The less precisely regulated, even somewhat mercenary-like and slightly *déclassé* position in the voluntary associations of the *Freikorps* was a substitute for the blocked career path in the German armed forces, shrunk to a fraction of their earlier strength.

These mercenaries had highly ambivalent feelings towards the German military, whose leadership excluded them from the longed-for position as officers in the regular army. In the early post-war years, although they had no great sympathy for it, these military leaders opposed all attempts to put an end to the parliamentary regime by force of arms. But it was not possible for the outsiders in the *Freikorps* to fight against the army. In the end, the latter was a patron and an ally; the *Freikorps* officers quite often relied on its help. It was similar for the middle-class or aristocratic civilian groups who, like the *Freikorps*, saw themselves as 'nationalist', and especially for the nationalist associations and parties. The mercenaries, who had reverted to a wilder lifestyle, may have despised the staid burghers, the often rather corpulent nationalist middle class, but they, too, were a powerful partner whose protection and financial help were in many cases essential. The latent generation conflict in the relationship between the relatively young *Freikorps* leaders and their followers, on the one hand, and the older establishments of army leadership and top groups in the nationalist associations and parties, on the other, could not be physically lived out. The hierarchy of German army officers might block entry to their desired career for the *Freikorps* officers; the insecure young middle-class man in the officer's uniform of a *Freikorps* might not have too much time for the staid, patriotic old bourgeoisie; but the struggle of the younger outsider groups against the older established ones for the opening of constricted life chances and chances for meaning could not be resolved on this level.

Despite all difference of interest among them, these younger and older generations nevertheless presented a common front. The common opponents of both were the upwardly mobile groups which had won new power-chances through the defeat of the imperial establishment, above all, the numerically very large organized working class and the numerically very small Jewish middle-class circles which, in the total structure of German society, formed, so to speak, a middle class of second rank. Together with the small democratic-liberal wing of the German middle class, these groups, whose representatives had now for their part become part of a republican establishment, formed the main target in the struggle of all those who could not reconcile themselves to Germany's defeat, whose entire hopes were directed towards restoring the glory of the empire and its good society. Also fighting against the new republican establishment and the circles supporting it were what one can perhaps call the extra-parliamentary opposition of the Weimar Republic, to which the *Freikorps* belonged.

This case is not without significance as a model for a theory of social conflict between the generations, centring on reopening and widening channels to life chances and chances for meaning which have become dried up or narrowed. The protest of a younger group against its own establishment blocking its path to desired life chances may, under certain circumstances, turn from this goal and be displaced on to other groups. In addition, the example shows very clearly how the struggles of younger, predominantly middle-class generations for the opening of career and political chances can interweave with each other.

Indeed, it was Hitler who succeeded, at first through extra-parliamentary strategies and then through the adept use of parliamentary channels of upward mobility, in ripping open for certain cohorts of younger generations the path to political command positions and thereby to desired life chances and chances for meaning which had been closed to them by the Weimar party establishment. The class conflict which was expressed in the fight of both the *Freikorps* and the National Socialist movement against the Weimar regime was thus bound up most closely with an inter-generational conflict.

8

A generation conflict was also involved in the case of the movement out of which the terrorists of the Bonn Republic arose. Here, too, members of a younger generation turned against older established groups whose authority they took to be an oppressive choking-off of what seemed to them to be meaningful and worth living for. There was no shortage of attacks aimed at opening up previously constricted or closed career channels in the professions. The extension of access to teaching posts in the universities and the demand for participation in decision-making regarding university appointments were among the demands of the student movement in the late 1960s and early 1970s. But the struggle against the older political establishments had a more central meaning. It was the pressure of the party establishments that the younger generations opposed through the organization of an extra-parliamentary opposition which was thus at the same time also external to the opposition operating in the existing party organizations.

Parties easily congeal into hierarchical associations ruled by an older leadership group, with the consequence that, within them, younger generations can often rise only at a very slow pace. Of course, in multi-party states, where the competition between parties acts to relax the situation, this restriction of the chance of rising politically through the predominance of older establishments is a little less perceptible than it is in dictatorial one-party states. In many cases, the topmost representatives in one-party states are only prepared to give up some of the power which is so extremely meaningful and fulfilling to them when ill health or the frailty of old age compel them to. In any case, the constitution of such states does not usually require any publicly controllable rules of succession. But in multi-party states, too, despite the inter-party competition, there is a noticeable tendency for intra-party channels of upward mobility to be reduced or blocked and accordingly for younger generations to be excluded from political positions where more or less independent decision-making is possible. This situation leads time and time again to the dampening of younger party members' willingness to disagree, contributing considerably thereby to the pressure towards intra-party conformity. In this way, extra-party, extra-parliamentary forms of opposition often offer younger generations the only chance to express political and social objectives which, in the framework of the existing party organizations and therefore also of parliamentary institutions, can neither be expressed nor gain a hearing. Perhaps people ought to be more aware than they are today of the character of such movements as a sign of the narrowing or choking-off of political life chances and chances for political meaning for younger generations of party members.

In order to understand the dynamics of an extra-parliamentary movement, account has to be taken of the fact that, in the parliamentary states of our times, career channels in the framework of firmly established institutionalized party organizations represent the only path to effective political activity – yet, particularly in longer periods of peace, they are very narrow and, for large numbers of people in the process of growing up, inaccessible. If the command positions of the parties and, with them, the chances of exercising governmental functions are occupied for many years by older party establishments, members of the younger generations accordingly have hardly any leverage for carrying through their political goals. This is one of the structural peculiarities of the relationship between generations in multi-party states which goes at least some way towards explaining the feeling of younger people of living in an oppressive society, although it is not the whole story. When young people enter as newcomers onto the scene of public life, they often have a very strong feeling that much in their society should be different. But they have only meagre opportunities in the framework of existing institutions to work towards an effective change in what they perceive to be weaknesses.

The meaning of this blocking of effective participation is that much greater because, in the twentieth century, political doctrines have more than ever before become an integral element of that which is meaningful for people and which accordingly enables meaning to be bestowed as well as removed. I have already pointed out that the meaning-giving functions which, in earlier times, were associated with other-worldly, religious creeds shifted increasingly in the course of the great wave of secularization to this-worldly political creeds. Struggles over political faith in the twentieth century therefore have often had the same emotional intensity as the religious struggles of earlier centuries. The religious zeal, the affective involvement with which the young middle-class leadership groups of the extra-parliamentary movement in the 1960s and the conspiratorial terrorists in the 1970s stood up for their society-transforming goals and with which they denounced the existing state – which they saw as to a very high degree embodied in the ruling party establishments and as involving a morally valueless and oppressive system – cannot quite be understood as long as this meaning-bestowing function of the battle for one's own political ideals is not simultaneously taken into account.[66]

Indeed, probably one of the strongest roots of the distress and actions of the young opponents of the Federal Republic in the 1960s and 1970s was that, in the context of a party state in which party organizations claimed the monopoly of access to all political activities, they found themselves excluded from any political activity whose goals seemed at all meaningful to them. Seen in this light, the organization of an extra-parliamentary opposition brought out into the open something which is latent in every society with a monopolistic party regime: the existence especially of young outsider groups who are politically highly motivated, and who – however they themselves care to interpret it – care deeply about the public problems of their society, without, however, the official institutions giving them any opportunity to express this interest.

Forms of extra-party, extra-parliamentary opposition are therefore normal manifestations of parliament-ruled state-societies. Protest movements related to those in the Federal Republic formed in many of the more advanced industrial societies of the world, such as the USA, France and Britain. In all these countries, people of predominantly middle-class origin banded together in an attempt by extra-parliamentary means to turn upside down a regime dominated by old middle-class groups. In many cases their enterprise had long-term consequences for the relationship of the older to the younger generations, especially in the universities. But in every country it was a failure when judged in relation to the great hopes entertained in the circles involved at the high point of the movement.

If this struggle had been successful, the regime of the grey hairs over the political institutions would have been broken. The narrow or congested channels of political upward mobility would have been opened, and there would have been new, initially still wide and flexible channels. The men and women of the older generations would have stepped down and would have been replaced by members of the younger generations. As a rule, however, the power-chances of such movements are extraordinarily slight compared with those of party organizations, especially the pinnacles of a party hierarchy, the party establishments. As long as there is no severe crisis in their society to assist them, the members of such movements hardly ever have the chance to acquire access to effective political activity related to their political goals.

It was just such a crisis which eventually enabled the extra-parliamentary opposition of the Weimar Republic to intervene effectively in the political struggle between the parties. For the members of the extra-parliamentary opposition of the 1960s in the Bonn Republic, there was no such corresponding opportunity. It drew a great deal of support; the mass demonstrations awakened high expectations; the simultaneous student movement had considerable success in its attempts to alter the balance of power between the established older generations of professors and the outsider generations of students and young non-tenured lecturers in favour of the latter, thereby opening up or widening a series of career channels for them. All this generated a feeling of elation among the participants. Their dream of realizing their ideals, of emancipating all the oppressed people in the Republic, and especially the younger generations who participated in this struggle, seemed on the point of being fulfilled. And then, unexpectedly, this dream was shattered. The euphoria was followed by depression and a hardening of the struggle.

Pre- and Post-War Generations: Differences of Experience, Ideals and Morality

9

The frustration of a politically motivated younger generation which felt itself pushed aside by the monopoly position of older generations, not only from access to all bodies where political decisions were made, but also for a long time from active participation in political decision-making generally, certainly contributed a great deal to the demonizing of the existing state which showed itself in many circles of Federal Germany's extra-parliamentary movement of the 1960s and 1970s. But other peculiarities of their experience, and thus also other, more specific aspects of the generation conflict, worked in the same direction. One of these was the different attitudes of the older and this younger middle-class generation to the National Socialist incursion into German history, and to its causes and consequences.

It may be helpful to put oneself in the place of these young people when they, so to speak, entered the scene and looked around at the political landscape of the Federal Republic fully consciously for the first time. What strikes one first is how great the difference was between the world experience of the newcomers and of the older ones who occupied all the leading positions – those who stood at the pinnacle of both political and occupational career channels, including those of the parties and the universities, and from there determined the fate of the German state-society and of its members who were growing up.

For the older generations of the middle class who had lived through the transition from the Weimar Republic to the dictatorship of the National Socialist Party and then the ensuing war, the question of the personal guilt or innocence of individuals – including, of course, themselves – played a quite decisive role in the debate over this decivilizing incursion into German history. Most of them had been cleared by the Allies' denazification commissions of having personally had any, or any considerable, part to play in the atrocities of the Nazi period. In this way, the problem of 'coming to terms with the German past' was, for them, to a considerable degree solved. Officially, they had nothing to fear and nothing to regret. Their consciences may have plagued them now and then. But in public life, so it appeared to the leading men of this generation, the nightmare of the Hitler years could be buried. Over and above the issue of individual membership or non-membership of National Socialist organizations, the question of what peculiarities of the German state-society and its specific tradition had enabled that outbreak of brutality and inhumanity to occur lay by and large beyond their horizons. Conscious of being more or less free from the stain of belonging to the now stigmatized group, they sought to continue the German state tradition, which led through numerous old bourgeois and noble family chains from the *Kaiserzeit* through the Weimar Republic into the new Federal Republic. In many respects they carried on as if nothing had happened.

The management of German internal affairs by representatives of the victorious powers, as can be seen here, had a markedly retarding effect on the development of the Federal Republic. The leadership groups of the post-war era, typified by the symbolic father figure of Adenauer, concentrated their efforts above all on securing reconciliation with the victors and constructing a stable state edifice in the style of the liberal-conservative tradition of the pre-war era. Through that, the young German Federal Republic would be able to present itself as a trustworthy partner of the Western powers, and thus also as a legitimate recipient of huge amounts of economic aid. Because of the consequences of the defeat and the long duration of the reconstruction, the debate among the younger, rising generations about the attitudes and ideals of the ruling older generations was postponed. The explosiveness with which this debate was then carried out in the 1960s and 1970s was partly the expression of a catching-up effect.

For the young middle-class generations who were then entering the political arena, the problem of the nation's past appeared quite different from how it had to their fathers' and grandfathers' generations. Born late in or after the Hitler period, they were certain that they were not in any way guilty of the atrocities of the Hitler regime. But they were aware, perhaps with a certain astonishment, that the world at large blamed the German people for the creation of a violent regime which went far beyond the normally bearable forms of inhumanity. In other words, they found that the stigma attached not only to individual people who had been personally involved in the acts of violence of the Hitler period, but to the entire nation. Every German felt the force of that when he or she met foreigners, even if their youth acquitted them of any participation in the stigmatized events. If the fathers' generations had seen the problem of being cleansed of the past primarily as a matter of individual guilt or innocence, for the generation of the sons and daughters the social problem of the origins of the Nazi regime surfaced to a much greater degree. For them, who lived later, it was clearer than for their fathers that the nightmare of the past would not let itself be buried quite so quickly, and so on their part the generation conflict broke out with especial force – of course, not necessarily as a family conflict, but above all as a wider social conflict.

The usual competitive situation between younger outsider groups and older established groups who monopolize the life and meaning chances of the younger group for years on end became, in this case, quite exceptionally sharp. It is common enough for sons and daughters to feel the fathers' generation to be authoritarian and oppressive because it blocks access to life chances. But this perhaps not quite clearly articulated feeling now combined, for a large number of young middle-class people, with the awareness that these self-same fathers represented the generation which was directly or indirectly responsible for the rise of Hitler and his supporters. Far more expressly than before, this generation demanded an answer to the question of how the victory of the National Socialists – or, as they also called them, the 'fascists' – could have come about in Germany. They also demanded the assurance that what had happened would never happen again.

From the experience of this situation it is easy enough to explain the concern about the approach of a new dictatorship in Germany, and the readiness to interpret current forms of oppression as the forerunners of a second period of fascism. These worries played a central role in the plans and actions of the extra-parliamentary opposition groups and later also in those of the conspiratorial terrorists. From it arose the needs that Marxism promised to satisfy, especially for young people of middle-class origin with intellectual leanings. Expressed roughly, Marxist teachings and their derivatives had a four-fold function for the young middle-class generations of this period: they served them as a means of purification from the curse of National Socialism; as a means of orientation through which to interpret the social character of the Nazi period as well as of contemporary society; as a vehicle for fighting against the older, established generations, against their fathers, the bourgeoisie; and as a model of an alternative society, a meaning-giving utopia against which one could critically expose one's own society's defects.

For one brief historical moment it seemed possible, to the leading groups of these middle-class young people in Germany, to escape the constraints – seen by them as economic – of the existing social regime, and to realize the goal they dreamed of: an end to capitalist domination and the transition to rule by the working class. The time had nearly come, they felt, when the Bonn Republic of the entrenched establishment could be transformed by the forward-surging outsiders into another, freer, more meaningful social system, which they usually denoted by the concept of 'socialism'; and the ghost of fascism would thereby be exorcized once and for all.[67] When the dream was not fulfilled, when for this young generation, too, the great hope began to shatter, the dynamics of protest led to an intensification of violence in the collision between rebellious groups and the representatives of the state monopoly of force. It led in the end to the formation of secret organizations which sought to topple the ruling apparatus – which was obviously not going to be shaken by relatively non-violent strategies – through systematic acts of violence.

In trying to explain terrorism in the Federal Republic, one can scarcely overlook the fact that the countries where opposition movements of younger people led to the formation of violent groups are principally those where, in the recent past, a decisive part was played by forms of more or less arbitrary rule by violence, outside the control of law, of the type characteristic of fascist or National Socialist regimes. Evidently the same social conditions and traditions which favoured the emergence of violent dictatorial types of rule in Germany and Italy also contributed to the emergence of violent anti-fascist counter-movements. In both these countries, moreover – and possibly in Japan as well – the fear of a new violent authoritarian dictatorship was, for understandable reasons, particularly great and particularly strong, in line with the sensitivity of sections of the young post-war generations towards any apparent sign of the return of such a regime. And once the bonds are broken which, in more developed state-societies, normally restrict the arbitrary use of physical violence as a means of settling conflicts, then the fire continues to smoulder and the fear of a return to the rule of violence more easily drives the opponents, too, to use violence as a preventative measure or in retaliation. Whatever else is brought into the explanation of terrorism in the Federal Republic, account has to be taken of the fact that, in other countries ruled by parliaments, extra-parliamentary opposition movements have not led to the formation of conspiratorial terrorist groups when such movements lost their impetus and their hope of rapid change in the existing regime which they felt to be oppressive.

It was their tragedy that some members of these younger generations, in their efforts to bring about a better, warmer, more meaningful kind of human social life as a counter-image to the National Socialist regime, were driven in their turn to more and more inhuman acts. And perhaps not only *their* tragedy, but also that of the state, the society, which they sought to transform; and of older generations, who, in possession of all power-positions, represented society and state. For their part, these older established elements had certainly attempted – in accordance with the transformed power relationships – to moderate the harsh inheritance of the absolutist authoritarian state which had survived in the republican successor states of the thousand-year German monarchy, not only in many nooks and crannies of the state organization itself, but beyond that in the recesses of the personality structures of German people. The catastrophe of this German tradition had brought to an end the hard-fought-for unity of the state; and, as a result, the will and desire was certainly reinforced among the surviving leadership groups who led the post-war reconstruction to build a less authoritarian state and to make corresponding reforms to the state apparatus and educational institutions. But limits to their will for change were set by their fear of revolutionary doctrines infiltrating from neighbouring countries which, although internally they continued and developed further the pattern of autocratic absolutism, in their propaganda addressed to other countries, called for freedom and the overthrow of the existing order.

Sections of the younger generations felt that the limited reforms of their elders, who themselves still bore the stamp of pre-war times, were inadequate. Despite the parliamentary institutions, despite the multi-party system, they still discovered in the reformed state many traits of the traditional autocratic authoritarian state. Special difficulties were created by their frequent use, as a tool of intellectual critique, of the edifice of Marxist ideas which present and reject the state as factually being an instrument of the ruling class. For one thing, wherever these teachings had been put into practice, the result almost without exception was the formation of highly autocratic and oppressive states. For another, however, Marxism acted as an infallibly provocative irritant to the older established groups of their country. Although they had long since decided to give wide scope for free competition between the major parties, following the model of their Western allies – and in view of the changed power relations within the state – it nevertheless awoke in them feelings and attitudes which were related to those of earlier German ruling strata.

This only confirmed the suspicion of the young middle-class groups who had joined together to form an extra-parliamentary opposition that the inclination to use physical violence, which in the case of the Weimar Republic had led to the setting up of an autocratic and violent regime, could assert itself once more in the Bonn Republic, too. Plagued by the vision that tendencies on the part of the ruling strata towards violent dictatorship could once again prevail under the second German parliamentary republic, sections of these younger generation opposition groups intensified the fight against the older generations who held all the power positions in the parties and thus in the government, and whom they regarded as susceptible to having resort to dictatorship and police violence.

In fact, the fear that a new violent dictatorship might be imminent never left these young people. And it was not just a fear. They also drew a great deal of their reforming or revolutionary energies from the idea that, behind the mask of their parliamentary multi-party state, a new dictator was already lurking with his henchmen, waiting for his hour to strike, and that the police of the Federal Republic were his vanguard. This conviction that the great enemy, 'fascism', had not been totally destroyed but might rise up again at any time is a kind of leitmotif which runs through their testimonies time and time again. It followed that one had to bring the opponent out of his hideout and into the open light of day. The tendency of these younger people's organizations to provoke the state authorities into revealing themselves in their true fascist nature for everyone to see was strengthened in the course of their confrontation with the state apparatus.

The question here is not whether it was correct to see the Federal Republic as a highly oppressive state, and as the forerunner of a fascist regime. The young middle-class people who led an extra-parliamentary struggle against the Weimar state in the 1920s were also deeply and sincerely convinced that that republic was something absolutely rotten and evil, and that one had to attempt to overthrow it using any means. The same now also held for the young middle-class generations of the

1960s and 1970s. In both cases, this conviction was based on a dream, on the idea of the possibility of a better and more meaningful society; in the Weimar period, the dream was a form of nationalism which directly or indirectly led towards a fascist dictatorship; under the Bonn Republic, the dream was of a just, humane form of society, free from constraints, social inequality and oppression, through which the Western successor state of the German Reich could cleanse itself once and for all from the defiling memory of the fascist state. Even though neither the Federal nor the Weimar Republics corresponded to the image their young opponents held of them, in both cases the existing state to a large extent blocked the path to life chances which the opponents understood as meaningful. In neither case did the young opponents have a clear picture of the form of society which could satisfy their desire for meaning. But they knew exactly what they did not want.

10

One of the differences between the young extra-parliamentary opposition groups of the 1920s and 1960s was that the former shared the ideals of their fathers, whatever different nuances there may have been, whereas the latter did not. The *Freikorps*, like the National Socialists, shared with the old middle-class establishment of their time the national ideal, the dream of the unique greatness and destiny of Germany. Nevertheless, however much they were excluded from the positions of power held by their fathers' generation, and however much these young middle-class groups in consequence also belonged to the outsiders in their society, their bitterness was not channelled into a conflict against the older generation of their own class, but instead against the others, the strangers – above all, the workers and the Jews.

For the young middle-class groups who grew up after the Second World War, it was, on the contrary, the very ideals of their fathers which were tainted and from which they wanted to dissociate themselves – the ideals of nationalism and everything connected with it. Broad circles of the German middle class and not a few workers had allowed themselves to be beguiled by the attractions of the nationalist ideal and to be inspired into enthusiastic support for Hitler and his movement. Their renewed endeavour to realize the national dream of the supremacy of Germany in Europe and the world had brought shame and dishonour to the country and all its citizens. For young rising generations of the middle classes, the nationalist ideal as a vehicle for obtaining meaning was bankrupt. In this situation, the socialist ideal embodied in Marxist teachings promised refuge.

Without doubt the devaluation of the national ideal was particularly strong in Germany, and the turn to the counter-image of the socialist ideal especially intensive. But justice cannot quite be done to this process if it is understood merely as a specifically German event. It is not adequate to assume that the extreme form taken by the socialist ideal of the struggle against inequality and oppression in the terrorist movements in the Federal Republic was just a matter of the pendulum swinging back after the extreme nationalism of the Hitler movement. For in a toned-down form, an analogous development of the struggle between generations also took place in other multi-party states of Europe and North America.

It is perhaps useful to regard the relationship between the nationalist and the socialist ideals as means of giving meaning and orientation to broad sections of the population in contemporary states, as a question of balances. In the spectrum of legitimating political ideologies, exclusive reference to one or the other is characteristic only of the most extreme cases. Normally one encounters mixtures in which the one tendency outweighs the other.

In attempting to determine rather more closely the distinctive characteristics of the two ideal types, it can be said that it is a matter of the different 'norming' of the relationships between human groups. Nationalist ideals mobilize pleasure and happiness in people in the name of the fame and greatness of their own group. The interests of one's own nation justify the struggle against and, if need be, the oppression and destruction of other human groups. The liberal ideal, that the optimal human order arises from the untrammelled pursuit of the self-interests of individuals, and the nationalist ideal, which accords centre place in the behavioural code to the unrestricted striving for the interests of one's own people, thus both belong equally to the genus of egoistic, self-centred ideals.

At first glance, the same holds good for the socialist ideal. In the Marxist version, at least in the first instance, it emphasizes the interests of a particular class, the working class, over those of their structural opponents, the capitalist class. Beyond that, however, Marx attributed a special moral meaning, a special 'virtue', to the egoistic ideal of the working classes and the striving for its realization because it was the egoism of an oppressed and exploited class. In a further flight of his imagination he saw in the conflict between the two industrial classes, so to speak, the last battle of human history in the great fight of the oppressed against the oppressors. To a degree he equated the interests of the workers with the interests of humankind, and prophesied that, after the victory of the workers over the capitalists and after the removal of this form of oppression of one human group by another, humanity would enter a phase of freedom without either oppressors or oppressed. In that context, the self-centredness of individual groups of people as a principle of their action would and should disappear.

The factual course of development has shown that the path towards the reining in and subduing of group self-centredness in the dealings of people with each other is very much more difficult, and takes a lot longer than Marx had thought. His romantic idealism – the idealism of the materialists – blocked his view of the simple fact that the victorious oppressed for their part very quickly become the oppressors, and that the group egoism of their members can be asserted just as ruthlessly as that of their structural opponents.

In spite of that, the Marxist system of thought was able to serve the young post-war middle-class generation in the Federal Republic – and in fact, in many other industrial states of Europe and North America – as a guiding thread for orientating themselves in the social world in which they found themselves. There was nothing else like it – no other theory which described the human world from the perspective of the disadvantaged and the oppressed in one broad stroke and was relatively close to reality. They did not need to concern themselves with the difficulties and contradictions which came to light in attempting to realize his ideal model of a society without oppressors and oppressed. The socialist ideal corresponded to their needs. That Marxist teachings carried within themselves the seeds of a new oppression under the name of the 'dictatorship of the proletariat' was easy to overlook.

One can understand why the need for such an ideal was so strong especially among the young German middle-class intellectual groups of the post-war period. It arose from a process of collective learning: the entry of the German Reich in 1871 into the centuries-long battle for hegemony among the European states had led to the defeat of 1918. An extremely strong ability on the part of broad circles of the German middle class to suppress unwelcome facts from their consciousness enabled them to reinterpret this event as treachery by their class opponents. That relieved them of the trouble of realistically probing, as a means of orientation for the future, the reasons for the defeat. Once again, a German government succeeded in mobilizing the mass of the German people, especially the middle class, for an armed encounter in the name of the nationalist ideal. The hard blow of the second defeat and the excesses of the Hitler period which had been justified by national egoism did indeed then drive a learning process forward. The taken-for-granted character of the egoistic ideal was now shattered, not by argumentation, but by the factual course of social events. As the shock effect of the defeat and its painful aftermath began to die down, it was probably too late for the older generations to attempt a new orientation through which they could have come to terms with the bitter lessons of reality. But the generation of their sons and daughters was not only ready for a new orientation, it demanded one. They recognized very well that one of the tasks which the German past had left to them was to fight against the self-centredness of human groups in their dealings with other groups, and to strive to bring about more humane, less oppressive forms of relations between people.

It is more difficult to grasp that it was not only in the Federal German Republic that the lesson of the excesses of National Socialism influenced the thinking and feelings of young intellectual groups. It had an even broader resonance in other European countries once their victory over Germany turned out very rapidly to be a pyrrhic one. It was not only Germany's dream of national greatness and hegemony which crumbled in the Second World War but the global supremacy of Europe in general – especially of the great imperial countries, Britain and France. In other European states, too, younger generations were growing up who, under the pressure of this crumbling away of national greatness, observed the deeds and ideals of their fathers' generations with critical eyes. Even in the North American states and Japan the example of the second great war in the twentieth century left deep marks, if perhaps in a toned-down form, in the thinking and feeling of the younger generations.[68]

Certainly the balance between national and social ideals, between the dream of greatness for one's own nation and the desire for a less unequal, less oppressive and authoritarian type of social life in human groups, has its peculiarities in every country. But by and large, one can say that, in the more developed countries outside the Soviet Union's sphere of influence, a far-reaching difference with respect to national ideals exists between the experiences of the older generations and those of the generation who grew up in the 1950s and 1960s. As in Germany, the past also throws a shadow over political deeds and thoughts in other European industrial nations. The guilt complex of the younger generations may be particularly pronounced in Germany because of the atrocities of the fathers, but one also encounters it, in degrees and shades which vary according to national historical circumstances, in Britain, France, Holland, Belgium, and perhaps in other European countries. The power-loss which they suffered – the end of European supremacy in the world and the relative rise of previously subordinate and dependent states – led there, too, to attitudes and ideas among their respective younger generations which can be considered as a type of distancing and purification ritual in relation to the sins of their fathers. Their fathers' generations – the ruling Europeans – experienced themselves in the way that established groups are accustomed to doing, not only as more powerful, but at the same time as better and more worthy in human terms; and as a counter-attack against this attitude to power the young post-war generations were in many cases inclined to regard just those groups who are oppressed as better and more worthy in human terms.

Without doubt, the murder of peoples in many European countries in the two great wars of the twentieth century has left a legacy of decided mistrust towards the high-sounding national and patriotic slogans in whose name the peoples went for each other. The mistrust is particularly strong in the Federal Republic. As a reaction to the halo with which the German middle class surrounded the word 'national' up to the end of the Hitler period – as a symbol of their own supremacy within the state as well as of the greatness of their nation in relation to others – the use of this word and its derivatives had now, through mere association with the term 'National Socialism', fallen into such disrepute that one could scarcely use it in the public life of the Federal Republic without rousing the suspicion that one was a latter-day ally of the nationalistic fathers. But even among the younger generations of the middle classes in other countries who are not burdened to the same extent as the Germans with the traumatic memory of past nationalistic excesses, the glorification and taking for granted of one's own nation, and the unbridled pursuit of national self-interest which was previously regarded as the highest rule in dealings between states, have become very subdued since the National Socialist example brought home the dehumanizing consequences of this doctrine if raised to the level of absolute validity.

The rather more critical stance of younger generations of intellectuals towards the unconditional subordination of all other goals to the interests of one's own nation goes, with great regularity, hand in hand with heightened sensitivity to forms of oppression and inequality in the interactions between humans both as groups and individuals. The increased sensitivity in this respect can, but need not, find its expression in adherence to one or another variant of Marxism. Basically, however, this is not simply a question of the adoption of one pattern of thought or another, but is in fact rather a kind of collective learning, a small step in the direction of a less egoistic means of overcoming human problems as a reaction to a terrible explosion of national egoism. This small step can, of course, like any step forwards in the collective learning of humanity, also go into reverse gear again.

Perhaps one should add that the only group of relatively more developed industrial nations which seems so far not to have shared in this learning process (as far as can be ascertained, given their relative impenetrability) is the Soviet Union and its allies. The peculiar intertwining of socialist and nationalist objectives which has occurred in this case apparently enables national interests to be followed unrestrainedly in the name of a socialist ideal. One of the reasons for this is that in those countries generation conflicts are not often openly expressed and hardly any forms of extra-parliamentary opposition can arise. Accordingly, signs of the difference in attitudes and experience between pre-war and post-war generations are only rarely and fleetingly seen there.

11

If, in seeking better understanding for oneself, one attempts to reconstruct what was experienced by the generations in the Federal Republic from which the leading men and women of the left-wing extra-parliamentary opposition and later of the terrorist groups arose, then a peculiar picture emerges. Already at school, so it seems, their sensitivity towards the atrocities of people in their relations with each other, towards the suffering people can inflict upon one another through violence, was sharpened to a considerable degree by their memory of Germany's most recent history. The question of an explanation of their country's shame, which had now become their own shame, weighed upon their consciousness. They felt intensified sensitivity not only towards the atrocities and cruelties which had been committed in Germany's name, but also – if one can for once express it as naïvely as it was perhaps actually experienced by these young people themselves – towards the wickedness of the world in general. Horst Mahler, looking back at this early period of his generation, summed it up on one occasion using Hegel's words 'Anxiety for the well-being of humankind' [*Herzklopfen für das Wohl der Menschheit*], suggesting that he and his age group had, as it were, constructed their own morality. Sensitized by the atrocities of their fathers, they went, as if already fully aware, from school into the wider world and saw that this world was itself full of atrocities:

> The world is bad, every day endless suffering, murder, homicide. We have to change that. It can only be done through violence; it requires sacrifices, but when all is said and done fewer sacrifices than the continuation of the existing conditions.[69]

Here can be seen to some extent the kernel of the experiences which led to terrorism. What emerges is more like an old-style tragedy than a simple crime. The tragic aspect lies in the fact that in a generation of younger people who had begun as selfless idealists, some groups became hardened in the escalating confrontation with the older generation, embodied in the state and police authorities, and at the same time these older people, too, felt pushed into taking increasingly hard and sharp measures against the younger groups. In this case as in others, the self-escalating double-bind process had the effect that each side came more and more to correspond to the negative image which the opposing side had of it. The harder the adults – the police and the courts, but also the law-making parliament and the parties – struck, the more they resembled the demonized image of an inhumane oppressive apparatus. And the more the restless young people fought – in the name of humaneness, social justice and the equality of all people – against a state they felt to be a violent regime of oppressors, the more violent and inhumane they themselves became.

What is easily lost sight of is the fact that both opponents legitimated themselves in their actions by a code of norms, a type of morality. For both, the conviction that they were doing what was morally correct was of great importance. But the content of their normative precepts and the way in which they behaved in terms of them was so different that for each side the other's morality seemed to be the pinnacle of immorality. This conflict was by no means limited to the relatively small groups of politicians and terrorists. This example makes clear a difference between the older and younger generations which was and is responsible to a great extent for the communication difficulties between them.

Older people have, as a rule, made a pact with the imperfection of the human world. They have grown accustomed to compromises with evil. They know about the half-measures of social life, the constant compromises with people's greed and self-interest. They know that nothing in human communal life is done as it actually should be done, that all goodwill remains stuck in the mire of interests, more or less far from the goal. Adults for the most part have tacitly made their peace with the lukewarm compromises of social life. They already know, or believe they know, that one can do nothing about all the evils of humankind.

But these Germans of the younger generations, who went to university after the worst after-effects of the war had been overcome, did not yet know that, or did not want to know it. What they wanted to know was why these awful things had happened in their country and how one could prevent their recurrence, not only in Germany but in the world as a whole. In contrast to the adults, they were not yet prepared to hush up the evils of the world, make compromises with them and shrug their shoulders.

It can be said that the tendency towards uncompromising absolutism in thought and action is a characteristic of young people in general. That is certainly not untrue; but in the case of the generations in the Federal Republic which are under discussion here, this tendency became especially marked and sharp because they had to free themselves from the blemish of their national past, because they found that their uncompromising stance stood in contrast to that of the generations of their fathers who seemed to have made a thousand compromises with the terrible past, who had apparently reconciled themselves to evil. It should not be forgotten that the political structure of the time played a role in this feeling. In the eyes of politically motivated youth, the rule of Adenauer and Erhard still belonged to the old days. But from Brandt and his Social Democrats they expected help in their desire for an uncompromising debate about the violence of the Hitler period, for a thoroughgoing opposition to the traditional ruling classes and an effective reform of the existing regime. The 'grand coalition' government of the two big parties destroyed this hope.

In the conversation between Minister Baum and the former terrorist Mahler, from which I have already quoted a number of times, the memory of this experience still comes out very vividly. The politician had the merits of compromise in mind, the harmfulness of absolute morality. He asks why the middle-class people of the younger generation, who at the time formed the extra-parliamentary opposition, withdrew from discussion with the parties. As he sees it, they were in that way withdrawing themselves from reality:

BAUM   You, Mr Mahler, withdrew into a theoretical discussion then and distanced yourself from reality. You lost touch with real politics, perhaps out of deep disappointment, and you established the incompatibility between your moral demands and reality. You did not consider that moral claims always lag behind reality, everywhere and at all times. The more rigorous they are, the more they lag behind. From this theoretical discussion, individual groups then created the downright cynical desire to provoke the state and to represent it as something they would liked to have had – as fascist.

MAHLER: And the state let itself be provoked.[70]

Here, we gain a momentary glimpse behind the scenes and see how there was set in motion the double-bind process in the course of which groups representing the state and others which feel themselves outside the state drive each other mutually into an escalation of acts of violence.[71]

The difference between the generations does not lie only in the willingness of the older generations to compromise and the relatively uncompromising character of the younger. Their mutual lack of understanding also points to a deep-rooted structural change with respect to what is regarded as morality.

For the older generations, what they understood as morality related centrally to the private sphere of human life – to the sphere in which each individual can make decisions for him- or herself alone. Correspondingly, regulation of sexual behaviour played a particularly important role for them in this connection. Even today, the term 'immoral' seems to a large extent to denote transgressions against codes in the sexual sphere. It is often used synonymously with 'indecent'. But over and above this, it is primarily directed towards the standardization of individual behaviour. On this level, too, so it seems, moral principles can perhaps be regarded as absolutely binding, as uncompromising in their applicability.

The middle-class code of morality with reference to individual behaviour was once very strict, and perhaps still remains so today. But in public life, as any experienced adult knows – and Gerhart Baum, politician and minister, explicitly says so – uncompromising behaviour according to rigorous principles is impossible. It is unrealistic. According to the minister, the more one attempts to master political problems on the basis of absolute moral principles, the further from reality one's behaviour becomes.

The criticism of the younger generations begins at this point. This is where the difference is manifest between what they understand as moral and immoral, and the moral understanding of the older generations. Mahler indicates this indirectly. The willingness to compromise, which the politician defends as realistic, is to Mahler – and in this respect perhaps he is speaking for the younger generation in general – 'the hypocrisy of the politicians':

> As someone who is affected by it, I can only say that the hypocrisy of party politicians, with whom we tried to talk, made a decisive impression on us. Our experience is simply that, although politicians time and time again fall over backwards in approving of the values we stand for, when it comes to political action – even if it were only in the form of consciousness-raising and registering disagreement – they backed off with the flimsiest of excuses, dropped us and betrayed us.[72]

The difference between the two moral codes – originally a generational difference and a focus of a generation conflict – is very significant. What I can say about it here is limited to broad outlines.

A key position in this change is held by the shift in the balance between private and public morality. Without doubt, a standardization of individual behaviour in private situations has been taking place among the younger generations. But one of the most striking differences between the generations is that the importance of the norms regarding people's sexual behaviour has decreased considerably within the total behavioural code. Even if norms in relations between the sexes among the younger generations have by no means disappeared, many norms of the older generations have most certainly either disappeared or been relaxed. The dead weight placed on relations between the sexes by the conventional notion of sin has diminished, and the burden of guilt in this area has become correspondingly lighter. In relations between the sexes, however, new norms are always being formed, and the stronger tendency of younger generations to live together in groups increases the influence of group opinion about what is proper and what is not. This is just one example among many.

What has to be emphasized above all in this connection is the growing significance which the morality of social relations in the public life of states is achieving in contrast to the morality of individual relations in the private sphere. Among the younger generations, problems of social inequality and oppression have moved increasingly to the centre of moral commitment. The absoluteness of the categorical imperative which formerly concentrated on the standardization of individual behaviour is now to be found in the absoluteness of the moral demands made on the behaviour of groups towards other human groups. This is one of the main roots of the misunderstanding between the generations. The quotations from the conversation between the minister and party politician and the former member of the extra-parliamentary opposition and of one of the terrorist groups illustrates these communication difficulties. They illustrate at the same time the peculiar compulsiveness of fate which drives people to actions because of what are – for them – inescapable moral convictions but which are regarded by people generally as immoral and criminal.

Problems of the Extended Youth of Middle-Class Groups

12

I have attempted to show that extra-party political movements, whether of a violent or non-violent type, such as those which emerged in the 1960s and 1970s, arose basically from generation conflicts. In the Federal Republic, the differences in the experience of the pre- and post-war generations, and accordingly also the communication difficulties between them, were particularly large, especially in the middle classes. The tendency of many social scientists to speak of 'the middle classes' or the 'bourgeoisie' as if they were a social formation removed from the diachronic change of society, and accordingly – to express it metaphorically – timeless, hardly does justice to the observable facts. And a good part of the struggle against the bourgeoisie, theoretically much discussed at the time, was in fact a fight of young middle-class outsider groups, not so much – and certainly not necessarily – against their individual fathers and mothers, but instead against the established generation of their fathers and mothers.

It is not easy to perceive the peculiarity of such conflicts in more complex societies. Societies of this type are less bound to tradition than are peasant-agrarian societies and find themselves undergoing transformations accelerated by revolutions and wars. Because they take so many forms, the differences in the needs of younger and older groups in these societies, and the consequent clashes between them, are more difficult to comprehend as generation conflicts. And people today are perhaps also reluctant to see the relationship between the different interdependent generations in a state-society as a process which nearly always entails open and latent struggles for power rather than as the smooth and natural transition often depicted in traditional thinking.

In many simpler societies, these battles have their high point fixed institutionally and sanctified by tradition in *rites de passage* during which, frequently through the fear and suffering to which the elders expose them, the younger members of a society learn very forcibly to submit to the constraints and rules of adult life, whether through self-constraint or through fear of others. In this case, the individual civilizing process, in which the relatively unnormed drive-behaviour of the small child is remodelled in accordance with the rule-pattern of adult behaviour, is crowned by a conversion ceremony which is shrouded in fear, often painful and therefore powerfully impressive, but narrowly limited in time.

By contrast, in the differentiated and complex industrial nations of our times, this process of socially and psychologically becoming adult stretches without a specific institutional framework over a comparatively very long period. The decisive reason can be stated quickly: societies like ours require a very much more all-round civilizing remodelling of drive structures than do simpler societies. The extent, durability and differentiation of drive-controls required for a reasonably successful life as an adult are considerably greater than in societies at an earlier stage of development. The outward sign of the length and complexity of this individual civilizing process which people have to go through in the more developed industrial societies of our era is the unusually long period of learning required of them, and the unusual length of what is considered to be youth. While biological maturity, within a certain margin of variation, is preordained by nature, many young people in our societies do not socially have quite the character of adults ten to fifteen years after this natural stage of growth; that is, they have not quite reached social maturity, and this gap between biological and social maturity has widened further in the course of the twentieth century.

Not so long ago, the temporal discrepancy between the two lines of development led to particular difficulties, because no love relationship was regarded as legitimate unless it was linked to marriage and starting a family. That was especially true for women, but also for men – if less strictly for them. In short, to be socially acceptable, such relationships were linked in middle-class circles to the conditions of social adulthood. The discrepancy between biological and social adulthood at that time brought specific personal problems for young people from good middle-class families, including the problems – which were often understood as purely biological – of the social extension of puberty. If they have not quite vanished, these problems have at least been ameliorated with the spread of coeducational schools and the relaxation of sexual taboos. Other social problems connected with the extension of youth, as well as of old age, are now coming all the more decisively to the fore.

To a great extent this is a question of class-specific problems, or at any rate of problems which are especially strongly pronounced in young university-educated middle-class groups. In these groups, from whose ranks the incumbents of the higher positions in industrial nation-states are increasingly drawn, it is not at all exceptional for young people to be in the position of preparing for their future career until the end of their third decade of life and sometimes for even longer. Even in their careers, 39-year-olds often count as young, if not as youthful. It is frequently regarded as unusual for a person to move into one of the established, commanding positions in the professional or political sectors before the age of 45 or even 50. Often people from this group spend no longer than fifteen to twenty years at the height of their career.

In other words, hand in hand with an extended old age – a consequence of the increased physical security in relatively highly developed industrial societies – there goes an extended youth. It is, to a certain extent, the counterpart of the closure or narrowing of professional as well as political career paths by older, established generations discussed above.

The peculiarity of this long 'youthfulness' and the problem of its social bases perhaps first become fully apparent when it is remembered how different this structuring of human life is from that at earlier stages of social development.[73] In warrior societies, for example in the Arabic, Norman or Turkish armies of conquest, an 18- to 25-year-old could already be a full-blown warrior who had completely absorbed the normative pattern of the adults of his society, its pattern of drive- and affect-controls. The process of remodelling individual drives and affective impulses, the individual civilizing process, was accordingly relatively short. This process lasts so much longer in twentieth-century industrial societies – especially in their higher ranks – because of the increased demands for the remodelling of elementary animalic drives and for the internalization of adult norms required equally by both men and women for life in such a complex and differentiated society.

A peculiar problem comes to light if a connection is made between the younger generations' experiences and ways of behaving, expressed in extreme form in the formation of terrorist groups, and the special qualities and above all the length of the individual civilizing process in contemporary societies. The predominant tendency in coming to grips with such connections social scientifically focuses attention on the acquisition of the older generations' patterns of behaviour and feeling by the younger generations. The concept of 'socialization' is typical of this tendency. It implicitly involves taking it for granted that the adults' edifice of rules is appropriate for those who are growing up. Its acquisition is treated almost exclusively as the problem of the single individual; the central question is whether and to what extent every single member of a younger generation adopts this set of rules as his or her own. Such a perspective hardly facilitates the understanding of generation conflicts as they have been brought out here. For conflicts of this type are lost sight of if one focuses attention on each representative of a younger generation as if he or she could in any sense whatsoever be regarded as a single being existing in isolation.

Characteristic of what happened in the Federal Republic, but also to a degree in other more developed industrial states of Europe and America in the years after the Second World War, is precisely that there appeared on the scene younger generation groups predominantly of middle-class origin who revolted against the older generations and especially against their corpus of norms. They trained their critical sights against the ways of life and the ideals of the older middle-class generations. Instead of taking over their pattern of behaviour and feeling, as the concept of 'socialization' leads one to expect, they began to set up their own pattern in opposition to it.

The younger generations' new patterns were not in any sense created all at once. They were also partly concealed by conventional patterns of thought which could serve as an expression of opposition against the established older middle-class generations. As independent patterns of behaviour and feeling of the young, they usually took form only slowly and rather hesitantly. Certainly, they did not develop solely as the prod-uct of purely intellectual effort, in the form of theoretical doctrines set down in books. To a large extent they grew from people's experiments in their actual life together, often in what they called 'communes'. Such experiments had become necessary because some people were finding the older patterns of life unsatisfactory and because other patterns which might be more satisfactory not only as ideas but also, above all, in practice could only be found through a long process of trial and error.

Seen in this light, the waves of terrorism represented one of these experimental blind alleys. They were an expression of despair by groups of younger people about the resistance of the older generations and about the hopelessness of their battle against the latter's ways of life.

Doubtless in earlier times as well there were social conflicts between the generations, in the course of which a younger, rising generation attempted to rebel against the established code of behaviour and feeling, which was watched over vigilantly by the older generations, and to oppose it with a new code. But as in the current case, the perception of such conflicts as being generation conflicts is made difficult by the fact that the people involved themselves interpret their clashes in a purely impersonal sense – for example, as confrontations between antagonistic or at least incompatible doctrines and ideals. That it is a conflict between adult and younger people may appear marginal at most. The age difference between the main protagonists of the different viewpoints is well known, yet it is not usually recognized that the differences in opinions and ideals are connected with differences in the experiences and interests of older and younger generations.

13

In fact, in the case at hand, the peculiar nature of this conflict only becomes apparent to the researcher when account is taken of the special social situation and the corresponding experiences of the young middle-class generations from the circles of which the extra-parliamentary movement and later also a large proportion of the Federal Republic's terrorists were recruited. One aspect of their social situation, related in turn to structural characteristics of the wider society, needs to be emphasized: the fact that most members of these groups underwent an extended civilizing process which can be observed everywhere in more highly developed industrial societies where direct confrontation with the constraints of occupational work and earning is postponed to between the ages of 25 and 30 or even later. Even today, that is characteristic mainly of people of middle-class origin.

These young men and women, then, had behind them a rather longer period at school than most of their age-peers from working-class homes; and because many of them transferred straight from school to university, their life course was different in a distinctive way from that of working-class children. For the latter, the path from school led more or less directly to a position within the adult world – even if it was a position of very low rank, such as an apprentice. The majority of offspring from workers' families are already seeking paid employment before the age of 20 and – when jobs are available – are accordingly exposed to the peculiar constraints of occupational work at this relatively early age.

By contrast, the young sons and daughters of the middle class who went to university continued to live for the most part on a kind of island of young people: already more or less independent of the parental home, but still outside the realm of adult occupational functions and their particular constraints. That gave them a better chance of organizing themselves as a generation, and of closing ranks with their own goals, ideals and patterns of behaviour against the older generations.

In many cases, their studies were financed by the state – by the society.[74] This money was generally sufficient but meagre, and was often supplemented by paid employment during the holidays. As a group, the students were not poor as they had been in former times. They were not at risk of going hungry and in addition their income was completely secure. They were also covered by social security with regard to illness, accident and every form of inability to work. None the less, they had to make do with relatively little money and with less than their age-peers in the factories. Sometimes, their time at university was one in which their standard of living fell in comparison with that enjoyed in their parents' middle-class home. Thus, their income was one of the lowest in their society; on the other hand, their expectations for their own future, and also the status they claimed, were among the highest.

A further distinguishing feature of the situation of these students was that, in relation to the older-generation established groups of their society, they represented an outsider group. To a limited extent they were able to increase their power-potential by organizing themselves in groups, or taking action *en masse*. But, as already remarked, one of the structural givens of industrial societies – and indeed of most societies – is that all decisive positions of power and command are reserved for the older generations, and that the younger generations, even when they unite, remain relatively powerless outsiders.

One cannot help thinking that the growing sensitivity to social problems – particularly those such as poverty and oppression – and the greater willingness to identify with outsider groups were, among other things, also determined by this peculiar situation – by the situation of a group of people who were provided for, adequately but meagrely, by an anonymous society with which they had impersonal dealings via civil servants and often incomprehensible regulations.

The problems emerging from all this made themselves felt in the

Federal Republic when the economic reconstruction after the destruction of the war had progressed sufficiently far. The young generations of this period had a better chance than their predecessors to debate the fate and significance of their country. Through the memory of the recent past, they were particularly sensitive to authoritarian constraints, to oppression of one human group by another. In addition, their own state had a very long tradition as an authoritarian and police state. This tradition was deeply ingrained in the personality structure of its members, and therefore in their behaviour in their dealings with each other. Because they felt themselves to be free from any share of the blame for the offences committed by their fathers, it was accordingly to some extent easier for the post-war generations which were growing up when things were improving again for the defeated country to distance themselves from this inheritance and to confront the established older generations on a number of fronts, especially at the universities and on the level of state and party politics in an open, at first non-violent, power struggle.

To the younger generations, striving to rid themselves of the stigma of their nation, all members of the older generations, the middle-class establishments in business or the universities, in the state or in the parties, seemed suspect even if they had personally had no part in the shameful acts of violence of the past. Collectively, as the younger people saw it, they shared the blame for not preventing the advent of the inhumane regime. If the development in the direction of a violent state should ever be repeated, would the older generations who had failed last time now know better how to counter the danger? And what they were striving for socially and politically, was it not simply just an improved version of the Weimar Republic – that is, a return to the same forms of political life which had given the dictator his chance and so led to catastrophe? Their moral authority was also weakened in the eyes of the rising generations because they were unable to come up with any new way forward.

Sensitive to all signs of authoritarian oppression, these younger groups saw such signs in all the constraints to which they were exposed. In the Western successor state of the old Reich, just as in other states, there was no shortage of such constraints.

14

The relative freedom from the constraints of paid occupational work which was characteristic of a growing number of young people of middle-class origin by no means meant that they were free from social constraints in general. In their case, these were of a different sort. The constraints arising from law-makers distributing student grants like an anonymous financier, the constraints imposed by the institutions of higher education or the distant Ministry of Education which laid down curricula and examinations – these differ quite considerably from the constraints imposed, for example, by office work in constant, direct reach of superiors and colleagues. Compared with office workers, students have considerably greater scope for the individual pursuit of knowledge and their own ideas.

The men and women of our time who pursue their studies from the end of the second decade of their life, often until the end of the third decade, form their own kind of society – a student society which has no less specific structures than, for instance, a court society – the development of which can be traced back into the Middle Ages. Its members, as far as can be seen, have always found themselves in a peculiar state of suspension, a state of expectation: they have already left their families, their childhood and early youth behind them, and become people who more or less look after themselves and have to find their own way through the labyrinth of social life. But although released from the close bonds of their family, they are not yet chained to other people through the almost equally close bonds of an adult occupation and its constraints. For both men and women, the centre of their social-convivial life lies within their circle of age-peers and fellow students, where a distinctive subculture develops with a code of behaviour and feeling which can either agree in all particulars with the established code of the older generation in their country or be in sharp contrast to it.[75] And they are still busy learning.

The length of their period of learning or apprenticeship is a consequence of the fact, too often taken for granted, that knowledge in many fields has both expanded and become more complex and differentiated. Through its increased diversity, the demands on what is called in German *Bildung* rise at the same time: demands for the broad orientation which, in large and complex societies such as ours, every specialist needs over and above his or her specialist knowledge. This circumstance, too, contributes to the lengthening of the period of learning. Although the academic institutions themselves, thanks to a tradition of extreme specialization, are hardly adequate for fulfilling this function, so that much is left to the initiative of individuals, they nevertheless offer – at least to those students who are ready for it – considerable opportunities for learning and thinking on their own and a not inconsiderable amount of spare time in which to do so.

Something else is especially characteristic of the peculiar constraints to which students are subject. The adult occupations for which they are preparing require not only a very broad and comprehensive knowledge but, over and above this, the acquisition of a type of knowledge which those who are learning cannot acquire if they are driven to work only by the fear of others. It is, in other words, a type of knowledge the acquisition of which requires, besides all external constraints, a high degree of self-constraint in addition. This accords with the organization of the universities, which does not make the transition any easier for the young people: schoolteachers concern themselves a great deal with whether their pupils work or not, university teachers comparatively little; and examinations, which certainly represent external constraints, belong to a type of external constraints which are only effective if they are supplemented by very strong self-constraint.

For those who have at their command enough self-discipline, for instance in the form of intellectual concentration, there beckons the chance of an adult profession ranking relatively high – in prestige, and usually in income too – in the occupational hierarchy of their society. But the route from the peculiar intermediate stop in the universities where these young people find themselves to the destination of their later occupations is full of risks, traps, uncertainties and dangers. The adult positions for which they are striving may be occupied for many years by older people, and thus career paths leading to them may be blocked. Or the individual student may fall behind in the overt or covert competition with his or her companions. Or the self-constraint necessary for concentrating on work may suffer under the special temptations of student sociability.

Moreover, whatever those concerned themselves say and think, student existence is not just an intermediate stop, a first-class waiting room in which one lingers awhile until the train continues its journey. As an educative and formative period, it does indeed have its own, highly autonomous value, insofar as it gives young people, independent from their families for the first time, the opportunity to put both the world and themselves to the test, and to discover for themselves their own general orientating principles. In the past, these principles of orientation to the world were primarily religious and philosophical; even in the social and political debates of the time, the position a person adopted often took on a religious guise. In the present, it is usually quite directly the principles of this-worldly education, an orientation in the seemingly higgledy-piggledy structures of the human world, that are developed in this period of life.

It is precisely in this respect that the relationships and conflicts between the older, established generations and the younger, outsider generations at the universities play a significant role. Understandably, these relationships are nearly always ambivalent. The mere fact that they involve mutual, but unequal and highly complex, dependencies contributes to this. The older generations, here as elsewhere, have control over chances of access to resources and opportunities which can serve to satisfy the needs of the younger. They have at their disposal a kind of monopoly of these chances. Among them are, above all, parts of the fund of knowledge of their society. But something else which lies in the hands of the older generation, and constitutes one of the means by which younger people's needs can be satisfied, is the positive or negative human image which those who teach – following on from the parents – present to those who learn. So, too, does their function in the individual civilizing process as fear- or anxiety-provoking assistants in the development of self-constraints on the part of the students.

Conversely, however, the teachers and older generations of a society are in general dependent on the up-and-coming generations precisely because it is on them that the future of their society depends. The younger are quite literally the future of the older. They will occupy tomorrow the adult positions occupied today by the older generations. The social decisions which are today characteristically reserved for members of the older generations will be taken tomorrow by members of today's younger generations – unless the division of power between the generations changes radically. And although at present the older generations' power superiority is so great because many power positions are open only to them, their power-ratios are nevertheless limited by the fact that all their efforts and work will be in vain if the members of the younger generations who will take their place tomorrow devalue the results of their efforts and work by making wrong decisions.

Viewed statically, the younger generations may seem to be highly dependent in the social structure on the older; viewed dynamically, the imbalance in the power-ratios between them is nowhere near so great. But the tendency of many human groups to exploit here and now the power chances that fall their way because of their position, without thinking about the future of the group, can often be observed in the relationship between older and younger generations. That is especially true in a state with such a strong and long-established tradition of command and obedience as Germany. In the relationship between the generations, too, the revolt by groups of younger people against the norms of their elders, and their emphatic rejection of many of the rules of the political game, can easily seem to be an intolerable provocation to state authority. In the trials of strength between older representatives of state authority and rebellious groups of young people, the former often forget that the latter are among those who will be involved in the life of their society when they themselves are dead.

Terrorism, National Pride and National Civilizing Patterns

15

There are generational chains in which the older and the younger clearly have the same orientation culturally and politically, and others in which the younger generations deliberately set new patterns of orientation in opposition to the patterns associated with their established older counterparts. The extra-parliamentary opposition and the terrorists of the Weimar Republic are an example of the first type, those of the Bonn Republic an example of the second.

I have already said that the generation conflict over orientations, beliefs and political ideals in the Federal Republic cannot be fully understood if one does not keep in mind that analogous conflicts can be observed in nearly all the more developed non-dictatorial states, especially in the industrial nation-states of Europe.[76] They are largely related to the fact that the Second World War in certain respects signified a deeper break in the development of this group of states than did all earlier European wars and revolutions. In its wake not only the smaller and middling European states but also the largest and most powerful experienced a radical change in their position in the global hierarchy of peoples; they lost the hegemonial position among the peoples of the world which they had until then occupied for centuries, and sank to become at best powers of the second rank. How such a loss of status affects the people who form these states cannot be discussed in detail here. It must be enough to continue the line of thinking begun earlier into the significance that it had for the relationship between the older and the younger generations.

The national pride of the older generations was often scarcely affected by the change in their country's power-ratio and status. They had received their education and their personal stamp before the war. Their we-image as British, French, Italians or Germans had been formed at this time, and since such a we-image is built deep into individuals' sense of self-esteem and personality structure, even in this case it remained relatively uninfluenced by changing reality. Their coolly rational knowledge of their country's decreased status and its reduced power-ratio relative to others hardly affected their warm national consciousness; their national pride remained by and large intact. It was otherwise with those who were born during or after the war. Yet there were considerable differences between the particular European nations in this respect.

The British post-war generations, for example, were certainly aware of their country's changed power position in the world after the war of 1939–45, and this knowledge certainly influenced their self-esteem as British people.[77] But in Britain, the high sense of worth people felt in belonging to the nation was particularly stable – perhaps more stable than in any other European country. This collective awareness of their own worth was not like a political idea to be stirred up by party propaganda. It referred and refers to a widespread and taken-for-granted feeling that it is better to be British than French, German or whatever – a feeling that does not need any reasons and also no special emphasis.[78] Its emergence was linked to a centuries-long and continuous process of state-formation, and with the country's increasingly powerful position and rising wealth. The growing interdependence and integration of the various strata and regions also played a decisive role in the double process of nation-building and development of a feeling of solidarity which encompasses the nation. In addition, this feeling in British people receives special support and confirmation from a highly pronounced but comparatively unobtrusive behavioural code, which in the end serves as a shibboleth: it can be used to test the reactions of a stranger, and people who react correctly are recognized effortlessly as British, those who react differently as foreigners.[79]

This has to do with a national pattern of behaviour and a closely connected we-image, deeply anchored in the individual personality structure, which represents at the same time both an integral element of the identity of each person, a reliable symbol of a person's belongingness to a group, and also the common identity of its members. This behavioural pattern and we-image also play a part in the conscience, insofar as it incorporates certain precepts as to how one should and should not behave as a British person ('it isn't done').

The British example of the relationship between national sentiment, national behaviour patterns and national conscience-structure allows me to introduce into the discussion of the sociogenesis of terrorism in the Federal Republic a problem which could easily escape attention if one looked at German terrorism in isolation. One needs also from time to time to cast a glance at the question of just why it was in Germany – in contrast with Britain, for example – that protest groups of the post-war generation opted for violent forms of political activity. What I have to say about this is a suggestion – or, if one insists, an hypothesis – which is perhaps worthy of more detailed examination.

Murder, arson and robbery as vehicles for achieving political goals mean a breaching of the state monopoly of physical force, the maintenance of which guarantees that people within a state can live together relatively peacefully and free of violence. A high degree of internal pacification is a prerequisite for the complex framework of functions of an industrial nation-state. The violent strategy of terrorist groups was a deliberate attack on the continued existence of the state monopoly of force, and was directed as it were at the heart of the state, for when this monopoly becomes unable to function and crumbles, then sooner or later the state will crumble too.[80] But breaching the monopoly requires at the same time the breaching of individual barriers against violent actions inside the state, incorporated as part of the normal pattern of conscience-formation in each and every member from childhood onwards. And since the necessity to abstain from violence within states is one of the fundamental elements of what we call 'civilized behaviour', and since civilizing processes and state-formation processes are in fact intimately interwoven with each other, terrorist movements represent regressive movements in the context of the civilizing process. They have an anti-civilizing character.

This statement certainly contains nothing that the terrorist groups themselves would have accepted as a counter-argument to their way of acting. Their argument was that the Federal German state and its civilization deserved nothing more than to be destroyed by any means available. Since they believed they could reach this goal only with the help of acts of violence, they became terrorists.

In Britain, too, young middle-class groups appeared on the scene with more or less revolutionary ideas. They, too, most decisively rejected and fought against their social order because of its injustice. But to my knowledge, none of them went as far as the German terrorists. There was no movement which sought to shake the structure of the state through hostage-taking, murder, arson and robbery. My hypothesis is that the limiting of extra-parliamentary opposition groups in Britain – just as in France or Holland, for instance – to more or less non-violent and to that extent legal forms of opposition is linked, among other things, to the unbroken stability of national feeling in these countries. What a man like Orwell, for example, stated with reference to the first decades of the twentieth century – that in Britain there is a very solid feeling of nationality transcending all class conflicts and a shared national pride besides – still probably holds for the 1980s, although under the pressure of the reality-shocks which have robbed Britain of much of its earlier glory, the protective covering of civilization seems to be coming loose. No one can foresee if and for how long the traditional form of British national pride will survive these blows. But for the time being one has the impression that the feeling of great value attached to a person being British remains intact. Apparently it also remains intact for the younger groups who are highly critical of the country's existing social order. There is still a clear connection between national pride and civilizing self-restraint, which does not allow the idea of murder and robbery as vehicles of political struggle to come to the surface.

National pride and the civilizing transformation of the individual person stand in a curious relationship with each other. Even in simple tribes, the civilizing remodelling that leads from the free run of drives in small children to the acquisition of the drive-control pattern of adults entails considerable difficulties, all sorts of anxieties, sufferings and torments; and in the more developed societies this process is not only especially long, in line with the relatively high level of civilization, but also especially arduous. The risk involved is always considerable. What is decisive in the end is, to put it briefly, the balance between the denial of drives imposed upon a person in the course of the individual civilizing process, and the gain in pleasure facilitated or opened up by this. If all the needs and wishes of a small child could be immediately fulfilled, it would remain a small child as a person even when it grew physically. Reward and denial – the carrot and the stick – both play a role in the impetus of the formation of an adult person capable of controlling and modifying impulses and drives according to the norms of the adult world. Maintaining the civilizing self-controls once they have already developed also requires pleasurable rewards of one sort or another as a counterweight. National pride, a more encompassing form of self-love, can serve as one such reward. Britain is just one of many examples of this complementarity between national pride and the following of a specific national pattern of norms in behaviour and feeling.

The solidly based and highly distinctive patterns of civilization which developed in countries like Britain and France over the centuries in the course of notably long and continuous state-formation processes and which led gradually to great power status – despite all the problems of declining in power in the period after 1945 – enabled even the post-war generations to see themselves as part of the national chain of generations, and to attach meaning and value to this taken-for-granted national identity. The emotional reward which the individual received from his or her share in the collective value of the nation may have become less, and, compared with what those who grew up before the war were endowed with, perhaps also somewhat more dubious. Nevertheless, despite all upheavals, the value and meaning of a national identity and the corresponding pattern of civilization remained relatively unproblematic in these countries. Only experience will reveal what the longer-term effects of the fading of meaning-fulfilment connected with belonging to a nation will be, whether and to what extent national ideals and patterns of conscience – together with the self-denials they impose on each person – can retain their strength if the affective rewards of national pride are reduced. Up till now, the continuing conflict between pre-war and post-war generations which also occurred in Britain and France has made a break in the continuity neither of state-formation, nor of the development of the national pattern of civilization.

In Germany, too, as in all highly industrialized nation-states, adult life requires a far-reaching civilizing transformation of the structure of individual drives. But the pleasure premium which plays a role in many other more developed states in the maintenance of civilizing self-constraints and denials, the reward given by a feeling of the special value of being a member of a nation remains, in the case of citizens of the Federal Republic, fairly limited – insofar as it exists at all. In the upper ranks of the world's hierarchy of states, there is hardly another state whose members have such a vague and relatively colourless we-image as the Federal Republic's. Germany is, in this respect, an unfortunate country.[81] Two fateful waves of nationalism that went far beyond the actual capacities of the country, and two serious defeats, have left an inheritance of confusion and, in many cases, a negative national sentiment. After the extreme nationalism of the Hitler period and the excessive self-satisfaction of national pride – the collective narcissism – which it offered and allowed the German people, there followed after the catastrophe a hardly less extreme reaction in the other direction. What followed was not really a cool taking stock of things. Instead, there came a period of disorientation, with a strong tendency to self-stigmatization and in some cases self-hate.

It is not improbable that the completely unrestricted damnation of the Federal Republic by members of the extra-parliamentary opposition, especially the terrorist groups, is related, among other things, to this loss of a positive national we-image: 'For us', declares Horst Mahler for instance,[82] 'the state was the absolute enemy.' Along with the disappearance of the loaded expression 'nation' – or even 'national consciousness' and 'national' – from publicly acceptable ways of talking, the matter of a national we-image had almost totally disappeared from the younger generation's store of experience.[83]

I do not believe that it would have been impossible to bestow a positive meaning on the West German state for its younger generations. One could imagine a movement whose members said to each other, 'States throughout the world are apparatuses of compulsion; and since at the present stage of development one cannot depend on all the members of a state having the self-discipline necessary for a flourishing life together, one cannot for the moment do without the police and similar organizations of external constraint to safeguard German social life. But the best way to purify and free us from the memory of the cancerous growth which the German state became in the Hitler era is to create an exemplary and humane state – a state which values educating people to awareness of the fact that a peaceful and friendly co-existence of millions of people is not possible without a considerable degree of self-discipline and mutual consideration and in which not even the police let themselves be provoked into inhumane acts of violence by the inhumanity of criminals.' Certainly, this sort of thing could not be achieved in a day or a year. But a decisive break with the tradition of the authoritarian state, an unwavering experimental humanizing of all aspects of the state – the parties, the bureaucracy and the military included – would certainly have been just as useful and welcome as a means of cleansing the state of the stigma of the past. It would at the same time have served as a vehicle bestowing meaning on state and nation in the present and the future. A humane state – really there is still no such thing in the world.[84]

16

Even in those European countries which had undergone a continuous state-formation process and rise towards great power status, there were undoubtedly signs of an incipient erosion of the national pattern of civilization and symptoms of its crumbling. The strength of their pattern of civilization was related above all to the length and continuity of the state-formation process in the context of which it had been formed. But the reversal of the direction of this movement after 1945 – when a decline set in, even if it still remains moderate – entailed a shock in these countries too, and led to evident and to some extent quite serious conflicts between the younger post-war and older pre-war generations. In these countries, too, members of the younger generations demanded a partial revision of taboos which appeared sacrosanct to many members of the older generations.

So far as the differences or even the contradictions between the respective normative patterns in this deep-seated generation conflict are concerned, remarkable similarities exist in all the European countries in which it can be observed. Especially in the field of sexual morality, the younger generations oppose the code of the older with their own pattern. But the moral commitment of the younger generation regarding questions of social inequality is also greater to an extraordinary degree. Everywhere they show a deliberate neglect, perhaps also a certain contempt, for the subtleties of form in social intercourse – for instance in the precise gradation of bows and curtsies – especially insofar as these formalities seem to symbolize differences of power, rank and prestige.[85] Finally, a more intensive support for the cause of the oppressed in their fight against oppressors, for the weaker against the superior power of the stronger, is another element in the syndrome of norms which weigh more heavily with the post-war generations than with those who grew up before the war.

This change in the moral commitment of European generations is easily understandable. To summarize once again what has already been said: the grandfathers and fathers who grew up before the war had an individual morality which related to the behaviour and feelings of persons, especially in private life. The hegemonial position *vis-à-vis* less powerful groups in other countries or in one's own country scarcely fell within the field of moral demands, or did so only insofar as it related to individual behaviour. These generations mostly accepted power differences in the relationships between groups, including their own social supremacy and the advantages it incurred, as self-evident, without critically examining them. The loss of European predominance in many parts of the world forced the post-war generations to examine recent history. Involuntarily in doing so, sons and grandsons sat in judgement upon their fathers and grandfathers. They themselves often began their independent paths in life as outsiders and dependants. For them there was no longer any chance – or only a much reduced chance – of treading in the footsteps of their fathers as lords and masters over other human groups. As members of European countries whose power-ratios in relation to other peoples had visibly diminished, they experienced the dominance of their fathers as an injustice that had been perpetrated on less powerful groups. In the confrontation with their fathers, the sons stood firmly and unambiguously on the side of the oppressed.

17

In view of these elements which the different countries have in common, the question arises as to why the eventual impasse of the predominantly young middle-class opposition movement – after some considerable partial successes – led in two nations, Italy and Germany, to the emergence of terrorist groups which sought to force through by violent means the goal of a transformation of society which was unattainable by peaceful means. And why, in other countries, despite a structurally similar generation problem, did the step into illegality, the transition to the use of physical violence – in short, the formation of indigenous terrorist groups – not occur? It is this question, so it seems to me, which one cannot answer without referring back to the different patterns of state-formation processes and the related differences in national civilizing patterns.

Italy and Germany are the two latecomers in the group of European great powers – latecomers in the process of state centralization and unification as nations. This process was delayed in both of these successor states to the Holy Roman Empire of the German Nation, in contrast particularly with Britain and France, because the extraordinary size of this medieval empire had favoured the formation of independent units in the form of kingdoms, duchies, free city-states, and so on. The consequences were deep and far-reaching.

In both cases the integration, desired especially by urban middle strata, was fundamentally achieved by kings and their armies, by the use of violence of one sort or another. In both – like a hat with which one keeps one's hair in place, or like iron scaffolding around a ruined building – the state was regarded as an autonomous social edifice existing outside and beyond the citizens, as 'they' and not as 'we'. Since they succeeded in entering the phase of highly centralized nation-states only very late and with extreme effort, Italians as well as Germans suffered from an almost chronic uncertainty over their own self-worth as nations. This was frequently expressed in extreme vacillations between over-valuation and under-valuation. Accordingly, the dialectical sinking of the national sense of self-worth in the extra-parliamentary opposition of the Federal Republic in the 1960s, after its over-elevation in the pre-war years under Hitler's rule, is only one example of many. In both countries, moreover, pacification was recent, again in accordance with the fate of latecomers. Just as labile as national pride was the pattern of self-control supported by external state control, which held people back in their dealings with each other from the use of physical violence in the case of conflicts. Nothing illustrates the fragility of built-in civilizing controls against the use of violence better than the fact that, in both cases, social conflicts largely arising from tensions between the middle class and organized workers were ended by the use of violence.[86]

In their struggle during the First World War to catch up and gain a 'place in the sun', Germany and Italy lost out, and this setback in the elimination struggles of the nations left behind, especially in the middle classes of both states, a considerable amount of bitterness and resentment. Mussolini was the first to understand how to mobilize this wounded national pride or national resentment for his own rise to power, and Hitler undoubtedly learned from the experiences of Italian fascism. But in practice, in his attempt to profit from the Italian example, something else came about – something that was characteristic of the specific pattern of development of the German state and the tradition of feeling and behaviour linked to it.

Besides the similarities, there are also in fact very significant differences between the two successor states of the medieval empire.[87] Even at the height of their power, Mussolini and his followers did not receive anything like the enthusiastic reception from the mass of Italian people that Hitler and his followers did at the height of theirs in Germany. Above all, it must be said that the Italian fascist movement, certainly violent enough, never brought into play the same extent of methodical violence as its German counterpart. The apparently completely unemotional, coolly planned murder of millions of people that has entered history as the hallmark of the National Socialist movement was not one of the traits of Italian fascism.

The peculiarity of what developed in Germany was not the systematic, illegal use of violence *per se* by an initially extra-parliamentary organization. Nor was it the further use of physical violence after the seizure of power in order to strengthen the regime and destroy its foes. There are precedents for this in all other states. What is unique, and for which a convincing explanation is still lacking, is precisely the extent of the planned murder of people who could offer no resistance; murders, moreover, for which even today it is scarcely possible to recognize any reason that could be called 'realistic' or 'rational' – for instance in the sense of a benefit or advantage for the society or the regime that measured up to the costs necessarily incurred in the organization of the killing. What remains a problem, and for which we still lack an explanation, is the enormous mass murder in the service of something that has been called either a theory or a political creed and ideal, that is to say, mass murder in the service of a utopia, the dream of a great empire in Europe under the rule of the Germans or people of German descent. This mixture of quasi-scientific, pseudo-rational ideal and absolutely uncompromising violence – whose human victims were for those who perpetrated the violence really only impersonal things, treated like materials in a factory in order to turn them into useful objects such as soap, bone-meal or animal food, and were basically only symbols in a theory for those who killed them – remains an open question to this day.

Recalling this problem is not irrelevant, because a related mentality is found in some terrorist groups of the later period. Among them, too, the feeling that their victims were human beings, the ultimate identification of a person with his enemies, was lost in the course of time. In this case, too, for the perpetrators of the violence the victims merely represented symbols in the framework of a theory – representatives of a collectivity no longer experienced as humans but perceived only as symbolic representatives of a social category which has been proved by a specific system of argumentation to deserve destruction.

In order to explain this peculiar feature of National Socialism and later also of Federal German terrorism, it is necessary to broaden the perspective to take into account the peculiarity of the German pattern of development and its related pattern of civilization. One then immediately becomes aware of how far from linear, how full of spurts backwards and forwards, is German development. In contrast, for instance, to Britain, the historical fate of the Germans has prevented a long, continuous process of state-formation in one direction; and, in the struggle between centripetal and centrifugal interest groups, between tendencies towards state integration and disintegration, first one and then the other has gained the upper hand. Here, too, the structure of state development and that of national traditions of behaviour and feeling are very closely bound up with each other. This can be seen particularly clearly if one looks at the relationship between, on the one hand, state-formation processes and the pacification of the citizens of a state, and, on the other hand the stability of the built-in mechanisms of self-control which regulate and perhaps prevent the use of violence in case of conflict. Admittedly, the difficulties arising from the partial discontinuity of German development have contributed to the fact that the development of the German pattern of civilization has remained relatively unresearched. For the moment, it is only possible to offer suppositions on this score.

What soon becomes apparent is the contrast between the relatively low evaluation of warlike deeds, military virtues and violent behaviour generally by the circles who set the tone of the German middle class in the second half of the eighteenth century, the period of the great classical German poets and thinkers, and the comparatively high evaluation of warlike deeds and other state-sanctioned forms of violence in the period of the *Kaiserreich* and then during the rise of the Third Reich. It seems as if the entry of the unified Germany into the elimination contests of the great powers may have weakened the civilizing barriers of self-constraint against the use of violence in human relations. The importance of duelling – which was not limited to serious affairs of honour, as for instance in France, but was part and parcel, so to speak, of the daily life of most members of the student associations – was only one symptom of the strength of the tradition of military violence which was embedded in the specifically German pattern of civilization as it developed especially after 1871. The connection with the pattern of the German state-formation process, the late unification through force of arms, is obvious.[88]

Above all, however, the battle for national causes justified every use of acts of violence. It brought into the German tradition of behaviour and feeling, so it seems, a note of calculated brutality in the service of a cause.

In the age of the military aristocracy's predominance, this calculated brutality was still restrained by the obligations of the code of honour of the upper classes. For Hitler and his helpers, who were not born in the purple and who had struggled hard to rise, such gentlemanly barriers no longer played any role. They went unconditionally on the hunt for power and greatness, using every means and at any price. This included the unconditional use of physical violence, unhampered by gentlemanly codes and scruples of conscience. In their striving to realize their dream of the Third Reich – note, the Third *Kaiserreich* – all civilizing constraints of honour and morality became inconsequential.

Italian nationalism legitimated itself by an appeal to the greatness of the ancient Roman Empire and the culture of Roman antiquity; German nationalism legitimated itself by an appeal to the Germanic tribes of the time of the great migrations, who, as barbarians had played a part in the downfall of the Roman Empire. This difference in the models which embodied the respective national ideals is not without significance for the level of civilization of the two dictatorial movements, Fascism and National Socialism. In the one case, an imperial state and its culture were held up as a model for the leading men; in the other, it was the idea of a race destined by nature to rule the world which they took as their model. The desperate mobilization of the entire population to fight for the great prize of the global empire dreamed of by Germany's last 'monarch', this *parvenu* 'Kaiser', then led on the political level to the abandoning of all self-constraints, even against the most inhumane acts of violence, as long as they appeared to be serving the desired goal, the building of a racially pure German empire.

The appeal of this dream-goal to national self-love also makes it understandable why the mass of the population so willingly subordinated themselves to the command of the great Führer and his staff. The way the German people were almost totally brought into line in the framework of the Hitler regime is not explained solely by the use of all the means of enforcement that were available to those in power at that time against those who did not conform; it is explained above all by the gratifying rewards National Socialism promised its followers in return for the often severe sacrifices they made in its service. For those who obeyed the Führer's orders, there beckoned the great prize of ruling over all other peoples of Europe as a member of a new European elite, a new aristocracy. This promise made the self-denial of individuals, including their complete submission to the command of higher-ranking superiors and ultimately of the Führer himself, seem worthwhile. In other words, in this state structure, command by the Führer took the place of personal conscience in all political affairs.

18

The personality structure of people whose self-regulation is to a large extent dependent on external constraints, that is, on directives from other people, and who for their part are accustomed to pass on directives in the form of orders to others, is often described and discussed in the framework of a theory of the authoritarian personality.[89] The implicit fundamental assumption of this theory is that people, as a result of a specific family structure when they are growing up, develop the syndrome of the character structure corresponding to it. This explanation does not need to be discarded but it is not adequate. The authoritarian family structure is itself very closely linked with the authoritarian structure of the state. In order to recognize this, it is necessary to look at the state organization as an organization in the process of becoming, as an aspect of a long-term process.

Germany was subject to absolutist rule until 1918 – despite some limitations on this in the unified Reich after 1871, when political parties gained in power. The personality structure of the Germans was attuned to this absolutist tradition, unbroken through the centuries. In addition, military forms of superordination and subordination, command and obedience, served widely as models for human relationships in other spheres. They were perceptible in the behaviour of the civil service hierarchy, the police, and most definitely also in the family. In all these, and some other areas too, the models of the authoritarian state played a central role.

Only when one is clear how deeply the behaviour and feeling of the Germans in their relations with each other were pervaded by models of the authoritarian state, and what sort of key position in this structure was held by the man at the top, the highest commander, can one quite appreciate the difficulties of the German people after the Kaiser's abdication in 1918. Before the First World War, the Kaiser/King still possessed many of the prerogatives of an absolute ruler: he decided on war and peace, he nominated the senior military men, the top of the administration, and above all the members of the government. The repugnance felt by many Germans when, after his disappearance, they were confronted for the first time with the task of deciding, without the supreme commander-in-chief, without orders from above, by whom they should be ruled did not arise solely from horror that the 'poor', the workers, now also had a right to participate in government and that, accordingly, men of low rank were exercising government functions. Their reaction was at the same time an expression of the fact that, suddenly, a central figure in the social scene to whom their personality structure was attuned was no longer there. His place was taken by figures who corresponded to neither their emotional needs nor their type of behavioural code. The Kaiser had served not least as a symbol of one of the many positive feelings woven into their we-image. Ebert as German president could no longer fulfil this function, and this was the case in many respects with the new regime as a whole. It had great instrumental meaning – or, more precisely, it could have had if, to begin with, the German people had placed any importance on an institution-alized form of self-government serving a purpose as best as possible. But the emotional satisfaction, the satisfaction it offered to the longing for a symbolic protector figure, a supreme father or mother, was minimal.

The strength of the emotional opposition to the parliamentary arrangements, an opposition which had already emerged a few months after the end of the war, was certainly very closely connected with specific class conflicts. But to explain them, it is not enough to point to quasi-rational interests or a lack of clear insight into the advantages of a 'democratic' system of government. In order to understand the deep antagonism of many Germans to the Weimar Republic, one has to take into account the fact that, for a parliamentary regime to be able to function effectively, quite specific personality structures are a precondi-tion and that these form only gradually in connection with the practice of parliamentary politics itself.

The transition from the still semi-absolutist regime of the Kaiser/King to the parliamentary regime of the Weimar Republic came very suddenly. For broad circles of the population, it came quite unexpectedly and with highly unpleasant associations with a defeat in war. Basically, many Germans abhorred a form of government geared to struggles, nego-tiations and compromises between parties. They hated the 'talking shop' of parliament, where – so it seemed – all was words and no action. Freedom or no freedom, they yearned for the comparatively much simpler and uncomplicated form of rule in which all important political decisions were made by the strong man at the top. One could quietly leave worrying about Germany's weal or woe to him. It was enough if one limited oneself to one's own private life. From the first beginnings of the Weimar period, many men and women did indeed long for the man at the top, whether prince or dictator, who made the decisions and gave orders. They craved for such a man as for a drug. They were accustomed to it, and the withdrawal came much too quickly.

The characteristics involved in being attuned to a parliamentary regime are easily overlooked if, as often happens, this form of social life is viewed ideologically, solely with regard to its rational advantages over, for instance, dictatorial forms. Becoming accustomed to doing without an order of things in which a symbolic ruling figure bears the responsibility for a nation of subjects, and adjusting to a regime which lays however limited a responsibility on each person, is a lengthy process that requires conditions that are as crisis-free as possible and takes at least three generations. There are many examples in European history of the difficulties of such a reorientation. One of the few countries in which, so far, a parliamentary state structure and an individual personality structure have become attuned to each other in a comparatively friction-free way is Britain. The long process through which this attunement was reached can be clearly traced in British history. In fact, it has been happening very slowly since the time when the son of the puritan dictator had to give up the reins of government to the newly installed king who, however, inherited considerably reduced power-chances.[90]

Some thoughts on why this adjustment between political and personality structures is so difficult may be useful. Here again, the theory of civilizing processes points the way. A personality structure attuned to an absolutist-monarchic or dictatorial regime allows great scope for a readiness in the individual person to accept orders, to allow him- or herself to be guided by external constraints. The individual citizen is then spared the heavy burden of having to participate in debates with people of different opinions. The ruled do not need to decide in favour of one side or the other. The order comes from above; the decision has been made. Under a regime of this type, the individual person still remains in a child-like status in relation to the state. Parental orders are certainly not always comfortable, and the same is also true of the orders of aristocratic princes and dictators. But in the end one trusts them. And if one does not obey, the military or the police, which are among the main pillars of the organization of a monolithic autocratic state, will quickly step into action. The personality structure of the individual person may be adapted to a hierarchy of command and obedience; but in order to make quite sure, autocratic rulers usually use their unrestricted right of disposal over the state's monopoly of force to create the most airtight surveillance apparatus possible, an apparatus of external constraint that ensures that the individual does not go astray.

If one looks at autocratic forms of government of a monarchic or dictatorial type and parliamentary forms of government with at least two competing parties as phases of an interwoven state-formation and civilizing process in the course of which the power relations of different human groups change in a blind and unplanned way, then it becomes clear that they represent different stages. An autocratic regime requires a relatively simple personality structure on the part of both those who command and those who obey. This fact explains why, time and time again over thousands of years, a single man – along with a small, inner group – has been able to establish and maintain his rule over the many; this has been the case at least since the time when the pharaohs brought Upper and Lower Egypt under their control and set the double crown on their heads, or since the Chin princes won overlordship over the heartland of today's China, to the times of the German, Austrian, Russian monarchs up to 1918, and then, in the form of dictatorships, into our own times. Compared with such regimes, a multi-party parliamentary system is a considerably more complex and difficult governmental form which requires a correspondingly more complex and more differentiated personality structure.

This difference between the two forms of government is linked to the fact that a multi-party parliamentary regime legitimates *conflict* between people or groups of people. Conflicts are not relegated to the category of the extraordinary, abnormal and irrational, but are instead treated as normal, indispensable aspects of social life. In this respect, one could say, democracy contradicts the laws of classical rationality, which equate order with harmony, that is, with lack of conflict.[91] The task of a democratic state is to regulate the resolution of a society's most important group conflicts via special institutions which facilitate both struggles between opposing groups and their resolution. Strife is limited to non-violent forms of struggle fought out primarily in the form of discussion or word duels, the resolution of which depends on all the participants adhering to certain rules.

Wishful or ideal images of human social life, literary or academic utopias for example, are mostly based on the idea that an ideal regime, an ideal form of society, would have to be absolutely conflict-free and harmonious. This idea is an expression of the fact that conflicts between people jar the nerves, so to speak, that they are disturbing and that, for many people, a condition of complete quiet and perfect peace is seen as the ideal. I do not share this view. A conflict-free social life, as far as I can see, is simply inconceivable, and therefore it makes no sense to devise ideal images of a society – which are after all meant in some way to be models to orientate and guide behaviour – without taking into account the constituting significance of conflicts for human societies. A conflict-free society may appear to be the pinnacle of rationality, but at the same time it is also a society of the silence of the tomb, of the most extreme emotional coldness and utter boredom – a society, moreover, without any dynamic. In any society we may desire, as in the one we have now, the task is not to do away with conflict – that is a futile undertaking – but instead to regulate it, to submit the tactics and strategies of conflict to rules – rules which themselves can never be regarded as final. These rules keep the tension of conflicts at a medium level like a fire which must be neither too hot, so that it consumes itself and all around it, nor too feeble, so that it gives neither heat nor light.

A regime of the parliamentary type which presupposes such moderate conflicts, however, requires a degree of self-control from the people belonging to it, a measure of self-restraint which is not easy to introduce and which far surpasses the comparable demands made by a dictatorial regime. It is precisely this point which leads to the conclusion that, in the context of a civilizing process, a multi-party regime represents a higher level than an absolute monarchy or a dictatorship. A regime of the absolutist type – even though it certainly contributes to the formation of self-constraints – depends, on balance, on the primacy of external constraints over self-constraints. One of the central traits of a multi-party parliamentary system, by contrast, is a higher degree of self-constraint. External constraints have not disappeared; they are not absent in any state-society. But a parliamentary regime breaks down if the firm lid of self-control, which prevents all individuals involved from resorting to violence in their struggles with opponents or from violating the rules of the parliamentary game, bursts or breaks. The disintegration of self-control in political battles means *ipso facto* the end of the multi-party system and its probable transformation into a dictatorial or monarchical autocracy. There, the requirement to keep oneself permanently in check in clashes with opponents is absent. In this respect, a multi-party parliamentary system resembles a football match: it is fought out, but according to strict rules, the observation of which also requires a high degree of self-discipline. If the struggle becomes too heated, if the football match degenerates into a comparatively unregulated brawl, it ceases to be a football match. The function fulfilled by the players' self-control is then taken over by the external controls, represented, for instance, by the police.

This example may be a bit feeble but it illustrates something fundamental. Like all forms of society, absolutist states, whether of a monarchic or dictatorial type, also have their specific structural conflicts. However, they remain behind the scenes of public life. Officially, life in states of this sort is harmonious. Conflicts on the lower levels are quite simply decided by orders from above – by external constraints – and those on the highest level of command are pursued *in camera*, behind the scenes.[92] Many of the people in such societies may well know that such conflicts exist. But they have no place in the institutional framework. And the official state ideology does not recognize them either.

The fact that a multi-party parliamentary system makes considerably greater claims on the ability of the members of a state-society to impose constraints on themselves than does an absolutist regime is one of the most important reasons why the transition from a regime of the absolutist type to one of the parliamentary kind is an extremely difficult process. Many people whose destiny it is to participate in such a transition are not able to cope with these demands. Accustomed to simple superordination–subordination relationships in which external constraints are dominant, and to an apparently harmonious hierarchy in which everyone except the highest rulers and military commanders receives orders from above and gives orders to those below, they find the contest of the parties in a multi-party system irritating if not absolutely unbearable. Even under the most favourable circumstances, as I have said, a chain of several generations is usually needed in the life of a people for completion of the transformation of personality structures which facilitates the secure functioning of a multi-party parliamentary regime. In every country that has undergone such a process, institutional and civilizing fluctuations typically occur until the society gradually becomes attuned to a more even course of development, both in its parliamentary institutions and in the modes of renunciation of violence – that is, civilizing self-controls – that go with it.[93]

Completely public conflicts between different groups, even where the use of violence is renounced and there is not much expression of hatred or too provocative verbal abuse, still jar on the nerves. How far can one go before opponents lose their self-control, before the moderate contest according to parliamentary rules turns into a brawl, a revolt, a double-bind process of mutually escalating violence? Is not the emergence of terrorist groups also an aspect of the long and difficult process in the course of which a society at an earlier level of civilization (at which the members keep themselves in check out of fear of the strong hand of a king or dictator) works its way up to a level of civilization at which the members are able to disagree with political opponents and still restrain themselves and submit to the generally accepted rule of the contest almost without external constraint?

19

If one says that a multi-party parliamentary regime requires a higher degree of self-constraint than an autocratic-monarchical or dictatorial regime, and in this sense represents a higher level of civilization, this is a purely factual statement. It does not in any way imply that the current way such a regime copes with conflict is the final and ideal form, as it is often made out to be. In the form that has been reached so far, multi-party parliamentary states are a milestone in the state-formation and civilizing processes; reaching it has entailed a reduction of the power-difference between the rulers and ruled and an increase in the civilizing self-controls of both groups. But, just to emphasize one single point, it is not in the least necessary to assume that the central conflicts which determine the formation of parties must or will always be the same in character as they are today – that is, conflicts between classes or strata. Other types of conflict which are at present widely disguised and submerged by the pressure of class conflicts – conflicts such as those between men and women, between younger and older generations, or conflicts of regional and ethnic origin – can also serve as the basis for party formation.

Quite generally, the idealization of the multi-party parliamentary system, which gives rise to constant external political conflict between states of this type and dictatorial states, hinders public discussion of structural problems and leads to recurrent difficulties. It also disguises, for example, the difficulties which people of the rising generations have from time to time in coming to terms, in the framework of their individual civilizing process, with the peculiar realities of a parliamentary regime.[94] Official teachings give them for the most part only a knowledge of the stereotypical ideal image of democracy. Often they only learn about the real conditions of the practice of parliamentary politics, not without certain astonishment, through their own experience. This astonishment, the discovery that what the parties do in practice is not always congruent with the ideal image of their principles, probably played a not insignificant role in the stigmatization of the state seen among terrorists in the Federal Republic.

The practice of politics in a multi-party parliamentary regime constrains all participants again and again to compromise with their opponents. It leads to negotiation in which precise knowledge of the opposition's power-ratio and a corresponding willingness to make concessions are an advantage. Now there are in all societies, but especially in highly differentiated industrial societies, specific differences between the civilizing patterns of the younger, rising generation and the older, established ones that have already been discussed. In the political life of multi-party states, they are expressed among other ways in the younger generations tending more to favour uncompromising and radical solutions to acute conflicts than do the older. In almost all parties there is a gradient from the relatively unconditional nature of the demands of the younger generations, to the greater preparedness of their older counterparts to adjust their objectives to the often complex balance of power between the various party groupings. In the eyes of people on the outside – and particularly of a critical, intelligent and sharply observant younger generation – such compromises easily appear to be betrayals of the ideals and principles a party professes. The entire party regime then seems to the young members of opposition groups to have nothing to offer that can awaken their affection or hope. That this feeling was so comparatively strong in the Federal Republic may once again have something to do with specific German traditions.

The renunciation of violence in the relations of different interest groups entails forms of give and take which can often only be denoted in German by words which have a negative flavour. The German *Feilschen* ['haggling'] sounds a lot more unpleasant than the British *bargaining*. Complete determination, absolute loyalty to principles, uncompromising adherence to one's own convictions, still sound particularly good in German. Compromise, on the other hand, is somehow slightly pathetic. Here, too, it is military values which have once again grown deep roots in the German tradition of behaviour and feeling. In regard to his own honour, the honour of his country, his Kaiser, his Führer, the officer cannot make any compromises. He looks down with contempt at the merchants who bargain with each other, who allow this or that to be negotiated away from their initial strong position. In this way, the German language still contains many values from the autocratic centuries, values held in earlier forms of state and society which run contrary to the conditions of life in a parliamentary and industrial society. The living communicate with each other in a language that is to a large extent moulded by the dead. In this way, the dead are revenged on the living for breaking with their values.

In fact, the arrangements of a multi-party parliamentary regime place a high value precisely on those things which in a military tradition are held in low regard. In place of violent fighting, which in the end is a matter of life and death, they stress negotiation and the renunciation of violence. Instead of absolute obedience, even to principles (*Prinzipien-treue*), there is now the search for the middle way, for mediation and compromise. It is easy to find one's way in a landscape where there are only proscriptions and prescriptions; it is far more difficult in a landscape where one has to gain through experience a certain sensitivity for how far one can go in a specific situation and how far one must hold back. The strategies of compromise, of tact in putting out feelers as to where one can press forward and where one has to retreat, which are among the elementary forms of life under parliamentarianism, are certainly still quite some way from gaining a high place in the German scale of values. For that probably a few centuries of growing accustomed to them are required.

IV
The Breakdown of
Civilization

1

On the face of it, the Eichmann trial was simply the trial of an individual, with the former SS man as the accused and his Israeli accusers, a contingent of witnesses, some of them survivors of the concentration camps, and an invisible international public following the statements of the two trial parties and judging. Over the months, however, as news of the trial spread throughout the world and penetrated the conversations, thoughts and feelings of people in many countries, it seemed to become something more than the trial of just this one individual. It began, on a small scale, to assume the character of a landmark. Like the two German wars, it contributed to the growing mass of experiences which challenge the image we have of ourselves as civilized societies. On the surface, the issue was parochial; deeper down it was of considerably wider concern.

The fact that the National Socialists had inflicted evil on the Jews was not unknown. But before the Eichmann trial, the enormous human capacity to forget painful things, especially if they have happened to

---

The following text originated (in English) in 1961–2. In the original typescript, references to the Eichmann trial are in the present tense. [German editor's note]

other, relatively powerless people, had already begun to do its work. The memory of how a modern state had sought to exterminate a hated minority had slipped more from people's minds. The trial in Jerusalem brought it back sharply into focus once again. All discussion about whether or not it would have been better to let the memory of the murdered and murderers fade into obscurity, with, at most, a few paragraphs here and there in a history book as an epitaph, became invalid. The memory had come back. And the circumstances of its return were instructive.

Generally speaking, the victims of history, the less powerful groups who have been defeated, have had only a small chance of being remembered. The principal framework of what is remembered as history remains to this day a state, and history books are still largely the chronicles of states. What we have here is a living example. The memory of the murdered Jews was reawakened thanks to the new Jewish state and its power resources.

With it have returned the many questions which this memory provokes. How was it possible that people could plan and execute in a rational, indeed scientific way, an undertaking which appears to be a throwback to the barbarism and savagery of earlier times – which, leaving aside all differences of population size and provided one is allowed posthumously to grant slaves the status of human beings, could have taken place in Ancient Assyria or Rome? It would not have been out of place in a feudal society where landowning warriors lorded it and had powers of life and death over their serfs, or when crusaders robbed and burned to death the Jews of their time. But in the twentieth century people no longer expected such things.

Looked at closely, the main problem raised by the mass murder, in the name of a nation, of men, women and children from an alien group, does not lie in the act itself but rather in its incompatibility with the standards which have come to be regarded as distinguishing marks of the most highly developed societies of our time. People of the twentieth century are often inclined implicitly to see themselves and their age as if their standards of civilization and rationality were far beyond both the barbarism of earlier times and that of the less developed societies of today. In spite of all the doubts which have been cast on the belief in progress, their self-image remains permeated by it. Yet their feelings are contradictory, a blend of self-love and self-hate, pride and despair – pride in the extraordinary capacity for discovery and daring of their age and the humanizing advances it has seen, despair about their own senseless barbarities. Numerous experiences convey to them the idea that they are the highest stage of civilization. Other experiences, among them the endless series of wars, nourish their doubts. The Eichmann trial, with everything it brought to the surface, belonged to this second category. Facts which had been available for a long time were made conspicuous by it and brought to light in a personal and authoritative manner. People could no longer look away. As it unfolded, many of them heard the terrible tale as if for the first time and with shocked incredulity. They did not want to believe that such things could have happened in a highly developed industrial society, among civilized people. That was their fundamental dilemma; and that is the sociologist's problem.

The most obvious way of coping involved the tacit assumption that the mass killing initiated by Hitler was an exception. The National Socialists, one might have said, were a cancerous growth on the body of civilized societies, their deeds those of people who were more or less mentally ill, rooted in the irrational hatred of Jews on the part of people who were particularly wicked and immoral or perhaps in specifically German traditions and character traits. All these explanations represent the cold-blooded, methodical mass murder according to plan as something unique. Normally – that is the implication – such barbarities cannot take place in the more highly developed societies of the twentieth century.

Explanations such as these shield people from the painful thought that such things could happen again, that such an outbreak of savagery and barbarism might stem directly from tendencies inherent in the structure of modern industrial societies. They offer a measure of comfort. But they do not explain very much. It is easy enough to point to unique historical aspects of the events which led to the attempted extermination of the Jews in Europe. Other aspects, however, were not in any way unique. Many contemporary events suggest that National Socialism revealed, perhaps in an especially blatant form, what are common conditions of contemporary societies, tendencies of acting and thinking which can also be found elsewhere. Just like scientifically conducted mass wars, the highly organized and scientifically planned extermination of whole population groups in specially constructed death camps and sealed-off ghettos by starvation, gassing or shooting does not appear to be entirely out of place in highly technicized mass societies. Instead of taking comfort from the idea that the events called to mind by the Eichmann trial were exceptional, it might be more fruitful to investigate the conditions in twentieth-century civilizations, the *social* conditions, which have favoured barbarisms of this kind and which might favour them again in the future. How often, one cannot help thinking, must such horrors be repeated before we have learned to understand how and why they happen, and before powerful people are able and willing to apply such knowledge in order to prevent them?

It is common today to confuse the social need to make people individually responsible for the damage and pain they have inflicted on others with the social need to explain sociologically and also psychologically how and why the pain and damage came about. The second need does not extinguish the first. Both have their place in the course of human affairs. Even if one is completely orientated towards blaming, one must nevertheless explain; and the attempt to explain is not necessarily an attempt to excuse. The Eichmann trial has momentarily lifted the veil which hides the darker side of civilized human beings. Let us take a look at what has been revealed.

2

The final decision physically to destroy all Jews in Germany and the conquered territories was taken by Hitler and the inner circle of the state and party leadership, so it seems, in September 1939, shortly after the invasion of Poland.

Jews had been killed earlier, of course – together with members of other persecuted minorities such as communists, Jehovah's Witnesses, homosexuals and resisting Christian pastors and priests – in concentration camps and occasional manhunts. But the main thrust in that period had been directed not against the lives of the Jews but rather against the bases of their income and employment. The Nazis had sought then, above all, to dispossess the Jews of the bulk of their assets – commercial and industrial firms, houses, bank deposits, jewels, works of art, etc. – and to drive them from all professional and other activities which could bring them into contact with the non-Jewish population. Approximately 1 per cent of the total German population were Jews. Although the Jews formed a largely urban minority concentrated in commerce, industry and the professions, the Germans in general stood to gain only small economic advantages from expropriating them. Of course, as in the case of any forcible transfer of the property and occupations of one social group to others, there were certainly German families who obtained direct gains from this attack. Considerably more enjoyed the humiliation of the Jews and still others derived from it the hope for a better future. In each of these respects, the persecution of the Jews had a strong element of realism and rationality. In any case, up until that time Jews had still been allowed to leave Germany alive if they could find a state willing to grant them asylum and if they did not feel too old to be uprooted from the country which had come to be their home. They had even been allowed to take with them part of their personal belongings and, for a while, also a limited sum of money.

In retrospect, the decision taken by the Nazi leadership in 1939 to kill off all the Jews in their power may appear to have been predictable. In fact, in the 1930s when the National Socialists came to power, it was still quite inconceivable for most people in Europe and America that the Germans could kill millions of men, women and children in cold blood. The decision of the National Socialist power elite was kept under the strictest secrecy. For its implementation, the Department of Jewish Affairs was responsible. It was run from 1940 to 1945 by Lieutenant-Colonel [*Obersturmbannführer*] Karl Adolf Eichmann. Even after the goal had been set, the way for reaching it was still far from clear. German advances in the West and East brought more and more Jews under German control. There were no models for the organized murder of several million unarmed people. A good deal of thought and experimentation were required before the most effective and economical methods of killing were discovered. A growing administrative apparatus was needed to plan and supervise the various measures aimed at the destruction of the Jews. The larger it became, the more frictions and conflicts with rival departments began to pile up.

The National Socialist state apparatus consisted of a series of semi-autonomous, quasi-feudal sectors, each headed by a Führer of second rank, men like Ribbentrop, Goering, Himmler and Goebbels, and each with its subordinate organizations which stretched across the country. Each of the sectors formed an official domain on whose usefulness for Hitler and the Party the prestige and status of its leading men depended. And since the balance of power between these second-rank Führers was kept unstable, each of them was suspicious of the others as was Hitler himself. The rise of one could mean the ruin of another. People who are prepared to use violence and murder as normal instruments of politics can never be free of the fear that others might use the same instruments against them. In this way, behind the apparently smooth functional efficiency of the Hitler state one hits upon an extraordinary mass of tensions, jealousies, status-manoeuvring, with the corresponding squandering of resources and strength. The dictatorial state apparatus with its rival overlords of quasi-autonomous official domains was primarily held together and in check by their common dependency on the Führer and by the common beliefs which they held in varying degrees of orthodoxy.

As in many other dictatorial states, the secret police was one of these formations. It belonged to Himmler's official domain. With all its branches, it was a central organ of the SS, the mainstay of its power. From early on, the SS leaders had been champions of a militant National Socialist orthodoxy. The decision to kill the Jews, which was Hitler's own, was supported emphatically by them. That meant a gain in power for them in relation to rival cliques in Hitler's court. For one thing, it secured for them an enormous expansion of the sphere of activity of the Gestapo's Department of Jewish Affairs. Furthermore, the planned extermination of the Jews or, to give it its official name, 'The Final Solution of the Jewish problem', had always been one of Hitler's overriding aims. Men like Himmler, Eichmann and their subordinates, now entrusted with carrying it out, could count on the Führer's sympathy and support. In the context of the Nazi state, that strengthened their position and their prestige.

But the full realization of this policy took time. Suitable technical means and administrative systems had first to be developed. Pogroms, the traditional way of persecuting Jews, had died out in Germany. The National Socialists had begun to revive them. Now, under the leadership of the SS, they were organized more thoroughly and on a grand scale. Already in 1941, as the German armies advanced towards the East, the SS and other units of troops were systematically killing all the Jews in occupied towns and villages they could capture. About 32,000 Jews were violently killed in Vilnius, 34,000 in Kiev, altogether some 220,000 in the former Baltic states. Wherever German troops appeared in Poland, Russia and to a lesser extent in the Balkans, Jews were methodically hunted down and as far as possible killed.

As a means of extermination, however, pogroms had their deficiencies. They were liable all too often to arouse unfavourable comment. They were messy, awkward and not very effective. A number of Jews could always escape. In order to reach the goal of total annihilation, a cleaner, less public and less haphazard technique of mass murder was required. This meant an overall organization which was so tightly knit that not a single Jew in German-occupied Europe could slip through the net, an organization so highly structured that every step within it could be unequivocally controlled by the leadership of the Gestapo and their Department of Jewish Affairs without interference from *Wehrmacht* officers or outsiders. In this way, in addition to the older, military methods of shooting and various other forms of direct physical violence, the highest officials in the responsible parts of the Gestapo developed a new, less awkward and messy method of killing which, properly organized, required only a minimum of direct force and which made it possible, through the turning of a tap, simultaneously to kill hundreds of people, and which allowed the officials themselves to steer and supervise the whole proceedings from a distance. That was the killings in gas chambers.

Compared with pogroms, and with military procedures, this new form of extermination meant an advance of rationalization and bureaucratization. Experiments with poison gas for the fumigation of camps, or for the quick murder of people seen by the National Socialists as unfit to live, had already pointed the way.[1] Besides, as early as 1925 in *Mein Kampf*, Hitler, who had himself been a victim of gas attacks in the First World War, had recommended the use of poison gas for the mass killing of Jews. After some experimentation, the first actual gas chambers were installed in a camp near Poznań towards the end of 1941. Others followed. While direct, military killing continued, the main burden of the extermination policy was shifted to a small number of concentration camps with special installations and from which there was no escape. By means of the gas chambers the destruction of the Jews from the whole of occupied Europe could be speeded up. It could be concentrated in a few places, hence easing the tasks of administrative control. Jews were now sent to a camp under the direct supervision of the Gestapo's Department of Jewish Affairs. The increase in competence and prestige which was achieved in this way continued to create difficulties in relation to other branches of the state apparatus. It took a certain time before – in addition to the material techniques – suitable administrative techniques for the well-regulated murder of hundreds of thousands of people had been developed. These administrative difficulties, among them even the question of who was to be counted as a Jew, were finally resolved at a conference of the inner circle called together by Himmler's deputy in January 1942. It was at this meeting that the final guidelines for the extermination of the Jews were laid down. The responsibility of Eichmann's office was defined more clearly and its authority strengthened. His department remained in full operation until October 1944 when Himmler – not completely successfully – ordered the killing of the Jews to be stopped and conditions in the death camps to be improved. By then, it was already clear that Germany was losing the war. Himmler evidently hoped that the Allies might leave him in peace if he handed the remaining Jews over to them alive. To Austrian gauleiters at the beginning of 1945, he explained that the Jews were his most valuable asset.

All in all, between the end of 1939 and the beginning of 1945, 9 to 10 million Jews came under the control of Nazi Germany. Of these, around 5 million were shot, gassed, starved or otherwise put to death.

3

The attempt to wipe out the entire population of Jews in the lands under German rule remained half completed only because of Germany's defeat. It was not by any means the only regression to barbarism in the civilized societies of the twentieth century. Others could easily be pointed out. But of all these regressions, it was perhaps the deepest. Hardly any other example shows the vulnerability of civilization so clearly or reminds us so strongly of the dangers of contemporary growth processes and the fact not only that processes of growth and decay can go hand in hand but that the latter can also predominate relative to the former.

One of the reasons for the slowness with which people are beginning to recognize the treatment of the Jews by the National Socialists as a symptom of one of the severest breakdowns of civilization in recent European history is a concept of civilization that is flawed. Many Europeans seem to be of the opinion that it is part of their nature to behave in a civilized manner – more or less in the manner in which aristocrats used implicitly to consider their specific manners and ways of behaving as inborn. Sometimes they even characterize themselves in their speaking and thinking as members of 'civilized races' in contrast to 'uncivilized races', as if civilized behaviour were a genetically inherited attribute of specific human groups and not of others. It was partly due to this idea of civilization as a natural inheritance of the European nations that many people reacted to events such as the open relapse of the National Socialists into barbarism at first with incredulity – 'that cannot happen in Europe' – and then with stunned surprise and dejection – 'how was it possible in a civilized country?' The experience seemed to justify the many voices which had been murmuring about the inevitable decay of Western civilization and threatened to drown out completely the fading belief in its eternal progress and superiority. And in fact, people who as children had been brought up in the idea that their own, higher civilization was a part of their 'nature' or their 'race', might very well have fallen into despair and been driven to the opposite extreme when, as adults, they noticed that this flattering belief was contradicted by events. Every war was clearly a regression to barbarism.

Up till then, however, European wars had always been relatively limited regressions. Certain minimum rules of civilized conduct were generally still observed even in the treatment of prisoners of war. With a few exceptions, a kernel of self-esteem which prevents the senseless torturing of enemies and allows identification with one's enemy in the last instance as another human being, together with compassion for his suffering, did not entirely lapse.

In the attitude of the National Socialists towards the Jews none of this survived. At least on a conscious level, the torment, suffering and death of Jews did not appear to mean more to them than that of flies. Along with the whole way of living which the SS allowed themselves in the concentration camps and that which was forced on the prisoners there, the mass murder of Jewish people, as has been said, was probably the deepest regression into barbarism in twentieth-century Europe.

One might think that the Nazis decided on these measures because of the war. However, although it took place during the war and was partially facilitated by it, the extermination of the Jews had little to do with the conduct of the war. It was not an act of war. Eichmann and others have compared it with the killing of Japanese civilians through the first American atomic bombs. But the Japanese had attacked the United States; Pearl Harbor came before Hiroshima. The attack by the National Socialists on the Jews was almost entirely lacking in the reciprocity which, according to present conceptions, lends an element of realism to enmity and group killings during a war. Their hatred towards the Jews was, at that stage, an unrequited hatred. For the majority of Jews, it would have been difficult to say why the Germans treated them as their worst enemies. The only sense which they could give to these experiences came from their own tradition. They had been persecuted since time immemorial. Hitler was a new Haman, one of a long line, perhaps a little more menacing than his predecessors. The military usefulness of the pogroms and gas chambers was absolutely nil. All population groups in the conquered territories of Europe constituted a certain danger for their German masters and exploiters, that of the dispersed Jewish groups hardly more than others. Their death did not free land for German settlers. It did not in the slightest increase the political power of the Nazis inside Germany or that of Hitler's Germany among the states of the world. Nor did it any longer have the social function in the tensions and conflicts between various sections of the German people which attacks on the Jews had undoubtedly had for the Nazis in their struggles before they seized power. Its propaganda value was in this phase trivial or negative. In no way was the considerable outlay of labour power and resources which the transport and killing of millions of Jews involved rewarding – at the height of the war when both were growing more expensive.

Indeed, the more one learns about the facts, the clearer it becomes that our standard explanations have failed.

4

The question why the Nazi leadership decided at the beginning of the war to exterminate all the Jews under their dominion has an answer which is simple and ready to hand. However, it almost seems as if, in the eyes of many people, this answer does not make any sense. Apart from some incidental reasons – such as, for example, the reinforcement which it gave to Himmler, the *Reichsführer SS*, and his faction in the continuing manoeuvring for position which took place at the top levels of the party and the state – the decision to implement the 'Final Solution of the Jewish problem' had no basis of the kind which we are accustomed to describing as 'rational' or 'realistic'. It was simply a question of the fulfilment of a deeply rooted belief that had been central for the National Socialist movement from the beginning. According to this belief, the present and future greatness of Germany and the whole 'Aryan race', of which the German people were the highest embodiment, required 'race-purity'; and this biologically conceived 'purity' required the removal and, if necessary, the destruction of all 'inferior' and hostile human groups who could contaminate 'the race', above all people of Jewish stock.

Hitler and his followers had never concealed the fact that they regarded the Jews as their own and Germany's worst enemies. For this, they required no specific proof. It was simply their belief that this had been decreed by nature, by the world order and its creator. They believed that the Jews, on account of their inborn racial characteristics, were bound to hate the superior, Aryan-Germanic people, and, if they were allowed to, to destroy them. Whoever wanted to save the crown of humanity, the Aryan race, from destruction by the Jews and other inferior 'races' had therefore to see it as his noblest task and mission to destroy the Jews themselves. The speeches of Hitler and many other Nazi leaders, together with the whole National Socialist literature, testify to the strength and consistency of this doctrine. One could read there how all the misfortunes experienced by Germany, including the defeat of 1918 and the iniquitous impositions of the Treaty of Versailles could in the last instance be traced to the machinations of the Jews.[2] One could read how a Jewish conspiracy prevented the renewed rise of Germany after the defeat, how, after the First World War, Jewish warmongers had repeatedly tried to sow the seeds of increasing discord between Germany and other countries, how their plans were foiled in 1938 when Chamberlain came to Munich, how world Jewry reacted to this failure with an outcry of fury, redoubled their efforts and in 1939 finally succeeded in unifying a number of neighbouring nations to attack Germany in the interests of the Jews. All of this had been said with different words again and again. To end the conspiracy of the Jewish race was the often declared goal of Hitler and the National Socialist movement. Since the early days of the movement it had found popular expression in slogans such as 'Croak, Judah' or in the lines which anticipated the great volte-face, 'when Jew-blood spurts from the knife'.

Uninhibited threats and the systematic use of physical violence – in a society in which many people were still contemptuous of non-violent forms of politics – were among the most important factors to which Hitler owed his eventual success. Although the 'racial purity' of Germany and the elimination of 'inferior' groups, above all of people of Jewish stock, were central to the political programme of the National Socialists, they had refrained from a fully logical pursuit of their aims so long as they regarded it as necessary to take account of the potential effects of their actions on public opinion in other countries. The war removed these constraints. Inside Germany, the National Socialist rulers were now firmly in the saddle: they were the undisputed leaders of a nation at war. Under these favourable circumstances, Hitler and his closest collaborators decided to put into practice what they believed in and had long since preached. They decided to destroy all people of Jewish stock, regardless of their religion, once and for all. After the war there was to be in Germany – and in the 'great German empire' [*großdeutsches Reich*] they were striving for – no Jewish conspiracy and no more pollution of German blood by Jewish blood.

The question why, in 1939 the path was taken towards the murdering of all Jews is thus not difficult to answer. The decision itself and its implementation followed directly from a central doctrine of the Nazi belief system. Hitler and his followers had never made a secret of their total and irrevocable enmity towards the Jews or of their wish to destroy them. It is not surprising that, when the risk no longer seemed too great, they finally began to translate this destruction-wish into fact.

What is more surprising is the fact that for a long time only a few people, and above all only a few statesmen from leading countries, were able to imagine that the National Socialists might one day put into effect what they had announced. There was then, and there still is today, a widespread tendency to underrate political and social beliefs, to see them as mere froth – as 'ideologies' which have as the only real substance at their basis the interests of the carrier groups as these are defined in their own understanding. According to this assumption, the actions and aims of social units must be explained in the first instance by reference to current 'group interests', while expressed goals and doctrines only have a secondary explanatory value insofar as they serve these interests which they often conceal.

Numerous attempts to explain the murder of millions of Jews correspondingly proceed from the expectation that it is possible to discover a kind of realistic 'interest' which this policy served. The search is for grounds that can be regarded as more or less 'rational', as derivable from a 'realistic' goal other than the fulfilment of the belief itself, and which point in this sense, for example, to the elimination of potential economic competitors and the opening of new income-chances for party members, the cementing of the unity of one's own followers through the channelling of all dissatisfactions on to an external scapegoat, or, purely and simply, to the improvement of one's chances of victory in the war by the killing of as many enemies as possible.

It is certainly not unjustified to suppose that some of these or other, similarly 'realistic' interests played a part as driving forces of the anti-semitic propaganda of the Nazis and as reasons for their adoption of anti-Jewish measures in the phase of their ascent to power or later when Hitler ruled Germany but his power was not yet secure. However, there is little evidence that the decision to kill all the Jews and to undertake the sustained and costly effort necessary to achieve this goal, which was taken during the war, that is, when Nazi rule had been secured, was based decisively on 'realistic interests' of this kind and for which the anti-Semitic beliefs served merely as an ideological smokescreen. In the final analysis, it will be found that the mass murder of Jews did not serve any purpose which one might call 'rational', and that the National Socialists were driven to it above all by the strength and unshakeable character of their belief itself. It is here that the lesson to be drawn from this experience lies.

This is not by any means to imply that professed irrational beliefs are *always* to be taken at face value as the primary factors in group actions, but only that there are *also* figurations where they do work as primary determinants.[3] Professed aims and beliefs are quite often at most secondary impulses to action and perhaps merely an ideological weapon or an ideological screen which hides other, more narrowly sectional interests which today, lacking more adequate concepts, we describe as 'realistic' or 'rational'. In these cases, the explanation of group actions in terms of such aims and doctrines is deceptive, illusory or at least highly incomplete. Sometimes, however, a course of action is determined by nothing stronger than a goal derived from a set of professed beliefs. The beliefs in question may, as we say, be extremely 'unrealistic' and 'irrational'. They may, in other words, have a high fantasy content so that the fulfilment of aims demanded by them promises the acting group a high degree of immediate emotional satisfaction. As a result – at the level of social reality and in the longer term – such a fulfilment brings the carrier group no advantages other than the realization of their belief. It may even harm them. The attempt of the National Socialists to destroy the Jews belongs to this category. It was one of the most striking examples of the power which a belief – in this case, a social or, more properly, a national belief – can gain over people.

It was this possibility for which in the 1920s and 1930s many people inside and outside Germany were hardly prepared. Their conceptual equipment led them to the idea that human groups – especially groups of people in power, including the rulers and statesmen of the world – however fantastic their professed beliefs were, would in the long term always orientate themselves towards hard 'reality', towards their so-called 'real interests'. No matter how savage their creed, no matter how absolute the enmity they preached, in the end they would recognize the merits of moderation and come to conduct their affairs in a more or less 'rational' and 'civilized' way. Evidently something was very wrong with a way of thinking which blocked the insight that a nationalistic movement in whose programme the use of violence and the total destruction of enemies loomed large, whose members ceaselessly emphasized the value of cruelty and killing, might in fact commit savage acts and kill.

It is not usual to hold an inquest in order to test in the light of the factual course of events what was wrong with one's own earlier ways of thinking and acting. If one were in this sense to investigate the systems of ideas, dispositions and beliefs which led so many people to be so ill-prepared for events such as the Nazi concentration camps and the mass murder of the Jews, then one would have to place at the centre the basic flaw in the dominant conception of contemporary civilization that has already been mentioned. Contemporaries did not then conceive of civilization as a condition which, if it is to be maintained or improved, requires a constant effort based on a degree of understanding of how it works. Instead, like their 'rationality', they took it for granted as one of their own permanent attributes, an aspect of their inborn superiority: once civilized, always civilized. So, in Germany and elsewhere, and at first with a shrug of the shoulders, they swept the barbaric doctrines and deeds of the Nazis under the carpet because it seemed to them unimaginable that people in a civilized country could behave in such a cruel and inhuman way as the adherents to National Socialist beliefs had announced they were going to act, proclaiming it to be necessary and desirable in the name of their country. When members of tribal groups such as the Mau Mau in Kenya unite in a belief which demands the killing of others, people are fully prepared by the beliefs they hold about them for the possibility that they will do what they say and hence take the appropriate defensive measures. When the members of more advanced industrial societies, such as the National Socialists, unite in a no less barbaric belief, people are led by their conceptual inheritance to the judgement that they have an 'ideology', that they will not act as brutally as they talk.

That was the position. Because of their conceptual equipment, observers of the German scene before but also after 1933 did not reckon with the possibility of a genuine recrudescence of barbarism in their own midst. They had at their disposal specific techniques for dealing intellectually with the wilder and more strongly emotionally laden beliefs which they encountered in some political movements. Hitler and his people were classified as 'agitators' who used the Jews in their propaganda as 'scapegoats' without, however, themselves necessarily believing everything that they said about them. 'Underneath it all,' such commentators seemed to imply, 'these Nazi leaders know as well as we do that much of what they say is rubbish. When it gets serious,' that was the implicit assumption, 'these people think and behave just like us. They simply need all this propaganda talk in order to gain power. That is why they do it.' The belief was seen as the means to a rational end. It was conceived simply as an instrument which the Nazi leadership had developed in order to gain power. And the goal of gaining power appears to people all over the world who have power as eminently 'rational'.

Then as now numerous people, among them certainly many statesmen, had no understanding of a mentality that was different from their own. They could not picture to themselves that, in civilized countries, anything other than an at least moderately civilized belief system could be seriously advocated by its adherents. If a social creed was inhuman, immoral, revolting and demonstrably false, they thought it could not be genuine: it was a made-up goal of ambitious leaders who wanted to gain a mass following for their own ulterior ends. Perhaps they were vaguely aware that the National Socialist movement was mainly led by half-educated men. But they did not, so it seems, wake up fully to the fact that Hitler and his closest collaborators believed deeply in most of what they said.

Even in the most advanced industrial societies of our age, the gap between the highest and the lowest educational levels is extraordinarily wide. The number of illiterates has declined, that of 'half-educated' people has increased. A great deal of what is regarded as characteristic of twentieth-century civilization carries their stamp – as a consequence of the deficiencies of contemporary educational systems with all the frustrations and wastage of abilities they entail.

Among the more or less surface factors in the rise of the National Socialist movement were the peculiar social characteristics of its elite. The majority of party leaders were, in fact, 'half-educated'. They were – and this is in no way unusual for a movement of this type – outsiders or failures in the older order, often filled with a burning ambition which made it impossible for them to bear their inadequacies and admit them to themselves. The Nazi belief system with its pseudo-scientific varnish spread thinly over a primitive, barbaric national mythology was one of the more extreme symptoms of the moral and intellectual twilight in which they lived. That it could not withstand the judgement of more educated people, and with few exceptions had no appeal for them, was probably one of the reasons why such people often underestimated the seriousness of the belief itself and the genuineness of the feelings vested in it. Few of the social and, especially, the national myths of our age are free of similar falsehoods and barbarisms. The National Socialist doctrine shows, as if in a distorting mirror, some of their common features in a glaring form.

That Hitler and his helpers were masters of dissimulation and the spreading of deliberate lies, that their preachings contained a strong dose of hatred, humbug and hypocrisy, was in no way incompatible with their fervent belief in the ultimate truth of their creed. In fact, National Socialism combined many of the traits of a religious movement with those of a political party. To see it as such, as a movement resting on a very sincerely held belief, is one of the first preconditions for understanding what happened. The movement began as a sect. Its leader believed from early on in his messianic mission, his mission for Germany. So did many of its members. And, carried miraculously to the top on the crest of a prolonged crisis, their certainty that their beliefs were true, their methods justified and the success of their mission preordained became absolute and unshakeable.

It is understandable that many representatives of the older educated elite experienced the extent of the regression under the Nazis as a shock out of the blue, because they could not discern beneath the lies, the propaganda tricks and the deliberate use of falsehoods as a weapon against enemies, the sincerity with which the standard-bearers of the movement believed in ideas which appeared to them themselves as doubtful or patently absurd. They were also inclined to understand the kernel of the Nazi belief system, especially its wild and extreme anti-semitism, as propaganda or as a well-planned means for unifying the German people, but not as a deep conviction of religious strength.

Even today the gulf separating the 'educated' higher strata, whose ways of thinking steer their interpretation of social events, and the great mass of 'less educated' people, whose interpretation of such events is often quite different, leads recurrently to the former perceiving the latter in a distorted form. One can understand better why so many 'educated' people, brought up on the tacit assumption that civilized behaviour would continue in European societies without any effort on their part, were so ill prepared for the forthcoming breakdown of this civilization, if one looks into some of the conditions in Germany which gave the National Socialists their chance.

5

The rise of the Nazi movement and its belief system remains incomprehensible if, as so often happens, one focuses attention solely on relationships in Germany at the time. Specific short-term developments which favoured its rise, such as the severe economic crisis around 1930 and the intensification of class conflict which resulted, come immediately to mind and have been previously discussed on many occasions. However, in order to understand the conditions for the peculiar success of this movement, it is above all necessary to consider the pattern of Germany's long-term development. In conversation, the question is often raised of why the strongest resurgence of barbarism in a highly industrialized nation-state so far happened in of all places Germany. Explanations of the same type as cultivated by the Nazis – that something in the 'nature' of the Germans, a 'racial' or biological inheritance, was responsible for the course of events – can be discounted as fantasy-constructs. The answer has consequently to be sought in the direction which we inadequately describe through the concept 'historical' – that is, process-sociologically, in terms of the development of Germany as a society.

Problems of this sort are not often researched. Although the *de facto* development of Germany offers many clues, they have largely remained unused. The task of systematically investigating which factors in the long-term development of Germany and of the so-called German 'national character' contributed to the rise of the Nazis is still to be undertaken. At the present stage in the knowledge of such long-term processes, it is not possible to do more than sketch a theory, to propose a consistent hypothesis. Perhaps one should also start by saying that it is not the long-term developmental factors themselves which are specific to Germany so much as their coincidence in time and the pattern which resulted from that fact.

Let us start with some of the peculiarities of the territories settled by the Germans. They have certainly constituted one of the lasting determinants of Germany's development. Both to the east and west of the Elbe, the German territories – like those of the Poles but unlike those of other neighbouring groups – were difficult to defend. Furthermore, the starting point of the German national state, the first empire ruled by German Kaisers, was very large. The enormous extent of the territories which were seen as German by the Germans was doubtless one of the reasons why the development first of a unified dynastic state and then of a unified nation-state was realized more slowly and later in Germany than in the case of other European dynastic and nation-states whose starting point was smaller.

The number and spread of the sub-divisions of the first German empire and the corresponding strength of centrifugal forces in it had as their consequence that, for centuries, the Germans fought with each other. They were permanently disunited and hence remained relatively weak and powerless at a time when unification and centralization were steadily progressing in many neighbouring states. This whole factual constellation left deep traces in the picture which Germans had of themselves and which other peoples had of them. Here lies the root of the burning desire for unity which recurrently came to the fore in Germany in crisis situations, since the precarious balance between centripetal and centrifugal forces there has tended to favour the centrifugal. It is not necessary in this context to explore how such continuities of self-image, attitudes and beliefs and their transmission from one generation to the next are to be explained. The fact is that, despite the discontinuities and changes which are placed at the centre of attention by present methods of history writing, such continuities do play their part in the development of nations.

The cumulative experiences of fragmentation and the corresponding self-image of the Germans as people who are not capable of living together without discord and quarrelling also found expression in the longing for a sovereign, a monarch, a strong leader who would be able to bring them to unity and consensus. As elements of the German self-image, these complementary traits – this fear of their own ability to find a peaceful way of living together and this longing for a powerful central authority who would bring an end to all this dissension – changed their character and function over time. But, together with other persistent patterns of the German tradition of beliefs and attitudes, they prepared the ground for a predisposition to react in a specific way to the traumatic experience of disunity – the feeling, which asserted itself again and again, that the make-up of the Germans means that they are destined to remain disunited unless a strong man – a Kaiser or a Führer – appears among them who is able to protect them from themselves no less than from their enemies.

In the recent past, this heightened sensitivity of the Germans with regard to fighting and quarrels among themselves found expression in an aversion to parliamentary democracy with its ceaseless tensions and conflicts between different parties. Parliamentary party states can only function among people who have, to a degree, learned to bear and deal with conflicts in their midst, who obtain satisfaction or even pleasure from the restrained competition between different parties, seeing it as something which gives meaning and direction to their personal ambitions and adds spice to life. Many Germans, however, in correspondence to their traditions of thinking and behaving, experienced the conflicts and fights between social strata, the parliamentary struggles between political parties, as emotionally repellent or unbearable. They had no inherited models of their own to show them how far they could go when they fought among themselves and which compromises they could accept without betraying their convictions. And since they lacked strict internalized rules for fighting and reaching compromises among themselves, they implicitly feared that their conflicts would get out of control, that if left to themselves, they or their opponents would fall into licentiousness or corruption.

The longing for external control by a strong ruler, which often grew stronger in critical situations, was closely bound up with the insecure standards of self-control which were passed on to the Germans by their traditions. One could still hear in the 1920s and 1930s sentences such as: 'Without monarchy anarchy breaks out.' One met many highly educated and cultivated people who said with a knowing smile: 'Parliamentary democracy may be all well and good for the Americans and the British but it is not for us. It is unGerman. We need a strong man to keep us disciplined and in order.' They always had a kind of unity in mind about which the Germans had dreamed for centuries, a unity so complete that it excluded every trace of discord.

Although the desire for total unity and oneness now related to the quite different framework of a highly industrialized nation-state, the longing for an ideal unity continued as a recurring leitmotif of national feeling. At its root over the centuries had lain the fact that the German emperors had been weak and the many German princes strong. The antagonism with which wide circles in Germany viewed 'this party business' stood in direct descent from the antagonism against the division of the Reich into dozens of rival state-units. Earlier, it had been for centuries a Kaiser, a prince, an hereditary monarch of whom countless Germans had dreamed as saviour of their unfortunate and disunited nation. Under the different conditions of the 1920s and 1930s, countless Germans dreamed of a strong leader as such, whether noble or not. And as it happened, the nobles had had their day. Continuities of a national tradition of attitudes and behaviour, of a 'national mystique', reinforced through the repetition of similar national experiences, are a powerful determinant of actual behaviour. The longing for unity which had once been expressed in the dream of Frederick Barbarossa underwent a change of form with changing circumstances and fastened onto other leader figures. The last in the line so far was the strong man for whose coming many Germans worked in the twilight of the Weimar Republic in the hope that he would end what they experienced as repulsive and intolerable: the party strife among Germans and the injustices which, as they saw it, had been inflicted on the German nation by its enemies in 1918.

In contrast to the currently dominant picture of Germany among the nations of the world as a particularly strong and potentially dangerous power, from the fifteenth and sixteenth centuries to the second half of the nineteenth, the country counted, both in Germany itself and abroad, as comparatively weak. The potential weakness of the German Reich in this time and the relative strength of some of its member states may give the impression that one can hardly speak of Germany prior to 1871. Yet as far as one can see, the Germans never ceased to feel themselves as German and were perceived as such by members of other nations, whether they came from Prussia, Hanover, Bavaria or other parts of the Reich.

However, the image which the Germans had of themselves as Germans was profoundly affected by this centuries-long powerlessness of their country. Between them, their continuing identification as Germans and the relative weakness of Germany strengthened the dream-like character of the German self-image and the aura of unreality which often surrounded it. In this way, the tendency to build up an ideal picture of Germany was promoted, a we-ideal that was more idealistic and more divorced from sordid reality than in the case of practically every other country. At the same time, this constellation contributed in no small measure to the contradictions and fluctuations that are typical of the national self-feeling of the Germans. The inherited feeling of inferiority in the hierarchy of the European states and the resentment, the feeling of humiliation which often accompanied it, had their counterpart in the exaggerated stress on their own greatness and power after 1871. And the fluctuations in the self-esteem of Germany followed similar patterns after the two German wars of the twentieth century. Although the self-image of a nation may vary considerably from generation to generation and from social stratum to social stratum, even if one compares it to the corresponding images of other nations, one can recognize very clearly both the continuity and the distinctiveness in the development of each of them.

The use of the term '*Reich*' in Germany is a further example of continuities of this type.[4] The British and French equivalent, 'empire', meant in those countries something towards which the earlier dynastic kingdoms had gradually developed. In Germany, the word, '*Reich*' meant something that had been lost. Germans kept the great German empire of the past alive in their thoughts. Concepts like '*Reich*' helped to perpetuate the memory. Later forms of the state were presented as renewals of the old empire. That the ideal image of a 'Third Reich' appealed to many Germans shows how strong the memory was of the old 'First Reich' as a symbol of Germany's vanished greatness. It formed an integral part of the image which Germans had of themselves.

The selective outline of their own history which found its place in the construction of the national self-image of the Germans had a structure which was different from that of most of the other larger European nation-states. It began with a large and mighty empire which experienced reversals, lost its cohesion and gradually shrank. Only in 1871, centuries afterwards – and later than most other European nations – did Germany attain a new level and, on a smaller scale, yet again a form which approached the ideal image of a 'Reich'. This new state, unified at last, for a short while assumed its place as a European great power, of which many Germans had dreamed; but then, in 1918, it suffered defeat once more, followed, as many Germans experienced it, by the decadent years of the Weimar Republic. In accordance with this historical self-image, the idealized 'Third Reich' represented the third attempt to break the spell which seemed recurrently to be preventing the Germans from achieving the greatness for which they were destined. It was the last and in many ways the most desperate attempt yet again to resurrect the 'Reich' which the Germans had dreamed of over the centuries and which had always eluded them. Like so many of the earlier attempts, it ended with a shrinking of the territories of the Germans. And it led to the splitting-up of Germany into two unequal halves.

The French, the British and even the Russians have all had longer experience of state-unification. They have also all until recently been in their own ways fundamentally expansionist states. Germany for the greater part of its history has been not only a weak state but a shrinking one as well. Its most recent break-up into two parts is only the last link in a chain of similar events in the course of which territories whose inhabitants spoke a variant of German and who at one time or another had belonged to the German Reich, for example the Netherlands, Flanders and parts of Switzerland and Austria, broke away from the main body of the Reich or were driven out. In the High Middle Ages, the German Reich had stretched towards the East. Apart from this first massive wave of colonization and expansion, it had undergone a process of increasing fragmentation. The break in Germany's linguistic development between Middle High German and New High German was symptomatic of a break in the whole German behavioural tradition caused by a shift in the centres of power away from the older western and southern territories towards the more recently colonized territories in the East. In the first half of the seventeenth century, Germany became the cockpit of Europe. In many ways, the German line of development has probably been more disturbed than that of any of the other great European countries. Even a cursory overview shows the effects of this disturbed development on the beliefs, behavioural traditions and self-image of the Germans.

6

However one may want to evaluate it, the national pride, the collective self-esteem of the Germans has always been more fragile than that of peoples like the British and the French who have had a more continuous and even development.

Above all in Britain, whose development from a dynastic state to a nation-state took place in a particularly undisturbed manner compared with that of other countries, national pride and self-respect reached an unusually high degree of firmness and stability. If one were to investigate through a series of case-studies what the relationship is between the patterns of development of different state-societies as wholes and those of their dominant traditions of behaviour and belief, then on a hypothetical scale Britain might form almost the opposite pole to Germany. In both cases, as is typical of nations generally, people grew up with ideas of the worth and significance of their nation which far exceeded any sober, factually grounded assessment. As elsewhere, realistic pride in national achievements and characteristics shaded imperceptibly into pride over exaggerated or wholly imaginary attainments and attributes – into a national hubris based on collective fantasies about being greater and better than all the other people in the world. In Britain, however, for better or worse, national pride as well as national hubris were so firmly rooted that the British could poke fun at themselves and, within limits, tolerate the jokes and laughter of others about them. In Germany, the balance in national self-consciousness between pride and hubris remained relatively insecure and vulnerable. To joke about matters which touched on national pride was here, unless one deliberately wanted to hurt, taboo. Whenever it came into play, German national pride was a solemn and deadly serious matter. Given their insecurity, Germans felt themselves easily wounded. They were inclined to suspect others of looking down upon them. They almost seemed to expect it and were inclined, with or without reason, to become indignant and, as a counter, to lay especially strong emphasis on their own superiority. Even in their own feelings, they tended to fluctuate between a marked under-evaluation and a marked over-evaluation of themselves. The self-image of the British had its swings of the pendulum and contradictions, too, but by comparison they were small.

As in the case of other nations, the self-image of the British contained idealizations of the national past, present and future. Their we-ideal told individual British people what was British and what was not, what it meant to be British, and how as a British person one ought to be. This ideal was not unattainable. It imposed upon those brought up according to it an obligation to behave in a prescribed British way. At the same time, it gave them a reward: the proud and pleasurable feeling that they were acting in accordance with their ideal. National ideal and national reality were not poles apart.

British patriotism was not romantic. Like the Germans, the British often sought guidance in the past. But in their image of Britain, until recently, past and present coalesced. The past was not felt to be a very much greater period than the present. It did not stand out as a time of greatness which was lost for ever, as an unattainable ideal which, by comparison, made the present feel small. Thanks to the unbroken continuity of a firm but relatively flexible tradition, the past in British people's image of Britain and Britishness was able to merge with the present. Slowly adjusted to changing conditions, this image offered to individuals at any given time a very clear idea of their identity as British men and women and very clear guidelines as to what British people ought and ought not to do over almost the whole range of life-situations.

What was and was not German, what it meant to be German and how as a German one ought to behave was far less clear. Compared with the self-image of the British, Germans had only an indeterminate image of their country and its national characteristics. There was no 'way of life' that counted in thinking and speaking as specifically German. The most that was specifically German was a *Weltanschauung*, an overall view of the world. One knew, one felt, that it was of great value to be German; but of what this value consisted remained somewhat vague. Opinions about it differed widely. In the past, as long as Germany was weak, the national pride of the rising German middle classes had been based on common achievements in science, literature, philosophy and music – in short German *Kultur*. Later, when talking about the values of being German, people referred more to common feelings and not so much to common achievements, let alone to achievements which had significance beyond the borders of Germany – significance for humanity as a whole.

The German self-image hardly gave any guidance to individuals when they were thrown back on their own resources. It was not linked to a specific code of conduct which provided individuals, as did the British self-image, with a moderately firm yardstick, internalized as a layer of their own conscience, by which they could judge others as well as themselves. Since the national consciousness of the mass of the Germans was primarily activated on feast days and public holidays and above all in crises and dangerous situations, they were in everyday life, even though no less German, less *conscious* of being German than the British were of being British. The mere sound of the word '*Deutschland*' seemed for Germans to be laden with associations that were out of the ordinary, with a charisma that bordered on the holy. In ordinary life, being German entailed few obligations except in relation to power-holders and persons in authority. For the rest, people could allow themselves to be guided far more by their spontaneous feelings whether friendly, hostile or whatever.

The pride and with it the felt obligation of being British showed itself in ordinary as well as extraordinary situations. National pride was linked here with a form of self-respect – whether in ordinary or exceptional and extreme situations. If one were British, there were things one did and did not do. It went together with an elaborate code of conduct stratified according to class yet unified enough to serve as a collective shibboleth: by it, the British recognized each other. The precisely defined constraints which this code imposed became to some extent second nature, a part of the individual conscience and I-ideal.

Like members of other national groups, the British, too, fell short again and again of the standard embodied in the collective code of rules which they had erected in their own conscience, in their ideal image of how the British ought to behave. But their code, their national ideal itself, took human shortcomings into account. It left room for deviations from the norm as well as for individual eccentricities. And the scope for such deviations, the span between formally demanded and informally tolerated behaviour, the degree to which people were allowed to fall short of the ideal without falling foul of their own self-respect and the respect of their compatriots, was for a given time and in a given circle quite precisely framed. In short, the ideal image which the British had of themselves was a little larger than life but not very much. It was not impossible to live up to. One always had the feeling that Britain left a lot to be desired, as was in fact the case. One grumbled about its shortcomings and thought that this or that had been better in the past or would have to be better in the future. But in the final analysis, the actual life of the country rarely fell too far short of what British people held to be right and proper. And because in general they did not expect perfection, they had less trouble than the Germans in living with each other – provided, that is, that the highly developed British restraints with their many, situationally specific nuances and gradations had been well integrated into a person. Accustomed from childhood onwards to a specific tolerance of human frailties, they made allowances for the fact that even the British were not perfect.

The German ideal, the German code of behaviour, made no concessions to human imperfections and frailties. Its demands were absolute and uncompromising. Nothing less than total compliance with its norms provided satisfaction. During centuries of absolute rule, the Germans had developed an unspoken yearning for national ideals, beliefs, basic principles and standards which could be obeyed absolutely. It was a question of all or nothing. The imperative was categorical. But because the German national ideal was experienced as meaningful, as an object of pride and hence as a source of deep satisfaction only when people were convinced that it was perfect, that it held good unconditionally and absolutely, they could never really live up to it except occasionally for a short while in extraordinary circumstances, especially in times of national crisis.

In normal times, the great ideal picture of Germany remained in the background. It brought some glitter into the life of the German people on holidays. And it cast its shadows, too. It was so exalted that many Germans found the day-to-day business of political life by contrast to be stale and insignificant. In the light of this national ideal, parliamentary matters often appeared to be very sordid affairs. In Britain, the United States and a few other countries where parliamentary democracy formed a centrepiece of the historical legacy, people were able to bear and even enjoy the strains and stresses of party life, the recurrent elections and party controversies, not only because generations had been brought up accustomed to party government, but also because people identified with it and were proud of it. Parliamentary democracy formed part of the ideal picture which people had of themselves as a nation and as persons – of the ideal picture of which they said 'we'. And because people identified with it, because the majority were reasonably well attuned to a tradition of parliamentary behaviour, they also played the great parliamentary game well enough. For many Germans, on the other hand, as for the members of other countries with a long autocratic tradition, parliamentary democracy was not an institution with which they automatically identified when it came in 1918. The considerable demands it made for specific forms of self-control and for precise judgements as to how far it is possible to go in party battles and parliamentary struggles without destroying the nation were not compensated, as in Britain and America, by a feeling of pride in institutions which were seen as specifically their own. Among Germans, the party structure did not fuse with their national ideals; and because, in the eyes of many Germans, politics belonged to an everyday life which was rather humdrum and often sordid, political practice in Germany was often sordid in fact.

In this respect, too, the deep gulf between ideal and reality, between extraordinary and ordinary situations, had far-reaching consequences: the latter were devalued as trivial and meaningless, while approximations to the ideal in extraordinary situations were accompanied by such strong emotional pressure that such behaviour could rarely be kept up for very long. The German national ideal was like a brilliant star high up in the sky. In everyday life it hardly played a role as a guiding thread for action or as a meaningful goal. Here the Germans could loosen the reins. Whether for better or worse, they were far more able than the British to let themselves go. They could relax and allow themselves to do what they wanted as long as they did not violate the external controls, the controls by other people which had been set up in society at large. Especially among the middle and higher strata of the German people, it was a common idea that all people in everyday life simply pursued their egoistic interests. The suspicion: 'Someone must have gained personally from this' was always close at hand. It was frequently justified, yet not always. Only in an hour of crisis, or so it seemed, are people truly lifted above themselves and capable of selfless acts.

Built into this German tradition was thus a latent or open yearning for the spectacular, the out of the ordinary. In this respect, too, German traditions of behaviour and belief were expressive of a highly extreme development of dispositions which, in other industrial countries, were normally observable in a much milder form. A desire for extraordinary situations in which the routines of everyday life are broken is characteristic of all industrial societies. But in most of them the contrast between attitudes in routinized and extraordinary situations was not quite so glaring as in Germany and the underlying tensions not quite so great.

For the less individual self-restraints are supported in everyday life by common norms and goals, the less people are able to live up to their ideals in their day-to-day existence. Thus it is more likely that they will fall back on extraordinary occasions as means of satisfaction which appear capable, on the one hand, of freeing them from the isolating slavery of their selfishness, and, on the other, of promising them a community of feeling in their devotion to common ideals. In pre-Nazi Germany, the latent and often half-conscious longing for the extraordinary event with the power to take people out of themselves, which would tear down the barriers between individual and individual and between ideal and reality, and permit the reconstruction of a true 'community' [*Gemeinschaft*], was the reverse side of the particularly sharp contrast between the traditional national ideal and the day-to-day practice of a parliamentary industrial society. When the crisis came, this longing for the extraordinary was thus available to be used by the most discontented sections of the German people in their struggle for power. Compared with this ideal the goals of ordinary life seemed humdrum and its norms uncertain. Thus, in contrast with Britain, the national ideal fulfilled neither a restraining nor a guiding function in daily life.

Because Germans were brought up with a more strongly exaggerated we-ideal than the British, it was often difficult for them to decide which shortcomings in people, institutions and private and public relationships it was more sensible to tolerate and which it was not. In their work, their striving for perfection stood them in good stead. In their wider social life, particularly their politics, the wide gap between ideal and reality, the quest for perfection, the yearning for an ideal community – the dream Reich – had its counterpart in feelings of emptiness and often of indifference, apathy or criticism; if the ideal could not be reached, it was hardly of importance what one did and how one did it.

7

This German tendency to search for a common ideal outside of daily life was reinforced and, indeed, continually reproduced by the image of supposedly lost national greatness, through the idealized image of the powerful *Kaiserreich* of former times which every German absorbed as part of his or her identity and formed part of the answer to the question: 'What am I as a German?' An analogous image of the national past also formed part of the self-image of the British and the Americans. But in the German case, where it imparted the feeling of a decline which had only been temporarily interrupted, it frequently had a depressive effect. And while the past of other nations often gave their living members the choice between contrasting and antagonistic national heroes – such as Cromwell and King Charles, Lincoln and Jefferson, Louis XIV, Marat and Napoleon – the national heroes in the German pantheon, figures like Frederick the Great or Bismarck, all stood on one side, in accordance with the autocratic tradition and the monolithic structure of the German national ideal. They were all figures, often very much larger than life, who owed their fame to a contribution to the making of the Reich. The only other heroes to enter the collective self-image of the Germans were men like Goethe and Beethoven – culture heroes outside politics, but not 'makers' of 'history', not counter-heroes on a national scale.

In this form, with the glory of the past overshadowing the present, the idealized image of the German Reich was kept alive not only by the teaching of history or by the changes Germany underwent on the map (probably the most vivid representation of a national image) but also by direct or indirect acquaintance with all the groups who spoke a variant of German but who were not citizens of the present state – by the discrepancy between this German state and the 'German *Volk*' which comprised so many larger and smaller groups who were scattered over the territory of the former Reich and beyond. It was this Reich, this ideal image of Germany, which recurrently became a focus for real actions in critical situations. It formed a symbol under which the Germans rallied. It mobilized strong emotional forces; the real and the ideal Germany came closer; sometimes for a short while they became almost one. In such situations, the absolute and uncompromising character of the German national ideal came fully into its own. Where it was a question of the restoration of Germany's old glory, it was possible, as in the case of the pursuit of other absolute ideals, to take no account at all of circumstances – in this case, of the actual political situation. Concessions were out of the question.

Specific characteristics of the Germans which have often been regarded as dangerous were not, as many observers have supposed, the expression of their being naturally endowed with a larger dose of aggression and destructiveness than other peoples. They rested rather on a tendency conditioned into Germans, not only by their behavioural tradition but also by the combined efforts of recurrent historical experiences, schooling and propaganda – on a tendency in crisis situations, when they had been summoned in terms of their exaggerated we-ideal, to act in the name of Germany as unquestioningly as their high ideal demanded, that is, regardless of what others called 'hard reality', independently of the consequences for others and themselves. In the service of the ideal Germany, everything seemed possible and allowed. It was here, in the compelling force of an exclusive belief, of an unconditional national and social belief which momentarily gave to its followers a feeling of omnipotence and which had to be pursued at any price, that the danger lay which later came to be given such extraordinarily virulent expression in the Nazi movement.

Of course, beliefs, ideals and behavioural tendencies of this sort can be found in other nations and other social movements, too. However, the cumulative effect of Germany's disturbed history – a history marked in the long term by defeats and consequent power losses, and which gave rise correspondingly to a broken national pride, a national identity very uncertain of itself, a backwards-looking national ideal which involved the projection of a fantasy picture of the greater past into the future – facilitated the emergence of a particularly malignant variant of beliefs and behavioural tendencies which also arose elsewhere. It was a question of a particularly extreme and dangerous form of devotion to *a priori* ideals, to creeds or principles which were absolute, unyielding, unalterable and could be neither questioned nor modified in the light of new experiences or reasoned argument – in short, to the type of creed which has been characteristic of nationalist and many other social movements since the beginning of the nineteenth century, and before that of countless religious movements in the narrower sense of the term.

Since the beginning of the nineteenth century, a strong tendency has been observable for a high value to be placed on the pursuit of social ideals *per se*. The word 'idealism' came generally to be associated with positive overtones, as something 'good', and the same held true often enough for words like 'belief', 'principle' or 'conviction'. People valued others who had 'firm beliefs' or 'firm principles', who 'stood up for their convictions' or behaved 'idealistically'. It was not always established, however, why the beliefs, principles and ideals in question necessarily had to be 'good'. Whatever one understands by 'good' or 'bad', it is at any rate conceivable that they were 'bad'. Whether a social, political or any other kind of ideal is 'good' or 'bad' evidently depends on the *kind* of ideals, beliefs or principles which prevail at a given time. There are many examples which show that long-term goals and directives in the form of absolute, unchangeable ideals and beliefs can be just as responsible for bitter conflicts and struggles between people as they can for friendliness and advances in co-operation. Their rigidity and exclusiveness, their tendency to be impervious to reasoned arguments or contradictory facts, have proved in many cases to be a potential or actual source of danger. They have certainly been among the principal factors involved in the production of absolute and irreconcilable enmities between different human groups.

The Nazi ideal of a German Reich which was totally free of Jews drove its adherents particularly far in the consummation of the hostility which it instilled in them. But in some ways it differed more in degree than in kind from other *a priori* ideals which produced absolute enmities in the past and continue to do so today. It was particularly extreme in its exclusive character and in its restricted orientation to a single nation or 'race'. In other cases, such as those of Russian and Chinese national communism or American national capitalism, the exclusiveness of the ideal and the enmity which is inspired in the adherents are no less absolute; but they are to a certain degree tempered and modified by the concern for a better future not only of a single nation or 'race' but of humanity as a whole.

Perhaps a clearer distinction should be drawn, as is already customary in the case of magic, between creeds, principles and ideals which are beneficial for people and others which are harmful – between 'white' and 'black' beliefs, 'white' and 'black' ideals. As has already been said, one basically misunderstands the meaning and particular character of the National Socialist movement and Hitler's Germany if one fails to appreciate the sincerity and compelling force of their collective convictions. Both the victory and the failure of the National Socialist movement remain incomprehensible if account is not taken of the strongly idealistic element in their beliefs which often made the Führer and his followers blind to considerations other than those dictated by their creed, occasionally allowing them to see the world entirely in the light of their own hopes and wishes. Their devotion to an ideal as such stands out clearly from the documents and records they have left. But their idealism shows in almost exemplary form the characteristics of a 'black idealism': the constructive side of their beliefs was massively overwhelmed by its destructive and barbaric aspects. It was this basic character of Nazi rule which, together with other, similar factors, played a fundamental role in the breakdown of civilization in Germany, culminating in such events as the cruel treatment of prisoners of war and the setting up and operation of concentration camps and gas chambers.

In the normal course of political conduct, preconceived and dogmatic national beliefs and ideals coalesce and blend in the decisions made by national leaders with more realistic and flexible considerations related to the long-term conditions under which all nations have to live. But there are situations in which preconceived and dogmatic beliefs gain the upper hand. Especially in national emergencies such as wars, they gain a momentum of their own, the strength of which will vary according to circumstances, not least according to national behavioural traditions. Some nations incline more, others less to this total surrender to an exclusive we-ideal. It would be quite unjustified to imply that the rise of a movement such as the National Socialists followed necessarily and unavoidably from the German national tradition. But although not necessary, it was certainly one of the possible developments implicit in this tradition. In some respects, National Socialism bore all its characteristic hallmarks.

8

Among the continuing characteristics which deserve to be mentioned in this connection – and which are understandable in the light of German history – is the tendency for people in times of national emergency to submit themselves, at least for a while, to an extremely rigorous discipline and rule when they were imposed in the name of Germany. An absolute, unquestioning obedience was held in such situations to be a national duty of every individual. If one had to destroy others, they had to be destroyed. If the sacrifice of one's own life was required, one had to die. Few other peoples had in their national mystique, in their poetry and in their songs so many allusions to death and self-sacrifice as did the Germans. Schiller's 'Guten Kamaraden' [Good Comrades], in which a soldier is depicted as marching and fighting side by side with the best friend he ever had until a fatal bullet struck him, was a favourite song of German soldiers and the German people generally. Other examples are Heine's song of the 'Lorelei' who enchanted the fisherman so that he forgot the dangers around him and drowned; or Herwegh's songs 'Soldaten: Morgenlied', in which the red dawn lights the singer's path to an early death, or 'Reiterlied', about the men riding through the dark night 'to their death, to their death'.[5]

These songs were sung with fervour, again and again; they had a strange fascination for the Germans. The lessons of history had taught them of the greatness of Germany – a greatness which was lost. They had learned that it was the duty of a German to uphold this greatness, to restore it if the occasion arose, and without more ado to march to victory whatever the consequences might be for one's self or for others.

But, at the deepest levels of their thinking and feeling, the memory of the lost generations, of the upsurge of hope followed by destruction and death, could never be fully extinguished. While the British, in accordance with the lessons of history, seemed to be convinced at the deepest level that they would win the last battle, even if they suffered a defeat (a conviction which helped them, in fact, to win), the Germans, even when they were victorious, never seemed quite able to silence the feeling that they would lose the last battle (which contributed in no small measure towards their eventually losing it).

Yet independently of what Germans felt in ordinary life, in times of national crisis their specific national belief system exercised strong pressure upon them: it compelled them to follow leaders who proclaimed it to be the duty of Germans once more to take the field against the common foe. They could not easily escape the demands made on them in the name of Germany since these demands were strengthened by their own conscience and we-ideal, by their ideal image of themselves – their images of how a German ought to behave. Not only external but also inner compulsions, their pride, their identity, their value-consciousness as Germans, all acted upon them in such a situation. In their Fatherland's hour of need, they had to obey the call to arms for better or for worse. And while marching against the enemies of their country whom they hoped to defeat, they were burdened by the memory of earlier generations who, like them, had marched loyally, unquestioningly and with similar faith in Germany's victory, towards defeat and death. The sad German songs about people going to meet their deaths as if under a self-sacrificial spell – *morituri te salutamus* ('those who are about to die salute thee') – gave expression to this mood. They reflected a pattern of history and society as well as a pattern of ideals and conscience.

Few other nations were as inclined as the Germans to give a place in their national pantheon to heroes who died in defeat – heroes like the '*Schillschen* officers' who were court-martialled and shot after rising up against Napoleon in a vain attempt to free Prussia from the French occupation. Then there was the widely read ballad, reprinted in many schoolbooks, of Alaric, King of the Goths, who, defeated and killed in battle, was buried by his loyal warriors in the bed of a river whose waters had been diverted and were then allowed to return after his burial so that no enemy could defile his corpse:

> And a chorus of men sang:
> 'Sleep in your hero's honour!'

No Roman's base greed
Shall ever soil your grave!'

Today this poem reads like a rehearsal for the death of Hitler, who, defeated and killed by his own hand, was secretly burned and buried so that, in his case, too, no enemy should lay a hand upon his corpse.[6]

The 'heroic death' was a standing motif not only of German songs but also of German history itself, or at least of what remained alive as such for later generations. The gradual achievement of the status as national heroes of the brave men who tried to topple Hitler and to kill him, a large proportion of whom were barbarically executed, corresponds yet again to the traditional German pattern according to which heroism and sacrifice for 'the Fatherland' end in disaster and defeat. In this case, however, there is something new. If they are remembered, they will be the first Germans to be remembered because they fought in the name of Germany against the ruler of the German state. Apart from that, their example, too, will teach every schoolchild the recurring lesson of German history, namely that heroism, unflinching devotion to 'the Fatherland' to which one is obligated as a German, regularly leads to defeat and death. Nowhere was this lesson formulated explicitly. Rather it was implicit in the German heritage and passed on from one generation to the next.

9

Comparison with other peoples shows that they, too, in correspondence to the lessons of history and the self-images which emerge from these lessons, each have their own peculiar development of patriotism and nationalism. All these variants include forms of loyalty-bonding which are typical of specific social formations and share a number of basic common features. Despite many claims to the contrary, patriotism and nationalism, although often separated conceptually, in fact form a continuum. They differ from each other by degrees and not in qualitative respects. They differ, for example, in terms of the degrees of superiority, exclusivity and enmity towards others which they involve. Both concepts signify a feeling of personal bonding, identity and belonging in relation to one's country, an unquestioning belief in its pre-eminent value as something which must be defended at any price in times of need, even at the cost of one's own life, a belief which has as its correlate the external obligations which every country imposes on its individual members.

Everywhere in modern nation-states, the external compulsion which is imposed on people in times of national need has its counterpart in a feeling of loyalty and duty towards one's country which is more or less firmly anchored, so to say, in the 'inside' of individuals as a pattern of conscience. It is also anchored in a belief that the survival of the nation is the highest value. Everywhere in national crises and quite often in times of peace as well, people are urged, as soldiers or performing other functions, to join the armed forces and subordinate their own ambitions, goals, hopes, even their own survival, to the survival of the society to which they belong. One can speak of 'individualism', prize the 'freedom of the individual' as the highest social value and proclaim the primacy of 'the individual' in relation to 'state', 'nation' or 'society' – in times of national need individual freedom is everywhere curtailed; the survival of individuals is put at the back of the queue, behind that of society. And even in peace-time, many organizational and educational measures taken by a modern nation-state – in terms specific to the national belief system, a special kind of social religion – are directed towards war.

Organized life-and-death struggles between different societies are nothing new. But in their present form as a state-wide event, the subordination of individual to social demands is very recent. The 'people's army' is a relatively late development. Before the French Revolution, and in many countries more recently, the conduct of war was a matter for nobles and career officers, together with units from the ranks of the poor who were recruited into military service for pay. The view that, as private citizens not serving with the forces, nobles and gentlemen had nothing to do with their country's wars was not wholly extinct, at least in Britain at the time of the Napoleonic Wars, and one or two indignant voices were raised when Napoleon molested British people in Paris because he found himself at war with Britain.

The present forms of patriotism and nationalism are closely bound up with the rise to power of the industrial middle and working classes. Their emergence was also closely connected with the fact that particular countries came to rely for attack and defence increasingly on their citizenry as a whole. The formation of secular national belief systems – involving the idea of one's own country as the bearer of such high worth that all inhabitants are expected to give up their lives for it – and the inclination of individuals of all classes to identify with their country, that is, to regard their membership of a country as an integral component of their self-image, was bound up with the increasing democratization of state-societies and with the need for people's armies. It was not only in Germany but in all the more highly developed industrial nation-states that members of the upper and middle classes and, depending on the degree to which social integration gained ground, members of the working classes, too, came to be tied to their country as much through 'inner' ideas and beliefs as through 'external' controls.

Admittedly, nowhere does the conflict between the wish for individual survival and the wish for the survival of the nation take the simple form of a conflict between 'the individual' and an 'outer' power called the 'state' or 'society'; it is always a question simultaneously of an 'inner' conflict between different compulsions of one and the same individual. The rules and norms of a nation-state, together with the system of attitudes and beliefs which is supported through the external constraint [*Fremdzwang*] of the state, have their counterpart in the inner constraint [*Selbstzwang*] which individuals exert on themselves in the form of their conscience and their we-ideal.

One may incline towards the view that the pattern of the 'outer' and 'inner', of external constraint [*Fremdzwang*] and self-constraint [*Selbstzwang*] simply complement and augment each other. One finds such an idea in Durkheim: the society, so he seems to have thought, projects its norms and rules into an individual. Freud and many of his followers assumed an equally static correspondence, even if in their case it often appears as if it is 'the individual' who projects his or her pattern of conscience into the 'society'. And so long as the model from which one begins is simply of a society at a particular point in time, so long as it is fundamentally a static model, there will hardly be any possibility of handling matters in anything other than one of these two ways. By proceeding thus, however, one cannot handle the many problems which the relationship between the organization and patterning of personal and social controls throws up. One can only begin to grasp them when static models are replaced by dynamic models, when societies as well as individuals are seen as processes of development.

From such a starting point, it becomes easier to detect the changing degrees of correspondence and non-correspondence between patterns of state-control and conscience-control and to explain them. If one simply asks what they are at a particular point in time and how they are connected without asking how they have developed and how, in the course of their development, they have come to be combined, their correspondences as well as their discrepancies will remain obscure. The accompanying means of speaking and thinking will also remain inadequate. It is usual to express everything that exerts 'external' constraint on individuals with concepts such as 'society', and everything which can be internalized by individuals through concepts such as 'culture', as if both these aspects of social development were not only different but also separate data. Distinctions are made without clear models of connections. One cannot, *de facto*, clearly recognize the connections between – whatever it is – 'society' and 'culture', 'state' and 'individual', 'external' and 'internal' steering mechanisms, unless one conceptualizes them as something in movement, as aspects of social processes which are themselves processes, indeed as functionally interdependent processes involving varying degrees of harmony and conflict.

The change-relationships between these aspects are complex. It is flatly not the case that one of them is the prime motor of social development while others only have secondary effects or passively follow. As aspects of a social process most of them have both active and passive functions. They form and are formed, drive and are driven or are active through the sheer resistance with which they oppose changes beyond themselves. To be sure, the degree to which they are able to influence each other and the development of society as a whole varies. On account of their peculiar properties some of the many part-processes which we tend to represent as 'spheres' in the development of a country – the 'economic', 'cultural', 'political' spheres, etc – are more powerful agents of change than others. But their power in relation to each other is by no means always the same in all types of society, at all stages of social development. And they are, moreover, not always so sharply separated as our present-day terminology makes it appear. This terminology has become more differentiated as society itself has become more differentiated and complex.

Complexity is increased by differences in the degree to which people at this or that stage of development are able to control and manipulate these particular social spheres or part-processes. State-institutions in recent times, for example, have not infrequently been consciously and systematically changed. Up to now, however, 'culture' or the peculiarities of a 'national character' have been far more resistant to planned manipulation. Many of the conceptual distinctions that we are accustomed to encountering rest simply on differences of this sort. Labels for particular social 'spheres' which we see as their eternal properties often represent nothing more than our greater or lesser capacity to control them. In the political sphere, the progress is clear enough. The protagonists of the American and French revolutions in the eighteenth century set about changing the political institutions of their countries with greater clear-sightedness and reflection than the supporters of Cromwell in the seventeenth; and the range of knowledge, the degree of deliberateness with which Russian power elites in the twentieth century pursued their revolutionary enterprise was greater yet again in comparison with the earlier revolutions in America and France.

So long as differences in the degree of conscious control which people at a given stage are able to wield in different spheres of their social life are not recognized as such, it will not only lead to the formation of false and muddled concepts but also create specific problems of social development. One of the chief problems of German development after the First World War was of this kind.

Through the defeat of 1918, it became possible in Germany to transform political institutions in the direction of a parliamentary democracy in a highly conscious way. With the help of these institutional changes, people tried to stabilize specific transformations in the intra-state balance of power. Germany's traditional upper and middle classes and their representative power elites had suffered a loss of power as a result of the defeat; the rising working classes and their power elites, together with relatively small liberal sections of the old middle classes, among them many Jews and the liberal and socialist intelligentsia, had gained through the change. But the national traditions of belief and behaviour of these different groups in German society were less touched by the change than were the political institutions. At that time in Germany and elsewhere people did not have a clear idea of how 'national characteristics' perpetuate themselves; and, correspondingly, people did not know how these characteristics could be influenced in a desired direction. They were far less accessible to planned control than political and other social institutions. As a result, Germans in this period experienced a fairly abrupt spurt in the development of institutions and power relationships without experiencing an analogous spurt in the development of their 'national character'. While the institutions underwent a noticeable change in the sense of greater democratization, the power relationships retained much more the authoritarian imprint which they had acquired in the centuries of autocratic rule. It was one of the more fantastic expressions of the ahistorical rationalism of this century that people then supposed (as many still do today) that a democratization of attitudes, beliefs and convictions would follow in the footsteps of the establishment of democratic, parliamentary institutions.

10

In most of the German states, the habituation of many centuries had produced a tradition of attitudes and beliefs which was attuned to strong rule from above with very little or no participation at all from the ruled. People had become more or less accustomed to all decisions touching on the control of the state being in the hands of small, autocratic elites who held the reins of power in a far-reaching system of control. To a certain extent, as always happens, this pattern of external control had been internalized. (As a result of broader education, such a pattern is more evident in dictatorial national autocracies than in pre-national monarchical ones.) The personality structure, conscience-formation and code of behaviour had all become attuned to this form of regime. Private persons could only make decisions in spheres where the state did not appear to reach and in which there were no direct state-controls, for example in areas such as philosophy, literature and music. For the rest, people who did not belong to the ruling power elites were cut off from all public responsibilities and decisions. The burdens, as well as the pleasures, of ruling remained alien to them. And even when sections of the intelligentsia demanded greater political participation, the skills, patterns of conscience and codes of behaviour which are necessary for a (limited) exercise of self-rule began to grow in a direction different from the demand. They did not develop automatically and immediately when institutions were changed. A number of peculiarities of the German development worked against such an adaptation.

Among these peculiarities were not only the long time during which Germany had been fragmented and ruled autocratically, or the dream-like, demanding, unconditional type of ideals and the philosophical manner of thinking that resulted from it, but also the form and manner in which the unity of the country was finally brought about in 1871. One of the most important distinguishing marks of the German sequence of development was the fact that national unification and the whole epoch of early industrialization, with its power-increment for the industrial middle class and working class, took place within the framework of a still mainly autocratic regime.

The process of transformation through which the autocratic-dynastic states of an earlier period became nation-states began, in Germany as elsewhere, above all in conjunction with an increase in the power-potential of the middle classes and a heightening of their self-consciousness. As in France, the transition to a nation-state stage was first accomplished when the 'third estate', thanks to increasing commercialization and industrialization, gained in power and became aware of that fact. But in contrast to most other European countries, the 'third estate' in Germany was unable to translate its greater power-potential into effective common action against the old autocratic establishment. In particular, the fragmentation of Germany into a multitude of kingdoms and princedoms made it more difficult for the German middle class and working class, in comparison with what happened in more strongly centralized states, to form unified organizations which at least embraced the country's largest cities. There was no dominant capital city such as London or Paris which could serve as a decisive focal point for action. In addition to this, when in 1848 a chance arrived, the division of the third estate into a middle class and a working class was already more advanced than it had been in the late eighteenth century. The self-awareness of groups of what was now the 'fourth estate', the pressure which representatives of the working classes exerted on representatives of the middle classes, had grown. The German middle classes saw themselves in that context as hemmed in between two fronts. Their revolt against the traditional noble and bureaucratic elites was counter-checked by their fear of the ascendant working classes and their elites. Standing literally in 'the middle', they were incapable of decisive action against the ruling order.

As a result, in the end the German middle classes had to obtain fulfilment of their national dream at the hands of their autocratic rulers. Even in the first great phase of industrialization during which the power-potential of the German middle class and also of the working class grew, their political power remained extremely limited. As the dream of a unified German nation became a reality, the German state remained in great measure still an authoritarian state and the idea which the majority of subjects had of their nation and of politics at a national level remained, just as before, fixed on unrealities. The national ideal of the Germans was not, as in the case of many other European countries, bound up with victorious reform and revolutionary movements against an autocrat and his regime. It included no images of counter-heroes who could be counterposed to royal or noble hero-figures. It offered no models which showed how one can fight for social dreams, how one can test them in reality and successfully translate them into fact. Even after its realization, which came about as a gift from above, this ideal preserved its strongly autocratic character, bathed in a twilight of fantasies. The habit of being ruled from above remained virulent; the idea that one could lean on a superior authority and entrust it with the responsibility and power of command retained its force of attraction.

As long as the mass of the German people – it was similar in other countries, too – lived in dynastic states where everything turned on the court of the ruler and the cleft which divided the people from the privileged power elites was very great, membership of the organization which we call 'the state' resembled more something about which one would say 'you' and less something about which one would say 'we'. When Germany was unified under the Prussian rulers, both images – that of the German state which still remained to a large extent an organization of the privileged and which was experienced by the mass of the people as 'you', and that of the German nation with which the middle class and later also the working class could identify and about which they said 'we' – slowly began to fuse. And so it came about that the self-image of the nation as a 'we-unit' absorbed the association with an autocratic central power instead of, as in many other cases, shaking it off.

Among the symptoms of this fusion were expressions such as one mentioned before: 'We Germans need a strong man who keeps us firmly in hand.' It was reflected in half-comic anecdotes such as the story of the old Saxon before 1914 who every evening on his way home passed the royal castle and, seeing the light on in the king's chamber, would go to bed with the soothing feeling: 'the king is watching over and working for us.' Subjection to an authority found its reward in the satisfaction that one did not need to worry about matters of state – that one could leave the responsibility in the hands of others. As an example, one can cite the classic German rhyme: 'I thank God every new morning that I don't need to bother about the Roman Empire' ['*Ich danke Gott an jeden neuen Morgen daß ich nicht brauch' fürs Römisch Reich zu sorgen*']

The growing-up process of the broader population in which they undergo the transition from autocracy to active participation in the affairs of state, and with it the building of a nation, was or is not in any country so simple a process as many people seem to think. To be sure, to be ruled and to leave to others the responsibility and the right of command is quite often experienced as threatening and unpleasant; but it also has, for autocratically ruled adults as for children, its deep gratifications. It is a situation which people seldom give up without considerable pressure. The course of events may push the mass of a people in this direction. Yet as a rule, those affected follow the pressure of events with clearer ideas of what they are fighting against than of what they are fighting for. Subordination to autocratic power elites, whether of a monarchical or a dictatorial kind, becomes a deeply embodied habit. People who have acquired it – even when they are highly dissatisfied with their rulers – for the most part find it difficult to be ruled in any other way. The transition to a non-authoritarian regime requires the learning of new social techniques and skills which make greater demands on people's independence and self-control and ability to make judgements of their own. As a rule, people emerge only gradually from a long era of autocracy in which the related habits have taken root, and the inclination in the transitional phase to revert to a phase of autocracy in every serious crisis is very widespread.

The German process of development in this respect was not in any way exceptional. The only peculiarity was the degree to which the habits and images of autocracy flowed – without counter-images – into the national code and the national self-image, and the particularly demanding, unconditional and, in this sense, particularly oppressive character of the authoritarian-state tradition which found expression in the we-ideal of the German nation.

11

Identification with a social unit which has massive compulsion-functions, even love for such a unit and identification with the oppressor at the level of conscience and ideals, was not limited to Germany alone. At the present level of human development, it is a feature of all nation-states.

Their descent from autocratic states ruled by princes who made war on each other can be traced in the continuation of this princely tradition. Just as was earlier the case with dynastic states, so nation-states remain guided by the belief that differences of interest and opinion have to be settled by war. But in great dynastic states, it was not to the same degree either possible or necessary for people of all classes and regions to be bound together by a unified, impersonal and strongly internalized system of beliefs which entered into the self-image of every individual. The maintenance of what we call the 'morality' of a people or of fighting troops was achieved to a great extent through external pressure and constraint, and secularization had not yet advanced so far that non-religious justifications of war by reference to 'national interests', 'social ideals' and so forth had become convincing for the mass of the people.

In more democratized industrial nation-states where the urban middle and working classes had, potentially or actually, more power at their disposal, it was a question of developing common national values, beliefs and doctrines which still continued to include the idea of what was the *ultima ratio regum*. It was regarded, first of all in Europe and later in the rest of the world, as an essential means for protecting the integrity of a nation that every individual should be prepared in times of emergency to kill the enemies of the nation and sacrifice his own life. Through the creation of this disposition, such national doctrines, which, even in peace-time, prepared the majority of the population in all nations of the earth for war and the submission of individual existence to the state, contributed quite a bit to the never-ending series of wars. Exclusive national religions and the absolute enmities which they mutually produced and nourished became one of the main factors responsible for the recurrent breakdown of civilization in the form of wars.

Of course, the tragedy was sharpened by the particular character of the internalized oppressor which the image of a nation that could demand one's life in an emergency obtained in Germany. There are two points to stress in this connection.

On the one hand, there was the unusually strict and demanding character of the German ideal. As far as matters of the nation were concerned, no compromise appeared to be permissible. Whatever there was to do, it had to be done unconditionally. Consideration of real circumstances was often judged to be the product of a cold, calculating reason, of a kind appropriate in business and commerce but not in the affairs of 'the Fatherland'. The particularly oppressive features of the national tradition of conscience and behaviour in Germany were closely bound up with the high fantasy content of the German national ideal, with the highly idealized imprint which it had obtained over the centuries during which the national reality was unsatisfactory and a testing of the reality of the collective ideal was either not possible or, through fear of disappointment, not desired. For the stronger the fantasy-impulses in the demands made by people's conscience, the less are these demands accessible to modification through critical testing with the help of facts, the less people are able to escape them and the harsher, more menacing and tyrannical they become.

And the compulsive, inescapable and unrelenting character of such demands is increased when they derive not only from the conscience and ideals of every individual but are, beyond that, imposed mutually on each other by a number of individuals. Collective pressure in the same direction, towards which the conscience and ideals of individuals also push, the *mutual reinforcement* of internalized voices, whether recognized or not, sets in motion a specific form of group dynamics which can be frequently observed in present-day societies and about which more will be said later: its working within the National Socialist leadership, above all after the outbreak of the war, is easy enough to see, at least if a conceptual model of it is worked out and put into use. Social reinforcement makes even more difficult the renunciation of fantasy demands of conscience and ideals, which, at best, individuals might be able successfully to achieve on their own. It paralyses even more critical judgement and the capacity to perceive contradictory facts for what they are. It allows these demands, however fantasy-laden they may be, to appear self-evident, normal and highly realistic. Above all in times of crisis, people are driven through reciprocal reinforcements more and more to exaggerate the demands of their 'inner voices', their beliefs and convictions, their moral principles, ideals or whatever, and to obey them more and more uncompromisingly. In such a situation, groups, social movements or whole nations can become caught in a dynamic of escalation which increasingly stresses their collective fantasies, leading them into increasingly reality-blind behaviour until, finally, the great crash comes which – usually with a high loss of human life – brings them back down to earth, more clearly revealing in retrospect the emptiness of their compulsive idealism.

Leaders who come to the fore while such a process is in motion usually follow the trend and exploit it. In the struggle for leadership positions, the most likely victors are those contenders who, whether of the first or second rank, are best able to embody the trends towards radicalization and give expression to the common beliefs, doctrines and goals in their more extreme form. For leaders are not simply, as is sometimes said, 'father figures'. In order to be accepted as leaders, they have to correspond more or less to a leader-image which belongs to the tradition or, to express it in static terms, the 'culture' of those whom they wish to lead. A leader must be capable of fulfilling a role in the ideal image which a nation or other grouping has of itself – its national self-image. The scope which this image allows for variations and contradictory types of leader may be greater or smaller. For its part, the leader image can be changed through the acts and behaviour of individual leaders, especially when they are successful. But all variations, contradictions and changes will be specific: they will be stamped by the development of this particular nation or other collectivity.

When, therefore, in a nation, or some of its powerful sections, forms of belief, conscience and ideals – in short, levels of control within the personality itself – are traditionally particularly strict and authoritarian, as was the case in Germany, people will, in all probability, turn to leaders with similar characteristics. In fact, differences between the types of leaders which tend to predominate in the historical pantheons of particular nations can serve as indicators of differences between the traditional leader-images and the ideal self-images, the 'we-ideals' of these nations.

The fact that national developments produce not only specific social institutions but also specific national beliefs, doctrines, patterns of conscience and ideals which become part of the personality of individuals contributed considerably to the fact that, in Germany as elsewhere, specific properties of a common tradition of beliefs and behaviour could be continued over the generations – so long as the nation as a whole or its ruling groups did not suffer drastic defeats which forced a reorientation of the collective self-image and, with it, of the collective beliefs, moral ideals and goals. When a nation such as Germany, with a traditional inclination to an autocratic pattern of conscience and a we-ideal which subjected the future to a dream-image of a greater past, became caught up, during a national crisis, in a dynamic of escalation in which, first of all, the ruling power elites and later wider social circles drove each other through mutual reinforcement to a radicalization of behaviour and beliefs and a progressive blocking of reality-perceptions, then there was an acute danger that the traditional autocratic traits would intensify into tyrannical harshness and that the fantasy-dominance, although previously moderate, would grow stronger and stronger.

12

The other peculiarity of the German identification with an oppressor was connected with the fact that, apart from its particularly disturbed course, German history over the centuries was, with many ups and downs, a history of decline. The compensation for the exercise of compulsion-functions by the state which the members of other nations received – the satisfaction from a cumulative gain in power, pride and fame – was only granted to the Germans for short periods. In most phases of their history, these compensations were denied them. Even today, in France and Britain images of Louis XIV or Napoleon, Henry VIII or Elizabeth I have their place as symbols of success in the self-images of their peoples. In Germany by contrast, a long tradition of autocratic rule went hand in hand with relative lack of success. Over the centuries, exemplary victories were thinly spread in comparison with defeats, gradual decline and repeated spurts of power-loss relative to other, rising states. Whether it was a question of the end of the Hohenstaufens or the Hohenzollerns or finally of the end of Hitler and his regime, the result every time was a weaker or smaller Germany.

It is probably also necessary in this connection to seek an answer to the problem of what is often described as the German inclination to sentimentality and self-pity. The 'Fatherland-ideal' which a growing proportion of the German people absorbed into their conscience in the nineteenth and twentieth centuries as a more or less automatic self-steering mechanism in their behaviour, especially in situations of tension and conflict with foreigners, represented the demands of a state whose image was sufficiently great and glorious to justify the sacrifice of one's life but which appeared simultaneously to be condemned to decline and failure so that the sacrifice was in vain. The ideal contained the promise of a fate as glittering as only love can be, accompanied by a foretaste of catastrophe and hopelessness which was as bitter as death.

Many features of the German tradition of belief and behaviour are best explained by reference to the peculiar pattern of German history as a history of decline. In that way, it is not least seen somewhat more clearly which of the many potentials that lay hidden within such a tradition coalesced in the origins of such a cruel and barbaric movement as the National Socialists. The rise and fall of this movement marked the point in which a whole period of German history came to an end – the period in which Germans had a feeling of greatness orientated primarily to their past, symbolized through the concept of an 'empire' [*Reich*].

Nearly all European nations were drawn sooner or later into the competition for an empire. But their energies were for the most part directed, at least in recent times, towards an empire overseas. The Germans were practically the only ones who had as part of their tradition of beliefs and behaviour the image of an empire in Europe. They were bound to this tradition all the more strongly by the fact that, in the struggle for an overseas empire, they lagged so far behind on both internal and external grounds.

The National Socialist movement came on the scene at a time when the traditional dream of restoring the German empire was more strongly threatened than ever by the factual course of events. Some groups of German people were increasingly worried because the dream of a great German empire in Europe, and, with it, a great deal of what they found most meaningful and valuable, appeared to be more and more incompatible with Germany's real situation. Until the defeat of 1918, the dream had lived on. Now, however, the history of Germany had almost reached a point where the Germans, who for centuries, despite their actual weakness, had seen themselves as a great and powerful, leading nation, would have to open their eyes to the fact that their country was no longer a first-rank nation or a potential centre of a far-flung empire. The National Socialist episode marked the moment in Germany when it became almost unavoidable to recognize that the imperial dream was the echo of a past which had gone for ever and of a greatness which would never return. Whatever else was responsible for the barbarity of the Hitler period, one of its grounds was certainly the refusal to see and accept this development. The strength of the downwards trend was reflected in the extreme brutality of the means with which people sought to check it.

Other European nations faced the same problem at the same time or later. Everywhere a painful reconstruction of the national self-image and feeling of self-worth was demanded; everywhere a difficult re-arrangement of traditions of belief and behaviour was required. For Germans, however, this task was particularly hard because the reality of their national existence had only seldom come up to their expectations, to their ideal image of themselves as Germans.

Britain was struck less abruptly by the shock which a nation experiences when its members become aware of their loss of power, of the reduction of their international status. In the British case, the unavoidable turbulence of the transition from the status of a world power to a power of second rank where people have to recognize that their dream of an empire is over was noticeably more muted. However, even in this case one could hear voices which complained bitterly and angrily over the course of events. For example, the following manifesto appeared in *The Times* of 1 January 1962. It read:

- All pretensions of world leadership have slipped away from us
- Our foreign policy is almost non-existent . . .
- Our share of world trade is declining . . .
- Taxation is rising
- Bureaucracy flourishes and becomes ever more arrogant
- Monopolies and restrictive practices bedevil industry and free enterprise
- The standard of education is falling

- Our traditional pride of craftsmanship is disappearing
- Nationalization and the selfishness of the miners have between them killed our export coal trade . . .
- Crime and violence are on the increase, and no longer receive proper punishment
- The Trade Unions openly hold the country to ransom and have become a state within a state
- Electricity, our key industry, is still largely in the grip of Mr Frank Foulkes, Communist President of the [Electrical Trades Union]
- Death and injury on the roads, caused by drunkenness and selfishness are increasing
- Children are brought up to believe that the world owes them a living
- The moral standard of the nation is lower than it has been for more than 200 years
- Patriotism and loyalty are out of fashion.[7]

The 'National Fellowship' which announced itself to the public with these words, said of itself that it had:

Taken upon itself the tremendous task of endeavouring to give Great Britain a lead in restoring our moral standards and returning to our former greatness. We believe that despite many errors of omission and commission Great Britain has contributed more to the advance of civilization than other nations and that the world still needs our leadership.

The historical situation, the phase of development in which Britain found itself around 1960, had many things in common with that of Germany at the time of the rise of the National Socialists.[8]

In both cases we encounter the decline of national power, the dawning realization of loss and the burning desire for restoration of the old greatness. Nevertheless the reaction to a comparable situation was, in correspondence to the different tradition of beliefs and behaviour, in many respects different, too. One senses how enormously difficult it is, after having been for centuries a leading power, to come to terms with a lower status in the international ensemble. In Britain, the older, more established power elite also used this difficulty to an extent as a weapon in its struggle against the broader distribution of power which is both a concomitant of and a condition for industrialization. It also used it against the social reforms which are necessary so that such a process can continue and enable a nation to maintain the same rank in the competitive struggle with other advancing nations. There was the same feeling as previously in Germany that one's own nation was superior to all others, even if in the German case this was justified in terms of the unexplained natural fact of racial superiority and in the British by reference to a unique contribution to civilization. There was the same pressure for the restoration of former greatness in the face of the corrosive influence of the trades unions, the miners and, above all, of all social groups that people felt hostile towards; but in one case the return to former glory was bound up with the earlier moral standard, whereas in the other it had to be reached without any consideration of morals and humanity. There was the insider-blindness for everything which did not affect one's own group, the mutual reinforcement of wishes and hopes, and the mutual persuasion that the irretrievable could and must be brought back, that the old greatness, the leading role in world politics, could and must be restored.

But although this can serve as an omen for future adjustment-difficulties, Britain was nevertheless one of the few great European nations that tried to adjust to a loss of power without using violence in a final recrudescence and without resisting the threatening change in the balance of power between states through a war. Compared with the bloody rearguard actions of numerous countries, the few occasions on which Britain tried to preserve its earlier position by force, such as the Suez crisis for example, seem like small indiscretions. Evidently a national tradition came to the help of the British which enabled them to a considerable extent to judge and revise their national ideals in terms of a fairly realistic diagnosis of factual events.

Furthermore, centuries of power and glittering achievements had created in Britain a feeling of national self-worth that was far more secure than in most other European countries, especially Germany. The British system of national beliefs had, since time immemorial, legitimated their claim to superiority at least partially through Britain's service and achievements for others, for humanity and civilization. The claim to a leading role in world politics – a frequent leitmotif of the British national ideology – was characteristic of the form and manner in which the sights of British people were directed by their belief system to the world outside Britain. In it was reflected the experience of a people who, for centuries, had traded with and colonized great parts of the world. By contrast, the German national ideology was turned in on itself. A claim which rested on the superiority of one's own race could not be justified in terms of service for other people, even for their leaders. British people, just like the Germans, used the word 'race' in a sense which established their superiority. But when the former said 'the British race', the expression was filled with a feeling of superiority which no longer needed to be especially stressed. People perpetually form hierarchies; but politeness towards others and service to them were among the things which were necessary for one's own well-being.

The German national ideal was much more ambitious and far more removed from real events. As a result, its tyrannical and oppressive character emerged in a situation of decline much more blatantly. Its compulsive character permitted no corrections on grounds of anything so unimportant as the real course of events. Realities had to be altered without considering losses and adjusted to the national ideal. With a national tradition of the kind which had formed in Germany, the shock of finding themselves once more as a second- or third-rate power was far more difficult to bear. There were many factors which favoured the extremism of German social movements in the 1920s and 1930s. One of the most powerful among them was the attempt to avoid at any price the shock of recognizing Germany's altered position, and the burning desire to reverse the process of development which was threatening to plunge Germany into second- or third-rate status. In part, the attempt turned out to be so wild and barbaric because, in comparison with the ideal, with the dream empire which the National Socialists set out to restore, the factual resources of Germany were already very small.

13

The last train of thought cannot properly be taken further without once more turning to some of the broader implications of what has been said for one's image of human beings. Much of it, or so it may appear, contradicts the usual idea of the relationship between 'individual' and 'society'.

What was observable in the national character of the Germans as a tendency towards self-pity and sentimentality was, at least in part, like other German peculiarities, the symptom of a deep conflict. It was the heightened version of a typical basic conflict which one encounters in one form or another among the members of all great nation-states with a highly individualized population. In Germany, through the special pattern of the country's development as a nation-state, it was given a special twist.

It was not simply a conflict of the kind which Freud seems to have postulated and which results from the development of individuals on their own. At first glance, it appears to be a conflict between the desire of an individual for personal survival and his or her wish for the survival of the society to which he/she belongs – a social unit to which the individual is bound through a feeling of identity and which at the same time transcends him or her. The more kinship groups such as families and clans lost their function as carriers of the identity of persons stretching beyond death, the more the same function was strengthened for other social formations. For a time in Europe, specialized religious organizations such as churches which grew up alongside state-organizations and which were often their rivals in the struggle for power were the principal foci towards which the twin desires for an identity and a value, a belongingness and a meaning stretching beyond an individual's life-span were directed. More than the dynastic states of their day, if also often in unison with them, the social representatives of such supernatural traditions of belief and behaviour promised the individual a value and a meaning which survived his or her physical existence. And the fear that this value could be destroyed, the dread of a loss of meaning in their case, too, aroused feelings of total enmity so strong and so compelling that the believers, in the name of their exclusive supernatural religion, were ready – as was the case later in the name of such social religions as class religions and national religions or whatever – to make war against the adherents of other, opposed belief and value systems, and, if possible, to destroy them in order to secure the survival or the supremacy of their own religious organization and the traditions represented by it.

In more recent times, especially in the nineteenth and twentieth centuries, such feelings have been linked to an increasing degree to social products of a purely secular kind and to the corresponding traditions of belief and behaviour; units such as classes or nations have now become the principal foci for needs of this kind. They have taken over more and more the function previously performed by smaller descent-units such as families, clans and other kinship groupings as guarantors and symbols of an identity and a value which, simultaneously, were quite personal and transcended personal life. Today, the recording, teaching and learning of one's own national history has widely taken the place occupied in simpler societies by the oral transmission of an in many ways secret fund of knowledge – the names and deeds of ancestors, legends, rituals, etc. – which imparts to individuals a feeling of identity and solidarity with a group and a lasting meaning and value in relation to other people.

So the basic conflict mentioned before, which appears at first glance and on the surface to be simply a conflict between the survival-wish of individuals and their wish for the survival of their nation, proves on a deeper level to be a conflict between the desire of a person for physical survival and his or her desire for the survival of that which helped to ensure the meaning and value of their existence. With regard to one's nation, as previously in relation to one's estate, one's occupational group, one's church, one's tribe or one's clan, one was faced with a choice between the continued existence of that about which one said 'I' and that about which one said 'we'. The alternative to risking one's own life often appeared to be a mere physical survival which had been robbed of its value, pride and meaning. And there are few experiences which strike a person so painfully and traumatically as the loss and destruction of that which they feel to be the value and meaning of their lives.

What that is in particular can vary. It can be filled with strong affects yet consciously experienced only in a blurred and unfocused way. In societies so peculiarly individualized as ours, it is easy to forget that even the value and meaning which people attach to their own lives in a purely personal and individual sense is always a value and meaning in relation to others, to something beyond one's own person, whether real or imaginary. Without functions for others, without social functions however they may be dressed up, a human life remains empty and meaningless. Thus life can become meaningless for a person when their love and affection for another is no longer reciprocated or when the loved one dies. For the giving of love, even though it may be a compelling personal need, is no less a social function than the receiving of love. The main source from which a person derives their value, their meaning in the longer term, can be the skilful practice of a profession. For others it can be their wealth, their birth, their stamp collection or the unconditional, demanding love of a small child; or the experience of an answered prayer and the knowledge that the grace of God has touched one. Societies such as ours offer the most varied sources from which people can create in their own personal way a feeling of their own individual value and meaning in life but they also generate constant threats to these sources and destroy personal meaning and value.

The feelings of satisfaction or dissatisfaction which people in highly individualized societies experience in a purely personal form as a result of their need for value and meaning seldom remain completely untouched by the feelings of satisfaction or dissatisfaction, the pleasures or the disappointments, which flow into their lives from the development, the successes and the failures of the social units with which they identify. At the present level of human development, the weal and woe of the country, the nation to which one belongs, is coming to play an increasingly central role as a factor in the fulfilment or destruction of that which, in his/her own eyes, confers meaning and value on the life of a person. In normal times, one does not need to pay too much attention to this connection. In fact, one may be hardly aware of it. One may first notice the invisible bond which ties the meaning and value of one's own individual existence to the fate of one's country or another social unit when developments on the national or international level endanger what one feels to be meaningful and valuable in one's individual life. But whether one is aware of it or not, failures and successes at the national level, or at any level between the individual and the national, also have a function as permanent sources of personal satisfaction and disappointment, individual pleasure and depression which can considerably strengthen or weaken feelings from more personal sources.

In the present-day world, nations in their relationship to one another, in their rank-order, appear to have become the dominant and most powerful of all these supra-individual influences on people's feelings of meaning and value. On the national and international levels, the interdependence of individuals is growing ever closer and more compelling. And individual people are becoming ever more conscious of the degree to which practically everything which they experience as direction-giving and meaning-conferring in their lives is bound up with the survival of social units on the national level, that it cannot continue in existence without the countries with which they identify. They are coming to recognize more and more clearly the function of nations or national groups as the guarantors, guardians, embodiments or symbols of a great part of that which they perceive as of lasting value in their individual existence. And the fact that the nation-states of the twentieth century, perhaps more than any earlier form of state, are 'we-states' – organizations with which all social strata in varying degrees identify – that in their case solidarity and loyalty are secured, probably more than ever before, through the inculcation of an exclusive belief system with built-in feelings of enmity towards strangers who do not share in the common national religion and identity, strengthens the effectiveness of all the other factors which contribute to enmities and conflicts between states.

14

At this point there arises a particularly difficult problem: the peculiar significance of that which people experience as meaningful and valuable seems often to be connected (if not quite caused by) its exclusiveness, its restriction to part-groups of humanity and built-in hostility towards others. The value and meaning which people confer upon themselves as members of a nation-state is an example – perhaps the most revealing example which can be pointed to in modern times.

Because the exclusiveness, a built-in polarity, a latent or manifest enmity towards others counts among their characteristic attributes, present-day forms of value and meaning usually contain within themselves the seeds of their own destruction. It is for the members of nation-states meaning-conferring and highly valuable to belong to one nation and no other. The value and meaning of their individual lives appears in the last instance to depend on the preservation of the integrity of their country And the fear of the destruction of this integrity, the fear of the destruction of that which appears meaningful and valuable for their own lives, is expressed almost automatically in open or hidden threats to destroy that which appears meaningful and valuable to the members of other nations – who are, for their part, caught in the same dilemma, that the deep insecurity which they feel in relation to the preservation of their own country or group of countries and, with it, the preservation of highly esteemed values and articles of belief generates an enmity towards other countries or groups of countries which for their part feel themselves threatened and correspondingly insecure on the same grounds. On this level, too, one encounters processes of reciprocal amplification. They are not restricted to the amplification of common beliefs and ideals *internal* to particular nations. In the relations between nations they reveal themselves particularly clearly in the reciprocal character of their threats to and their fear of one another. At both levels, such processes can result in a dynamics of increasing escalation. And whenever that happens, civilization goes into reverse and approaches its breakdown.

In such situations, even people who are otherwise hardly aware of it gain a sharper realization of the fact that their individual self-image contains an image of their nation. In ordinary life, identification with one's nation, consciousness of belonging to it, the voices of a national conscience and of national ideals as levels in the conscience and ideals of individuals, often remain mute. They are dispositions to a specific form of experience and action which emerge from their more or less unconscious latent condition in reaction to specific signals. These signals, planned or not, are given in specific situations.

A process of reciprocal reinforcement of individual national feelings in a nation is one of these occasions. As a rule, it is bound up with an intensification of fears and threats between nations, especially between those who form the chief axis of tensions in a balance of power system. The reciprocal strengthening of threats to and fears of one another on an international level can reach a point at which none of the participants can stop the process any more, at which an inexorable dynamic of escalation drives both sides towards armed struggle and mutual destruction. And in such situations the latent voices of the national conscience and ideal in individuals become particularly loud. Mounting threats and anxieties on the international level can serve as a trigger which activates in the individual members of the nations involved the disposition to act in conformity with their national ideals and norms. When these feelings grow on an individual level, they can reciprocally reinforce one another and the boiling-up of national feelings can intensify the tensions and fears on the international level. Personal dispositions to identify with one's country which come to life in such an international situation are not, as may at first glance appear to be the case, factors outside – they are a part of the situation. The mutual reinforcement of national ideals, doctrines and beliefs on an intra-state level contributes in one way or another to the mutual reinforcement of threats and fears on the international level, and vice versa.

The fact that these processes of reciprocal reinforcement can be set in motion on at least two levels of a system of nation-states more or less simultaneously makes it even more difficult for the units involved – for the nations concerned or their constituent groupings – to prevent the immanent drift towards armed conflict from getting out of control. An effective intervention to restrain such a process would require an authority which is not wholly identified with either of the two sides, armed with sufficient theoretical knowledge of the nature of such processes to be able to dismiss the idea of the sole guilt of this or that side, and with enough power to be able to work out and effect a relevant strategy.

The levels which the mobilization of national sentiments through reciprocal reinforcement and the concomitant deterioration of civilized conduct in dealings with opponents can reach varies between countries and situations. Many factors are crucial in this connection: the prevailing structure of ruling, the sharpness and form of internal conflicts, traditions of belief and behaviour, the past and present division of power, and many more. Whatever they are, however, it is never the immediate situation of one country alone which determines the strength and particular character of national sentiments or the degree of the barbarity of which a country is capable in its relations with those earmarked as its enemies. The pattern of its past, its chances and expectations for the future play just as great a role as determinants of a nation's conduct here and now as does the immediate present. In this as in other respects, the past leaves its imprint on the present order and ways of behaving. It does so implicitly as one of their conditions, explicitly through the image which living generations carry with them of their country's past. As determinants of behaviour, past, present and future work together. Lived situations, as it were, are three-dimensional.

While national beliefs may thus vary considerably in accordance with people's perceptions of the distinctive characteristics of the past, present and future development of a country, at the same time they also have many common features – although this only becomes clear if one stands back and looks at them from a distance. Different patriotisms and nationalisms often have a remarkable family-resemblance. They can stoke each other up because, as exclusive belief systems with their stress on the overriding value of a closed society, of a single nation-state, they resemble one another like twins. Situations in which the threats and the fear between nations are reciprocally reinforced nearly always have their intra-state correlate in an infection-like reinforcement of national sentiments. In fact, the recurrence of such situations on the international level is one of the main reasons, if not *the* main reason, for the persistence of national traditions of belief and behaviour which are concentrated exclusively on single nations in their function as guardians of everything that is considered meaningful, as the highest value to which everything, including the lives of individuals, is subordinated, and as the justification for hidden or open feelings of enmity towards the members of other nations and towards minorities, that is, strangers and outsiders, in one's own. And these exclusive traditions of belief and behaviour are, for their part, one of the chief reasons, if not *the* chief reason, for the recurrence of processes of reciprocal threat and fear on the international level and of the consequent wars.

In times when the national conscience and national ideals are mobilized in this way, the form and manner in which people perceive themselves also change in specific ways. It is one of the most elementary characteristics of humans that they do not have only an image of themselves as individual persons who can say 'I' but also an image of themselves as the members of groups of which they can say 'we'. In simpler societies, the I-experience and the we-experience in the self-image of their members are often hardly separable from one another. In more developed contemporary nation-states, the I-experience and we-experience are under normal circumstances sharply distinguished, and the former, the experience of oneself as an isolated individual separated from all others, stands sharp and clear in the centre of self-consciousness, whilst the perception of relationships experienced as 'we' remains more in the background. It is this form of self-awareness which finds expression in the everyday speech of today, for example when people speak of society as the 'social background' of a person. In situations of national emergency, however, the centre of gravity shifts for a shorter or longer time: the emotional content of the we-level in the self-image usually grows stronger and that of the I-level weaker. What the we-level gains in emotional loading is withdrawn from the I-level.

But such emergency situations are not by any means the only circumstances which show that, even in highly individualized societies, images of we-groups such as the nation belong to the self-image of individuals and that, at the same time, the personality structure of any individual represents one of countless variations on a common national pattern. Another situation in which the strength as well as the elasticity of the bond becomes clear, which links the patterning and self-awareness of individuals to their society, is when they change their nationality.

At least for adults, a change of national identity is hardly easier than a change of personality, and the chance of success is hardly any greater. More than just a change of passports is involved. A disturbance of national identity, of the national image embedded in the self-images of people, whether caused by a transformation in the life of a single individual or in that of a whole nation, always leads to a reorientation of behaviour and feelings. It requires a reassessment of a person's values and beliefs and a reorganization of their perception of self and others. However much the ability to make such an adjustment may vary from individual to individual, with adults it has definite limits as a rule. An adult Frenchman or German does not easily lose his basic character as such or forget his earlier identity if he becomes an American citizen. Nor, when its present situation changes, does a whole nation immediately lose the basic characteristics of its traditions of belief and behaviour. In the case of a nation, too, the past, the whole pattern of its development, decides whether and how far it can adjust to changed circumstances, whether and how far it can reorganize its traditional we-ideal and self-image.

15

It is only in the light of reflections such as these that the full significance which the history of the self-image of a nation has for the history and self-image of its individual members becomes accessible. Just as national conditions are one of the sources of meaning and fulfilment in the lives of individuals, so they can also contribute to the feeling that value and meaning are threatened or lost.

Germany offers an example of the curious relationship in which, given the world as it is, loss of power leads to loss of meaning and value. But the connection is not restricted to one specific country. It can be observed in many other nations – and not only in nations: threatened with a loss of power, ruling groups in all ages experience in the eyes of their members a corresponding loss of meaningfulness and value. Innumerable examples show that ruling groups of every type – tribes, elites, estates, classes or nations – whose power is dwindling seldom vacate the field without a fight even if the chances of maintaining their power and rule may be nil. The weaker they are, the more insecure and threatened their superiority is in fact, the crasser, the more reckless and unrealistic as a rule are the measures likely to be with which they seek to preserve their position.

There is a widespread idea that the members of declining social groups cling to power and often fight for it to the last mainly because they do not wish to renounce the 'material' advantages which they owe to it – for example, a higher level of consumption or the chances of physical services from their subordinates. And the loss of such advantages no doubt plays a part in the fears and visions of an unpleasant future which drive them to fight, often using crueller and crueller and more and more desperate means, even though developments beyond their control may be visibly tilting the balance of power against them. But the explanation of such behaviour in 'material' or, as it is often expressed, 'economic' terms is never more than a part explanation.

Whatever else it may mean, a threatened loss of power is invariably associated for the members of ruling formations with a serious disturbance of their self-image and often enough with a complete destruction of whatever it is which, in their own eyes, gives meaning and value to their lives; it threatens them simultaneously with a loss of their identity – a loss of self. And above all this, the threat to what they feel their identity, their value and social status to be makes it impossible for them to see their situation as it is and to adapt their identity, their goals, their feeling of their own meaning and value to their changed circumstances. Almost invariably they are defeated not simply by the greater physical or social power of their rising opponents but even more by their own feeling that life is no longer worth living if the old order in which they enjoyed supremacy disappears. Without the attributes of their social superiority, life appears to them to be devoid of value and meaning. If in such a situation whole groups of people resist the change to the last, if they are prepared, in order to preserve their supremacy, to fight and sacrifice their lives, it is not only because they fear an existence without the material comforts they are accustomed to: it is not, in the first instance, because the loss of their means of subsistence or their luxuries is threatened but because of the threat to their way of life as a whole. Above all, what is threatened is their self-esteem, their pride.

Perhaps there is a tendency today to underrate a little the significance which many things, including things of a 'material' or 'economic' kind, can have for people because they serve as symbols of their pride, the self-esteem and higher status which almost every adult and nearly all human groups on earth claim in relation to somebody or another. It is through the exploration of such connections that, sooner or later, the key will be found to the many problems which the curious relationship between loss of power and loss of meaning and value continues to pose. Members of more powerful social formations are willing to fight when their power is slipping away from them, and frequently under such circumstances no means is too rough or barbaric for them, because their power and their image of themselves as a great and splendid formation has a higher value for them than their lives. And the weaker, the more insecure and desperate they become on the road to their decline, the more they develop the sense that they are fighting for their supremacy with their backs against the wall, the more savage for the most part does their behaviour become and the more acute the danger that they will disregard and destroy the civilized standards of conduct on which they pride themselves. That is because, whatever other functions they may serve, civilized standards of conduct are often only meaningful for ruling groups as long as they remain symbols and instruments of their power.

As a result, power elites, ruling classes or nations often fight in the name of their superior value, their superior civilization, with means which are diametrically opposed to the values for which they claim to stand. With their backs against the wall, the champions easily become the greatest destroyers of civilization. They tend easily to become barbarians.

It is thus only if one includes in one's diagnosis of social decline the value- and meaning-conferring significance of power- and status-superiority that one can gauge the difficulties which are bound up with adaptation to a lower status. Such an adaptation is difficult enough in the case of individuals. In the case of powerful social formations – if they survive at all – it is so difficult that it can hardly ever be achieved in a generation. Normally, it takes at least three generations or more before a powerful nation (or some other once powerful social grouping) which survives such a loss of power is able clearly to recognize its lower status and accept it emotionally; before the image of the greater past ceases to hover in front of the present generation as a measure and a challenge; and before the latter have developed a new image of themselves as a social unit which offers them a source of pride and self-respect and in which they are able, despite everything, to find meaningful tasks for the future and goals worth living for.

The immediate effects of such a decline, of a loss in power and status, are usually feelings of despondency and disillusionment. Feelings of worthlessness and aimlessness interspersed with tendencies towards cynicism, nihilism and withdrawal into oneself can gain the upper hand. Strange though it may seem, one encounters the same effects with people who have lost their beliefs or whose ideals have been shattered by reality. They are reminiscent of the feelings and attitudes associated with mourning for a lost love, and have much in common with the processes which doctors, in their diagnosis of individuals, classify as 'regressions'.

If a process of decline takes place slowly, if the struggle to bring it to a halt stretches over the generations and remains undecided for a long time, if occasional upturns and recoveries from time to time rekindle hopes for the restoration of the old glory, if, in short, the decline never goes so far that people *have* to face up to it, then the ambiguities of a nation's status and the symptoms of a massive status-insecurity can sink deep into the make-up of its members and permeate their entire tradition of beliefs and conduct. This is precisely what happened in the case of the development of Germany. As has been said, our own age offers many examples of nations which – often rather suddenly and unexpected by them – are faced with a loss of power and status, and are accordingly compelled to adapt their national ideals, their self-image, their pride and self-esteem to the loss of their imperial role. Germany's adaptation to the loss of its imperial role after 1918 was especially complex because it involved a continuation of the traumatic process of decline which had already started far back in the Middle Ages. In the spectrum of different cases which show the connection between experiences of power-loss and loss of meaning and value, the pattern of Germany's decline was curious and perhaps unique. It was a case of lingering decline over the centuries with many ups and downs which never reached a point low enough to dispel the imperial strivings, rendering them obsolete and compelling a final adaptation among the German peoples to their lower status and initiating a reorientation of the German self-image and German national ideals.

What is in question here, the attempted extermination of the Jews by the National Socialists, is only one episode in the rise and fall of peoples. But in several respects it has a paradigmatic significance. It shows what the leaders of a civilized nation are capable of doing in their struggle for the restoration or preservation of their imperial role when a chronic feeling of decline, of being encircled by enemies and driven into a corner, awakens the conviction that only absolute ruthlessness can save their fading power and glory. It also makes clear to what extremes of behaviour people can be driven by the exclusiveness of a national belief system against those whom they experience as 'foreigners', as 'outsiders' who do not belong, as members of a different, potentially hostile group.

The degree of ruthlessness and barbarism to which the leaders of the German nation went on this occasion corresponded to the strength of the threats which they saw closing in on their hopes and aspirations for Germany. For the love of the Fatherland which they proclaimed and in the name of which they rallied large sections of the German people around themselves was no love of Germany as it was. It was no love of Germany as one among several nations on an equal footing and certainly not of Germany as a second- or third-rank power. It was a love for Germany as it ought to be according to their feelings, for a Germany which was greater than other European nations and in specific ways greater than all the nations of the world. It was the love for an ideal, not for the real Germany.

The efforts of the Nazi leaders and, in their wake, of large sections of the German people were aimed at the fulfilment of this ideal self-image; they were so monstrous, so desperate and so ruthless because, in comparison with the 'great German' [*großdeutsches*] empire they were striving for and the power-potentials of all other countries which would have to be fought or subjugated to achieve it, the resources of the actual Germany had already become quite small. The gap between the German national ideal and the German national identity was great and it was growing. Even Hitler regarded his own time as the last historical moment in which there still remained a hope of Germany regaining its imperial role and the world entering a chiliastic epoch of a German 'thousand-year Reich'. To achieve this end, as he repeatedly said, a total mobilization of German resources, a total war regardless of losses, a completely merciless and unscrupulous struggle, including the mass extermination of hostile, 'racially inferior' groups, would be required. If the Germans were incapable of restoring the greater empire which they thought they had lost, then, in Hitler's eyes, they might as well go down for ever. He, too, had no love for Germany as it really was; what he loved was the *fata morgana* of Germany and his own greatness. The National Socialist war, and, as part of it, the whole monstrosity of those years, was the desperate move of a nation which, in relation to other, more powerful nations was rapidly sinking to second- or third-rank status. It was undertaken as a last attempt to live up to its ideal image of itself as a first-rank world power.

One might think that the Germans could have learned to live with a less exalted image of themselves without the murder of millions of Jews. But only in rare cases when others are growing stronger and they are growing weaker do powerful social formations submit peacefully to a narrowing of their power, to a lowering of their social status and, with it, to a change in their self-image, their we-ideal, their identity – simply on grounds of a clear insight into the fact that the tide of development is running against them. Even if, for outsiders and perhaps for a few individuals and groups from inside the declining unit itself, the sociological diagnosis of such a development is clear enough, as a rule the overwhelming majority of those affected remain incapable of perceiving facts which would deeply wound their self-esteem and pride. Under such circumstances, they turn again and again to leaders who hold up in front of them the image of their superior greatness, who appeal to them in the name of their superior values and call on them to resist the threat, to fight for their collective superiority and the ideals that go with it. In such moments, insider-blindness, the incapacity of perceiving what one does not wish to perceive, the mutual reinforcement of a belief which – also contrary to the reality of their situation – corresponds to the common hopes and wishes current in their society, breaks out in all its strength and fury. Like wild animals, powerful nations or other powerful social formations are at their most dangerous when they feel cornered – when they have the feeling that the balance of power is going against them, that the power resources of potential rivals and enemies are becoming greater than theirs, that their values are threatened and their superiority slipping away. Under past and present conditions of human social life, developments of this kind are one of the most typical and frequent situations in which people are driven to the use of violence; they are one of the situations which lead to war.

16

Many factors contributed to the fact that the breakdown of civilizing restraints in the case of Nazi Germany was particularly profound, and that violence was directed with particular fury against the Jews. Some of these factors have been mentioned already; others remain to be discussed. From what has been said so far, it has perhaps become somewhat clearer that the attitudes and beliefs of the Nazis cannot be fully understood if one takes account of the German situation only at the time of their rise and under their rule. That in Germany an extreme nationalist, anti-democratic and anti-semitic movement with a strongly fantasy-dominated social religion and a tendency towards the use of brute force could come to power, in fact, the whole National Socialist episode, is bound to remain obscure if one fails to take simultaneously into account its place and function in the wider context of Germany's long-term development. Among the long-term developmental trends which contributed to the upsurge of movements of this type after the defeat of 1918, eventually favouring the seizure of power by one of them, Germany's lingering decline as a European great power, briefly interrupted after 1871 by the rise of the Second Reich, was one of the most important. In contrast to other, comparable European powers, Germany only experienced a few decades of greatness in which its real position came a little closer to the national ideal. After this interlude, ideal and reality grew further and further apart as before.

It has already been suggested that this trend was in some measure responsible for the peculiarly 'romantic' emotional stress of the German 'Fatherland' ideal and the concept of Germany's imperial role as symbolized by the term 'Reich'. It also helps to explain why broad sections of the German population were inclined to orientate their goals for the national future around their image of the greater past. It created a disposition in national attitudes towards what may be called in traditional terms 'romantic conservatism'. Furthermore, the high rank occupied in the German self-image by the idealized past, as the only time of national greatness, played at least a part as a determinant of the high rank which the concern with history – a specific type of history – gained in the value-scale of Germans.

Closely connected with that developmental trend were also specific elements of the German tradition of belief and behaviour which prepared the way for the extreme violence of the Germans at a time when the conflict between their traditional self-image and the factual course of events became sharper, threatening to force itself into their consciousness as the moment of truth grew closer. A highly characteristic example of these persistent dispositions was the idea of politics which found expression in the German word *Realpolitik*. At its root lay a whole part of German national ideology which can be summed up something like this: 'Whatever others may say, the only realistic view is that politics rest on the unbridled use of force. In particular, international politics is nothing more than the continuation of war by other means. For all the fine words which foreign statesmen may use, when it comes to the crunch, they, too, rely on their "power" in order to reach their political goals, and, like the Germans, they use it unscrupulously. The only difference is that the Germans are more honest.'

The German national belief in *Realpolitik* is connected with the general belief in war, with the use of armed strength as the means of last resort for settling conflicts between nations. It shows with particular forcefulness the descent of these beliefs from the traditions of pre-industrial, dynastic and usually absolutistically ruled states. The autocratic princes of predominantly agrarian states, with a largely uneducated population which lived at or just above a certain minimum subsistence level, could believe with a certain justification that all disputes with other princes could be settled in their favour by the use of superior military force. They could conquer territories, if necessary impose on their inhabitants their (the conquerors') own religion, if they wanted to, even force their language on them, and in this way absorb disputed territories, which were often simply territories with tempting riches or strategically more favourable borders, into their own realm.

German *Realpolitik*, as the war aims of Germany's leaders in both world wars clearly revealed, still stood very much in the line of succession of this type of policy of autocratic princes. The belief that 'God is always on the side of the strongest battalions', that currently all disputes between nations are decided in the last instance by the strongest and best led armies and that they always will be, survived even after it had become crystal clear that, in a world of increasingly interdependent industrial nation-states, military victors are not necessarily the greatest beneficiaries of their victories and the vanquished are not necessarily weakened or led to suffer more than their opponents. A belief in the efficacy of military force as the *ultima ratio regum*, which was not entirely out of place in the context of limited power balances between pre-industrial states with relatively little mutual dependence, was carried over almost as a matter of course into an almost world-wide power system consisting of more and more nation-states which were becoming increasingly and more closely interwoven. Growing levels of education, the growing national consciousness of even the lowest social strata, increasingly higher standards of living even for the very poorest people, all helped to make conquest and annexation (meaning the quick or gradual incorporation of foreign populations) increasingly difficult.

German *Realpolitik* in 1914 as well as in 1939 was orientated to war aims of this latter type. Many reasons contributed to the fact that the leading circles of an empire with a history such as that of the Germans were filled with so strong a belief in physical violence as the decisive instrument of politics. One of them was Germany's long-standing weakness. For centuries, Germans had been exposed to attacks and invasions by foreign princes. As members of a conglomerate of relatively weak states, they had ample opportunity to observe how others used their superior power and how ruthlessly they often did so. And the fact that first Prussia and then Germany itself owed their rise to a consider-able extent to a series of military victories – which was not unimportant for the survival of a landowning warrior aristocracy as the elite grouping – consolidated these tendencies in the German tradition of beliefs and behaviour. The one-sidedness of their perception corresponded to the pattern of their history. Aware of their earlier weakness and never quite sure of their strength after 1871, the Germans tended to place the power aspect of politics above all others. As a result, they were able concep-tually to grasp it more clearly than many other European nations whose leaders and representative thinkers treated power in a rather more taken-for-granted way.

Although Germans were highly sensitive regarding the role of physical violence and 'power' in the relations between states, they were less sensitive regarding the limitations on the use of superior power which had developed elsewhere. In European nation-states which could look back on a longer tradition of their own power-superiority, the role of power-chances and physical violence in social life was often – with exceptions such as, for example, Hobbes – conceptualized and articulated less concisely. Power resources were, rather, used in traditional ways, and the experience accumulated over many generations had contributed much to the springing-up of traditional rules which determined when it was useful to use superior power ruthlessly and when it was not. They had contributed, accordingly, to the cultivation of a feeling for the limits on the use of brute force as a means of practical politics and, in many cases, to the formation of a conscience which reined in the ruthless use of violence if people became conscious of it – which, even if it could not completely prevent it, acted as a brake. The German tradition of beliefs and behaviour, with its tendency towards absolutes, however, produced a willingness to undervalue such limits and restraints: quite often, it totally blocked the capacity to perceive them. With reference to this or that example of the naked use of force – which, of course, one finds everywhere – they saw in limits and restraints often nothing more than cunning camouflage, an expression of hypocrisy.

Thus, when the Germans themselves for a while became stronger and more powerful, their tradition of beliefs and behaviour embodied a pronounced tendency to regard the relations between nations as nothing but power politics in the most elementary sense of the term – as *Realpolitik*. The ruling groups of both the Second and Third Reichs were comparative newcomers on the stage of national politics. As heirs to a strongly autocratic tradition, they were particularly liable in their thoughts and actions to follow the example of successful princes such as the Great Elector or Frederick II, who had been able to absorb whole territories by conquest without feeling any need to consider the wishes of the populations concerned even if their languages and traditions were quite different. However, while the memory of Germany's past had heightened the sensitivity of its leading strata to power politics and led to a sharper articulation of the power aspects of politics than elsewhere, they had hardly any eye for, and few concepts relating to, the limits which are set in complex, multi-national systems on the use of power in general and military power in particular. It was, in fact, one of the fundamental paradoxes of the German tradition of beliefs and behaviour that the same people who followed an absolute, unconditional and often highly unrealistic national idealism at the same time boasted about what they believed to be their realism, their *Realpolitik*.

Like other forms of idealism, the national idealism of the Germans –
like that of nations generally – functioned as a lodestar which gave
direction, value, meaning and, occasionally, fulfilment to the actions of
individuals. Seen in that light, it was one of the necessary conditions for
the sacrifices which they made for their country. If one uses single
individuals as a frame of reference, national idealism, patriotism, nationalism – whatever one wants to call it – has some attributes which are
usually classified as 'morally good' behaviour and feeling. If the frame of
reference one uses is whole nation-states, national ideals have many
attributes which are usually classified as behaviour and feeling which are
regarded as 'morally bad'. In Germany, as elsewhere, collective national
idealism was an extreme form of collective selfishness. It had the
exclusive character of every national belief with its built-in hostilities
against out-groups. It became easily associated with power politics. The
use of violence in the pursuit of national ideals was only weakly hedged-
in by common norms and conventions.

And just as, in this sense, German national idealism was nothing less
than 'idealistic', so German *Realpolitik* was anything but 'realistic'. In a
period of dynastic agrarian states whose populations often placed greater
value on whether they were ruled by a good or bad prince than on
whether this prince came from Spain, Austria, Bavaria, France or Britain,
stronger battalions certainly had a role to play in the solution of unsettled
problems of balance of power rivalries. The victor could take land and
people, the principal sources of power and wealth, from the vanquished
until the latter had to withdraw from the contest. In a multinational
world society with a highly complex balance of power and increasing
mutuality of dependence, with growing checks against the snatching of
foreign territories and peoples – partly as a consequence of growing
national consciousness – the unrestrained, unconditional and uncompromising use of power by a nation, its use as a kind of magical device with
which all international problems could be remedied, hardly corresponded any longer – as Hitler's fate so clearly shows – to the realities
of international politics. In such a society, self-restraints on the use of
power, in particular of military power, were becoming more necessary
than ever for purposes of realizing the goals of a 'realistic' strategy.

17

Nothing shows the unreal quality of German *Realpolitik* better than the
German war aims. Although the leading groups in the two German wars

of the twentieth century differed considerably in terms of their social descent, their war aims were, in all essentials, practically the same. They were directed towards the creation of a German empire in Europe, perhaps with a few dependencies overseas. The continuities of an absolutist tradition combined with the image of the old Reich produced the vision of a future state which, in practice, was nothing other than a German colonial empire in Europe and beyond.

Besides the direct annexation of territories particularly in the East, among the German war aims in the First World War was the formation of a central European union comprising France, Belgium, Holland, Germany, Denmark and Austria-Hungary, with Italy, Sweden and Norway as associate members. Many territories in the East, including Poland and large parts of Russia, were to become colonies pure and simple. In Africa, too, an expansion of the German colonial empire was envisaged. The characteristic heading under which this and similar war aims were advocated was 'the politics of strength': this slogan used by Reichschancellor von Bethmann-Hollweg points to the connection with the belief in *Realpolitik*. As early as the beginning of the war, a German general, von Falkenhayn, had stressed that Germany was no longer strong enough for such a policy. The historian Fritz Fischer has shown in detail how unrealistic these plans were.[9] He came to the conclusion that, even if Germany had won in 1918 and tried to put its war aims into effect – that is, to erect the empire of its dreams and establish German hegemony in Europe, whatever name it went by – it would merely have delayed the ultimate collapse.

One does not need to assume that the German government had clearly developed ideas of what would be the implications of the war aims which they announced. Yet even a short glance at the numbers of people involved conveys an idea of the magnitude of the task which the Germans would have set themselves. If the official war aims of the First World War had been achieved, it would have resulted, estimated very roughly, in an empire of 400 to 500 million inhabitants, with a ruling group of about 60 million Germans. German rule would have had to be maintained in the first instance by denying many of the conquered peoples the right to have an army of their own. Besides this, many of them would have had to lose their own currencies. In short, in order to preserve the supremacy of the Germans and to maintain the character of the whole empire as German, a strict violence-monopoly and a whole series of economic monopolies would have been required in a territory as gigantic as this. At that time, perhaps unavoidably, it was not so evident as it is today that this pattern of conquest and empire-building was already becoming obsolete at the time of its conception, that it was very deeply influenced by the traditional stereotypes of pre-industrial, pre-national stages of social development. And the fact that traditionalistic power elites with pre-industrial, pre-national and even anti-industrial ways of thinking still had a large share in the shaping of German national politics, that their ways of thinking, in comparison with those of leading industrialists and other middle-class elites with whom they were allied, still dominated these politics or, to the extent that the two class groupings had fused, played a co-determining part in them, was presumably not without significance in contributing to the traditionalistic basic features of this vision of conquest and empire-building.

With the techniques of ruling they envisaged, the sovereignty of such a small minority over so vast and populous a territory could hardly have been maintained even if it had been a question of an empire consisting of simpler agrarian societies of the type which still predominated in Africa in those days. But in that case at least, the difference between the ruling minority and the mass of the subject population in what is often called their 'levels of civilization', in their capacity for controlling natural and social events, would have still remained very great. And that might have given the conquerors at least a temporary supremacy. In an empire of the type which the German leading groups of 1914 had in mind, rulers and ruled would have been more equal regarding their levels of knowledge and skill; the difference in levels of 'civilization' would have been at least much smaller and sometimes nil. Not only the unfavourable ratio of personnel but also their relatively small superiority in terms of education and training would have severely impaired the chances of the Germans creating any sort of lasting political structure through their imperial endeavours.

But one need not suppose that the German war leaders thought about these matters in particularly realistic, let alone sociological, terms. The leaders of a country at war are often so preoccupied with winning their war that they only perceive the problems of the post-war period, of the probable social structure after their victory, comparatively dimly. Then as now, people often seem to have imagined that, once victory had been achieved, all their hopes would be fulfilled and all their problems automatically solved.

In the First and then again in the Second World War, the German leaders acted as if, after victory, the empire would fall into their laps. The discrepancy between the traditionalistic remnants in their thinking and the factual task with which they were confronted may go some way towards explaining their actions and their fate. The idea that highly industrialized, educated and self-conscious nations, or even large peasant masses under the leadership of highly articulate and self-conscious elites, would allow themselves to be ruled for a long time by others was only conceivable either if the victors were far superior to the vanquished, at least in numbers, or if they were prepared deliberately to decimate and perhaps to exterminate subject populations in order to replace them by members of their own group. The first possibility was barred to the Germans. The second, so far as one can see, did not enter the minds of German war leaders during the First World War.

To the German leaders in the Second World War, it came very readily to mind. Hitler had already toyed with such an idea in the early 1920s. The problem which preoccupied him then was nothing substantially new. It had been posed often enough for the members of societies who had been toppled, as they saw it, from the pinnacle of their power into an abyss of defeat. In earlier centuries, the hardest hit had for the most part been high-ranking elites, princes and nobles. Now poorer people, even social outcasts, shared deeply in the humiliation of defeat as well. The reaction was simple and elementary. One denied the defeat. It had been caused by malicious deception, by criminals, by a plot, by the fighting troops being 'stabbed in the back' by internal traitors. A real defeat had never taken place. So the question arose of how one could make Germany great again. Hitler's whole way of thinking – and the same goes for the majority of Germans who were trapped in the national tradition – continued to bear a pre-industrial imprint. He thought first and foremost of the conquest of land for the settlement of farmers. 'Let us conquer Russia. Let us enslave or kill the native population. Let us settle the land with German farmers and Germany will become the greatest nation in Europe, indeed the whole world. In the future, there will be 250 million Germans.' That was the dream.

The reality looked different. The dream presupposed that the Western industrial nations, in particular Britain, would tolerate the German expansion and, as partner and ally, share world-rule with Germany. Hitler never had a proper understanding of the sensibility of British politicians in relation to the danger of one continental power being able to dominate the others. The balance of power problem that would arise with the expansion of Germany remained incomprehensible to him. As a result, like the German generals in the First World War, he had no chance of fighting a war on one front. In both cases, Germany had to fight simultaneously against its eastern and western neighbours – and not only against its European neighbours: the threat of German dominance in Europe, including dominance over Russia, was experienced as such a dramatic subversion of the existing balance of power that, both times, the USA was drawn into the war.

In this way, the simple, pre-industrial mind-set of Hitler and his generals was confronted with the reality of a war between industrial nations. The simple dream – 'let us kill the populations of the conquered territories' – which promised to decrease the human potential of enemies and to crush their will to resist, clashed not least with the hard facts of a war which increasingly over-stretched the human potential of the Germans and made them more and more dependent on the labour-power of foreigners. The destruction of hostile populations which, in pre-industrial societies with a surplus of peasants, would have been to the advantage of the conquerors proved in the conquest of industrial countries to be self-damaging. It weakened industrial productivity.

This was a dilemma with which the leaders of Nazi Germany saw themselves confronted during the war. They had no scruples about tolerating conditions which led to a decrease in enemy populations; sometimes, they created such conditions quite deliberately. But during the course of the war, the growing need for labour forced them to change their policy to some extent. The change in the treatment of concentration camp inmates after about 1942 was symptomatic of this need. It foreshadowed the problems which, if the dream had been realized, would have sooner or later materialized in a *großdeutsches Reich*. Unless the victors are able to replace enemy populations from the ranks of their own nation, the conquest of territories with highly industrialized and educated inhabitants by others at the same level of development is unlikely to lead to a reasonably stable and enduring structure. The replacement of such populations by one's own people is only feasible if one is numerically superior and has people to spare. The Germans were not, as the Chinese may be one day, in a position to follow such a course. Their conquest of industrial territories was useless unless the people who lived there were willing and able to collaborate in the high level production of goods and complicated services which is typical of industrial societies. The dilemma confronting the National Socialists during the war consisted, on the one hand, of the fear of the countless 'enemies' who surrounded them and their wish to compensate for their own numerical inferiority by killing as many of these enemies as possible, and on the other, of their need for labour power which forced them to keep alive as many of their enemies as possible. It was a dilemma which, had they remained victorious, would have been with them for the foreseeable future.

One cannot entirely dismiss the idea that the mass killing of Jews had something to do with this dilemma. Jews, too, could have been used as labour power. But in their case, the hostility of the National Socialists was so overwhelming and their hate so strong that so-called 'rational' considerations could not as a rule prevail against them. One sometimes has the impression that all the rage which the Nazis could not afford to discharge against their other enemies and victims because they needed their labour or because the groups involved were generally too powerful was released against the Jews, who, of all their declared enemies, were in power terms the weakest. With no other enemy groups were such systematic and purposeful efforts made to kill them, although in practical terms, in regard to their chances of victory and the establishment of a durable empire, the extermination of the Jews was far less significant than the elimination of enemies from other foreign groups. The Nazis acted like a man who, prevented from destroying his real enemies, discharged his pent-up rage against enemies who represented a predominantly imaginary danger for him.

To estimate the magnitude of the mis-match between the population of a German empire as the Nazis envisaged it and the population of Germany as the planned ruling stratum is not an easy task. The frontiers of the thousand-year Reich were not very sharply defined. If one adds the Austrian population to the German and estimates the empire as including continental Europe, Russia and parts of Africa, one could roughly say that a German group of some 70 to 80 million people would have formed the ruling class in an empire of 500 to 600 million inhabitants.

The Nazi leadership was not unaware of the problem of the relatively small German population which stood at their disposal in comparison with the size of the populations which they wanted to subjugate and rule. But their awareness of this problem was distorted by their social beliefs. Immediately after their seizure of power, the Nazis passed a whole bundle of measures to speed up Germany's population growth. They introduced bonuses and tax reliefs for large families, increased the taxes on unmarried people and founded breeding establishments for 'racially pure Aryans'. Later came the incorporation of German-speaking groups from other countries, the collection of children of 'Aryan-type' – sometimes even after they had already been destined for concentration camps – and their 'aryanization', their education as Germans and National Socialists. These and many other measures designed to increase as quickly as possible the numbers of potential rulers of the empire indicate how strongly the Nazis felt about the smallness of *their* 'chosen' population in comparison with the overwhelming number of enemies, of actual or potential subject-populations, by which they were surrounded. But their belief in the magical superiority of the Aryan race over other peoples was extremely unsuitable as a guiding thread for a population policy consistent with their imperial aims. Like other social religions, that of the National Socialists often defeated its own ends. It created blind spots and blockages of perception. The strategy which arose from it squandered human resources and was full of contradictions. This is an example. If on the one hand the National Socialist belief system led to population increase, on the other it led to heavy losses: it lay at the root of the measures which led millions of Germans to their deaths or to imprisonment.

18

The unsuitability of the Nazi belief system as an instrument of policy comes sharply into focus if one considers one of the other functions which it served. It was used as an instrument of empire-building, and then in consolidating and controlling the empire which had been built.

Their profession of a specific social creed which could be propagated and, so it was hoped, win followers not only among the German masses but also those of other highly developed industrial nations which were to be absorbed into the *großdeutsches Reich* was one of the characteristics which distinguished the Nazis as a ruling elite from the traditionalistic German elites at the beginning of the First World War. Such a belief system was symptomatic of the increase in the power-potential of the German masses after the old power elites of the *Kaiserreich* had been defeated in 1918. While in other respects, particularly regarding the character of their ideals, the Nazis still resembled the older elites and carried on their traditions, in this respect they came nearer to the new type of elite which arises sooner or later in all societies on the road to industrialization and democratization. The ruling German elites of 1914 entered the war still without feeling any particular need for a social creed which could serve as the rallying point for a mass movement. They, too, had to mobilize popular support; but for this purpose, it was enough to appeal to the then firmly established and internalized national creed, to the love for the 'Fatherland' and the traditional duty to support it buttressed through such then-current forms of external controls as compulsory military service. That the Nazis sought and achieved mass support based on a common belief and symbolized by a hybrid word derived from 'nationalism' and 'socialism' is indicative of the increase in the power of the broader population during the phase of German development which people have become used to calling the 'Weimar Republic'. The composition and mentality of the state and party leadership after 1933 reflected this power-gain as well as its limitations.

So long as armies were recruited mainly from the uneducated poor, it was enough that the officers should have convictions. And their convictions did not take the form of a general social creed, not even of a national belief; they were more personal and more specific. Noble officers fought for the prince, not for what they would have called the 'rabble' – not for the nation. What made them fight was their status-honour and a sense of duty to their prince. Their convictions were as a rule strictly those of a caste. More strongly unified national beliefs arose when military techniques required citizens' armies. They grew up even more decisively when wars ceased characteristically to be fought by soldiers alone and had, as a result of the growing interdependence of all social activities, to rely on the efforts of the nation as a whole, civilians as well as soldiers. Under these conditions it became more and more imperative to maintain morale through a collective belief in the value of one's nation and the justice of its cause; and since the continued existence of states depended on the morale and feelings of solidarity of all their citizens, nations would hardly have been able to survive without implanting in their individual members, even in times of peace, a deep feeling of belonging to and identity with the nation, together with an unshakeable belief in the value of its survival.

The National Socialist creed was an extreme example of a belief system of this type. It showed very clearly the double-edged character which all such belief systems possessed: they protected nations from dangers which they themselves had helped to produce. For the national beliefs, the social creeds of a power or a group of powers are usually experienced by others as a threat to their values and existence against which they have to protect themselves by propagating their counter-creed – which in turn is experienced by the first group as a threat. The intensification of their propaganda leads quite often to an intensification of the counter-propaganda until the vicious circle reaches its climax in a war.

Because the National Socialist belief system embodied the features common to all national religions in an extreme form, it illustrates some of these common features particularly well. As has been explained, in Nazi doctrines more realistic ideas were fused with views which were utterly fantastic. For the protagonists of the beliefs as well as for the mass of followers, it was often impossible to distinguish between the two. The latter appeared as convincing as the former. Both aspects expressed what the people to whom the doctrines were directed and who made them their own wanted and hoped. Pure fantasies appeared to be just as true as realistic ideas because the whole mixture flattered the self-love and pride of the believers. The Nazi creed represented the Germans as a people with a unique mission in the world, as the 'chosen people'. In accordance with the more democratic division of power which had been achieved since 1918, it allowed all the Germans, not only the nobles, the rich and the educated, to feel that they belonged to the elite of humanity – at least if they had the correct head and body-shape or the right ancestors, that is, belonged to the right 'race'. The introduction of a relatively unspecific quality such as 'race' – which excluded only people who were classified as 'Jews' or who definitely had the 'wrong' physical characteristics – created a broad ideological basis for a superiority claim capable of tempting the mass of the German people.

At the same time, however, the criterion of 'race' offered non-Germans a share in this superiority. The National Socialist authorities strove might and main to use their belief system as an empire-building instrument. They hoped, not entirely without success, that a common creed with strong anti-democratic and anti-semitic tendencies, with a racial myth which promised even people with a strong sense of their own inferiority a compensatory sense of superiority, which justified killing and torture as legitimate means of crushing 'racially inferior' opponents – that such a belief would bring them sympathizers from the subject countries to whom they would be able to delegate part of the responsibility for ruling these countries. In this way, the spread and exploitation of a common social religion formed an integral component of the organization and especially of the control system of the *großdeutsches Reich* as it was envisaged in 1939. With its help, an imperial ruling elite was to be gradually built up which would include, besides the German core group, members of other nations, too. They probably expected that the National Socialist creed, backed up by necessary force, would in time come to be accepted by more and more people in the conquered territories. And in that case it would in fact – as with the social religions of all twentieth-century empires which need mass support – have served as a unifying and consolidating factor in the process of empire-building.

The more traditionalistic German elites headed by nobles with a militaristic outlook, which led Germany in the First World War, still saw the task of pacifying and ruling a German empire in the first instance as a military and policing problem. Secondly, however, in correspondence to the rise of the industrial power elites who were allied with them, they also envisaged economic controls. Hitler and his people by contrast represented a democratizing thrust, a rise to power of broader social strata which hitherto had hardly had any access to it. And so, to the other instruments of ruling, they added another which is characteristic of mass societies: rule and disciplining by means of a social belief. They were not alone in doing so. The use of a new social religion as an instrument of empire-building, as a means for maintaining and stabilizing the rule of a minority over a subject-majority, was a general development of the times. Educated or half-educated masses who had learned to a certain extent to think for themselves could no longer be controlled solely by external constraints. More than ever before it was necessary for them, so to speak, to control themselves – with the help of their own beliefs. And since metaphysical religions had lost much of their earlier power as means of ruling, social religions came increasingly to take their place.

Of course, the Nazi creed, which taught that one specific race alone, with Germany as its centre, was destined to rule over humanity as a whole, could by its very nature have had only strictly limited appeal for the subject peoples of an empire, especially when, as in France, Holland, Italy or Norway, they already possessed a strong and vibrant national consciousness of their own. The protagonists of National Socialism as a belief system may have hoped that at least such negative aspects of it as the isolation and weeding out of Jews would find a broad acceptance among the peoples of Europe and that they would thereby attract helpers and converts from other nations who would recommend themselves as members of the empire's ruling caste and help to swell its all too meagre numbers. But although potential anti-Jewish feelings were widespread among the peoples of Europe, even this aspect of their beliefs did not win the Nazis very many converts. It could not prevail against indigenous national sentiments which were further heightened by the ruthless behaviour of the German colonizers in the occupied countries.

Moreover, the fantasy aspects of the Nazi belief system were so self-evident and crass that, in other countries even more than in Germany, its attraction was greatest among half-educated people and social outsiders. If it attracted some members of other nations, it repelled an even greater number. And the type of people of which the Nazi elite was composed were not particularly well suited to the task of propagating their creed among non-Germans. Like Hitler, they understood each other and in general their own people; but their approach to other nations rested to a large extent on the implicit assumption that they should behave and feel exactly like Germans. They had no sense of the differences between national traditions of behaviour and belief. Perhaps they might have been able to cow leaderless peasant masses in the East but they were not very effective colonizers of nations with a fully developed sense of their own uniqueness and a firm national pride.

Even if they had won the war, their chances of pacifying for any length of time the *großdeutsches Reich* which they envisaged would have been slender. In an epoch of 'awakening nations', an empire in Europe comprising in large measure nations which were already 'awakened', had far less prospect of maintaining itself than empires overseas.

There was thus the unfavourable numerical ratio between rulers and ruled. There was the official belief system of the rulers which met with the disapproval, if not of all, of the majority of the subject peoples. There was the lack of social tact and social skills on the part of the majority of the Nazi core group with their defective understanding of the feelings of others and their naïvely superior posturing towards conquered peoples. And there was Hitler himself with his certain insight into a narrow field, his flair for the successful use of power and violence from a superior vantage point and his deeply impaired sense of reality in almost every other respect. In all likelihood, the Third Reich, if it had really come into existence, would have had to fight increasingly against guerrilla groups and resistance movements – perhaps even inside Germany – which would have been supported by most of the major unoccupied countries of the world. And sooner or later, it would have disintegrated under this pressure, leaving behind a powder keg of suffering and hatred surpassing by far all the consequences of the Second World War.

19

But in this case, too, there is little to suggest that Hitler and his circle ever thought in realistic terms about the thousand-year Reich which they wanted to build. The inability of most war leaders to picture to themselves, clearly and realistically, the tasks likely to arise after victory was heightened in their case by the age-old readiness of Germans to do what their ideals demanded – regardless of whether the demands were achievable at all, whether there were any prospects of success. The National Socialist vision of a Third Reich was the culmination of a long tradition of beliefs and behaviour. In it was asserted yet again the German tendency to obey a national ideal and the leaders who represented it unconditionally. This basic characteristic was expressed in the attitudes of the state and party leaders no less than in those of the masses who followed them. The National Socialist episode showed the oppressive and tyrannical character of such an ideal with the utmost sharpness.

At the same time, it sheds clear light on the peculiar identification with the oppressor which has been spoken of already. In this case, it was a question of an extreme form of a more general pattern, namely identification with a master (or a group of masters); its early and often formative prototype in the life of an individual is the identification of a child with its parents. Simple examples of identification with the oppressor are offered by slaves and concentration camp prisoners who make the attitudes, beliefs and values of their masters or SS guards their own. In highly differentiated societies the relationships are often more complex.

The masses of the ruled in societies such as ours are often trapped, for example, between, on the one hand, interests and feelings which are antagonistic to those of the more powerful, ruling elite and, on the other hand, interests, feelings, values and convictions which they share with their rulers. National interests and beliefs, in particular, create – on account of their exclusiveness, the common front against foreigners (especially the arch-enemies of the moment) – a bond between all individual members and all sections of a state-society. Such feelings of togetherness which spring from national beliefs and ideals can, especially in situations where the tensions in relation to other nations are being experienced more sharply than the tensions and cleavages at home, attenuate the latter and often block their public expression altogether. In other words, national creeds cement a unity of conduct and sentiment between the ruling minorities, whoever they are, and the great mass of those whose access to the higher and more powerful positions in the land is mostly blocked. Through their adoption of these doctrines, the less powerful majority identify with the ruling circles who function as their representatives in relation to other nations and who take most decisions in that field. They identify with their masters.

When rule is autocratic and when, as was normally the case in the past and still is in many societies today, it is merely exercised primarily for the benefit of the rulers and more or less oppressively, the adherence in thinking, feeling and acting to the common national creed does, in fact, have the character of an identification with the oppressors. Even if one feels oppressed, the will and capacity to work for a lessening of or an end to the oppression is paralysed through identification with national ideals and the persons who embody it – persons who, on the one hand perform the indispensable task of representing the nation as a whole, and, on the other, often without being conscious of it, keep sections of it in bondage. The engagement of national pride in the defence and protection of collective values whose principal spokespersons and interpreters also have the function of rulers, in some cases of oppressive rulers, and in defence of shared idiosyncrasies and antagonisms in relation to foreign nations – in particular the canonized hate-objects, one's arch-enemies – impedes the capability of fighting effectively against the oppression.

In Germany, where most political achievements, above all the achievement of national unity itself, had been the work of autocratic or semi-autocratic regimes largely monopolized by relatively small, oligarchic social groups, the dilemma of the mass of subjects was correspondingly great. They found themselves in a situation in which their national pride and self-esteem as Germans, humbled and wounded by the long weakness of Germany in comparison with other powers, could only be satisfied if they swallowed their pride in relation to their rulers; for only these, so it seemed and as it proved for a number of decades to be the case, were in a position to lift them out of their insignificance and into the ranks of the great and mighty powers.

It was probably this dilemma which contributed to the 'lust for submission' which one encounters as a recurrent disposition among Germans, especially in crisis situations – contributing to their tendency to subordinate themselves almost enthusiastically and, as it often seems, with an ecstatic feeling of elation to the commands of strict patriarchal elites (in the case of their traditionalistic-autocratic elites) or also to harsher and more brutal leaders (in the case of newly risen and more democratized autocrats), as long as these commands were given in the name of Germany, their national ideal. If leaders appealed to 'the Fatherland ideal', one had to obey without questioning their goals or what the realistic chances of achieving them were. This submission was inescapable for Germans not only because of external constraints, because they had been forced into it by strict or tyrannical rulers, but also because of the pressure of their own inner voices, their strict and often tyrannical 'Fatherland ideal'. That was the trap in which they were caught.

The Nazi state was the most recent embodiment of a highly oppressive and tyrannical tradition of belief and behaviour in which it was customary to demand and expect that, in times of national crisis, individuals should subordinate themselves unconditionally – and more unconditionally than elsewhere – to state commands, that they should do their duty for the 'Fatherland' regardless of the consequences for themselves and the future, even if it led to their own downfall or national catastrophe. That was a recurrent theme in German soldiers' songs: 'One does one's duty for the Fatherland. One does it with joy and pride. One sacrifices oneself and death waits at the end of the road.' Nothing could be done about it. One was driven to it like the fisherman in the enchanting song of the Lorelei, like the children of Hamelin by the enticing music of the piper, like the gods in Valhalla who were driven to act as inexorably as they did, knowing full well that by doing so they were contributing to their own downfall.

The sense of doom among the Germans was never far from the surface even in moments of triumph, and it became stronger as defeat followed defeat – without loosening the spell of their oppressive ideal or diminishing the attraction of its promise: the deep satisfaction one would feel when, in times of crisis, one obeyed, together with one's fellow countrymen, the demands of the 'Fatherland'. Fulfilment of the national ideal also promised to many members of the nation an incomparable personal fulfilment. Failures and defeats left in their wake again and again disheartened 'lost' generations.

Inherent in the identification with strict or tyrannical rulers and ideals out of which a lust for submission could arise was a standard conflict. It took the following basic form.

Generally speaking, one can free oneself from oppression by resistance or rebellion against the oppressor. But that is only possible when subject peoples have an integrated system of ideals and values which they can oppose to those of their rulers or, if applicable, their oppressors. When their system of ideals and values is more or less identical with that of their masters, when their own conscience and we-ideal is on the side of the oppressors, the negative components of their feeling-set towards the oppressors cannot be directly and openly expressed. The tensions and conflicts between subjects and masters, oppressed and oppressors, become internal tensions and conflicts of the ruled and oppressed themselves. Hands which might otherwise be raised against the masters become paralysed. The hostility aroused by the oppression becomes impotent and inadmissible. The main battleground of the conflict shifts from the inter-human to the intra-human level. In relation to the oppressors, the conflict only becomes perceptible through a reinforcement of the opposite gesture, that is, in a 'lust for submission'.

There are many other forms in which the intra-human aspect of such a conflict can become manifest. For example, the 'lust for submission' is not infrequently supplemented by a 'lust for attacking' in another direction. The hostility which is blocked from consciousness and expression in relation to powerful superiors may show itself as resentment or hatred against people who are, or appear to be, socially inferior and weaker. In Germany, they had a characteristic metaphor for this kind of displacement. One spoke of certain kinds of people as *Radfahrer*, that is, cyclists, because they bend their backs before those above them and tread on those below.

Much of the hostility against the Jews was of this type. Already before 1933 many Germans had seen the Jews as a socially inferior group and it gave an edge to their negative feelings against them that the majority of German Jews acted as if they themselves were completely unaware of the lower status allotted to them. It would oversimplify matters rather too much if one were to explain the anti-Jewish feelings merely by saying that the rulers offered the Jews to the people as a 'scapegoat' in order to divert negative feelings from themselves. The Jews were favoured hate-objects of strata who lived under considerable social pressure from above, who, through their own ideals which mostly took the form of a nationalist belief system, identified with their superiors so that their reactive bitterness over their own factual inferiority was unable to find appropriate discharge on that front and sought all the more strongly for an outlet against people whom they held to be socially weaker and inferior.

As one would expect, the Nazi system was particularly conducive to the reinforcement of old and the production of new *Radfahrer*-mechanisms. A characteristic example of this displacement of feelings, directly connected with anti-Jewish attitudes, is provided by certain standard rituals of the SS guards in the concentration camps. 'Usually', wrote a former prisoner who survived,

> the standard initiation of prisoners took place during transit from the local prison to the camp. If the distance was short, the transport was often

slowed down to allow enough time to break the prisoners. During their initial transport to the camp, prisoners were exposed to nearly constant torture. The nature of the abuse depended on the fantasy of the particular SS man in charge of a group of prisoners. Still they all had a definite pattern. Physical punishment consisted of whipping, frequent kicking (abdomen or groin), slaps in the face, shooting or wounding with the bayonet. They alternated with attempts to produce extreme exhaustion. For instance prisoners were forced to stare for hours into glaring lights, to kneel for hours, and so on.

From time to time a prisoner got killed, but no prisoner was allowed to care for his or another's wounds. The guards also forced the prisoners to hit one another and to defile what the SS considered the prisoners' most cherished values. They were forced to curse their God, to accuse themselves and one another of vile actions, and their wives of adultery and prostitution. I never met a prisoner who escaped this kind of initiation which lasted at least twelve hours and often much longer. . . .

The purpose of this massive initial abuse was to traumatise the prisoners and to break their resistance; to change at least their behaviour, if not yet their personalities. This could be seen from the fact that tortures became less and less violent to the degree that prisoners stopped resisting and complied immediately with any SS order, even the most outrageous.[10]

One can certainly think of good practical reasons for this sort of initial treatment of prisoners. Over time, as a reaction, quite a few of them identified with the SS and submitted to them. In this case, too, the identification with the oppressor may have been to some extent deliberately induced as an especially suitable means of safeguarding the oppressors' rule and of saving them trouble.

Nevertheless there were in different countries very different methods of enforcing camp discipline among the great masses of prisoners who had been represented to their guards as enemies of their country. The functional similarities of the situation left considerable scope for national variations in the behaviour of the guards. If the behaviour of the Nazi guards was particularly cruel and barbaric, this was characteristic of their own identification with a particularly tyrannical and cruel master. In their case, too, the *Radfahrer*-mechanism was at work.

So far as we know, the guards came from the least educated strata. Many of them were probably young peasants. They had learned early in their young lives to submit to the hard and often callous pressure from above which permeated the whole regime. Used to being trodden under by others, as camp guards many of them probably experienced for the first time a situation in which they could trample on others. Hidden impulses which had previously been curbed by the need to repress all hostile feelings towards superiors and to submit cheerfully to the strict discipline demanded by the regime in the name of a harsh and oppressive idol, together with their self-protective identification with this regime, broke out with terrible force like steam released under high pressure in their behaviour against people whom they had to view as inferiors and who were utterly powerless. In relation to the prisoners, the guards themselves could play the role of masters and oppressors.

Their behaviour betrayed to an extent how, in their imagination, the oppressors with whom they identified could and perhaps should turn on people, including themselves, who did not obey orders unconditionally and immediately, who did not, as they themselves had to, nip every feeling of rebelliousness firmly in the bud. They had likewise to reckon on severe punishment and perhaps death if they forgot even for a moment to submit totally to their superiors and to show that *Kadaver-gehorsam* (a much used German word), that corpse-like obedience to Hitler and his representatives which was expected of them. So it is not surprising that, for their part, they enforced with zeal and even more roughly the corpse-like obedience of the prisoners. Every hint of independence, the smallest sign of rebellion, had to be violently stamped out. Nothing was permitted to a prisoner except absolute submission.

It may well be that the concentration camp guards derived enjoyment from all this. Perhaps they experienced it as a kind of liberation. But whatever was the case, the barbarities of the concentration camps were certainly not isolated events explainable primarily in terms of the particularly sadistic propensities of a number of individuals. They are indicative of the enormous pressure of the tensions and conflicts (inter- as well as intra-personal) behind the monolithic façade of a social system whose leading men had embarked, as it were with clenched teeth, on a gigantic task for which their resources were scarcely sufficient. They throw some light on the price which people had to pay for their identification with a highly oppressive national ideal and for their unconditional submission to a Führer who may have promised victory and a thousand-year Reich but who, at the same time, never ceased to remind his followers that they might be unworthy of him, that all their sacrifice might be in vain, and that this time, too, Germany's enemies might be successful. It was as if the whole mixture of thwarted and contradictory feelings for which the regime left few outlets elsewhere revealed itself in all its fury in the treatment of the concentration camp prisoners: 'For once the enemies are in our power. We have them in our hands and no one is watching. So long as it lasts, let us show them who the masters are.' And so they inflicted on them everything they had secretly wished to inflict on others. They did to them things which in ordered societies even children are forbidden to do and took revenge for all the disappointments they had suffered.

20

All these horrors happened with the approval of the one authority which, for many Germans, took the place of a conscience, namely the Führer, the highest authority in the state: they happened in the half-knowledge that it would not last and perhaps without too much worry about what would happen afterwards: 'The categorical imperative of action in the Third Reich', wrote one of the highest officials of the Hitler-state, Hans Frank, *Reichsminister* and Governor-General of occupied Poland,[11] 'is this: act in such a way that the Führer, if he knew of your action, would approve of it.' The Nazi system fostered identification with the oppressor. In the concentration camps one sees some of the results.

Frank's maxim was symptomatic of a tendency which had been common among the Germans – as among other people with a long and powerful autocratic tradition – long before 1933, and which the years of Nazi rule made more pronounced. The development and traditions of German society often produced a rather weak individual conscience. Even among adults, the functioning of an individual's conscience remained, at least in the expanding sector of more impersonal public affairs, dependent on someone outside watching and reinforcing the compulsion, the discipline which individuals were incapable of imposing unaided on themselves. And among the external authorities which many Germans needed in these spheres of life in order to be able to curb their purely selfish impulses and regulate their behaviour, the state and its representatives played a particularly large role. Left to the resources of their own conscience, they were not strong enough to erect stable limitations on disallowed, forbidden or dangerous urges. For purposes of self-control they needed the help of a strong state and, in crisis situations, often craved for precisely that. Above all in times of national emergency and war, many Germans cheerfully shed the burden of having to control themselves and shoulder the responsibility for their own lives. In such situations, the state authorities, and especially the symbolic figure at the head of the state, took the place, wholly or partly, of individual conscience, in that way further reinforcing an attitude of submissiveness and awe towards the head of state. People gladly left to the state authorities the decision over what to do and what not to do, over what was right and what was wrong.

Before the rise of the National Socialists, as long as Germany was a *Rechtsstaat* governed by the rule of law where even the most powerful people were subject to regulation by an impersonal code of law, where the administrators of justice had a high degree of autonomy and sought to base their judgements on firmly grounded principles, individuals in need of state support for the functioning of their own conscience received from the state instructions and models based on fairly developed standards of human decency and honesty. But when the state apparatus fell into the hands of people who lacked such standards, when the official rulers of Germany, including the head of state, encouraged what would previously have been regarded as asocial and criminal tendencies, the mass of Germans had no personal conscience strong and independent enough to have enabled them to act on their own. What qualms they may have had individually when it came to their ears that men, women and children were being terribly treated and killed in concentration camps were quickly suppressed and half-forgotten. Used to relying for reinforcement of their conscience on the representatives of the state, they experienced any conflict between the pattern of state-control and that of conscience-control as profoundly disturbing. Hence they strove automatically to blot out any event which threatened to produce such a conflict. They did not admit it – did not want to become aware of it. Afterwards it was often asked: 'But you must have heard of what went on in the concentration camps?' Again and again, the answer was: 'I did not know.' They tried as best they could not to perceive any unpleasantness. In the conflict between a powerful state and a relatively weak and dependent personal conscience, the former was bound to prevail. State-control superseded conscience-control.

The Nazi regime also differed from earlier forms of autocratic rule in Germany through its more deliberate efforts to undermine the reliance of people on their own individual conscience in public affairs. It distrusted people who claimed to have a conscience of their own, independent of Hitler and the party creed, and punished them if possible. It had little regard and left little scope for the exercise of a conscience based on anything other than the Führer-ideal and the Nazi *Weltanschauung*. Frank's recasting of Kant's categorical imperative simply expressed what was in fact a broad trend in the development of the Nazi system. It bred many Führers, great and small. And as so often happens, those on the lowest level of the hierarchy, small people like the SS guards in the concentration camps, were among the most ferocious oppressors of those under them.

Nor was the pressure by any means one-sided. The Führer, seemingly the spring and fountainhead of all oppression, was anything but a free arbiter of his decisions. He was himself subject to the dictates of an unrelenting ideal and a national belief which drove him from crisis to crisis to greater and greater exertions regardless of circumstances. The more people embraced the belief, the greater and more powerful the movement, the organization, the state which he led, the more they drove him on towards his fate. Once set on its course, the whole system with its Führer at the top and its *Weltanschauung* as a binding force developed a dynamic of self-perpetuation and self-reinforcement. Hitler was as little able to escape the demands his followers made on him as they were able to escape from his. He could not risk disappointing their expectations without endangering his position and, indeed, his life. The greater his pressure on them, the greater their pressure on him. As usual, the harshness and oppressiveness of the regime were proportionate to the counter-forces which threatened it. Under the smooth surface of discipline and efficiency on which the Nazi leaders prided themselves, the pressure of tensions, conflicts and rivalries was extremely great.

The powerful war-machine into which Germany transformed itself after 1933 and its initial successes in the swift conquest of the greater part of Europe often concealed from view the grim effort that lay behind them. The victories appeared then as the work of a genius and the brutalities as accidental. In the face of the successes, people forgot the price which had had to be paid. The fact that, in peace-time, other peoples were not ready to pay a commensurate price made the initial successes possible. The successes and the oppressiveness of the regime were complementary; they were apt to obscure the fierce determination with which Hitler and his men marshalled all the resources of their country with the single aim of achieving military superiority and possibly military hegemony in Europe. All other considerations were subordinated to this aim.

The techniques used by the Nazis to keep in check the counter-pressure engendered by their ruthlessness and brutality proved highly effective. In recent times, terror has hardly been used more effectively as a short-term instrument of rule than it was by the Nazis. Concentration camps did not only remove real and imaginary enemies from their potential field of activity but also contributed greatly to the intimidation of the remaining population. They were symptomatic of the pressure which made the German war effort possible. But this and many similar reasons would hardly have been so resoundingly effective in enforcing conformity and obedience had the Nazis not been heirs to a tradition of belief and behaviour which made Germans highly susceptible to discipline exacted by the state as a necessary corollary of individual self-control – if the German conscience-formation had not been of a type which, in order for individual conscience to function adequately in public affairs, a high degree of regulation and control by agencies of the state was required. It was this dependency which gave the German identification with nation and state – and if the state was oppressive, with the oppressor – its specific stamp.

In Germany itself it was often felt that no resistance against Nazi oppression was possible because the measures taken by the regime against any possible opposition or revolt were highly effective and all-embracing. In fact, no effective resistance from Germans was possible because, in addition to all the external controls which discouraged resistance against the state, the conscience, the self-control of the mass of German people in all matters of public concern, remained highly dependent on the state, whoever its rulers and representatives were. The intensive educational and propaganda techniques which the Nazis employed in order to ensure the absolute loyalty of the mass of the people to their state served merely to reinforce the characteristics of a personality structure which made the regulation of individual behaviour highly dependent on regulation by the state and which created in individuals a disposition to submit loyally to the demands of a head of state who could be looked up to and whose image could be internalized by people as part of their own conscience.

The one attempt which Germans with a strongly state-dependent conscience made to overthrow the 'legally' installed government by 'illegal' means showed some of these difficulties clearly enough. The participants who decided in the middle of the war to kill the German head of state were unable to take such a decision without severe conflicts of conscience. It was unprecedented in the history of Germany that people who regarded themselves as good Germans and who identified fully with the German national tradition and the accompanying ideals, nobles and military officers among them, should seek to raise their hands against the man who was head of state and try to kill him. Perhaps it was not quite as fortuitous as it seemed that the attempt failed.

21

How strong the identification with the oppressor remained despite all the hate and doubt which many Germans may have felt in their heart of hearts can also be seen from the fact that, throughout the war, there occurred no noteworthy breakdown of morale among either the fighting forces or the German people as a whole. If one looks back at the Nazi system with some awareness of the high level of tension and pressure under which its members lived, one can appreciate better how remarkable it was that the identification of the mass of the German people with their rulers and their belief in them remained more or less intact right to the bitter end. Even when enemy troops had penetrated Germany's borders in the East and West and were pressing towards the German heartland, the vast majority of Germans continued unconditionally to obey the commands of their state and party overlords so long as the orders came through.

This was certainly due to some extent to the fact that Hitler, and Hitler alone, seemed in the end to stand in the eyes of many Germans between them and total annihilation. They had no alternative. But in other countries, among other peoples, a halfway realistic assessment of the situation might have induced people to lose faith; feeling that further killing and sacrifice of life were useless, they might in despair have ceased to obey orders or perhaps turned angrily against the masters who had betrayed them. The Germans never ceased to obey. It is probably true to say that a large part of the German people continued to believe unshakeably in the Führer until he was dead, and perhaps for quite a time afterwards.

One of Hitler's greatest talents – and one of the main factors in his success – was his intuitive, emotional understanding of the needs which a leader of the Germans and his crew had to satisfy in a critical situation. His own emotional needs corresponded to those of his followers. He reacted, without much reflection, to their emotional signals, verbal or non-verbal, with the emotional signals which they demanded and expected of a leader if they were to trust that he would be able to save them from an apparently hopeless situation of danger and despair. His way of responding to their needs was not the only possible way. There were other potential Führers who might have filled the place of national 'saviour', offered by Germany's situation at that time, in a somewhat different way. And there were also a good many Germans who responded to his symbols and signals in a negative way.

However, the correspondence between Hitler's personality and the needs of many Germans was sufficiently great to allow him, once he had attained power, to play the role of a German leader successfully – a role that was quite specific and differed in some respects from that of a crisis leader in other countries. He filled the role of head of state so convincingly that he was gradually accepted as such by the vast majority of the German people. He was accepted by them, in other words, as the symbolic completion and representation of their own conscience and as the symbolic embodiment of their own we-ideal.

For many Germans, a fact which in retrospect stands out strongly is that Hitler was a Nazi but that, in the course of the war, that role receded into the background compared with his role as head of the German state, as the Führer of all the Germans. As such, he met emotional needs which none of the leaders in the Weimar Republic had ever fully satisfied. One of these needs, which became greater and greater, first with the mounting crisis of 1930 and then with the series of crises which the Nazis themselves helped to create, was the need for a man to whom they could submit blindly, who would magically remove the burden of responsibility from their shoulders and take it on his own, who would make himself responsible for all national hopes and wishes, all longings for an end to Germany's humiliation, for a new greatness, a new power.

In this respect as in others, Hitler can serve as the symbol of a basic feature which is common in the societies of today. Many of the most pressing problems of social life are at present still attacked in a manner analogous to the way in which, in simpler societies, problems of both realms which we separate and call 'nature' and 'society' are approached. One seeks to overcome them by semi-magical means. It is no figure of speech but a simple statement of fact to say that Hitler in Germany had a function and characteristics similar to those of a rainmaker, a witch doctor, a shaman in simpler tribal groupings. He reassured a distressed and suffering people that he would give them all that they wanted most, just as a rainmaker promises a people threatened with hunger and thirst by a long period of drought that he will make it rain. And like a tribal leader, he demanded material and human sacrifice. The Germans were thirsting for a new self-respect, a new greatness and a new pride. He promised fulfilment of their wishes. Doubtless, he himself believed in his ability to keep his promise. He was undoubtedly imbued with a deep sense of being all-powerful and he was able up to a point to impart this to his followers. However much he play-acted and lied, he was also completely sincere in his belief that he had been called to renew Germany's greatness and perhaps to dominate Europe if not the whole world.

In this way, Hitler uncovered needs in respect of which not only the Germans but also many other modern nations are hardly less simple and 'childlike' or, if one prefers, hardly less 'primitive' than tribal societies. In spite of the relatively high control of events on that level of the universe which we call 'nature', even in the societies which, up to the present, are the most highly developed, the degree of control which people have over themselves as societies is still very low. On this level, even today, people still think in many cases that they can control by magical means the course of events where adequate knowledge of factual connections is lacking, and the attitudes of leaders towards the social events in the widest sense of the word in which they are involved are to a large extent conditioned by those of the mass of the people. Particularly in critical situations, the masses of the population, even in the most 'advanced' nations, feel threatened by dangers whose nature they hardly understand better than the people in simpler, tribal societies understand the dangers of floods and thunderstorms, droughts or diseases. And like the latter, they are liable to fill the gaps in their knowledge with half-truths and myths.

Hitler was in essence an innovative political medicine man. Others may be more conventional in their procedures. And since the Nazi regime represented a particularly malignant form of social mythology and magical manipulation of society, it throws into fuller relief the stage of development reached in our time regarding the capacity of people to handle their own social affairs and to solve their own social problems.

The fact that the war-morale of the German people held up despite all the shocks and doubts shows how firmly they were bonded to the supreme sorcerer and his helpers – not merely by external coercion but also by their own needs and beliefs. Life would have been almost unbearable if people had had to look its uncertainties and their own helplessness fully in the face. Magical rituals and mythical beliefs act as a balm which protects people against the full impact of awareness, the shock of recognition of their powerlessness in the face of a course of events which threatens both their physical existence and their sense of the meaningfulness of life. At the same time, however, magical acts and mythical beliefs also contribute to the preservation and renewal of the very conditions which create the need for them, the conditions of human impotence and ignorance in the face of threatening events. They provide people with an emotionally satisfying palliative which prevents them from even conceiving the idea that a less mythical, more realistic way of thinking about the nexus of social events which threatens them and a less magical, more realistic way of acting in relation to these dangers might be possible.

That was the vicious circle which kept the Germans under the Nazis entrapped, like all other peoples with strong fantasy elements in their behaviour and thinking. Hitler and the Nazi faith helped to reproduce and reinforce the very uncertainties against which they seemed to their adherents to be a protection. The use of biological concepts such as 'race' in a largely magical and mythical sense was only one among many examples of the curious way in which, in our times, scientific ways of approaching 'nature' may be used in the service of a magical-mythical approach to 'society'; it was one example of the way in which concepts which are scientific in one context can become mythical in another.

The elementary simplicity of the belief of many Germans in the Führer as the symbol of Germany, and the closely connected firmness of German war-morale up to the bitter end, are often obscured by intellectual arguments which appear to suppose that the masses of German people (or of any others for that matter) had at their disposal an articulate and highly integrated system of beliefs of the kind expounded in books, that the Germans were either convinced National Socialists or, failing that, convinced anti-Nazis and democrats. But the belief in the Führer and the power which this exerted over the mass of the population right to the end can hardly be adequately explained in terms of such concise political categories. They were grounded essentially in the simple needs of simple people whose helplessness in the face of the great events of world politics made them turn to someone who, in their imagination, had the aura of a saviour, whose attributes and characteristics dovetailed with their needs and who, fortified by a machinery of external coercion, facilitated them in making all the efforts and sacrifices and bearing the oppression of a society geared for war without a serious breakdown of their weak and dependent self-control.

22

Perhaps one will understand the position of these people somewhat better if one listens to their own authentic voices. The following excerpts from civilian letters to the front which were written in the summer of 1944 may help to illuminate some of the problems which have been discussed so far in more general terms. They stem from a selection of around 300 letters which became available to the author by chance. Since such witnesses are not very numerous, their publication may have a certain documentary value. In what follows, all personal names have been changed or made unrecognizable. The spelling and punctuation have been carefully corrected.

6.7.44

My dear Robert,
The club has just received more bad news – Martin has fallen. I was almost torn to pieces when I heard it. . . . At Christmas we put on a Christmas party together, and then he was suddenly called up, and since then he has not been on leave. . . . It is so awful when one thinks that they don't all come back: one can hardly imagine it.

Today Anne-Marie was here swimming. She is in correspondence with Hubert Uhlich at the moment. That is my latest.

The swimming today was marvellous. The water was 22°. The children had great fun, too. It would be too lovely if you could come on leave and we could go swimming together every day. Sadly, however, we must both wait until the war is over and you are finally home again.

I will close now, my sweet, it is already late and my eyes are beginning to close. . . .

Your faithful,
Lilli.

19.7.44

I still haven't recovered from the shock; it is as if I have just got up after a severe illness. I am so tired, and I don't feel good in other ways.

Dear Hermann, the funeral was on Sunday. I was on duty, as I already wrote to you. Various people said that, if they had known what had happened at the funeral, they would not have gone. They were very annoyed at the brown [Nazi] theatre. The priest was rather unimportant. The mourners were so outraged, they could not cry. But that will all pass, just as it began.

(continued, 20.7.44)
. . . There was another air-raid warning; they flew over us on their way to N. [a large town]. There was a rather horrible droning. Fräulein Steiger has quite a good cellar.

People here are so agitated; I am really quite calm. Only when I have to walk by the ruins a few times each day, I feel so sorry when I think of the poor people who have lost everything. I think how easily my house could also be like that.

Now there have been exactly 63 deaths. I spoke yesterday with the layer-out. During yesterday morning's air-raid alert, Frau Franzen from the mill had a heart attack from the anxiety. Frau Leber, too, is so agitated that the day before yesterday she cried all day. Now she is crying, too, because they no longer have a church. On Sunday, the Protestant service was supposed to be at 9 a.m. I was there at about 7.45; the service had hardly ended and there was another alert. The all-clear came just before 10. Then the bells rang for the Protestants. The people streamed in, the organ started and there was yet another alert.

The radio is still playing but I don't want to listen to music at the moment. . . .

21.7.44

. . . only a few hours with you to see you, to kiss your mouth, your dear hands, I could not do more any longer. I am so terribly detached with my feelings. . . . Today we already had to go down to the cellar twice. . . . nothing but ash and fire. Alles kaputt. Quite terrible to have no rest at all. . . . it never stops. . . .

25.7.44

. . . the only ambition one can satisfy is to remain a true comrade of the soldiers at the front. If all the men, or at least all SS men, would think as I do one wouldn't have to worry. But my whole faith is still with the Old Guard. Even though I never met them, I knew from you what they were like and will swear by them because I know you. No man could set a better example to a woman than you, so proud, so noble, do you stand before me. My endeavour is, and will remain, to be worthy of you. . . . I know that for this attitude you will accept me still more as your wife later.

27.7.44

It is a pity that you are no longer quite in the picture. But the news of the attempt on the life of our Führer will probably have got through to you. And I also hope that this is Fortune's sign of a turning point. Last night Dr Goebbels spoke on the radio. We drove a few kilometres out in the country to listen to the speech. It was a good speech and there was a lot of truth in what he said. What one can't understand is that the party needed 11 years in order to say clearly that we are a National Socialist state. It strikes me as slightly ludicrous that just now in this war situation one thinks it is the right moment for putting people under the leadership of the Party. ... We two have said before that one day the decision whether Wehrmacht or party state will have to be taken. Now it has been taken it worries me. The party was not active enough in the war, the people have lost a good deal of their faith, and who can blame them. Still, I do believe that Dr Goebbels can do it. He is one of those who stand by the Führer 100 per cent as a full Pg.[12] And Pg Himmler to be responsible for the home reserves – that should work OK. At any rate the SS can now no longer laugh at the Wehrmacht. They, too, have to give the 'German salute'. Do you think they will do it? I should like to see their faces!

I can imagine your position in the army, my dear daddy, it is bad if one and the same family is split in two parties. We were nearly getting in the same condition as Italy. The people as a whole are sound. They are slowly learning to see that if we lost the war, we would be miserably finished for good.

23.7.44

My dear son Wolf,
Today is Sunday and at the moment I'm back home again completely on my own. Father has gone to the meeting of the veterans association. Anneliese is with Aunt Lina. Today we received with great joy another sweet letter from you, dated 14 July; sincere thanks for your lovely lines. My dear son, you write that, up to now, things have gone well for you, which I can also say about us. Yes, my dear son, you are now facing the enemy too, and I know, my dear son, that you will do your duty as befits a German soldier. May Almighty God protect you. Our dear German Fatherland is in great danger, attacked by enemies from all sides. And on 20 July the worst thing imaginable happened – people close to our beloved Führer made an assassination attempt on the Führer. But Almighty God did not want it to succeed and held His protecting hand over him, so that he was only lightly wounded. Yes, my dear son, what would have become of us if the Führer had been taken away from us in time of war. We will hope that, in the end, everything goes well nevertheless. Our dear Erich has also been wounded. Hopefully he will soon come somewhat nearer home. Now, my dear son, last year around this time, you, my dear son, you were with us and mowed our rye. This year you have another duty to perform. Hopefully next year things will be better. Now, my dear son, I will close. This week they're bringing in the harvest. Write and tell us where you are, in what city in the West.

Now, my dear son, may God protect you,
best wishes
from your dear mother,
Auf wiedersehen, God willing.

23.7.44

I have never had illusions about our present military situation and was completely clear that the mightiest efforts and the greatest sacrifices would be necessary to overcome it. Also the thought was never far away that now the enemies inside the Reich would think their hour has come. But that German generals would lower themselves to do such shameful work for our enemies was something no one expected. . . . And that is why the outrage is so enormous among the broad mass of the people. The mood here can be summed up in the sentence: Thank God that nothing happened to the Führer. Just now we must stand defiantly by him.[13]

But the confidence that, despite everything, our leadership and our armies will succeed in checking the push remains unshaken.

24.7.44

Are you still all right, my dear boy? Fritz is now in Z. but thinks they will move soon. He has got a tropical uniform and thinks he'll be going to Italy. Everything there is terribly expensive, a glass of beer 7 marks, a litre of wine 20 marks, a pair of shoes 1500, a pound of cherries 50 marks. . . . But it is much the same where you are, isn't it? And if I think back to our great inflation, these prices are really nothing. Because then we had to pay one billion for a loaf of bread, a figure one can hardly write any more today. And that would surely have happened again if the attack against the life of the Führer had succeeded. What did you all think of that at the front? Here, our hearts stood still, when we heard about it on the radio. We probably would not have a war any more if they had succeeded, but instead occupation, civil war and Bolshevism. One cannot imagine that there are still people who do not see that, and, above all, they should have learned from the last World War. We are lucky that the Führer is alive and in good health. But what this man has to go through, he is spared nothing. The French POWs here in B. have said that they would not have thought that a German officer would have done it. One must really feel ashamed for these fellows.

We're now having air-raids every day. The day before yesterday a bomb fell on a house in M. and there was a direct hit on the car-park of the SA hostel. . . . In R., a whole house was destroyed from the ground-floor up, there were two dead, both of them Frenchmen. . . . Yesterday was the funeral. A great part of the German population turned up. I wonder whether the French would turn up in the same way. We Germans simply won't learn. We are too good and the foreigners only laugh at us. . . .

We still have enough to eat. We must be strong in our faith that one day victory will still be ours. It is time for everyone to do his bit; there are still plenty of women running around who could be brought into action.

Sometimes one feels our party work has borne no fruit, but then again one finds proof that it has done some good and takes heart again.

With a vigorous Heil Hitler!

Your Mother.

26.7.44

A few days ago enemy planes came and dropped bombs on the station in E. but they didn't hit the station but only the street which was very badly damaged but should have already been repaired. Bombs were also dropped on L. and a house was destroyed with 16 victims. I wonder why the T.-works and the hut in O. haven't been bombed yet, since both are working day and night for the [. . .?] Probably our enemies lost their bearings. They'll be back again in any case. The newly built chemical plant in P., where petrol is made from coal, was recently completely destroyed along with all the houses around it, and the losses were pretty high. How long can this work of annihilation go on? One cannot call it war.

Because of the closure of our business I have lost all sense of purpose, and do all kinds of work chopping up wood, because one cannot get a worker to do it any more, although lots of people run around and steal the day from our Lord God, receive support and work is a minor matter.

27.7.44

Hopefully this year this war will come to an end. Because in the long run no one will be able to bloody well endure it! But we have to keep going, as is required.

30.7.44 *(from the German eastern territories)*

On principle, I haven't written about matters connected with the war, only I'd like very much to know what you really think about the East. I certainly hope that one day everything will take a turn for the better – but would it not be better if we left here? Papa made us quite mad when, two weeks ago, he suddenly arrived here and wanted to take us to Q. [in South Germany]. We didn't take the whole thing very seriously and so he drove off quite disconsolately but thought that, when the Russians are in Warsaw, we'll go there quickly enough. Early this morning, we got a phone call from him to say that, in any case, we should come to him on the estate. Now we haven't any idea what to do, there's so much for and against. . . . What mad times these are. One is always being posed new

*problems. What do you think about it? If we were really to go to Q. and
you were transferred here, then I would come to you alone and at least
we'd know the children were safe.*

30.7.44

*... The situation here is now beginning to get really serious – my cheerful
optimism is beginning to waver – they're almost in Warsaw and it's not
rosy on the Baltic either – I'm now directly curious about whether they're
going to chuck us out of here! – and if that happens, for sure, we'll only
be able to take very little with us – and with the little one I've already got
luggage enough. I will try and go to Irma, because it's better with people
you know than to be with little Hans with strangers. ...*

2.8.44

My own dear hubby,
*I'll just quickly write you a few lines. I've just come home from the field.
We mowed corn and wheat. My dear hubby, your father could have done
with you, and I, my darling, could also have done with you in bed, but
when will the time come? Yesterday, dearest hubby, the planes were with
us for four hours – but we've also had good luck again. That is, my own,
in K. [and the X. factory] ... it was burning, blazing everywhere. It rained
phosphorus and the station at K. is completely destroyed, the tracks are
standing straight up in the air. So, dearest, it wasn't anywhere near as bad
as yesterday. The trains aren't running and there's no post. It's lasted now
for days and everything's destroyed.*
    Many greetings from your darling. Heil ...
We had bean salad, it tasted wonderful.

6.8.44 (to a female addressee in the country)

*... But there's no sense in brooding. One man holds our time in his hands.
That's the only comfort now. Here a very dejected mood prevails, because
no one can do as they please any more. Yesterday I got the following
letter, delivered by a Hitler youth:*

*'For the Marhold operation (a false name) you are detailed to help in
the cooking place and do other women's tasks. You are begged to hold
yourself ready from Monday 7 August. ...*
    Mischke, District Women's Leader.'

*I enquired and learned this morning that it is to be a question of trench-
work, and that we have to cook for the workers. 150 boys from upper*

schools left yesterday for an unknown destination and I heard today by the alarm in the Lyceum that various deputy heads and graduate teachers have to be ready for deployment tomorrow (with their work clothes). All are upwards of 60 years of age and more (64). In all this sweltering heat! Things look really rosy! You know, everyone helps willingly where he can, but the 60-year-olds should not be sent. I absolutely can't stand the heat and spending the night under such primitive conditions any more.... I keep on hoping that things will change a little with me and that I'll be able to stay here....

8.8.44

My dear Otto,
Today I received the two letters from 30.7 and 1.8, many thanks. Here it's still very hot and often so sticky. Yesterday evening there was a thunderstorm but here it only rained a little. The harvest has now been brought in and it was good.... Herr Dahn, that's married to Schulze's daughter, was officially declared missing on Sunday – what are we going to hear about all the others that haven't written yet. From here there are 20–30, including Achim who hasn't written since 20 June, exactly as long as Herr Dahn. There's misery and wretchedness everywhere, with what one hears and sees, you sometimes want to keep away from people. At the moment, thank God, we're having a bit of a break from the bombers, if only it was also like that with you, I live all the time in anxiety about you. I'm so anxious generally at the moment that I hardly sleep soundly any more.
Love and kisses,
Your Alma and the children.

17.8.44

The war must come to an end sometime. But, dear Franz, they're breaking through everywhere, in East Prussia they're in our fields, we're down to the last reserves. If only they could stop the Russians, that's our worry. Our dear soldiers can't be blamed – only the leadership are at fault – for they give their utmost. It breaks your heart when you read so often how they're fighting for the homeland.

21.8.44

Why am I writing all of this to you? I just wanted to distract your attention for a half an hour from thoughts of your duties.... G. was also idyllic as one neither heard nor saw anything of the war, though there was a moaner and they had to shut him up. Often we were only surprised when we read the paper or heard the army news on the radio, but we took our cue from the women: that is happening in another world and is not affecting us. And that is the current situation in which we find ourselves, so deadly serious. The air superiority is not to be denied. You write: 'in a few weeks, it will all be different.' To me it's a puzzle how that will be possible, but you ought to know better! The enemy airmen are searching out our tank factories systematically and destroying them. The Y. factory could write a song about it . . . the manager told me it's been 60 per cent destroyed by enemy terror raids . . . the whole staff had to be employed temporarily in clearing up the ruined sheds . . . ; 90 per cent of the workers were foreigners . . . the V2 is now really ready for use, although lots of people are puzzled because we thought that the army high command had every reason to launch it, and it also seemed to many as if we'd already lost the war especially because, round here, all the women *have been called up for military service . . . without consideration for profession or status, all in fact between 15 and 50. . . . One day came the order and on the next they had to be ready to leave. I can only think that the trenches they're digging make more sense than the Atlantic wall they brag about so much. But one shouldn't grumble.*

I got a great boost yesterday from a letter that the son of our landlord wrote to his parents; he is a bailiff and about 40 years old and is at the northern end of the eastern front. He writes: 'Don't worry about us losing the war, the inexhaustible supply of men that Ivan had is exhausted, he's filling the gaps in his lines with 12-year-old boys, and when our tanks break through, they find no reserves, only the terribly wide open spaces, deserted by people. Why we don't turn the front here I don't understand but our leaders in whom we have boundless faith, will know why! . . .'

We have raids every day, often in the night, too. . . . When the radio, which is reporting all the time, warns exactly where the enemy planes are going to be (it really is a magnificent thing) we go immediately to the air-raid shelter. . . . I don't stay down there very long, though, but stand outside by the door; it really is a pretty sight when the anti-aircraft guns fire tracer ammunition and the tracer bullets light up the whole town like daylight. . . . We've just nothing more to lose in this world, life and whatever luck it might bring are behind us.

These extracts from letters convey a sense of the thoughts and feelings of ordinary people at a time when the factual course of events was making it more and more unlikely that the war could be won and defeat averted. They show something of the dawning awakening from a great, hopeful dream into the at first still unthinkable dreadful reality. Like the members of many other nations, if perhaps somewhat more strongly and less critically than most, the Germans had believed the promises of their leaders. And now these promises were being revealed as hollow and false.

Since Hitler's rise to power, the majority of the Germans had been more or less passive objects in the hands of a minority.[14] A period of almost complete political passivity and irresponsibility, a period, more-over, in which any attempt at independent political thinking would have been highly dangerous, had made them relatively helpless. As the illusion of victory faded and life became more difficult, changeable and uncer-tain, one's own home, family, personal friends and possessions gained greater importance than ever as the only remaining support. For more and more people, the wider world lost its trusted form. Their private worlds became increasingly the one firm element in their lives. Many Germans seem to have reacted to the evident worsening of the military situation with a growing 'privatization' of their interests.[15]

Naturally one finds in the letters numerous references to air-raids. All in all, they point, at least on a surface level, to considerable self-control. It is possible that people had been warned not to 'moan' to their relatives at the front; and that perhaps such measures by the authorities contrib-uted to a stabilization of the morale of the people, at least on the outside. Even in cases where destruction in the immediate neighbourhood and the deaths of direct acquaintances are being discussed, the reports remain clothed in factual language. Written hurriedly and visibly under great emotional stress, they nevertheless hardly contain open complaints and accusations. Only asides, for example about 'the poor people who have lost everything', betray something of the underlying tension.

On the other hand, general as well as more personal references to the increasing destruction are very frequent. They establish very clearly how people had scarcely been prepared for such experiences – and how little they were aware of the air-raids by German bombers on cities like Warsaw, Rotterdam or London. Even if they had heard or read reports of the destruction caused by the *Luftwaffe*, they probably lacked the powers of imagination and the interest to create for themselves an image of the consequences of the war in the air. The propaganda justification of German war actions will also have produced a certain insensitivity to the suffering which Hitler's *Luftwaffe* inflicted on the civilian popula-tions of enemy cities. As a result, when the war came to their own backyard the shock was all the greater.

There are many indications that the manifest discipline and self-control in relation to air-raids and the other threats of war which emerge from these letters arose not only from continuous pressure and constraint from the outside but also from the all-pervasive feeling that there was nothing people could do about it. One of the strongest impressions left by the above comments (and by others of a similar kind) is that of an obedient and anaesthetized people whose members have lost the capacity and the possibility to organize themselves and to grasp the initiative for common action independently of or against the official representatives of the state. The relatively pronounced restraint regarding public matters, the tendency towards 'privatization', was the reverse side of this incapacity.

Now, however, with the enemy armies advancing on them from East and West, it became increasingly difficult to separate their own interests fully from the course of public events. The excerpts from the letters show that reactions were varied. A not inconsiderable number of the writers, female as well as male, refuse, even at this late stage, to admit the possibility of defeat. And even those who saw the end coming evidently had the feeling that Germany's defeat would mean the end of all their hopes and wishes if not the end of their lives; they experienced the impending defeat as a catastrophe from which Germany would not recover in their lifetime and which would condemn them for the rest of their lives to misery and misfortune.

This extreme despair in the face of defeat points to a problem which cannot be completely ignored in this connection. Most people then – if they thought at all about what was in store for their country after a defeat – presumably expected that, for a long time, Germany would no longer be able to play a role of any note in world politics and that it would take generations before the Germans would recover from the defeat and once more be in a position to lead a satisfying and peaceful life. This is not the place to go more deeply into the question why such expectations were so fundamentally refuted by subsequent developments. But the fact that they were refuted, that Germany, although divided politically in two, recovered fully at least in an economic sense, is one of the most striking proofs of the meaninglessness and uselessness of war in our times.

This development, it is reasonable to conclude, confirms very clearly what was said earlier about the difference between war aims in pre-industrial societies and societies in an age of advanced industrialization whose populations have acquired the knowledge and the corresponding skills that are necessary for the maintenance of such a society. As long as the rest of the world was unwilling to wipe out the Germans, to resettle them or let them starve where they were, there was hardly any other possibility after the defeat but to help them out with the capital which they needed for the reconstruction of their industrial society.

Conclusion

Two sets of factors contributed mutually to the severe breakdown of civilization associated with the name of Hitler and National Socialism: the peculiarities of the long-term development of Germany and specific features of the stage which it had then reached in this process. Among the former must be counted, first, the exceptionally disturbed pattern of German long-term development, the creeping decline which made the long-lost Reich a symbol of Germany's greatness and its supposed restoration the highest goal for the future, and then the almost unilinear autocratic tradition which bequeathed to the majority of Germans a relatively weak and dependent conscience in public affairs. Factors such as these and the complications which followed from them did not, of course, lead necessarily to the breakdown, but they prepared the way for this specific form of a breakdown of civilization.

In addition, there were the immediate causes. Among them, a central role was played by the conflict between, on the one hand, the inherited aspirations and the national self-image of the more powerful German groups and, on the other, the renewed loss of German power after 1918. The crisis around 1930 brought this conflict to a head.

The classical danger situation which many powerful nations encounter in their history sooner or later does not occur so much when their power declines *de facto* as when their members are no longer able to avoid becoming aware of their relative loss of power and the threat which this implies for their position in the rank hierarchy of nations. That a man like Hitler and a movement like National Socialism came to power in Germany was symptomatic of such a situation.

Inside Germany, increasing industrialization was shifting the balance of power to the disadvantage of the old ruling cadres. Representatives of the German nobility, with the old Field Marshal Hindenburg as the figurehead, had tried, with the help of disappointed officers and other groups, to win back the power which was slipping away from them; and their fight, with their backs against the wall, against the more broadly founded Weimar Republic, their resolve not to give up their power and rank without one last fight, cleared the way for the National Socialists.

In comparison with other nations, the rise of the Nazis, whatever else may have happened in conjunction with their success, meant for large numbers of Germans above all a violent avoidance-reaction. In short, under the strain of a world-wide economic crisis, many Germans reacted to the thought and feeling that the once imperial greatness of their country was lost for ever. The realization that Germany's position among the peoples of the world had grown weaker had to be avoided at all costs. Hitler, the gifted shaman with his magical symbol, the swastika, invoked once more for the German masses the *fata morgana* of a superior German Reich.

Like so many great nations fighting with their backs against the wall for their earlier greatness, the German leaders in this situation threw all norms of decency, honesty and identification with other people overboard whenever it suited their purposes. The goal of saving Germany's vanishing glory appeared to justify anything. A reciprocal reinforcement of welcome ideas and rejection of views which were unwelcome allowed broad sections of the German people to wrap themselves in a cocoon of collective fantasies which should have protected them from the 'shock of discovery' – the shock which every powerful nation and, more generally, every powerful social formation experiences when its members can no longer avoid recognizing that their earlier power and superiority are irretrievably lost. Many Germans were not able to admit, not even to themselves, that Germany had suffered a clear defeat in 1918 or that the conditions of the Treaty of Versailles, irrespective of its particular qualities and defects, were very moderate in comparison with the conditions which the Germans would have wanted to impose on their enemies if they had won. The Nazis revived among the Germans the belief that they were still a first-rank power and had the necessary resources, that, like the medieval emperors, Germany's masters would rule over wide stretches of Europe. The degree of oppression, violence and barbarism which they used corresponded to the degree of effort which was necessary to give Germany once more the appearance of greatness and to avoid the shock of discovery that the days of German pre-eminence and the dream of a Reich were over.

V
Thoughts on the Federal Republic

1

If one regards the situation with a degree of detachment, one of the most astonishing and frightening discoveries which one can make in West Germany today is the enormous bitterness and enmity parts of the population feel with regard to other parts. Consciousness of the factual interdependence of all classes and regions of the Federal Republic, so it seems, is on the wane. One can sense in this connection a feeling of increasing helplessness: 'Where are we really going? Does the German Federal Republic still have a future? And if so, what sort of future?' The antagonism towards fellow groups, often imbued with undertones of hatred, is, as in earlier situations of recent German history, uncompromising and absolute. The feelings of total enmity towards domestic opponents are hardly controllable, and perhaps it would even be felt to be wrong, insincere and therefore un-German to control them. In this way, as in other cases, irreconcilable splits may be driving all parties in a nation collectively in a direction none of them intended nor wished for – in the direction, for example, of a police state or a party dictatorship.

The following essay was written between October 1977 and March 1978 at the request of *Der Spiegel*. I am grateful to Michael Schröter for his collaboration.

Some time ago in France the leader of the Communists declared that the Communists would be in the front line of defence if the country were threatened with attack.[1] In Britain, the feeling of common ground and of the high value of being British which pervades all classes and regions has by and large hardly been shaken at all despite all the upheavals and the experience of sinking from great power to second-rate power status that Britain shares with the other European nations. In Germany, the excessiveness of the self-praise of their own nation under the National Socialists, the bitter collision of their great collective fantasies with the hard reality of inter-state power relations in the post-war period, has triggered off, especially among younger people, an often equally strong swing of feelings in the opposite direction. The bombast of the National Socialists and the acts of violence they committed in the name of the German people have, if not completely destroyed the value of the name of Germany in the eyes of many younger groups, then at least diminished its value and dragged its former glory through the mud.

I have said elsewhere[2] that the turning of younger people, especially of intellectually relatively alert groups of middle-class origin, to Marxism, which reached its first peak in the events of 1968, is partly related to the desire to free themselves from being identified with a German past which is burdened with the stigma of National Socialism. I have been asked whether I could speak about this in greater detail. It is with some hesitation that I take up this request. I feel that I cannot evade the duty to do so. As a sociologist, one is used to examining and laying bare the broader relationships between social events. Perhaps it will help if they are made visible for the many people who, under the pressure of their own specialist work, look at daily happenings on a shorter time-scale. However, if I did not feel obliged to as a sociologist, I would not venture into the arena of daily events. For when one probes the broader connections between the most recent social events, then many of the short-term explanations turn out to be inadequate. I cannot just echo what other people – whether right-wing, left-wing or in the centre – are saying; and what meaning would my work have if I were to do that? I can only attempt to *explain* something of what is happening today in the society of the West German state, and to indicate some trends, especially dangerous trends, that I observe in this society. Perhaps one can still avert the disaster.

If one seeks to explain the deep division of the West German people and the waves of hatred and fear which are coursing through this people today, then it is not enough to keep one's eyes fixed on the immediate present. The violent acts of small, tightly knit terrorist groups in the Federal Republic and the counter-wave of the hunt for sympathizers merely have the function of a trigger which brings out into the open in one fell swoop the latent fracture points for all the world to see. The reasons for the brittleness of West German society go further back.

The National Socialist leadership, who owed their rise to a large extent to the active help of older aristocratic and grand-bourgeois groups, dragged the German people into the worst catastrophe they have suffered since the Thirty Years War. The mass of the German people, however, whether in the East or in the West, do not seem to have become aware of the magnitude of this catastrophe. They are certainly conscious of its most visible consequence; the division of the German people into two states. But other, no less serious consequences are not recognized as such. It is not easy to speak of them since much of what has to be said is certainly painful. One can therefore understand why broad circles in West Germany close their eyes to them. They are seeking to forget the historical catastrophe of their people, just because the attempt to explain it is embarrassing and painful.

Similarly, one could argue that the Adenauer regime did the right thing in its time when it allowed it to appear as if the National Socialist period was now in the past and as if nothing basically had changed. 'Germany has admittedly disintegrated into two parts,' so people seemed to think, 'but that can only be a temporary situation. One simply cannot admit that it is anything else. One may not speak of the "GDR" or of the "West German people". The unification of Germany will happen again, because it must happen. Nothing decisive has changed. Everything has remained as it used to be. Business as usual.'

The factual problematic, the real problems of a West German state, are thereby obscured. The shock was perhaps still too great, the wound too deep and too painful for people to be able to deal with it openly. Then came the 'economic miracle', and the relative prosperity also contributed to excluding from public discussion the dangerous inheritance which Hitler had left behind for the German people. Right up to the present, the relatively high economic efficiency of the Federal Republic serves to suppress from the public consciousness of the nation the need to look the severe non-economic problems of the West German people straight in the eye.

If one looks back today, then one can recognize clearly enough that this policy of concealment was mistaken. It is still difficult to hide that something irrevocable has happened. New generations are growing up in West Germany who are asking what the meaning and value of the society in which they live really is. One cannot simply fob them off by saying, 'Just wait a little while, then the old, great unified Germany will reappear.' In such a way, one only exacerbates one of the most severe problems which remains untackled in West Germany up to now – the crisis of identity. The far-reaching disorientation, the growing helplessness about the direction, worth and meaning of the Federal Republic which can be observed are a consequence of the attempt to hush up the fact that the disaster of National Socialism and the destruction of German unity which it brought about have created a new situation.

There were certainly at first quite solid grounds for arousing the pretence that, apart from the disappearance of the National Socialist Party, everything in Germany remained as of old. This attitude reflected the sincere belief of the old ruling strata of Germany under the leadership of the honourable old man that, after the removal of the horrid upstart, they were called upon, just as in former times, to continue guiding the destiny of the German people in the old manner. And the mass of the West German people, paralysed by the defeat, the destruction, the lingering suffering and the real hardship which they faced, were only too willing to trust their fate yet again to a father figure.

In earlier times, if kings or the leading groups of a people had proved their lack of judgement by leading their people from one defeat to another and eventually to the loss of part of their territory, then they usually lost the trust of their people. In our times, one might at least have expected that the traditional leading strata of Germany would have subjected themselves to a self-examination even if the mass of people for their part did not demand it. One might have expected that they would have asked themselves: 'What is wrong with our tradition, our attitudes, our political philosophy, that they have led to this national disaster?' The fact that Germany's leading strata did not subject themselves to such a self-examination, that they pretended that everything remained as of old, and thereby blocked even for themselves the understanding of the new problems thrown up by the creation of a West German state, contributed decisively to the difficulties of this new society. What this society needed more than anything else was a reform of the attitudes of its leading strata in the direction of greater humanity and tolerance, of an explicit solidarity with every class and generation of its people. I can well believe that it would have been better if, then or at some later time, a person to whom people listened had stood up and, with the same sincerity with which Churchill declared to his country at the beginning of the war that he could promise them nothing other than blood, sweat and tears, had said to the German people:

> A great catastrophe has afflicted us. The old Germany, as our fathers knew it at least since 1871, no longer exists. A new German state has come into being, and we must pull together so that within the borders of this state a people, and perhaps in future a nation, will form which continues the best of the old German tradition and at the same time creates its own tradition, so that for the younger generations and for those who will come after us it is pleasurable, exciting and meaningful to belong to this new Germany. Above all, we must show the world and ourselves that this is no longer the old Germany which gave birth to the inhuman regime of National Socialism. We must show that we are a new, humane Germany. For this, it is necessary to bury a number of hatchets, to fight against some of the old attitudes among us which found expression in the violence of National Socialism; they must be eradicated even in the family, the kindergartens and the schools. We must develop with full awareness new, decent attitudes of mutual respect for all human beings, whatever their age, their social position or their party.
>
> We cannot get rid of the opposition of interests between entrepreneurs and workers, and the resultant tug-of-war regarding the distribution of the national product. Up to now, no industrial society has been successful in finding a solution for such class conflicts. No one to date has drawn up a convincing plan for an industrial society in which the inequalities are less great than in capitalist–communist industrial societies. I am quite sure that that will only be possible if one changes not simply the relations of ownership to the means of production, but above all also the means of production themselves, that is, the factory character of industrial production. Nationalization of the means of production without this change in the means of production themselves hardly reduces the inequality between people at all, as the Marxist countries show clearly enough.
>
> We must therefore resign ourselves to the fact that there will continue to be class conflicts in the Federal Republic. But both sides stand to lose a great deal, if not everything, if, instead of fighting out these conflicts with conscious moderation, they drive themselves mutually ever anew through the violence of words and arms into a situation where there is no way out other than by attempting to gag the other side or to break them physically, either through a Federal German police state, or a Federal German party dictatorship of the political right or left. This is what we must avoid at all costs. In order to avoid it, there has to be a conscious moderation especially in relation to people who stand on the other side in internal disputes. Only when we are capable of doing that will this new, smaller Germany have a chance of surviving, prospering and thriving.

One could imagine that, if such thoughts had been further publicly developed by a group of determined people, they would have gained a hearing in many circles in the Federal Republic. Then, perhaps, a corresponding reform not only of the laws, but also of the norms of behaviour of the people, above all regarding how rival groups deal with each other, would have been able to give the younger generations to an increasing extent the feeling that it was rewarding to live in this Federal German society. No one can say for certain how many younger people in West Germany are lacking such a feeling today. But one has the impression that the lack of enthusiasm for the Federal Republic among them is growing at the moment. Is it necessary to say that everyone who contributes to this growing disaffection with Germany among the younger generations is placing at risk the future of their own people just for short-term satisfactions?

Other European states have suffered heavy defeats in recent centuries which have not only reduced their territory, but at the same time shaken their pride to its foundations and called into question their identity as peoples and as states. Denmark, Sweden, even France, are examples. In such cases, only seldom were movements of self-reflection entirely lacking. At first, vociferous groups usually clamoured for a revanchist war, in France after 1871, in Germany after 1918; it was unthinkable that their former greatness had been irrevocably lost. Then sometimes, perhaps after only one or two generations, the recognition broke through the deceptive national fantasy into their consciousness that the loss of their former greatness and thereby of their former national ranking was permanent. Poland after the various partitions, Denmark after the loss of Norway and Schleswig-Holstein – how did people on these occasions come to terms with the reality-shock?

In Denmark, besides the movement to restore the old, larger empire, there also gradually arose tendencies towards self-reflection. In accordance with the social structure of the country, they were geared amongst other things towards integrating into the smaller state the mass of the peasant population, who had stood outside the established strata as a for the most part still poor and uneducated class. Some Danes apparently recognized then that it was a social as well as national necessity to raise the living and educational standards of the people, thus giving a better chance of reducing the class gradient as well as of forming the consciousness of a common national destiny. Among other things, a network of rural people's high schools served this effort to bring about a national renewal after the defeat. It contributed to raising the level of knowledge and thus at the same time the standards of production and of living of the Danish peasantry. The gradual flourishing of Denmark after the defeats, and perhaps the survival of the country, certainly rested not least on this self-reflection and the related reforms. But one would probably not go astray if one supposed that, among all those endeavours, the insight that the defence of a country depends to a large extent on the well-being and feeling of belonging of all strata and in particular of the younger generations also played a part.

One of the peculiarities of the German Federal Republic is that this insight seems to be as good as completely absent, especially among many members of the leadership groups. For members of the generations of Adenauer, Brandt and Scheel who grew up before the war, identification with the German tradition is still anchored in their consciousness as something taken for granted. Accordingly they do not understand that this is not and cannot be the case with the younger generations, such as that of Rudi Dutschke, who grew up during or after the war, or that for them the most realistic solution to the problem of German disintegration seems to be careful *rapprochement* between West and East.

Those who have no taste for this solution ought really to understand that one is more liable to reinforce than lessen such convictions among members of the post-war generations if one lashes out, so to speak, with one's fists from above in a kind of panic. Excessive media campaigns, oppressive laws and above all use of the law as a means of party-political power by the authorities only gain new supporters for the conviction (and it is a *conviction* we are dealing with) that political slogans such as 'freedom' and 'democracy' are threadbare and that the creeping increase of oppression in West Germany is steadily approaching the degree of open oppression in the East. I know of younger citizens of the Federal Republic who have little sympathy for the East German regime but who say to me, 'What is the difference? There you are thrown out of your career if you are not a Marxist. Here you are thrown out of your career if you are or were a Marxist, and perhaps even an active Young Socialist or Young Liberal.' One wonders sometimes at the short-sightedness of those who grant untold sums for the most modern weapons for the defence of the Federal Republic but who at the same time irrevocably alienate not inconsiderable parts of the younger generations, that is, parts of those generations upon whose feelings of belonging and con-sciousness that their country is worthy of continued existence the effective defence of the country depends at least as much as it depends upon hardware. With patience, moderation, tolerance and conscious caring about the chances for fulfilment of those who are growing up, it would not even be particularly difficult to allow the generations on which the future of the Federal Republic depends to come to the conviction themselves that the Marxist countries have not by any means found the key to a more just, non-authoritarian and non-oppressive society. But patient self-control, moderation, humanity and especially understanding for people with different opinions have only rarely belonged to the strong points of Germany's leading strata.

2

There is quite a bit of confusion at present about the nature of the tensions which run through world society. This confusion is greatly increased by the fact that politically weaker groups of the most diverse types try to find orientation, allies and ideological justification by calling upon Marx's framework of ideas. Marx's theory referred, as is well known, to a quite specific type of conflicts: to conflicts between economic specialists who have at their disposal the means of capital, and others who are dependent on them since they possess nothing but their labour power. But bound to the sober analysis of figurations in Marx was a prophecy. He predicted the inevitable toppling of the existing order through the revolutionary victory of the proletariat – later often understood as the revolutionary victory of his followers and their dictatorship in the name of the industrial workers, with the necessary consequence of a social order without classes, social inequality and oppression.

I must refrain from examining here the manifold transformations of this prophetic theory of society, such as its transformation into a slogan of the emancipation struggles of national minorities, or in some cases even by oppressed ethnic majorities. I can only point out in passing that the Marxist body of thought currently plays a relatively minor role in the practice of the industrial struggles between workers and entrepreneurs in the richer industrial states, and that in this late – perhaps last – century of traditional factory work the hierarchical character of such work is no less great and perhaps even greater in the East than in the West. The Marxist system of thought has not changed this inequality in the factory in the slightest. On the contrary, it now plays an important role in another type of tensions and conflicts within the richer industrial states, a type of tensions and conflicts whose particular sociological character is often not properly understood. It has to to do with tensions and conflicts between the generations. In the chain of generations, wars are nowadays the dividing lines. The break between the worlds experienced by those who grew up before and after the war was, in the case of the great war of the years 1939–45, especially deep. This holds for large parts of the world. In particular, it holds for the imperial countries of Europe. But it is for Germany, however, that it holds to the greatest extent.

Britain and France went into this war still as great imperial powers. They came out of it as second-rate powers which bit by bit lost their colonial empires. To a corresponding degree, the power potential (if by no means always the economic potential) of smaller countries like Holland and Belgium or Hungary and Czechoslovakia was reduced.

It is seldom asked how the people of Europe are actually coming to terms with the declining power of their continent. As a result, a great deal of what is now happening in European societies cannot be explained. Among these inadequately explained occurrences is the student movement, which found its most striking expression so far in France, Germany, Britain and in some other countries in the events around 1968. I want to speak here above all about certain sociological aspects of the German student movement and the broader movement with which it was related. But this cannot be done without taking into consideration that this was a question of a European occurrence. The ability to see the explanation of what sometimes looked like a youth revolt is distorted if, in searching for an explanation, one concentrates only on one's own country.

The wave of tensions, whose high point up till now was the student movement around 1968, received and receives its central impetus, it seems to me, from the already mentioned conflicts between the generations. It is simple enough to diagnose and explain them. The first structural characteristic which strikes the eye is the social background of the leading people and of a considerable part of their followers: they are predominantly young people from the middle classes, and in addition a small number of socially rising students from working-class circles. These people of the post-war generations, for the greater part from middle-class families, saw themselves placed in a social world that was largely ruled by middle-class and partly also by aristocratic pre-war generations. De Gaulle no less than Adenauer belonged to them. The student movement was the vanguard of the still excluded generations and has remained so to this day.

Their champions emphatically repudiated the political values and, in a broader sense, the human ideals of the still dominating pre-war middle classes of their respective societies. They took stock of what their fathers had intended and done, and rejected it. The colonial empires, which as visible proof of the greatness and worth of their own nations had nourished the pride and self-esteem of the pre-war middle classes, had broken up. In the case of Germany, the desire for restoration of the empire, for a rebirth of imperial self-esteem, had turned out to be a fantasy far beyond their power and therefore self-destructive. It was similar with the never quite extinguished longing in grand-bourgeois circles for the restoration of unrestricted control over their businesses, which had found new nourishment in Germany through the economic policies of the Nazis. In the end, as those born after the war saw it, it was the generations of their fathers who had driven Europe and wide parts of the world dependent on Europe into the catastrophic war of 1939–45 for such oppressive ideals, and who were, in the last instance, to blame not only for the destruction and degradation of Germany, but also for the humiliation of most of the European victor states, for the loss of their former greatness.

It is not often that an attempt is made vividly to visualize the task with which the most intellectually alert young people of the post-war generations found themselves confronted. Not only in Germany, but also in many other European nation-states, the problem which arose for them is indicated in Germany by the idea of *Bewältigung der Vergangenheit* ['overcoming the past']. Not only the post-war youth of the German Federal Republic, but also many British, Dutch, French, Italian and Danish young people were confronted – perhaps with a little less urgency – with the problem of their own identity. The old national identity had not everywhere become so offensive and called into question to the same degree as in the divided Germany, especially in the Federal Republic. For the unwilling heirs of National Socialism, 'overcoming the past' was particularly embarrassing and difficult. However, in other countries, too, above all for the French and British with their far more stable and deeply anchored we-image and we-ideal – thanks to a centuries-long continuous development – the loss of their great power status meant a severe shaking of traditional national sentiments.

Germany's fall from great power status happened in two phases. Both were the result of unsuccessful attempts by aristocratic and middle-class ruling strata to win for Germany hegemony over all the other states of Europe and their dependencies in other parts of the world. In the second half of the twentieth century, it is not difficult to recognize that this competition among the European states sealed the destruction of

Europe's hegemonial position in relation to the rest of the countries of the world.

At any rate for Germany's leadership strata, orientated towards the tradition of the *Kaiserzeit*, the loss of great power status through the defeat of 1918 was all the more unbearable since they had only recently, in 1871, won this equality for their country with the older great powers, and now they simultaneously lost the chance of hegemony over Europe and supremacy in Germany. This double reality-shock which the representatives and successors of the leading strata of the defeated *Kaiserreich* suffered as a result of their simultaneous external and internal defeats was too painful and unbearable for them to be able to take in the insight that the time of their external and internal supremacy was gone forever. So, after 1918, they prepared – bit by bit with the help of popular upstarts such as Hitler, in whom they at first probably saw suitable tools for achieving their own objectives – to raise Germany again not only to the rank of an economic great power but to that of one which was powerful in military-political terms as well. At the same time, they sought to restore their internal power.

When the upstarts then seized the reins from their hands, these leading groups were caught in their own trap. The deeply rooted Prussian-German conscience-formation made it almost impossible for most of the ruling strata, raised in this tradition, to put a spoke in the wheel of the head of state, even if they recognized the enormous risks of his politics – and that was quite certainly the case for only a minority of them. In this way, any effective policy of resistance to the head of the German state was stifled – quite apart from the threat of acts of revenge – by the loyalty to the state which was deeply embedded in the conscience of the majority of members of these strata. As a result, he had the greater part of the older leading strata, together with his own new ruling strata, behind him in preparing for the second use of arms in the attempt to secure Germany's hegemony over Europe and its overseas dependencies. The enormous organizational and propaganda effort, the total mobilization of the German war potential which became necessary for that in the course of the war, gives an impression of how the contradiction between the fantasy goal of the supremacy of the great German empire and its actual power resources in comparison with those of its opponents, America and Russia included, gradually became perceptible. Thus the dream of German hegemony in Europe faded. At the same time and in this way, too, the hegemony of European powers among the nations of the world was unintentionally ended.

It was the clash with the dominant attitudes and ideals of their pre-war middle-class fathers and mothers which led many of the daughters and sons born after the war to an acute rejection of aspects of this middle-class tradition. They felt it to be inhuman and were led at the same time to an emphatic profession of a more humanistic ethos. They themselves often made – and still make – use of routines of speaking and thinking which go back to Marx. In truth, not only had leading middle-class groups, middle-class politicians and industrialists smoothed the way for the National Socialist organization in its rise to power, but so too had the traditional noble leading strata of Germany, that is to say, above all groups of aristocratic military men and large-scale landowners. But for the generations born after the war the structure of their society before the war was in the very distant past. The more militantly disposed groups of the post-war generations, especially, saw the pre- and post-war society of their country in shortened perspective, simply as a bourgeois society dominated by the class struggle with the proletariat. They were hardly aware that, behind this use of the concept of class struggle by predominantly middle-class groups of the post-war generations, was often hidden a more decisive generational struggle, a struggle of sons and daughters of middle-class origin against the bourgeois attitudes and norms of parents who had grown up before the war. Marx's edifice of ideas – which as an achievement of sociological synthesis and in its relative congruence with reality has few rivals – offered them a means of orientation which was both emotionally and intellectually satisfying in their struggle with the political and moral means of orientation of the fathers' generations which had so obviously and so catastrophically failed.

This passionate rejection of attitudes and norms of the fathers' generations, which was now conceived of as a rejection, lock, stock and barrel, of bourgeois attitudes and norms as such, gives an idea of the difference between the worlds experienced by these pre-war and post-war generations. (It was, incidentally, preceded by a comparatively much weaker but nevertheless analogous breach after the First World War.) Such a profession of a new ethos by those who grew up after a war is not by any means limited to groups who fight under the banner of Marxism. It is true that, thanks to the sociological systematics of Marx's work and its prophecy of a future, more just social order, Marxist groups possess a relatively closed means of argumentation and orientation which lends at the same time a special force and momentum to their programmes of action. But a new prevailing social-ethical mood, a feeling of the wrongness of many of the authoritarian attitudes which had been commonplace among the parent generations during the period of European hegemony, can be encountered fairly generally among people of the post-war generations, even among many who are not Marxists.

One of the most moving experiences of our times is to see the dedication with which, precisely in the richest industrial nations, sections of post-war youth are committing themselves to the struggle against injustice, oppression, exploitation of people throughout the world, for political prisoners of tyrannical regimes, for the protection of threatened animal species or the beauty of the unravaged earth. Their humanistic ethos is sometimes utopian, sometimes realistic and often a mixture of both. Moreover, their social-ethical commitment sometimes lacks the inseparable complement of an ethical commitment at the individual level, that is, the obligation to decency in personal relations which is often denigrated as a bourgeois-liberal principle, but which, examined more closely, is a social duty like the other. The creation of a less unequal and oppressive social order would have little meaning if people in their personal dealings were to lie to each other, cheat each other, if, in other words, they were to make no effort to be decent, friendly and reliable in their social relations.

Perhaps it is not pointless to recall that this kind of intense personal dedication to relatively impersonal ideals and principles, which is hardly inspired by the expectation of personal advantage, is actually to be observed only in richer, more developed societies. The Scottish philosopher Hume once remarked how astonishing it was that the parties of his era, that is to say, the Tory and Whig aristocracy and their followers in the country, differed from each other in terms of impersonal principles. Hume, who was also an historian, declared that this type of party division was as far as he knew unique in history, since party groupings usually arose in pursuit of the naked interests of various groups. This is a sharp and extremely illuminating observation. Even today in poorer countries where the inequality between relatively small groups of very rich people and the mass of the urban and rural poor, often living on the verge of starvation, is very much greater, one finds that party divisions are orientated relatively openly to the pursuit of self-interest, whether of single families, single tribes or particular regions. One does not need to conceal the pursuit of personal interests, because the mass of the population is poor, uneducated and by and large powerless.

One sees here at a stroke something of the paradox that lies at the bottom of the stigmatization of pre-war Europe by substantial segments of the European post-war generations who view it as exploitative and colonialist: the wealth of these nations – above all their high level *per capita* of capital investment compared with that in poorer nations – could hardly have been acquired without the power inequalities of the past. That is to say, it would scarcely have been possible without the exploitation of other peoples and classes by princely, aristocratic and middle-class ruling groups, which is one of the preconditions for the way of life which enables members of the post-war generations of these countries to reject the exploitative ethos of their fathers, and beyond that to reject injustice throughout the world.

This brief allusion to some of the common aspects of the new humanistic ethos which one encounters among many post-war generation groups in the richer industrial nation-states must be enough for present purposes. It makes it easier to understand the peculiarity of the relationship between the pre- and post-war generations in the Federal Republic. The break in the worlds experienced by these generations caused by the war of 1939–45 was considerably greater and considerably more difficult to come to terms with in Federal Germany than in other countries. The internal tensions to which it contributed became all the more acute when the leading groups, under whose leadership the first reconstruction took place, set special store on preserving continuity with the past. This compelled them to push into the background or to conceal altogether the new problems by which, in particular, the people born in the Federal Republic after the war found themselves confronted. This hushing up, however, in its turn reinforced the tension between the generations.

In the very new situation of the young Federal German Republic, one of the most urgently needed tasks was a public discussion regarding the meaning and value of the Republic, that is to say, a process of self-examination, a realistic debate about possible aims and objectives. Such a debate was owed not only to the present generations, but above all also to the future generations of the German people and beyond that to the deeply wounded enemies of yesterday, the partners of today and tomorrow. What was needed was to lay bare publicly and reform those traditions of ruling and behaving which had been responsible for the regression of the more complex multi-party state to the more primitive and autocratic one-party state, and responsible for the related breakdown of the standard of civilization previously reached in Germany. In that way, the rising generations of Germans and Germany's neighbours would not have needed to continue living in secret fear of a new relapse into autocratic party dictatorship, not only in East Germany but in West Germany as well, or in fear of a new breakdown of the standard of civilization achieved. One could have asked in this connection how the obvious lack of realistic judgement of Germany's leading strata in the twentieth century, or the persistent preference of large parts of the German people to be ruled from above without any individual responsibility or co-responsibility, are to be explained.

As a first step on the path to self-purification from the curse of unrestrained violence which Hitler had bequeathed to the German people, such an attempt at shedding light on the sociogenesis and psychogenesis of the 'Third Reich' and its rise and fall would have been quite indispensable. Perhaps it would have been useful to have set up an impartial official examination of such problems as a prelude to the much-discussed but never completed 'overcoming of the past', which, needless to say, would hardly have been able to begin without a determined public initiative by the government. 'The attitude of a nation to its past' according to a recent leading article about 'Britain's conscience' in *The Times*, 'conditions its responses to the present. If a nation sweeps its crimes under the carpet it heightens the risk of repeating them and perpetuates a false image of itself which is liable to distort its other perceptions.'[3]

The governments of all nations commit crimes. What distinguishes the German crimes under the Hitler government from those of other nations is their extent, their extraordinarily high fantasy content and relatively low reality content and, connected with this, the meaninglessness and disproportion which are characteristic of certain features of the German conscience-formation. That coming to terms with the past remained only a phrase in the new Federal German Republic; that insight into the way in which 'the present responses of a nation are conditioned by its attitude to its past' was lacking; that, quite to the contrary, in the early years of the Federal Republic the ruling groups issued the slogan that nothing essentially had changed – all these were perhaps understandable under the circumstances of that time and in connection with the Allied intervention. But the unreformed continuance of the country's business in the manner of Germany's old ruling strata was certainly one of the fundamental reasons why many young members of the rising generations had the feeling that nothing had basically changed and that they were still continuing to live in an authoritarian state. It did not matter whether this notion was right or wrong; the deciding factor was quite simply the fact that a considerable number of young people, who increasingly did not know the past from their own experience, came to this conviction. It is certainly the case that here lay one of the roots of their radicalization and therefore also in extreme cases of the later terrorism.

The crisis in which the Federal German Republic finds itself today rests not least on this failure to provide a clear explanation of the rise of Hitler and thereby also of the creation of the Federal Republic which points the way ahead. For as the generations who grew up before the war and had experience of it became older and fewer in number, and as the number of those who knew the old Germany only from hearsay grew, so the need among the latter, who were its heirs, became correspondingly greater to know how one could actually explain Germany's lost wars, the rise of National Socialism and Germany's downfall. For the consciousness and identity of these younger generations as Germans, open debate about the past became more urgent. But they were not helped in this by the fact that official politics largely avoided open debate about the past, thus contributing not only to banishing the dangerous inheritance of Hitler from the awareness of the West German population, but also in particular to forcing the intellectually more alert young people to seek their identity in Marxism, the only edifice of ideas which provided a ready explanation of fascism and at the same time gave them the possibility of feeling that they did not have anything to do with this past, that they were free of any blame.

That was also the way in which the new East German state sought to come to terms with the past. There, it became official policy to explain to the younger generations that the capitalist bourgeoisie found itself threatened by the growing power of the working class, that many large-scale entrepreneurs accordingly looked favourably on Hitler's rise, and that Hitler then crushed the workers' movements and established a brutal, violent regime, leaving an inheritance which is made clear to schoolchildren in visits to the empty concentration camps. Fragmentary though this explanation may be, it at least represents an attempt at an official examination of the traumatic past. To be sure, this attempt to enlighten is at the same time in certain respects also an attempt to obscure. It awakens the impression that the population of those parts of the old Germany which nowadays belong to the East German state had no part in the rise of Hitler. In addition, it obscures the faulty policy of the former Communist Party which described the late Weimar state as 'fascist', branded the then Social Democrats as 'social fascists', and thus contributed its part to the irreconcilable division of German workers' organizations and hence to the rise of German fascism.

There is an unmistakable structural relationship between the polarization of opinions then and now. Today once more, the most extreme among the groups who are alienated from the state, the Baader–Meinhof group and its terrorist successors, also declare, certainly too unjustly, that the existing German state – that is, no longer the Weimar, but the Bonn Republic – is already a fascist state which oppresses all nonconformist groups with the help of biased judges, police truncheons, a press which stirs up hatred and other means of violence and which one can therefore only fight and destroy by means of physical violence. Today, once more, powerful leading groups take the violent acts of these minorities as an occasion for using all means of state and verbal violence against groups and individuals whom they dislike, far beyond the level of their guilt. Just as previously the Jews served as a scapegoat against whom the deep internal social conflicts of the Weimar Republic were released, in the same way the excitement stirred up by the party fight over the terrorist murders was fixed to the word 'sympathizer' and applied completely unselectively even to groups who were opposed to violence of any sort. In conjunction with this wave of hatred, the active use of state violence against left-wing groups has been intensified to an increasing extent, even when the convictions of these groups lead them most sharply to condemn and fight acts of terror. And since in this way many young people are threatened with the destruction of their careers or are simply thrown onto the streets, the band of people who are alienated from the state and possibly of their sympathizers, too, is enlarged as an unplanned by-product of the passing of ever tougher laws.

No one can be more pleased with this development of the Federal German Republic than the terrorists themselves. They had always said that the freedom of Germans in the Federal Republic is a façade, behind which is hidden an authoritarian police state, if not actually a fascist one. Through the most recent developments in the Federal Republic, their ideology is gaining greater power of conviction than before. If one of the objectives of the terrorists was to intensify tensions within the Federal Republic, then they were successful. It may be that the death of their leader and the most recent wave of arrests have crippled their organization. But the reaction they triggered can only contribute to their conviction that they are in a position to accelerate the disintegration of the state which they hate or to speed up its open transformation into an authoritarian party dictatorship. And since, like some extremists in the Weimar Republic, they seem to believe that open fascism is to be preferred to the covert variety, they may feel that, in this respect, too, their strategy has proved its worth, and accordingly decide to continue it at all costs.

3

Tensions and conflicts between the organizations of workers and entrepreneurs, between parties of the left and right, are among the enduring social facts of highly industrialized nation-states. But those nation-states which are able to look back on a longer tradition of non-violent ways of dealing with such stratum or class conflicts, such as Britain or Holland for example, have learned to live with tensions of this kind as a normal fact of national existence. The members of these states possess as part of their national heritage a selection of behaviour patterns which enable and at the same time constrain them to keep their feelings more or less in check in the course of intra-societal debates and conflicts. The people who form nation-states with a relatively long unbroken tradition usually also have a certain feeling for the ultimate dependence on each other of the opposing groups which comprise their nation, for their common bond as heirs of a survival group who share a common destiny. Even when they passionately dislike each other, they are still able to see that they may never take clashes with each other to a point where their feelings of togetherness and solidarity, in the last instance their trust in each other as people who are British, French or Dutch, are called into question in the survival struggles of nations.

To be sure, except in extreme cases such as a natural catastrophe or a war, this bonding of a state's opposing strata is formed only over many generations. Only under quite specific conditions are the opposing strata and groups of a country in a position to break down their mutual distrust, their fear of violent acts by the other groups, and to gain enough trust in each other to be certain that the opponents will, just like themselves, keep the rules of the non-violent power struggle and, for their part, non-violently relinquish government positions, with all the power-resources which they make available to a group, if the rules of the game require it. One can follow in detail how and why in Britain – between about 1650 and 1750 – a transition took place from the violent fighting-out of group conflicts, and the constant suspicion that the other side was preparing to take over the government by force of arms, to a pattern of non-violent parliamentary fighting according to rules.

On German soil the bloodless fights of parliamentary parties, safeguarded by firm rules against violence, do not have a very long tradition. The personality structures of Germans, which are more important than laws and written constitutions for the functioning of struggles between strata in the non-violent parliamentary form, are, accordingly, still inadequately geared to this type of dealing with tensions and conflicts. In the nineteenth century, and in fact essentially until 1918, Germany was still ruled by absolute princes, that is, from above. This governmental form corresponded to a type of national character which is also to be found among other peoples who have had similar experiences. Basically, their personality structures are geared to being ruled from above. That means, among other things, that in Germany there has been too little time and opportunity to develop that sort of self-control, that form of conscience, which enables people individually, by themselves, to keep a tight rein on their antagonism towards other groups and strata of their own society – even if their insight allows them to recognize the need for such control. They have learned to keep a tight rein on their antagonisms only via external controls, via commands from above.

When the Kaiser, the imperial overlord, disappeared from the German scene in the year 1918, party hatred expressed itself immediately in an outbreak of violence. In this case, it was in particular the outrage of members of the old German ruling strata over the founding of the first German Republic which was vented in the acts of violence of the terrorists of those times, for example in the murders of Erzberger, Rosa Luxemburg, Rathenau and Liebknecht, but also of many less well-known people. Then followed the increasing polarization between right and left which at first found expression, for example, in the brawls and assembly hall battles of opposing party armies, and which eventually ended in the National Socialist dictatorship. It was a typical situation, similar in its basic structure to what was observable during and after the English revolution of the seventeenth century in the relationship between Royalists and Puritans, and later also in the relationship between Whigs and Tories: each of the polarized human groups fears being violently overcome by the other (or others) in a situation in which the centralized state monopoly of physical force is no longer able effectively to prevail. In order to prevent themselves being overcome by the others, each of the threatened and threatening groupings in the country mobilizes its means of violence to overcome the others. The escalation of mutual threats leads in the end to dictatorial rule based on the monopolization of all means of force by one or the other side.

In the Federal Republic today one encounters just such a mounting polarization. Many persons of the left are seriously concerned that a new fascist dictatorship is in the offing. Many in middle-class circles fear that a dictatorship of the proletariat will arise from the Marxist movement. Their fear has been intensified by the terrorists' acts of violence, and they demand sharper and sharper measures of repression by the state – especially for example by the police – which in turn increase the number of people alienated from the state and thus the reservoir of potential terrorist recruits. The irrationality of such an outbreak of witch-hunting in the Federal Republic becomes clearer if one compares the comments of German and British newspapers. Thus, *The Economist* wrote in 1977 that: 'The aim should be to destroy the core of active terrorists without increasing the size of the outer ring of alienated, indoctrinated or just plain muddled people who are willing to help the terrorists now and perhaps take their place later. It is a case for precision weapons, not blanket bombing.'[4]

The difference between the British and the German tradition of behaviour – especially of conservative ruling groups in the two countries – strikes the observer very clearly in a comparison between this statement in *The Economist* and the attitudes of comparable organs of the Federal German press. The traditional lack of proportion of Germany's leading strata, which has contributed so much to the misfortune of the German people, was shown very drastically in the 'blanket bombing' of 'sympathizers'. Even today, people still seem tacitly to assume that it will be enough simply to break away from the content of National Socialist doctrines without at the same time freeing themselves from the human attitudes which found their – certainly extreme – expression in National Socialism. In Germany there is a long tradition of shutting oneself off from outsider groups and rejecting them. That is a behavioural tradition which differs markedly from the long-practised tradition in Britain of limited step-by-step assimilation of outsider groups, for instance of native-born workers in the nineteenth century, and 'guestworkers' (often, though, with British passports) in the twentieth.

But however that may be, the fateful dynamics of the vicious cycle – in the course of which the violent acts of one side, even the mere announcement or fear of them, are played up by the other – are thereby kept in motion. As has been said, this can be encountered in the development of many states. A contemporary example is the terror and counter-terror in Northern Ireland. The violence of words – one should not forget this – contributes no less than the violence of arms to keeping such a vicious cycle in motion. The unplanned dynamics of such processes have already been set forth: if one group in a country fears the violence of another, then both ask themselves whether or not they should pre-emptively use violence in order to forestall the other side. If in this way, the fear of the other group's violence leads to the use of violence on their part and, as a response, to the use of violence by the former, then the probable outcome, which possibly neither of them intended to bring about, is the violent dictatorship of one or the other side. The dynamics of this vicious cycle were not particularly perceptible in the Federal Republic as long as the economic rise of the young state created and reinforced a feeling of common ground. However, if the economic outlook becomes more gloomy and the only symbol of common pride correspondingly crumbles, then the mutual enmity will come more undisguisedly to light and the vicious cycle of fear of the violence of those who are 'the others' at the time will begin its subterranean work once again.

At the same time the previously mentioned central problem of the Federal Republic, a problem which is currently obscured by 'the economic miracle', will reveal itself with greater clarity: the problem of national identity. At the current level of means of social orientation it often looks as though the worst thing that can happen to a nation is an economic crisis. In this respect, communists and capitalists stand on the same platform: both think that the economy is the central sphere of every society. I do not share the view of this capitalist–Marxist paradigmatic unity. An insidious identity crisis, such as has befallen the Federal Republic, is no less threatening than an economic crisis.

It is all too understandable that the disorientation regarding the meaning, worth and future of the nation is especially great in the Federal Republic – greater, it seems to me, than in any other contemporary nation-state in Europe. For the younger generations of this country, this is bad. People have said to me time and time again: 'In this society, there is nothing which could give meaning, worth and direction to life.' This is the gap which was filled for many younger people by Marxism. It gave direction and hope to people who found no other compass in their society. It is bad, so it seems to me, that today in other circles it is common to reproach the students for turning in such numbers to Marxism, or at least for not having any trust in their own state. In the excitement, people are content simply to accuse them antagonistically.

But they do not ask themselves how it is to be *explained* that this state has alienated such a large number of its most gifted people. Can it be that, in reaction to the enforced production of a feeling of national belonging under National Socialism, too little attention has been paid in the new West German state to the simpler problem of feelings of belonging, and that it is precisely because of this that people are helpless to confront the problem of the growing split within the Federal Republic?

It is certainly among the most difficult problems of the Federal Republic that the consciousness of belonging to a community which encompasses all groups and of sharing a common destiny seems to be missing. This lack is a common destiny of the Federal Germans and it is simply a social fact. It does not actually look as though many Federal Germans, Marxists or non-Marxists, would seriously wish to recreate German unity in the framework of the East German state and thereby within the Soviet bloc. It is only the consciousness of this unintended belonging together, this dependency on a way of life to which people are accustomed, of the dependency of their own social existence on the continued existence of the Federal Republic, which is missing in many people. By and large, people are inclined to sweep this problem under the carpet. Many older persons (who are gradually disappearing) seem to regard identification with the old German state, as it existed for instance after 1871, as something self-evident. But for younger people who know only the new Federal State from their own experience, and who know about the old Germany only from history books, this is hardly sufficient. The expectation that the old Germany will return in the foreseeable future is turning out to be more and more of a fantasy. East Germany, at least superficially united through its affiliation to the Marxist creed, is following its own path. There is no realistic ground for the belief that it could quit the Warsaw Pact in the foreseeable future and join West Germany. Perhaps people should look more closely at the consequences that follow from these facts. For when waiting for the restitution of the old, greater Germany turns out to be unrealistic, the problem of the identity of members of the Federal Republic as West Germans will gain a new urgency.

That public discussion of this problem has widely been avoided, that even the expression 'West Germany', which is increasingly being used in the other West European countries, was politically taboo for a while in the Federal Republic, contributes not a little to the fact that its citizens are mostly only vaguely aware, and often not at all aware, of how the various social (including regional) groupings of the Federal Republic are ultimately reliant on and interdependent with each other. The possibility of the deeply divided Federal German state disintegrating is certainly not to be dismissed out of hand. The centrifugal forces at play in the *Länder* of the Federal Republic may perhaps not yet be visible on the surface, although they can already be recognized unambiguously in the cultural foreground. They are, however, certainly very strong and without doubt reinforced by the harshness of the competitive struggle between both of the great political parties and by the smouldering aversion of their leading men for each other. Economic interests, one might say, keep the country together – but really only as long as the country is not affected by an economic crisis. Who can know whether in the course of time with the help of efficient party machines different *Länder* will become the unshakeable domains of particular parties? Who can say whether, under such circumstances, a future Bavarian premier would not feel himself to be firstly a Bavarian and only secondly a German?

Perhaps it is tacitly assumed that national sentiments are, so to speak, equally impressed onto every member of a nation by nature. Accordingly, the fact tends not to be perceived that the Federal Republic is one of the few European states in whose members, if one excludes the fragile pride in the 'economic miracle', the cement of a feeling of common identity is almost entirely lacking. And the especially large generation gap, between those who still knew the old Germany and those who know only the new Germany, the Federal Republic, contributes its part to the disunity and dismemberment of the country. People of the older generations may say, 'If a young person does not have this feeling of national identity, then he should simply go away; he is contemptible, a "Fatherland-less fellow."' But perhaps they have failed to recognize that, for the time being in West Germany, there is only the outer shell of a state organization. To say this does not by any means imply that the population of this state feel themselves to be a nation.

The abuse which the National Socialists committed with their appeal to German national sentiment, moreover, makes it much more difficult to couple the concept 'national' with a positive value. There is in German no word that quite corresponds to the British–American expression 'nation-building'. But it almost looks as if the Federal Republic may only have the choice between conscious integration and unplanned disintegration. In older states with a continuous development, a sentiment of national identity – 'I am French, I am Dutch, Italian, British', etc. – which incorporates all regions and classes has formed through an unplanned process in the course of centuries. In most younger states, there is a fairly conscious effort at nation-building. In the by no means classless society of East Germany the rulers are making every effort deliberately to build a nation. In the Soviet Union, too, there is a very deliberate cultivation of the feeling of national belonging to the Soviet mother country. Where such a policy is difficult, as in Belgium or Northern Ireland, the population lives for decades in the condition of a latent civil war, on the verge of disintegration. It is not out of the question that the Federal Republic will have to prepare itself for a similar type of existence.

After the experiences of National Socialism it is certainly no longer possible, within the framework of a non-dictatorial German state, to use the building of a nation and the development of a feeling of national belonging as camouflage for the supremacy of the old leading strata. Accordingly, the building of a nation in the Federal Republic is a particularly difficult task. It requires above all that one gives the younger generations, on whose good will and feeling of belonging the future of each and every country depends, the feeling that it is worthwhile to live in this society. The economic successes achieved by West Germany will quickly change to the opposite if the unity of the country is threatened or crumbles: if, for example, not inconsiderable parts of the younger generations are alienated from the state because they are unable to find a satisfying career or because every career-channel is blocked for them. To build a nation requires one to make an effort, in spite of class and party conflicts, to incorporate all classes and groups into the circulation of social life with equal rights, to integrate them into the nation even if one does not agree with the attitudes and ideas of these groups.

Much of what I have to say, I say primarily as a person who feels deeply bound to the European tradition. A disintegration of the Federal Republic or its transformation into a dictatorial regime – both possibilities which one must look squarely in the eye – would be a misfortune not only for the German people, but for European countries and the European tradition as a whole. Both possibilities would most seriously threaten the chance of a closer union of the European countries, and would be an evil omen for Europe's future. A Federal Republic permanently at odds with itself would have a weak voice in the European councils, and a second dictatorship, however disguised, would very quickly reawaken the only lightly sleeping distrust of Germany. People perhaps sometimes forget that the bitter internal political debates in West Germany are carried out in an open arena in front of a broad

European public, which, even if it comments with reserve, still feels directly affected.

4

So much of what in the Federal Republic is banished as far as possible from public discussion is spoken about publicly in other European countries, discreetly but as a matter of course. Would it not be more salutary to discuss painful problems frankly and openly in West Germany, too? I am thinking above all of the problem of the stigma and the guilt feelings bequeathed by National Socialism to subsequent generations. Despite all protestations to the contrary, it has never stopped burdening the German conscience. Much has been said about coming to terms with the past. But it is quite clear that this has only been repressed and in no way overcome. To speak about it is certainly not easy. I realize that by doing so, one touches an open wound in the we-consciousness of the Germans. But precisely because it has not healed, it is necessary to talk about it – not in order to accuse, but as a prelude to the effort to explain the temporary breakdown of human civilization in Germany. It seems to me that it is important for the health and future of West Germany (if the country does have a future) to draw the problem out of the oblivion into which it has sunk and into the public eye again.

I myself believed for a while that it was time to forget the past. The difficulty is that one can perhaps forget it in Germany; but everywhere else it is unforgotten, most especially in Germany's neighbouring countries. There, where people suffered heavily from the occupation by Hitler's war machine, it remains to this day a completely topical problem how this or that person conducted himself during the occupation. The relatively firmly entrenched national sentiment in countries like Holland, Norway or France continues to be manifested in that, from time to time but none the less regularly, the matter of a man's collaboration with the Nazis is brought out into the open, and the question of whether anyone else committed this type of treachery is intensely discussed throughout the country.

Young Germans are quite right when they say, 'But we had nothing at all to do with it. Why are we being made responsible for something our fathers did?' The truth is that in their dealings with each other, the people of different nations do not make such sharp distinctions. For them, a Briton is a Briton, a Frenchman a Frenchman, and a German a German, irrespective of his age. Here one is approaching the core of the problem. For a British, Dutch, Danish or French politician, it would mean the end of his career if only the slightest suspicion of having collaborated with the Hitler regime fell upon him. One was able to see the reality of this feeling of defilement, undiminished in the course of time, in France a short while ago, where charges laid against the leader of the Communist Party, Marchais, aroused the suspicion that he had not been forced but had gone voluntarily to do labour duty in Germany. Confirmation of this suspicion would have been enough to make him impossible as a political figure, and he, the Communist, defended himself – as a Frenchman.

The West German Federal Republic is today the only country in Europe in which it is no stigma and hardly an obstacle to a person's career that he was a National Socialist. The barbaric murder of Dr Schleyer has illustrated this problem all of a sudden. The conservative *Times* later reported accurately and matter-of-factly in its obituary that Dr Schleyer became a member of the Nazi Party in his early years, worked in the leadership of the Nazi students' organization, then became a member of the SS, was active as such in the economic administration of occupied Czechoslovakia, and finally, when the SS was classified as criminal, was interned by the Allies for three years. In the obituaries in German papers, this information was hardly to be found. Some of my British acquaintances were very upset by this information in *The Times*. 'It seems', said one of them, 'that in Germany everything has remained the same.' And without doubt there in the background was the thought: 'We have fought a hard war, and we believed we had eliminated the cancer in Germany and Europe – but perhaps the tumour is still alive?'

Those are not my thoughts. It hardly accords with my feeling of human decency not to forgive yesterday's enemies. I myself am an old man and find it inhuman that, to take one example, an old man like Rudolf Hess who can no longer harm anyone is still being held in solitary confinement. To me, it would appear to be a symbolic gesture of humanity if he were set free. What I mentioned above is simply a factual report. It indicates that the National Socialist problem is not a problem of the past; it has never stopped being a topical problem.

It seems to me to be a mistaken policy, mistaken especially in the sense of the future of Federal German society itself, to impose a secret taboo on the public discussion of National Socialism and its roots. People have a greater understanding nowadays than was earlier the case that a violent traumatic experience in an individual person's life causes severe damage if it is not raised to the level of consciousness through being talked about and discussed, hence giving the healing process a chance. I have been convinced for a long time that in the lives of nations too, and in fact of many other social groupings, there are collective traumatic experiences which sink deep down into the psychic economy of the members of these nations and cause severe damage there – damage especially to behaviour in communal social life – if one denies them the possibility of a cathartic cleansing and the associated relief and release which are associated with that. The situation today in the Federal Republic must remain incomprehensible without reference to the traumatic experience of National Socialist rule and the terrible consequences it had for Germany. That this trauma was allowed to sink from view, that public discussion declined and the associated chance of purification was missed, have been bitterly revenged. I am certainly not concealing from myself that there were social reasons for this. It was without doubt the honest opinion of the transitional generation which seized the reins of power immediately after the defeat that it would be possible to continue to pursue the business of Germany as though nothing had happened, and that the best thing for the German people would be to forget the National Socialist interlude. But it was an expression both of their claim to rule and their will to power that they believed they could draw a line under the past.

I have already spoken about how the society of the Federal Republic is in danger of being caught up in an escalation of fear, in a polarizing escalation of conflicts between those who fear the setting up of a communist dictatorship in West Germany and those who fear the return of a fascist dictatorship. The wave of terrorism can only be understood in this context. It, too, is a social phenomenon for which there are long-term bases. Not to see this connection, to explain the atrocities of the terrorists simply as the result of their personal evil, their criminal nature, is itself an attempt to suppress from consciousness the obvious fact that these barbaric acts of violence are long-term after-effects of the barbaric acts of violence of the National Socialists with an inverted sign, and even those certainly did not form the first link in the chain. The National Socialists had sympathizers, too, an incomparably larger circle of sympathizers than today's terrorists. Both sets of violence can be explained only in the long term in relation to the particular fate of the German people.

The Baader–Meinhof group lived, and its successors still live today, under the impression that fascism has returned to Germany, that the Federal Republic is a fascist state and that one can destroy the fascist rule of violence only through counter-violence. It is certainly a fantasy to call the Federal Republic a fascist state. But one cannot ignore the fact that these acts of terror fit into the context of the escalating conflict between anti-fascists and anti-communists of which I have just spoken. As in the case of the National Socialists, so, too, in this case collective fantasies form a part of social reality. One can master them only by looking this reality of collective fantasies in the face. They, too, are a long-term after-effect of the National Socialist trauma. If one attempts to present terrorism simply as the deeds of a few criminals, then one misunderstands its social meaning precisely because one is thereby seeking to repress from consciousness the long-term after-effects of that trauma on the further course of German development. I am certain that it would have a cleansing, cathartic effect if more were spoken about these connections, if these problems were discussed factually and with complete frankness above all at schools and universities, indeed everywhere where young people are learning.

Clashes between different classes and parties are unavoidable. An increase in the passion and excess of such clashes, however, is not unavoidable. There is, so it seems, no real communication between the enemy camps in West Germany today. The mutual ratcheting-up of fears, the unplanned process of escalation, remains hidden to both sides. Therefore I want to point out once more in summary the structure of this polarization.

On the left nowadays, especially among young people, one meets with a very serious fear that in the future they will be living in an increasingly rigid authoritarian state. Some call it a police state, some a fascist state – the name itself does not really matter. They have many quite sound reasons for this fear. There are leading persons on the right, who, although they are far from the National Socialist creed, have attitudes which in the eyes of the other side show an ominous similarity with the attitude of representatives of an authoritarian fascist state. This refers to men in high government and party positions such as judges, large-scale entrepreneurs and policemen. The excessive, hate-filled campaign against 'sympathizers' has understandably considerably strengthened the fear that Germany is heading in the direction of a *de facto* party dictatorship even within the framework of a nominally parliamentary regime. On the right, on the other hand, it is constantly being pointed out that their opponents are steering towards a revolution. That is on this side the central fear, and for this, too, there are sound reasons. Many Marxists use words such as 'revolution' or 'revolutionary' rather thoughtlessly, as if a revolution were a question of a happy trip into the countryside. In reality, a revolution is no less bloody and violent a matter than a war, and currently, as the experience in African countries shows, it is becoming less and less possible to separate these two forms of the use of organized violence from each other.

The threat of revolution and the fear of it, the threat of a dictatorial police state and the fear of that thus play their devilish game with each other. It is difficult to say whether the dynamics of this spiralling movement have already reached the point of no return. I hope that there is still time to brake the movement in this direction. If not – poor, self-destructive Germany.

Editorial Postscript

Michael Schröter

The present volume is a collection of the works of Norbert Elias on German development in the nineteenth and twentieth centuries. They revolve around two main interconnected problems: that of the national habitus, which he had already treated in the first chapter of his book *The Civilizing Process* ('Sociogenesis of the difference between *Kultur* and *Zivilisation* in German usage'), and that of the barbarizing thrust of National Socialism, the specific pattern of German state-formation and civilizing processes which facilitated it, and their after-effects.

The selection and compilation of the articles published here was approved by the author, but in the end it is the editor's responsibility. Certainly, most of the texts – as their titles indicate – were written about broader questions, and use German conditions to start with as material for discussion. However, the reference to Germany in them has such significance that it seemed appropriate to make it the criterion for selecting the contents of the volume, which thus gains a certain unity.

The articles were written over a long period of time (but particularly during the years of Elias's temporary return to Germany) and quite independently of each other. This circumstance may explain some repetition of trains of thought, but also provides the chance of following the continuity and development of a body of very original theoretical and empirical research.

With the exception of part III (excluding endnotes and the appendices), none of the texts published here was completed for publication by the author himself. Making a version suitable for publication therefore required editorial work to a greater or lesser extent, which was undertaken by the editor with the author's permission.

The introduction was written specially for the publication of this volume.

Part I arose in conjunction with a lecture given at the University of Bielefeld on 18 December 1978. Part I/A reproduces the prepared text of the lecture (with a new conclusion), part I/B the later working out of one of its central themes. In both cases, subtitles were added by the editor. There are different versions of the original manuscript together with textual emendations. What is offered here is an inclusive, editorially integrated selection. The main body has been organized into sections and in part also into paragraphs, carefully condensed and linguistically checked by the editor. The guiding theme has been to prepare a maximum of the original for publication in a coherent form.

Part II probably arose in the second half of the 1960s in connection with a plan to use part 1 of *The Civilizing Process* as the basis for an independent study in English of the sociology of knowledge. The original text was translated into German by the editor and consisted for the most part of clean, fair copy; some passages where fragmentary further work had been attempted were incorporated into endnotes; connecting passages and the organization of sections (from 16) were provided by the editor.

Part III arose in conjunction with an address given on 18 September 1980 at the Twentieth Congress of the German Sociological Association. The reworked lecture text was published in *Lebenswelt und soziale Probleme: Verhandlungen des 20. Deutschen Soziologentages zu Bremen 1980* [Lifeworld and Social Problems: Proceedings of the 20th Congress of the German Sociological Association, Bremen, 1980], ed. Joachim Matthes, Frankfurt and New York, Campus, 1981, pp. 98–122. It is published here in a form somewhat condensed by the editor. The sections have been reorganized and traces of the author's original lecturing style removed. In the first two sections, parts of a later version have been incorporated and, at the end of the third part, parts of an earlier version were incorporated. The appendices (with titles formulated by the editor) and the numerous endnotes were extracted from the various versions and strands of text of the original manuscript. The same principles guided this work as for part I.

Part IV arose in 1961–2. The original English text, divided into sections (from section 7) and translated by the editor, exists in fair copy with some handwritten alterations and insertions. The penultimate section comes from an unfinished part of a conclusion, the final section from a draft version.

Part V was written with the collaboration of Michael Schröter between October 1977 and March 1978 at the request of *Der Spiegel*. The text was published in *Merkur*, no. 39, 1985, pp.735–55 with some deletions, and is reprinted here unabridged.

Notes

Notes to the Preface

1 *The Civilizing Process*, trans. Edmund Jephcott, Oxford, Blackwell, 1994. Under the title *Über den Prozeß der Zivilisation*, the first German edition of Elias's *magnum opus* was published in two volumes in 1939 by Haus zum Falken of Basle, a publishing house which specialized in the publication of works by exiled German Jews. References throughout *The Germans* are to the first single-volume English edition of 1994, the appearance of which should limit the tendency for scholars not to recognize the integrated character of vols I and II. The 1978 English translation of vol. I was sub-titled *The History of Manners* by the publishers, Urizen, in the face of very strong objections from Norbert Elias. Elias's own sub-title in the German was *Wandlungen des Verhaltens in den weltlichen Oberschichten des Abend-landes*, and the direct translation of this – 'Changes in the Behaviour of the Secular Upper Classes in the West' – might have helped to avoid some misunderstandings. Confusion about the book as whole was compounded when, in 1982, the English translation of volume II was published under two different titles: *State-Formation and Civilization* in the British edition, and *Power and Civility* (to which Elias again objected) in the American edition.

2 Since the publication of *Studien über die Deutschen*, two full-length studies of the place of duelling in German society have been published: Ute Frevert's *Ehrenmänner: das Duell in der bürgerlichen, Gesellschaft*, Munich, C. H.

Beck, 1991 and Kevin McAleer's *Duelling: the Cult of Honour in Fin-de-Siècle Germany*, Princeton NJ, Princeton University Press, 1994. McAleer's book, though written with an irritating facetiousness, contains much relevant material; see especially ch. 4, pp. 119–58, on the fighting fraternities in German universities. Frevert emphasizes what she calls 'the feudalization' of the German bourgeoisie, but also argues that there took place an embourgeoisement of the aristocratic duel. McAleer criticizes Frevert, seeing a contradiction between the two tendencies; but, as Elias shows both in the present book and elsewhere (see, for example, *The Civilizing Process*, pp. 460–5, 499–513) the intermingling of cultural elements of different social provenance is common in modern societies. The discussion of duelling inevitably becomes entangled with the *Sonderweg* ('special path') debate among German historians since the Second World War concerning the peculiarity or 'exceptionalism' of the German path of development. A slightly earlier book, V.G. Kiernan's *The Duel in European History*, Oxford, Oxford University Press, 1986, contains much factual information on duelling in Britain, France and other countries.

3 See, for example, Pierre Bourdieu, *Distinction: a Social Critique of the Judgement of Taste*, trans. Richard Nice, London, Routledge and Kegan Paul, 1979. The term 'habitus' first appears on p. xi of the preface to the 1939 edition of *Über den Prozeß der Zivilisation*. It was apparently used quite commonly in German sociology between the wars. It has been somewhat misleadingly translated by Edmund Jephcott as 'psychical make-up'; see, for instance, p. xii of the 1994 English edition.

4 Anthony Giddens seeks – quite implausibly in our view – to deny that there is any connection whatsoever between a group's history and its present habitus. See Giddens, *The Constitution of Society*, Cambridge, Polity Press, 1994, pp. 241–2; for a rebuttal of Giddens, see Eric Dunning, 'Comments on Elias's "Scenes from the Life of a Knight"', *Theory, Culture & Society*, 4 (2–3), 1987: 366–71.

5 For a bibliography and summary of the main issues in this debate, see Stephen Mennell, *Norbert Elias: an Introduction*, Oxford, Blackwell, 1992 (1st edn, entitled *Norbert Elias: Civilization and the Human Self-Image*, 1989), pp. 241–6. The 'informalization thesis' has been developed especially by Cas Wouters, who describes its origins in his discussions with Elias in Han Israëls, Mieke Komen and Abram de Swaan, eds, *Over Elias: herinneringen en ankedotes*, Amsterdam, Het Spinhuis, 1993, pp. 7–19; although the article is in Dutch, Wouters quotes illuminating letters from Elias in English.

6 Elias, *The Civilizing Process*, pp. 339–45. This short 'excursus' does not seem to have been noticed by those critics of Elias who see him as having proposed some kind of 'unilinear' theory of social development. See, for example, R.J. Robinson, 'The civilizing process: some remarks on Elias's

social history', *Sociology*, 21 (1), 1987: 1–17, and Eric Dunning, 'A response to R.J. Robinson's "The civilizing process: some remarks on Elias's social history"', *Sociology*, 23 (2), 1989: 299–307.

7 Elias, *The Civilizing Process*, pp. 339, 343.

8 Norbert Elias, *What is Sociology?*, trans. Stephen Mennell and Grace Morrissey, New York, Columbia University Press, 1978, p. 159.

9 J.P. Arnason, *The Future that Failed: Origins and Destinies of the Soviet Model*, London, Routledge, 1993, is partly influenced by Elias's work.

10 *The Civilizing Process*, pp. 344–5.

11 Norbert Elias, *The Court Society*, trans. Edmund Jephcott, Oxford, Blackwell, 1983.

12 Norbert Elias, *Mozart: Portrait of a Genius*, trans. Edmund Jephcott, Cambridge, Polity Press, 1993.

13 Norbert Elias and Eric Dunning, *Quest for Excitement: Sport and Leisure in the Civilizing Process*, Oxford, Blackwell, 1986.

14 Norbert Elias, 'Studies in the genesis of the naval profession', *British Journal of Sociology*, 1 (4), 1950: 291–309.

15 Edward W. Said, *Orientalism*, New York, Pantheon, 1978.

16 See, for example, Lipset's survey of early research, in his *Political Man*, London, Heinemann, 1960, pp. 140–54.

17 Cf. F.L. Carsten, *The Origins of Prussia*, Oxford, Clarendon Press, 1954; E.J. Feuchtwanger, *Prussia, Myth and Reality: the Role of Prussia in German History*, London, Wolff, 1970.

18 Ralf Dahrendorf, *Society and Democracy in Germany*, London, Weidenfeld & Nicolson, 1968.

19 Hannah Arendt, *The Origins of Totalitarianism*, London, Allen & Unwin, 1967.

20 T.W. Adorno, E. Frenkel-Brunswick, D.J. Levinson and R.N. Sanford, *The Authoritarian Personality*, New York, Harper & Row, 1950.

21 For an up-to-date study and review of the literature, see Alison Palmer, 'Colonial Genocides: Aborigines in Queensland, 1840–1897, and Hereroes in South-West Africa, 1884–1906', unpublished PhD thesis, University of London, 1994.

22 Charles Maier, in Ralf Dahrendorf et al., *The Unresolved Past: a Debate in German History*, London, Weidenfeld & Nicolson, 1990, p. 4.

23 On the issues of the *Historikerstreit* ('the historians' dispute') see: Charles Maier, *The Unmasterable Past: History, Holocaust and German National Identity*, Cambridge, Mass., Harvard University Press, 1988; Richard J. Evans, *Rethinking German History: Nineteenth-Century German History and the Origins of the Third Reich*, London, Allen & Unwin, 1987; Dahrendorf, et. al., *The Unresolved Past*; Stefan Berger, 'Historians and Nation-Building in Germany after Reunification', *Past and Present* 148, 1995: 187–22.

24 Zygmunt Bauman, *Modernity and the Holocaust*, Cambridge, Polity Press, 1989.

25 Cf. Johan Goudsblom, 'The formation of military-agrarian regimes', in Johan Goudsblom, E.L. Jones and Stephen Mennell, *Human History and Social Process*, Exeter, University of Exeter Press, 1989, pp. 79–92.
26 Norbert Elias and John L. Scotson, *The Established and the Outsiders*, 2nd edn, London, Sage, 1994 (originally published 1965): c.f. T.J. Scheff, *Bloody Revenge: Emotions, Nationalism and War*, Boulder, Westview Press, 1994.
27 Bauman, *Modernity and the Holocaust*, pp. 12, 107, 224n.
28 Elias, *The Civilizing Process*, pp. 3–41.
29 This is our translation of the original German (Elias, *Über den Prozeß der Zivilisation*, p. 278). Edmund Jephcott has 'economy of instincts' for *Triebhaushalt* (see Elias, *The Civilizing Process*, p. 165). We have changed it because Elias would not have used the term 'instincts' in discussing human behaviour. A looser translation, less Freudian but in line with Elias's later terminology, could read 'the standards of the demands made upon emotion management are very gradually changed as well'.
30 Elias, *The Civilizing Process*, p. 253.
31 Norbert Elias, *The Symbol Theory*, ed. Richard Kilminster, London, Sage, 1991, pp. 146–7.

Notes to the Introduction

1 It is not without deliberation that I talk about 'processes' here, in a field of research which is conventionally regarded as 'history'. The traditional view of the past of societies as 'history' is on a low level of synthesis: it is usually restricted to short-term connections. In actual fact, the effects of social events are often felt first only centuries later. Models of long-term processes are therefore necessary to take account of them.
2 Norbert Elias, *The Civilizing Process*, one-volume edn, trans. Edmund Jephcott, Oxford, Blackwell, 1994 (originally published in German in 1939). [Translators' note]
3 Cf. Norbert Elias, 'Studies in the genesis of the naval profession', *British Journal of Sociology*, 1 (4), 1950: 291–309. [Translators' note]
4 Norbert Elias, *The Civilizing Process*, pp. 3–28. [Translators' note]
5 The Duchies of Schleswig and Holstein had been united since the Middle Ages, with the King of Denmark as Duke, although a large part of their population was German and Holstein had become a member of the German Confederation in 1815. When a member of a collateral branch of the royal family succeeded in 1863 as King Christian IX, his right to succeed also as Duke was disputed. After a brief war in the summer of 1864, the duchies were ceded, Holstein to be administered by Austria, Schleswig by Prussia. Finally, in 1920 under the Treaty of Versailles, a plebiscite was held in Schleswig, and the northern part where Danes were in the majority was incorporated into Denmark. [Translators' note]

Notes to Part IA

1 Japan in the 1970s is an example of the rapid transition from the first period of industrialization, orientated to high capital formation (in part through keeping mass consumption low), to the second, in which efforts have to be made to boost the domestic consumer market, and stimulate the consumer needs of the masses, in order to maintain economic growth.

2 By and large, one can say that the Weimar Republic was the scene of an intense struggle for supremacy between two establishments. To say that it was a struggle between a bourgeois and a workers' establishment is not exactly incorrect, but it is not sufficiently precise. With today's habits of thought, such a statement could be easily understood to mean we are dealing with one establishment whose members were bourgeois by social origin, and with another whose members were workers by origin. But this tendency, when assigning a person to a certain social stratum, to take as the decisive – often the only – criterion the person's social origin (that is, the stratum to which his or her family, and especially the father, belongs), is not fully in accordance with reality. It is quite well known that many leaders of the labour movement were (and are) of middle-class origin. In Germany, as in other countries, the heads of the bourgeois and workers' parties, which fought against each other for control of the central institutions of power in the state, differed from each other mainly in the codes of behaviour and feeling they upheld and represented. And the leaders of the workers' parties, irrespective of origin, were representatives of a different tradition of thought and behaviour from the leaders of the bourgeois parties. Their identification, their goals and ideals were different from those of the bourgeois parties.

This dissimilarity was all the more marked since in Germany the code of behaviour and feeling of bourgeois politicians also continued to be influenced to a fairly large extent by the tradition of behaviour and feeling of the German and particularly the Prussian nobility. Indeed, some aspects of the German warrior code upheld by the nobility penetrated behaviour in peacetime, serving as a model of behaviour among extensive circles of Germans.

A typical component of the noble tradition which had been adopted and adapted by the bourgeoisie is connected with the German nobility's special emphasis on its closure to socially lower classes, shown among other things in their unsullied aristocratic lineages. The entire family tree was polluted and some rights and privileges forfeited if even one woman of merchant background, or at any rate of lower rank, was to be found even four to five generations back among the ancestors. The singularity of this German aristocratic tradition is made particularly clear when it is compared with the British. The standing and status of British nobles among themselves was little marred by the existence in their ancestry of a woman whose own family had been in trade – or even Jewish – as long as the descendants observed the demands of the aristocratic code of behaviour and feeling. That the personality type fitted this code was the decisive consideration. In any case, except for the eldest sons, the descendants of a high aristocratic family sank bit by bit back into the middle class with the passing of generations. This favoured the preservation of the noble family's fortune. In Germany, in contrast, all sons and daughters of nobles carried the differentiating title and rank of their forebears. Therefore there were very many poorer nobles, who could legitimate themselves only through their descent, their 'blood'. In this way, descent was a more important criterion of membership than behaviour.

The aristocratic 'proof by ancestry' reappeared in a bourgeois form in the National Socialist code of behaviour and feeling. It transferred the notion of the 'purity of the blood', that is, unsullied descent to the fourth or fifth generation, to the entire population. The German people, purified as far as possible from admixtures of groups standing socially lower than themselves, were now, as the nobility of Europe so to speak, to take it upon themselves to rule over people of less pure blood. That this should be achieved through the conquest of other European countries was also an expression of the continuation of the aristocratic warrior tradition dressed in petit-bourgeois trappings.

3 *The Letters of Mozart and his Family*, trans. and ed. Emily Anderson, 2 vols, London, Macmillan, 1966, vol. II, p. 601. The translation of the ceremonious titles has been modified in light of the German text (*Mozart, Briefe und Aufzeichnungen*, ed. Wilhelm A. Bauer and Otto Erich Deutsch, Kassel, Bärenreiter, 1962, vol. 2, p. 462). See also Norbert Elias, *Mozart: Portrait of a Genius*, trans. Edmund Jephcott, Oxford, Polity Press, 1993. [Translators' note]

4 In a postscript to his letter of 4 November 1777 from Mannheim to his father in Salzburg, Mozart wrote:

> As for the targets, if it is not too late, this is what I would like. A short man with fair hair, shown bending over and displaying his bare arse. From his mouth come the words: 'Good appetite for the meal'. The other man to be shown booted and spurred with a red cloak and a fine fashionable wig. He must be of medium height and in such a position that he licks the other man's arse. From his mouth come the words: 'Oh there's nothing to beat it.' So, please, if not this time, another time.

(*The Letters of Mozart and his Family*, vol. I, pp.357–8). [Translators' note]

5 One of the standing debates in the literature on Mozart revolves around the

fact that in his letters he made jokes with the greatest of unconcern about such topics as the musical concomitants of flatulence which today produce awkward feelings of embarrassment rather than laughter. In the nineteenth and early twentieth centuries, these unwelcome parts of Mozart's letters and the unpleasant aspects of his personality which were thought to be expressed in them were glossed over; they were suppressed, since they did not really fit in with the ideal image of a German genius, and perhaps would have disturbed people's enjoyment of Mozart's music, which was always considered to be graceful and charming. In the more recent literature, the social informalization process is evident. The taboo on speaking directly about these indecent aspects of human existence has lost much of its severity. One consequence of this is that although the jocular preoccupation with the excremental and anal sides of human life, seen in particular in the famous Basle letters of the young Mozart, is mentioned and discussed, it is on the whole understood to be a personal idiosyncrasy, a type of neurotic fixation by the great man on problems of that phase of life when small children are encouraged to be clean and to fit their calls of nature to specific places and times.

This interpretation may or may not be correct. But in many cases, biographers are currently still concerned with the idiosyncracies of a particular person, as though he or she developed in a social vacuum. As long as that remains the case, it will not be easy to judge which of a person's ways of behaving and feeling are really unique features of this person, and which are social traits of the era which the person accordingly shares with other members of his or her society. In fact, a theory of civilizing processes is needed in such cases in order to be able to differentiate clearly between what aspects of a person's behaviour and feeling are at any one time representative of the standard of the society to which the person belongs and what are quite personal elaborations of this code.

6 Some of my Dutch friends and students have been especially interested in the problem of the modern trend towards informalization as an aspect of a civilizing process. One of them, Cas Wouters, actually introduced the concept of informalization in his essay, 'Informalization and the civilizing process', in Peter Gleichmann, Johan Goudsblom and Hermann Korte, eds, *Human Figurations: Essays for/Aufsätze für Norbert Elias*, Amsterdam, Amsterdams Sociologisch Tijdschrift, 1977, pp. 437–53; and further developed in the essay, 'Developments in behavioural codes between the sexes: formalization and informalization in the Netherlands 1930–85', *Theory, Culture & Society*, 4 (2–3), 1987: 405–20. Compare also Christien Brinkgreve and Michel Korzec, *Margriet weet raad: Gevoel, gedrag, moraal in Nederland 1938–1978*, Utrecht/Antwerp, Het Spectrum, 1978 (summarized in English in 'Feelings, behaviour, morals in the Netherlands, 1938–78: analysis and interpretation of an advice column', *Netherlands Journal of Sociology*, 15

(2), 1979: 123–40). All three authors use their material both to test and to develop further my theory of civilization.

[Additional note by the translators: For further contributions to the discussion of informalizing processes and the so-called 'permissive society' see Christien Brinkgreve, 'On modern relationships: the commandments of the new freedom', *Netherlands Journal of Sociology*, 18 (1), 1982: 47–56, and the following essays by Cas Wouters: 'Formalization and informalization: changing tension balances in civilizing processes', *Theory, Culture & Society* 3 (1), 1986: 1–18; 'The sociology of emotions and flight attendants: Hochschild's *Managed Heart*', *Theory, Culture & Society* 6 (1), 1989: 95–123; 'Social stratification and informalization in global perspective', *Theory, Culture & Society*, 7 (4), 1990: 69–90; 'On status competition and emotion management', *Journal of Social History*, 24 (4), 1991: 699–717.]

7 Norbert Elias, *The Civilizing Process*, trans. Edmund Jephcott, Oxford, Blackwell, 1994, p. 66. 'Thingis somtyme alowed is now repreuid', from Caxton's late fifteenth-century *Book of Curtesye*, p. 45 v 64.

8 Indeed, at first the problem of civilization appeared to me as a completely personal problem in connection with the great breakdown of civilized behaviour, the thrust towards barbarization, which was something totally unexpected, quite unimaginable, taking place under my own eyes in Germany. Under National Socialism, a latent tendency to let oneself go, to loosen the grip of one's own conscience, to roughness and brutality, which, as long as the external constraint of state control remained intact, could come out at most informally in the private interstices of the network of state control, became formalized and, for established groups, elevated to a type of behaviour both demanded and supported by the state. Even as the question of the German spurt towards barbarization was becoming such an urgent issue for me, even as I was beginning to write my book on civilization, it seemed to me to be totally inadequate to discuss this acute breakdown of civilizing controls simply as a problem for political scientists studying party doctrines – as a problem of fascism, as it would somewhat ashamedly be expressed today. That way, some of its central aspects could hardly be properly grasped. I was convinced that this could be done only if, as a social scientist, one could distance oneself sufficiently from the immediate situation, if one did not pose only such short-term questions as why did the standard of civilized conscience break down among a highly civilized people in the second quarter of the twentieth century?

First of all it seemed to me that we still knew absolutely nothing about how and why in the course of human development – and then, in closer focus, in European development – changes in behaviour and feeling took place in a civilizing direction. In a nutshell, one cannot understand the breakdown of civilized behaviour and feeling as long as one cannot understand and explain how civilized behaviour and feeling came to be constructed and developed in European societies in the first place. The ancient Greeks, for instance, who are so often held up to us as models of civilized behaviour, considered it quite a matter of course to commit acts of mass destruction, not quite identical to those of the National Socialists but, nevertheless, similar to them in certain respects. The Athenian popular assembly decided to wipe out the entire population of Melos, because the city did not want to join the Athenian colonial empire. There were dozens of other examples in antiquity of what we now call genocide.

The difference between this and the attempted genocide in the 1930s and 1940s is at first glance not easy to grasp. Nevertheless, it is quite clear. In the period of Greek antiquity, this warlike behaviour was considered normal. It conformed to the standard. People's conscience-formation, the structure of their personalities, was such that this sort of action seemed to them to be normal human behaviour. The way the conscience is formed in European societies – and, indeed, in large parts of humanity – in the twentieth century is different. It sets a standard for human behaviour against which the deeds of the National Socialists appear abhorrent, and are regarded with spontaneous feelings of horror. The problem I set myself to examine was, then, to explain and to make comprehensible the development of personality structures and especially of structures of conscience or self-control which represent a standard of humaneness going far beyond that of antiquity, and which accordingly make people react to behaviour like that of the National Socialists (or similar behaviour by other people) with spontaneous repugnance.

9 Andreas Capellanus, *De amore libri tres*, ed. E. Trojel, Copenhagen, Havniae, 1892, pp. 235ff.
10 Elias, *The Civilizing Process*, p. 248, n. 69; Norbert Elias, *The Court Society*, trans. Edmund Jephcott, Oxford, Blackwell, 1983, p. 48, n. 15.
11 'Crass foxes' were in some ways equivalent to 'fags' in the British public schools. Each new member of a fraternity had to perform services for an older student (his *Leibbursche*) in return for which he was inducted by the latter into the fraternity, receiving also a degree of protection. [Translators' note]
12 *Time Magazine*, 27 November 1978, 'America's new manners', Letitia Baldridge, p. 47.
13 *The Amy Vanderbilt Complete Book of Etiquette: a Guide to Contemporary Living*, revised and expanded by Letitia Baldridge, New York, Doubleday, 1978; quoted in ibid., p. 48.
14 Cf. Norbert Elias, 'The changing balance of power between the sexes in the history of civilization', *Theory, Culture & Society*, 4 (2–3), 1987: 287–316, especially pp. 287–90. [Translators' note]
15 *Bielefelder Universitätszeitung*, no. 108, 12 December 1978.
16 Wouters, 'Informalization and the civilizing process', p. 444.

Notes to Part IB

1 See Norbert Elias, 'The personal pronouns as a figurational model', *What is Sociology?*, trans. Stephen Mennell and Grace Morrissey, New York, Columbia University Press, 1978, pp. 122–7.

2 Heinrich Mann, *Man of Straw*, trans. Ernest Boyd, Harmondsworth, Penguin, 1984. The original German title was *Der Untertan* [The Underling], 1918; this is the first part of Mann's *Das Kaiserreich* trilogy. [Translators' note]

3 In the novel, 'Cimber' is the name of the fraternity to which Werner belongs. [Translators' note]

4 These were the colours of Werner's fraternity. Such student fraternities were often termed *farbentragenden Verbindungen* – 'colour-bearing fraternities'. [Translators' note]

5 Walter Bloem, *Der krasse Fuchs* [The Crass Fox], Berlin, Vita, 1906, pp. 73f.

6 Norbert Elias, *The Court Society*, trans. Edmund Jephcott, Oxford, Blackwell, 1983. [Translators' note]

7 See Norbert Elias, 'Studies in the genesis of the naval profession', *British Journal of Sociology*, 1 (4) 1950: 291–309. [Translators' note]

8 For the history and details of the various kinds of German student fraternity, see for example R.G.S. Weber, *The German Student Corps in the Third Reich*, Basingstoke, Macmillan, 1986. [Translators' note]

9 This remark is richer in German, since *Land* has the sense of 'province' besides the meanings of 'land' in English; the allusion here is to the independent and semi-independent principalities (etc.) such as Prussia, Bavaria, Hesse, and so on. [Translators' note]

10 'Particularism' is here being used mainly in a sense related to its specific political meaning, 'the principle of leaving political independence to each state in an empire' (*OED*); it is less directly being used in the more abstract and recent sociological sense (associated for example with Talcott Parsons), although something of that is also involved. In the German text, Elias in this passage uses both *Partikularismus* itself and *Vielstaaterei*, which can also be translated as 'particularism'. For Elias, of course, 'political principles' are more 'determined' by political practice than 'determining' of it. [Translators' note]

11 The standardization among students and officers of the code of honour, the rules for duelling, and everything connected with them, was a symptom of the process of forming a 'good society' comprised of those entitled to demand satisfaction. It made progress despite the refusal of the Minister of War, when approached by the leaders of the student fighting fraternities, to pass an official regulation because duelling was legally prohibited.

However, a convergence between the two groups on the code of honour and rules of duelling was reached by less official, more informally social routes.

The changes in the code of behaviour and feeling of the students belonging to colour-bearing fraternities (about which more will be said later) were therefore not just changes within a 'subculture'. The development of the code, to which young men of both noble and middle-class origin felt by honour bound, was symptomatic of the character of a German upper class which was in the process of being formed in this period and which bound aristocratic and bourgeois groups together in a hierarchical order.

12 The imperial court society in the broadest sense included the entire group of those eligible for presentation at court: not just those who held court positions, but all those who were regularly or periodically commanded to attend at court or who, after leaving their visiting cards with the Lord Chamberlain [*kaiserlicher Zeremonienmeister*] and being carefully scrutinized by his staff, were admitted to one of the imperial receptions or perhaps to a ball.

This court society spanned a rather broad group. Loyal members of the provincial aristocracy were all regarded as eligible for presentation at court. The 'season' became a regular institution under the empire, probably following the older London season (which went back to the seventeenth century), and with its abundance of glittering balls gave the provincial aristocracy, too, the opportunity to present their daughters to the imperial couple at court and to make their debut in society. The ceremonial developed here was a German version of the traditional ceremonials of the great courts of Europe. There were smaller courts in Bavaria, Saxony and many other parts of the empire, but the court of the emperor with its dazzling aura was more important than any of these as a centre for integrating the emerging German upper class and its modes of behaviour.

Although the nobility formed the kernel of court society, it was apparently the policy of the imperial court to invite deserving higher-rank public servants to attend certain court functions. I myself remember that, one year, the headmaster of my high school was one of the guests invited to accompany the Kaiser on his annual cruise aboard his yacht.

13 A few misalliances certainly did occur every year, particularly in the higher ranks of nobles, and society talked about them; but by far the largest part of the German nobility married amongst themselves. A few members of the high nobility allied themselves to entrepreneurs, and there was for example a count who renounced his title as a concession to the other side when he took over the management of a large factory. But such cases were relatively rare. The poorer nobles in particular were held back by their fear of the humiliation which going into business would inevitably mean in the eyes of their peers.

14 Hans-Ulrich Wehler, *The German Empire, 1871–1918*, trans. Kim Traynor, Leamington Spa, Berg, 1985, p. 69, gives the following data:

> After 1871, it is true, the time was past when, as in 1858, 42 per cent of all Prussian civil servants in the middle and upper grades had been drawn from the nobility. Even so, around 1910, 9 out of 11 members of the Prussian State Ministry, 38 out of 65 privy councillors, 11 out of 12 senior presidents, 25 out of 36 district presidents, and 271 out of 467 district administrators came from the nobility. In the senior posts of the Foreign Service in 1914 there were 8 princes, 29 counts, 54 nobles without a title and only 11 officials recruited from the middle class. At the same time, 55.5 per cent of all the administrative trainees (*Referendare*) in the Prussian government were nobles; in 1890 it had been 40.4 per cent and in 1900 the figure was 44.6 per cent. In 1918, 55 per cent of *Assessoren* were still recruited from the nobility.

15 Despite all their internal tensions, of which there was no paucity, at the beginning of the twentieth century these aristocratic and middle-class groups between them still formed the German establishment with the greatest power-chances and highest status, the establishment of those entitled to demand satisfaction. Compared with the central part this played in the running of society, the economy (as it would now be called) for the time being played only a secondary part.

Yet if the overall dynamics of society at that time are taken into account it becomes apparent that the power-chances of both economic groups – that is, of all the occupational groups who were interdependent as opponents and who specialized in the production and distribution of goods – were increasing relative to those of the upper classes. Superficially the court society of imperial Germany can easily make it seem as though the age of Louis XIV was not long past. The problem is, in hindsight, to depict the power-chances of the German upper classes in this period as neither too large nor too small. On the one hand, they were anything but the executive organs of the entrepreneurs or the functionaries of the bourgeoisie. On the other hand, their privileged positions of power were very much more under pressure and threat from the ongoing rise of both economic groups, the workers and the entrepreneurs, than had been those of the upper classes under the monarchy in previous centuries. One is led to ask oneself to what extent the leading lights of these upper classes, or even perhaps the majority of their members, were aware of their declining power and increasing defunctionalization.

16 The fact that, in contrast to France for instance, in Germany noble families had always sent some of their sons to university to prepare for a career in the civil service was of crucial importance in the development of the German student code.

17 A closer examination is required of the breakdown by profession of the

members of the alumnus societies, the Old Boys' associations [*Alte-Herren-Verbänden*], in order to establish when and how this gradual change in values took place.

18 Cf. Elias, *The Court Society*.

19 Norbert Elias, *The Civilizing Process*, trans. Edmund Jephcott, Oxford, Blackwell, 1994, chapter 1; see also Elias, 'Das Schicksal der deutschen Barocklyrik: Zwischen höfischer und bürgerlicher Tradition' [The fate of the German Baroque lyric: between courtly and middle-class traditions], *Merkur*, 41, 1987: 451–68.

20 I am conscious that here I am referring in far too compressed a way to a pattern of social development which really requires much longer exposition. I am contrasting the eighteenth-century phase of German development, in which the distinct middle-class movements achieved a relatively high degree of autonomy from the specifically court tradition of the time, with the path of development taken by German society during the *Kaiserzeit*, when sections of the German bourgeoisie submitted to the leadership of groups of the court nobility and absorbed elements of their cultural tradition. In drawing this contrast I am leaving aside what happened in the intervening period, from the beginning of the nineteenth century up to 1871. The development of the relations between nobility and bourgeoisie in that period certainly deserves more attention and more careful study. Nevertheless, the contrast is obvious: in the eighteenth century the duel was definitely not an integral component of the German bourgeois cultural tradition, but after 1871, in the *satisfaktionsfähige Gesellschaft*, it achieved significance as an integral part of the German *national* cultural tradition.

21 See the discussion of the 'royal mechanism' in Elias, *The Civilizing Process*, pp. 390–421, and *The Court Society*, pp. 146–213. [Translators' note]

23 For a fuller discussion of this, see pp. 26–40 of Elias's Introduction to Elias and Dunning, *Quest for Excitement: Sport and Leisure in the Civilizing Process*, Oxford, Blackwell, 1986. [Translators' note]

23 In France, the strength of the army, together with the size of the royal income, normally enabled the king and his generals to carry out their destructive wars for supremacy in Europe outside their own country. The French heartland and Paris in particular were never seriously threatened by enemy powers from the mid-seventeenth century to the end of the eighteenth.

24 One of the conditions which limited German princes' scope for power in relation to the high nobility was Germany's fragmentation into many states, and the alternative possibilities this offered those in the service of a prince. In *ancien régime* France, there was only one court which counted. A high-ranking courtier had no alternatives if he lost the king's favour. In contrast, in Germany when a man of rank lost the favour of a prince, or felt insulted by him, he could leave his court or service and find a place at the court or in the service of another German prince, without having to feel that he was

going into exile and that his life had lost all sparkle and meaning.

There are many examples of such alternative strategies. I can recount one from the Wilhelmine era (cf. Fedor von Zobeltitz, *Chronik der Gesellschaft unter dem letzten Kaiserreich* [Chronicle of Society under the Last Kaiser], 2 vols, Hamburg, Alster Verlag, 1922, vol. I, pp. 133ff). Wilhelm II loved to attract to his court men of the high aristocracy who would bring lustre to it. Among them was Prince Carl Egon von Fürstenberg. He was a member of the original German nobility, being descended in unbroken line from counts and landgraves since the thirteenth century, whose successors had been raised to princes of the Holy Roman Empire in the seventeenth century, until their principality of Fürstenberg was mediatized in the course of the Napoleonic Wars. The Prince von Fürstenberg of the Wilhelmine period, married to a Princess de Talleyrand-Périgord, was immensely rich, relished the good life of court society in Berlin and Potsdam, and was what was in those days known as an enthusiastic sportsman [*begeisteter Sportsmann*], who loved racing, gambling and the life of the smart set. The old Kaiser was very well disposed towards him and his wife. But some years after his accession, the young Kaiser Wilhelm II, who was hasty and impulsive, in the course of his attempts to limit the ever-increasing luxury of life at court and especially among the officers, made a denigrating comment that Prince von Fürstenberg took personally. Thereupon the prince turned his back on the capital, settled on his estates in southern Germany, and left, as people put it, a noticeable gap in Berlin society. The Kaiser attempted to bring the wealthy nobleman back to his court. To begin with, he gave him an honorary rank in the army, and then appointed him to higher and higher court posts. In the course of time the two men were reconciled, and Prince von Fürstenberg and his family returned to Berlin.

25 Where in accordance with its power structures, high value is placed in the behavioural code of a society on strategies of command and obedience, strategies of persuading and convincing people through discussion are understandably accorded low value. In such a milieu, the art of discussion has no great chance of developing, and skill in the use of appropriate strategies suffers. Very noticeable in the German tradition is the habituation to strategies of command and obedience – quite often through direct or indirect use of physical strength – and, until recently, the comparatively low level of skill in debate as a heritage from the long period of absolute or near-absolute rule. Unease with the relatively complicated restraint of affect which is required in solving conflicts solely through discussion, and, conversely, a feeling of ease with simpler command and obedience strategies, can still be observed today in Germany.

In my book *The Civilizing Process*, p. 482–3, I have illustrated a corresponding difference in social strategies using the example of two French opposition aristocrats at the beginning and end of the seventeenth century.

The Duc de Montmorency openly rebelled against the king and pursued his aims in the style of the warrior in bodily combat, whereas the Duc de Saint-Simon, in the style of the courtier, endeavoured to use intrigue and persuasion with the heir to the throne.

26 Ludwig Hassel, *Die letzten Stunden des Polizeidirektors von Hinckeldey: Beitrag zu seinem Nekrolog von einem Augenzeugen* [The Last Hours of Police-Chief Hinckeldey: a Contribution to his Obituary by an Eyewitness], Leipzig, Brockhaus, 1856. I am quoting the account of the affair given by Zobeltitz, *Chronik der Gesellschaft unter dem letzten Kaiserreich*, vol. I, pp. 208–10.

27 Cf. Norbert Elias, 'Zum Begriff des Alltags' [On the concept of the everyday], in Kurt Hammerich and Michael Klein, eds, *Materialien zur Soziologie des Alltags* [Materials on the Sociology of the Everyday], Köln, Westdeutscher Verlag, 1978, pp. 22–9. (Special Issue no. 20 of the *Kölner Zeitschrift für Soziologie und Sozialpsychologie.*)

28 Indeed, in early literature, no distinction was made between *duellum* and *bellum*; they are two forms of the same word. Only during the process of state-formation, with the increasing monopolization of the use of physical violence by a central ruler, do people come to be able to differentiate between war as an act of violence formally declared and organized from the lofty standpoint of a head of state, and the duel as a, so to speak, lower-level, privately declared and privately organized act of violence.

29 It is perhaps useful to add that in the course of the nineteenth century, and especially with the integration of high-ranking middle-class civil servants and professors into the court society of the *Kaiserreich*, the handling of affairs of honour came to permit a more tolerant interpretation of the code of honour, especially in the case of civilians. When at the beginning of 1894 the dashing Baron von Stumm-Hallberg challenged the well-known privy councillor Adolf Wagner to a duel, Wagner requested that a court of honour be set up. He declared he was quite prepared to take back those of his utterances which the Baron von Stumm felt to be insulting, if von Stumm would show the same willingness with respect to his own insulting remarks. As far as can be ascertained, the court of honour upheld his appeal: the duel did not take place. In the society in which Baron von Stumm moved, the conduct of the scholar was considered dishonourable, but since he kept strictly to the rules of the code of honour in his proceedings, they could not formally fault him. (From Zobeltitz, *Chronik der Gesellschaft unter dem letzten Kaiserreich*, vol. I, p. 10.)

30 Cf. W.H.R. Rivers, 'The psychological factor', in W. H. R. Rivers, ed., *The Depopulation of Melanesia*, Cambridge, Cambridge University Press, 1922, pp. 84–113.

31 Zobeltitz, *Chronik der Gesellschaft unter dem letzten Kaiserreich*, vol. I, pp. 138–40.

32 Ibid., vol. I, pp. 144.

33 Ibid., vol. I, pp. 124f.
34 Ibid., vol. I, pp. 77f.
35 Ibid., vol. I, pp. 5f.
36 Ibid., vol. II, p. 318.
37 Ibid., vol. II, p. 309.
38 Ibid., vol. II, pp. 351f.
39 *Koofmich* is a Berlin dialect word for *Kaufmann*, 'tradesman'. [Translators' note]
40 Zobeltitz, *Chronik der Gesellschaft unter dem letzten Kaiserreich*, vol. I, p. 69.
41 Cf. Hermann Haupt, 'Karl Follen', in *Hundert Jahre Deutscher Burschenschaft: Burschenschaftliche Lebensläufe* [One Hundred Years of the German Students Duelling Associations: Careers in the Associations], vol. VII of Hermann Haupt and Paul Wentzcke, eds, *Quellen und Darstellungen zur Geschichte der deutschen Burschenschaften und der deutschen Einheitsbewegung* [Sources and Accounts for the History of the German Student Duelling Associations and the Unification Movement], Heidelberg, C. Winter, 1921, p. 27.
42 Friedrich Ludwig Jahn (1778–1852), German nationalist agitator during the Napoleonic period, who tried to organize popular movements to spread national awareness and mobilize resistance to France. In 1811, in Berlin, he founded a gymnastics society, defining his intention as 'protecting young people from softness and excess in order to keep them sturdy in the coming struggle for the Fatherland' (quoted by James Riordan, in E.G. Dunning, J. Maguire and R.E. Pearton, eds, *The Sports Process*, Champaign, Ill., Human Kinetics Publishers, 1993, p. 247). His gymnasts were disbanded by the Prussian authorities after the Congress of Vienna. See also George L. Mosse, *The Nationalization of the Masses: Political Symbolism and Mass Movements in Germany from the Napoleonic Wars through the Third Reich*, New York, H. Fertig, 1975. [Translators' note]
43 Wilhelm Hopf, 'Turnte Turnvater Jahn?' [Did Jahn, the Father of Gymnastics, actually do gymnastics?'], *päd. extra*, 11, 1978, pp. 39ff.
44 Zobeltitz, *Chronik der Gesellschaft unter dem letzten Kaiserreich*, vol. I, p. 47.
45 With the changing position of the nationalist fraternities from being outsider groups in relation to the upper-class establishments of their society to being groups within the hierarchy of this establishment and sharing its outlook, there was a corresponding change in the relationship of the students in these corporations towards the older generations, especially to former members who were now in high positions. After 1871, increasing numbers of former fraternity members formed Old Boys' associations. From the 1880s onwards, these associations gradually won greater influence over the fraternities. They financed fraternity houses, which became more numerous as a result of the

pressure of competition among the fighting fraternities and of the improved economic situation of the relevant strata in the Wilhelmine period. Also as a consequence of the competition for status, the fraternity houses became increasingly luxurious. Georg Heer (in Paul Wentzcke and Georg Heer, *Geschichte der deutschen Burschenschaft* [History of the German Student Duelling Associations], Heidelberg, C. Winter, 1939, vol. IV, p. 65) writes, 'At first, these houses were still fairly simple. . . . From about 1900, they became ever more spacious and better fitted out; a true competitive zeal emerged amongst all student fraternities, not only the nationalist fraternities, to set up magnificent buildings.'

46 The training in duelling, that is, in a formal, precisely regulated type of violence, was certainly important in itself. It met the needs of young men, who in Britain during the same period for instance found satisfaction in competitive sports. But at the same time, it prepared them for a society in which, for men, the possibility of being challenged or having to challenge to a duel was ever-present. (Incidentally, it was only on 26 May 1933 that a law was passed legalizing student fencing matches with rapiers.)

47 *Einen* or *den Salamander reiben*: 'student usage [meaning] to scrape one's glass three times on the table, empty it, and after brief drumming put it down with a bang (as a mark of honour)', *Oxford Duden German Dictionary*, Oxford, Clarendon Press, 1990, p. 618. [Translators' note]

48 Wentzke and Heer, *Geschichte der deutschen Burschenschaft*, p. 47.

49 Ibid., pp. 82f:

> It was still exceptional in the 1870s for fencing matches to be discussed in the convocations of each fraternity. Later, it became common practice after every fencing match to convene a so-called fencing convocation which mercilessly punished every mistake that a member made, the judgement often resting on the opinion of a single observer. And the observers at the fencing competition hardly did anything else but watch with tense concentration how their own fraternity brother acquitted himself. . . . Anyone who fought in a way considered to be 'technically' or even 'morally' inadequate was punished, the first time usually only with a warning and a 'name-clearing match', but quite often with permanent expulsion. If the 'name-clearing' duel were also unsuccessful, or in general a later fencing competition inadequate, then the offender would be expelled.

50 Ibid., p. 82.

51 Ibid., p. 85.

52 There is also a clear-cut difference with respect to the duel: court ceremonial, which on the whole took place in the residence of the prince or in his presence, precluded open disputes. So even the formalized settling of disputes

in duels had there to take place behind the scenes. In contrast, among students, the mutual threat through conflict and matters of honour lay closer to the surface. Despite the legal prohibition, it was basically barely concealed.

53 Bloem, *Der krasse Fuchs*, p. 89.

54 Ibid., p. 11. Similarly, in the account of the Marburg Museum Association Ball (pp. 92f):

> And the mothers and headmistresses watched the goings on, smiling, peaceful ... the young things should enjoy life ... even if that meant the occasional rendezvous and a few kisses ... after all, the young ladies were not seriously in danger from the students ... for that, there were other girls ... easier, less dangerous possibilities.

55 Ibid., p. 13.

56 Ibid., p. 154.

57 Ibid., p. 158ff.

58 The fencing match by appointment (*Bestimmungsmensur*) is a good example of the transience of such convictions. In the light of further developments, it appears to be rather functionless, a product of the unplanned development of a code from which people bound by the code cannot escape. They are entrapped in it.

59 H. Pachnicke, *Führende Männer des alten und neuen Reichs* [Leading Men of the Old and New Empires], Berlin, Reiner Hobbing, 1930, p. 13; see also von Heydebrand, 'Beiträge zu einer Geschichte der konservativen Partei in den letzten 30 Jahren (1888–1919)', [Contributions to a History of the Conservative Party in the Last 30 Years (1888–1919)], *Konservative Monatsschrift*, 1920: 607.

60 This unconditional aspect of the behaviour of warriors, the expectation that warriors must fight to the end for their side in order to preserve their honour, is an ideal which has played a fairly central role in the European tradition. So it is perhaps interesting that the Japanese warrior code offered, to a man who found himself confronting in battle a superior power he obviously could not defeat, a way out that was not present in the European warrior tradition, or at least not part of the code. It was possible for Japanese warriors in a completely hopeless situation to join the former enemy and to serve him with the same total devotion as they did their former lord.

The extent to which warrior traditions can become national traditions can also be seen in this case. It seems obvious to think that Japan's extraordinary ability to assimilate to the victors of the Second World War was linked, among other things, with the fact that according to the traditional mode of superego formation, becoming more like an irrefutably stronger opponent as a life strategy was not charged with deep feelings of guilt and inferiority – this adaptation was, so to speak, one of the permitted life strategies.

61 See the discussion of the 'Sociogenesis of the difference between *Kultur* and *Zivilisation* in German usage', in *The Civilizing Process*, pp. 3–28. [Translators' note]

62 Friedrich Nietzsche, *The Antichrist*, ed. and trans. Walter Kaufman, in *The Portable Nietzsche*, New York, Viking, 1954, p. 570. [Translators' note: text slightly modified]

Notes to Part II

1 See Elias's discussion of 'process reduction' as an affliction of modern sociology in *What is Sociology?*, trans. Stephen Mennell and Grace Morrissey, New York, Columbia University Press, 1978, pp. 111ff; see also his castigation of the related but more general 'Retreat of sociologists into the present', *Theory, Culture & Society*, 4 (2–3), 1987: 223–47. [Translators' note]

2 Friedrich Schiller, 'Was heißt und zu welchem Ende studiert man Universalgeschichte?' [What does universal history mean and why do we study it?], in *Schillers Werke* [The Works of Schiller], Nationalausgabe, Weimar, Herman Bölhous Nachfolger, 1970, vol. 17, part 1, pp. 365, 367ff.

3 Ibid., p. 370.

4 Jacob Burckhardt, *The Civilisation of the Renaissance in Italy*, trans. Middlemore, Oxford, Phaidon, 1945. (Originally published in German in 1860.) [Translators' note]

5 Eberhard Gothein, *Die Aufgaben der Kulturgeschichte* [The Tasks of Cultural History], Leipzig, Duncker und Humblot, 1889, pp. 2 ff.

6 Dietrich Schäfer, *Deutsches Nationalbewußtsein im Licht der Geschichte* [German National Consciousness in the Light of History], Jena, Fischer 1884, pp. 1ff.

7 Particularly strong expressions of this change in identity feelings can be clearly observed during the French Revolution. One of the best known literary expressions of this transition to a value and belief system which lifts the image of the nation to the highest rank can be found in E.J. Sieyès, *What is the Third Estate?*, first published 1789, here quoted in the translation by M. Blondel, London, Pall Mall Press, 1963. A characteristic expression of the new stress on the nation is this:

The nation is prior to everything. It is the source of everything. Its will is always legal; indeed it is the law itself. Prior to and above the nation, there is only the natural law.

Sieyès represents the rising middle classes in the literal sense of the word, the classes in the middle between the privileged estates – in France, the nobility and the clergy – and 'the poor' who did not earn enough to contribute to the upkeep of the state. Theoretically Sieyès still held firmly to the ideal of the equality of all human beings which was used as a weapon of the rising middle classes in their struggle with the privileged estates above them. But in practice, in his proposals for the new constitution, he wanted to limit the right to vote for the national assembly to those citizens who could contribute at least three livres a year in taxes. The main front on which Sieyès as representative of the 'classes in the middle' fought, though, was in the revolutionary situation the front against the privileged ruling classes, against kings, nobles and clergy: 'What then is "The Third Estate"? All; but an all that is fettered and oppressed' (p. 57).

Sentences such as this show clearly how the beginnings of an identification with the 'nation' already heralded specific changes in the emotional atmosphere. One encountered here – in an age whose mode of thinking in many areas was becoming more realistic or 'rational' and less emotional – the rise of a new mystique, related not to 'nature' but to 'society', the rise of a new belief system centred on an ideal image of one's own nation, a compound of fact and fantasy. The difference in atmosphere becomes particularly clear if one compares these and other expressions of the rising nationalist belief system with the attitudes of authors such as Machiavelli to the relations between dynastic states which were not yet conceived as nations.

8 In a chapter of *The Prince* which has the heading, 'In what manner Princes should keep their faith', Machiavelli wrote:

> You must know, therefore, that there are two ways of carrying on a contest; the one by law and the other by force. The first is practised by men, and the other by animals; and as the first is often insufficient, it becomes necessary to resort to the second.
>
> A prince then should know how to employ the nature of man and that of beasts as well. This was figuratively taught by ancient writers, who relate how Achilles and many other princes were given to Chiron the centaur to be nurtured, and how they were trained under his tutorship; which fable means nothing else than that their preceptor combined the qualities of the man and the beast, and that a prince, to succeed, will have to employ both the one and the other nature, as the one without the other cannot produce lasting results.
>
> It being necessary then for a prince to know well how to employ the nature of the beasts, he should be able to assume both that of the fox and that of the lion; for whilst the latter cannot escape the traps laid for him, the former cannot defend himself against the wolves. A prince should be a fox, to know the traps and snares; and a lion, to be able to frighten the wolves; for those who simply hold to the nature of the lion do not understand their business.
>
> A sagacious prince then cannot and should not fulfil his pledges

when their observance is contrary to his interest, and when the causes that induced him to pledge his faith no longer exist. If men were all good, then indeed this precept would be bad; but as men are naturally bad, and will not observe their faith towards you, you must, in the same way, not observe yours to them; and no prince ever yet lacked legitimate reasons with which to colour his want of good faith. Innumerable modern examples could be given of this; and it could easily be shown how many treaties of peace, and how many engagements, have been made null and void by the faithlessness of princes; and he who has best known how to play the fox has ever been the most successful.

(From *The Living Thoughts of Machiavelli*, London, Cassell, 1942, pp. 65–6.)

9 Nationalism, as an expression of love towards, pride in, and identification with a particular we-unit, is different from the apparently similar ties of traditional aristocratic groups. Bismarck, for instance, is often taken as the prototype of German nationalism. In fact his love was directed in the first instance to king and country, not to the German nation as a symbolic representation of the mass of the German people as a whole – although, since he lived in a period of transition, he had to pay belated lip-service to it as an ideal when the need arose.

10 Henri Bergson, *The Two Sources of Morality and Religion*, trans. R. Ashley Audra and Cloudesley Brereton, with the assistance of W. Horsfall Carter, London, Macmillan, 1935. (Originally published in French in 1932.)

11 Ibid., p. 20.

12 Machiavelli, *The Living Thoughts of Machiavelli*, pp. 65–6.

13 Kingsley Davies, *Human Society*, New York, Macmillan, 1965, pp. 10ff.

14 Even Victorian Britain, often regarded as a society ruled by the industrial middle classes, had a much more complex power structure. Only from the viewpoint of the country's industrial working classes could its industrial middle classes appear as the leading groups. Seen in the context of British society and its development as a whole, tensions and conflicts between the rising middle and the traditional upper classes were hardly less great than those between the latter and the groups who were referred to by contemporaries as 'the masses' or 'the workers'.

So far as inter-state politics are concerned, the precedence of dynastic-aristocratic traditions in Victorian Britain in comparison with continental states had a different stamp only insofar as, in the British power strategy, a navy and not a land army played to a large extent the more important role. In addition, the army did not consist of conscripted citizens but, as in previous centuries, of mercenaries who were recruited, mainly voluntarily, from the circles of the poor. Besides, thanks to its naval superiority, the principal expansionary thrust of Britain was directed at the acquisition or control of territories outside Europe. Small troop contingents, supported by warships, superior weapons and superior knowledge, were enough for the conquest of vast territories inhabited by societies at a less advanced level of development.

These and other aspects of the special position occupied by Britain in the context of European inter-state rivalries are responsible for the fact that the nationalization of the British people in the proper sense of the term began somewhat later than the comparable processes in Germany and France. As long as the expansion and the wars were directed at less developed, non-European societies and executed using mercenary armies, the mass of the British people were not too much affected. The middle-class intelligentsia could still understand these wars under the sign of a 'civilizing mission' as defined by Matthew Arnold: 'Civilization is the humanization of man in society' (M. Arnold, *Mixed Essays: Works*, London, Edition de Luxe, 1904, vol. 10, p. vi). Or if they were familiar with features of the British colonial expansion which contravened the standards of middle-class humanism, they could still criticize their country with a freedom which would have made outcasts or traitors of members of continental societies such as Germany and France, where, largely in conjunction with contingencies connected with reasons of state, the nationalization of feelings and ideals had already gone much further. An example is provided by the bitter outburst of Wilfred Scawen Blunt against the failure of Britain's policy in Egypt ('The wind and the whirlwind', 1883, in *The Poetical Works of Wilfrid Scawen Blunt*, London, Macmillan 1914, vol. 2, p. 233):

> Thou art become a by-word for dissembling,
>   A beacon to thy neighbours for all fraud.
> Thy deeds of violence men count and reckon.
>   Who takes the sword shall perish by the sword.
> Thou has deserved men's hatred. They shall hate thee.
>   Thou hast deserved men's fear. Their fear shall kill.
> Thou hast thy foot upon the weak. The weakest
>   With his bruised head shall strike thee on the heel.
> Thou wentest to this Egypt for thy pleasure.
>   Thou shalt remain with her for thy sore pain.
> Thou hast possessed her beauty. Thou wouldst leave her
>   Nay. Thou shalt lie with her as thou hast lain.

What appeared in the eyes of the people brought up in the tradition of middle-class morality to be hypocrisy, deceit and violence was, in fact, a normal distinguishing mark of a dynastic and aristocratic warrior tradition. In the interests of one's own rule and one's own country – for princes and noble ruling elites, and the two were inextricably related – all these means counted as necessary and unavoidable weapons in the permanent struggle with other rulers and other countries in accordance with the traditional upper-class code. Such weapons were used in inter-state relations in a quite taken-for-granted way. Only in an age when rising industrial classes, with middle-class elites as their vanguard, were fighting the traditional upper classes on a broader front for equal status and a share in governmental power did the former begin to turn openly and in many cases with considerable sharpness against the Machiavellian means of statesmanship. Presumably in Britain there are more examples of open conflict between the spokespersons of a humanistic, moral code and those of a Machiavellian code than is the case in continental countries where the pressure to conform with the nationalistic credo and the frowning upon nonconformity began earlier.

The first great wave of nationalism in Britain seems to have been connected with the Boer War and the siege of Mafeking. There took place at that time the formation and spread of a unified belief system which moved the nation as symbol of an unarguable value into the centre and in which the, as the people then saw it, indispensable requirements of statecraft were more or less successfully combined with the expectations of the educated masses from the middle and working classes that the nation, that the state and its representatives, would satisfy the ideal form of a moral and humanistic standard of the kind they had to follow in a less perfect form in their domestic social dealings.

15 Cited in John Drinkwater, *Patriotism in Literature*, London, Williams & Norgate, 1924, pp. 244–5.

16 The perception of long-term changes of this kind is often obscured by a lack of clarity regarding the criteria to be used. In many cases, a sharp enough distinction is not made between the rise of an individual from one estate or class into another, without any change in the relative positions of these strata, and a change in the positions of superordination and subordination of different social strata as such. As a result, the two types of occurrence are not clearly researched in their relation to each other. Such a distinction is crucial for investigation into the traditions, 'cultures', specific norms, standards and beliefs of different strata. Individual rise normally has as its consequence that the upwardly mobile individual gives up the 'culture' of his/her 'stratum of origin' and takes on that of the stratum to which he/she aspires. Or rather, it is the upwardly mobile family which thus crosses over in the course of two or three generations into another culture. ('It takes three generations to make a gentleman.') By contrast, the rise of a whole social stratum, its increase in status and power relative to others, may indeed involve a further development of its 'culture' but it does not unconditionally involve a break with its traditions. It is quite consistent with a continuity in

the development of traditional norms, standards and beliefs, even when the absorption of elements of the tradition of a previously superior stratum or a fairly extensive mixing of cultures are involved. In this latter case, the specific process of change in the relative power-chances of the rising and falling strata is decisive for the form and manner in which the two cultures influence each other and for the type of mixture which finally results.

Notes to Part III

1 If, as here, one contrasts civilization with violence, with the sort of violence people inflict upon each other in wars, in political struggles, in private life, or whatever, then one narrows the image one has of civilization from the beginning. One delimits the concept in such a way that actually only one of its aspects is considered: the non-violent co-existence of humans. But living together in a civilized way includes very much more than just non-violence. It includes not just the negative aspect implied by the disappearance of acts of violence from human relationships, but also an entire field of positive characteristics, above all the specific moulding of individuals in groups which can only take place when the threat that people will attack each other physically, or force others through their stronger muscles or better weapons to do things they would not otherwise do, has been banished from their social relations. The civilizing moulding of individuals in pacified territories is reflected in the arts with which people please each other, in the sport-games with which they put each other to the test without injuring each other, in travelling and wandering through pacified regions, and in many other things. No pacification is possible as long as the distribution of wealth is very uneven, and the power ratios are too different. And, vice versa, no long-term affluence is possible without stable pacification.

2 Asking the wrong sort of questions is also linked to the currently widespread tendency to attribute the conflicts between people, and the inner conflicts which arise from them, to an inborn aggressiveness of humans. The idea that humans have an inborn drive to attack other humans, an aggressive instinct, which is similar in structure to other inborn drives, such as the sexual drive, is unfounded. Humans possess an inborn potential for automatically switching their entire bodily apparatus to another gear if they feel they are in danger. Sometimes it is called an alarm reaction. The body reacts to the dangerous experience with an automatic adaptation which prepares it for intensive movements of the skeletal muscles, especially for fight or flight. Human impulses which correspond to the model of an instinct are triggered off physiologically, that is, as it is often put, 'from within', relatively independently of the given situation. The switching of the bodily economy into preparedness for fight or flight is determined to a far greater extent by

specific situations, whether they are present here and now, or remembered.

The potential for aggression can be activated by natural and social situations of specific types, above all by conflicts. As a deliberate challenge to Konrad Lorenz and other researchers who attribute to humans an instinct of aggression analogous to the sexual drive, I would like to suggest, perhaps somewhat bluntly, that *it is not aggression which triggers conflicts, but conflicts which trigger aggression*. Our habits of thought lead us to expect that everything we have to explain about humans can be explained by reference to an isolated individual. The attunement of thinking, and thus of what one expects an explanation to look like, to the way in which people are bound together in groups (that is, to social structures) is evidently difficult. Conflicts are an aspect of such structures, that is, of the living together of humans with humans. Furthermore, they are an aspect of humans' life together with animals, plants, moon and sun, in short, with non-human nature. Humans are geared by nature towards this life together with people and nature, and the conflicts which are part of it.

3 Put briefly, the form of social life within a state and the pacification which it entails are themselves based on violence. The polarity between civilization and violence, which might seem too absolute at first glance, is revealed on closer examination to be relative. What is hidden behind it is the difference between people who threaten others with violence or use weapons and brawn in the name of the state and protected by the law, and people who do the same without permission of the state and without protection of the law.

4 I have presented an explanatory model of its development in *The Civilizing Process*, trans. Edmund Jephcott, Oxford, Blackwell, 1994.

5 On this matter and this concept, see Norbert Elias, *Involvement and Detachment*, Oxford, Blackwell, 1987; see also Norbert Elias, *Humana Conditio*, Frankfurt am Main, Suhrkamp, 1985.

6 But these specialists in violence can also be deployed to support a social stratum or specific party in their struggles with others in intra-state conflicts. As I have already said, the violence-monopoly is Janus-faced.

Besides, it is the very same people who are, on the one hand, brought up to a relatively high level of civilization, to a comparatively strong aversion to the use of physical force in intra-state relations, and who, on the other hand, for instance as conscripts in the armed forces, are trained to become specialists in killing in inter-state affairs. The difference in the level of civilization in domestic and foreign relations of today's state-societies is accordingly reflected in specific personal imbalances and conflicts of those affected. It is expressed in their personality structure. In times of peace, within the pacified spaces where acts of violence are punished, people are trained for war in which acts of violence are allowed and demanded. The survivors return from war, in which they have grown used to all sorts of violence, to the pacified spaces of their state-societies. It is expected of them that they will adjust themselves in a flash to the non-violence demanded there. But often enough that cannot be done so quickly. The flood of violent wars carries waves of violence into the pacified state-societies often over generations.

7 This code had been formed in the officers' practice, extending over several generations, of an aristocracy which was often not very well-off. That war was a bloody business was taken for granted in these groups. One killed enemies, when necessary burned down their houses, lived off the land, and most certainly also plundered. But for officers, there were at the same time certain rules, a code of behaviour which was also observed in relation to enemies, especially those of one's own class. For the nobility, war was a type of profession. However much one might hate one's opponent, conduct towards him was by and large determined by a relatively uniform gentleman's code which remained binding for as good as all officers of European states into the nineteenth century, and perhaps into the early twentieth century.

8 Not only individual people but also groups of people such as classes or nations learn from their experiences. As a correlate of inter-generational continuity there is therefore something like a collective memory in social groups. One of the fundamental collective experiences of wide sectors of the bourgeoisie of the Wilhelmine empire was the memory that the long-cherished unification of Germany was not accomplished peacefully, through reason and a bourgeois revolution against the supremacy of the princes and the aristocracy, but instead through a military victory over France under the leadership of the aristocracy. The about-turn which occurred in considerable parts of the German bourgeoisie because of this collective experience can be expressed, perhaps at the risk of a degree of oversimplification, in the following way. It was as though many of its members said: 'All our beautiful ideals have been of no use to us. What has brought us out of the depths up into the heights and thus to the goal for which we had striven for so long was military force, military violence. Obviously, this is what counts in the end in human affairs. The beautiful, great words of Schiller, Goethe and the others, with their appeal to humankind and humanity – all that helped us very little. In the end, what helped was only fighting, the will to power and firmness of resolve.'

9 Walter Bloem, *Volk wider Volk* [Nation against Nation], Leipzig, H. Fikentscher, 1912, pp. 326f.

10 I myself, just 17 years old, experienced these feelings as something strange and not quite comprehensible. But I had schoolfriends and acquaintances who, unlike me, shared this prevailing mood.

11 *Kriegsbriefe gefallener Studenten* [Letters from Active Service by Fallen Students], ed. Philipp Witkop, Munich, Müller, 1929, pp. 7f.

12 By and large, for many members of the old ruling strata it appeared to be a break with German tradition, a narrowing of their own rights to rule, that

representatives of these groups which had previously stood clearly below them now took over governing functions. The parliamentary regime in line with Western models – which was condoned and supported by the Allies, the enemies of yesterday – appeared to them to be doubly reprehensible: because it was promoted by the Western enemies, and because it seemed designed to secure for representatives of the working class lasting access to governmental positions and thus to open up to them power-chances which they had never possessed in Germany.

One can understand this contrast as an expression of a class conflict – but not a class conflict as portrayed in books. The often civil-war-like tensions accompanied by violence in the early part of the Weimar Republic between different camps in the German population do not correspond exactly to the rather simplified image of such conflicts outlined by Marx. In his scenario, factories stand at the centre-point of class conflicts; they form the focus of the tensions between the bourgeoisie and the working class. At their core, these tensions seem to be simply an expression of the opposing economic interests of industrial entrepreneurs and industrial workers. In Marx's time, that was perhaps an adequate diagnosis, although, of course, even then the factory was an apparatus for ruling and the struggles for economic opportunities formed one aspect – albeit a very central aspect – of a power struggle. In the course of the twentieth century, however, tensions and conflicts on the political level gained increasing significance relative to those on the factory level. And access to ruling positions, as to a whole series of other positions in state and city administration, which representatives of the workers had attained in Germany (as in Britain) after the 1914–18 war, played a considerable part in the division of power-chances between these two social groups.

When in an established–outsider relationship with a steep power gradient the distribution of power weightings shifts somewhat in favour of the outsider groups, without eliminating the power superiority of the established, then with great regularity the tension between the two camps is sharpened – though often not obviously. The fact that the previous subordinate groups, including in this case the representatives of workers' parties, had won access to the deciding command positions of the state, and through this to many middling and lower positions in the administrative hierarchy, was not perceived in many bourgeois-noble circles of the old establishment as a significant step towards the integration of the working class into the nation, but merely as a restriction of their own leading position, as a reduction of their self-worth, as a destruction of their ideals.

13 Both goals, the domestic as well as the foreign one, had hardly anything to do with the factual power relations, and thus had to a large degree the character of wishful thinking. With the increasing industrialization of Germany, the power-ratio of entrepreneurs and other capital-owning groups,

but also of the industrial working class, had risen. It would require extraordinary conditions – such as a particularly severe economic crisis accompanied by high unemployment – in order to succeed in destroying the central power-resources of the working class, their professional and political organizations. Whether that would have been possible in the longer term under conditions of relative peace remains a moot point. It is just as questionable whether, in a period in which the rise of the United States to a position of global supremacy was already heralded, the power-ratio of Germany would have been sufficient to win hegemony in Europe against the resistance of America and its allies. That course of action was most certainly out of the question if the German leadership acted in a way so as to drive the professed rivals, Russia and America, into each other's arms in order to fight Germany together.

When the seductive dream of the destiny of one's own land becoming great and holding a position of world-supremacy, or having a mission encompassing all people, takes hold of the ruling groups of a nation and all those who identify with them, then there is seldom any other humanly less wasteful path than social and military defeat. In that way, the groups in question can be woken from their dream and the narcissistic delusion of the superior worth of their nation, compared with all other peoples, and the related striving for hegemony, can be extinguished. That in Germany two severe defeats of its self-aggrandizing leading strata were necessary in order to lower the pitch of the national image and the corresponding goals of German politics to a more realistic level was certainly partly related to the attraction that the goal of world power possessed especially for a nation which had long suffered from weakness.

14 Pseudo-Xenophon, *Athēnaiōn politeia*, 1, 5, in *Xenophon* (Collected Works) VII, *Scripta minora*, London and Cambridge, Mass., 1968 (Loeb Classical Library 183), pp. 476f. On the general pattern of such established–outsider relationships, see Norbert Elias and J.L. Scotson, *The Established and the Outsiders: a Sociological Enquiry into Community Problems*, London, Frank Cass, 1965; 2nd edn with a new theoretical introduction, London, Sage, 1994 (the quotation from Pseudo-Xenophon is on pp. xxv–xxvi).

15 Emil Julius Gumbel, *Verschwörer* [Conspirators], Vienna, Malik-Verlag, 1924, p. 14.

16 Ibid., p. 45.

17 The guerrillas had a well-known song:

> Shoot down Walter Rathenau,
> The god-damned Jewish sow!

They had sung it and then done it. The cult of brutality and the high value accorded to physical violence, which had already started to flourish among the bourgeois youth of Wilhelmine Germany, was now a full-strength part of the culture of the *Freikorps*. They represented to the highest degree the anti-civilization, anti-moral standards of that neo-bourgeois tradition which idealized violence. Under the National Socialist regime it found its consummate expression. There are also signs that the young German terrorists of our time fit into this tradition.

18 Gumbel, *Verschwörer*, p. 29.

19 Ibid., p. 27.

20 Friedrich Wilhelm von Oertzen, *Kamerad reich mir die Hände* [Comrade, Give Me Your Hands], Berlin, Ullstein, 1933, p. 156.

21 Ibid., pp. 158f.

22 In the comments of the upper strata at this time, the lower strata appear again in two guises: as the people, who are in principle good-natured, friendly and obedient, rather like the loyal and subordinate non-commissioned officers and men encountered by army officers in the war; and at the same time as the people, who, after the war, proved to be rebellious, antagonistic or even violent and dangerous. This difference between the two guises of 'the people' was then explained by maintaining that the fundamentally good-natured people had been stirred up and incited mainly by Bolshevik agitators.

23 Ernst von Salomon, *Die Geächteten* [The Outlaws], Berlin, Rowohlt, 1931.

24 Ibid., p. 69.

25 Closer examination reveals three levels in the guerrillas' dreams which were intertwined in a complex way. The guerrillas needed a livelihood, an income, a career; they needed a *group*, which offered the youth of mobile societies which were less dependent on family cohesion a second home, a shield against loneliness, an answer to the need for love, friendship, confirmation of self-esteem through the affection or regard of other people; and they needed the feeling of having a task over and above their own existence, a task *which could create meaning*.

26 The *Wandervögel* were a youth movement in Germany before the First World War, and the *Pachants* were one of their sections. [Translators' note]

27 Salomon, *Die Geächteten*, p. 109.

28 Ibid., p. 110.

29 Many Germans, and therefore most of the guerrillas, hated the new state and the new society, because quite simply it contradicted their concept of the greatness and pride of Germany to stand there as losers. The old vision of a united and strong Germany which eventually came true in 1871 made it impossible for them to recognize that their country had succumbed to superior military power and was not defeated because of some internal betrayal.

Furthermore, the legend of the so-called 'stab in the back' was a very effective pattern of stigmatization which served at the same time as an alibi, as a means of exonerating the old German establishment, and as a weapon in the fight against the rising outsider masses of the working class. It freed Hindenburg and the entire regime of the Kaiser from any responsibility for the defeat and its consequences for the German people; and it laid the blame for the defeat firmly on the shoulders of groups of people who were regarded as of lower social standing and who had now, as an unintended consequence of the war, gained a considerable increase in power. As in other cases, the forces of the stigmatization corresponded to the power-ratio in the relation between the established and the outsiders (cf. Elias and Scotson, *The Established and the Outsiders*).

One asks oneself if some things in the development of Germany might not have turned out differently if the high military men, particularly Hindenburg in person, had publicly taken responsibility for the defeat and for the decision to sign the Treaty of Versailles. Instead, they dissociated themselves from the decision to sign the treaty, and thus kept open the option for a new armed encounter when the time was ripe. Symptomatic of this is the episode when Ebert telephoned Hindenburg and wanted to know from him whether the government should accept the conditions of the peace treaty, or whether the supreme military command thought there was still a chance for military resistance. Hindenburg left the room, and it was left to his deputy, General Groener, to inform the president that, in the opinion of the supreme military command, military resistance was not possible (for the details, cf. Gordon A. Craig, *The Politics of the Prussian Army*, Oxford, Clarendon Press, 1964, pp. 372f). Ebert and the other party representatives whose unavoidable duty it was to sign the treaty were widely stigmatized for a decision which in the end should have rested with Hindenburg.

30 For example Oertzen, *Kamerad reich mir die Hände*, p. 131.
31 Salomon, *Die Geächteten*, pp. 144f.
32 It is no coincidence that in the course of the 1920s the leadership of the terrorist extra-parliamentary fight against the parliamentary German republic passed from the *Freikorps*, with their still perceptible tradition of the Wilhelmine officer society, to the armed bands of the National Socialist Party. In highly differentiated industrialized nation-states, the power potential of the broad mass of the population in relation to the government is already too large for a government to be able to fulfil its functions without the ideological concurrence – whether manipulated or not – of considerable parts of the ruled. Concurrence is achieved and maintained by means of a party organization incorporating large sections of the population, at the top of which stand those who are the rulers at any given time. The multi-party parliamentary and one-party dictatorially ruled republics are forms of social organization at the same level of development of human society. The necessity of mass parties as linking, bridging organizations between rulers

and ruled did not exist in territorial states in earlier centuries, and is symptomatic of the compelling character of the process which I have called 'functional democratization' (cf. Norbert Elias, *What is Sociology?*, trans. Stephen Mennell and Grace Morrissey, New York, Columbia University Press, p. 63).

33 Much of what is characteristic of the later wave of terrorism can also be shown in the example of the earlier one – perhaps even a bit more clearly because one is able to view the social situation in the earlier period with a higher degree of detachment. In looking at the later events, their implication in acute party struggles can easily distort recognition of the key issues regarding the reasons for the emergence of terrorist groups and the explanation for their development. In particular, the simple fact is more easily brought to light with respect to the Weimar period that one must take into consideration the specific social situation in which such organizations develop in order to explain their emergence. It would perhaps sound rather strange if one were to content oneself with explaining the acts of violence of German terrorists of the 1920s using the same model as has often been used to explain the terrorism of the 1970s, that it is, for example, a result of reading certain books or of the ideas of certain teachers.

34 A little researched and hardly noticed change in our society is reflected in the mirror of the terrorist movement: breaking through the state monopoly of force has, up until recently, been a male privilege. The female terrorist is, with only a few exceptions, something new. It is not just a question of acts of violence committed under the spontaneous or repressed pressure of a personal hatred – there have always been those among women as well as men. It is a question of relatively impersonal, coolly thought out acts of violence executed by women and men together.

35 This different positioning on the political spectrum was connected with a further difference between the two terrorist movements: the financing of their plans was not quite as difficult for the terrorists of the Weimar Republic as it was for those of the Bonn Republic. The numbers of affluent sympathizers were far larger in the Weimar period.

36 To argue about which of the opponents ensnared in such a process should take the blame for what is happening is rather futile. Both sides mutually turn the screw. The question is how one can damp down and perhaps halt the escalation. Normally, the more powerful side in such a process is much more capable of doing this than the weaker one.

37 In both cases the transition to the formation of violent conspiratorial terrorist organizations, which sought to shake and if possible destroy the existing regime through pointed breaches of the state monopoly of violence, took place in a situation where attempts by other means to bring about change in a desired direction in an existing political order, which was experienced as without meaning or value, had failed.

38 Jochen Steffen, 'Nachwort' (Epilogue) in K.R. Kohl, *Fünf Finger sind keine Faust* [Five Fingers Do Not Make a Fist], Cologne, Kiepen, Heuer & Witsch, 1977, p. 452.

39 Hans-Joachim Klein, *Rückkehr in die Menschlichkeit* [Return to Humanity], Reinbek, Rowohlt, 1979.

40 Michael Baumann, *Wie alles anfing* [How it all Began], Munich, Trikont, 1980, p. 13.

41 Ibid., pp. 10f.

42 Rudolf Herzog, *Hanseaten* [Hanseatic Merchants], Stuttgart and Berlin, J. G. Cotta, 1923, pp. 126f.

43 Ibid., p. 99

44 Bloem, *Volk wider Volk*, pp. 400f.

45 Ernst Jünger, *In Stahlgewittern: ein Kriegstagebuch*, Berlin, E.S. Mittler und Sohn, 1926 (originally published 1922), p. 166. (English translation, *The Storm of Steel*, trans. Basil Creighton, London, Chatto & Windus, 1929.)

46 Ibid., p. 288.

47 Ibid., p. 256.

48 Ibid., p. 257.

49 Ibid., p. 142.

50 In his *A History of the Weimar Republic* (trans. I.F.D. Morrow and L. Marie Sieveking, London, Methuen, 1936, p. 105), Arthur Rosenberg argues that:

> True revolutionaries would, above all, have faced the danger that threatened from the army. The National Assembly might have declared in the manner of the [French Revolutionary] Convention that the Republic was in danger. It might have called all Socialists and Republicans to arms to save their country. A general armament of the people would have rendered the Free Corps harmless, would have nipped in the bud any danger of individual *coups*, would have secured the eastern frontier against the Poles, and might even possibly have strengthened the position of Germany in face of the Entente at the peace negotiations.

Rosenberg is referring to the models of the French and English Revolutions. He sees the regularities of revolutionary processes exclusively as sequences of intra-state events. He accordingly fails to recognize the foreign political situation of the young German republic. It is extremely unlikely that the Allies would have simply accepted such a *levée en masse* of the German population, arms at the ready. Such a mass uprising – even if the national army would have stood for it, even if the weapons had been available – would have been possible only with overt or covert revolutionary slogans. The Russian revolutionary movement was already getting badly on the nerves of the Western Allies. A similar movement in Germany would have been the signal for them to invade.

51 The *Reichswehr* gave its support at this point not from sympathy with the parliamentary republic, but because it considered this first attempt to overthrow the government and the subsequent proclamation of a dictatorship to be premature. Its policy was to bide its time. However much its hopes and wishes resembled those of the rebels, the older and more experienced leaders of the officer corps saw clearly that the time had not come for rearmament, nor for doing away with the multi-party state in favour of a regime with the strength and popularity to undertake rearmament. This hesitation on the part of the *Reichswehr* was partly responsible for the fact that it was not until 1933 that a party dictatorship arose, and that this came about by means of the formal parliamentary path, bringing with it, among other things, the dissolution of the existing parties and trade unions.

52 The following quotation usefully illustrates how much this belief contributed to the failure of its opponents, especially the intellectuals among them, to recognize the political potential of the Hitler movement. As early as 1924, Emil Julius Gumbel had written in his book *Verschwörer*:

> National Socialism can only be understood instinctively. It contradicts even the most primitive standards of rationality. It is a passion, created from economic necessity and the bitterness of the soul that it leads to. It has nothing to do with realistic forms of politics. Its entire rationale comes from romanticism. . . . [The] idea of a racially pure state cannot possibly be put into practice, of course, and the demands for this are naturally merely mouthings, but they find support among the youth. . . . Such ideas lead naturally to a direct way of realizing them: attacks against Jewish people on the street, destruction of newspapers and so on, since this level corresponds to the lowest, most violent instincts. . . . (pp. 177f)

These remarks make clear why the pattern of thought nowadays known as 'rationalism', with the related concept of human reason as a natural endowment – which formed in close relationship with the wave of pacification in developing absolutist states and later within nation-states which furthered internal pacification – makes it difficult for its exponents to incorporate into their picture of humanity the control or non-control of violence in dealing with conflict between humans as a universal problem of social life. In line with the level of civilization expressed in concepts such as 'intellect', 'reason' or 'rationality', their upholders do not yet reflect upon the civilizing conditions of their respective concepts. They therefore do not know that a high degree and peculiar form of pacification are among the conditions for the movement they call 'rationalism', and thus also for their concepts of 'reason' or 'understanding'. The use of violence as a social fact is then quite simply relegated to the realm of the irrational, if not the anti-rational, and thus remains in principle incomprehensible.

53 Salomon, *Die Geächteten*, pp. 297–8.
54 *Völkischer Beobachter*, 14 July 1934, cited here from Max Domarus, ed., *Hitler: Reden und Proklamationen, 1932–1945* [Speeches and Proclamations], Neustadt, Verlagsdrucker Schmidt, 1962, vol. 1, pp. 411f. [English translation by Mary Gilbert, *The Chronicle of a Dictatorship*, London, I.B. Tauris, 1990, vol. 1, pp. 487–8.] Cf also Robert G.L. Waite, *Vanguard of Nazism*, Cambridge Mass., Harvard University Press, 1952, pp. 280f.
55 In the majority of the working class, the generation problem seems to be manifested comparatively weakly. Up to now, in industrial societies of both the capitalist and communist types, the opportunities for the mass of workers' children, the chances of rising out of industrial work, have been relatively limited. Such opportunities are accessible only to a small minority. The majority, as the drop-out and social climber Baumann puts it, are 'adapted' (*Wie alles anfing*, p. 8). The sons and daughters of working-class parents live and work by and large like their parents, even taking improvements in the standard of living into account; they remain in the cultural and social traditions of the working class. Largely on the strength of its relatively taken-for-granted character, this tradition satisfies the desire for meaningfulness of people who, as individuals, at work as in the private sphere, are embedded in community life as a group to a high degree.

It is different for the bourgeois middle-class groups of the rising generations. As individuals, they are isolated and left to themselves to a much greater extent – even when they attempt to dispel or at least limit their isolation, as sometimes happens today through the formation of secondary groups based more on conscious reflection, such as by sharing living accommodation. Correspondingly, the problem of personal meaning-fulfilment acquires a far greater urgency and actuality – often, as I have noted, in the area of politics.
56 In the German, I have introduced the adjective *arbeiterlich* ['worker-ly'] because it seems to fill a gap in the German language, as in most European languages.

The adjectival use of other class designations, so that one speaks of 'aristocratic' and 'bourgeois' classes, is self-evident. In accordance with the social relations of power, the designation of the respective lower classes usually has a negative taint. Those with more power can effectively stigmatize those with less power. The pejorative undertones that are easily connected with the term 'bourgeois' or 'middle class' originate in their use by aristocrats. It was only with their deliberate use in the class struggle by an increasingly powerful working class that these terms acquired the social character of stigmatization from below.

The missing adjective corresponding to the term 'worker' was apparently first felt to be a gap in the vocabulary by Marx and Engels. They filled it with the adjectival form of the formerly pejorative word 'proletariat', which they attempted to transform into a word of praise. But for my taste, the term 'proletariat' has clinging to it a type of positive or negative political evaluation making it unusable for pure research work. It seems to me that the missing expression *arbeiterlich* better fulfils the research requirements of sociology.

57 Baumann, *Wie alles anfing*, pp. 92f.

58 In an age in which longer-lasting military conflicts demand the mobilization of the entire population, a war brings much more clearly to light the dependence of ruling classes on the less powerful, ruled groups than is evident in times of peace. It was characteristic of both great mass wars of the present century that the population was promised high rewards after victory. And although the promises were never quite kept, both post-war periods did show at first a clear move to the 'left', as one says in the political language of today – that is, an increase in the power-chances of less powerful groups, especially the working class. The further development of this democratization then followed the pattern of a famous procession: three steps forwards, two steps back.

59 The following portrayal by a participating eyewitness speaks for itself (Ralf Reinders, 'Schlußwort im Lorenz-prozeß' ['Closing words in the Lorenz trial'], *die tageszeitung*, special edition of 11 October 1980, p. 60):

> Our revolt thus had an important political starting point. That was the Easter March Movement. ... The Easter March Movement was the starting point of the APO [*außerparlamentarische Opposition* – extra-parliamentary opposition]. APO, three letters which then spelt hope for a generation .... it was exactly what the three letters say, an extra-parliamentary opposition in which all classes of the younger generation were represented.
>
> And the general political expression of the rebellion was the wish and will to be able to determine one's own fate, collectively and alone. It was the attempt to structure our lives ourselves, freely, and no longer to let some idiotic authorities and lobbyists of capital to determine them for us. ...
>
> What made us so euphoric then was the fact that we were not fighting alone. The fight against capitalism, imperialism and encrusted power structures raged throughout the whole world. In Vietnam ... even in America ... in France ... in China. ... We've learnt a lot since then.

This is one of the statements which convey to people living later a picture of the trains of thought that moved many members of the extra-parliamentary opposition in the Federal Republic at that time. Despite the assurance that it was a movement involving youth from all strata, this short excerpt already shows how decisive an influence was the global view of young bourgeois intellectuals. The reference to Marx met their great need for theoretical orientation. Marx's intellectual edifice, however, was restricted to analysing a specific power gradient within states. Meanwhile, a whole series of other established–outsider relationships, above all those between states, had entered the field of vision of groups that were sensitive to the problems of power inequality and oppression. But they lacked the ability to develop further the limited nineteenth-century theory of oppression in accordance with the extended field of experience of the twentieth century. So they poured their new wine into old bottles.

60 This conflict appears in the framework of the Marxist schema and its descendants not solely as the theoretical model for, but also as the real root of, all other social conflicts. The difficulty is that, although the conflict of the two great industrial classes did indeed have a fairly central significance as a motor of social development in the nineteenth and twentieth centuries, at the same time there are a number of other central conflicts which in twentieth-century social development most certainly have not played a lesser role, and in some cases have played a considerably larger one, than economic class conflicts. The defective orientation to which the economistic explanatory monism of all versions of Marxism gives rise simply has to be corrected, thereby also pointing out Marxism's ideological function.

   Of the conflicts that fall prey to being obscured by this monism, three will be focused on more sharply in this study, partly directly, partly indirectly: (1) the conflict between rulers and ruled (this proceeds differently in multi-party states than in one-party states, and here we will be talking almost solely about the former); (2) the conflict between states; and (3) the conflict between the generations. This list is not exhaustive. In particular, the conflict between the sexes, seen as social groups, remains neglected in this context, although it most certainly belongs on the list. Conflict between states will also be stressed less than would accord with their actual significance.

61 *Der Minister und der Terrorist: Gespräche zwischen Gerhart Baum und Horst Mahler* [The Minister and the Terrorist: Conversations between Gerhart Baum and Horst Mahler], ed. Axel Jeschke and Wolfgang Malanowski, Hamburg, Rowohlt, 1980, p. 32.

62 Baumann, *Wie alles anfing*, p. 86.

63 In addition, there is another shift in emphasis that has taken place in the twentieth century, and which now often seems to be self-evident, although it is not in the least so. The existing social order is seen as the cause of all the constraints that make it difficult if not impossible for the adolescent to find fulfilment of his or her desire for meaning. In the nineteenth and early twentieth centuries, the idea that it was an invisible inner barrier in each person which hindered his or her fulfilment played a considerable role (cf. Norbert Elias, *The Society of Individuals*, ed. M. Schröter, trans. Edmund

Jephcott, Oxford, Blackwell, 1991, e.g. pp. 120ff). Since then, there has evidently been a change of emphasis in this respect. The explanation of oppressive and fulfilment-denying self-constraints is now sought first and foremost in the oppressive external constraints of the society, which must therefore be changed or even destroyed in order for people to be able to 'find' themselves and satisfy their desire for meaning.

64 The structural change in this conflict in the course of social development makes nonsense of any attempt at explanation in terms of a causal sequence. People's expectations are still largely directed towards the idea that the explanation of this intensification of the conflict between the generations has just one cause, or perhaps ten causes. But there are no absolute beginnings, and therefore no causes, in continuing processes; there is actually only a complex human web, in unbroken movement and transformation as a whole.

65 Iring Fetscher, 'Thesen zum Terrorismusproblem' [Theses on the terrorist problem], in *Der Minister und der Terrorist*, p. 116.

66 The paradox in this is that such an open generation struggle as that fought in the 1960s by the extra-parliamentary opposition and the student movement was possible only in the framework of a social structure which gave its members relatively wide scope for the expression of disagreement between groups – including generations – with contrary political ideals. In the totally oppressive absolutist states of the present day, whatever their political flag, there may be latent generation conflicts, but they have little chance of becoming manifest – even if for this very reason they smoulder much more fiercely under the surface. The fact that generation conflicts can appear and be fought out so undisguisedly as happened in the German Federal Republic in those years was thus a sign of the relative elasticity of its political institutions, of the relatively minimally oppressive character of its regime.

67 One of the most astonishing aspects of the testimonies of participants in this movement was the total fixation on what they saw and felt here and now in their presence. They were obviously so carried away by the strength of their wishes that they hardly ever concerned themselves with details of what would happen once the capitalist state had been removed. Concepts like 'socialism' were enough for them to be sure that getting rid of the existing state would be a deed well done. Their belief in the necessity of destroying the contemporary state-society never quite ceased to be a group dream supported by overpoweringly strong affects.

68 This also holds for the United States, although the after-effects of the most recent European war were rather obscured there by the particular form of American nationalism. The Vietnam experience may have pushed in the same direction.

69 Cf. *Der Minister und der Terrorist*, p. 16.

70 Ibid., p. 19.

71 Yet another point is worthy of attention in this connection: today, if one retrospectively reads comments made by people involved at the time as spokespersons or as leaders in the fight of the younger against the older generations, then what impresses one time and time again is the strength of their moral conviction in the justice of their cause and their lack of understanding of the means of power of the state, the parties – in short, of all the political and economic groups they challenged to a power struggle by their actions. On the other side were people of an older generation, who in many cases were no less concerned to distance themselves from the theory and practice of social inequality and oppression as they were embodied in the National Socialist creed. But through long experience, they were attuned to extreme caution in political activity. Schooled by the constant collision of goals which may have seemed desirable to them and the power of human groups opposed to their being carried through, they were hampered and paralysed from the outset in their standing up for desired goals.

72 *Der Minister und der Terrorist*, p. 20.

73 See also Norbert Elias, 'Die Zivilisierung der Eltern' [civilizing parents], in Linde Burkhardt, ed., ... *Und wie wohnst Du?* [... *And How Do You Live?*], Berlin, IDZ, 1980, pp. 21f.

74 This is a further similarity between the young middle-class outsider groups who formed an extra-parliamentary opposition after the First and Second World Wars. For both (and at the beginning also for the *Freikorps*) the state was, if not their exclusive financial backer, then the most important one. But they were hardly aware of this.

75 The situation in the Weimar Republic was remarkable in this respect. The student culture of that time, especially the student associations, still orientated itself on the whole towards the code of the Second Reich. Its decisive normative structure coincided correspondingly with that of the conservative old bourgeoisie.

76 There are certainly fairly acute generation conflicts, too, in the less developed states which are going through an earlier phase of the modernization process. They differ from the generation conflicts of the more developed countries, however, and this difference is highly instructive in understanding the relationship between the structure of social development and the structure of generation conflicts. In both cases the older generation incline more towards tradition and the unchanging continuation of things as they are, whereas the younger ones are more open to change. But the so-called developing countries are societies whose younger generations – justifiably or not – feel that things in their countries are looking up. They want to escape from a situation of economic poverty and political humiliation, and for them the tradition that their generational predecessors uphold and want to protect carries with it in may ways the stigma of national humiliation. The younger ones counter this with the pride of their new-found self-esteem, pride of nation as standard-

bearer of the progress of their land. Especially in the relatively highly developed nation-states of the non-dictatorial parts of Europe, the situation is almost the reverse.

77 It is questionable whether one should denote such a feeling of self-esteem simply as 'nationalism'. For this expression can refer to a purely cerebral system of argumentation, to a predominantly intellectual action programme or to a party ideology behind which are hidden specific class interests. Perhaps it would be useful to distinguish between nationalism thus understood and something not always intellectually sharply articulated, namely the feeling of belonging to a nation or national consciousness.

78 This has held at least since the excess of 'jingoism' (as its British opponents called it) in the early twentieth century.

79 In one of his essays George Orwell has described some aspects of the British feeling of nationality ('England, your England', in *Inside the Whale and Other Essays*, Harmondsworth, Penguin, 1957, pp. 72–4; I am indebted to Cas Wouters for drawing my attention to this volume). A necessarily brief excerpt may illustrate this:

> It is quite true that the so-called races of Britain feel themselves to be very different from one another. A Scotsman, for instance, does not thank you if you call him an Englishman.... But somehow these differences fade away the moment that any two Britons are confronted by a European.... Looked at from the outside, even the Cockney and the Yorkshireman have a strong family resemblance.
>
> And even the distinction between rich and poor dwindles somewhat when one regards the nation from the outside. There is no question about the inequality of wealth in England. It is grosser than in any European country.... Economically, England is certainly two nations, if not three or four. But at the same time the vast majority of the people *feel* themselves to be a single nation and are conscious of resembling one another more than they resemble foreigners. Patriotism is usually stronger than any kind of internationalism. Except for a brief moment in 1920 (the 'Hands off Russia' movement) the British working class have never thought or acted internationally....
>
> In England patriotism takes different forms in different classes, but it runs like a connecting thread through nearly all of them. Only the Europeanized intelligentsia are really immune to it. As a positive emotion it is stronger in the middle class than in the upper class.... In the working class patriotism is profound, but it is unconscious.... The famous 'insularity' and 'xenophobia' of the English is far stronger in the working class than in the bourgeoisie.... During the war of 1914–18 the English working class were in contact with foreigners to an extent that is rarely possible. The sole result was that they brought

back a hatred of all Europeans, except the Germans, whose courage they admired.... The insularity of the English, their refusal to take foreigners seriously, is a folly that has to be paid for very heavily from time to time. But it plays its part in the English *mystique*.

80 'True, the state is not demoralized by it or even heavily shaken, it's not that easy. But its monopoly of violence was broken. It simply had to be broken . . .' ('Schlußwort im Lorenz-Prozeß', Reiners, p. 63).

81 If people do not see these relationships more clearly, it is primarily because of the tendency to seek short-term explanations when only long-term explanations can provide convincing conclusions. And only when one takes account of the latter is it perhaps also possible to overcome the problems concerned in practical action and policy.

82 *Der Minister und der Terrorist*, p. 16.

83 In this regard things are easier for the dictatorial state of the German Democratic Republic, where there is a state monopoly of the means of orientation with the aid of which at least the façade of a unified state consciousness can be created. The cross between nationalist and socialist ideals permits the social creed of Marxism superficially to be made into the centrepiece of state consciousness and perhaps of a dawning national awareness. What lies behind this façade is difficult to say at present.

84 It is only fair to add that there has been no lack of attempts to achieve this. But they have remained too weak and diffuse, the resistance too great for them to have acted as nuclei for the crystallization of consciousness of the positive meaning and value of this state.

85 The development of this stance has been called 'informalization'; cf. Part IA in this volume, especially pp. 443–4 n. 6 above.

86 The reference to class struggle as it is contained, for instance, in the Marxist theory of fascism is inadequate as an explanation for the rise of Mussolini and his followers in Italy, or of Hitler and his supporters in Germany. For conflicts of this sort also occurred in many advanced industrial countries, including France and Britain. One has therefore to ask further why these conflicts did not lead elsewhere to the formation and in the end to the dictatorship of what started out as extra-parliamentary parties which rose to power through terror and the use of violence, and why it was just in Germany and Italy that this was the case. If one poses this question, then one can see clearly that such fundamental differences cannot be explained solely by taking economic structures into account. Here, long-term processes which, in the framework of short-term economic analyses, are usually swept under the carpet play a most decisive role. Central in this connection are state-formation processes, civilizing processes and the processes of pacification that are closely connected with them.

87 One must ask whether it is fruitful and useful for understanding the social

development of Europe to obscure the differences between the two national-populist dictatorships of Hitler and Mussolini by calling them both 'fascist'.

88 It was no coincidence that the largest of the princely courts, that of the Kaiser in Berlin, had a strong military stamp. In states like Britain and France, pacification took place considerably earlier than in Germany – correspondingly, one of their symbols involved restriction of the wearing of military uniform to martial occasions. Already at the time of Louis XIV it was no longer customary to appear at court in a military uniform. The British attitude is yet again best illustrated by a quotation from Orwell's essay ('England your England', p. 69). In this connection, one has to keep in mind the model-setting function of the German officer corps and the uniform-loving imperial court up to 1918:

> What English people of nearly all classes loathe from the bottom of their hearts is the swaggering officer type, the jingle of spurs and the crash of boots. Decades before Hitler was ever heard of, the word 'Prussian' had much the same significance in England as 'Nazi' has today. So deep does this feeling go that for a hundred years past the officers of the British army, in peacetime, have always worn civilian clothes when off duty.

89 Best known is the study published by T.W. Adorno, E. Frenkel-Brunswick, D.J. Levinson and R.N. Sanford under the title *The Authoritarian Personality*, New York, Harper & Row, 1950.

90 Cf. Norbert Elias, 'Introduction', in Norbert Elias and Eric Dunning, eds, *Quest for Excitement: Sport and Leisure in the Civilizing Process*, Oxford, Blackwell, 1986, pp. 26f.

91 In fact, a dictatorial regime is much more consistent with the notion of a perfectly rationally organized order of human living than is a parliamentary multi-party system – everything goes like clockwork from the top downwards in complete harmony and with optimal efficiency. A well-organized dictatorial state would be, in other words, the incarnation of rationality.

Perhaps it is no coincidence that a philosophy which places the concept of rationality at its centre, as is the case with Kant, for instance, found its highest expression in an epoch of absolutism. Deep in his heart, Kant was himself rather more critical of the royal dictatorship. This dictatorship itself, the state of the Hohenzollerns, was anything but perfect. But the ideal of an order subject to the strictest logical consistency of general laws which Kant read into nature and the moral world of humans certainly found strong support in the ideal state image of enlightened despotism as represented, for instance, by Frederick II of Prussia in his youth.

Just to reiterate the point: for classical rationality there are no conflicts. Accordingly Kant saw the natural world as well as the world of morals as areas of the highest harmony. Conflicts may really occur among people, he might have said, but if all people were to act rationally, if every person were to follow the laws of the state as they did the laws of nature, then there would be no more conflicts, for conflicts are abnormal; they are disturbances in human social life, which, if it really corresponded with the laws of rationality, would proceed harmoniously and without friction.

92 Information about differences of opinion and conflicts in the highest places leak out to the mass of the people at most indirectly through rumours or gossip. By and large, the establishments of autocratically ruled states show a closed and united front to those over whom they rule.

93 The transformation of an absolutist or dictatorial regime into a parliamentary regime seems to be represented by many theories in political science simply as a result of an intellectual decision in favour of a freer and more rational form of social life within a state. If it is viewed this way, ignoring the related civilizing problem, it is easy to lose sight of the difficulties faced by contemporary societies undergoing transformation from a traditional tribal structure to integration on the level of a nation ruled by a parliament, or from a long-established dictatorial one-party regime to a multi-party regime.

94 A further difficulty which could be mentioned is that the level of affect control on the parliamentary level itself is often far higher than it is in the broader public, to whom the elected members of parliament constantly have to justify their actions. For this and other reasons, one of the peculiarities of the parliamentary regimes in our times is a discrepancy between the factual power struggles which take place on the parliamentary and governmental levels and which run their course along relatively restrained paths, and the ideal images, the artificial affectivity of the catchwords and slogans presented to the public by politicians in their writings and speeches and which appeal far more strongly to the emotions. In this way, the problem becomes poignant precisely because political debates in today's societies often have functions resembling those of religious battles in earlier times. But the resonance found by such emotional needs in the factual course of parliamentary struggles, with their restraint of personal affects, is small.

Notes to Part IV

1 See, for example, G. Reitlinger, *The Final Solution: the Attempt to Exterminate the Jews of Europe, 1939–1945*, London, Vallentine, Mitchell, 1953.

2 See, for example, Dr W.F. Könitzer and Hansgeorg Trurnit, eds, *Weltentscheidung in der Judenfrage: der Endkampf nach 3,000 Jahren Jugendgegnerschaft* [World Verdict on the Jewish Question: the End-Game after 3,000 Years of Opposition to the Jews], Dresden, Zwinger-Verlag, 1939.

3 The general problem of what sorts of beliefs can have this function and under what conditions lies beyond the framework of the present study. But even a limited study such as this may help people to see it in the right perspective and to appreciate its urgency.

4 See the article 'Reich' in Waldermar Besson, ed., *Geschichte* (vol. 24), Frankfurt am Main, Fischer-Lexikon, 1961.

5 Georg Herwegh (1817–75); see Ludwig Reiners, ed., *Der ewige Brunnen: ein Volksbuch deutscher Dichtung* [The Eternal Spring: a People's Book of German Poetry], Munich, Beck, 1955. [Translators' note]

6 Hitler's 'political testament' contained the words: 'Neither will I fall into the hands of enemies who need a new play, staged by Jews, for the entertainment of their inflamed masses. I have therefore decided to remain in Berlin and there of my own accord to choose death at that moment when I believe that the seat of Führer and Chancellor can no longer be maintained' (quoted in Max Domarus, ed., *Hitler: Reden und Proklamationen, 1932–1945*, Munich, Süddeutscher Verlag, vol. 11/2, 1965, p. 2237).

7 From an advertisement for the 'National Fellowship'.

8 Another striking example of the same situation is offered by the recent history of Portugal. A report from a *Daily Telegraph* correspondent of 20 December 1961 under the headline 'Fall of Goa stuns Lisbon: radio dirges for end of an empire' vividly describes some of the typical aspects of the moment of crisis in which the factual course of events comes cruelly into collision with the collective fantasies of traditional elites and how this reality-shock is released. The moment of truth has come. Previously trapped in their insider-blindness and the mutual reinforcement of their beliefs, they are now compelled to look the fact in the face that their empire and the dreams of eternal greatness and superiority connected with it have been lost:

> Lisbon was completely cut off tonight from its own sources of news from Goa. The radio messages picked up in Karachi speaking of 'continued heroic resistance in Panjun and Masmagao' were not confirmed by the government.
>
> But everyone believes that if fighting is not yet over it will be very soon. Thousands attended a special Mass for Goa tonight in the fifteenth-century church of the Jerominos celebrated at the same altar that Vasco de Gama took with him on his voyage of discovery to India.
>
> All day long Portuguese radio programmes confined themselves to solemn music. It sounded like, and it was, the funeral of an empire.
>
> *A Myth Dies*
> This is the day when the Portuguese have realised for the first time that they are not in any sense an imperial power. The sudden loss of Goa destroys once and for all the myth that for years has sustained the Salazar regime.

It is an assumption that Portugal, though militarily and economically weak, possesses a peculiar spiritual strength to enable her, alone among European nations, to remain in Asia and Africa in the furtherance of a non-racial, Christian civilizing mission.

It is this faith that has enabled the Portuguese to fight in Angola a colonial war that to the rest of the world looks utterly hopeless. One wonders whether they will now have the heart to continue it.

9   Fritz Fischer, *Germany's Aims in the First World War*, trans. Lancelot L. Farrar, Robert and Rita Kimber, London, Weidenfeld & Nicolson, 1975.

10   Bruno Bettelheim, *The Informed Heart*, Glencoe, Ill., Free Press, 1960, pp. 123ff.

11   Hans Frank, *Die Technik des Staates*, 2nd edn, Cracow, Burgverlag Krakow, 1942, pp. 15ff.

12   'Pg' is short for *Parteigenosse* – that is, a member of the party. [Translators' note]

13   Despite the necessary cautions which must be entered in relation to isolated remarks of this kind, a problem nevertheless arises here which perhaps deserves to be raised. In France and other countries, the resistance against the Nazi regime had the support of broad sections of the population because it united the members of different social strata in revolt against the foreign oppressor and welded together adherents of different political convictions in opposition to a common enemy. By contrast, the German resistance movement lacked a broad basis in the population. It rested on an alliance between remnants of the pre-Nazi elites, among whom the old military elites played a dominant role. It is not unlikely that the fact that officers and nobles were the chief actors in the attempt on Hitler's life would have strengthened the sympathies for Hitler among the mass of the German people because compared with the old ruling strata Hitler was certainly to a far greater degree a 'man of the people'.

14   (Addition 1984.) If one considers the development of states in this century, one becomes aware again and again how helpless the mass of the population really are in relation to the relatively small established groups, in particular the occupants of government positions, who make decisions over the weals and woes and, at times, the life and death of the people over whom they rule. Very often, these decisions turn out to be disastrous mistakes. But even had they known this, the rulers would have hardly been in a position to change things. Their power-resources would not have been sufficient. And, in most cases, they were not aware that they were the victims of wrong decisions, were perhaps even jubilant about them. Protest movements, in the main, only show the powerlessness of ruled people – not only in relation to their own government regime but also in relation to the decisions of other governments on whom the fate of their country depends.

That is how it is today. Why should it not clearly be said for once that all the people in the world today are dependent on decisions made by government elites in Moscow and Washington? Awareness of one's own powerlessness should not lead to the idea that the governments of the two world powers on whose decisions the fate of almost the whole of humanity depends are people who make their decisions with the help of a more comprehensive knowledge than the people over whom they rule or that they make these decisions freely and unhindered by external and internal compulsions. The knowledge-chances and scope for decisions of great power governments are greater than those of the people who depend on them. But even they see the intra-state and inter-state contexts for which a clear picture is needed in order to make decisions through the spectacles of their social ideologies and personal values. They, too, make decisions under the pressure of social constraints which they do not understand and whose mere existence is for the most part hidden from them. The chances of those over whom they rule to get to know and understand the unplanned processes on which their future fate depends are even fewer.

15 The excerpts from letters cited above, which were chosen in part with respect to political comments, obscure this trend a little.

Notes to Part V

1 Cf. *Der Spiegel*, 1977, no. 42, p. 188.
2 Norbert Elias, 'Adorno-Rede: Respekt und Kritik' [Adorno Address: Respect and Criticism], in Norbert Elias and Wolf Lepenies, *Zwei Reden anläßlich der Verleihung des Theodor-W.-Adorno-Preises 1977* [Two Addresses on the Occasion of the Award of the Theodor W. Adorno Prize, 1977], Frankfurt am Main, Suhrkamp, 1977, p. 61. [The first Adorno Prize was awarded to Norbert Elias in 1977 – Translators' note]
3 'On Britain's conscience', *The Times* of 20 February 1978, p. 15. The article continues:

> One of the darkest blots on the British record is the forcible repatriation of Soviet citizens at the end of the Second World War. Some committed suicide rather than return. Many were murdered the moment they reached Soviet soil. Many more died in camps in appalling conditions. A few survived.

4 *The Economist*, 17 September 1977, p. 13.

Index